THE PRISON AND THE GALLOWS

Over the past three decades the United States has built a carceral state that is unprecedented among Western countries and in U.S. history. Nearly one in fifty people, excluding children and the elderly, is incarcerated today, a rate unsurpassed anywhere else in the world. What are some of the main political forces that explain this unprecedented reliance on mass imprisonment? Specifically, why didn't the construction of the carceral state face more political opposition? Throughout American history, crime and punishment have been central features of American political development. This book examines the development of four key movements – the victims' movement, the women's movement, the prisoners' rights movement, and opponents of the death penalty – that mediated the construction of the carceral state in important ways. It shows how punitive penal policies were forged by particular social movements and interest groups within the constraints of larger institutional structures and historical developments that distinguish the United States from other Western countries.

Marie Gottschalk is associate professor of political science at the University of Pennsylvania. She has a PhD in political science from Yale University and an MPA from Princeton University's Woodrow Wilson School of Public and International Affairs. She is the author of *The Shadow Welfare State: Labor, Business, and the Politics of Health Care in the United States* (2000). She is a former associate editor of *World Policy Journal* and a former associate director of the World Policy Institute in New York City. She also worked for several years as a journalist.

D1016295

CAMBRIDGE STUDIES IN CRIMINOLOGY

Editors

Alfred Blumstein, *H. John Heinz School of Public Policy and Management, Carnegie Mellon University*

David Farrington, *Institute of Criminology, University of Cambridge*

Other books in the series:

Series list continues following the Index.

The Prison and the Gallows

The Politics of Mass Incarceration in America

Marie Gottschalk
University of Pennsylvania

![Cambridge logo] **CAMBRIDGE**
UNIVERSITY PRESS

CAMBRIDGE UNIVERSITY PRESS
Cambridge, New York, Melbourne, Madrid, Cape Town, Singapore, São Paulo

Cambridge University Press
40 West 20th Street, New York, NY 10011-4211, USA

www.cambridge.org
Information on this title: www.cambridge.org/9780521864275

First published 2006

Printed in the United States of America

A catalog record for this publication is available from the British Library.

Library of Congress Cataloging in Publication Data

Gottschalk, Marie.
   The prison and the gallows : the politics of mass incarceration in America / Marie
Gottschalk.
   p.   cm. – (Cambridge studies in criminology)
Includes bibliographical references and index.
ISBN-13: 978-0-521-86427-5 (hardback)
ISBN-10: 0-521-86427-5 (hardback)
ISBN-13: 978-0-521-68291-6 (pbk.)
ISBN-10: 0-521-68291-6 (pbk.)
   1. Prisons – United States.   2. Imprisonment – Government policy – United States.
3. Capital punishment – United States.   4. Prisoners – United States – Civil rights.
5. United States – Politics and government. I. Title. II. Series: Cambridge studies in
criminology (Cambridge University Press)
HV9471.G67   2006
365'.973 – dc22   2005031115

ISBN-13   978-0-521-86427-5 hardback
ISBN-10   0-521-86427-5 hardback

ISBN-13   978-0-521-68291-6 paperback
ISBN-10   0-521-68291-6 paperback

In loving memory of Sally Gottschalk

CONTENTS

LIST OF FIGURES AND TABLE

Figures

Table

PREFACE AND ACKNOWLEDGMENTS

Toward the end of my two-year stint teaching in Xian, China, in the 1980s, I thought I was inured to shocking scenes. And then I was shopping at the local outdoor produce market on a glorious sunny day in late spring when I heard a racket of loudspeakers. I looked up to see an aging flatbedded truck slowly winding its way through the crowded streets. In the back were about a half-dozen men with shaved, bowed heads, nondescript baggy uniforms, and blank faces. Watched over by crisply dressed police officers, each man slowly shuffled forward as his name was called. The blaring loudspeakers recited his alleged crimes and pronounced his sentence: death.

Over the previous months, my students had told me stories about witnessing executions at crowded outdoor stadiums. And Xian had been peppered with posters with big red X's scrawled across the mug shots of people rounded up in the "strike hard" campaign against crime, some for violations as egregious as petty larceny. Yet witnessing the punitive, unforgiving, and seemingly invincible arm of the state directly in action in the everyday setting of a bustling market deeply unsettled me.

After working for more than six years on this book about mass imprisonment in the United States, I remain similarly shocked and unsettled. The United States today has an incarcerated population that dwarfs that of China, a country that is several times larger and has at best only democratic aspirations and pretensions. The shock is all the greater in the U.S. case not only because of the enormity of the American carceral state, but also because of its invisibility – the invisibility of the numerous prisons that dot rural America and the desolate outskirts of urban areas; the more than two million men and women locked up on any given day; the hundreds of thousands released from prison each year with stunted employment, economic, educational, and social prospects; and the millions of families and children unhinged by the carceral state.

Most striking of all is that this vast, unrelenting, and costly punitive thrust in public policy has not been a central topic of political debate and political analysis. While politicians and public officials still regularly invoke the war on crime, the carceral state and its far-reaching consequences for U.S. society, economy, and polity have not been a leading political concern. Nor has the fact that disadvantaged groups in the United States, especially blacks and the poor, disproportionately shoulder the crushing weight of the carceral state.

As I was completing the final revisions for this book, I took a week off to participate in the intensive training for faculty interested in teaching in the Inside/Out Prison Exchange Program. Originated by Lori Pompa at Temple University, Inside/Out takes college students behind prison walls to study alongside imprisoned men and women in a semester-long course on some specific topic. Much of my Inside/Out training took place at Graterford Prison, a maximum-security facility for men about an hour from Philadelphia, with members of the prison's "Think Tank." Nearly all of the men in the Think Tank are lifers. In a state where "life means life," they are likely to live and die behind prison walls. Despite their bleak prospects, a number of them expressed optimism about their potential – and the potential of those of us on the outside – to fundamentally challenge the carceral state in our lifetimes.

This book is my modest contribution to that cause. Writing it has been a bleak, sobering experience. Yet if the lifers in Graterford can somehow keep alive a sense of hope and political efficacy, then those of us on the outside also must not succumb to fatalistic despair as we excavate and consider the formidable political and other forces that built the carceral state and sustain it.

Acknowledgments

I am deeply grateful for the generous intellectual and other support I received for this project. I benefited enormously from constructive critics in my disciplinary home of political science and further afield in sociology and criminology. The following people provided critical feedback at various stages of the project: Fran Benson, Ann Chih Lin, David Garland, Paul Rock, Carroll Seron, Larry Sherman, Rogers Smith, the members of the Graterford Think Tank, and the anonymous reviewers for Cambridge and other presses. The comments, questions, and expressed skepticism of numerous seminar and conference participants also helped make this a much better book. Mary Fainsod Katzenstein, Desmond King, James Morone, and Austin Sarat read the entire manuscript and provided detailed, thoughtful suggestions that went far beyond the call of duty. An extra special thanks to Mary Katzenstein, who was a kindred spirit every step of the way and provided invaluable intellectual support and camaraderie. My editor at Cambridge, Ed Parsons, eased publication of this book with his unflappability, straightforwardness, and amazing ability to turn big problems into small ones.

This project was completed sooner rather than later because I received generous leave and financial support for my research. In addition to my regular sabbatical leave, Penn gave me an extra semester off courtesy of a Faculty Research Fellowship. Penn's Alice Paul Center provided me with important financial help for my research, as did the School of Arts and Sciences and the Penn Research Foundation.

The Russell Sage Foundation, which made me a visiting scholar in 2001–02, provided me with enormous intellectual, infrastructural, and research support. I will always treasure the year I spent there, especially the friendships and intellectual connections I made with some of the other visiting scholars. Nicole Radmore and Katie Winograd of RSF's information services deserve a special mention for their invaluable help and dogged persistence in tracking down materials.

I am grateful to all the research assistants I have had the good fortune to work with: Christine DeChiaro, Willie Gin, Stefan Heumann, Ayanna London, June Lee, Eric Lomazoff, Julian Millikan, Sabina Neem, Meredith Wooten, and Veronica Zapasnik.

This project was punctuated with great joy and sadness. It coincided with the death of my mother Sally Gottschalk, who succumbed to breast cancer in February 2002. I dedicate this book to her in admiration of her great strength in the face of all the adversity she faced during and at the end of her life. In the course of writing this book, my daughter Tara went from being a struggling, ill infant to a thriving six-year-old who has boundless good cheer and who is more aware of prisons than she probably ought to be at her age. My deepest love and thanks to Tara and Atul, my toughest and most forgiving critics.

December 2005

1   THE PRISON AND THE GALLOWS

The Construction of the Carceral State in America

I N 1850, Nathaniel Hawthorne suggested that prison is a necessary but not entirely desirable social institution. He described prison as "the black flower of civilized society" and implied that prisons were durable weeds that refused to die.[1] Over the past three decades, this black flower has proliferated in the United States as the country has built a carceral state that is unprecedented among Western countries and in U.S. history. Three features distinguish the U.S. carceral state: the sheer size of its prison and jail population; its reliance on harsh, degrading sanctions; and the persistence and centrality of the death penalty.

Nearly one in fifty people in the United States, excluding children and the elderly, is behind bars today.[2] In a period dominated by calls to roll back the state in all areas of social and economic policy, we have witnessed a massive expansion of the state in the realm of penal policy. The U.S. incarceration rate has accelerated dramatically, increasing more than five-fold since 1973.[3] Today a higher proportion of the adult population in the United States is behind bars than anywhere else in the world.[4] The United States, with 5 percent of the world's population, has nearly a quarter of its prisoners.[5] America's incarceration rate of 714 per 100,000 is five to twelve times the rate of Western European countries and Japan.[6] Even after taking into account important qualifications in the use of the standard 100,000 yardstick to compare incarceration rates cross-nationally, the United States is still off the charts (see Figure 1).[7]

The reach of the U.S. penal state extends far beyond the 2.2 million men and women who are now serving time in prison or jail in America. On any given day, nearly seven million people are under the supervision of the correctional system, including jail, prison, parole, probation, and other community supervision sanctions. This constitutes 3.2 percent of the U.S. adult population, or one in every thirty-two adults, a rate of state supervision that is unprecedented in U.S. history.[8] If one adds up the total number of people in prison, plus parolees, probationers, employees of correctional institutions, close relatives of prisoners and correctional

employees, and residents in communities where jails and prisons are major
employers, tens of millions of people are directly affected each day by the
carceral state.[9]

These overall figures on incarceration belie the enormous and disproportionate impact that this bold and unprecedented social experiment has
had on certain groups in U.S. society, especially young African Americans,
Hispanics, and the growing number of incarcerated women who are parents of young children.[10] Blacks, who make up less than 13 percent of
the U.S. population, now comprise more than half of all people in prison,
up from a third twenty years ago and from a quarter in the late 1930s.[11]
The number of black men in prison or jail has grown so rapidly over the
past quarter-century that today more black men are behind bars than are
enrolled in colleges and universities.[12]

Unlike other major state-building exercises like the New Deal and the
Great Society, the construction of the carceral state was not presented
as a package of policies for public debate. The carceral state was built
up rapidly over the past thirty years largely outside of the public eye
and not necessarily planned out. While the explosion in the size of the
prison population and the retributive turn in U.S. penal policy are well
documented, the underlying political causes of this massive expansion
are not well understood. Clearly, why the United States created such an
extensive and punitive penal state is a complex question. Penal policies
and institutions are formed not from a single factor, but instead by a
whole range of converging forces.[13] Still, it is important to sort out the
more important from the less important factors. The central question of
this book, then, is what are some of the main political forces that explain
this unprecedented reliance on mass imprisonment and other retributive
penal policies? Specifically, why didn't the rise of the carceral state face
more political opposition? The absence of such opposition, as will be
shown, provided permissive conditions for political elites to construct a
massive penal system.

Explanations for the rise of the carceral state vary enormously, but many
of them do have one thing in common. They adopt a relatively short time
frame as they try to identify what changed in the United States over the
past thirty to forty years to disrupt its relatively stable and unexceptional
incarceration rate and to bring back capital punishment with a vengeance.
The half-dozen major explanations – an escalating crime rate, shifts in
public opinion, the war on drugs, the emergence of the prison-industrial
complex, changes in American political culture, and politicians exploiting
the law-and-order issue for electoral gain – concentrate on developments
since the 1960s.

This focus on recent developments to explain the rise of the carceral
state makes some sense. After all, from the mid-1920s to the early
1970s, the U.S. incarceration rate was remarkably stable, averaging about

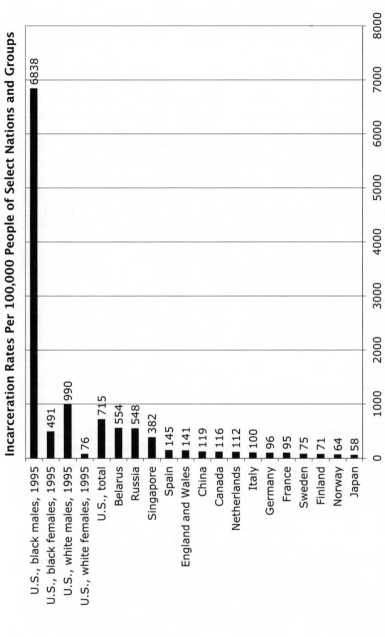

Incarceration Rates Per 100,000 People of Select Nations and Groups

Figure 1. Incarceration Rates for Select Nations and Groups. *Source:* Ann L. Pastore and Kathleen Maguire, eds., *Bureau of Justice Statistics Sourcebook of Criminal Justice Statistics – 2001* (Washington, DC: U.S. Department of Justice, 2002), p. 486, Table 6.13; and International Centre for Prison Studies, "Entire World – Prison Population Rates per 100,000 of National Population," http://www.kcl.ac.uk/depsta/rel/icps/worldbrief/highest-to-lowest-rates.php (accessed November 30, 2004).

110 state and federal prisoners per 100,000 people (see Figure 2).[14] From the 1960s to the early 1970s, the prison population was slowly but steadily shrinking by about one percent a year. While the U.S. incarceration rate historically has been higher than that of other Western countries, it was not until the 1970s and 1980s that it began radically to exceed them. Likewise, until the 1970s, the United States appeared to be traveling down the same path as Western Europe and Canada toward abolition of the death penalty. The annual number of executions dropped steadily beginning in the late 1930s, bottoming out with the decade-long de facto moratorium on the death penalty that began in 1967. After the Supreme Court reinstated capital punishment with the 1976 *Gregg* decision, the number of executions began its grim rise, first hesitantly and then with steady regularity. Given these patterns of imprisonment and use of the death penalty, it appears logical to locate the trigger for the carceral state in the relatively recent past.

Explanations of the construction of the carceral state that emphasize recent developments challenge some of the central premises of how we understand American political development. If correct, they suggest that this may be an instance of a major expansion of the state and a radical shift in public policy that has shallow historical and institutional roots. In short, history and institutions do matter, but only in the broadest, most general sense.

A central contention of this book, instead, is that contemporary penal policy actually has deep historical and institutional roots that predate the 1960s. Just as prisons are all around us but we choose not to notice them,[15] crime and punishment have been central features of American political development but we choose not to notice. Both state capacity to incarcerate and the legitimacy of the federal government to handle more criminal matters were built up slowly but surely well before the incarceration boom that began in the 1970s. Understanding the specifics of how this came about is a necessary precondition for understanding the construction of the carceral state. Explanations that concentrate too narrowly on the recent past overstate the historical, political, and institutional discontinuities, and understate important continuities or preconditions. As such they present an incomplete picture of why the prison-building boom of the past three decades and the wider use of vengeful, degrading, dehumanizing sanctions like chain gangs, supermax prisons, and capital punishment did not face more political opposition.

The United States has a long history of active political concern about issues related to crime and imprisonment. Throughout American history, crime and punishment have been central concerns not just at the local and state levels, but at the national level as well. This past helps us understand how institutional capacity, especially state capacity to pursue mass imprisonment as public policy, was built up well before the 1970s. It

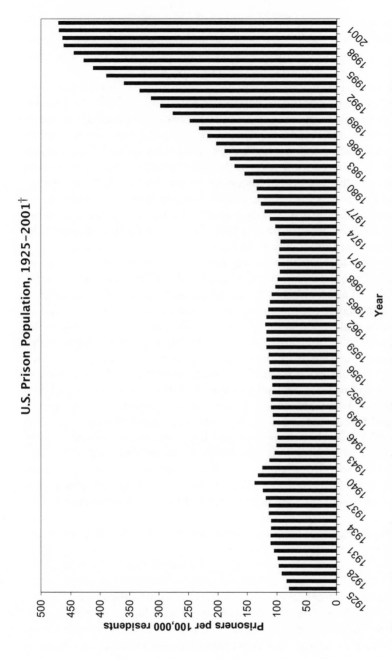

Figure 2. Prison Population per 100,000 Residents, United States, 1925–2001. *Source:* Ann L. Pastore and Kathleen Maguire, eds., *Bureau of Justice Statistics Sourcebook of Criminal Justice Statistics – 2001* (Washington, DC: U.S. Department of Justice, 2002), p. 494, Table 6.23.

† Includes number of federal and state prisoners per 100,000 residents. Does not include inmates in local jails.

also illuminates how the ideologies that legitimated such policies were constructed. While the history of crime and punishment has been a ripe field for social historians, their insights and findings have had little bearing on discussions of the politics of contemporary penal policy in the United States.[16] This is unfortunate because, as Norval Morris and David Rothman forcefully remind us, prisons do have a history: "In the popular imagination, institutions of incarceration appear so monumental in design and so intrinsic to the criminal justice system that it is tempting to think of them as permanent and fixed features of Western societies."[17] For anyone seeking to either explain or reverse the country's appalling incarceration rate, understanding the deeper historical context out of which contemporary penal policy was forged is essential. Furthermore, by comparing the institutional and political development of the United States with other Western countries, we can have a better idea of why the carceral state emerged here but not elsewhere so far.

Analysts who identify politics as a central factor in explaining the transformation of penal policies in the United States generally emphasize the role of political elites aided by conservative interest groups in fueling the nation's enthusiastic embrace of incarceration and other get-tough penal policies. While taking these factors into account, this book takes a broader look at the political and institutional context to understand what fueled the law-and-order debate ignited by political elites. After all, as discussed in Chapter 3, political elites in the United States have a long history of raising law-and-order concerns in an attempt to further their own political fortunes. And Americans have a long history of periodic intense anxiety about crime and disorder. Yet only recently have these concerns and anxieties resulted in such a dramatic and unprecedented transformation of penal policies in a more punitive direction. By understanding the subtleties of this institutional and political context, we can begin to grasp why elite political preferences for a war on crime had such profound consequences for penal policies despite contemporary public opinion polls showing that Americans can be quite ambivalent about the crime issue. Politicians alone cannot forge the public mood on law enforcement issues.

The Past as Prelude

Explaining the political reasons for the development of the carceral state – defined by its reliance on mass imprisonment and degrading punishment and its fierce attachment to the death penalty – is the central task of this book. Chapter 2 surveys and critiques the major existing explanations for the creation of this extensive and unforgiving carceral state, including what I term the law-and-order argument. While law-and-order explanations differ in significant respects, they share several important features. These accounts portray political elites as key catalysts in the politicization of the crime issue and the creation of a more punitive public. They suggest that the politics of law and order, that is, the "public contestation of the dynamics of crime, disorder, and their control," is a relatively recent phenomenon, dating back to the 1960s.[18] Prior to that the crime issue is assumed to have been largely insulated from partisan politics, at least at the national level. Belief was widespread that "crime, like the weather, is beyond political influence; and that the operation of the law and criminal justice should be above it."[19] In addition to analyzing and critiquing the law-and-order accounts, Chapter 2 discusses alternative explanations for the rise of the carceral state, including changes in the crime rate and the illegal drug trade, the emergence of a prison-industrial complex, shifts in public opinion, and changes in American political culture. While each of these explanations has considerable merit, they are not very political in the sense that they do not explain why political opposition to the carceral state was so muted. In short, as the give-and-take of interest groups is such a central aspect of American politics, why didn't liberal groups and others mobilize to resist mass imprisonment?

Chapter 3 uses historical evidence to challenge several key premises of the law-and-order argument: that the nationalization and politicization of the crime and punishment issue are relatively new phenomena; that the public's recent concerns about crime are unprecedented; and that we can safely ignore inherited institutions in any discussion of the politics of crime and punishment before the 1930s or even later because of the absence or late development of the basic federal crime control institutions. This critical evaluation serves as a vehicle to develop one leg of an alternate explanation, namely that the state structures and ideologies that eventually facilitated the incarceration boom and other contours of the carceral state were built up well before the 1970s.

With each campaign for law and order and against certain crimes and vices in earlier eras, state capacity accrued, as evidenced, for example, by the growth of the Federal Bureau of Investigation (FBI) and the federal prison system, and by the militarization of crime control. As each campaign receded, the institutions it created did not necessarily disappear. Rather, the institutional capacity of the government expanded over time. Thus the periodic calls for law and order and the attacks on the designated vices of the moment were more likely to result in concrete policies with real ramifications. The politics of law and order became less symbolic and expressive and more substantive and instrumental. Politicians' strategic use since the 1960s of calls for law and order as a political mobilization strategy is not a new phenomenon in U.S. history. But unlike earlier tough-on-crime campaigns, the latest push for law and order resulted in wide-ranging changes in penal policies that have had concrete consequences for the millions of people behind bars in the United States today and for the tens of millions who have a direct connection to the criminal justice apparatus. The consequences have been different because of the vastly different institutional and political context in which the campaigns against crime have been carried out since the 1960s. That institutional and political context not only has encouraged mass imprisonment and capital punishment as the preferred policies, but has also impeded the mobilization of countervailing groups to challenge the carceral state.

Social Movements, Interest Group Politics, and Institutions

This is not to argue that the punitive turn toward more prisons was entirely the result of increased state capacity at the national, state, and local levels. Something significant did change from the 1970s onward, but even that had historical and institutional roots. In addition to public officials and candidates championing the politics of law and order, numerous new groups began to mobilize around criminal justice issues and alter the political context. The role of conservative groups in promoting a more hardline position on crime and punishment is well documented. Left largely unexamined is why these conservative groups did not face more political opposition to their law-and-order crusades. What has been overlooked is the role of other groups, some of them identified with progressive and liberal causes, in facilitating – often unwittingly – a more punitive environment conducive to the consolidation of the carceral state. This book examines the development of four key movements and groups – the victims' movement, the women's movement, the prisoners' rights movement, and opponents of the death penalty – that mediated the construction of the carceral state in important ways.

Critical new factors were the timing and manner in which these groups organized and mobilized, but their formation and mobilization cannot be understood in isolation from history. While many of these groups and movements were new, they did not come out of nowhere. The prior history of U.S. crime and punishment in American political development and the particular political and institutional context in which these groups emerged circumscribed their strategies and opportunities and affected the debate over criminal justice policy in significant ways.

Another major argument of this book, then, is that penal policies are forged by particular social movements and interest groups within the constraints of larger institutional structures.[20] Most explanations for the escalating incarceration rate in the United States that emphasize the role of interest groups or social movements tend to stress the importance of conservative groups like the National Rifle Association (NRA), the consolidation of a powerful victims' rights movement, or the influence of organizations that have strong economic incentives to support an ever-expanding penal-industrial complex, like Corrections Corporation of America and Wackenhut Corrections Corporation, the largest of the for-profit prison firms. Liberal or progressive groups have not been left out of the picture entirely. The prime focus here has been on how growing liberal disillusionment with the rehabilitative ideal, and specific sentencing practices like indeterminate sentencing beginning in the late 1960s and 1970s, provided an important opening for conservatives to push penal policy in a more punitive direction.

The role of progressive penal reformers and their temporary allies on the right who were dissatisfied with the criminal justice system, but for different reasons, is an important part of the story. Liberal disillusionment with rehabilitation and attacks on sentencing policy from the right and left certainly provided a significant opening for penal policy to shift radically in the United States. But we need to look more systematically at groups and movements that are not the usual suspects in penal policy and yet have played pivotal roles in making public policy more punitive. Furthermore, we need to consider how the institutional context, not just conservative law-and-order politicians like Barry Goldwater and conservative groups like the NRA, facilitated a major shift in penal policy such that incarceration became the punishment of choice, justified in the name of deterrence and retribution without any pretense of rehabilitation.

By the 1990s, the elite consensus in favor of get-tough penal policies had become a formidable and defining feature of contemporary American politics, even as the extraordinary extent of the carceral state remained largely invisible and unexamined. The tenacity of this elite consensus should not lead us to assume that all-powerful political authorities operating in a political and ideological environment largely of their own making were single-handedly responsible for the creation of the U.S. penal state. The need for political and economic elites to legitimate control and coercion is an age-old theme in politics.[21] What's new here is identifying the particular features of the institutional and political landscape in the United States that mediated the emergence of a powerful elite consensus in favor of the carceral state over the past four decades or so. In short, whether state elites co-opt or facilitate social movements that challenge the status quo is historically contingent on particular political and institutional forces, as Charles Tilly reminds us.[22]

Just because political or economic elites desire a certain type of social control (such as massive imprisonment of African Americans in the wake of the rebellions of the 1960s and the deteriorating economy of the 1970s) or seek to create a new electoral base by igniting the law-and-order issue does not mean they automatically get what they want. A variety of political and institutional factors can stymie or facilitate their goals. This book identifies certain historical factors – such as the weakness of the American welfare state and a pattern of roundabout state-building induced by morally charged crusades – and some important contemporary ones (namely the role of several key interest groups and movements)

to explain why the creation of the carceral state did not face more political opposition. Women's groups, prisoners' rights organizations, and the
anti-death penalty movement faced seriously constrained political circumstances. While these groups did not instigate the law-and-order crusade,
they helped to facilitate it once elites declared war on crime and criminals.

My analysis challenges the view among some social control theorists
and other analysts that public support for more punitive policies was
unproblematic and automatic in the face of a political elite mobilized and
united behind such policies from the mid-1960s onward.[23] The politicization of law and order was more complex and contingent than is commonly assumed. Elite support for the policies that led to the development
of the penal state was initially more fragmented, fitful, and tentative,
even among reputed hard-liners like Richard Nixon and Ronald Reagan.
While conservative Republicans are most closely identified with the politics of law and order, liberal Republicans and Democrats have been key
architects of the penal state.[24] Despite Nixon's stress on law-and-order
themes in the 1968 presidential campaign, rates of imprisonment fell during his first term in office. On the eve of the prison-building boom, prison
reformers and analysts were cautiously optimistic about the prospects for
decarceration, especially in light of the successful campaign for the dein-
stitutionalization of the mentally ill.[25] Even as imprisonment rates began
to turn upward in 1973, the Nixon administration's National Advisory
Commission on Criminal Justice Standards and Goals was recommending
a ten-year moratorium on penal construction and closing existing facilities for juveniles.[26] Furthermore, the Nixon administration initially sat
on the sidelines of the national dispute over capital punishment.

Political opportunism and ideological zeal do not on their own explain
why the penal state was constructed. That opportunism and zeal were
mediated in important ways by interest groups and movements, many of
them not usually identified with conservative policies, and by an exceptional institutional context that turned out to be highly receptive to the
establishment of the carceral state. This helps to explain why the countervailing tendencies were not stronger. As Jonathan Simon and others suggest, we need to look at more than just the ideological and electoral relationship between state power and penal policies. We need to consider the
resources, the discourses, and the expertise political elites employ to promote certain policies.[27] Building on this, I argue that resources, discourses,
and expertise are best understood by examining them in the context of specific state and nonstate institutions and certain interest groups and social
movements that can serve as facilitating or countervailing forces. This
book attempts to identify meaningful analytical relationships between
interest groups and movements that are usually treated in isolation from
one another and that are usually examined through lenses other than their
contribution to the carceral state.

Politicians in other countries also attempted to exploit the law-and-order issue for electoral gain. For a variety of political, historical, and institutional reasons discussed in Chapter 4, a powerful conservative victims' movement emerged to help penal hard-liners in the U.S. case but not elsewhere. This movement viewed the rights of the victim and the rights of the accused and convicted as a zero-sum game. While political elites seeking to ensure electoral success or to contain rebellious populations exploited this movement, they did not single-handedly create it.

Using comparative and historical evidence, my analysis highlights specific aspects of the institutional and political development of the United States that favored the emergence of this potent, conservative, victims' movement founded on the compelling call for victims' rights. Being for victims and against offenders became a simple equation that helped knit together politically disparate groups ranging from the more traditional, conservative, law-and-order constituencies mobilized around punitive policies like "three-strikes-and-you're-out," to women's groups organized against rape and domestic violence, to gay and lesbian groups advocating for hate crimes legislation, to the Million Moms pushing for gun control.[28] "If the postmaterialist politics tends toward issues of good and evil, crime is a natural metaphor for evil," Caplow and Simon suggest.[29] Zimring, Hawkins, and Kamin echo this view when they argue that punishment policy has become a "zero-sum competition" between crime victims (good) and criminal offenders (evil). Citizens no longer have to calculate the costs and benefits of various policies. All they have to do is choose sides. Because the "implicit assumption is that anything that is bad for offenders must be beneficial to victims," the offenders lose out every time.[30]

Women and women's organizations played a central role in the consolidation of this conservative victims' rights movement that emerged in the 1970s in the United States. Chapters 5 and 6 analyze the relationship of feminism to the emergence of the victims' movement. For a variety of reasons, feminist groups – many of whom initially were skeptical of employing state power to further their goals – became champions of state intervention to address problems like rape and domestic violence. In doing so, they ended up reinforcing the stance of conservative law-and-order champions. Institutional factors, including the shallow roots of the U.S. welfare state and the distinct organizational structure and political base of the U.S. women's movement, help explain why the movements against rape and domestic violence in the United States were more vulnerable to being captured and co-opted by the law-and-order agenda of politicians, state officials, and conservative groups.

Chapter 7 analyzes the exceptional nature of the prisoners' movement in the United States. This movement was ignited behind prison walls. In its formative years, it was closely associated with broader issues involving race, class, and various struggles around injustice. The movement transformed several American prisoners into national and international celebrities, including Angela Davis, Eldridge Cleaver, Huey Newton, and George Jackson. Offenders became starkly associated in the public mind with controversial issues related to race and rebellion. As such, it became harder for a victims' movement to emerge that did not pit the rights of victims against the rights of offenders. These factors help explain a striking anomaly of the U.S. case: The United States, which had the most vibrant and extensive prisoners' movement in the 1960s and '70s, ended up facing the least political resistance to the rise of the carceral state in subsequent decades.

Capital punishment was also pivotal to reframing the politics of punishment so as to bolster the carceral state and further the consolidation of a conservative victims' movement. Chapters 8 and 9 analyze how the contentious politics surrounding the push to abolish capital punishment transformed the broader politics associated with criminal justice and law enforcement. The issue of capital punishment was anchored for several decades in the judicial system prior to the landmark *Furman* and *Gregg* decisions in 1972 and 1976 that, respectively, suspended and then reinstated the death penalty. The courts played a decisive role in the legal and political framing of capital punishment long before the consolidation of the contemporary anti-death penalty movement in the 1970s. Unlike in other countries, the battle about capital punishment would be played out primarily in the courts, not the legislature.

The more recent legal wrangling around the death penalty bolstered three tendencies conducive to the expansion of the carceral state. First, it legitimized public opinion as a central, perhaps *the* central, consideration in the making of penal policy. Second, it helped to embolden the deterrence argument – that is, the controversial contention that harsher sanctions greatly deter crime – which had been discredited in many other countries. Finally, it helped to enshrine a zero-sum view of victims and defendants in capital and noncapital cases that has been such powerful fuel for the consolidation of the conservative victims' movement in the United States. This political and legal reframing of capital punishment did more than just give the death penalty a new lease on life. It also helped to deflect critical attention away from the state's towering role in the making of penal policy and from a central question about state sovereignty – what should be the limits of the state's power to punish and kill?

In short, this book attempts to show what we miss by ignoring the long history of penal policy in our efforts to explain the rise of the carceral state. This rediscovery of the past should not come at the cost of slighting the particularities of the past three to four decades. Earlier institutional and ideological developments were important preconditions for the eventual rapid "take off" in the incarceration rate. A full explanation of the latter also requires attention to the "trigger" that eventually facilitated these rapid increases. The manner in which certain interest groups and social movements mobilized around crime and punishment issues from the 1970s onward was an important component of that trigger.

Qualifications to the Argument

Lest my argument be misunderstood, I offer several important qualifications. First, my analysis focuses primarily on national trends and developments in penal policy rather than regional or state ones, even though the diversity of imprisonment rates across the fifty states is enormous, far greater than what exists across Western Europe. For example, Louisiana and Texas, at the top of the list, incarcerate their citizens at four to five times the rate of Maine and Minnesota, which are at the bottom.[31] This great variation and the fact that crime control in the United States is primarily a local and state function, not a federal one, suggest that state, local, and perhaps regional factors might be more significant than national developments in explaining U.S. penal policies. A number of scholars have ably demonstrated how certain institutional and political factors at the state level are central to understanding a state's degree of punitiveness.[32] Others have shown how differences in socioeconomic variables, demographic factors, and crime rates help explain some of the state-by-state variation in incarceration and criminal justice policies.[33]

State-level differences are important and a ripe field for further investigation. However, the construction of such an expansive and unforgiving carceral state in the United States is also a national phenomenon that has left no state untouched, which justifies my focus on national developments. Despite the highly decentralized character of the U.S. criminal justice system and wide variations in regional and state incarceration rates, penal trends have converged significantly across the country. All fifty states have experienced a sizable increase in their incarceration rates over the past thirty years or so.[34] Between 1995 and 2003, the average rate of change in the incarceration rate was negative in only two states, Massachusetts and New York.[35] While the incarceration rate in Massachusetts dipped after 1995, in the late 1980s and early 1990s state legislators in this deep-blue state were seized by penal populism. They enacted a series of tough law-and-order initiatives, including adding thousands of cells to a prison system that had already tripled in size since 1980, and nearly succeeded in bringing back the death penalty to the Bay State.[36] Minnesota, widely credited for years with resisting the pull to punish, saw its imprisonment rate jump by more than 10 percent in 2003. Its incarceration rate of 155 per 100,000 surpasses Spain and the United Kingdom (England and Wales), which are at the top of the list in Western Europe (see Figure 1).[37]

Furthermore, while the federal government remains in many ways the junior partner in criminal justice policy, its role has expanded considerably. It sets the ideological climate, directs much of the research money on criminal justice, and provides important carrots and sticks to prod local communities and states to shift their criminal justice policies in a certain direction. Notable examples of this vast expansion of federal authority and institutional capacity in law enforcement include "truth-in-sentencing" legislation, which rewards states with federal money for ensuring that offenders spend at least 85 percent of their sentenced time in prison; the enormous growth of the Federal Bureau of Prisons, which was warehousing about 10 percent of the national prison population by the 1990s; and the growing use of the U.S. military for civilian law enforcement, notably in the war on drugs.[38]

The second qualification to my argument concerns my choice of cases and the question of whom is to blame. I focus here on four social movements and related interest groups – victims, women, prisoners, and death penalty activists. This is by no means an exhaustive list. For example, more work needs to be done on how the legal profession and legal organizations affected penal policy. And while I discuss the role of the National Association for the Advancement of Colored People (NAACP) and other civil rights organizations, most notably in my chapters on the prisoners' rights movement and capital punishment, more work needs to be done here as well.

Let me also emphasize that I am not blaming the women's movement, the prisoners' rights movement, and opponents of the death penalty for the rise of the carceral state and the consolidation of a powerful victims' rights movement. My analysis underscores how these movements were *highly* constrained by historical and institutional factors, and some strokes of bad luck and bad timing. In some cases, they may have had a real choice to pursue another path. But in many instances their choices were sharply constricted by factors that were beyond their control. Their immediate political and strategic choices had many long-term consequences, some of which could not have been predicted at the time.

Identifying the political factors that help us understand the construction of the carceral state beginning in the 1970s is not the same as identifying all the factors that sustain it today. It may well be that the political dynamics driving the carceral state over the past three decades is not a unitary phenomenon and thus no one explanation will suffice. For example, Franklin Zimring suggests that the period be broken up into three separate eras characterized by different politics and policies. In the current phase, vested financial interests like private prison companies and prison guards' unions may be more critical in explaining the ongoing growth of the carceral state than in the previous two eras he identifies.[39]

The longer historical view I adopt is distinct from a couple of other explanations for the carceral state that, in my view, overemphasize the deep past at the cost of slighting the particularities of the more recent past. The history of crime and punishment in American political development is complex. In digging back into the past to demonstrate how issues of law and order have been integral to American political development, I do not mean to suggest that the United States has had a deeply punitive political culture from early on, traceable perhaps to its Puritan roots or the "culture of honor" in the South, of which the carceral state is the latest manifestation.[40] Political culture matters in my alternative explanation, but in a more nuanced way. The critical factor is not that the United States has a deep-seated history of moralism and punitiveness. Rather, as demonstrated in Chapter 3 in particular, Americans have been habituated throughout much of their history to indulge in a politics of moralism and law and order in the context of a state that, until recently, had rather limited capacity and legitimacy in the area of law enforcement. Thus, the politics of law and order were largely but not entirely symbolic for much of U.S. history. Nonetheless, they provided an important means to build up the law enforcement apparatus slowly and subtly in an environment where distaste for the targeted crime and criminal of the moment had to compete with distaste for a real state with normal policing powers. As state capacity accrued, this overheated rhetoric had more concrete consequences.

The argument of this book is also distinct from some social control explanations for the carceral state that stress the deep past to the near exclusion of the present. While imprisonment and capital punishment are the ultimate social control mechanisms, it is a mistake to view the creation of the carceral state as merely the latest chapter in a book that began with slavery and moved on to convict leasing, Jim Crow, and the ghetto to control African Americans and other "dangerous classes."[41] While there are similarities between these institutions, it is important not to flatten out their differences and the variations in the political, institutional, and economic context that created and sustained them. Treating these social control institutions as one and the same minimizes the unprecedented nature of the incarceration boom in the United States since the 1970s. For all the horrors of the convict-lease system, relatively few blacks were subjected to it in the decades following the Civil War, though many more feared it. Today's incarceration rate of nearly 7,000 per 100,000 African-American males dwarfs the number of blacks imprisoned in the South under convict leasing.[42] Although today's policies of mass imprisonment are undeniably about race and social control, it is important to look more specifically at the political and institutional context that sustains them.

This brings me to the final qualification of my argument – the question of what weight to give race in any explanation of the construction of the U.S. penal state. Certainly American political development is exceptional because of the twin and related legacies of slavery and race. But the United States did not end up with the carceral state merely because racial cleavages have been so central to American political development. Prisons became one of the main arenas to respond to the unrest of the 1960s and 1970s because of the way race interacted with a complex array of other specific political and institutional developments elaborated in Chapter 7 and elsewhere. As Cathy Cohen and Michael Dawson remind us in their critical overview of the study of race in American politics, every time we use race as an explanation we need to problematize and contextualize it.[43] That is what I have tried to do here.

In this sense, race is just the starting point of the explanation. If it is not bound to a particular political, historical, and institutional context, race explains everything about American political development and thus explains very little. If we are to unravel the political causes for the rise of the carceral state, we have to be drawn intensely back both to the long past of the last couple of centuries and to the more recent past of the last three to four decades. The more recent past needs to be viewed alongside the long history of the politics of law and order and alongside the ongoing and epic tension between the two orderings that King and Smith identify as central features of American politics and American history – the "white supremacist" order and the "transformative egalitarian" one.[44]

In short, an extraordinary outburst of political activism and unrest gripped the United States, Europe, and other countries in the 1960s and 1970s. Looked at more closely, this tide of unrest was hardly uniform from one country to the next. The social movements that burst forth in the United States during this period developed in distinctive ways because of important differences in the historical and institutional context. These differences help explain why it has been more expedient for U.S. politicians and public officials to stoke society's and victims' punitive impulses rather than respond to concerns about crime by emphasizing prevention, rehabilitation, services for victims, fundamental economic and social changes, and, yes, social justice. The differences also help explain why, as the United States began voraciously incarcerating its residents at unprecedented rates and brought back state executions with a vengeance, this vast expansion of state power went largely unchallenged.

The Future of the Carceral State

Today the United States has a deeply entrenched carceral state that is "long on degradation and short on mercy."[45] Like many historical-institutional accounts of the development of social policy, this one can be read as highly pessimistic about the prospects for changing that reality.[46] After all, institutions and interests tend to be deeply embedded. Once social policy veers off on one path, it is hard to shift it to another. Political leaders, whatever their intentions and strategic preferences, are highly constrained by the institutional landscape. Their actions tend to have unanticipated consequences that can make matters worse. However, there is another central feature of my analysis to keep in mind – that political outcomes can still be highly contingent. As Raymond Aron observed, major historical events are always "born of general causes [and] completed, as it were, by accidents."[47]

If we are to begin to dismantle the U.S. carceral state, it is important to focus a spotlight on the more than two million people behind bars at this moment and on the millions of Americans who are marked for life because they have a felony conviction, or they have a parent, child, or sibling sent up the river. We also need to unlock the doors to both the distant and the more recent past to understand the complex institutional and political context out of which the carceral state was forged.

The final chapter briefly highlights the analytical contribution of this work to the study of American political development. But its central focus is more prescriptive than analytical. It speculates on the future of the carceral state. Unlike the earlier chapters, Chapter 10 focuses more intently on contemporary penal policy. Building on some of the insights from the preceding chapters, it focuses on the political prospects for building a strong reform coalition in the near future to challenge the carceral state.

Certainly institutions can be highly constraining and the policy paths are rather fixed. But political openings do occur, and then the political future is less constrained by the institutional past and present. These moments are usually few and far between, but they can have profound political consequences. And all the political ferment and mobilization in anticipation of that opening help determine whether major public policy reforms succeed or not.

2 LAW, ORDER, AND ALTERNATIVE EXPLANATIONS

"Seek simplicity and distrust it."

– Alfred North Whitehead[1]

T HE PROBLEM OF THE PRISON was central to major political theorists of the eighteenth and nineteenth centuries. The role that punishment and imprisonment served in maintaining social order, legitimizing the state, and reforming the soul were key concerns of thinkers like Mill, Bentham, Kant, Montesquieu, Tocqueville, and Francis Lieber, the first named professor of political science in the United States. Years ago prisons also transfixed the public. American penitentiaries were a prime sightseeing destination for foreign and domestic tourists. Prison officials charged entrance fees and put prisoners on view as if they were in a zoo, sometimes hosting thousands of tourists in a single day.[2] Charles Dickens reportedly told the warden of Cherry Hill prison after a visit: "The Falls of Niagara and your Penitentiary are two objects I might almost say I most wish to see in America."[3] By contrast, the contemporary carceral state has been largely invisible. What caused the country's incarceration boom and the political, social, and economic consequences of this unprecedented experiment in public policy have not been a major focus of social science research or public concern.

This chapter critically analyzes half a dozen of the contending theories of the origins of the carceral state. It takes as its starting point that the penal system in any society cannot be understood as "an isolated phenomenon subject only to its own laws."[4] Rather, it is deeply embedded in a particular social, political, historical, and institutional context. Reductionist explanations for the rise of the carceral state that examine the country's penal system in isolation from other institutions and broader political currents are inadequate. So are ones that exclusively emphasize narrow variables like fluctuations in the unemployment rate or demographic shifts separate from the wider political context.[5] After first outlining the extent of the carceral state, this chapter critically evaluates the most popular reductionist explanation – the claim that more crime causes more prisons. It then examines five competing explanations that have some merit but are still inadequate: changes in public opinion; the rise of the prison-industrial complex; the illegal drug trade; the politicization of law and order by politicians and public officials; and major shifts in American political culture. It points toward an alternative and complementary explanation that builds on these other accounts, particularly law-and-order explanations, but shifts attention more squarely to the institutional inheritance and to the role of social movements and interest groups.

The Contours of the Carceral State

The carceral state has been a largely invisible feature of American political development, not a contested site of American politics. Any full analysis of how this carceral state was built must begin by acknowledging that the United States now has a carceral state and by noting its central features. The extent of the carceral state is breathtaking and defies any characterization of the United States as a weak state.

Imprisonment has become a "pervasive event" in the lives of the poor and of blacks, Hispanics, and other minorities.[6] About half of the growth in U.S. incarceration since the early 1970s has been fueled by removing more African Americans from their communities.[7] While the proportion of blacks among those arrested for violent crimes dipped slightly from the mid-1970s to the early 1990s, the proportion of blacks in prison skyrocketed.[8] By the mid-1990s, the combined incarceration (prison and jail) rate for adult black males in the United States was nearly 7,000 per 100,000 compared to about 1,000 per 100,000 for adult white males (see Figure 1, p. 3).[9] Today three out of four prison admissions are either African American or Hispanic.[10] Members of minority groups and the poor also comprise a disproportionate number of people on death row. The United States is currently imprisoning black men in state and federal prisons at about five times the rate that black men were incarcerated in South Africa in the early 1990s on the eve of the end of apartheid.[11] If current trends continue, about one in three black males and one in six Hispanic males born today in the United States are expected to serve some time behind bars.[12] Young black men must routinely contend "with long terms of forced confinement" and the "stigma of official criminality in all subsequent spheres of social life, as citizens, workers, and spouses," according to Bruce Western. The "profound social exclusion" they experience significantly undermines "the gains to citizenship hard won by the civil rights movement."[13]

Nationally, women are the fastest growing sector of the incarcerated population. The number of women in U.S. prisons has risen more than eight-fold since 1980.[14] The annual growth rate of female prisoners has averaged 5 percent since 1995, amply exceeding the 3.3 percent increase for incarcerated males.[15] The total number of women locked away in U.S. prisons and jails is now more than double the *entire* prison populations of France or Germany.[16] An estimated two-thirds of incarcerated women and one-half of incarcerated men are parents of children under age 18.[17] More than 1.5 million children in the United States have a parent in state or federal prison, or about triple the number in the mid-1980s.[18] Many of these incarcerated parents lose contact with their children or even knowledge of their whereabouts.[19]

The expansion of the carceral state has been a costly drain on government budgets, soaking up money that otherwise would be available for public services like higher education and health care. In 2001, the United States spent a record $167 billion on the criminal justice system, an increase of 165 percent in constant dollars from 1982 and about a three-fold increase since the early 1970s.[20] The criminal justice system accounted for 7 percent of all state and local government spending in 2001, an amount roughly equal to what was spent on health care and hospitals.[21] In the 1990s, spending on corrections grew more quickly than all other line items in state budgets except health care.[22] Brooklyn has thirty-five "million-dollar blocks" where so many residents have been sent to state prison, at an average annual cost of at least $30,000 each, that the total cost of their incarceration will exceed $1 million. For one Brooklyn block, the expense will surpass $5 million.[23] For about a decade now, states have spent more on building prisons than on building colleges and universities.[24] In a number of states, notably California, New York, and Florida, there has been a direct inverse relationship between increased outlays for prisons and decreased outlays for higher education.[25]

Despite record spending on corrections, many prisoners in the United States are housed in overcrowded, disease-infested facilities where they are subjected to violent, unhealthy, even deadly conditions. Prisoner-on-prisoner rape is endemic.[26] The millions of people who cycle in and out of the correctional system each year are exposed to deadly infectious diseases, including HIV/AIDS, hepatitis C, and drug-resistant strains of tuberculosis and staph, which are at epidemic proportions in some prisons. Fearful of being required to treat huge numbers of infected prisoners at crushing costs, some penal facilities have actually cut back on testing for these diseases.[27]

Numbers alone do not fully convey the distinctiveness of the U.S. carceral state. In short, "American punishment is comparatively harsh, comparatively degrading, comparatively slow to show mercy."[28] Some European countries have moved recently toward harsher sanctions in specific areas, including drug-dealing, terrorism, and certain types of violent crime. But the overall thrust in Europe has been toward milder penal policies that are strikingly at odds with the harsh, degrading treatment that permeates the U.S. carceral state and would be unthinkable in many European countries.[29] One notable exception may be Britain, which over the last dozen or so years has become more enthralled with the American style of punitive justice.[30]

The idea that the punishment should be proportional to the crime remains a cornerstone of the criminal justice system in many other Western countries, but not in the United States. The U.S. Supreme Court permits police to jail drivers overnight for not wearing seat belts, and it ruled that life sentences for minor infractions like the theft of $150 in videotapes under California's "three-strikes-and-you're out" law are constitutional.[31] Property offenders and drug users rarely find themselves incarcerated in France, Germany, and other European countries, while nonviolent offenders comprise more than half of the jail and prison population in the United States.[32] After nearly two decades of get-tough policies in France, average time served was still just eight months in 1999, roughly a doubling since 1975. In 1996, the average time served in U.S. state prisons was fifty-three months.[33] Violent offenders in the United States spend five to ten times as long in prison as those in France.[34] Nonviolent offenders accounted for more than three-quarters of the growth in U.S. admissions to state and federal prisons between 1978 and 1996.[35] In 1998, the number of nonviolent offenders incarcerated in the United States exceeded one million people for the first time.

Physical and sexual abuse comparable to the degrading abuses at the Abu Ghraib prison in Iraq that sparked worldwide condemnation when they were exposed in April 2004 is not unheard of in U.S. jails and prisons.[36] Some human rights experts contend that conditions at Guantánamo Bay, where the United States is holding "enemy combatants" captured in Afghanistan and elsewhere, may actually be better than those in many state prisons.[37] The United States has witnessed a revival of punishment practices that had almost disappeared in the West, including public shaming and degrading public labor, like the return of the notorious chain gang.[38] In 1994, Governor Fife Symington of Arizona boasted about the cruelties of a new prison planned for his state. "It will be a hell-hole [to which] no man will ever want to go," he said.[39] At penal farms in the South, prisoners, many of them African American, do backbreaking work as field hands in the blazing sun. Trailed by packs of hounds, they are watched over by armed guards who are authorized to shoot to kill and are addressed as "Boss" in a convention dating back to the days of slavery.[40] Alabama continued until 1998 the practice of chaining prisoners who misbehaved to hitching posts – something no state had done for a quarter of a century – and required prisoners caught masturbating to wear special flamingo pink uniforms.[41] Oklahoma and Louisiana still host prison rodeos where, as members of the public look on, prisoners compete in dangerous events like wresting a tobacco sack from between the horns of a Brahman bull released into an arena.[42]

The U.S. carceral state does not just reach back into the past for its punishments. It has the dubious distinction of being at the leading edge of new punishment technologies and techniques. The United States is the forerunner of penal innovations like boot camps for young offenders, electronic monitoring, and supermax prisons, where offenders are kept nearly round the clock in windowless, spartan cells designed to eliminate virtually any human contact and interaction.[43]

U.S. penal practices starkly underscore that offenders are not just like everyone else. The practice of "civil death" is widespread in the United States. Prisoners and former prisoners are denied a wide range of civil and political rights, like the right to vote and to be licensed in certain professions, including hairdressing in some states.[44] Many ex-felons are ineligible for social services such as public housing, student loans, and welfare benefits.[45]

By contrast, the guiding principle in much of Europe is that life in prison should approximate life on the outside as much as possible.[46] While European countries vary in how much they live up to this ideal, the dominant idea that pervades European debates over penal policy is that convicted criminals and prisoners should not be considered lower status persons. As such, the prison and the whole community should be enlisted to give the offender "a real chance to become a free citizen again."[47] For example, German prisoners are expected to work at jobs comparable to those in the real world. They enjoy far-reaching protections from arbitrary dismissal and are even entitled to unemployment benefits and four weeks of vacation a year.[48] While bright day-glo uniforms are commonplace in the United States, French prisoners generally do not wear uniforms, and German prison uniforms are supposed to resemble street clothing as much as possible.[49] In U.S. prisons, there is no assumption of privacy. Prisoners are routinely housed in barred, locked cells that afford them no privacy and are regularly subjected to body cavity searches and unannounced searches of their cells. By contrast, one of the liveliest controversies in German prison law recently was whether guards should be required to knock in all cases before entering prisoners' cells.[50]

The persistence of capital punishment is another key feature of the U.S. carceral state. The retention of capital punishment and the long shadow that the death penalty casts over U.S. politics, culture, and society are the starkest examples of how singularly unforgiving the U.S. carceral state is. Western Europe had its last state execution in 1977, and Europe today is a death-penalty-free zone. By contrast, support for the death penalty has remained strong in the United States since the country resumed executions in 1977. This is evidenced by public opinion polls, the rising tide of executions in the 1980s and 1990s, and the approximately 3,400 people sitting on death row today. The United States is the only advanced industrialized country besides Japan that actively retains the death penalty. In Japan, the practice of capital punishment is cloaked in extreme secrecy and has not been a central issue in local or national politics.[51] By contrast, the enthusiasm with which U.S. politicians and public officials began embracing the death penalty so as to demonstrate their law-and-order credentials is nothing short of remarkable.

By the 1990s, it was hard to find prominent candidates for national or statewide office who publicly opposed capital punishment. The death penalty also became a major factor in judicial elections, especially in states that retained capital punishment and permitted judges to override a jury's sentence of life imprisonment and impose the death penalty.[52] Candidates who opposed the death penalty, notably Massachusetts Governor Michael Dukakis in the 1988 presidential race against Vice President George H. W. Bush, and Democratic Governor Mario Cuomo of New York in his 1994 race against George Pataki, were vilified by their political opponents and in the press.[53]

This enthusiasm for the death penalty puts the United States at odds with global trends. Since 1985, more than 50 countries have abolished capital punishment (for a total of 118) and only 4 have reinstated it.[54] While 78 other countries and territories retain the death penalty, the actual number of executions in any year is concentrated in a handful of countries. In 2003, 84 percent of all known executions took place in just four countries – China, Iran, the United States, and Vietnam.[55]

More Crime, More Time

The United States is distinctive not only because of the existence of a vast punitive carceral state, but also because of the vast gap between criminal justice policies and politics on the one hand and empirical knowledge about crime and punishment on the other.[56] For example, a 2001 report by the National Research Council found that data on the consumption, markets, pricing, and distribution of illegal drugs was so inadequate that it was impossible to formulate effective policies to deal with drug abuse.[57] By the mid-1990s, federal spending on criminology research comprised less than one percent of national crime expenditures.[58] Public officials at the national and state levels have been reluctant to fund studies that examine the relationship between crime and more punitive policies, such as mass imprisonment. Until recently, federal research funding agencies devoted nearly all their resources to studying other criminal justice issues.[59] In California, hard-liners opposed funding any study of the impact of the state's "three-strikes-and-you're-out" law. They feared the data might show, as Franklin Zimring and his colleagues eventually demonstrated, that this draconian penal policy, which is likely to result in a sizable bulge in the prison population fifteen to twenty years after its enactment in 1994, had no significant effect on lowering the crime rate.[60]

The gap between penal policy and empirical knowledge is most apparent in the widespread acceptance of the claim that an ever-escalating crime rate is to blame for the prison buildup. This explanation rests on two main pillars. First, that the number of people in prison rose over the past thirty years because the United States became an increasingly violent, crime-ridden country. Second, other Western countries have lower incarceration rates because they have less violence and less crime. Both of these contentions wither under closer scrutiny.

As a preface to any discussion of crime trends, one needs to keep in mind how politicized and unreliable U.S. crime statistics can be.[61] The FBI's Uniform Crime Reports (UCR), which are based on data supplied to the agency by local police, often provide a distorting and misleading picture of crime trends and have a bias toward maximizing the appearance of crime.[62] For example, the FBI instructs local police departments to record as "murder" any instance in which a dead body is found and the police officer believes the person was murdered. The incident remains classified as murder for the UCR even if the coroner later determines it was a suicide or the prosecutor eventually determines it was justifiable homicide or accidental death. In Sweden, by contrast, "a death is not officially recorded as a murder *until someone has been found guilty in court of having committed the crime.*"[63] Under the FBI regulations, if five people are attacked by one person in a bar fight, each attack is counted as a separate assault, even if the legal definition of assault is not met, no one is arrested, and no one presses charges. The FBI crime reports do not distinguish between attempted and completed crimes, nor between felony theft and misdemeanor theft. For a long time the FBI statistics did not even distinguish between statutory and forcible rape.[64]

Although the UCR and the National Crime Victimization Surveys, an alternative measure of crime developed in the early 1970s to compensate for the UCR's shortcomings, are problematic, a consensus exists about broad trends in crime and imprisonment in the United States.[65] Most experts in criminal justice basically agree that "there is no general relationship between crime rate trends and the rate of incarceration."[66] The steepest increase in crime in the United States occurred during the 1960s, when the rate of imprisonment was falling. After that, crime rates rose in the 1970s, declined in the early 1980s, rose in the late 1980s, and declined from the early 1990s onward. During this entire twenty-year period, the incarcerated population was continuously increasing.[67] State-level developments also cast doubt on any simple correlation between higher crime rates and mass incarceration. States "with high crime rates sometimes also have high rates of imprisonment, but sometimes they do not."[68] The most striking example is the Dakotas. South Dakota imprisons its residents at about two times the rate of North Dakota, even though the two states have similar demographics, geography, and crime rates.[69]

There is some relationship between the crime rate and the incarceration rate, but it is slight. Analysts using a variety of methodologies have found that the deterrent and incapacitation effects of incarceration in bringing down the crime rate are small, and that the offenses avoided through greater use of prisons tend to be nonviolent rather than violent crimes.[70] A 1993 report by the National Academy of Sciences that was commissioned and paid for by the Department of Justice under the Reagan administration noted that the average prison time per violent offense tripled between 1975 and 1989, without any appreciable effect on the level of violent crime.[71] After reviewing several of the leading studies on the relationship between crime and incarceration in the United States, William Spelman concluded that only about a quarter of the drop in violent crime over the last twenty-five years or so could be attributed to the prison buildup.[72] Bruce Western's recent research concludes that mass imprisonment has had a more modest effect on the crime rate. He demonstrates that only 10 percent of the serious drop in crime between 1993 and 2001 was due to the gigantic growth in the state prison population. The remaining 90 percent most likely would have happened anyway due to other factors, like changes in city policing.[73]

These findings are consistent with studies of long-term patterns of crime in the United States and Europe. Violent crime fell significantly from roughly the mid-nineteenth to the mid-twentieth century, when it began to rise steeply but never reached the peak of the previous century. While scholars of criminal history disagree about why crime rates tumbled for a century, virtually none of them attribute this backward J-curve to innovations in criminal justice, such as changes in sentencing policies or increased reliance on imprisonment.[74] Comparative studies of contemporary penal trends in Europe also indicate that crime and incarceration rates move quite independently of one another. Some European countries reacted to higher crime rates since the 1960s by relying more on imprisonment. Others underwent a substantial decarceration.[75]

While some European incarceration rates have been on the rise in recent years, they remain well below the U.S. rate (see Figure 1, p. 3). This has prompted the popular belief that differences in the incarceration rates between the United States and Europe are the result of differences in their crime rates. After all, U.S. rates of death and life-threatening injury from intentional attacks are four to eighteen times as great as in other developed countries. But lethal violence makes up just a small percentage of total crime.[76] Thus it is hard to see how violent offenders alone could be responsible for such a massive increase in the U.S. prison population.[77] With the exception of lethal violence, the rates of serious forms of crime are not dramatically higher in the United States.[78] Some studies indicate that the United States actually lags behind many other countries in most of the major crime categories.[79]

This is not to say that the high levels of lethal violence are insignificant factors in explaining why the U.S. has such high levels of incarceration. Franklin Zimring and Gordon Hawkins contend that the relatively large amount of lethal violence in the United States prompts citizens to fear excessively many forms of criminal behavior because they mistakenly "imagine them all committed by extremely violent protagonists."[80] Here the media are also partly to blame, as they have misrepresented crime trends, the causes of crime, and who is most likely to be a victim. The media have contributed to the exaggerated public fear of crime and promoted simplistic solutions based on emotion and the most heinous crime of the moment rather than sound public policy.[81] With some notable exceptions, the media have also ignored the existence of the carceral state and its many negative consequences.[82] It is not obvious, however, that the U.S. media have been radically different from media elsewhere. One of the problems is that most of the literature on the effects of the media on the politics of crime and justice is based on the U.S. case. The comparative work that does exist suggests that the media, especially television, have been instigators of punitive penal populism in many countries, not just the United States.[83] In short, if the media in the United States are not that exceptional, and if lethal crime makes up only a small proportion of total crime in the country, it is hard to see how violent crime is driving the massive rates of incarceration. The fact is that mass imprisonment is only weakly related to the underlying crime rates.

A More Punitive Public

Despite ample evidence to the contrary, many policy makers continue to subscribe to a very simple explanation for the growing prison population – more crime. Their "solution to this is equally simple: expand prison capacity."[84] They portray the rising prison population as an act of fate over which they have little control. A slightly more complex version of this argument attributes tougher penal policies to a tougher public. A central contention is that the U.S. public is more punitive than it once was and more punitive than people elsewhere. Policy makers are portrayed as merely responding to an increased demand from a rational and fearful public for tougher policies in the face of a dramatic increase in crime.[85]

A number of public opinion surveys offer compelling evidence that public attitudes in the United States have hardened on criminal justice matters even though they have liberalized on a range of other issues, such as sexual behavior, abortion, and civil liberties. In her study of popular views of crime, Kathlyn Gaubatz notes that criminals are the only remaining group in society that it is acceptable to hate.[86] Rising support for the death penalty,[87] for imposing capital punishment for retributive rather than deterrent reasons, and a growing belief that the courts are too lenient with criminals are all evidence of a more punitive public.[88]

A hardened public certainly has contributed to the tougher penal policies, but explanations that focus primarily on public opinion are problematic. While public attitudes about crime and criminals appear to have hardened, it is misleading to portray the public as overwhelmingly punitive. The role of public opinion in penal policy is extremely complex. For all the talk about a more punitive public mood, the public's anxiety about crime is "subject to sudden, dramatic shifts, unrelated to any objective measure of crime."[89] The widespread impression that public concern about crime skyrocketed in the 1960s with the jump in the crime rate and the general uneasiness associated with the riots and demonstrations of those years is not solidly supported.[90] Ironically, the public began to identify crime as a leading problem in the mid-1990s, just as the crime rate was dramatically receding (see Figure 3).[91]

The public certainly "accepts, if not prefers" a range of hard-line policies like the death penalty, "three-strikes" laws, and increased use of incarceration.[92] But support for these more punitive policies is "mushy," partly because public knowledge of criminal justice is so sketchy.[93] The public consistently overestimates the proportion of violent crime and the recidivism rate.[94] Possessing limited knowledge of how the criminal justice system actually works, people in the United States and elsewhere generally believe the system is more forgiving of offenders than it really is.[95] Overly simplistic public opinion surveys reinforce the "assumption of an unflinching punitive 'law and order' tilt of U.S. public opinion on crime" and mask "large and recurrent" differences between the views of blacks and whites on the criminal justice system.[96] Moreover, policymaking elites also appear to misperceive public opinion on crime, viewing the public as more punitive and obsessed with its own safety than is in fact the case.[97]

Some of the more sophisticated surveys and focus groups reveal a potentially more forgiving public.[98] Polls in the United States and elsewhere consistently show that when people are asked broad questions about whether they believe judges are too lenient, the overwhelming majority answers yes. Yet when respondents are asked to choose an appropriate sentence after being given the details of a specific crime, the offender, and the judge's reasoning, the sentence lengths they choose generally correspond to what judges choose, or in some cases are shorter than what criminal justice officials recommend.[99] While it is commonly assumed that public support for rehabilitation has vanished, surveys show that support for rehabilitating offenders remains deep, sometimes exceeding the public's enthusiasm for punishment.[100]

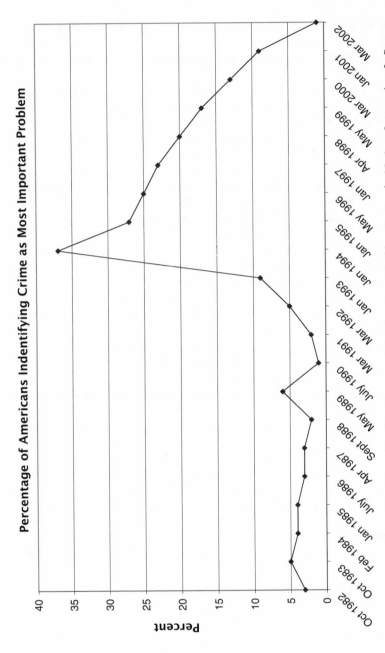

Percentage of Americans Indentifying Crime as Most Important Problem

Figure 3. Percentage of Americans Identifying Crime as Most Important Problem Facing the Nation. *Source:* Ann L. Pastore and Kathleen Maguire, eds., *Bureau of Justice Statistics Sourcebook of Criminal Justice Statistics – 2001* (Washington, DC: U.S. Department of Justice, 2002), p. 100, Table 2.1.

Prison-Industrial Complex

Many activists seeking to reverse the nation's penal policies single out the emergence of a powerful prison-industrial complex – not the crime rate or public opinion – as the main engine driving the nation's prison-building boom.[101] The prison-industrial complex argument has two main prongs. First, that "penal Keynesianism," or what Mike Davis calls "carceral Keynesianism," is serving as an economic stimulus package for local communities hit hard by deindustrialization and other recent major economic shifts.[102] Second, that powerful economic interests are promoting the penal state in order to line their own pockets. Joseph T. Hallinan and others attribute the "race to incarcerate" to the emergence of powerful private groups like the Corrections Corporation of America (CCA) that stand to make enormous profits from prisons (especially privately run prisons) and to local communities, many of them in rural areas, that have latched onto prisons as a way to perk up their depressed economies.[103]

The wide range of individuals and corporations profiting handsomely from the burgeoning corrections industry is well documented.[104] Telecommunications companies have their eyes on the estimated $1 billion in telephone calls that people in prison make each year. In Tamms, IL, citizens so loved their new supermax prison, which cost $120,000 per cell to build, that a local sandwich shop renamed its specialty dish the "supermax burger." Like the prison, it came with "the works." The stock for CCA, the country's oldest and largest prison company, soared over 1,000 percent after its inception in 1983.[105] In Wallens Ridge, VA, the electronically armed fence that surrounds the new $77.5 million prison is a source of pride for prison officials. It is identical to the sophisticated sixteen-foot-high fence used by the Israeli government in the Golan Heights, according to the warden.[106] The American Jail Association promoted its 1995 conference with the crass slogan, "Tap Into the Sixty-Five Billion Dollar Local Jails Market."[107] Hallinan portrays the annual convention of the American Correctional Association (ACA), the largest private correctional organization in the country and once the epicenter of prison reform activities in the United States, as largely a corporate-sponsored trade fair for penal gadgets and services.[108]

Warden after warden told Hallinan that running a prison today is like running a business. Prison administrators now do time in the public sector, then cash in on their experience and connections to become "prison millionaires" at private firms servicing or operating prisons. The revolving door between the public and private sectors and the increased pressure to run prisons like businesses have fueled corruption and distorted public priorities.[109] One of the most lucrative areas for the corrections industry is contracting out prison labor at minimum or sub-minimum wages to private firms engaged in all sorts of commercial activities, from manufacturing designer shirts to making airline reservations and assembling computer circuit boards. The American Federation of Labor-Congress of Industrial Organizations (AFL-CIO) reported that tens of thousands of inmates working at below-market wages were generating more than $1 billion in sales by the mid-1990s.[110]

While the carceral state is certainly lucrative for some, there are several problems with primarily economic explanations for the prison boom. Hallinan includes numerous testimonies by enthusiastic prison administrators, corrections staff, and members of the community but provides little hard evidence about how prisons have actually buoyed local economies. Some analysts and activists involved in the burgeoning movement against mass incarceration contend it is a myth that prisons comprise a critical public works program for economically distressed communities.[111] Ruth Wilson Gilmore's research shows that, all things being equal, counties without prisons did better economically than counties with them.[112] Craig Gilmore, who helps citizens in rural California organize against the construction of prisons in their communities, says that local residents are often suckered into becoming boosters for penal facilities and that the purported economic windfall does not materialize.[113]

Much of the wrath of activists fighting the penal state is directed at companies that build and administer private prisons. While the private corrections industry is certainly a significant player in penal policy today, for-profit prisons are a relatively new phenomenon. The first private prison opened in 1983, a full decade into the current prison expansion. For all the talk of privatization, by 1997 there were only about 140 privately run penal facilities in the United States, holding 64,000 inmates, or a minuscule 3 percent of the entire population of confined adults.[114] While the corrections industry has become a major champion of the carceral state and is an important obstacle to dismantling it today, the prison-industrial complex was not the primary trigger of the prison boom.

The Illegal Drug Trade

Earlier periods of public alarm over crime, for example during Prohibition in the late 1920s and the "crime wave" of the late 1930s, resulted in relatively modest increases in incarceration rates. Contrary to the pattern of the last thirty years, incarceration rates did not climb continuously higher, but were cyclical. They retreated after peaking in 1931 and then again in 1939. "For political mobilization around law-and-order to produce a sustained increase in imprisonment, other conditions must be present," according to Caplow and Simon.[115] One important condition is the illegal drug trade, in their view.

The war on drugs launched in the mid-1980s is certainly a major factor in the construction of the carceral state. Both the number and proportion of drug offenders in prison exploded in recent decades. In 1980, the drug incarceration rate was 15 drug offenders in state and federal prisons per 100,000 adults. By 1996, the rate had increased more than nine-fold, to 148 per 100,000, "a rate greater than that for the entire U.S. prison system in the fifty years to 1973."[116] Despite the huge increase in law enforcement power in the 1990s, the total number of arrests in 2000 for any crime at the state or local level fell back to the 1991 figure. But the percentage of total arrests attributed to drug law violations soared by 50 percent.[117]

Some argue that political and economic elites launched the war on drugs, directed disproportionately at poor Americans and minority communities, so as to contain the social instability resulting from vast changes in the U.S. political economy.[118] Some of the data on drug arrests appear to support their claims. Between the mid-1970s and early 1990s, the overall percentage of those arrested for violent crimes who were black fell from 47.5 percent to 44.8 percent. But the percentage of prisoners who were black increased sharply after 1980, largely because of the disproportionate impact of the war on drugs.[119] While studies show that blacks are no more likely to use drugs than are whites, the percentage of blacks among drug arrests increased from slightly over 20 percent in the late 1970s to 42 percent in 1989.[120] If convicted of a drug offense, blacks were more likely to serve a longer sentence because of sentencing irregularities. The most notorious example is abuse of crack cocaine, a drug used primarily by poor urban blacks and Hispanics, which is punished 100 times more severely than abuse of powder cocaine, the drug of choice for middle-class whites.[121]

While significant, the war on drugs begun in the 1980s does not explain the birth of the carceral state. First, this drug war was not unprecedented. The country has periodically been convulsed by crusades against illegal substances, most notably in the Progressive era, the 1930s, and again in the 1950s.[122] Furthermore, the incarceration binge was well under way prior to the start of this latest war on drugs. The number of drug arrests increased sharply from the 1960s to the early 1970s, yet the total prison population held steady or decreased slightly. From the early 1970s to the mid-1980s, the number of drug arrests fluctuated while the prison population began its steady climb. It was only in the mid-1980s that drug arrests and the prison population began to increase in tandem.[123]

Second, public alarm over drug abuse does not automatically morph into more punitive policies. Germany and the Netherlands provide a good point of comparison. Confronted with the drug wave of the 1960s, public opinion in Germany and the Netherlands was overwhelmingly hostile and punitive to users. But the initial public policy response was quite different. Whereas German legislators enacted more repressive drug laws, Dutch officials softened sanctions against drug abuse for a complex set of internal reasons.[124] Another good example is Mormon-run Utah, which was liberalizing its drug laws in the 1970s during the so-called panic over drug abuse.[125]

Some suggest that it was not public alarm over drug abuse that prompted the massive lockup, but rather changes in the nature of the drug trade. In the 1980s, the scale of drug enterprises expanded rapidly with the introduction of new drugs and distribution strategies, most notably for "crack." Caplow and Simon argue that the rise of a large retail drug sales force furnished a nearly unlimited pool of offenders to be imprisoned. But they may be overstating the degree to which changes in the drug trade independently fed the politics of mass incarceration. A potentially unlimited pool of offenders is always available because "deviance is not a property *inherent* in any particular kind of behavior." Rather, deviance is a property conferred upon a certain behavior by the majority or by the powerful.[126] Moral panics or crime waves, such as the war on drugs, do not necessarily entail increases in the volume of deviance. Such moral panics involve "a rash of publicity, a moment of excitement and alarm, a feeling that something needs to be done."[127]

The war on drugs so dominated the public debate about crime and morality from the mid-1980s onward that it is easy to forget that illegal drugs were not integral to the early calls for law and order. The Nixon administration and the U.S. Congress initially treated marijuana and casual drug use as benign deviances not worthy of serious punishment. Similar to what happened during Prohibition, they sought to go after the major drug sellers and not to stress criminalization of possession and use.[128] In 1970, leaders of both parties applauded when Congress eliminated almost all federal mandatory minimum sentences for drug offenders.[129] The Nixon administration subsequently shifted its emphasis from treatment of hard-core users to punishment for both casual users and addicts. It did so in order to protect its right flank after Governor Nelson Rockefeller (R–N.Y.) declared that addiction had become a plague that threatened the lives of innocent middle-class children, and pushed through his draconian drug laws in 1973.[130] Nixon's new drug policy also provided a convenient cover to reorganize various agencies of the government to better serve the electoral and perceived national security needs of his administration.[131]

U.S. incarceration rates began their upward climb at the start of the second term of the Nixon administration. They continued to climb steadily during the 1970s, even though the country appeared ready to decriminalize marijuana on the eve of the 1976 election and the Carter administration took a more tolerant attitude toward drug use.[132] Presidents Reagan and George H. W. Bush subsequently declared war on drugs and pushed for much tougher penalties for drug offenders beginning in the mid-1980s, despite evidence of continually falling drug use.[133] They were prodded in part by the emergence in the late 1970s of a powerful grassroots movement of suburban parents bent on shifting the terms of the debate over drugs from public health to morality, fueling the zero-tolerance stance that has since undergirded drug policy.[134] Some black leaders also supported the war on drugs, at least for a time. After All-American basketball player Len Bias died in 1986 of a cocaine overdose, the Rev. Jesse Jackson, Sr., endorsed Reagan's drug war, calling drug abuse, "a threat to our culture greater than any ideology ever could be."[135] While the war on drugs certainly served as a major source of new prisoners, we need to understand the deeper political and institutional factors that help explain why the war on drugs, once initiated, faced so little public or political opposition.

Law-and-Order Explanations

When drug use was at its peak in 1979, very few Americans identified drugs as a pressing national problem. After President Reagan declared war on drugs in 1982 and renewed the call to arms in 1986, fewer than 2 percent of those polled identified drugs as the most important problem.[136] It was not until 1988 that the public identified drug abuse as a leading problem.[137] Given such volatility of public opinion on illegal drugs and other crime and punishment issues, some analysts emphasize the role of public officials in propelling the nation's enthusiastic embrace of mass imprisonment and other get-tough penal policies. They argue that the 1960s were a watershed period for law enforcement, as politicians truly nationalized the crime issue for the first time by staking out a tough law-and-order stance for electoral and ideological purposes. Prior to that, the argument goes, the federal government's involvement in criminal justice matters was limited, because crime was viewed primarily as a local or state issue, not a national one.[138] They suggest that politicians and policy makers are active architects of the more punitive public mood and not just passive transmitters of it. As such, crime policy is a product of the actions of political elites and not merely a reflection of the fears and anxieties of citizens.

These analysts tend to single out the 1964 presidential candidacy of Barry Goldwater as a major turning point. They contend that the politics of law and order initiated by Goldwater and promoted by subsequent aspirants to the White House – notably George Wallace, Richard Nixon, Ronald Reagan, and George H. W. Bush – politicized and nationalized the crime issue. As a result, legislators, law enforcement officials, and the public adopted a "get-tough" stance. They turned sharply away from the rehabilitative ideal and embraced punishment and retribution as the new goals of penal policy. Americans subsequently were far more willing to countenance a massive expansion of the prison system and greater use of the death penalty.

Some researchers have refined this theme. Katherine Beckett, for example, attributes the expansion of the criminal justice system and the law enforcement apparatus to a broader "conservative project of state reconstruction: the effort to replace social welfare with social control as the principle of state policy."[139] John Dillon Davey focuses on the politics of law and order at the state level. He attributes vast differences in state incarceration rates to whether individual governors succumbed to or resisted the law-and-order politics promulgated at the national level.[140]

In another version of the law-and-order argument, Caplow and Simon attribute the more punitive public and more punitive policies to the "governing through crime" strategy politicians pursued beginning in the 1960s to shore up their electoral base.[141] That base was weakened, in their view, due to shifts in the underlying structure of American politics, including the erosion of broad-based political parties, the emergence of single-issue interest groups, and the waning of public confidence in the government. In order to win elections, politicians ignited and inflamed the crime issue.

A related strand of the law-and-order argument concerns race. Conservatives and Southern Republicans, and later New Democrats like Bill Clinton, are charged with using the issues of crime and welfare to woo whites, because in the minds of many white Americans, both of these issues are identified negatively with blacks.[142] This strategy was fruitful not because of the inherent punitiveness of the American public at the time, but because it resonated with broader social conflicts, racial antagonisms, and shifts in the structure of American politics and the U.S. economy.[143]

This earlier work by Beckett, Caplow and Simon, and others is pathbreaking, because it highlights the role of elites in penal policy and draws our attention to some of the important broader contemporary political developments that facilitated the incarceration boom. My argument builds on this earlier work as it attempts to explain why these elites were so successful in shifting the discourse on crime and punishment so as to facilitate construction of the carceral state. In short, why didn't political elites face more countervailing pressures and opposition? To repeat, my account stresses the role of a broad range of groups and social movements and identifies some key features of the political and institutional landscape that played a significant mediating role. In short, it shows how the politics of law and order are propelled by more than just the shrewd electoral and ideological calculations of political elites.

Changes in American Political Culture

Some analysts point to deeper changes in American political culture to explain the embrace of the penal state. In particular, they single out the public's response to the apparent growing weakness of the state. They suggest that declining public confidence in social welfare programs and state interventions in the national economy are evidence of that weakness, as are periodic surges in the crime rate that sowed deep doubts about the ability of the state to perform its most traditional obligation – maintaining civil order. The decline in public confidence in social welfare programs has removed an important set of tools that the state could once use to tackle pressing social problems. Intensification of crime-control activities is an attractive way for the state to burnish the image of its competence and restore its sense of purpose.[144]

This theme is most fully articulated in David Garland's work. Garland identifies fundamental changes in the culture of the United States and Britain that he associates with the "coming of late modernity" to explain the rise of the penal state. In doing so, he presents a more nuanced and sophisticated analysis of the role of the public and political elites in constructing the carceral state. According to Garland, major transformations in the structure of capitalist production and markets, technological advances, the restructuring of the family, the emergence of suburbia, the rise of the electronic mass media, and the democratization of social and cultural life created a widespread sense of insecurity that undermined "penal-welfarism," the ruling framework for penal policy and social policy more broadly for much of the twentieth century. The penal-welfare state that took shape more than a century ago was premised on two central beliefs: that growing affluence together with the social reforms we now associate with the modern welfare state in the advanced industrialized countries would reduce crime; and that the state was responsible not just for the punishment and control of offenders but also for their care and rehabilitation.[145]

Rising crime rates in the postwar period in the context of the enormous social, political, and economic dislocations Garland associates with the arrival of late modernity brought about a crisis for penal-welfarism in the United States and Britain. Criminal justice experts and more lenient politicians and state officials were discredited.[146] As a consequence, penal-welfarism began "to collapse under the weight of a sustained assault upon its premises and practices," resulting in far more punitive policies and discourses that comprise the new "culture of control."[147] Garland emphasizes that these more punitive practices were not inevitable. He suggests that politicians and other public officials served as key intermediaries between the structural developments he identifies and the harsher penal policies that emerged.

To its credit, *The Culture of Control* forces us to think big. For Garland, the problem of crime and crime control is not a narrow one best examined within the specialized confines of criminological theory. Rather, he locates the study of crime and punishment at the center of social scientific and historical analysis. He ably identifies significant cultural trends that help explain recent major shifts in penal policy. In this respect, Garland's work is a much welcome corrective to other analyses that stress how hard-line penal policies are largely the creation of manipulative political elites who single-handedly generate hysteria and moral panics over crime to serve their own electoral and ideological needs.[148]

While Garland acknowledges that political factors played important mediating roles, he does not discuss these factors in any great detail. His focus on the big picture and broad cultural trends naturally comes at the cost of not examining in depth the specific factors that help explain why the United States and Britain, in his view, have responded to the arrival of late modernity with such harsh penal policies while other developed countries have not. At least not yet. The main political variable he identifies is that the United States and Britain, faced with the challenges of late modernity, embraced free-market neoliberalism and social conservatism to a degree not found elsewhere, resulting in more punitive penal policies.[149]

My analysis is both an affirmation of and a departure from Garland's "culture of control" argument. While political elites have been able to exploit the general culture of anxiety created by the economic, social, and political transformations Garland describes, the combination of elite behavior and broader cultural trends are insufficient to explain why the United States embraced imprisonment and other get-tough policies so wholeheartedly and enthusiastically.

At a very high level of generality, Garland is correct that the "politics of crime and punishment may well be about the form and future of the liberal state."[150] But there is another story to be told, one that focuses more specifically on the politics and governing institutions of developed liberal states confronted with the strains of late modernity. After all, the responses to these strains have been quite varied. Such a nuanced focus reveals that the politics of crime and punishment that built the carceral state were more fluid, multilayered, and less deterministic than is commonly assumed.[151] In subsequent chapters, I attempt to trace how some of the major social changes Garland identifies got funneled through different interest groups and institutions in the United States and elsewhere and thus had dissimilar consequences from country to country.[152]

In doing so, I use Britain, and to a lesser extent other advanced industrialized countries, as an important point of comparison. Garland places the United States and Britain together at the sharp end of the punitive stick. Britain certainly deserves the dubious distinction of being among the most punitive countries in Western Europe. But its penal apparatus, despite a significant prison buildup recently, is still skeletal compared to that of the United States. As I demonstrate in later chapters, U.S. and British penal policies have some striking dissimilarities due to major differences in their interest groups and social movements and the environment they operate in.

Interest Groups and Social Movements

Analysts have not entirely ignored the role of interest groups and social movements in building the carceral state. They have demonstrated, for example, how the NRA, victims' organizations, and other conservative groups like the American Legislative Exchange Council (ALEC) have been instrumental in pushing penal policy in a more punitive direction with the help of supportive political elites.[153] Liberal or progressive groups have not been left out of accounts that stress the role of interest groups. The prime focus here has been on how growing liberal disillusionment with the rehabilitative ideal and specific sentencing practices like indeterminate sentencing beginning in the late 1960s and 1970s provided an important opening for conservative groups and conservative public intellectuals like James Q. Wilson and Ernest van den Haag to move penal policy in a more punitive direction.[154]

The rehabilitative model, which first took hold in the Progressive era, is based on the idea that the main purpose of incarceration and other penal policies is to change the attitudes and behavior of convicted offenders so as to reduce recidivism and other antisocial behavior and improve the welfare of offenders.[155] Indeterminate sentences, which reward offenders for good behavior, were a cornerstone of the rehabilitative model. From the emergence of the prison system in the beginning of the nineteenth century until the early twentieth century, most states had determinate sentencing systems. Offenders generally served out a fixed term decided by the judge at the time of sentencing. With the rise of psychological, medical, and sociological explanations of criminal behavior in the early 1900s, prison reformers successfully pushed to have much of the control over the length of prison terms turned over to administrative authorities, usually parole boards. These boards individualized sentences based on the offender's capacity for and evidence of rehabilitation.[156]

Struggle for Justice, a 1971 report by the American Friends Service Committee, is the starkest and best known expression of liberal disillusionment with indeterminate sentences and the rehabilitative model. That report charges that the rehabilitative model was "bankrupt" after "a century of persistent failure."[157] It condemns individualized treatment because it gives the state enormous discretionary power to "control not just the crimes but the way of life" of offenders."[158] The report charges that the rehabilitative model perpetuates race and class discrimination by giving criminal justice professionals, the majority of whom are white and middle class, enormous power to decide who has been "rehabilitated" and who has not, and thus who is deserving of early release and who is not.[159] Reports like *Struggle for Justice* and books like Judge Marvin Frankel's *Criminal Sentences: Law Without Order*, which argues that sentencing discretion needed to be curbed because of great disparities in time served, prompted prominent liberal politicians, notably Senator Edward M. Kennedy (D-Mass.), to push for new federal sentencing guidelines and the abolishment of indeterminate sentences to address alleged sentencing disparities.[160]

In claiming that the rehabilitative approach neither reduced recidivism nor prevented crime (two of its main goals), liberal politicians like Kennedy and progressive groups like the American Friends Service Committee played into the hands of conservatives, some charge. At the time conservatives were attacking judges and parole boards for other reasons, notably their perceived leniency. Liberals and progressives unwittingly paved the way for a wholesale assault on the penal system and on the legitimacy and expertise of criminal justice professionals and experts. This provided an important opening for penal policy to become highly politicized at a time when the broader political environment was moving in a more conservative direction.[161]

Liberals' growing hostility toward indeterminate sentencing and their declining faith in the rehabilitative ideal reportedly made it easier for the federal government and individual states to enact mandatory minimum statutes, which inevitably led to increases in time served, David Rothman and others argue.[162] Liberals also came under fire for their unfounded conviction that transferring sentencing authority from judges and parole boards to newly created sentencing commissions would somehow insulate sentencing decisions from politics and populist pressures. This reportedly paved the way for the creation of sentencing commissions that increased time served, with a couple of notable exceptions, like the commissions established in Minnesota and Washington State.[163]

The argument that liberal disillusionment with the rehabilitative ideal was an important precondition for the creation of the carceral state is problematic in several respects, however. As Garland notes, the theoretical, philosophical, and political criticisms lobbed at the rehabilitative model in the 1960s and 1970s were nothing new. They had been around since the model began to take shape in the late nineteenth century and were buttressed by negative research findings beginning in the 1930s.[164] Furthermore, research in the 1970s had not demonstrated unequivocally that rehabilitation was a failure. Even Robert Martinson's infamous "Nothing Works" article was not a blanket condemnation of rehabilitation, even though it was widely characterized as such at the time, especially in the popular media.[165] In fact, Martinson quickly retracted and qualified some of his original claims, which were subjected to considerable criticism.[166] Andrew von Hirsch takes explicit exception to Rothman's claim that the chief vehicle for increasing sentencing levels throughout the country were mandatory-minimum sentences that were the product of liberal reforms. He notes that the draconian Rockefeller drug laws ushered in the widespread use of mandatory-minimums in the early 1970s, well before liberals began pushing hard for sentencing reform through the creation of sentencing commissions and other measures.[167] Prison populations began rising in many states long before determinate sentencing laws were enacted. Moreover, states that did not enact determinate sentencing laws nonetheless experienced substantial increases in their prison populations.[168] Indeed, for all the talk about the end of indeterminate sentencing, this model remains the most prevalent one in the United States, with some thirty states using a version of it.[169] Texas, whose incarceration rates are regularly near the top of the charts, built its expansive prison system out of indeterminate sentencing.[170] Furthermore, disillusionment with the rehabilitative model was not confined to the United States. Britain, Canada, Australia, Sweden, and other countries experienced similar backlashes against rehabilitation but did not subsequently experience exponential increases in their incarceration rates.[171] While Western Europe experienced a comparable loss of faith in rehabilitation, European bureaucrats did not abandon rehabilitative programs.[172]

Dissatisfaction on the right and left with U.S. sentencing practices certainly provided a political opening for wide-scale changes in penal policy. This dissatisfaction did not foreordain, however, that penal policy would take a hard right, beginning with the abandonment of rehabilitation as a goal, or that an overhaul of the sentencing framework was necessary to address concerns about equity in sentencing. Compelling arguments could still be marshalled on behalf of rehabilitation and indeterminate sentencing. Arguably, rehabilitation had yet to be given a fair hearing because of implementation issues like inadequate funding, poor staff training, tensions between the custodial and treatment staffs, and the failure to identify suitable offenders for treatment.[173] Furthermore, the charge that indeterminate sentences discriminated against minorities, the poor, and other disadvantaged groups rested more on anecdote and intuition than hard evidence. The issue of sentencing disparities had not been widely studied at the time and the existing evidence was inconclusive.[174] As Norval Morris and Nigel Walker suggested years ago, the problem of sentencing disparities for disadvantaged groups could be addressed by moderate changes in sentencing practices without scrapping the existing sentencing framework.[175]

Liberal disillusionment with rehabilitation and attacks on sentencing policy from the right and left certainly provided a significant opening for hard-line conservatives to hijack penal policy. The role of progressive penal reformers and their temporary allies on the right who were dissatisfied with the criminal justice system, but for different reasons, is an important part of the story. But the role of liberal and other groups in the development of the carceral state is more complex than explanations that focus on the fall from grace of the rehabilitative ideal suggest. The attack on rehabilitation may have momentarily united sworn enemies on the right and left. But this does not answer the question of why criminal justice policy took off in a direction that favored conservative approaches and why alternative proposals premised on reducing as much as possible the use of incarceration as a punishment were left in the dust.

As shown in the coming chapters, a remarkable transformation took place in the interest groups and social movements involved in criminal justice policy making. While concerns about law and order have been a central and abiding feature of American political development and national discourse since the founding, the actual construction of the penal-welfare state from the late nineteenth century to the late twentieth century was largely an elite-led, top-down project.[176] Its primary engineers were law enforcement professionals, experts on criminology, and select public officials who monopolized criminal justice policy.[177] With the decay of the penal-welfare state over the last four decades or so, criminal justice policy became a central area of concern for a wider range of groups. The main analytical focus of scholarly analyses has been on how conservative groups mobilized by law-and-order politicians took penal policy in a more punitive direction. But a closer look reveals that a whole range of new groups entered the law-and-order arena, including social service organizations and reform-oriented groups spanning the left–right spectrum and, on criminal justice matters, not always comfortably or consistently located on a single spot on that spectrum. These groups operated in a complex institutional environment that helped predispose them toward policies and political positions that undergirded the carceral state. That environment had deep historical roots, to which we now turn in Chapter 3.

3   UNLOCKING THE PAST

The Nationalization and Politicization of Law and Order

> "History is like waves lapping at a cliff. For centuries nothing happens. Then the cliff collapses."
>
> – Henry See[1]

CRIMINAL JUSTICE POLITICS AND POLICIES have been a major, not a minor, theme in American political development. It is striking how often public officials throughout U.S. history have latched on to the crime and punishment issue to further their own political agendas and fortunes. Numerous national figures and presidential aspirants, from Thomas Jefferson to Theodore Roosevelt to Joseph McCarthy, played the crime card long before Barry Goldwater highlighted the issue in the 1964 presidential campaign. Furthermore, while direct federal involvement in crafting penal policy was minor and intermittent for much of U.S. history, the federal government did step in at key junctures (often by orchestrating or responding to national campaigns organized around crime-related concerns) that had important long-term consequences for the development of the carceral state.

These periodic campaigns, undertaken when criminal justice and law enforcement institutions were undeveloped, habituated Americans to indulge rhetorically in a politics of moralism that was not that costly for a long time. Americans could use penal politics to indulge their moralism and express their fears and anxieties because, while their law-and-order campaigns had enormous symbolic significance, the skeletal law enforcement apparatus checked their actual consequences. This is not to minimize the enormous consequences these campaigns had for some individuals, be they the 20 people hanged in the Salem witch trials in 1692 or the 30,000 women rounded up during World War I on suspicion of prostitution. For politicians and public officials, these moralistic campaigns were a useful way to construct, via the back door, in a context where citizens greatly mistrusted extensions of state power, the law enforcement institutions (such as the FBI) associated with a "normal" state. State authorities used the crime and punishment issue to engage in bursts of state-building. As in Western Europe, law enforcement institutions were used "not merely to hold off threats to public order, but to define 'disorder,' create 'disorder,' and press their rights to suppress some 'disorder.'"[2]

In the U.S. case, this use of the legal apparatus to build the state occurred in a more fitful, roundabout, and morally charged manner. This is due to an extraordinary feature of early American political development: the absence of any significant interest in creating federal or even state-level law enforcement agencies. Colonial justice was a "business of amateurs," with lay magistrates and no real police force.[3] After the Revolution, the United States was slow to establish the institutions that constitute a modernized criminal justice system. The office of the attorney general was created in 1789, but for the next quarter of a century, the position was held by lawyers who did not reside in the capital, infrequently attended Cabinet meetings, and did not give up their lucrative private law practices.[4] The Department of Justice was not established until 1870, nearly a century after the American Revolution and in the midst of the passionate battle over Reconstruction, which crippled the department for years.[5] The Justice Department did not have even a rudimentary detective service until 1909, when the Bureau of Investigation was created. The special agents of the bureau, which eventually became the FBI, were not allowed to carry guns, serve warrants and subpoenas, and make seizures and arrests until more than two decades later.[6] Prior to the twentieth century, only two states – Texas and Massachusetts – had statewide police forces.[7] And the United States did not create a federal prison system until 1930.[8]

One should not conclude from this absence or delayed development of the institutions commonly identified with the nationalization of criminal justice that until very recently crime and punishment were trivial issues in national politics or exclusively a local or state matter. A closer look at U.S. history calls into question the widespread claim that the depth of public concern in recent years about crime, violence, and law and order is something new in American politics, as is the emergence of crime as a major issue to be exploited in national electoral politics. It is true that before the twentieth century, the actual making of criminal justice policy was overwhelmingly the business of individual states or local authorities. Yet penal reform was often a national concern that was integral to debates over the leading issues of the day, including the meaning of the American Revolution, the founding of the republic, slavery, Reconstruction, the modernization of the South, economic development, and race relations.

Furthermore, as shown later in the chapter, the United States was periodically convulsed by intense campaigns waged against specific crimes and criminals in the late nineteenth and twentieth centuries, including family violence, prostitution, alcohol, gangsters, lynchings, ransom kidnappings, sexual psychopaths, juvenile delinquents, and organized crime.

An examination of these campaigns shows that what has changed significantly over time is what constitutes a crime, the meaning of "law and order," and the state's growing institutional apparatus to pursue more punitive policies. These campaigns, like the late eighteenth- and early nineteenth-century debates over capital punishment and the establishment of the penitentiary, were infused with basic political questions about what should be the proper bounds of the state's power to imprison and kill. In striking contrast, these issues of state sovereignty have been incidental to more recent debates about law and order.

Many of these earlier campaigns were carried out with moral fervor, much as a sense of righteousness has propelled the contemporary war on drugs. But in earlier periods, the state's skeletal criminal justice institutions kept a check on these moral crusades, as did the country's racial, ethnic, and regional divide. Because these earlier campaigns resulted in, by today's standards, insignificant increases in the incarcerated population, it is easy to dismiss their significance in explaining the origins of the carceral state established over the past thirty years. But these campaigns were important state-building exercises, and left in their wake increasingly fortified law enforcement institutions.[9] They bolstered the legitimacy of the state, especially the federal government, to take law and order into its own hands.

Convict Nation

Crime and punishment have been integral to the history, politics, and identity of the United States, right back to the voyage of Columbus, whose crew of ninety included at least four convicts. The role of convicts in establishing the New World is much greater than commonly acknowledged.[10] After a royal commission in England declared that most felons could be legally transported to the New World to become servants on plantations, many roundups of children and prisoners from county jails took place under official encouragement at all levels of the British government and at the highest levels of the British church beginning in the early 1600s. By the middle of the seventeenth century, "most British emigrants to colonial America went as prisoners of one sort or another."[11] They were either forcibly kidnapped, arrested, tricked, or bound as servants. An estimated one-quarter of all British emigrants to America during the eighteenth century were convicts.[12] By the 1720s, all colonial cities and almost all counties had at least one house of detention. Most had several. Indeed, America had more jails than public schools or hospitals. In the decades prior to the American Revolution, the transportation of convicts to the New World and impressment (the Royal Navy's controversial practice of recruiting seamen by force) were important areas of dispute between the colonies and the King.[13] Abuse of prisoners was also a key feature of the war, during which more Americans perished while prisoners of Britain than were killed in combat.[14]

This is not to argue that the United States, founded by a goodly number of convicts, was destined to be a more punitive country. Rather, this discussion seeks to highlight how integral the issues of penalty and incarceration were to the early history of the United States and how they set the context for the extensive debates over crime and criminal law that took place in the founding era. The leaders of the Revolution explicitly identified British oppression with abuse of criminal law. Reforming the law to make it conform to the perceived ideals of the American Revolution was a central task of the founding era. In his study of the rise of the penitentiary, Adam Hirsch ties the birth of the republic directly to the birth of the penitentiary. The Revolution, in his view, stirred Americans to reexamine their existing laws and pushed them to consider new ways to improve the legal system.[15] Some penal reformers argued at the time that independence had liberated the former colonies to experiment with penal innovations like the penitentiary that had been suppressed under British rule.[16]

It is tempting to present the founding era as insignificant for the development of contemporary penal policy and American political development more broadly, because the key provisions of the Bill of Rights were not activated, so to speak, by the courts until a century and a half later. While the controversial Bill of Rights, added to help ensure ratification of the U.S. Constitution, "contained a minicode of criminal procedure," the federal courts largely ignored these protections until the milestone decisions of the Warren Court that extended procedural rights to defendants.[17] Until the mid-twentieth century, the courts took a hands-off approach to prisoners' rights and prison conditions, viewing people in prison as "slaves of the states" who had no constitutional rights and were not entitled to a legal forum to express their grievances.[18] Yet the lively political debates about criminal punishment in the late eighteenth and early nineteenth centuries were in many ways "a guide to the political principles that were most influential during the founding."[19] During the first three decades, states restricted the use of capital punishment and bodily punishments, eliminated hard labor in public by offenders, established comprehensive legal codes to supplement common-law traditions, and built the country's first penitentiaries. Although most of the penal reforms of this era were enacted and implemented by local or state authorities, many leading public figures of the day considered them to be issues of national significance and vigorously debated them. These penal reforms had a wider symbolic significance as well. Where one stood on various penal reforms signaled where one stood on broader issues of governance.

The ideological inheritance from this period is complex. The conventional view is that opposition to the death penalty and other bodily punishments like whipping and pillorying was rooted in ideas about criminal justice inspired by the rationalism of the Enlightenment and the spread of religious humanism.[20] The leading Enlightenment thinkers on criminal justice, including Hobbes, Bentham, and particularly Cesare Beccaria, rejected the idea that criminal law should rest on a moral foundation.[21] In their view, the purpose of punishment was not to "do good" or make a statement about morality, but rather to protect society. Milder punishments, if enacted swiftly and with certainty, served that purpose, thus obviating the need for capital punishment for most if not all crimes. They argued that utilitarianism – that is, society's self-interest – should be the basis for punishment and called for punishments that were proportional to the seriousness of the offense. They contended that the certainty of punishment rather than its severity was most important to ensure deterrence.[22]

Several historical works on the colonial and founding periods contend, however, that multiple legal traditions, not just the Enlightenment and the common law system inherited from Britain, influenced early American legal culture.[23] Some of them specifically challenge the contention that Enlightenment ideas about utilitarianism were the primary influence on discussions of criminal justice at this time.[24] These works suggest that the debate over criminal justice was broader and more fluid than previously assumed. It was animated not just by Enlightenment ideas about utilitarianism, but also by competing concerns about morality and broader political concerns about republicanism, how to maintain law and order in the country, and the future of slavery.

This was most apparent in the debate over capital punishment, which was a "subject of extensive public conflict" from the founding to the eve of the Civil War.[25] Some of the most prominent figures of the founding era favored restricting the use of capital punishment and other punishments of the body. At the same time, they opposed what they viewed as the excessive use of executive pardons and other mechanisms like the "benefit of clergy" that gave the guilty a reprieve from their death sentences.[26] Some of their opposition was based on pure utilitarian concerns. They rejected the expansive lists of crimes punishable by death because capital sentences were capriciously applied. The widespread use of executive pardons and the "benefit of clergy" made the promise of punishment uncertain, thus undermining the deterrent effect of the death penalty. Thomas Jefferson, for example, argued that keeping people in prison rather than sentencing them to death benefited society more. The imprisoned, in his view, served as "living and long-continued spectacles to deter others from committing like offenses."[27] For those who committed lesser offenses, a stay in the penitentiary promised to reform the offender, thus serving society by preventing future crime.[28] Killing offenders weakened the state, in Jefferson's view, because it eliminated people who could eventually become productive citizens.[29]

The death penalty and pardoning power were both associated with the detested features of the vanquished monarchy – notably "naked authority" and "uncontrollable discretion."[30] For penal reformers in the new republic, the gallows were a powerful symbol of what was wrong with European governments – capricious, unchecked state authority that privileged the interests of the state over the individual. The penitentiary represented an attractive alternative – state power that was accountable, predictable, and harnessed to reform the individual.[31]

Robert Vaux, a Philadelphia gentleman and philanthropist, epitomized these sentiments in his remarks to the crowd in 1823 at the laying of the cornerstone of Eastern State Penitentiary, the largest, the most expensive, and one of the most sophisticated public buildings of its day. He praised Pennsylvania and its legislators for rejecting "those cruel and vindictive penalties which are in use in European countries." Vaux applauded them for substituting "milder corrections" such as "the most strict solitary confinement" in penitentiaries where the community "wisely and compassionately sought to secure and reform the criminal."[32] All of this was in keeping with Enlightenment ideas about order, progress, and rationality. As Michael Meranze argues, the penitentiary was complementary to, indeed integral to, liberalism and Enlightenment ideas – not antithetical to them – because it was seen as restraining the "directly violent power" of the state. The rejection of bodily punishments was critical to bolstering penal reformers' contention that the "modern" penitentiary had nothing in common with pre-Revolutionary penal practices.[33]

Concerns about maintaining law and order also prompted Jefferson, Benjamin Rush, and other national figures to oppose the expansive use of capital punishment. They looked with dismay at the drunken, raucous crowds, many of them sympathetic to the condemned, who gathered on hanging day in a festive atmosphere to witness whether the prisoner would indeed hang from the gallows or would get a last-minute reprieve.[34] Rush and other penal reformers came to view an alternative to the gallows – hard labor in public – as also problematic for public order. Prisoners charged with public tasks like street cleaning often escaped and fought their keepers. Crowds gathered, sometimes to taunt, sometimes to give aid to the prisoners, subverting the very distinction between vice and virtue that the punishment was supposed to demarcate. This threatened the fragile public order and the authority of the incipient state. Rush was a strong advocate of removing punishment from the public view, believing that this would force citizens to focus on the moral lesson of the penal process rather than on the particulars of any individual offender.[35]

Utilitarianism, liberalism, and law-and-order concerns alone do not explain the origins and direction of the penal reform movement in the founding era and subsequently. As Ronald J. Pestritto, Louis Masur, and others have shown, a complex, sometimes contradictory, synthesis was at work that had strong moralistic and retributive elements.[36] Penal policies were heavily influenced by religion, for which utilitarians like Beccaria had no use. This is not surprising, given that the early colonists, especially the Puritans, made virtually no distinction between sin and crime and established a criminal justice system that "was in many ways another arm of religious orthodoxy."[37] Ministers, notably Quakers, dominated the early leadership of the Philadelphia Society for Alleviating the Miseries of Public Prisons, which was established in the late eighteenth century and is considered the first major modern prison reform organization.[38] Quaker and Protestant beliefs about how each individual had the potential for self-reform were important to the establishment of the penitentiary system. The penitentiary was founded on the Quaker idea of saving souls by isolating them in silent cells where they could reflect on the error of their ways, do penitence, and emerge as better people.[39] As one warden of San Quentin succinctly observed in the nineteenth century, "Every man has within him a germ of goodness."[40]

Several of the founders, including Jefferson, Washington, Madison, Hamilton, and Rush, believed that criminal law should be founded on a higher moral law.[41] They contended that punishment had a retributive purpose, that punishing criminals was inherently good, even if it does not result in any reduction in crimes. Evidence of the moral role the founders expected criminal law to play was evident from the start in the 1790 Crimes Act, the first criminal statute of the federal government. The act listed the crimes punishable by hanging and included a provision that the bodies of the executed were subject to dissection at the discretion of the court.[42] Opponents of dissection denounced it as "barbarous revenge" and "savageness." James Madison defended the practice, arguing that it was important to make the punishment proportional to the offense. If run-of-the-mill murders required the death penalty, he reasoned, then especially heinous crimes called for something more.[43] Jefferson, though widely identified with the ideas of the Enlightenment, also had his own Taliban-like moments. In 1779, he proposed modifying the state law in Virginia to restrict use of the death penalty to treason and murder. For men who committed rape or sodomy, he proposed castration as an alternative punishment. He suggested drilling a hole at least a half-inch in diameter through the noses of women found guilty of sodomy.[44]

Crime, Punishment, and the South

Penal policies and practices were integral to discussions of one of the other dominant issues of the founding era and the preeminent issue of the antebellum decades – slavery. The penitentiary was fiercely debated in the South from the 1790s to the 1850s. It was a powerful and contested symbol in Southern politics and in political disputes between the North and the South. The complicated and contradictory inheritance of the early penal reform movement was most apparent in its relationship to slavery. Many of the same people who advocated so forcefully for the construction of penitentiaries and so forcefully against capital punishment were at the forefront of the antislavery movement.[45] Leading abolitionists like William Lloyd Garrison and Wendell Phillips saw the two struggles as inseparable. Early advocates of the penitentiary went out of their way to show how incarceration was not like slavery. They could love the former and loathe the latter because penitentiaries, unlike the institution of slavery, provided convicts with an opportunity to improve themselves and be rewarded with emancipation. By contrast, Southern slavery, in their view, was not a "prelude to freedom of any sort."[46]

Not surprisingly, the South erected fewer penitentiaries in the antebellum years because, among other things, advocates of the penitentiary were identified with the abolitionist cause. Furthermore, the South lacked the vast network of penal and other reform societies that proliferated during the early nineteenth century in the North.[47] Also, the institution of "slavery made it ideologically difficult to acknowledge the existence of a white criminal class and to legislate for its control."[48] The association in the South of crime with race made it impossible to embrace rehabilitation, the purported *raison d'être* for the penitentiary.[49] The only consistent support for constructing penitentiaries in the South came from state governors, who were motivated by patronage and law-and-order concerns.[50] They battled with legislators and voters, many of whom viewed penitentiaries as a real threat to freedom, and not as a sign of enlightened government.[51] Many Southern legislators and citizens looked askance at the penitentiaries of the North, seeing them as unwelcome examples of excessive state intervention in local affairs. Although penitentiaries were more controversial in the South, most Southern states eventually erected them in the antebellum years. The only holdouts were the Carolinas and Florida (which was virtually unoccupied at the time). While most Southern states built penitentiaries, they generally used them far less extensively than did the North.[52]

The roots of the penitentiary were shallow in the South, however, and the Civil War uprooted them.[53] Many Southern penitentiaries suffered severe damage during the war. Most states of the old Confederacy opposed building new penitentiaries or repairing existing ones after the war because they were short of funds and they identified such large-scale public projects with the corruption of the carpetbaggers.[54] The collapse of state finances, the weakening of state governments, the rise in lawlessness, growing apprehension about the control of blacks with the end of slavery, and the demands of economic development and modernization prompted the South to adopt an alternative means of punishment – the convict-lease system.[55] Convict leasing actually predated the Civil War and was not invented in the South. But it was not used widely until after the war, when it took hold in the South but not the North.[56]

For more than half a century after the Civil War, controversies over the convict-lease system were a defining feature of Southern politics. Under the lease system, state authorities and prison officials hired out convicts to private contractors who exploited their labor in coal mines, turpentine farms, sawmills, phosphate pits, and brickyards under appalling conditions for a fixed sum.[57] Most states initially did not monitor or attempt to regulate the living and working conditions of the leased convicts. As one Southern convict manager explained, "The State turned over its charges body and soul, and thenceforth washed its hands of them."[58] The leased convicts overwhelmingly were blacks who had received lengthy sentences for petty crimes. Guarded by overseers with guns and bloodhounds, they labored under conditions that were in some ways more brutal than the antebellum plantation.[59] The leasing system in Florida was described as "the American Siberia."[60] Across the South, poorly fed and clothed convicts often slept at night shackled in open-air cages made from modified railway cars. The private contractors had no incentive to invest in the well-being of the leased convicts. After all, if a convict died, the state supplied another one for the same bargain price. Mortality rates were extraordinarily high.[61]

Several studies of the convict-lease system demonstrate that it was integral to the political and economic life of the South for decades after the Civil War. It was not a reincarnation of slavery, but rather an important bridge between an agricultural economy based on slavery and the industrialization and agricultural modernization of the New South.[62] Public officials, planters, industrialists, and prison officials promoted and defended leased-convict labor as a vital resource to develop the South.[63] The South's new industrialists relied on convict labor to provide a predictable cheap labor force to develop swamplands, forests, and mines. The planters viewed the lease system as a way to tame free black agricultural workers who risked being arrested and leased out to the highest bidder for minor transgressions. Mine operators saw convict laborers as a way to depress the wages of free miners and stymie unionization efforts.[64] State governments relied on payments from convict leases to put their budgets on sounder footing.[65]

Convict labor was associated with some of the most politically charged issues of the late nineteenth and early twentieth centuries in the South. Fights about convict leasing played a critical role in the history of organized labor in the South. These battles united blacks and whites in crucial biracial coalitions and prompted the establishment of formal political alliances between organizations that represented small farmers and urban workers. In the early 1890s, the "convict wars" convulsed mining communities in the eastern and central parts of Tennessee as thousands of people rebelled against the leasing of convicts. These violent rebellions eventually brought about the end of the convict-lease system there in 1895, but at the cost of weakening Tennessee's mining unions and the electoral appeal of Populism.[66]

In Tennessee and elsewhere, opposition to convict leasing was a key test of the strength of the Populists and of the Redeemer Democrats who came to power after Reconstruction.[67] Louisiana completely terminated its lease system in 1901 because of fears that the issue threatened to divide the new ruling faction of the Democratic Party, to the benefit of the Populists and black Republicans.[68] The convict-lease system challenged not only the political authority of the Redeemer Democrats but also their moral authority. The appalling conditions under which the convicts worked and lived undermined the Redeemers' claims that the South's tradition of paternalism gave them the moral authority to "settle the race problem and 'deal with the Negro'" without interference from the North.[69] Penal policy was a bone of contention between the North and the South as Southern defenders of the leasing system attacked Northern penitentiaries as inhumane.[70]

In the 1890s, the convict-lease system came under increased pressure. Facing difficult economic conditions, farmers and workers pressed state authorities to take a more activist view of government and pushed the Democratic Party to abandon the Bourbon program of low taxes and limited government services. In Texas, the Populists sought to remove convict labor from competition with free labor. There and elsewhere, they believed that the state should directly exploit the labor of the convicts rather than rely on private contractors who acted as middlemen and pocketed most of the profits from penal labor.[71] The appalling conditions under which leased convicts labored received increased attention in the press at this time, as did the rampant corruption associated with the leases. This prompted organized labor and middle-class urban reformers associated with the emerging Progressive movement to intensify pressure to end convict leasing.[72]

Banning the leasing of prisoners was one of the major reforms of the Progressive era. Texas called a special legislative session in 1910 to end leasing. Abolition of convict leasing was the first plank in the platform of the initial meeting of the Southern Sociological Congress, organized in 1912 to study how to improve economic and social conditions in the South.[73] That same year, the Governors' Conference at Richmond devoted a great deal of time to penal issues. Governor George W. Donaghey of Arkansas attacked the convict-lease system as one that "murders men alive." Governor Coleman L. Blease of South Carolina defended his controversial pardon record, especially his practice of releasing blacks who had received long sentences for trivial crimes rather than see them perish from being sentenced to hard labor.[74]

By the mid-1920s, nearly all the states in the South had banned convict leasing.[75] The reform was the result of a conservative strand of Progressivism.[76] In Georgia, Texas, and elsewhere, Progressive reformers argued that convict labor should be exploited directly by the state for economic development. As the economy improved in Texas and elsewhere in the late nineteenth and early twentieth centuries, states had more money to build penitentiaries and purchase large tracts of land to develop state penal farms where convicts could labor for state profit. Progressives contended that the state should also put prisoners to work building roads, constructing railroads, and performing other tasks to develop the South's infrastructure and economy. They were joined by organized labor, which feared direct competition with convict labor under the lease system, and farmers and commercial interests, who wanted good roads. Roads in the South improved dramatically with the expansion of the chain gang under state auspices.[77] Ironically, the public chain gang became the symbol of a more enlightened public notion of economic development in the Progressive era.[78] According to an old Georgia folk saying, "Bad boys make good roads."[79]

Progressives pushed for banning the convict-lease system not only for economic reasons, but also for racial ones. They contended that a ban would further their modest racial agenda by ending the racial repression and brutality associated with convict leasing and by reclaiming the state's duty to constrain and uplift blacks.[80] Yet chain gangs and county road gangs became notorious for their terrible conditions and the horrendous punishments meted out to prisoners.[81]

The development of the chain gang and road work gang was not a purely local or state matter. The federal government was critical. The U.S. Department of Agriculture's Office of Public Roads spearheaded the "good roads" movement. Up until the early 1930s, the federal government, under pressure from the South, agreed to allow Southern counties to use convict labor as a matching grant to federal aid programs for road improvement. Following enactment of the Federal Road Aid Act in 1916, a substantial amount of highway work financed by federal money was performed by convicts.[82]

The chain gang enjoyed the dubious distinction of being one of the few interracial institutions in the Jim Crow South. As the number of white convicts in the Southern penal system increased, the sight of blacks and whites laboring side-by-side chained to each other in the Jim Crow years discomfitted Southerners and made juries hesitant to punish whites. The higher visibility of white prisoners started to erode the public's belief in the advantages of convict labor. With the arrival of the Depression, concerns mounted that convicts laboring on public works were depriving unemployed workers of jobs. Bankrupt counties, no longer able to afford chain gangs, remanded their prisoners to the state. During the 1930s, the federal government mandated that states could not use convict labor on projects financed by federal emergency appropriations for unemployment relief. Despite these developments and numerous reports about the widespread use of corporal punishment and torture to discipline prisoners serving on chain gangs, the chain gang lumbered on in pockets of the South until the civil rights movement forced its dismantling in the 1960s, only to be revived again three decades later.[83]

To sum up, issues of crime and punishment were integral to the early political development of the United States. While the actual making of penal policy was primarily the work of state and local governments well into the twentieth century, penal matters informed and shaped debates over some of the leading national issues of the day. I have not provided an exhaustive history of early U.S. penal policy. Rather, several stylized examples substantiate the broader analytical point about the crucial role of penal policy in the early political development of the United States. The United States had an early identity as a convict nation. Penal concerns informed broader debates about republicanism, utilitarianism, and law and order during the founding decades. Disagreements over the establishment of the penitentiary were tied up with disputes over slavery and abolition in the antebellum years. After the Civil War, the convict-lease system was pivotal in the politics of Populism, Progressivism, race relations, and the economic development of the South. In short, crime and punishment were nationalized and politicized early on in American political development, and many of the early debates over law and order hinged on differing views about the proper extent of state power.

Public Anxiety and the Police

When it comes to crime and punishment, Americans have had an anxiety-ridden history. This is apparent in the creation of the penitentiary in the Jacksonian era, as discussed earlier, and in the controversies surrounding the establishment and development of municipal police forces and private police agencies in the nineteenth and early twentieth centuries. While these campaigns eventually petered out, they left a mark on the criminal justice system. They helped construct the institutional scaffolding for the more punitive policies of the carceral state. They augmented the state's capacity in the area of criminal justice and legitimated its role to define morality and to wage war on the designated criminal or vice of the moment. Furthermore, they provided politicians and public officials with an opportunity to play the crime card in national politics for electoral advantage.

In the 1700s, Americans did not view crime or poverty as critical social problems or as indicators of deeper flaws in society.[84] Crime mattered in the eighteenth century to the extent that criminal law, as discussed earlier, came to be regarded as a tool of repression closely identified with the hated monarchy. By the Jacksonian era, however, the extent of crime, poverty, insanity, and delinquency prompted a "crisis of confidence" for Americans. In the antebellum period, Americans "intently pondered the origins of deviant behavior."[85] The penny press, which first appeared in the 1830s and 1840s, exploited the public's fascination with crime and the underworld.[86] President Andrew Jackson cautioned, "This spirit of mob-law is becoming too common and it must be checked or, ere long, it will become as great an evil as service war, and the innocent will be much exposed."[87] In 1838, Abraham Lincoln warned about "the increasing disregard for law which pervades the country" and the "worse than savage mobs."[88] In his famous Lyceum speech, Lincoln singled out two notorious and gruesome instances of mob violence.[89]

From the 1830s to the 1870s, Northern cities were gripped by massive disorders, including gang warfare, race and ethnic riots, Election Day mob violence, and pitched battles between competing fire companies racing to be the first to put out a fire.[90] "The extent of these disorders was truly remarkable, even by the standards of the 1960s," observes Samuel Walker in his study of the history of the municipal police.[91] Between 1834 and 1844, New York City was seized by more than 200 major gang wars.[92] Newspapers, popular magazines, and pulp novels were filled with sensational accounts of mob violence and heinous crimes.[93] During this period homicide became institutionalized for the first time "as a 'popular' form of entertainment, as a spectator sport."[94] Fearful that social disorganization was imminent, Americans in the age of Jackson began building penitentiaries and mental asylums in earnest.[95] Bereft of public police forces, anxious rural communities established local protection associations and private antitheft societies.[96]

Public attention focused on the need to create police forces that were separately administered and on the public payroll of the criminal justice system. The massive urban disturbances were a catalyst to establish or strengthen public police forces in major U.S. cities in the face of widespread doubts that tougher laws were the best way to deal with the moral challenge of urban areas.[97] While the London Metropolitan Police were a model for some elite reformers in the United States, many others opposed the creation of a centralized police force. Faced with rising working-class and other unrest in the early nineteenth century, the British Parliament created the London Metropolitan Police in 1829 at the instigation of Home Secretary Robert Peel after years of agitation.[98] The new police force was designed to be an elitist, highly centralized agency that was essentially an extension of the Home Office and thus the national government. The London Metropolitan Police force was founded prior to the emergence of widespread suffrage and in the absence of fierce partisan infighting at the local level.[99] British police were expected to be "impersonal and neutral agents of 'the Law'" and national authority.[100] From early on, the citizens of London were not granted any effective means of controlling or influencing police practices.[101] To ensure their objectivity, London police officers were deliberately selected from outside the city. They were encouraged not to mix socially with the citizens they supervised and to live in different neighborhoods. And they were denied the vote, as were most Englishmen at the time.[102]

By contrast, the early debate over police reform in the United States took place simultaneously with the blossoming of the Age of the Common Man in the 1830s and in a fiercely partisan political atmosphere. U.S. police forces developed with the expectation that police officers should be politically active residents and voters. From early on, U.S. police forces were "never fully controlled from outside or above." The decentralized governments of nineteenth-century American cities "were incapable of enforcing real direction along a hierarchical chain of command as in the London or military models" of policing.[103] Indeed, even the question of having police officers wear standardized blue uniforms was extremely controversial in the United States.[104]

Police officers in the United States "exhibited much more 'organic involvement' in the communities which they policed than did English police."[105] They were responsible for a much wider range of functions – everything from maintaining weather records to providing temporary housing for the homeless to running soup kitchens.[106] They mirrored and reinforced local partisan and ethnic cleavages. Ward leaders in major cities used the police force to provide employment and upward mobility for their supporters and to consolidate their power bases.[107] Operating with little outside supervision and training in a highly decentralized system, the cop on the beat in the United States had much more discretion on the job, which resulted in more corruption and brutality on an ongoing basis.[108] Police in the United States also were less insulated from the communities they served than police were elsewhere because they had to contend with the persistent extension of the penal code into areas of widespread public disagreement. These included "victimless" crimes like public drinking, consensual sexual relations, drug use, and gambling, as well as political activities like labor organizing.[109]

A central issue for urban reformers for decades to come was how to create a more professional police force independent of local partisan concerns and accountable to a central authority.[110] The unreliability of metropolitan police, with their strong local and partisan ties, prompted major businesses and industrialists to establish the Pinkertons and other private police forces. The Pinkertons ultimately functioned as a de facto national detective and policing service until the 1920s, when the FBI finally came into its own. At the start of the twentieth century, the Pinkertons were the largest police business in the world. Allan Pinkerton, its founder, and his sons wrote many popular books that sensationalized the crime issue and they were treated as national spokespersons for criminal matters in the United States.[111] Robert and William Pinkerton forcefully lobbied in Washington for the creation of a government-funded national detective service and they were critical in the establishment of a national association of police chiefs in the United States. In its early years, the FBI modeled itself after the Pinkertons and other private police agencies.[112]

The role of private police agencies in suppressing organized labor in the 1880s and 1890s provoked a national debate about private police and the role of government more broadly in maintaining law and order. The Pinkertons' controversial role prompted charges that the private police agency represented a regression to the lawlessness of the Middle Ages, when the absence of public police prompted the establishment of feudal armies.[113] Prominent Populists like Thomas Watson of Georgia and three-time presidential candidate William Jennings Bryan objected to using private police agencies to preserve public order.[114] The Pinkertons' involvement in the violent suppression of the 1892 Homestead strike sparked a series of House and Senate investigations of private police agencies and a wider national debate over the constitutional use of police power.[115] Pinkerton officials and representatives of other private police agencies defended their profession, arguing that the inadequacies of the public police were responsible for the expansion of private police agencies in the country. In his testimony before Congress, Robert Pinkerton warned in dire terms, "We have reached a point in the history of the State where there are but two roads left to us to pursue. The one leads to order and good government; the other leads to anarchy." He went on to say, "The great question which now confronts the people of this country is the enforcement of the law and the preservation of order."[116]

To sum up, this brief history of the early development of the police and various reform efforts in the nineteenth and early twentieth centuries demonstrates a persistent unease about the police and the role of the state in fighting crime. Police forces in the United States have been subject to political and partisan winds and concerns in a way that police forces elsewhere, notably Britain, have not. All of this had a profound effect on the subsequent emergence and development of interest groups and social movements related to law enforcement, to be discussed in later chapters.

The State and "White Slavery"

Urban unrest and the police were not the only sources of public concern and anxiety about criminal matters in the late nineteenth and early twentieth centuries. From about 1874 to 1890, the country embarked on a major campaign to criminalize family violence. Family violence came to be regarded in a new light as a crime that not only threatened its victims but also the social order.[117] During this period, hundreds of societies for the prevention of cruelty to children were founded and more modest efforts on behalf of battered women and victims of incest were undertaken.

After the campaign to police family violence petered out, the United States focused more intently on policing sexuality. In the early twentieth century, prostitution emerged as a major social issue as the country engaged in what one historian described as a "spectacular vice crusade" whose "scope and intensity were unprecedented."[118] The campaign against prostitution was not marginal to Progressivism, but rather integral to how Progressives defined themselves and their broader mission.[119] Like many other Progressive reforms, it was founded on "fundamental trust in the power of the state to do good" and led by women activists.[120] Women reformers in the Progressive era helped to expand the surveillance and control of young women by policing their sexuality. Delinquent girls and women had to submit to invasive medical examinations, humiliating interrogations about their sex lives, and incarceration for sexual offenses.[121]

Like the women's prison reform movement and campaign against family violence of the nineteenth century (see Chapters 5 and 6), the crusade against prostitution had a lasting impact on penal policy for ideological and institutional reasons. All three movements were led by social feminists who complemented rather than challenged the dominant ideals of the Victorian age. In a pattern that would become all too familiar in subsequent discussions of penal policy, these women reformers did not make a radical critique of existing gender roles, social structures, or racial norms. Instead, they reinforced the Victorian view that women – white women, that is – inhabited a special domestic sphere. As such, they had a special responsibility to purify society. The maternalist tradition of women reformers was problematic in many respects. It legitimized an uncritical acceptance of the state in the area of social control and the greater use of various state-sponsored institutions to reform women and, by extension, men who strayed from traditional norms.

Alarm over prostitution was pervasive during the Progressive era. Prominent Americans, including Theodore Roosevelt, Emma Goldman, and Walter Lippmann, focused their attention on this "social evil," as did a range of women's clubs and organizations.[122] Roosevelt called for "the most relentless war on commercialized vice," and John D. Rockefeller, Jr., commissioned and funded two important investigations of prostitution.[123] The moral reformers defined prostitution so loosely that potentially any sexual activity outside of marriage could be characterized as a crime. At one point, a physician prominent in the war against vice made the extravagant claim that there were over 1.6 million prostitutes in the United States if one counted public prostitutes and women he termed "clandestine" ones.[124] Between 1910 and 1917, forty-three cities conducted formal investigations of prostitution. In 1907, Congress appointed a commission to investigate "the importation of women for immoral purposes." Immigration was considered a major cause of prostitution, even though there was no solid evidence to support that claim. Prostitution was a central concern of the United States Immigration Commission. The commission's 1909 and 1910 reports bolstered the widespread view that a well-organized network of "white slavery" existed in the United States that involved the importation of prostitutes from abroad and the seduction of young American women for immoral purposes.[125]

These national and municipal investigations and the general hysteria about immigration and the white-slave trade prompted important new national legislation. The Immigration Act of 1910 toughened up regulations related to prostitution.[126] It subjected immigrant women to arrest, prosecution, and possible deportation for merely being found at music halls, dance halls, and other places "frequented by prostitutes."[127] Shortly after enacting the Immigration Act of 1910, Congress passed the White Slave Traffic Act, better known as the Mann Act. This measure sailed through Congress, despite some concerns that it illegally usurped the policing power of the states.[128] In promoting the bill, Rep. James R. Mann (R-Ill.), its chief sponsor, and other supporters argued that the alleged trafficking in white women for immoral purposes was more grievous than the previous enslavement of blacks.[129] The Mann Act vastly extended federal policing powers by permitting Washington to prosecute anyone suspected of transporting women across state lines for any "immoral purpose."

Enforcement of the Mann Act was predicated on two powers explicitly granted to the federal government in the Constitution: the power to regulate foreign and interstate commerce, and the power to enact enabling legislation for international treaties approved by the United States. Purportedly designed to protect women, the Mann Act ended up being used primarily to prosecute the "voluntary and ordinary immoralities" of women.[130] One important consequence of the Mann Act was the prosecution of noncommercial sexual relations as a crime. The number of convictions under the Mann Act was not huge – averaging about 350 per year between 1911 and 1928 – yet this act and the campaign against prostitution had broader significance.[131]

The battle against prostitution reached its zenith during World War I as the "prostitute was cast as the enemy in the home front."[132] Shortly after war was declared, the federal government created the Commission on Training and Camp Activities (CTCA), which was granted far-reaching powers to suppress prostitution in communities near the military training camps.[133] Unlike the vice commissions, the CTCA had significant federal authority to implement repressive policies. Under the "American Plan," the government could arrest any woman within five miles of a military cantonment.[134] Women could be legally detained by the federal authorities if their behavior (observed or rumored) indicated they might have a venereal disease.[135] The military campaign against prostitution, like the wider war effort, was viewed as an "extension of the progressive emphasis on purity and morality in American life."[136] By the end of the war, an estimated 30,000 women had been held without due process, trial, or legal representation.[137] The antiprostitution campaign during World War I was a remarkable extension of federal police power. In Philadelphia, the military essentially took over the police department in 1918 as part of its effort to stamp out prostitution. At the end of the war Raymond D. Fosnick, who led the antivice campaign, could claim that every red-light district had been shut down in the United States.[138]

By the end of the 1920s, the "morals crusade" unleashed by the Mann Act and World War I began to dissipate.[139] Prostitution was never again the dominant issue in national politics that it had been for two decades during the Progressive era. Yet the battle against prostitution had lasting consequences for penal policy and American political development more broadly. It set a precedent for the federal government to legislate morality and to associate immoral behavior with criminal activity. As Ruth Rosen explains, "the state, rather than the clergy or the community, became instrumental in labeling and ostracizing society's deviants."[140] The campaign against prostitution also bolstered interest in using state institutions to correct behavior that deviated from traditional roles. These institutions included reformatories, special training schools for female delinquents, and women's courts, where women were denied jury trials and their cases were decided by judges who were granted extraordinary powers.[141] This campaign also was a catalyst for the gradual "professionalization" of the state and local police discussed earlier.[142]

The war against prostitution also helped to establish a national police force. Immediately after passage of the Mann Act, Attorney General George H. Wickersham created a special organization of agents charged with enforcing it.[143] Over the years, supporters of the new Bureau of Investigation used the act to transform the bureau into a national police force.[144] The Mann Act legitimated an expanded federal role in policing that had been the exclusive purview of states. The 1913 Supreme Court ruling (in *Hoke v. United States*) that the Mann Act was constitutional opened the way for other legislation granting the federal government broad policing powers under the interstate commerce clause of the Constitution. These included the 1919 Dyer Act prohibiting the interstate transportation of stolen motor vehicles and the wave of federal crime legislation enacted during the 1930s.[145] In the crusade against prostitution, the police and other authorities experimented with and refined new law enforcement techniques, some of which would soon become part of their standard arsenal – notably entrapment and the use of fingerprinting to identify recidivists and punish them more severely. The war on prostitution during World War I also legitimized the widespread use of preventive detention without any procedural guarantees when national security was deemed at risk.[146]

Lastly, the war against prostitution during the Progressive Era demonstrated the salience of the law-and-order issue for national electoral politics. The battle against vice and crime more broadly was a defining feature of the Progressive era. Theodore Roosevelt, the most renowned Progressive, had an interest in crime and vice from early in his career. As a young state legislator in the 1880s, he led the opposition against the "spy bills" that would subject private detective agencies to greater regulation.[147] During the two years he served as a member of New York City's Board of Police Commissioners, Roosevelt used the board as a bully pulpit to rail against vice, lawlessness, and police corruption, and would single out for sharp criticism judges who, in his view, were too lenient toward offenders.[148] He doggedly sought to create a professional, nonpartisan police force in New York City modeled after the military and subject to civil service procedures.[149]

Roosevelt was not as obsessed with the vice issue as some of the other moral reformers of his day. Nonetheless, law and order, police reform, and morality were important issues for him. He ascended to the presidency following the assassination of President William McKinley, whose violent death in 1901 fueled public concerns about crime and disorder.[150] As president, Roosevelt defied the wishes of Congress by signing an executive order on July 1, 1908, to create an independent Bureau of Investigation, arguing that the country needed a national detective service.[151] Concerns about crime and disorder were a central theme of his third-party run for the presidency in 1912 as a Progressive in the Bull Moose Party. The massive 400-page report *The Social Evil in Chicago*, published by the Chicago vice commission in 1911, appears to have influenced his famous "Confession of Faith" speech at the Progressive Party convention the following year. In that speech, he called for an "endless crusade against wrong" and concluded: "We stand at Armageddon, and we battle for the Lord."[152]

Gangsters, Prohibition, and Herbert Hoover

While public anxiety about prostitution subsided in the 1920s, public anxiety about crime did not. "During the decade following World War I uncontrolled crime had become one of the most serious threats to democracy," Virgil W. Peterson observes in his study of crime commissions.[153] As attention shifted from the prostitute to the gangster following World War I, many Americans came to believe that rampant crime had become a defining feature of their society.[154] As one contemporary commentator put it: "The United States is the most lawless nation on the globe, barring only Russia under Bolshevik rule."[155] Dozens of cities established commissions to investigate crime, often at the instigation of prominent business executives. In August 1925, the National Crime Commission was organized in New York City in the office of Elbert H. Gary, then head of U.S. Steel Corporation. Its executive committee included Franklin D. Roosevelt, Charles Evans Hughes (the former secretary of state and former justice of the U.S. Supreme Court), and other prominent figures. With the help of a "sophisticated and emotional" public relations campaign, the commission called for an increased federal role in law enforcement.[156]

The apparently explosive growth in lawlessness in the 1920s provoked a heated discussion in the media that centered on the gangster. The popular media portrayed gangsters as powerful, technologically sophisticated crime executives who vanquished corrupt, inefficient cops and impotent federal agents. Gangsters were the subject of numerous newspaper and magazine articles, novels, plays, and more than a hundred Hollywood movies.[157] These portrayals of criminals highlighted the weakness, ineptitude, and corruption of government officials.

Prohibition greatly contributed to the image of a toothless, ineffective, corrupt state. The "Ohio Gang" of the Warren Harding administration (1921–23), which included his attorney general, was known for dropping many federal prosecutions of liquor law violations and selling federal enforcement jobs.[158] The Federal Prohibition Unit (renamed the Prohibition Bureau in 1927) was comprised of a small group of poorly paid, inefficient government agents. At the time, Walter Lippmann likened the government's capacity to combat liquor to fighting the devil with a wooden sword.[159] The bureau only had about 1,500 federal agents to enforce Prohibition nationwide, many of whom were incompetent and had criminal records.[160] In many parts of the country, the enforcement agents were so careless and reckless that citizens were afraid to drive their cars at night for fear of being shot at by the authorities. A popular window sticker at the time was: "Don't Shoot. I'm Not a Bootlegger."[161]

Although Prohibition ultimately failed, as evidenced by the repeal of the Eighteenth Amendment in December 1933, at another level it was a great success. It provided an opportunity for the federal government and public officials to take decisive hold of the crime issue and refashion it. In doing so, they created a new image of a federal government capable of responding to pressing national problems like crime and therefore entitled to greater powers to combat crime. The two Hoovers – Herbert and J. Edgar – were critical to this outcome, as was Franklin D. Roosevelt.

Prohibition put enormous stress on the system and provided an opening for a wider discussion about law and order in the United States. The 1928 presidential contest between Herbert Hoover and Governor Alfred E. Smith (D-N.Y.) was pivotal. In that race, Hoover talked a great deal about Prohibition, but not in a simple, moralistic, wet versus dry way. While Smith favored revision of the Eighteenth Amendment to permit states to decide on enforcement of Prohibition, Hoover solidly supported Prohibition. But Hoover reframed the Prohibition question into a larger issue about the responsibility of citizens and government officials alike to observe the law. This inoculated Hoover from the charge that he was a narrow-minded moralist, even though he ended up supporting some draconian antialcohol legislation like the Jones Act.[162]

James D. Calder challenges the "do nothing" stereotype of Hoover and contends that his administration actually marks the origins of federal crime control policy. He demonstrates how Hoover was obsessed with criminal justice issues from early on, beginning right with his inaugural address, whose first major topic was "The Failure of Our System of Criminal Justice."[163] Hoover was philosophically comfortable with widening federal enforcement power, but within limits. He argued that the federal executive's role should include investigation of social problems like crime and the implementation of model federal programs in the area of criminal justice that states could then copy.[164] This was not the first time that crime and punishment were raised to the status of national issues. However, this was the first time that a president explicitly and repeatedly made the case for using federal crime control policies to ameliorate social problems.

A Progressive committed to rigorous scientific investigation of social problems, Hoover created the National Commission on Law Observance and Enforcement to conduct the federal government's first comprehensive study of crime and law enforcement in the United States. Hoover told the assembly of experts at the first meeting of the commission, which was appointed in March 1929: "No nation can for long survive the failure of its citizens to respect and obey the laws which they themselves make."[165] The commission, which was chaired by George H. Wickersham, studied a range of issues, including the collection of crime statistics, crime by immigrants, and lawlessness by government officials. It heard from thousands of citizens, who wrote in to offer information and advice and to propose their own reasons for the apparent spread of lawlessness.[166]

Of the fourteen volumes the Wickersham Commission produced, its report on the police drew the most attention. "The Lawless Enforcement of the Law" documented widespread use by police of outright torture and other abuses, commonly referred to as the "third degree," and likened the behavior of the police to that of "law-breaking gangs."[167] This scathing indictment of police brutality galvanized public support for new legal controls over the police and other law enforcement officials and fueled the growing movement for better trained, more professional police officers.[168] While the Wickersham Commission did not recommend outright repeal of the Eighteenth Amendment, it did concede that Prohibition had encouraged widespread lawlessness in the country and cast great doubts over the policy's future.[169]

During his first year in office, President Hoover revamped the leading federal agencies charged with the administration of criminal justice to make them more efficient and professional and to raise the stature of federal law enforcement in the eyes of the public. He transformed the enforcement of alcohol and narcotics regulation under the Volstead and Harrison Acts by creating elite investigative units. In 1930 Hoover pushed Congress to pass the Prohibition Reorganization Act, which transferred the Prohibition Bureau from Treasury to Justice. That summer, he signed legislation to establish the Federal Bureau of Narcotics in the Department of the Treasury. To counteract congressional and public opposition, he described the creation of this special narcotics force as a necessary effort to combat the importation of drugs from overseas. Hoover also worked to remove incompetent and corrupt government attorneys and to improve federal court procedures.[170] In 1930, a full decade after the Volstead Act became law, all Prohibition personnel were finally covered by civil service procedures.[171]

Other presidents had paid attention to issues related to penal reform in general, but the Hoover administration was the first to focus specifically on federal prisons and prisoners. Hoover viewed the severe prison overcrowding problem (which was partly the result of Prohibition) and the wave of prison riots in the summer of 1929 as an opportunity to finally establish a federal prison system (see Chapter 7). In creating the Federal Bureau of Prisons in 1930, the Hoover administration was quite conscious of how federal penal policy could be used as a model for state and local efforts. Members of his administration stressed the need for choosing strong, innovative people to manage the federal prisons, eliminating abusive and unprofessional prison practices like corporal punishment and torture, reducing crowding by building new facilities, and expanding prison industries to reduce idleness.[172]

While Prohibition barely outlasted the Hoover administration, in trying to save it, Hoover profoundly altered the federal government's role and capacity in the area of law enforcement and criminal justice. Federal agents were no longer seen at best as Keystone Kops and at worst as corrupt thugs, but increasingly as competent, efficient, straight-shooting professionals. Likewise, a new image of wardens and superintendents took shape, that of nonpartisan, humane, professional managers rather than political hacks and administrators of torture. Even the reputation of the Prohibition Bureau improved dramatically, thanks to the exploits of agents like Eliot Ness.[173] Perhaps most significantly, the courts granted the police new wide-ranging search-and-seizure powers that long outlasted Prohibition. The Supreme Court ruled that the authorities were permitted to search vehicles without a warrant if they could show probable cause and could seize property used in illegal activities, even if the property belonged to innocent third parties. The Court also ruled that wiretaps did not violate the Fourth Amendment, a decision that was not overturned until four decades later in 1967.[174]

In raising the level of integrity of law enforcement officers, prison administrators, and the courts, Hoover furthered public acceptance of a more extensive role for the federal government in law enforcement and penal policy. Hoover and his administrators keenly recognized the importance of public opinion in mobilizing support for what they were doing. In speeches, radio addresses, and appearances before Congress, William D. Mitchell, his attorney general, Sanford Bates, his superintendent of the Bureau of Prisons, and Hoover himself appealed directly to the public for support to revamp the law enforcement system.[175] While members of the Hoover administration courted public opinion on criminal justice matters, there were real limits to how far they would go. Hoover overhauled the prison system, reorganized the federal criminal justice system, and remade the image of federal agents. But he was uneasy about the push by some Progressives and hard-line conservatives to further federalize crime control in the face of weak public support, especially in the South.

Lynchings and Kidnappings

Southern opposition to greater federal law enforcement powers was rooted in the segregationist Jim Crow system and, in particular, in fierce resistance to any kind of federal antilynching legislation.[176] For most of the first half of the twentieth century, lynchings and antilynching campaigns were a leading – and highly controversial – issue in national politics. Because lynchings and other organized violence against minority groups are often treated primarily as racial or civil rights matters, their impact on the development of the law-and-order state has been underappreciated. This is symptomatic of a more general failure to look more systematically at the role of violence in American political development.[177] In an ironic twist, the abiding controversy over federal antilynching legislation and other efforts to end this heinous practice served for decades as a check on the development of federal law enforcement powers and the carceral state.

When federal antilynching legislation was first introduced in 1920, opponents claimed it would turn states into "vassals" of the national government. They attacked the concept of federal policing power and equated lynching with murder, plain and simple. Federal authorities had no special right to enter their state and interfere in what they viewed as ordinary homicide cases.[178] Southerners on both sides of the lynching debate viewed it as central to a whole range of issues related to the development of the legal system. Southern moderates who mobilized against lynchings often cast this issue as primarily a law-and-order matter, not a matter of racial justice. The Association of Southern Women for the Prevention of Lynching (ASWPL), a voluntary organization of Southern white clubwomen and a leading opponent of lynchings, emphasized how this odious practice discredited the legal process and undermined respect for law enforcement officials.[179] Founded in 1930, the ASWPL also challenged lynching on gender grounds, in particular the contention that lynching was necessary for the defense of Southern womanhood.[180] The white middle-class clubwomen initially opposed federal antilynching legislation and focused instead on attempting to use their social and political influence on sheriffs and county officials to stem mob violence.[181] Jessie Daniel Ames, the association's founder, worked behind the scenes to defeat federal antilynching legislation, which was the centerpiece of the NAACP's activities in the 1930s and 1940s. In her attacks on the federal legislation, she echoed widespread concerns in the South about permitting a larger federal role in local law enforcement.[182]

The kidnapping of the young son of Charles and Anne Lindbergh in March 1932 dramatically altered the public's view of what the federal government's role in crime control should be. It helped to overcome some Southern resistance to federal crime legislation, but not antilynching legislation. This crime and a few other spectacular ones around this time created a sense of national emergency. Prior to the Lindbergh kidnapping, waves of ransom kidnappings periodically gripped the nation, sparking public hysteria.[183] These ransom kidnappings became national events and raised concerns that citizens would take the law into their own hands. After the body of fourteen-month-old Lloyd Keet, the son a wealthy Springfield, Mo., banker, was found at the bottom of a well in 1911, *The New York Times* reported: "Springfield tonight was a city in which any eventuality seemed a possibility." The mayor ordered all saloons closed, banned cars in the street, and put the infantry on alert. Thousands of people paraded the streets and demanded the lives of the six people suspected in the child's death.[184] Between 1900 and 1919, legislatures in nineteen states and the U.S. Congress created or modified their kidnapping legislation.[185]

By the early 1930s concern was growing in some quarters that these laws were insufficient, as a pattern began to emerge of kidnapping gangs preying on wealthy families, largely in the Midwest. Tougher laws to combat kidnapping remained stalled in the House and Senate, however, despite the entreaties of business executives and legislators from the Midwest. The Lindbergh kidnapping galvanized the nation and created a sense of national emergency.[186] President Hoover, who held a modified states' rights position on criminal matters, resisted mobilizing public opinion for an all-out war on crime after the Lindbergh kidnapping and murder. William D. Mitchell, his attorney general, went on national radio to warn the public not to expect too much from the proposed federal kidnapping legislation. Despite these warnings, Congress enacted the Lindbergh Law, which made kidnapping a federal offense, and a second statute that made it a federal crime to send ransom demands through the mail. Notably, Congress resisted calls at the time to make kidnapping a capital offense.[187] Hoover reluctantly signed the two statutes.[188]

In short, Hoover had some reservations about expanding the reach of the law enforcement arm of the federal government at the expense of states' rights. Nonethelesss, he laid the groundwork for the vast expansion of the law enforcement capacity of the federal, state, and local government that took place under Franklin D. Roosevelt and his successors. By the time he left office, Hoover had initiated the construction of six new federal prisons to help relieve serious overcrowding, due in part to the more than 40,000 people held for liquor law violations.[189] Prohibition ended up being an opportunity for federal agents and local police to perfect and secure judicial sanction for intrusive policing practices that have since become a standard part of their arsenal, including surveillance, wiretapping, and use of informants.[190] Hoover and his attorney general established that the executive branch was the legitimate national spokesperson on crime and penal policy. By "professionalizing" federal agents and prison superintendents, he set an example for police and wardens at the state and local levels. As the law enforcement authorities became more reputable in the eyes of the public, citizens became more willing to let them take the law into their own hands and were more likely to side with them, not the accused. Hoover also was instrumental in the creation of the Federal Bureau of Narcotics in 1930. Under its despotic director Harry J. Anslinger, the bureau grew over the years into a drug control bureaucracy that dwarfed the Prohibition Bureau, which had the far more formidable task of prohibiting liquor. For more than three decades, Anslinger used the bureau as a perch to incite national hysteria about drugs.[191]

The New Deal and the Law-and-Order State

Elected in a landslide just a few months after the Lindbergh murder, Roosevelt had far fewer compunctions than Hoover about exploiting sensational crimes to advance his administration's broader agenda of extending federal jurisdiction in the area of crime control. As William Leuchtenburg suggests, the crime control policies of the Roosevelt administration were a microcosm of the New Deal in many ways. FDR and members of his administration appealed directly to the public on a number of occasions for greater coercive powers to tackle the crime problem, which they presented as a dire issue.[192] Roosevelt and his first attorney general, Homer Cummings, contributed to the "supercharged anticrime climate."[193] Soon after taking office, FDR declared war on kidnapping and expressed his wish to establish a national police force akin to Scotland Yard. In June 1933 he signed an executive order creating a special division of investigation within the Justice Department. FDR also temporarily transferred Raymond F. Morey, a key member of his brain trust, from the State Department to the Justice Department, where he was responsible for conducting a special survey of crime prevention measures.[194] In his annual message to Congress in January 1934, Roosevelt pointedly singled out "crimes of organized banditry, cold-blooded shooting, lynching and kidnapping" as violations of law that "call on the strong arm of the Government for their immediate suppression; they call also on the country for an aroused public opinion."[195] Roosevelt directly linked the fight against crime with the struggle for economic recovery during the Depression.[196]

Despite the Lindbergh Law, fear grew in the early 1930s that the nation was in the throes of a "kidnapping epidemic" and that local governments were powerless to deal with crime, as gangs equipped with Thompson submachine guns and high-powered cars crossed and recrossed jurisdictional lines.[197] Samuel Walker categorizes the 1930s as the "law-and-order" decade, one in which the country "witnessed a virtual revolution in the political dimensions of the crime problem."[198] During this period, there were grisly examples of the public taking the law into its own bloody hands.

One of the most notorious cases was the November 1933 lynchings of Thomas J. Thurmond and John M. Holmes, two white men accused of kidnapping and murdering Brooke Hart, the twenty-two-year-old son of a wealthy department store owner. A mob of San Jose citizens dragged the two defendants from jail to a city park, where they were stripped, beaten, and hanged from trees.[199] James Rolph, the governor of California, lauded the actions of "those fine, patriotic San Jose citizens who knew how to handle such a situation." He acknowledged he had denied a request from the authorities in San Jose to call in the National Guard to restore order before the lynchings.[200] His statements caused a wave of reaction across the country, much of it initially favorable. Two days after the lynchings, however, Herbert Hoover, now out of office, publicly lashed out at Rolph, a fellow Republican, as did a number of other prominent Americans. Roosevelt's response was more restrained and came ten days after the event. In an address to a religious group, he condemned the lynchings and those who endorsed the attack, but avoided mentioning Rolph by name. Roosevelt underscored that the answer to crime was "quick and certain justice" meted out by the judicial authorities.[201]

FDR was an aggressive proponent of expanded federal powers in law enforcement but he never became an outspoken proponent of antilynching legislation. At the time of the Thurmond and Holmes lynchings, a task force in his Department of Justice was preparing a comprehensive crime package that included some draconian proposals, including universal fingerprinting, tripling the personnel of the FBI, and eliminating the requirement of a unanimous jury verdict in criminal cases.[202] Concerns about antagonizing the South – not qualms about an expansion of federal law enforcement powers – prompted FDR to remain silent about antilynching legislation in public. The 1942 lynching of Cleo Wright in Sikeston, Mo., finally drew the U.S. Department of Justice directly into civil rights issues for the first time. Decades of pressure, first from black clubwomen and the NAACP, and then the strains caused by fighting fascism, death camps, and communism abroad while ignoring lynchings and other abuses at home, provided an opening for the Justice Department to use expanded federal law enforcement powers to address lynchings and other civil rights violations.[203] While this helped to establish a new role for the federal government in the area of civil rights, it also legitimized a greater role for the federal government in law enforcement more widely, an important precondition for the rise of the carceral state.

Homer Cummings, FDR's attorney general from 1933 to 1939, was a forceful advocate of expanding federal law enforcement authority and the prison system. Shortly after assuming office, Cummings promised that the administration would combat the "warfare which an armed underworld is waging upon organized society." Under Cummings, the federal government began to use aggressively the new powers granted in the 1932 crime package while it developed a crime package of its own.[204] "To put it bluntly we had outgrown our law enforcement system and it had broken down under the strain," Cummings declared. In his view, criminals were exploiting the no-man's-land between federal and state jurisdictions where "there existed a kind of twilight zone, a sort of neutral corridor, unpoliced and unprotected, in which criminals of the most desperate character found an area of relative safety."[205] Roosevelt's attorney general told bureau agents under his command: "Shoot to kill – then count to ten."[206] Cummings promoted Roosevelt's crime package in a series of radio appearances and public speeches and sought to make the Department of Justice a "nerve center" of local, state, and federal law enforcement activities in the country.[207]

In May 1934, Congress, without even making a record of its vote, approved six major crime bills requested by Cummings and drafted by his Justice Department.[208] A handful of legislators regarded these bills, which greatly extended federal authority, as an alarming usurpation of states' rights.[209] Roosevelt's signing of the six bills was front-page news. FDR called the enactment of the legislation "an event of the first importance" and proclaimed that he stood "squarely behind the efforts of the Department of Justice to bring to book every law breaker, big and little."[210]

Cummings was also a partisan of prisons. Shortly after taking office, he pushed for creating a "special prison" in a remote place, like an island or Alaska, where the incarcerated would be totally isolated from the outside world. Months later, the Bureau of Prisons announced that it had taken over the military prison at Alcatraz in northern California and would be turning it into a civilian prison. There the rules would be strict, the privileges minimal, and the rule of silence, abandoned elsewhere in the prison system, would be enforced.[211] Cummings used funding from New Deal programs to further his penal agenda. He secured money from the Works Progress Administration to undertake the first comprehensive nationwide survey of parole practices.[212] Public Works Administration money was used to repair county jails and build new ones. The Federal Bureau of Prisons also used PWA funds to construct new federal facilities.[213]

Upon assuming office, Roosevelt and Cummings encouraged J. Edgar Hoover, the director of the Bureau of Investigation, which was then a small and obscure division in the Justice Department, to develop and mobilize the bureau's investigative resources and publicity department.[214] Cummings was behind a grandiose public relations campaign to turn the G-men into public heroes. Hoover, who had been appointed in 1924 after a series of massive scandals involving the Bureau of Investigation,[215] was reluctant to use the vice issue in the 1920s to rehabilitate the bureau's image. He was well aware that his agents would be just as vulnerable to the lure of corruption as the cop on the beat.[216] He had fewer reservations, however, about exploiting public fears about organized crime and gangsters.

Beginning in the 1930s, the public relations department of the FBI under Hoover's direction convinced newspapers to portray criminals like John Dillinger, Bonnie and Clyde, Pretty Boy Floyd, and Ma Barker as major threats to society. As legislators in Washington debated FDR's crime package in early 1934, the country was riveted by the exploits of Dillinger, who had escaped from an "escape-proof" jail in Indiana and managed to stop for a haircut, buy cars, and have Sunday dinner with his family while 5,000 law enforcement officers were in hot pursuit.[217] Shortly after FDR signed his crime package into law, the FBI killed three of its most wanted – Dillinger, Pretty Boy Floyd, and Baby Face Nelson – in separate bloody incidents. Hoover's G-men became the heroes of the day as they killed or apprehended outsized criminals. Books, films, and magazines, which had once emphasized the corruption and incompetence of federal agents, now "echoed a new theme: 'Crime Doesn't Pay' so long as Hoover's elite 'G-men' were around."[218] In 1936, Cummings proudly declared: "No longer does the public glorify the gangster."[219] While professional criminologists at the time doubted the country was in the grip of a crime wave, Hoover, with the help of the Roosevelt administration, created the popular impression of a society standing at the abyss with only the G-men to save it.[220] *The New York Times* regularly published kidnapping box scores on the front page that summarized the accomplishments of Hoover's agents.[221] *The Times* and other papers also gave high-profile coverage to a number of kidnapping cases, making them national events.[222]

Hoover controlled the image of crime and crime fighters not just by cajoling movie producers, radio executives, journalists, and novelists, but by controlling the national crime statistics. The decision in 1930 to designate the Bureau of Investigation as the clearinghouse for criminal statistics handed the FBI a potent weapon to control the image of crime in the United States and to politicize it selectively. The Wickersham Commission had warned in its final report in 1931 of the danger of having law enforcement agencies responsible for collecting and disseminating crime data because of their vested interests.[223] At the time, Harvard law professor Sam Bass Warner argued in favor of the Census Bureau because it was independent of law enforcement interests. The revitalized International Chiefs of Police strongly opposed him and successfully advocated for legislation empowering Hoover's Bureau of Investigation to collect the crime statistics.[224] Over subsequent decades, Hoover and his successors at the FBI manipulated the crime statistics to serve their own political and institutional needs.[225]

In the mid-1930s, the nation became obsessed with fingerprinting at the start of an intense national campaign to get all Americans to submit their fingerprints to the FBI. Hoover proposed a voluntary fingerprinting program and enlisted the support of hundreds of prominent Americans.[226] Some communities enthusiastically embraced universal fingerprinting as a civic cause and involved nearly every community organization in the mission. One of the most enthusiastic supporters was Berkeley, Calif., which succeeded in fingerprinting nearly half of its population.

The 1930s were a wildly successful period for the FBI. The 1934 crime package vastly expanded its authority. In 1935, it opened the National Police Academy, and top FBI officials began organizing and participating in dozens of state and local law enforcement conventions. Publicity about the FBI's new police academy emphasized weapons training, especially the firing of machine guns from moving vehicles.[227] Between 1932 and 1936, the academy's budget doubled.[228] In the late 1930s the power of the FBI increased enormously as Roosevelt gave the bureau authority over all domestic espionage. In 1940 Hoover revived the notorious General Intelligence Bureau and began collecting secret files on anyone loosely defined as a threat to national security.[229] During this period the bureau ingratiated itself with the Roosevelt administration by monitoring the activities of its critics. At times, Roosevelt and the FBI could be at odds over the bureau's approach to fighting communists and "subversives." However, they saw eye-to-eye on the crime issue, as evidenced by the major crime package Roosevelt's administration pushed through Congress, support for an amendment to the 1932 Lindbergh Law that made interstate kidnapping subject to the death penalty, and the significant increases in funding for the FBI to battle kidnapping and other crimes.[230]

Sex Crimes and Juvenile Delinquents

National concern about the wave of bank robberies and kidnappings receded in the 1930s, and the 1936–37 national drug scare threatened to divert attention and resources to J. Edgar Hoover's main rival, the Federal Bureau of Narcotics. Hoover responded by discovering new enemies with which to burnish the image of the FBI and to keep his agency aglow in the national spotlight. Hoover was one of the leading instigators of the sex-crime panic that began in the 1930s, lost steam during World War II, and revived in the postwar decade. The FBI and other law enforcement agencies, together with the media and citizens groups, created a wave of national hysteria over sex crimes. They implored politicians to address the problems of rape and the sexual murder of children despite paltry evidence that the incidence of these crimes was on the rise.[231] This panic about sex crimes rivaled in intensity the national hysteria about child molesters in the 1980s and 1990s. Dozens of states passed sexual psychopath statutes in the mid-1930s and the mid-1940s. These statutes were never applied to large numbers of people, suggesting that their primary purpose was symbolic rather than substantive. For many years, those laws "were cited as a model example of failed legislation called forth by politicians pandering to ill-focused public fears but that had done nothing to reduce crime or detain the truly dangerous."[232] Nonetheless, these early campaigns against sex crimes had a lasting effect on the development of contemporary penal policy.

The laws provoked a backlash by liberal jurists, psychiatrists, and scholars who challenged government claims about the extent and seriousness of the sex crimes issue. Scholarship on rape, incest, and molestation at this time "presented the plight of the abuse victim in language that seems stunningly callous to modern ears."[233] Court decisions and academic works "depicted existing sex laws as relics of prudery" and shifted the focus of judicial and public concern away from victims.[234] This callous shift away from victims of sex crimes created a counterbacklash. It helps explain why the victims' rights movement that emerged in the 1970s took such a strident antioffender stance and why feminists found themselves in alliance with hard-line conservatives on many law-and-order issues when violence against women reemerged as a central national issue in the 1970s, as discussed in Chapters 4, 5, and 6.

Hoover was also instrumental in the creation of a national panic over juvenile delinquency after World War II. During the war, Hoover warned that the social disruptions wrought by the war would result in a sharp increase in juvenile delinquency. He used hyperbolic language to predict a postwar crime wave by juveniles. "Like the sulphurous lava which boils beneath the slumbering volcano – such is the status of crime in America today," he warned.[235] Each year the Uniform Crime Reports compiled by the FBI showed that juvenile delinquency was on the rise. After the war, Tom Clark, President Harry Truman's attorney general from 1945 to 1949, bolstered Hoover's claims that juvenile delinquency was spiraling out of control. Clark kept public attention riveted on this issue. In 1946, the Justice Department convened a national conference on juvenile delinquency, out of which was born the Continuing Committee on the Prevention and Control of Delinquency. The Justice Department and the FBI battled with the Children's Bureau for control of the issue. The Children's Bureau fought unsuccessfully to prevent the issue of juvenile delinquency from becoming captive of other agencies or part of a national law-and-order crusade.[236]

The "widespread impression that vicious and bored youth turned to murder and mayhem for amusement" prompted the Senate to begin major hearings into delinquency in 1953 that continued on and off for a decade.[237] Despite sensational media reports of brutal acts committed by teenagers, it does not appear that juvenile crime increased enormously during this period.[238] Nonetheless, politicians and the public singled out the mass media and popular culture as culprits in the juvenile delinquent crime wave. Comic books in particular were crucified for appearing to glorify crime and mayhem.[239] Across the country, communities held elaborate bonfire ceremonies in which they burned comic books. By 1955, legislatures in thirteen states had enacted laws regulating the sale of comic books.[240]

Organized Crime

The concurrent agitation at the time against juvenile delinquency, organized crime, and communism created the impression that American society was coming apart.[241] Many comparisons were made between crime and communism, and similar language was often used to explain the threat each posed to the United States.[242] During the Prohibition years, "organized crime" was regarded as a homegrown, localized phenomenon, one that brought together producers, distributors, politicians, and law enforcement agencies to "make crime pay." At the time "[n]o one tried to pretend that organized crime was an alien conspiracy."[243] Subsequently, with the help of ambitious politicians and law enforcement officials, organized crime was regarded as a vast, larger-than-life network run by gangsters who terrorized American society and were not considered organic to it. Waging war against this vast conspiracy became the ticket to national fame in the 1930s, '40s, and '50s for a number of politicians.

As a special prosecutor and then district attorney in New York City, Thomas E. Dewey became a household name in the 1930s with his prosecutions of gangsters with colorful names like Dutch Schultz, Waxey

Gordon, and Charles "Lucky" Luciano. Dewey artfully manipulated the press, especially on crime issues. Thanks to Dewey, Luciano, an important Manhattan racketeer unknown outside of New York, became the most famous gangster in the country, credited with nearly boundless power and influence. The New York *Daily Mirror* described his conviction in 1936 as one "hailed throughout the country as the definite beginning of the end of gangsterism, terrorism, and commercialized criminality throughout the United States" and that "blasted open the road to clearing the country of the terrors of gangsters everywhere."[244]

Dewey used his war on racketeering and vice to burnish his image as a righteous crusader, even as he established troubling precedents in the area of civil liberties. His career as a prosecutor launched three successful campaigns for the governorship of New York and two failed runs for the White House as head of the Republican ticket in 1944 and 1948. After he retired from public life in 1954, Dewey remained a power behind the throne in the Republican Party. He was the political patron of Richard Nixon, who enshrined the law-and-order issue in his 1968 and 1972 presidential campaigns.[245] Penal policy was also important to the political identity and aspirations of Earl Warren, who shared the Republican ticket with Dewey in 1948. Warren served as governor of California from 1943 to 1953 during a period when the state was recognized nationally as an incubator of penal innovation. With his eye on the White House, Warren wavered at key moments on the issue of capital punishment, which cost the anti-death penalty coalition dearly, and people on death row like Caryl Chessman even more dearly.[246]

This is not just a simple story of opportunistic politicians with presidential aspirations latching onto law enforcement issues to launch themselves into the national spotlight and in the process nationalizing the crime issue and legitimizing a larger role for the federal government in law enforcement. Truman tried to ride out the hysteria over crime by issuing some modest bureaucratic directives and expressing his willingness to cooperate with state and local authorities on law enforcement issues. He initially characterized crime as largely a local problem, best dealt with by cultivating the "gentler forces" of church and home life. He warned against using the crime issue for personal gain and about the potential vulnerability of civil liberties in the face of crime crusades.[247]

Local officials, especially mayors, were critical in maneuvering the Truman administration and other federal authorities into taking a more aggressive approach to crime, in particular organized crime. They shrewdly manipulated the crime issue to deflect attention away from their own shortcomings. As president of the American Municipal Association, Mayor de Lesseps S. Morrison of New Orleans used the organization as a platform to promote his ideas about the existence of a national conspiracy of organized crime. Morrison and other mayors provided a critical opening for public officials at the national level to seize upon the crime issue. Pressured by Morrison's national crusade against crime, J. Howard McGrath, Truman's attorney general from 1949 to 1952, sponsored a conference of mayors and law enforcement officials in early 1950s to study the issue. In his opening remarks, McGrath looked to local communities to lead the charge: "The stage is set for you to capture the popular imagination in a stirring campaign to crush organized crime in your communities."[248] But the mayors regarded the conference as an opportunity to press the point that organized crime was just too big a problem for them to handle and that the only solution was a greater federal commitment, including the enactment of more federal laws and the extension of the law enforcement capacity of the federal government. In doing so, they deflected attention away from corruption in their own backyards and other lapses in municipal law enforcement. This conference and the publicity it generated are credited with rescuing a bill that called for a congressional investigation of interstate crime, which was sponsored by Estes Kefauver (D-Tenn.), an ambitious freshman senator.[249]

The crime issue was critical to the national ambitions of Kefauver and another freshman senator, Joseph McCarthy (R-Wisc.), who competed for authority to wage a crusade against organized crime.[250] Searching in early 1950 for a big issue to propel his 1952 reelection campaign, McCarthy was weighing crime and communism as two possibilities. Kefauver outmaneuvered McCarthy on the crime issue. With public pressure building from the American Municipal Association, the media, and elsewhere to do something about organized crime, Kefauver secured Senate approval in May 1950 for the establishment of the Special Committee to Investigate Organized Crime in Interstate Commerce. He ended up chairman of this committee, which was expected to embarrass his own party because the Democrats controlled most of the big cities that the committee would investigate. In pushing for this committee, Kefauver implied that the federal government – that is, the Truman administration – had been negligent and must be forced to take action.[251] McCarthy had to settle for communism as his issue – and the rest is history.

The crusade against communism and the rise and fall of McCarthy in the early 1950s have overshadowed the significance and drama of the Kefauver investigation. During its fifteen-month lifespan, the committee convened hearings in fourteen major cities that riveted national attention on crime and Kefauver. The hearings were short on evidence but high on drama. The final hearings took place in New York City in 1951. They were an unprecedented media event, as an estimated twenty to thirty million people tuned in nationwide. The public interest in the hearings outstripped interest in the World Series. Newspapers reported that Con Edison had to turn on another generator to meet the spike in demand for electricity, and that stores and movie theaters were deserted as people stayed home to watch the hearings. Kefauver's televised drama was a template for McCarthy's later use of television during his crusade against communism.[252]

Although his committee received enormous publicity, Congress did not enact any of the various measures Kefauver recommended in 1951. Nonetheless, these hearings were a watershed for the politics of crime and punishment and for contemporary penal policy. They transformed Kefauver into a national figure, "a modern Sir Galahad crisscrossing the country in search of evildoers upon whom to wield the fatal sword of public exposure."[253] The hearings demonstrated for all to see the potency of the crime issue for national electoral politics. In 1952, Kefauver stood second only to Truman in opinion polls as the Democratic choice for president. While he never succeeded in his goal of heading the Democratic ticket, he did serve in 1956 as the vice-presidential candidate on Adlai Stevenson's ticket. The battle against organized crime became a signature issue for President John F. Kennedy and his brother and attorney general, Robert F. Kennedy, who intently mobilized to fight what he called the "enemy within."[254]

The Kefauver hearings recast the organized crime issue. In the 1920s organized crime was characterized as largely a local homegrown affair, and in the 1930s as a vast economic network akin to a corporation. By the 1950s it was considered an alien, ethnic conspiracy that "originated outside of American society and was imposed upon the public by a group of immoral men."[255] The economic, legal, and social conditions that gave rise to crime – which had been important areas of research and public concern in the Progressive era, the 1920s, and the 1930s – were overshadowed in the public debate about crime in later decades. Now crime was increasingly cast as a law enforcement issue, not a sociological one, and criminals were portrayed as somehow outside of American society, not organic to it.[256]

Conclusion

More than in other areas of American history and politics, we have incredible amnesia when it comes to the history of crime and punishment. Graduate students in American politics are expected to be familiar with Tocqueville's *Democracy in America*. Yet few political scientists know that prisons, not democracy, were what initially brought Tocqueville to the United States. Pressured by the Chamber of Deputies to hasten reform of France's penal system, the Minister of the Interior awarded a commission to twenty-six-year-old Tocqueville and his traveling companion Gustave de Beaumont to study the American penitentiary, which had become world famous by the 1830s. Tocqueville collected notes for his classic study of the social and political conditions of the new republic as he and Beaumont traveled from prison to prison, interviewing wardens and prisoners and collecting data about everything from the living conditions to the disciplinary policies and practices.[257] Tocqueville's paeans to democracy in *Democracy in America* are widely cited. Yet his and Beaumont's dark observations about the connection between the penal system and American democracy are seldom noted, except by a small circle of criminologists. Tocqueville and Beaumont warned: "While society in the United States gives the example of the most extended liberty, the prisons of the same country offer the spectacle of the most complete despotism."[258]

This chapter shows what we miss by ignoring the long history of penal policy in our efforts to explain why the relatively recent establishment of the carceral state did not face more political opposition. Its close examination of the role of crime and punishment in American political development underscores the importance of not evaluating the last three to four decades by the yardstick of some precious "golden age" that never existed in the United States.[259] It helps disabuse us of the notion that deep public angst about crime, violence, and disorder are something relatively new in American political development and in national politics. In fact, the country has an anxious past. Periodically the United States has embarked on reform movements or crusades that have fitfully contributed to the consolidation of carceral power. The absence of or limited development of some of the basic criminal justice institutions channeled the development of these movements and crusades. Likewise, these movements and crusades had a reciprocal effect on the development of criminal justice institutions. For much of U.S. history, the country's racial, ethnic, and regional divisions acted as a check on the development of criminal justice institutions at the national level, as evidenced, for example, by the crippling of the Department of Justice after Reconstruction and the intense, decades-long dispute over antilynching legislation. But those divisions also promulgated fears that could, under certain conditions, result in greater criminalization, as laid out in compelling detail in James Morone's *Hellfire Nation*.

What changed so profoundly from the 1960s onward was not that national politicians finally discovered the crime card, but rather how they played it. Once the South reached détente with the rest of the country over the racial divide in the postwar decades as Jim Crow came tumbling down, federal law enforcement capacity expanded. Opportunistic local politicians egged on federal officials to expand federal policing and punishment powers. The debate over law and order no longer hinged, as it had for so much of American political development, on fundamental questions of state power. Instead, the main issue for politicians with greater political ambitions was divining and defining the public will on penal policy. As shown in the next chapter, victims of crime came to embody that public will, which had profound consequences for the rise of the carceral state.

Previous campaigns for law and order were hampered not by a lack of zeal, but by the limits of the state's law enforcement institutions to wage war on the enemies of the moment, be they prostitutes, drug abusers, bootleggers, gamblers, pedophiles, juvenile delinquents, psychopaths, pornographers, common thieves, or comic books. These prior campaigns were significant because they bolstered the state's capacity and legitimated its role in defining morality, running the punishment apparatus, and waging war against the criminal and the immoral.

The earlier institutional and ideological developments excavated here were important preconditions for the eventual construction of the carceral state beginning in the 1970s. They help explain why long-standing concerns about the reach of state power in law enforcement receded even as the United States embarked on an unprecedented expansion of state power in the realm of penal policy. A full explanation requires attention to why the political environment was so permissive for the rise of the carceral state from the 1970s onward. The following chapters focus on more contemporary developments, in particular the manner in which certain social movements and interest groups mobilized around crime and punishment issues over the last three to four decades.

4   THE CARCERAL STATE AND
THE WELFARE STATE

The Comparative Politics of Victims

"Revenge is a kind of wild justice, which the more men's nature runs to, the more ought law to weed it out."

– Francis Bacon

T HE UNITED STATES gave birth to a formidable victims' movement in the 1970s that was highly retributive and punitive. Victims became a powerful weapon in the arsenal of proponents of the law-and-order agenda. In a way not seen in other Western countries, penal conservatives successfully framed the issue as a zero-sum game that pitted the rights of victims against the rights of offenders. This contributed significantly to a hardening of the penal climate against those who break the law. Whereas a concern for victims initially emerged in the 1950s and early 1960s out of progressive impulses in the United States and other countries, conservative impulses were clearly ascendant in the U.S. case by the late 1970s.

The dominant ideological current running through the U.S. victims' movement was retributive and focused on criminal justice concerns. Its guiding principles included a strong belief that offenders should be punished based on how much punishment they inflict on society and on individual victims; that victims should be given more power in decisions about prosecution and sentencing; and that the criminal justice system exists largely to satisfy the victim's "desire for justice, moral vindication or revenge."[1] This retributive criminal justice view of what victims deserve established such a tenacious hold in the United States by the 1980s that it is easy to overlook alternative perspectives that initially helped to spur an interest in the plight of victims in the United States and that continued to predominate in other countries.[2]

These alternative frameworks are generally associated with progressive rather than conservative political forces. The first is the "care ideology," which is rooted in the basic premises of the welfare state. The guiding principle is the idea that the community, as much as possible, should attempt to alleviate severe hardships. Just as the state extends the social safety net to people who get injured on the job, become unemployed, or fall seriously ill, so it should extend its social protections to those who fall victim to crime.[3] The second alternative view is premised on the idea of rehabilitation and the needs of offenders. Here the basic premise is that crime should be regarded largely as a conflict between two parties, both of whom need to be treated. The aim is to involve the victim in the criminal justice process not as a way to exact revenge or retribution, but to help rehabilitate the offender and heal the victim through programs like restitution and mediation.

The third alternative has its roots in the abolitionist penal movement and is at the polar opposite of the criminal justice approach to victims. Proponents of this view, notably the Norwegian criminologist Nils Christie, lament, as do many penal conservatives, the declining role and power of the victim with the development of modern criminal justice systems.[4] They part ways with conservatives, however, in arguing that this marginalization of the victim has had adverse effects on *both* victims and offenders. They favor creating an entirely new system to deal with most crime that would be based primarily on the principles of civil law. The state criminal justice authorities would intervene as little as possible in settling disputes. Instead, the primary locus for dealing with criminal behavior would shift to neighborhood and other local social groups, who would rely on mechanisms like mediation, reparations, crime prevention, and services and aid for victims.

The central issue addressed in this chapter is why the criminal justice perspective on victims came to dominate in the United States but not other Western countries. Many analysts single out the behavior of political elites to explain this outcome. In their accounts, the U.S. victims' movement raced off in a more punitive direction as conservative politicians discovered the political rewards of fanning the public's fear of crime and strategically juxtaposed the rights of victims to the rights of offenders in the wake of a number of court rulings favorable to suspects and prisoners.[5] This proved to be an effective means to harvest votes, build support for a hard-line agenda, and construct a new political base as the New Deal Democratic coalition decayed and the Republican Party sought to establish itself as the dominant political force in the South for the first time since Reconstruction. The conservative victims' movement, with its stress on victims' rights, ended up having such traction because of these seismic shifts in the governing bases of the political parties, so the argument goes. By the mid-1980s this growing social movement was comprised of thousands of groups at the local, state, and national level devoted to victims. The call for victims' rights also resonated so powerfully because it complemented the country's liberal, rights-based political tradition and stood in contrast to the prisoners' rights and other penal reform movements that took the rights of the accused, the convicted, and the condemned as their starting point.

There is good evidence to support this view that political elites were key in seeding and promoting the victims' movement, and that the country's liberal tradition provided a particularly hospitable environment for a rights-based victims' movement to emerge and flourish. Major political figures, notably Republican presidents followed by leading Democrats playing catch-up, elevated the issue of victims and their rights to a stature not previously witnessed in American politics. In accepting the GOP presidential nomination in 1968, Richard M. Nixon proclaimed that freedom from violent crime is "the first civil right of every American."[6] In his special message to Congress on crime in 1975, Gerald R. Ford declared, "For too long, law has centered its attention more on the rights of the criminal defendant than on the victim of crime. It is time for law to concern itself more with the rights of the people it exists to protect."[7] Ronald Reagan designated victims a cornerstone of his crime policies and promised to overhaul the federal code to "redress the imbalance between the rights of the accused and the rights of the innocent."[8] During the 1996 campaign, Bill Clinton appeared at a Rose Garden event with family members of crime victims to declare that "the only way to give victims equal and due consideration" is to amend the Constitution.[9]

The contention that the strategic calculations and resulting political behavior of political elites explain why such a virulently punitive victims' rights movement emerged in the United States is not so much wrong as it is incomplete. Such a focus fails to explain why elites in the United States were more inclined to adopt such mobilization strategies and why they were more likely to succeed here than elsewhere. The United States was more conducive to the coalescence of a powerful victims' movement centered on ratcheting up the penalties for offenders and granting victims more "rights" in the criminal justice process because of several important institutional differences. The varying institutional settings help us understand why politicians and public officials in the United States tended to pursue punitive options and why these options found more receptive soil in the United States than elsewhere.

First, the weakness of the welfare state in the United States was consequential. Britain and other advanced industrialized countries first discovered the victims issue in the late 1950s and early 1960s. The greater development of and consensus around the welfare state left an important mark on victim-related policies and politics in Europe. Extending a hand to victims was seen from the start as primarily an extension of the welfare state rather than just a new twist in penal policy. This was not so in the United States, due in part to the shallower roots and exceptional character of the U.S. welfare state.

In the 1980s, victims began to receive renewed attention in several European countries, notably Britain, Germany, and the Netherlands.[10] However, given the stickiness of institutions, the nascent victims' movements in these countries did not become powerful springboards for more punitive penal policies. The movements in Europe tended to push for improvements in services to victims rather than expanding victims' rights at the cost of the rights of the accused. In most European countries, "the idea of forcing change through the claiming and establishment of victims' rights was considered impractical, unlikely, and even unthinkable."[11]

Given the weakness of the U.S. welfare state, some specific attributes of crime-related institutions also molded the development of the victims' movement. Two important contemporary institutions were especially consequential: the pioneering, large-scale social survey research on victims carried out in the United States; and the establishment of the Law Enforcement Assistance Administration (LEAA) in the U.S. Department of Justice. But there were also other institutional factors that one might consider to be deeper and more historical. The United States, which is generally regarded as a weak state, was a pioneer in the establishment of a strong public prosecutor and in abandoning reliance on private prosecution in the nineteenth century. This had important consequences for penal policy as interest in victims surged in the late 1960s. Additional institutional factors include: the adversarial common-law legal system that prevails in the United States and Britain but not in continental Europe; and significant differences in the legal training, professional norms, and career paths of prosecutors, judges, and other judicial administrators in the United States and Europe.

Initial Interest in Victims

Interest in the needs of victims emerged in other Western countries before it did in the United States for several reasons. In the case of Britain, for example, the key factors were elite-level leadership and the greater development of and consensus around the welfare state in that country. Elite interest in victims came primarily from two quarters – opponents of the death penalty, and penal reformers concerned about the plight of offenders.[12] As Britain edged away from the death penalty in the face of strong public support for retaining it, lawmakers and others pushing hard in the 1950s and 1960s for the abolition of capital punishment viewed giving greater attention to the needs of victims as a way to mollify the public.[13] Margery Fry, the first secretary of the Howard League, Britain's leading penal reform organization, was pivotal in publicizing the plight of victims beginning in the 1950s at a time when no organized group of victims was seeking redress. Fry argued that greater attention to the needs of victims would actually help offenders by neutralizing vigilante sentiment. Fry was intrigued by reparations schemes, seeing them as a way to reintegrate offenders back into the community by allowing them to make amends to their victims. By 1959, some form of aid to victims was an official part of the Conservative Party's platform, though the emphasis had shifted from offender reparations to providing victims with compensation from the state.[14]

Influenced by the work of Fry and others in Britain, New Zealand became the first country to establish a victim compensation plan. New Zealand already was a pioneer in the development of the modern welfare state with passage of its Old Age Pensions Act in 1898 and a string of other social welfare legislation. In September 1963, New Zealand's ruling National Party proposed legislation to compensate victims of violent crime. The party had recently abolished capital punishment and was pushing other progressive reforms, including the greater use of halfway houses. It promoted the victims legislation to neutralize criticism of its penal reforms and to respond to growing public concern about crime. The legislation, which was enacted with little controversy and went into effect on January 1, 1964, was inspired by the New Zealand Workers' Compensation Act of 1956.[15] Both acts were premised on the idea "that fault is immaterial to the award of benefits." Just as employers "are held responsible not because they are at fault but because it is socially desirable that compensation be provided to injured workers; similarly, state payments to victims of crime is justified not because the state is at fault but because compensation is socially desirable."[16]

The practice of maintaining a rough parity for all compensation payments prompted New Zealand to establish a Royal Commission in 1966, headed by Sir Owen Woodhouse, to take a comprehensive look at all of the country's economic security programs. The 1967 Woodhouse Report recommended that New Zealand establish a single, comprehensive, state-run insurance system.[17] The commission explicitly rejected having any compensation "be regarded as a legal issue." Rather it was to be considered "part of the general responsibility that rests upon any strong and developed country to provide a system of income maintenance, a support for the living standards of citizens who have suffered as the random victims of 'social' progress."[18] Many of the recommendations of the Woodhouse Report became law in 1972. Under the Accident Compensation Act, injured workers and automobile accident victims essentially gave up their right to sue in exchange for universal guaranteed benefits. Over the next few years the scheme was expanded to include a wide range of other misfortunes, including criminal victimization, mishaps on the athletic field, medical malpractice, and sexual harassment.[19]

By including crime victims in the radical overhaul of its social welfare system, New Zealand firmly anchored victims of crime in its expansive welfare state rather than in its criminal justice apparatus. In doing so, it denied them a powerful political identity independent from that of other victims of misfortune. This in turn helped rob the crime-victim issue of some of its political salience. It opened up an important avenue to be supportive of crime victims by bolstering the welfare state rather than by expanding the criminal justice system.

A similar process took place in Britain as Fry and other early British advocates of victims' compensation schemes promoted these measures by characterizing them as extensions of the welfare state.[20] They made explicit comparisons with social legislation like Britain's Workmen's Compensation and Industrial Injuries Compensation Acts. Their arguments were persuasive with civil servants in the Home Office, who were instrumental in the development of the Criminal Injuries (Compensation) Bill, which was presented to Parliament in late 1959.[21] In 1964, England, Wales, and Scotland set up Europe's first state compensation scheme by administrative fiat.[22] Notably, the Home Office, while it supported the idea of compensation, explicitly rejected from the outset the notion of "victims' rights." According to a 1964 Home Office White Paper on the subject of victims' compensation, the government explicitly repudiated the view that it was "liable for injuries caused to people by the acts of others." The White Paper went on to argue that the government nonetheless supported the concept of compensation out of a recognition that the public felt "a sense of responsibility for and sympathy with the innocent victim."[23]

There are several things to note about the origins of this first wave of concern for victims in Britain and New Zealand that distinguished it from the victims' movement that emerged later in the United States. First, it originated with elite penal reformers concerned foremost about the plight of offenders and broader penal reform issues. Second, victims themselves did not wage a mass campaign. Indeed, they were largely "mute, invisible, and unorganized."[24] The creation of the victims' compensation scheme in England was primarily the result of elite-level politics without any significant public input. Finally, victims' compensation was viewed as a social welfare issue, not primarily a penal one. Reformers sought to bestow compensation on victims much as the expanding welfare state bestowed housing, education, and medical services on its clients. The main preoccupation in Britain and New Zealand was on providing compensation to victims, not rights.[25] Britain's Criminal Injuries Compensation legislation funnelled only minimal amounts of money to victims.[26] Its greater significance was in how it reinforced the view that victims were primarily a social welfare issue, not a penal one, and that victims had no special rights. "From the start, the emphasis in Britain has been on the plight of the victim as an individual who has suffered from crime, rather than as a potentially useful witness for the prosecution," explains Lord Windlesham.[27]

This initial wave of agitation on behalf of victims that began in the late 1950s in Britain and New Zealand and peaked in the early-to-mid-1960s provoked some, but not much, interest in the United States.[28] One proponent of greater help for U.S. victims suggested at the time that expanding private insurance to compensate crime victims might be the only realistic option. He lamented that this was the only realistic option because the U.S. welfare state was "decades behind that of other countries," and Americans were "so far from public acceptance of state compensation."[29] Ironically, victims' compensation in the United States was initially associated with leading liberals, not conservatives. In 1965, Senator Ralph Yarborough (D-Tex.) proposed a victims' compensation bill in Congress based on the New Zealand plan.[30] Six years later, Senator Mike Mansfield (D-Mont.), the majority leader of the Senate, introduced a federal compensation scheme for victims, but his bill also made little headway.[31]

In the mid-1960s several states began experimenting with victims' compensation schemes.[32] In 1965 California became the first U.S. jurisdiction to establish such a program, but used the term "aid" rather than compensation or restitution.[33] California created a highly restrictive program that equated aid to victims with welfare laws designed to help the poor. Like many other early victims' compensation schemes developed at the state level, the California program was not viewed as a critical extension of a universal safety net, such as Social Security. Rather it was considered more akin to public-assistance programs like Aid to Families with Dependent Children (AFDC) that targeted the poor. Most of these early state-level compensation programs excluded victims who were deemed "undeserving" and emphasized the needs of "innocent" victims.[34] Because victims of violent crime tended to be poor, the early compensation schemes were also seen as a way to reduce urban unrest.[35] In 1967, the California program's connection to social welfare concerns became even more tenuous when the legislature transferred it from the Welfare Department to the State Board of Control.[36]

Mass Surveys of Victimization in the United States

This first wave of interest in victims quickly dissipated in the United States, partly because the comparative underdevelopment of the U.S. welfare state did not provide a good environment to sustain it. A second wave took off in the 1970s in the United States. By the 1980s, concerns about victims had blossomed into a full-fledged social movement that diverged even more sharply from developments in Britain and other countries. Two related factors propelled this new interest in victims in the United States – the widespread use of the victim survey and the creation of the LEAA within the U.S. Department of Justice.

More so in the United States than elsewhere, crime surveys provided "a methodological tool to fuse the discourses of law and order to anxieties about personal safety."[37] Social surveys date back to at least the early twentieth century and have been widely used in the United States and other countries since the 1920s. But the idea of using social survey methods to study crime and its victims did not emerge until the mid-1960s.[38] The United States was a pioneer in the use of large-scale survey research on crime-related issues beginning in the 1960s with the work of P. H. Ennis and others.[39] Mass victimization surveys intended to reveal "the unreported 'dark figure' of crime" supplanted earlier micro-studies of individual victims.[40]

Lyndon Johnson's President's Commission on Law Enforcement and Administration of Justice gave pivotal institutional support to the development of large-scale victimization surveys.[41] The commission carried out three important pilot studies of victims in 1965 that became landmarks in the study of crime.[42] The U.S. surveys discovered, among other things, that the level of victimization was much higher than previously indicated by the standard indices of crime, the FBI's Uniform Crime Reports (UCR).[43] This promoted the belief that much crime went unreported and thus unprosecuted. Concern began to grow that the lack of cooperation by victims and witnesses was undermining the efficiency and operations of the criminal justice system.[44] LBJ's crime commission recommended the establishment of a clearinghouse for crime-related statistics, including victim surveys. After Congress created the LEAA in 1968, the new agency and the Census Bureau together developed a national program of victimization surveys that began in earnest in 1972 after several pilot programs. This heralded the widespread use of mass victimization surveys, most notably the National Crime Surveys sponsored by the Bureau of Justice Statistics.[45]

Research on victims developed differently in Western Europe and thus had different political consequences. In Britain, for example, apart from a valuable pilot project in 1977, there was no serious survey of victimization until 1982, when the first British Crime Survey was conducted. As a consequence, victim-related policies developed in a different context, one largely devoid of concerns, backed up by survey research, about the large proportion of crime that went unreported and unprosecuted.[46] It was only with the first national British crime surveys in the early 1980s that the wider public became aware of the high levels of previously unidentified crime, and public fears of crime began to outstrip the actual risk of being a victim.[47]

The Nordic countries began victimization research in earnest in the 1970s. Unlike in the United States, Nordic research on victims did not spawn a whole new discipline of victimology separate from the traditional field of criminology. Most Nordic criminologists found such a separation artificial. Studies of victims stayed anchored in the field of criminology which, in the Nordic case, is dominated by concerns about the excessive reliance on prisons as a social control mechanism.[48] Furthermore, the study of victims in the Nordic countries did not become an alternative site for political activism around the cause of victims, devoid of broader penal and other social concerns (a charge leveled by some at the burgeoning field of victimology in the United States).[49] None of the Scandinavian countries promoted "victimagogic penal bills."[50]

Despite the growing public and political interest in victims in the 1980s and the proliferation of mass victimization studies, there was relatively little rigorous research on key aspects of victimization. "Victimology," a subfield of criminology, had existed only since the late 1940s. Decades later, when the U.S. victims' movement was coming into its own, information about the experience and psychology of victims was still slim. Policy makers, politicians, activists, and the public assumed many things about crime victims without actually knowing much about the experience of victimization and its effects. Research focused on other issues, like who is most likely to become a victim and how best to measure the victimization rate. Many of the new public policies supposedly intended to help victims were based on "a new mythology of victimization" that failed to hear victims' concerns.[51] Researchers exhaustively documented how much crime goes unreported, which led many to conclude that victims do not go to the authorities because they are somehow alienated from the criminal justice system. Yet research on victim alienation was limited and left numerous questions unresolved.[52] Research was also scarce on the question of whether greater victim involvement in criminal proceedings would reduce their alienation, thus leading more victims to report crimes to the police.[53] The accepted wisdom was that victims were punitive, even though the limited psychological evidence available seemed to suggest that retribution and tougher law enforcement (two of the central demands of the victims' rights movement) failed "to address the experience and real needs of past victims."[54] In short, major projects aimed at fulfilling victims' needs were bolstered by these surveys without regard to, or a good understanding of, victims' real needs.[55]

The Creation of the LEAA

In the U.S. case, improving the efficiency of the criminal justice system became the basis for government funding of many victim and witness programs.[56] Whereas crime and law and order have been central features of American political development since the United States was founded (as shown in Chapter 3), until the 1960s little federal money was actually spent on crime control. Passage of the Omnibus Crime Control and Safe Streets Act in 1968 prompted a dramatic shift. Called the "master plan for the national war on crime," it created the LEAA, an appendage of the Justice Department.[57] A central mission of the LEAA, which was established in response to the recommendations and findings of President Johnson's crime commission, was to fund projects that would improve the criminal justice system's handling of victims and witnesses.[58] The agency provided a mechanism for channeling huge amounts of federal money to state and local law enforcement agencies and was one of the first significant expressions of the New Federalism that Nixon later extolled.[59] At the time a stalemate existed between conservatives, who argued that crime could be reduced by increasing the capacity of law enforcement to capture, convict, and punish offenders, and liberals, who contended that the causes of crime were rooted in the social structure. The Safe Streets Act was a compromise measure that established a process for distributing funds through an "unusually complex" block-grant structure.[60] It gave state and local law enforcement authorities enormous discretion to use federal funds as they saw fit without providing them with a "coherent definition of and attack upon the crime problem."[61]

By the time Congress pulled the plug on the LEAA in 1979, it was widely discredited.[62] Vexed with divided authority, diffuse responsibility, and no clear mission statement, the LEAA came to be viewed as a giant pork-barrel operation that allowed state and local law enforcement agencies to go on huge shopping sprees as they purchased all kinds of policing and military hardware and established special units, most notably SWAT teams.[63] Its budget blossomed from $63 million in 1968 to nearly $1 billion-a-year in its heyday in the 1970s.[64] The agency was by many measures a failure, according to Malcolm Feeley and Austin Sarat in their detailed institutional history of the LEAA. It did not lead to the creation of new institutions with the "authority and expertise to significantly alter crime fighting strategies."[65] But by other measures, the LEAA left an enduring mark on penal politics, one that outlived the agency itself.

The LEAA was more than just Santa Claus to hard-pressed state and local law enforcement agencies. Congressional dismay over the pork-barrel excesses of the LEAA and its apparent sense of drift belie the agency's profound effect on penal politics. The LEAA's dogged embrace of the victims' cause provided a way out of the impasse between conservatives and liberals over crime policy. The LEAA was pivotal in the creation of not just a victims' movement in the United States, but a very particular kind of victims' movement, one that viewed the rights of victims as a zero-sum game predicated on tougher penalties for offenders.

Administrators at the LEAA saw the victims issue as a vehicle to reclaim the initiative in crime policy from the states and from cities led by Democratic mayors. They also viewed it as a way to improve the efficacy of the criminal justice system. LEAA's block-grant mechanism initially stymied the Nixon administration's desire to be seen as the main avenger of crime and to bypass the State Planning Agencies established under LBJ's Safe Streets Act. Because the grants tended to filter down to large cities led by Democratic mayors, LEAA administrators became more critical of state block grants and more supportive of grants made directly to law enforcement personnel and other groups.[66] By 1974, Congress wanted to reassert some federal control over crime policies vis-à-vis the states and cities and was interested in funding new and different "social programs" to combat crime.[67] In response to this coincidence of interests, Donald Santarelli, the top administrator of the LEAA, created a new unit called the Citizens Initiative in 1974. Its main goals were to enlist more citizens in the "war against crime" and to promote greater concern for victims and witnesses in the criminal justice system.[68]

The LEAA funded some of the pioneering studies of victims. In response to concerns about the need for better statistics to tackle the "war on crime," the LEAA sponsored the first truly national survey of crime victimization in 1972, as well as an important study of the criminal court system that examined its effectiveness, in particular its conviction rates. These studies appeared to bolster claims that many victims and witnesses were reluctant to come forward to the authorities and cooperate with the criminal justice system. In response, the LEAA established its Crime Victim Initiative, which provided crucial funding to victim and witness programs designed to increase cooperation with authorities. By 1980 it was funding hundreds of such programs nationwide, many of them located in prosecutors' offices.[69] After the LEAA was disbanded in 1980, the Crime Victims Fund (which was created under the Crime Victims Act) and state block grants provided by the Justice Assistance Act of 1984 became the primary sources of federal support for crime victims.[70]

In addition to funding hundreds of victim and witness programs, the LEAA and the federal government had a significant impact on the victims' movement in other ways. In the United States there has been a greater tendency to conceive of social problems in terms of individual traits and personalities in need of therapy rather than as a consequence of deeper social and economic problems.[71] This fed the belief that specially trained paid professionals were best suited to deal with victims. The LEAA supported the premise that social service workers and victims' advocates needed special training to deal with victims and it sponsored a number of major training and educational conferences. These conferences led to the creation of the National Organization for Victim Assistance (NOVA) in 1975, which became the nucleus for the victims' movement.[72] That same year, the American Bar Association created for the first time in its history a victims committee within its criminal justice section. From the start, that committee was extremely active.[73]

Most NOVA participants worked for LEAA-funded projects.[74] Over the next few years, NOVA was transformed from a volunteer-run public-interest group into a professionally staffed organization, thanks to critical funding from the LEAA and other grants from the Department of Justice and National Institute of Mental Health. NOVA was an outspoken advocate of federal support for victims' services and viewed such grants strategically, seeing them as a way to embolden a broader social movement.[75] Its annual conference became the "Mecca of the victim-rights movement."[76]

NOVA was and is an umbrella organization that shelters a range of groups, programs, and causes, not all of them reflective of a conservative, hard-line approach to criminal justice. For example, beginning in the mid-1980s, NOVA designated crimes against racial minority groups and against lesbians and gays – hardly popular causes with the right – as two of its top priorities. That said, U.S. victims' groups tend to emphasize "rights rather than needs and the presentation of victims problems as part of a law-and-order problem," which complements the interests of penal conservatives.[77] NOVA's stated policy was "to take no policy positions on the death penalty and other punishment issues."[78] But at its conferences and in its publications NOVA gave a prominent platform to national figures who staked out tough law-and-order stances and who explicitly equated protecting victims with passing tougher criminal statutes. For example, in his keynote address at NOVA's annual conference in 1992, Attorney General William P. Barr credited the victims' rights movement with spearheading the restoration of "proper balance" in the criminal justice system. "This movement is helping to bring *justice* back into our justice system," Barr said. "We should not forget that justice is done when people get what they deserve."[79]

By the early 1980s, interest in the plight of victims was intense, resulting in a flurry of legislative and other political activity, thanks in part to government-supported organizations like NOVA. If the "success" of a movement is measured by legislation passed, organizations created, and major shifts in public attention to and conceptions of an issue, then the U.S. victims' movement was remarkably successful.[80] Victim advocacy groups played a prominent role in the formation and passage of measures that enlarged victims' rights and toughened penalties for offenders.[81]

Indeed, as early as 1983, a major newspaper proclaimed that the "so-called victims' movement seems to be making faster progress than any previous civil rights thrust in United States history."[82] In the executive branch, Attorney General Edwin L. Meese III, who had a deep and abiding interest in victims dating back to his years as a public prosecutor in Oakland, Ca., was a champion of victims in the Reagan administration.[83] After just three months in office, Reagan inaugurated National Victims' Rights Week. In 1981 he also created the President's Task Force on Victims of Crime, the first such presidential commission in U.S. history. Its final report in 1982 became a blueprint for major pieces of national and state legislation regarding victims. The task force made sixty-eight recommendations aimed at preventing victimization and providing assistance to those who are victimized. By 1989, the administration and Congress had acted upon three-quarters of those recommendations.[84]

Even before the presidential task force released its final report, Congress anticipated some of its recommendations and enacted the Victim Witness Protection Act in 1982, which authorized victim restitution and the use of victim impact statements in federal cases. It also required the attorney general to issue guidelines for the development of additional policies covering victims and witnesses. Two years later, Congress passed the federal Victims of Crime Act. VOCA established a fund to make grants to states for victims' compensation and assistance programs, and for child abuse prevention and treatment.[85]

This federal legislative activity was matched at the state level. In 1982 California became the first state to amend its constitution to explicitly recognize victims' rights. Three years earlier Wisconsin enacted the first bill of rights for victims. By the time Reagan left office, legislatures in nearly every state had enacted some version of a victims' rights statute.[86] Victims secured all sorts of rights, including the right to a speedy disposition of their case, a voice in sentencing, notification of parole hearings, input in parole decisions, restitution, and compensation. Legal rights for victims became so extensive that the American Civil Liberties Union in 1985 published a handbook devoted to the rights of victims.[87] Victims' rights expanded in 1990 with the passage of the Victim Rights and Restitution Act, which gave crime victims in federal cases numerous new rights to participate in judicial proceedings. The 1994 omnibus Violent Crime Control and Law Enforcement Act further expanded the rights of victims in federal cases by, for example, giving them the opportunity to speak out at sentencing hearings. It also made restitution mandatory in sexual assault cases and increased the amount of federal money available for local victim services.[88]

For all the publicity they garnered, federal and state compensation programs provided little substantive assistance to individual victims, and many victims had trouble securing the rights they had been given statutorily.[89] Compensation and other federal programs were pivotal, however, in transforming the politics surrounding victimization and shifting the broader penal climate in a more punitive direction. Funding from VOCA became an important source of money for grassroots victims' programs.[90] In response to VOCA, the Reagan administration established the Office on Victims to administer funds that Congress had appropriated to assist victims and victims' organizations. The number of such organizations skyrocketed, from 200 in the early 1980s to more than 8,000 by the early 1990s, according to a directory published by NOVA.[91] Most of these victims' organizations were small, local operations, but some had a formidable national presence with extensive local chapters. The most notable example is Mothers Against Drunk Driving. Established in 1980 by the mother of a thirteen-year-old struck and killed by a repeat offender, MADD grew to over 600 state organizations and chapters. MADD was, according to one account, instrumental in the passage of more than 2,500 anti-drunk-driving, victims' rights, and underage-drinking-prevention laws. It sought to educate the public that death and injuries caused by drunk drivers were "the most frequently committed violent crime" in the United States.[92]

After Reagan's Task Force on Victims of Crime issued its final report in 1982, some important figures in the victims' rights movement formed an ad hoc committee to study its recommendations. They were particularly interested in the task force's proposal to change the Sixth Amendment of the Constitution so as to guarantee crime victims the right to participate in all stages of the judicial process. They discussed ways to gain support for the measure in state legislatures in order to build national momentum to amend the U.S. Constitution. In 1985, the children of Sunny von Bulow, the Rhode Island heiress who fell into a coma under suspicious circumstances, agreed to fund their efforts. This resulted in the establishment of the Sunny von Bulow National Crime Advocacy Center with key personnel who had been active in MADD. Victims' rights became the cornerstone of the center's activities, in part because it was an effective issue around which to unite a disparate movement. At the time, a national survey of about 300 small, community-based victims' organizations and career activists found there was general agreement that offenders had too many rights while victims had too few. Yet this did not automatically translate into overwhelming support for the idea of reducing crime by locking up more criminals. The survey found considerable support for using rehabilitation as a way to reduce criminality.[93] Other research indicated that activists in victims' organizations tended to be "overwhelmingly White, female, and middle-aged – a group demographic that is hardly representative of crime victims in general."[94] These activists generally were more supportive of the death penalty and of the police, prosecutors, and judges than were victims not active in these organizations.[95]

The U.S. Department of Justice provided critical grant support for the von Bulow center. It used its considerable financial clout to assert control over what had been a "pretty un-unified" movement by funding certain groups and programs associated with the center, and not others.[96] One of the central concerns of the von Bulow center, which changed its name to the National Victim Center in 1988, was that police, prosecutors, and the courts were reluctant to enforce the numerous victims' bill-of-rights statutes that had been enacted. This helps explain why the center built up close relationships with law enforcement groups, including the National District Attorneys Association, the National Sheriffs Association, and the National Association of Attorneys General. It also had close relations with advocacy groups like MADD and the Center for Missing and Exploited Children.[97] Federal money was critical in transforming the National Victim Center into a key umbrella organization that, like NOVA, had a national presence and stressed victims' rights. In 1986 the center created the Crime Victims Litigation Project, the only data base in the United States concerned specifically and exclusively with victims' rights.[98]

The Historical Development of the Public Prosecutor

This selective federal support for organizations stressing victims' rights coupled with the political opportunism of law-and-order conservatives certainly helps explain why the issue of victims' rights became so politically salient, so punitive, and so capable of uniting disparate groups. It is too simplistic, however, to portray the victims' rights issue as largely the creation of conservatives identified with the rise of Reaganism who craftily transformed this cause into the golden key that hijacked the victims' movement and took it in a more punitive direction with the help of state money doled out by the LEAA. Victims' rights became such a potent and politically charged issue because of other deeper historical and institutional factors as well that made the relationship between the criminal justice system and victims in the United States significantly different from that of other Western countries, including its common-law cousin, Britain.

One important difference is how the office of the prosecuting attorney, a "uniquely American institution," developed in the United States.[99] Prosecutors, who were only minor local court functionaries in the colonial and early founding period, grew into offices that enjoy "an independence and discretionary privileges unmatched in the world."[100] Notably, they possess "an unreviewable discretionary power to prosecute" that the courts have consistently left largely unchecked in three key areas: the initial decision to press charges or not; the level at which to charge an individual; and the termination of prosecution when deemed appropriate.[101]

This particular institutional and political inheritance of the United States made the victims' movement more vulnerable to being co-opted by conservative crime-control proponents emphasizing victims' rights. The United States was a forerunner in establishing the concept of the public prosecutor and abandoning reliance on private prosecution. It ceded a prominent role to the state early on at the cost of a greatly diminished role for the victim, which has had far-reaching consequences for contemporary penal politics. Victims in the United States have encountered prosecutors who are far less accountable to the rest of the criminal justice system because of the early creation of the independent public prosecutor and rejection of private prosecution.

One of the central developmental milestones of any modern state is the establishment of a professional police force and a criminal justice system to take over responsibility for the pursuit, prosecution, and punishment of criminals from private individual victims and their kin. In the process, criminal law is transformed from a mixture of public and private law "to law of an exclusively public nature."[102] The state increasingly monopolizes police powers and the right to punish wrongdoers in exchange for assuming a broad responsibility to protect citizens from criminal offenders.[103] In short, the emergence of the modern state dispossesses victims of much of their power, as crime is increasingly defined as an offense against society and the state, not the individual.

While the United States and other Western countries traveled down this same developmental path, they reached this milestone through institutional and political arrangements that had subtle but significant differences. In an irony of development, the United States, traditionally understood to be a comparatively weak state, underwent the transformation from private prosecution to public prosecution earlier on and more extensively. As a consequence, the state came to monopolize the prosecution process to a larger extent, leaving the victim far more marginalized in the criminal justice system. Early on, the United States decisively rejected the British common-law system of private prosecution. The creation of the elected, highly autonomous public prosecutor was an important innovation of colonial and nineteenth-century America.[104] The idea of private prosecution, which is founded on the supposition that crime is essentially a private matter between an offender and victim, is "alien to modern America."[105] While important vestiges of private prosecution remain in other countries, the United States most fully embraced the view that criminal acts were first and foremost occurrences in which society as a whole was the ultimate victim.[106] To understand how this came about, it is necessary to look briefly at the historic role of the victim and of the state in prosecuting and punishing criminal acts in early Europe and the United States.

After the collapse of the Roman Empire, "the victim and the criminal process were intimately linked" in England and continental Europe.[107] Because formal government structures did not exist, blood feuds were the primary mechanism for achieving "criminal justice." Victims and their kin exacted vengeance and payments from perpetrators and their relatives. As English government and society developed, blood feuds became more regulated. Gradually a complicated system of monetary payments replaced the blood feud as the primary means to enforce the criminal law.[108] While this system appeared to acknowledge a victim's right to restitution, in actuality victims seldom received compensation. Criminal acts increasingly were seen as offenses against the crown rather than the individual, further diminishing the role of the victim in the judicial process. However, victims retained an important prerogative, for they or other interested private parties were permitted to bring charges and prosecute a case against a criminal offender. In the seventeenth and eighteenth centuries, the system of private prosecution prevailed in England. No public official was designated as a public prosecutor (though local justices of the peace sometimes took on that role). The state's prerogative to prosecute was limited. The attorney general was permitted to initiate prosecutions, but only in cases that were of special interest to the crown.[109] The state also retained some power to contain the excesses of private prosecution through the writ of *nolle prosequi*.[110]

Initially, criminal procedures in the American colonies were modeled after those in England.[111] Each colony had an attorney general who could represent the crown in criminal and civil matters, but criminal prosecution was largely a private affair. Victims or hired "informers" investigated the crime and sought the offender. The victim paid public officials to arrest the culprit and hired a private attorney to prosecute the accused.[112] Gradually, a system of public prosecution superseded private prosecution, for a variety of reasons. Private prosecution appeared increasingly ill-suited for the vastly different circumstances in the colonies. Poor communications and transportation and the enormous distances to be traveled made private prosecution more expensive. As the population and crime rate increased, the single criminal court of each colony appeared inadequate and was replaced by a system of county courts and county attorneys. Public prosecutors were seen as more compatible with the ideals of the burgeoning democratic society because they helped ensure that poor victims had equal access to justice. Furthermore, they came to be viewed as important buffers against other abuses, "most specifically, the uneducated impulses of juries and grand juries."[113] The United States thus became a forerunner in the introduction of the public prosecutor to replace "a system of private prosecution that was viewed as inefficient, elitist, and sometimes vindictive."[114]

Over time these county prosecutors were viewed more as local public officials rather than as agents of the central colonial authorities. In most of the colonies, public prosecution was superimposed over private prosecution. In a few places it emerged more directly.[115] By the time of the American Revolution, each colony had some form of public prosecution at the local level, while in England private prosecution still predominated. As these public prosecutors began to supplant private ones, they seldom had an explicit monopoly on the power to prosecute in the early years of the new country. That changed as the public's stake in criminal prosecution rose. Private prosecutors were seen as partisans, while public ones were considered defenders of the public interest. In the first couple of decades after the founding, prosecuting attorneys were generally minor judicial officials. During the 1820s, however, this office experienced a major transformation, as did many legal and governmental structures, with the rise of Jacksonian democracy and the "Age of the Common Man."[116]

A number of scholars have identified the 1820s and 1830s as a formative moment in American state-building. In a period characterized by extreme anxieties about social conflict, extraordinary public fears about crime, and a spate of labor and ethnic violence, the courts stepped in to fill a governing vacuum in early America when the state was relatively weak and fragmented. Stephen Skowronek and others have demonstrated how judicial decision making and court procedures were transformed during this period so as to establish the primacy of the judiciary, which subsequently played a leading role in American state-building.[117] During the nineteenth century the prosecutorial arm of the state underwent a radical transformation as well, one that left a distinct mark on the American state and that continues to have important implications for penal politics and policies to this day. Much of the scholarly literature has ignored the emergence of a strong, autonomous public prosecutor in the United States, which was a paradoxical development in American state-building.[118] Given how the fear of concentrated state power has been such a persistent theme of American political development, "it is surprising that the power of the prosecuting attorney has been left intact as it is today."[119]

No longer a minor official of the local court, public prosecutors became powerful members of the executive branch during the Jacksonian era as "the judicial and prosecutorial functions were clearly separated."[120] The election of judges was introduced as a way to break the perceived lock that elite, publicly unaccountable judges had on the judicial system. Local election of prosecutors was a by-product of this push to make judges electorally accountable.[121] In 1832, Mississippi became the first state to amend its constitution to authorize popular election of district attorneys. Almost all the other states soon followed suit by amending their constitutions or changing their statutes to authorize the election of local prosecutors.[122] Some states subsequently abandoned the election of judges because such contests impinged on "judicial impartiality." Elections were retained for local prosecutors, however, out of a belief that elections made the public prosecutor "more truly a lawyer for the people."[123] Over the years, this decentralized, partisan system for electing prosecutors periodically was criticized on grounds of incompetence, political opportunism, and corruption.[124] Nonetheless, most states continued to elect their prosecutors. In a handful of states they were appointed, usually by the governor.

Unlike in the United States, prosecutors in continental Europe "display a strong affinity with the judiciary." This closer relationship between prosecutors and the judiciary has deep historical roots. The public prosecutor in continental Europe "was created from the rib of the judge." Under the traditional inquisitorial system of justice that prevailed on the continent until the nineteenth century, judges were responsible for investigating the case, preparing the charges, and determining guilt or innocence. Mounting charges of conflict of interest in France under this system prompted the separation of functions between judges and prosecutors. This new model of judges as neutral arbiters spread from France to other

European countries in the 1840s. Although the judiciary and prosecutor were formally separated, their roles remained less distinct than in the United States.[125]

Local district attorneys in the United States were regarded as the ones best equipped to evaluate the evidence and defend the public interest. They came to enjoy an "unusual degree of independence" from judges, administrative superiors, and grand juries.[126] The decision to initiate prosecution was vested "almost exclusively in a designated public official" firmly anchored in the executive branch in the United States.[127] Prosecutors' status as members of the executive branch, combined with their status as elected officials, "served to consolidate prosecutorial power and discretion in the office of the public prosecutor."[128] Over the years, U.S. courts have bolstered prosecutorial independence. They generally have been unresponsive to claims by victims trying to compel prosecution of a case against the wishes of the district attorney's office.[129]

Periodically, the vast discretionary power of the local district attorney has come under attack in U.S. history. In response to a wave of concern in the Progressive era and again in the 1920s, dozens of states enacted measures to assert some judicial control over prosecutors. But this reform movement had little practical effect because the judiciary remained reluctant to curtail established prosecutorial prerogatives like the freedom to dismiss or reduce charges and strike plea agreements.[130] Attempts by victims and other private parties to compel prosecution "have also been uniformly denied."[131] Until the advent of the contemporary victims' rights movement, the victim's role in the legal process was largely confined to that of a witness in a criminal proceeding.

Prosecutors in continental Europe do not enjoy the vast discretionary powers common in the United States. As a result, victims have had much more say in the legal process to begin with.[132] The narrow formal role that crime victims have historically been assigned in the U.S. criminal justice system is the exception. In many other countries victims have enjoyed considerable rights to participate in the prosecution of a case or pursue civil claims within the criminal process.[133] In France, victims are permitted to bring suit for civil damages in criminal court. Prosecutors are then obliged to proceed with criminal action if a civil action has been filed against the accused.[134] Victims in France acting through their own counsel are permitted to be actively involved in prosecuting the accused and asserting their own rights to civil damages. Organizations in France that represent the interests of particular victims are also allowed to initiate private prosecutions, which are extremely popular in France and serve as a meaningful check on the prosecutor's discretionary powers.[135]

Victims in Germany have extensive rights to begin with, including the right to the assistance of an attorney and the right "for the victim's

attorney to inspect the prosecution file if the victim's need to do so out-
weighs the interests of requiring secrecy."[136] Victims of certain crimes,
including most sexual offenses, "may join the prosecution as auxiliary
prosecutors" who have "rights almost equivalent to those of the public
prosecutor."[137] Certain offenses require that public prosecutors secure the
victim's explicit permission to prosecute, which "in effect, gives the victim
a veto over public prosecution."[138] German law also allows for judicial
review of a prosecutor's decision not to pursue a case and denies prosecutors significant discretionary powers in other ways.[139] A number of other
countries, including Austria, Scotland, and Denmark, have comparable
mechanisms to push reluctant prosecutors to pursue a case.[140]

While Michigan and several other states permit some kind of judicial
review of a prosecutor's decision not to pursue a case, prosecutors generally enjoy unbridled discretion in the United States.[141] A number of
states do allow victims to retain an attorney to assist the public prosecutor. However, in many jurisdictions this right is secured only with the
approval of the public prosecutor or trial court.[142] The primary avenue
for victims and their kin to seek redress in the United States is in civil,
not criminal, court. Those who can afford a lawyer have the right to sue
a defendant (and even someone who has been acquitted) for wrongful
death or injury in civil court, where the standard of proof is much lower
than in a criminal trial (as in the O. J. Simpson case).[143]

Victims and the Common-Law System

The common-law system that prevails in the United States and Britain
has compounded the marginalization of victims in the legal process. This
accusatorial legal system demands more of victims and incites greater ani-
mosities than the inquisitorial, less adversarial legal system that prevails in
continental Europe.[144] In the United States and Britain, the prosecution
and the defense have equal standing before the courts, which are relatively passive in developing the case. Defense attorneys go to war with
prosecutors as they attempt to tear apart the state's case. In the process,
victims and their claims are often put on trial as well. In the Anglo-Saxon
system, the focus is on eliciting the facts relevant to determining guilt or
innocence. Elsewhere, for example in the Netherlands, the public trial
mainly serves as a check on whether the investigations have been carried
out properly. A greater portion of the trial is devoted to understanding
the personal circumstances and why the offense occurred, and victims are
rarely present at trials.[145] In the European continental system, judges play
a more active role in shaping the case by controlling the legal proceedings,
including the calling and questioning of witnesses and the like.[146] In the
Netherlands, for example, professional judges try both criminal and civil
cases, and jury trials are unknown.[147]

In Germany, victims and witnesses are not subject to the grueling cross-examinations that can be so trying for them in the U.S. legal system.[148] Presiding judges conduct most of the questioning of victims in a neutral manner. While defense attorneys in Germany retain expansive rights to question the victim, they tend to be less aggressive than their American counterparts. The German criminal justice system is less taxing on victims in other respects. Routine cases demand far less of the victim's time in Germany. The number of contacts between the victim and the court system are far fewer because the German system does not have the burdensome pretrial proceedings that are commonplace in the United States. The U.S. practice of deposition hearings, where the defense has the opportunity to question the victim in closed-door sessions prior to prosecution, has contributed to the widespread perception that U.S. victims of crime are alone and defenseless.[149] Victims' court obligations in Germany are far more limited. They typically involve giving a statement to the police and testifying in court when asked to. Only rarely do they appear before prosecutors or an investigating magistrate before trial.

While Germany has been slower to accord victims special rights beyond the rights of a typical witness in the prosecution of a crime, its criminal justice system demands less of victims to begin with. "Thus, the German victim's need for orientation and protection is less strong than that of his American counterpart," according to Weigend.[150] That said, Germany has established some influential organizations for victims, like the Weisser Ring, formed in 1976 and comprised of ex-police officers and other criminal justice professionals.[151] Despite some noise about victims' rights in Germany, the overall thrust has been toward milder sanctions for offenders. Safeguarding victims, according to the German criminal code, means encouraging mediation between offenders and victims as a way to avoid prosecution.[152]

To sum up to this point, the push by conservatives and others for "victims' rights" touched a political raw nerve in the United States that did not exist to the same extent elsewhere, because the U.S. criminal justice system had a different political and institutional inheritance. The U.S. public prosecutor in particular had a complex and paradoxical inheritance. The office of the public prosecutor developed in ways that made it highly autonomous from the wishes of victims and insulated from other pieces of the state, such as judges. U.S. prosecutors have been well-situated to resist the particular demands of any victim in a single case because of their well-established and enormous discretionary power. As a consequence, victims were comparatively more slighted and marginalized in the criminal justice process to begin with, which helped to make victims' rights such a central and effective rallying point in the war on crime. Once the victims' rights movement coalesced, prosecutors, many of whom are elected in the United States, were forced to respond to this movement or risk being voted out of office.

Differences in Legal Training, Norms, and Career Paths

Differences in the legal training, professional norms, and career paths of prosecutors, judges, and other judicial administrators are another reason why the U.S. criminal justice system has been more vulnerable to political winds whipped up by politicians and social movements. As previously discussed, most prosecutors, like many judges in the United States, are either elected or nominated and confirmed through a political process that makes them more dependent on public approval and more vulnerable to political pressures. The United States has resisted creating a legal system founded on career prosecutors and career judges with special training and education. As late as the mid-1930s, only half of the states required prosecuting attorneys to be licensed lawyers.[153]

Unlike U.S. officials, who bounce back and forth between the public and private sectors and academia, criminal justice administrators in many European countries are career civil servants appointed by the Ministry of Justice. The judicial appointment process is far less politicized in Germany, for example, because judges "are appointed as civil servants with tenured positions, early in their professional career, and usually according to academic achievement tests." In Germany, as in Austria and France, "[y]oung prosecutors and judges receive their legal education and training together and thus share attitudes and perceptions."[154] German law requires that all new lawyers, not just future judges and prosecutors, do a two-year internship in which they rotate among various public and private legal positions. Toward the end of the internship, they take the bar exam. State justice administrators choose judges and prosecutors from those who score in the top quarter. During the next three years, those who are selected work at various court levels and receive extensive training and supervision before being given tenure as either judges or prosecutors.[155]

Prosecutors in Germany traditionally have been empowered to play a broader public policy role that reconciles criminal justice concerns with competing policy goals.[156] That role was expanded in the aftermath of reunification. A March 1993 law permits prosecutors to dismiss a case if the offender's guilt does not necessitate a penalty. The greater economic burdens associated with German reunification, including the cost of rebuilding the criminal justice system in the East, prompted this push to streamline the judicial process to reduce costs. Many cases can be settled through simplified written proceedings. For example, if a prosecutor concludes that guilt can be readily established and that a day fine is an appropriate sanction, he or she may propose this penalty to the judge. If the judge concurs, the accused receives a penal order by mail, which he or she is entitled to appeal.[157]

Another key difference is German legal training. Sociology of the law, with its emphasis on the importance of the social, economic, and cultural context for understanding legal norms and other aspects of the law, has greater sway with legal scholars and law students in Germany.[158] Criminology is a core part of the law school curriculum in Germany. A large number of German law school students who are interested in criminal justice are familiar with the findings of empirical criminology. One leading German criminologist suggests that this might explain why German criminal judges "use the prison sentence in an essentially more reserved manner" than U.S. judges and overwhelmingly oppose the concept of deterrence via the death penalty.[159] John Graham attributes the significant and persistent decarceration Germany engineered in the 1980s to a "radical change in the practice of public prosecutors and judges, which in turn has been brought about by a shift in their perceptions of the efficacy and legitimacy of incarceration."[160]

Criminal justice policy in Germany is also less vulnerable to political pressures and radical shifts because academic experts rely much less on policy-making institutions and political agencies for their funding.[161] In the United States, the state largely created the fields of criminology and criminal justice. It allocated federal funds via the LEAA, beginning in 1968, to enable law enforcement agencies to raise their educational requirements and to provide tuition and other financial support for law enforcement officers to obtain higher-education degrees. Hundreds of undergraduate and graduate degree programs in criminology and criminal justice were created in the decade after the University of California at Berkeley established the nation's first nonsociological degree program in criminology in 1966.[162] Researchers affiliated with criminology and criminal justice programs in the United States tend to focus on topics and theories suggested by the state, according to Joachim Savelsberg and others. Furthermore, research findings based on funding provided by state agencies are more likely to reflect the concerns of the state.[163]

For all these reasons, criminal justice policy in Germany is generally the product of bargaining within a relatively insulated set of government actors and thus is less vulnerable to swings in public opinion and media hype over sensational crimes.[164] By contrast, the views of U.S. administrators "on policy issues are more influenced by loyalty to the current administrative leadership or to outside institutions, law firms, and academic or business institutions to which they may return than to political parties and the political bureaucracy, as in the German case."[165] These differences in the institutionalization of political and legal decision making between the United States and Germany help explain Germany's relatively low incarceration rate of 90 per 100,000, which is less than one-sixth the

U.S. rate.[166] Germany has experienced several major reductions in its prison population, while the incarcerated population continued to grow in the United States and other European countries.[167]

The Netherlands, which has maintained one of the lowest incarceration rates in Europe, provides an interesting complement and contrast to the United States and Germany on the question of prosecutorial discretion and the relative insulation of prosecutors and judges from political pressures and public opinion. On the one hand, Dutch prosecutors are accorded enormous discretionary powers that exceed even those of U.S. prosecutors – so much so that they have been called the "spider in the web" of the Dutch criminal justice system.[168] While concerned parties are permitted to appeal to the Dutch Supreme Court when the public prosecutor decides not to prosecute a case, this option is rarely used. Parliament technically holds the minister of justice responsible for the activities of the public prosecutor's office, but in practice the minister and legislators have little influence. "The overall result is a highly autonomous body acting 'in the public interest' with little control from its political overseers (parliament and minister) and almost no feedback from the people," according to one expert on the Dutch legal system.[169] Dutch prosecutors are permitted to waive prosecution not just for technical reasons, but also on policy grounds. In 1971, the so-called "principle of expediency" was reinterpreted in the Netherlands "to mean that prosecution should be waived unless public interest demanded it."[170] Dutch prosecutors are thus empowered to act as catalysts of policy and yet are far more insulated from politics than U.S. prosecutors. The same is true of justices who sit on the Dutch Supreme Court. The lower house of the Dutch Parliament appoints them to "a highly politically active highest court" through a process that is largely nonpolitical and nonpartisan.[171]

In explaining why the Netherlands has one of the lowest incarceration rates in Europe, David Downes emphasizes how the Dutch "culture of tolerance" needs to be understood within a particular institutional context and set of professional norms and training.[172] He contends that the "Dutch criminal justice system approximates to the Fabian ideal of small, highly trained elites getting on with their jobs without undue public interference (though with a due regard to public opinion and the public interest)."[173] While judicial autonomy has been under assault in the United States, judges in the Netherlands and elsewhere retain enormous discretion. In the Netherlands, the statutory minimum term of imprisonment is one day and applies to all crimes regardless of the seriousness of the offense.[174] As in Germany, prosecutors and the judiciary have evolved a distinctive occupational culture. Their legal training exposes them to criminological research showing the negative consequences of imprisonment and to the work of abolitionists who challenge the use of prison as a penalty.[175] The so-called Utrecht School in the Netherlands inculcated the view among the most influential elites that the best way to combat crime is through social and institutional changes rather than through penal measures.[176] As a result, the concerns of victims have been a low priority for Dutch prosecutors and other members of the criminal justice system. Unlike in the United States, this neglect went largely unchallenged until recently because prosecutors and the judiciary are far more insulated from politics and public opinion.[177]

The Movement for Victims in Britain

The Netherlands, Germany, and other continental countries have several distinct institutional and political features that help explain why a powerful conservative victims' movement centered on rights did not emerge.[178] The harder case to explain is why a punitive victims' rights movement did not take root in Britain. After all, Britain shares a number of relevant institutional and political features with the United States that, if the preceding argument is correct, should have served to nurture such a movement. On the political side, the rise of Reaganism was matched by a parallel conservative shift with the election of Margaret Thatcher in 1979. On the institutional side, Britain has a common-law system, the writ of *nolle prosequi*, and a significant voluntary sector and voluntary tradition, especially in the area of criminal justice.[179] Furthermore, unlike in France, Germany, and elsewhere, where victims have considerable rights to participate in the prosecutorial process, the role of victims has been highly circumscribed in Britain.[180] It has been confined largely to serving as a source of evidence for the prosecution, even though Britain has a longer and more established tradition of private prosecution.[181]

While the United States abandoned private prosecution relatively early, England has retained remnants of private prosecution right up to the present day. Britain did not create a Director of Public Prosecutions until 1879. Over the years various efforts were made to restructure the private prosecution system that resulted in ceding more authority to the state with respect to public and private prosecution.[182] While the bulk of criminal prosecutions continued to be considered private, this is misleading because most of them were initiated by the police "ostensibly acting in their private capacity."[183] Britain has been reluctant to dispense with private prosecution altogether because "the initiation of a crime action by a private citizen seems to be viewed as an important constitutional guarantee against abuse of prosecutorial discretion by public officials."[184] The 1985 Prosecution of Offenses Act, which established the Crown Prosecution Service, preserved the rights of private individuals to initiate and conduct criminal proceedings. While such prosecutions are rare, they still exist.[185]

Despite this historic reverence for private prosecution, victims in the legal process in Britain were marginalized much as they were in the United States, creating a gap between the ethos of private prosecution and the reality of how the legal system serves to marginalize victims. But a powerful and punitive victims' rights movement did not step into this gap and steer penal politics in a more hard-line direction in Britain. The British state, at least until the early 1990s, was far more effective at resisting demands made on behalf of or by victims for the curtailment of prosecutorial discretion and for greater influence on matters like the length of prison sentences.[186] This is so for several reasons, including significant differences in how the victims issue evolved and developed in the United States and Britain; in state structures, notably the Home Office and the judiciary; and in how Thatcherism and Reaganism were implemented.

As discussed earlier, British interest in victims emerged in the 1950s when confidence in the welfare state and sympathy for offenders were still high, and conservative law-and-order forces were not yet a significant factor in national politics. The second wave of British interest in victims occurred in the late 1960s and early 1970s. Here again, sympathy for the plight of offenders propelled a parallel concern for victims. Professionals and reformers with a long history of involvement with offenders were again at the forefront of drawing public attention to victim-related issues.

The National Association for the Care and Resettlement of Offenders (NACRO), which was founded in 1966 and replaced the earlier National Association of Discharged Persons, led the charge for the rediscovery of victims. In the early 1970s, NACRO began to take an interest in victims at the prodding of the National Victims Association (NVA), which was established in 1973 and was an offshoot of NACRO.[187] These two organizations viewed the issue of victims as a way to break the perceived deadlock in penal reform at the time. Members of NVA argued that the state and criminal justice system had methodically abolished the rights and dignity of victims. The demise of social concern for the victim had caused, in their view, a backlash from the public, which sought to satisfy its anger at the neglect of the victim by imposing more severe punishments on offenders. Feeling marginalized at the time, penal reformers calculated that the "victim connection is the key to public attitudes towards the criminal. [It] is the key to penal reform now," according to Philip Priestley, one of the founders of NVA.[188] Once again, penal reformers calculated that support for victims would be a way to neutralize calls for vindictive retribution against offenders.

NACRO took up the cause of victims, but in a particular way that helped prevent the emergence of a highly politicized victims' rights movement pitched against offenders. Organized as a wide federation of projects, hostels, and voluntary societies for offenders, it worked closely with the Home Office. Neither a pressure group in the traditional sense nor an official part of the government, NACRO was a large federation and a major recipient of Home Office and other government funding to provide services for offenders. It had a broad mandate and acted as the unofficial research and development agency for penal policy in Britain. Not formally part of the state yet intimately associated with it, NACRO could undertake certain experiments in policy that the Home Office could not, for fear that any failure would be embarrassing to the government.[189]

NACRO was a key supporter of one of Britain's pioneer victims' support schemes, which took hold in Bristol around 1971 and had no stridently political or partisan aims. The primary objective of this and other programs modeled after it was simply to serve as a "good neighbor" or "good samaritan" to crime victims.[190] The successful experience of the Bristol experiment and the hundreds of other programs like it that sprung up around Britain helped convince NACRO that, just as there was a need for a national federation for offenders, there should be a parallel one for victims. NACRO provided an organizational model for the National Association of Victims Support Schemes (NAVSS) and helped it secure funding early on.[191] NAVSS took shape in the early 1980s at a time when concerns about law and order were rising in national politics and the elite political consensus about not politicizing penal policy was eroding.[192] Nonetheless, NAVSS did not become the nucleus of an aggressive, politicized victims' movement that pitted victim against offender.

The unique institutional history and culture of the Home Office help explain why. Born at the time of the terror during the French Revolution, the Home Office is one of the oldest institutions of the modern British state.[193] Over the centuries, the Home Office developed an institutional culture that is cautious, conservative, and characterized by "a special brand of stuffiness."[194] Hierarchical, bureaucratic, dominated by precedent, and not wont to consult with outsiders in policy development, it is a highly insular bureaucracy "that could have been designed by Max Weber."[195] From the start, the NAVSS was put in the position of trying to prove itself with a Home Office that was mistrustful of new causes, like feminism and victims' rights, and of outside voluntary groups, particularly ones that received widespread media and public attention and were associated with zealots in its view. Civil servants in the Home Office looked down upon colleagues who became evangelists for a cause, such as the rights of victims. As one civil servant in the Home Office told Paul Rock, "it is definitely not done to manifest enthusiasm."[196]

While the Home Office was supportive of the idea of reparations for victims – seeing them as a way to empty prisons and reduce the court caseload – it initially opposed expanding government programs to provide more services directly to victims.[197] The country's long history of private prosecutions probably reinforced the government's initial tendency to keep victims at arms length. Over the centuries, the long-established practice of private prosecutions had contributed to an unfavorable image of victims as undisciplined, self-interested, capricious, and unreliable.[198]

The Home Office was slow to embrace NAVSS and the idea of victims' support.[199] NACRO, with its commitment to "sobriety and restraint" in penal policy and to eschewing the politicization of penal policy in order to gain support and respectability from the government and the public, provided an important model for NAVSS to win over the Home Office.[200] The early leaders of NAVSS came primarily from established organizations and professions that had been active in working on behalf of offenders. The first head of NAVSS was Helen Reeves, a senior probation officer in London who had not previously been identified with victim-related issues. Reeves, who assumed her post in January 1980 with the strong support of the Home Office, was an attractive appointment because she "did not enter NAVSS as an evangelist, an ideologist, or as a political activist."[201] Reeves eschewed using NAVSS as a platform to express views on controversial penal matters like the proper treatment and sentencing of offenders.[202]

NAVSS "adopted a 'social provision' rather than a 'social movement' emphasis."[203] It self-consciously situated itself as an alternative to Victims of Violence, an organization whose membership consisted primarily of actual victims of crime. Founded in 1976, Victims of Violence emphasized the threat of crime, particularly to the elderly. To the sober professionals in NAVSS and the Home Office, Victims of Violence "seemed to be the terrifying victim-vigilante come to life" as it sought to use victims for political ends.[204] NAVSS avoided sensationalizing accounts of victims at all cost. Even when it was desperate for funding, NAVSS turned down many opportunities to heighten its public profile by dramatizing the plight of particular crime victims, in contrast to many victims' organizations in the United States.[205] Even though funding for local victim-support schemes was haphazard and inadequate, NAVSS resisted imposing surcharges on convicted offenders as a way to fund victims' services, which was a growing practice in the United States. Victims' advocates in Britain feared that such surcharges would polarize victims and offenders. They held fast to the belief that victims' services should be seen as an essential public service, like the police or the fire department, and thus should be funded on a regular basis as part of the state's obligation to protect its citizens.[206]

After a courtship of several years in the early 1980s, the Home Office became convinced that NAVSS was not a "stalking horse for angry vigilantes or hostile radicals."[207] Prodded by Parliament's Home Affairs Select Committee, the Home Office rewarded NAVSS with a major grant in 1986 to develop services for victims, the beginning of an important stream of funding for the organization.[208] Many of the victims' support schemes depended on funding from the metropolitan councils, which were significant sites of radical opposition to Thatcherism. Once Parliament abolished the councils in July 1985, the Conservative government was more predisposed to providing funds for victims' support schemes.[209]

To sum up, at each stage, the Home Office was reasonably successful in steering and co-opting the growing concern for victims, thus making the cause of victims less vulnerable to the more strident law-and-order forces that emerged and gathered strength in the 1970s. Britain's elite interest in victims was fueled initially by ongoing concerns about the plight of offenders. As shown in the next two chapters, this interest preceded the emergence of wider concerns about the victims of rape and domestic violence. The main preoccupation in Britain was with providing special services for victims, not special rights. The expressed concern for victims did not galvanize a victims' movement comprised of a large number of groups and organizations. A single organization, NAVSS, monopolized the victims issue in Britain. NAVSS shrewdly aligned itself with a Home Office that by history and temperament is disdainful of crusades that whip up public sentiment for a particular cause.[210] Furthermore, thanks in large part to NAVSS and the absence of a strong therapeutic tradition, the dominant ethos in Britain was that volunteers, not specialists, could most effectively deal with the social and emotional needs of victims. Thus, there was less pressure in Britain than in the United States to have the state step in to develop and fund expensive programs for victims run by professionals, as in the case of the LEAA and NOVA.

Thatcherism, Reaganism, and Victims

Another factor that explains why a punitive victims' rights movement and a comparatively punitive penal climate were slower to develop in Britain than in the United States has to do with differences in Thatcherism and Reaganism. With their commitment to cutting the size of the government, rolling back state regulations, liberating the market through neoliberal economic policies, and upholding law and order, Thatcherism and Reaganism are generally understood to be cut from the same cloth. For all the similarities in their rhetoric and stated policy commitments, however, Thatcherism and Reaganism had some strikingly different consequences on the ground in the area of economic and social policy, as Paul Pierson has shown.[211] This is no less true with respect to criminal justice policy. One needs to guard against fixating on the "horrors" of Thatcherism at the cost of ignoring concerted efforts to reduce the prison population during Prime Minister Margaret Thatcher's tenure that had no parallels in the United States under Reagan or subsequent administrations.[212]

Like Reagan, Thatcher rode the conservative law-and-order wave into office and campaigned on a call for the revival of state authority.[213] The broad postwar consensus in Britain over basic aspects of law enforcement and penal policy had been eroding for about a decade prior to the 1979

General Election that installed Thatcher in 10 Downing Street for the first time. While the Conservative Party had been positioning itself for years as the "party of law and order," the Thatcher campaign "lifted that banner to new heights."[214] During the campaign, Thatcher bluntly declared: "The demand in the country will be for two things: less tax and more law and order."[215] In the campaign, Thatcher sought to use street crime as a powerful symbol "of the general moral and economic decline of the nation," and the Tories conflated Britain's industrial disorder and labor unrest with street crime.[216]

Early on in her tenure, Thatcher lived up to her memorable promise to provide "the smack of firm government."[217] Committed to widespread cutbacks in the public sector, she initially made an exception for the police, who took an active part in the 1979 campaign.[218] She quickly put money into policing, increasing the salaries of all ranks and making more funds available for police departments and police equipment.[219] Thatcher backed the Criminal Justice Act of 1982, which called for having more offenders serve short sentences in militarized detention centers, or what the Tories liked to hail as the "short, sharp shock."[220] The measure also gave magistrates more powers vis-à-vis social workers to take a tough stance against juvenile offenders. In the early 1980s, the government embarked on a major prison-building program to add twenty-five new facilities that would house an additional 21,000 inmates.[221] It backed the Criminal Justice Act of 1988, which gave prosecutors the right to appeal court sentences that were "over-lenient" in their view. The act also abolished the defense's right to challenge prospective jurors without cause and restricted the right to trial by jury for a range of offenses.[222] All of these measures helped to solidify the common view that Thatcher was the "iron lady" of criminal justice policy.

Yet a more careful examination reveals that competing ideological, institutional, and personal concerns forced Thatcher and the Conservative Party to retreat and compromise on law-and-order concerns in ways that Reagan and other public officials in the United States did not have to. For this reason, Conservative penal policy in the 1980s actually had a "Jekyll and Hyde" character.[223] The 1982 act, for all its bluster, included an important provision that limited the power of the courts to sentence young offenders to custody. The 1988 act also encouraged greater use of noncustodial penalties like community-based sentences. Even though Thatcher campaigned on the law-and-order issue, she generally did not take a great interest in the specifics of criminal justice policy. During her eleven years as prime minister, the privatization of prisons and remand centers and the contracting out of certain criminal justice services were the only significant penal issues in which she played a decisive part.[224]

For ideological and institutional reasons, the Thatcher government was forced to reconcile its penal policies and its neoliberal economic policies to an extent that Reagan and subsequent administrations did not have to. At the ideological level, the Conservative Party took more seriously the competing concerns of Thatcherism, notably the commitment to cutting the public sector and rolling back state expenditures. As the crime rate continued to rise despite increased spending on law enforcement, the government began by the mid-1980s to back away from the view that equated more government spending with less crime. The police were no longer immune from the dominant Thatcherite concern to cut the size and cost of the public sector. This prompted a reevaluation of the role of the police and spurred greater interest in what local communities could do on their own to prevent and detect crime.[225]

Institutional factors also prodded the Conservatives to make some important retreats in the battle for law and order. Because Britain has a more unitary, coherent state, economic and social policy making is more centralized in London. From the start, Thatcher's Treasury, concerned primarily with reducing government spending, remained unpersuaded by repeated calls for costly increases in police personnel. The Home Secretary was under constant pressure from Treasury and later the prime minister's office to cut expenditures for prisons, law enforcement, and criminal justice.[226] In the federal U.S. system, economic and social policy are far more fragmented. Each state essentially operates its own criminal justice and prison system, while the federal government has its own prison system and law enforcement bodies, such as the Justice Department and the FBI. Neoliberal rhetoric at the national level did not necessarily act as a check on law enforcement and penal expenditures in the U.S. case because of the absence of a coherent state where penal policy making and expenditures are centralized at the national level.

The dominant neoliberal ethos of Thatcherism does not entirely explain the de-escalation of law-and-order rhetoric and retreat from some notable hard-line policies during Thatcher's tenure. Once again, career civil servants in the Home Office played a pivotal role and exercised an important check on penal populism. David Faulkner, a senior official in the Home Office responsible for criminal policy, sought to build bridges with academics, journalists, and groups in the voluntary sector, including leading penal pressure groups like the Howard League for Penal Reform and NACRO, through regular meetings.[227] Faulkner effectively exploited the reality that home secretaries are rarely free to pursue their own fresh policy ideas.[228] Through a remarkable number of speeches at seminars, meetings, and special conferences between 1980 and 1991, Faulkner sought to build a consensus around penal reform policy at a time when views on penal policy appeared increasingly polarized. These meetings and conferences became important sites to address not just the issue of prison overcrowding, which dominated penal discussions in the 1980s, but to ask deeper questions about what was the purpose of prison and what sort of offenders belonged there. They also served as important forums to acknowledge how penal policy was inextricably linked with other social policies. For example, there was growing acknowledgment that increased spending on criminal justice meant that less money would be available for other social needs like public education.[229]

All of this prepared the way for a remarkable shift by the Conservatives on penal policy. After Thatcher was returned to power for the third time in June 1987, Douglas Hurd returned to the Home Office. He had been a key player in drafting the Conservative Party's manifesto that took a surprisingly moderate view of crime and criminal justice. The Conservatives argued that the government needed to mete out tough prison sentences to offenders who pose a risk to society, but also had to do more to keep out of prison those who did not. An extraordinary White Paper in 1990 concluded: "For most offenders, imprisonment has to be justified in terms of public protection, denunciation, and retribution. Otherwise it can be an expensive way of making bad people worse."[230] A string of major prison riots that year served to cast further doubt on excessively relying on incarceration to reduce crime. The most unsettling of these riots was the disturbance at Strangeways prison in Manchester, the largest and most serious riot in British penal history.[231]

The White Paper formed the basis for the Criminal Justice Act of 1991, which was a striking expression of political consensus around a moderate stance toward penal policy that is quite at odds with the stereotyped view of hard-line Thatcherism and with the tough stance that prevailed in the United States at the time. The act attempted to construct a coherent, comprehensive approach to sentencing that would encourage proportionality between the seriousness of the offense and the harshness of the penalty. To that end, greater use was to be made of punishment in the community and of more equitable financial penalties. Prison was to be viewed as a last resort for offenders who posed a threat to society. A key feature of the act was reining in the untrammelled discretion that English judges had long enjoyed in sentencing.[232] The 1991 act, which did contain some concessions to hard-liners, such as longer sentences for violent and sexual offenders, was nonetheless surprisingly moderate. It went further than any modern British sentencing legislation in attempting to impose a structure for sentencing decisions on the courts.[233] It marked the high point of the Conservative government's decade-long evolution away from the law-and-order platform that initially swept it into office.

At this point, British and American penal policy were at strikingly different places. After the initial lurch to the right in the early 1980s, British penal policy was dominated for most of the decade by concerns about how to bring down the escalating prison population and develop fairer and more rational penal policies. The U.S. prison population continued to rise unabated during this period, while Britain, after some sharp increases, experienced significant drops.[234] Meanwhile the United States continued blithely to construct more and more prisons without a wider public discussion or narrower discussion among elites about the economic, social, and other costs of mass imprisonment. In short, enlightened civil servants together with competing Thatcherite pressures to trim the public sector and the cost of government acted in Britain as major brakes on populist penal rhetoric emanating from elected politicians and their appointees. Important political and institutional differences between Britain and the United States served to hold penal populism at bay in Britain and to create a climate conducive to a major drop in the prison population.

A New Hard Line in Britain

The climate became significantly more punitive in Britain after passage of the 1991 act because several institutional and political factors collided with fate. Faulkner describes the dramatic shift in penal policies in 1992–93 as "the most sudden and the most radical which has ever taken place in this area of public policy."[235] Reports of the 1993 abduction and murder of two-year-old James Bulger in Liverpool by two assailants who were just ten years old sparked a moral panic and calls for tougher juvenile offender laws.[236] The Bulger murder came at a time when the Conservative Party no longer enjoyed a commanding position in British politics and was perceived as vulnerable to an electoral upset. The Labor Party, and Tony Blair in particular, seized on the issue of juvenile crime after Bulger's death. Blair succinctly set out Labor's new crime agenda shortly after the Bulger killing, when he promised that Labor would now be "tough on crime, tough on the causes of crime."[237] This stood in marked contrast to a year earlier in the General Election when Labor was remarkably disengaged from the crime issue.[238] Penal politics also became more polarized because of the elimination of nonpartisan mediating institutions, most notably the Advisory Council on the Penal System (ACPS), which was set up in 1966 and served as a clearinghouse to assess various penal proposals.[239]

All of these developments provided an opening for opponents of the 1991 act to undo it with passage of the Criminal Justice Act of 1993 and then the Criminal Justice and Public Order Act of 1994.[240] Among other things, the 1993 measure established new detention centers and long custodial sentences for juvenile offenders. It also curtailed defendants' expansive right to silence in court and restricted their access to bail.[241] The legislation was "notable not just for its particular clauses," but also for the strident, punitive rhetoric used by its supporters.[242] At the 1993 Conservative Conference, Home Secretary Michael Howard affirmed his strong commitment to greater use of incarceration, in a remarkable contrast to the deep doubts that Hurd and the Conservatives had expressed about prison just a few years earlier. Howard declared: "We shall no longer

judge the success of our system of justice by a fall in our prison population.... Let us be clear. Prison works ... it makes many who are tempted
to commit crime think twice."[243] In addition to supporting mandatory
minimums, Howard embraced many other get-tough measures that had
proliferated in the United States, including boot camps, supermax prisons, and greater restrictions on judicial discretion.[244] This was not just an
instance of penal hard-liners adroitly seizing the moment given to them
by fate (in this case the Bulger murder), the Conservative Party's eroding
electoral support, a new Labor Party prepared to cash in on the crime
issue, and the disappearance of the ACPS. A crucial additional factor was
the judiciary.

The British courts are uniquely positioned to play a constructive role in
stemming penal populism but, under certain circumstances, they can be
an agent of it. That is what happened in the early 1990s. At the highest
rungs, the British judiciary is well-placed to exert rationality and restraint
on British lawmakers and is thus theoretically well-situated to act as a
check on punitive penal populism. At the lower rungs, however, the judiciary is highly vulnerable, under certain conditions, to populist pressures
because of the recruitment patterns and norms of the judiciary. The peculiar composition of the House of Lords permits the highest levels of the
judiciary to participate in the legislative process and yet stand apart from
party politics.[245] The Lords of Appeal, the Lord Chief Justice, and Master of the Rolls all sit in the House of Lords. Because of their judicial
obligations, these law Lords do not regularly speak in general debates.
By convention, they sit at the cross-benches. "Yet they are not in any
sense supernumerary," according to Windlesham.[246] Bereft of electoral
legitimacy, these Lords use their special knowledge of criminal policy or
the administration of justice to justify their parliamentary role.[247] When-
ever any criminal justice legislation comes before the House of Lords,
the law Lords, and sometimes the Lord Chief Justice, will express their
views, especially on issues concerning sentencing and the prerogatives
of the courts to deal with offenders. Over the years, the law Lords and
the House of Lords have been at the forefront of some of the most progressive penal reforms and have served at times as a significant bulwark
against measures that would restrict the wide discretion the British judiciary enjoys in criminal matters. For example, in the late 1980s the Lords
pushed for the abolition of mandatory life sentences, a move that the
House of Commons successfully resisted.

Beginning in earnest in the 1980s, the judiciary actively involved itself
in public debates over sentencing policy. It increasingly relied on the media
to get across its views on important penal issues.[248] Prominent judges in
Britain engaged in some fierce public struggles as government ministers
and Parliament sought to stake out a tough law-and-order position and
restrict judicial discretion through measures like mandatory minimums.

Judicial opposition forced Parliament ultimately to make some concessions to the judiciary's concerns about the Conservative Party's initial
hard-line stance on certain penal matters.[249] Home Office ministers and
the Lord Chief Justice worked together to press the case for reducing the
reliance on custody as punishment.[250]

The British judiciary is not immune to penal populism, however. Indeed,
under the right circumstances, it is highly vulnerable to law-and-order
pulls. The first factor is the norms and recruitment patterns of the British
judiciary, which are more similar to those in the United States than to
those on the continent. The second and related factor is the extreme reverence with which judges and magistrates regard judicial discretion in
Britain. The most distinctive feature of the British sentencing system is
the wide discretion conferred on judges and magistrates, many of whom
have little legal training or special judicial training.[251] Adult offenders convicted in magistrates' courts are typically sentenced by lay magistrates who
are unpaid and generally untrained.[252] Full-time professional magistrates
supplement lay benches. Between them, the lay and full-time magistrates
handle 95 percent of the criminal cases tried. The decisive factor in sentencing decisions in magistrates' courts is not the law or guidance received
from other professionals. Rather it is the "sentencing culture" into which
new recruits are socialized, according to Michael Cavadino and James
Dignan.[253] That culture emphasizes the uniqueness of the magisterial role
in each individual case. It explicitly rejects consistency in sentencing as a
virtue. Instead, magistrates are socialized to view sentencing as a craft or
mystery that should be immune to outside control. "The law is the most
extreme British example of a closed and self-regulating community, with
all its strengths and weaknesses," according to Anthony Sampson.[254]

Defendants convicted in Crown Court are sentenced by judges who are
legally trained, unlike lay magistrates. While they may have spent most of
their careers as practicing barristers, they typically do not receive much
special training as judges, except for a three-day seminar for new recruits
and a refresher course every five years. This stands in sharp contrast to
judges on the continent who are recruited immediately after law school
and specially trained to serve on the bench. Like the magistrates, the
Crown Court judges are under the sway of an indigenous judicial culture
that reveres judicial independence. Judges and magistrates traditionally
have enjoyed "largely untrammelled sentencing power" and have fiercely
resisted efforts by Parliament to impose mandatory penalties or develop
a coherent set of sentencing practices and policies. As a result, the use of
custody as a penalty has varied greatly. Cavadino and Dignan go so far
as to say that the principle of judicial independence in Britain "has been
inflated into a much more extreme dogma." Britain's Court of Appeals has
not been inclined to formulate a coherent set of sentencing guidelines. The
magistrates' courts and Crown Courts have varied greatly in their use of

sentences, which created a policy vacuum that civil servants in the Home Office, members of Parliament, and various penal reform groups eventually sought to fill with measures like the Criminal Justice Act of 1991.

Not surprisingly, then, the 1991 act, which sought to curb judicial discretion and impose a sentencing structure on the courts, ignited a fierce judicial backlash. Many members of the judiciary did not see the purpose of enacting such a comprehensive statute and were committed to regarding the measure as a confirmation of the existing judicial approach.[255] The judiciary's efforts to maintain its expansive discretion fed into the efforts of penal conservatives who were committed to undoing the 1991 act for other reasons. The judiciary was particularly opposed to provisions in the measure that restricted its discretion to take into account previous convictions when meting out a sentence. At the time, the Lord Chief Justice complained that judges had been cloaked in an "ill-fitting straightjacket."[256]

By opposing the 1991 act, the judiciary helped bolster the more conservative penal climate. Ironically, through its opposition to the 1991 act, the judiciary paved the way for measures that hamstrung judicial discretion even more. These included the Criminal Justice Act of 1993, which amended key provisions in the 1991 act, and the Criminal Justice and Public Order Act of 1994, which altered the power of the courts to mete out custodial sentences to juvenile offenders, and the Crime (Sentences) Act of 1997, which established mandatory minimums. Parliament approved this last measure in spring 1997 shortly before the Conservative government fell.[257] Taken together, these measures signified a remarkable curtailment of the expansive judicial discretion judges had come to expect in the British legal system.[258]

In the 1990s, Michael Howard, the home secretary in John Major's Conservative government, and the judiciary, including the Lord Chief Justice, engaged in intense public battles over the introduction of mandatory minimums. Senior members of the judiciary began to use the mass media to rebut Howard's claim that sentencing was so lenient in some instances that mandatory minimums were warranted.[259] While the courts waged this battle with Howard over mandatory minimums, they were not entirely unresponsive to the tougher public mood. To maintain their own legitimacy as they attempted to fend off Parliament's attempts to curtail judicial discretion, judges felt that their sentences increasingly had to stay in tune with the more punitive public mood, according to Ashworth.[260] Without explicit prodding from the legislature, the judiciary began to increase its reliance on imprisonment. Between 1993 and early 1997, the prison population increased by 50 percent, from 40,000 to 60,000 – a remarkable rise.

All of these developments raised concerns and fears that Britain would go the way of the United States, with its tough line on crime and enthusiastic embrace of incarceration as the solution.[261] Taken together, these political and institutional changes eroded the delicate "joint moral community" that Faulkner and others had sought to build and sustain over the previous decade in Britain.[262] The "joint moral community" is extremely fragile.[263] Comprised of those who are responsible for shaping a society's criminal justice policies, it rests on four pillars: skepticism about prisons as well as other criminal justice and law enforcement tools to decrease crime; insistence on empathy with offenders and a capacity to see oneself in another person's place; rejection of the view that offenders are some kind of special breed of person; and recognition of an informal set of minimal standards considered decent in meting out punishment.[264]

While this "joint moral community" eroded in Britain, it did not collapse entirely. The conditions remained inhospitable for the emergence of a strident victims' movement premised on victims' rights. The new Labor government headed by Tony Blair increasingly pushed the victims issue, including granting victims formal rights in the legal system.[265] But it faced persistent resistance from probation officers, the Crown Prosecution Service, the judiciary, and professional organizations of solicitors. They continued to view victims "with an ambivalence, nervousness, and suspicion."[266] Time and again, the Home Office and prime minister faced "stout opposition" from these other pieces of the state who saw themselves as the guardians of defendants' rights, of professional, unemotional trials, and of the doctrine that crime is primarily an offense against state or society, not an individual.[267] NAVSS, the main voluntary organization for victims, remained reluctant to politicize the victims issue out of a concern that offenders would become the targets of law-and-order campaigns. It was not an enthusiastic supporter of victim-related measures that were popular in the United States, such as victim impact statements.[268] In short, no organized victims' movement emerged to complement and propel the Labor government's increased focus on law and order and its intensified calls for victims' rights. Furthermore, the ongoing chilly relationship between British women's groups and the criminal justice system continued to act as a check on more punitive policies (see Chapters 5 and 6). In short, Britain was able to maintain the "Maginot Line" of opposition to granting victims a formal place in criminal procedures.[269]

Conclusion

Certain combinations of political, historical, and institutional factors are more conducive to sustaining the "joint moral community" than others. This community does not erode and whither away merely because key politicians and public officials decide to play the crime card. Rather, one needs to consider the institutional casino in which they attempt to play the law-and-order card.

Britain shares some important political and institutional features with the United States, including an adversarial common-law system, the writ of *nolle prosequi*, and a significant voluntary sector and voluntary tradition. It also shares some important political factors, for instance the emergence of a powerful conservative movement under Thatcher committed to creating a law-and-order society and new neoliberal economic policies designed to shrink the state and grow the free market. Yet after an initial burst of enthusiasm in Britain for more prisons and police under Thatcher, Britain began to chart a course of penal pragmatism aimed at reducing the reliance on custody as punishment. Britain set off in this dramatically different direction because of significant differences in other state structures, notably the Home Office, the judiciary, and the welfare state. The victims issue evolved and developed in strikingly different ways because of these differences in state structures. Furthermore, the Conservative Party's efforts to reconcile its neoliberal commitments with its commitments to a law-and-order society served, at least for a time, as a check on penal populism in Britain.

By contrast, the push to expand the power to punish continued largely unabated in the United States. In the U.S. case, the laws of neoliberalism were suspended in the area of penal policy. The United States was particularly vulnerable to the call of penal conservatives because of the way the victims' movement was ignited and how it developed. The important long-standing institutional variables that distinguished the United States were: the comparatively underdeveloped U.S. welfare state; the highly developed and autonomous public prosecutor; and the adversarial common-law system. The contemporary institutional factors include the establishment of a new federal agency, the LEAA, to deal with crime; and pioneering social survey research done in the United States on victims.

The distinctiveness of the historical development of the U.S. state and polity helped give birth to a distinctive victims' movement that was remarkably in sync with the ascendant conservative forces and relatively immune from critical examination.[270] Ironically, the cause of victims' rights came to dominate penal politics to an unparalleled extent in the United States even though the victims issue emerged belatedly here. In the U.S. case, elite interest in victims took hold later and did not originate primarily out of sympathy for the offender. Furthermore, this elite interest in victims emerged almost simultaneously with the mobilization of women's groups against rape and domestic violence, which had important consequences for penal policy, as shown in the next two chapters.

5 NOT THE USUAL SUSPECTS

Feminists, Women's Groups, and the Anti-Rape Movement

"There will be no gallows, no dungeons, no needless cruelty in solitude, when mothers make the laws."

– Elizabeth Cady Stanton[1]

W OMEN'S GROUPS AND FEMINISTS in the United States have a long and conflicted history on issues related to crime, punishment, and law and order. Periodically, they have played central roles in defining violence as a threat to the social order and uncritically pushing for more enhanced policing powers to address law-and-order concerns. If one looks back at the history of penal policy and reform, it is striking what an uncritical stance earlier women reformers took toward the state. The women's reform movements and waves of feminist agitation that have appeared off and on since the nineteenth century in the United States helped to construct institutions and identities and establish practices that bolstered conservative tendencies in penal policy.

The contemporary women's movement in the United States helped facilitate the carceral state. Demands by the U.S. women's movement in the 1970s and 1980s to address the issues of rape and domestic violence had more far-reaching penal consequences in the United States than in other countries where burgeoning women's movements also identified these two issues as central concerns. Ironically, some of the very historical and institutional factors that made the U.S. women's movement relatively more successful in gaining public acceptance and achieving its goals for women were important building blocks for the carceral state that emerged simultaneously in the 1970s.[2]

The distinctive institutional arrangements and historical formation of the U.S. polity help explain not only the strong role of women in the development of social policies like mothers' pensions and public health programs, as Theda Skocpol has shown, but also the significant impact women have had on the development of penal policy.[3] Several key institutional variables include: the greater permeability of the U.S. Department of Justice to outside political forces compared to, say, the Home Office in Britain; once again, the relative weakness of the welfare state in the United States; the greater presence of diverse mass membership organizations like the National Organization for Women (NOW); the expansive role of the courts in the United States; and the decentralized and fragmented nature of the U.S. political system. Several ideological variables also conditioned the wider political context in which these institutions developed and operated, most notably the stronger liberal equal-rights tradition in the United States and the weaker influence that Marxism, socialism, and other radical traditions have exerted on feminism here. These institutional and ideological factors help explain why the U.S. women's movement did not act as an effective check on the law-and-order thrusts of conservative politicians but indeed helped hard-liners hit their mark. As a consequence, women's groups and the women's movement became a vanguard of conservative law-and-order politics in the United States but not in Europe.

Women's Groups and Early Prison Reform

Beginning with the emergence of the prison system in the early nineteenth century, crime and punishment were major concerns of women reformers, arguably second only in importance to suffrage in releasing feminist and protofeminist energies in the five decades after the Civil War.[4] Middle-class women who had been abolitionists and health-care workers during the Civil War shifted their attention to new forms of social activism after the war. They joined campaigns for "social purity," suffrage, and temperance; they battled juvenile delinquency, family violence, and prostitution; and they took a particular interest in the plight of female offenders.[5] These agitations to purify society had enormous consequences for penal policy more broadly as women reformers repeatedly pressed for an enhanced state to address their concerns. Chapter 3 discussed in detail how women reformers were heavily involved in the battle against prostitution in the late nineteenth and early twentieth centuries. This chapter begins by looking at some of the lasting consequences for penal policy of two other campaigns: the push to establish separate prisons and reformatories for women after the Civil War; and the movement against family violence in the late nineteenth century.

During the Second Great Awakening in the 1820s and 1830s, women reformers in the United States first discovered the plight of female prisoners.[6] Their concerns did not coalesce into a full-blown movement until after the Civil War. However, these reformers did succeed in getting a number of states to hire female matrons to supervise imprisoned women, many of whom were physically and sexually abused by male guards and subjected to dire prison conditions.[7] Prior to the 1870s, the various waves of prison reform, which were predicated on rehabilitating offenders through measures like enforced silence, isolation, and hard labor, focused primarily on male offenders. Incarcerated women escaped notice because of their small numbers and because of the impossibility of enforcing rules of silence and other rehabilitative punishments, given the lack of adequate penal accommodations for women. Another factor was the widespread belief that female offenders were "fallen women," so depraved as to be beyond the possibility of redemption.[8] Francis Lieber, one of the leading nineteenth-century theorists of crime, articulated this widespread disdain for female offenders when he remarked, "A woman once renouncing honesty and virtue passes over to the most hideous of crimes which women commit, with greater ease than a man from his first offense to the blackest crimes committed by his sex."[9]

Infused by Victorian sensibilities, a new wave of women reformers in the late nineteenth century argued that these "fallen women" were not beyond hope. The state could make them into "true women" by creating separate penal facilities for women where their distinctive feminine needs could be met.[10] They advocated, among other things, the establishment of reformatories where women, primarily white women, would be taught to be good wives and mothers and could learn the skills necessary to be good servants in middle-class homes upon release.[11] The reformatory movement "re-tooled the image of the female offender from that of a morally depraved monster to that of an errant child," according to Nicole Hahn Rafter. In the process, the "criminal justice system became a mechanism for punishing women who did not conform to middle-class conceptions of femininity."[12]

The reformatory movement had enormous consequences not just for the relatively small number of women offenders but also for male offenders. In 1869, Michigan enacted the country's first indeterminate sentencing law. It authorized the state to incarcerate women convicted of prostitution for up to three years. This measure, according to Rafter, marked an important turning point in penal policy by singling out women for special treatment and establishing the precedent of indeterminate sentencing. Women were now eligible for extended sentences based on the belief that prostitutes could be rehabilitated. Michigan and other states began to mete out long sentences to women found guilty of misdemeanors and lesser offenses. Previously, women who committed transgressions like vagrancy, drunkenness, prostitution, and giving birth out of wedlock served short sentences in local jails, if they were incarcerated at all.[13] Reformers successfully made the case that it was now acceptable to ignore the norm of proportionality because the aim was to treat offenders, not punish them.[14] When Michigan enacted its indeterminate sentencing law, it initially refused to extend this penal innovation to men.[15] Shortly thereafter, at the inaugural meeting of what became the National Prison Association, participants endorsed indeterminate sentencing for men, which became an increasingly widespread practice over the following decades.

The prison reform movement for women was surprisingly successful on its own terms.[16] By the late nineteenth century, nearly every state had opened a separate custodial unit for women. These facilities were often within or close to penitentiaries for men and staffed by female rather than male guards. Between 1870 and 1900, only four reformatories specifically for women were opened. But over the next thirty-five years, seventeen states, primarily in the Northeast and Midwest, established such facilities.[17] The reformatory movement had enormous and lasting consequences for the differential treatment of women in prison, especially black women.[18] It also had a wider impact on penal policy. While the first phase of the reformatory movement (1870–1900) was different in important respects from the second phase (roughly 1900–1935), both had some common threads.[19] The reformatory movement generally took an uncritical view of the state in penal policy. It did not question the fundamentals of the prison system nor whether many of these women ought to be considered criminals at all. It authorized the state to police new areas of behavior and to sanction tougher punishments for acts that previously had been overlooked or subject to mild rebukes. It contributed to the spread of indeterminate sentencing and to erosion of the norm of proportionality in punishment. It also legitimized the practice of using institutions like reformatories to "'correct' deviations from traditional roles."[20]

The Late Nineteenth-Century Movement Against Family Violence

Women's concerns about "social purity" and rising anxiety about criminal matters were manifest in other ways in the late nineteenth century. From about 1874 to 1890, women were at the helm of a major campaign to criminalize family violence, the first such effort since the 1600s, when the Puritans enacted the world's first laws against wife-beating and what they termed "unnatural severity to children."[21] Family violence came to be regarded in a new light as a crime that threatened not only its victims, but also the social order.[22] The violent crime rate soared in the late nineteenth century, and the press was filled with accounts of notorious sex crimes and serial killings. Concern grew that neglected and abused children would grow up to swell the ranks of the "dangerous classes" and threaten public security.[23] There was also a greater willingness to trust a strong centralized government to enforce middle-class morality and punish criminals. Hundreds of societies for the prevention of cruelty to children were founded, and some modest steps were taken on behalf of battered women and victims of incest. New laws and court decisions gave these societies extraordinary police powers to prosecute abusive, neglectful parents and terminate parental guardianships.[24] Women's groups were integral to these child-welfare campaigns.

The campaign against wife-beating was far more modest than the child-welfare campaigns, arguably because the women's movement chose to focus on suffrage and refused to challenge the conventional family structure.[25] This early effort in the United States to mobilize around the issue of violence against women had some modest achievements, like expanding tort protection for battered women and establishing the rudiments of legal aid for them.[26] But its primary consequence was to reinforce a zeal for law and order at a time when fears of violent crime and the dangerous classes were growing.[27]

Initially, American feminists took a more radical stance on violence against women, one that did not rest largely on ratcheting up the punishments for men but emphasized instead increased protection for women. Leading feminists like Elizabeth Cady Stanton and Susan B. Anthony charged that abuse of wives resulted from a husband's ownership of his wife as property. The solution, they argued, was to reform the institution of marriage and liberalize divorce laws to protect women from physical and other kinds of abuse. But after 1870, Stanton and Anthony began to downplay the issue of crimes against women as they sought to regain suffragist support lost because of their association with impassioned attacks on marriage and with several sex scandals. Also, the 1873 Comstock Law, which prohibited the dissemination through the mail of information about birth control and pornography, stifled open discussion of rape and incest.

Feminists spanning the range from liberals like Anthony and Stanton to conservatives like Lucy Stone and Henry Blackwell pushed for stiffer, often severe, criminal penalties for male offenders.[28] In 1879, Stone introduced a bill in the Massachusetts legislature that gave assaulted wives the right to apply for legal separation, financial support, and the award of child custody. After the protection bill failed to pass for the second time, Stone began to favor the criminal punishment of abusers as a solution, rather than the protection of their victims.[29] Some women reformers called for bringing back the whipping post to punish wife-beaters. Between 1876 and 1906, bills to restore the whipping post were introduced in twelve states, the District of Columbia, and the U.S. Congress; the bills passed in three jurisdictions, indicating that this was a national issue, not just a local or state one.[30] Some women active in the social purity movement and the Women's Christian Temperance Union advocated castration for rapists.[31] Stanton and Anthony supported the death penalty for rapists.[32] This was a particularly controversial position because it came just as black women were mobilizing their own women's clubs to participate in the antilynching campaign, which was premised on exposing the widespread myth that most lynchings involved allegations of the rape of white women by black men.[33]

The early movement against family violence in Britain provides a striking contrast to the U.S. movement. Whereas feminist interest in crimes against women began to diminish by the 1890s in the United States, it remained a central issue for British feminists, suffragists, and the British state for two more decades.[34] British suffragists "continued to cling to social purity ideas with a vehemence that had disappeared elsewhere."[35] However, British feminists resisted the temptation to address wife-beating primarily through law-and-order solutions like bringing back the whipping post. They made a connection between wife-beating and other volatile political issues, like demands for women's suffrage and divorce law reform.[36] Frances Power Cobbe, an ardent champion of women's rights, focused national attention on the horrors husbands inflicted on their wives and successfully pushed for passage of the Matrimonial Causes Act (1878).[37] The measure, which sailed through the House of Commons and was a model for the bill Lucy Stone initially sought in Massachusetts, permitted abused wives to secure protection orders that would have the effect of a judicial separation.[38] Throughout, Cobbe resisted pressures to rely primarily on law-and-order solutions to address the problem of family violence. She emphasized that parliamentary acts alone would not end violence against women. Rather it was necessary to upend conventional attitudes about women's inferiority and end the social subjugation of women, in her view.[39]

The central government in Britain had greater authority, resources, and capacity to address issues defined as national concerns in the area of criminal justice. While the Home Office was not sympathetic on the whole to the plight of abused women, if pushed to act by leading public officials, it could serve as an important resource. At the prodding of Colonel Egerton Leigh, who spoke out against wife-beating in the House of Commons in 1874, the Home Office initiated an inquiry into the subject. A number of prominent figures in British criminal justice conducted the inquiry. Their final report documented the brutal abuse women were subjected to and the inadequacy of existing laws to protect them. Cobbe's seminal article "Wife-Torture in England" was based on this study.[40] In 1889, the Home Office put out another important report, "Assault on Females."[41] Martin J. Wiener makes the provocative argument that from the mid-Victorian era onward, Britain, especially the British courts, began to take violence against women seriously because "treatment of women in Britain and in the burgeoning empire became a touchstone of civilization and national pride."[42]

To sum up, even at this early stage, women reformers in Britain and the United States took sharply different approaches to the issue of violence against women, which had important implications for the broader development of penal policy. As the suffrage movement began to flourish in the United States, white suffragists shed more controversial, less popular issues like violence against women and the movement for social purity, according to Elizabeth Pleck.[43] Hailing from a more militant tradition and having deeper ties to more radical political movements like socialism and Marxism, British feminists resisted centering their campaigns against family violence on calls for tougher sanctions, such as bringing back the whipping post for wife-beaters, that would bolster conservative interests more generally.[44]

Origins of the Anti-Rape Movement

The issue of violence against women petered out in the United States in the early twentieth century. It reemerged as a women's rights issue in the 1970s, and sustained momentum through its association with law-and-order issues, much as it had a century earlier. The contemporary movement was broader and more national in scope than the earlier one. It also was relatively more successful by certain measures, including its legislative achievements, shifts in public and official attitudes toward rape and domestic violence, and the explosion of resources and services available for abused women. Police, prosecutors, and the public no longer ignored rape and domestic violence.[45] But there was a disturbing undercurrent to these achievements. In striking contrast to what happened elsewhere, the issues of rape and domestic violence developed in ways that complemented the tough law-and-order policies that certain political elites, backed by conservative interest groups, were pushing and thus contributed to the construction of the carceral state.

The ultimate ascendancy of the equal rights strand of feminism over more radical strands in debates about rape and domestic violence in the United States helps explain why the U.S. women's movement was more vulnerable to being co-opted by crime-control proponents than were feminists in other Western countries. To understand this outcome, we need to look in detail at the origins and development of the mobilization of the contemporary women's movement against rape and domestic violence in the United States and make some comparisons with the women's movement in other countries. While the ascendancy of the equal rights strand was not entirely unexpected, the profound implications that this outcome had for penal policy have been largely unexamined.

By the early 1970s, feminism in the United States had developed into two main branches. One stressed women's rights – that is, focusing primarily on gaining for women the same rights and opportunities held by men. The second branch, while supportive of the goal of equal rights, made a more radical critique of the place of women in American society and attacked such things as the unequal gender division of labor and the myriad ways women were denied control of important aspects of their lives.[46] This second branch called not just for equal rights, but a wholesale restructuring of societal values and the reorganization of institutions to end the subjugation of women. The issue of violence against women reemerged in the early 1970s in a political and institutional context that was already biased toward the equal rights approach due to the historical dominance of the liberal political tradition in the United States.[47] The powerful example of the civil rights movement, which had made such significant strides by mobilizing around the cause of equal rights, bolstered this bias toward liberal solutions among some feminists.[48] But the ultimate ascendance of the liberal approach to deal with the problem of violence against women (which would prove to be so compatible with the law-and-order approach to penal policy more broadly) was not foreordained by the dominance of the liberal political tradition. We need to consider the particulars of the ideological, institutional, and political context at this time and not just assume that the engine of liberalism ground on.

In the U.S. case, the anti-rape movement, and the movement against domestic violence that followed on its heels, originated in the radical wing of U.S. feminism, with its oppositional rather than reformist ideology. These movements were founded on several radical notions: that violence against women was a fundamental component of the social control of women; that abused women needed to be transformed from victims into survivors; that reliance on the state for solutions risked co-optation; and that the ultimate solution to rape and domestic violence rested on overhauling the relations between men and women.[49] Founded on deep skepticism toward the state, these movements ultimately became champions of state intervention, though elements of the oppositional ideology persisted.[50] Over time, the primary goals became more modest – providing services for abused women in professional therapeutic settings and fighting for tough legislation to make it easier to convict and punish men accused of rape or domestic violence. This is in sharp contrast to movements elsewhere, for example in Germany and Britain, that maintained their distance from state structures and did not make tougher penal punishments a central demand. They retained their radical, oppositional ideology such that they could not be readily co-opted by political elites ratcheting up the call for law and order.

While the mobilizations against rape and domestic violence in the United States had their origins in the radical wing of American feminism, they soon attracted a more diverse following. As a result, pressure mounted to compromise their founding notions. From the start, the U.S. women's movement was more ideologically diverse overall, which predisposed it more to compromising. It included women previously politicized by the progressive movements of the 1930s and 1940s and later by the civil rights movement and New Left. It also included women who were being drawn into politics for the first time, as well as veteran elite reformers who had been mobilized by the state and later formed the nucleus of NOW, an elite-led, diverse, mass membership organization for women not found elsewhere.[51]

Whereas state actors in Britain and other countries generally kept an arm's length from feminists, in the United States public officials were important catalysts, sometimes unwittingly, in mobilizing and organizing the contemporary women's movement. As a consequence, the U.S. women's movement had from the start an important foothold in elite politics. This made women's groups more responsive – for better and worse – to shifting political winds, in particular growing conservatism on penal and other issues. In 1961 President John F. Kennedy signed an executive order creating the President's Commission on the Status of Women, which became an important elite institutional building block for the U.S. women's movement. The commission generated a number of task forces that began documenting gender discrimination in a wide range of areas. By 1969, all fifty states had set up similar commissions. These formal organizations served as a crucial elite-level network for women activists.[52] Congress's decision to add a ban on sex discrimination in employment to Title VII of the 1964 Civil Rights Act, which prohibited discrimination in employment based on race, religion, or national origin, further galvanized elite women activists. Dissatisfaction with the Equal Employment Opportunity Commission, which was charged with administering Title VII, helped spur the creation of NOW. Liberal government officials confidentially told leading women's rights activists in 1966 that the best way to exert pressure on the administration would be to create a national women's organization comparable to the major civil rights organizations. NOW was officially born in June 1966 at the Third National Conference of State Commissions on the Status of Women.[53]

From the start, the U.S. women's movement was riven with internal tensions. During its formative period in the late 1960s and 1970s, elite women reformers contended that the system could be changed quickly through a bipartisan approach aimed at sympathetic officials. They advocated a strategy based on exploiting their connections with the political and policy-making elite. Other women favored a more confrontational, separatist approach modeled on the protest tactics developed by the civil rights and radical student movements. They expressed doubts about how much could be accomplished by concentrating on legislative lobbying and by working with the established political parties. Internal papers and documents from NOW and the lobbyist group Women's Equity Action League (WEAL) document these organizations' disenchantment with the growing strand of militarism within the women's movement.[54]

Interest in the issue of rape and, later, domestic violence originated in the more radical, militant wing of the U.S. women's movement.[55] In January 1971, the New York Radical Feminists held a "Speak-Out on Rape," apparently the first time women in the United States gathered publicly as a group to disclose that they had been sexually assaulted. Three months later they followed up with a full day of workshops on rape.[56] Shortly thereafter, women in a number of cities established grassroots rape crisis centers. The founders of the pioneer centers in places like

Berkeley, Boston, Detroit, and Washington, D.C., envisaged them as social change organizations that would express the new feminist politics. They were suspicious of state involvement and rejected traditional service delivery methods founded on organizational hierarchies. They self-consciously maintained a distance from law enforcement agencies, hospitals, and conventional social services and assumed a militant stance toward professionals in such organizations. Early on they were particularly skeptical about accepting funding that would require them to work too closely with state agencies, especially law enforcement.[57] Instead, they stressed self-help for women who had been raped. A number of feminists involved early on in the anti-rape movement looked askance at the punitive arm of the state. Rather than pushing women to file reports with the police, for example, the Bay Area Women Against Rape, California's first rape crisis center, would post flyers in the community describing rapists and their patterns.[58]

NOW and the Women's Political Caucus were critical in catapulting the rape issue onto the national political agenda.[59] Under pressure from its radical flank and the many new chapters of WAR, or Women Against Rape, NOW took up the issue of rape. At its annual meeting in February 1973, it voted to establish the National Task Force on Rape.[60] State and local groups followed suit, creating 300 task forces nationwide between 1973 and 1976.[61] In 1974, women in Washington, D.C., formed the Feminist Alliance Against Rape (FAAR) to make the movement more visible and to improve communications among activists.[62] While NOW was the best known of the women's groups involved in the rape issue, other groups emerged that had a more single-minded focus. The Women's Crusade Against Crime was active in several Midwestern cities. Unlike NOW, which had to straddle a diverse set of interests and concerns, the Crusade had one main goal: "to support, assist, and augment the criminal justice system in doing its job." The Crusade considered it counterproductive to denounce the practices of police, prosecutors, and hospitals because this might discourage women from reporting sexual assaults to the authorities. Members of the Crusade tended to be older and to have closer ties to the political establishment than did rape crisis center volunteers and activists. They campaigned for items near and dear to law enforcement, like bond issues to purchase new equipment for police.[63]

The LEAA and the Transformation of the Anti-Rape Movement

Over the years, the anti-rape movement went through a remarkable transformation. This was evident in the changes in the rape crisis centers themselves, as well as in the movement's greater focus on lobbying for legislation that would make it easier to convict and punish rapists. Despite initial concerns about becoming too closely associated with the growing conservative law-and-order movement, the founding feminist notions of the anti-rape movement were overrun by law-and-order approaches more akin to the Women's Crusade Against Crime. Increased national attention on the rape issue through the activities of NOW, grassroots groups, and the federal LEAA (whose origins were discussed in Chapter 4) created new opportunities for public funding of rape crisis groups. The LEAA's Crime Victim Initiative provided an important mechanism to co-opt the women's movement and enlist it in the war against crime and the criminal. While support from the LEAA was critical in this development, it is important to note that the anti-rape movement exhibited some punitive tendencies early on.

The LEAA and the state were initially at odds with many feminists, in particular with the founding notions of the anti-rape movement. As the LEAA and other arms of the state became more involved in the issue of rape, they successfully "recast the feminist definition of rape as a political issue into the problem of an individual victim" in need of adequate services from the state so as to increase her willingness to help in the successful prosecution of her case.[64] The LEAA sponsored some pathbreaking studies of the special problems women faced in the criminal justice system as offenders, victims, and law enforcement employees.[65]

A fifteen-month study completed in 1974 by the LEAA, *Rape and Its Victims*, supported some of the central claims that feminists had been making regarding the treatment of rape victims and provided an important bridge between the LEAA and the movement. The LEAA report concluded that rape victims were victimized twice – first by the initial assault, and then a second time by police, prosecutors, and hospitals, whose responses were often "poor," "inadequate," and "haphazard." The report found that law enforcement and other institutions successfully resisted reforms introduced to help rape victims. It recommended the establishment of new local programs and procedures so as to improve the treatment of rape victims by the authorities and thus increase the likelihood of successfully prosecuting these cases.[66] But the report also questioned the approach and message of the rape crisis centers, suggesting that they should be less feminist. "The message must often be expressed in different, more conservative terms than that published in the feminist or even popular press," it concluded.[67]

With the help of LEAA money and other public financing, the government successfully absorbed many of the independent rape crisis centers and services, with their radical, volunteer, grassroots orientation, into its professional, hierarchical bureaucracy. Federal policy encouraged the creation of programs for rape victims in established community agencies through incentives like grants. These new programs placed less emphasis on peer support and self-help.[68] By 1981, only 200 to 300 independent rape crisis centers were still in operation, compared to 600 to 700 five years earlier. A third of the surviving centers consisted of little more than a hotline.[69] By the mid-1980s, about half of all centers surveyed did not engage in any political action work, excluding lobbying, according to one study.[70]

The LEAA heralded those rape crisis centers that contributed to increases in the reporting and conviction rates for sexual assault. In 1979, it lauded a rape crisis center in Baton Rouge, La., because of its "overall effectiveness in reducing crime" and its "cost effectiveness." A LEAA-sponsored report credited this center with an increase in the reporting and conviction rates for rape. It singled out the placement of this rape crisis center in the district attorney's office and the hiring of a program director from outside the prosecutor's office as key factors in its success. These measures reportedly enhanced the center's credibility and legitimacy with other law enforcement agencies and the wider community.[71] Left unsaid in the report is that in 1976 the Baton Rouge district attorney ordered the director of the Stop Rape Crisis Center to withhold services from victims who refused to file reports with the police. When the center's administrator objected, the district attorney dismissed her. The whole staff resigned in protest and was replaced by employees of the criminal justice system.[72]

While federal and state funding was uneven and unpredictable, it was nonetheless critical to the development of the anti-rape movement.[73] The National Center for the Prevention and Control of Rape, which was established by the National Institute of Mental Health in 1976 and disbanded in 1985, provided important services and information and sponsored training conferences. However, it was reluctant to fund feminist rape crisis centers.[74] The Mental Health Services Act provided federal funds for centers in 1980. Between 1981 and 1987, centers received support from the Public Service Health Act. From 1984 onward, they qualified for funding under the new Victims of Crime Act. VOCA provides block grants to states out of the Crime Victims Fund, which is financed through fines and restitution payments from offenders.[75]

LEAA funding was so controversial that many organizations refused to apply for it, especially those with strong feminist ties. Nonetheless, the LEAA had an important impact even on those rape crisis centers and services that rejected direct LEAA funding. By legitimizing some of the feminists' complaints about the police's and prosecutors' indifference to rape victims, the LEAA underscored that rape reform entailed significant law enforcement reforms. This provided an opening to stress law enforcement solutions at the expense of the deeper social and political critique developed by the radical feminists who initially raised the rape issue. It helped dull the edge of the skeptical stance the anti-rape movement initially took toward the state and law enforcement. Furthermore, while the early rape crisis centers eschewed direct grants from the LEAA, they often accepted funding from the state-level Offices of Criminal Justice

Planning established to administer the LEAA block grants. State granting agencies generally preferred to fund services for victims rather than political activities that challenged how police, prosecutors, and judges handled sexual assault cases, which had a significant effect on the anti-rape movement.[76]

In her study of six rape crisis centers established in the Los Angeles area between the early 1970s and 1984, Nancy Matthews details the process by which this occurred.[77] In its early years, the L.A. anti-rape movement was distrustful of the state and generally refused to accept financial support that required it to work closely with state agencies, especially law enforcement. It emphasized alternative forms of organization, especially nonhierarchical collectives. Funding pressures eventually prompted the centers to start emulating conventional hierarchical structures and to embrace more of the goals of state agencies, notably social services, mental health, and law enforcement.[78] The centers sought to appear more legitimate so as to share in the windfall of new state and federal money available to combat crime by aiding victims. Paradoxically, as social services began to shrink in the 1980s due to the tax revolt, the recession, and the Reagan revolution, services for crime victims, including rape victims, expanded.

Begun under the liberal administration of Democratic Governor Jerry Brown, funding for rape crisis centers continued to expand under successive Republican administrations. California's Office of Criminal Justice Planning (OCJP), funded by the LEAA, transformed many of the rape crisis centers from shoestring operations into social service agencies. While the oppositional ideology that characterized the first rape crisis centers was not completely lost, it was significantly muted.[79] Through the OCJP, the LEAA provided California with the institutional template to view the rape issue primarily through a criminal justice lens and to abandon the deeply critical political lens employed by the feminists who founded the anti-rape movement. Through its control of the purse strings, the OCJP put pressure on rape crisis centers to behave more like apolitical social service agencies, going so far as to terminate funding of groups found to be uncooperative or hostile to its approach.

After Congress phased out LEAA funding in 1980, the California state legislature directed the OCJP to continue developing criminal justice programs. The legislature created the Sexual Assault Program within the OCJP. The first head of the new Sexual Assault Program hailed from the mainstream of the anti-rape movement. Previously she had been the director of a rape crisis center with a history of accepting sizable amounts of LEAA funding. During the 1980s, most of the victim and witness services in California, including child abuse, crime watch, shelters for battered women, and rape crisis centers, were transferred to and consolidated within the OCJP. By locating the Sexual Assault Program in the OCJP, the rape crisis centers profited from being affiliated with law enforcement during a period when attacks on social spending were rife. (In Massachusetts, by contrast, rape crisis centers continued to be located under social services and experienced major cutbacks during the same period.) But this was a costly association.

Rising support for the Sexual Assault Program at the OCJP had little to do with support for the founding principles of the anti-rape movement. It was primarily the result of efforts to wage war on crime, and on criminals in particular. The Sexual Assault Program was funded largely as a result of the OCJP's decision to crack down on crime by enforcing penalty payments to the state by convicted criminals.[80] In California, funding for rape crisis centers increased dramatically, but at the cost of increased state regulation. In the process, "the feminist political agenda of relating violence against women to women's oppression was marginalized, ridiculed, and suppressed by various means."[81] As a consequence, the anti-rape movement no longer served as an ideological bulwark against the rising conservative tide. Indeed, anti-rape activists increasingly joined conservative coalitions and played the crime card in California and elsewhere.

Rape, Race, and the State

Playing the crime card served to attract money for rape crisis centers and also to broaden the base of the movement from middle- and upper-class white women to Hispanic and black communities. Blacks and Hispanics had been alienated by the style of the radical feminists and were unwilling to compromise some of their own goals and strategies in order to meet the standards of radicalism established by white feminists.[82] Emphasizing the crime card turned out to be an effective way to diversify and depoliticize the anti-rape movement in important respects. Marilyn Peterson, the first director of the OCJP's Sexual Assault Program, strategically used the crime issue to secure additional funding for rape crisis centers and to build bridges with minority communities. "I was always trying to think of new angles to get money. . . . So I came up with this idea, well, let's look at it in terms of high crime area and minority representation, and mainly with Republicans you talk high crime," she explained.[83]

The OCJP set up a target grant program for communities that had high rape rates. These grants were pivotal to the establishment of new anti-rape programs in predominantly black areas in South Central Los Angeles and Compton. In contrast to the pioneering centers, these two rape crisis centers were started with considerable state money and did not have strong ties to the feminist community. Instead, they had links to hierarchical, bureaucratic organizations like the Young Women's Christian Association and the Southern Christian Leadership Conference. From the start, these centers were generally not suspicious of the OCJP money and identified more closely with the growing victims' rights movement. "The broader emergence of a crime victim's rights ethic in the U.S. was the bridge by which rape crisis services came to Black communities," according to Nancy A. Matthews.[84]

This had mixed results. Without state assistance, rape crisis centers might never have been established in predominantly black and Hispanic communities. However, these new centers were bureaucratic and hierarchical. They had strong, uncritical links to the state, and only tenuous ties with the feminists who initially propelled the anti-rape movement.[85] They exhibited a more conservative orientation toward rape and crime, akin to the emerging victims' rights movement. Unlike the pioneering rape crisis centers, they did not serve as separate, alternative spaces in which to develop and nurture an oppositional ideology. Nonetheless, they were more sensitive to some of the racial and ethnic issues associated with combatting sexual assault and other violence against women within the black, Hispanic, and other minority communities.

Here again the diversity of the women's movement helps explain this outcome. Many of the pioneering radical feminists were insensitive to the complex racial and ethnic issues associated with violence against women. For example, the early anti-rape activists tended to play down or ignore how the charge of rape had been used historically to reinforce white supremacy and the color line in the United States.[86] That said, they initially viewed the anti-rape movement as an alternative to the criminal justice system and many of its shortcomings.[87] These early anti-rape activists increasingly had to contend with liberal, middle-class, primarily white women who viewed the state as an institution that, if properly reformed, could be counted on to control violence against women. These women assumed that the police could be successfully pressed to do their jobs. They largely ignored or were insensitive to the concerns of black and Hispanic women, who had more direct experience with the problems of the police and the criminal justice system, and, for various reasons, were less willing to endorse a radical, separatist stance.[88]

Many of the first rape crisis centers had few minority women on their staffs, and these centers were "unknown in minority communities," according to one LEAA-sponsored report.[89] Slighted by the anti-rape movement and desperate for funding and resources, black and Hispanic women subsequently established community rape crisis centers that had stronger ties to the state and thus to law enforcement. These centers, not surprisingly, had modest goals that turned out to be in some ways quite compatible with the growing conservative movement against crime. They sought to press "the state to fulfill its function of managing violence" and eschewed any broader critique of its role in waging the war against crime.[90] In the process, rape was increasingly redefined as an individual, psychological trauma.[91] This seemingly apolitical view of the rape victim complemented the growing conservative view that attributed the increase in crime to the pathologies of individual criminals and not to wider structural problems in society. It was compatible with the proliferation of dehumanized images of criminals, best exemplified by the infamous Willie Horton ads of the 1988 presidential campaign. Such images "restrict[ed] any type of public empathy toward those who break the law" and reinforced among all women the dominant image of criminals as "out-of-control evil strangers who randomly attack their victims."[92]

This is not to say that the anti-rape movement was uniformly insensitive to or ignorant of the particular concerns of blacks and other minority groups. In a special 1980 issue on "The Offender, The Abuser, and The Harasser" that appeared in *Aegis*, the flagship publication of the Feminist Alliance Against Rape and the National Communications Network, Laureen France and Nancy McDonald questioned the championing of the prosecution of rapists under the current criminal justice system. They noted that those who are convicted and incarcerated tend to be poor and members of minority groups. Other articles in the special issue also questioned whether incarceration was a solution to rape.[93]

Over the next decade some feminists began to make racial concerns a more central feature of their campaigns against rape. In her detailed analysis of the anti-rape campaign launched by black feminists in the St. Louis area during the highly publicized appeal of the rape conviction of boxer Mike Tyson in 1993, Aaronette M. White shows how feminists there sought to educate the black community about the racist and sexist myths surrounding crimes like sexual assault and domestic violence. At the same time, these activists acknowledged the limitations of a strategy premised on merely increasing the number of rape convictions. In attempting to educate blacks in the St. Louis area about the seriousness of the problem of violence against women, they expressed concerns about the criminalization of blacks, Hispanics, and other groups at the hands of an ever-expanding penal system.[94]

Rape Law Reform

In addition to establishing hundreds of rape crisis centers, the anti-rape movement succeeded in convincing state legislatures to overhaul their rape laws. One observer characterized the legislative achievements of the rape law reformers as "bold, dramatic and sustaining."[95] By 1980, six years after Michigan's enactment of the country's first comprehensive rape reform legislation, nearly every state had revised its sexual assault laws. These new measures typically redefined the offense of rape and introduced new state statutes that limited the admissibility of evidence concerning the character and sexual history of the victim.[96] In some instances, reformers sought to reduce the penalties for rape and introduce a gradation of penalties for various degrees of sexual assault. They sought to lower the penalties because of the unwillingness of juries to convict for rape when the punishment was capital punishment. Furthermore, in those rare instances when the death penalty was imposed for rape, it was used overwhelmingly in cases of black men convicted of raping white women.[97]

These legislative measures affected the public discussion of crime in significant ways.[98] On the positive side, the public and state authorities, including law enforcement, began to accept that rape was a significant social problem and not simply the consequence of a woman's behavior, character, or manner of dress. There also was growing acceptance that conventional policing, prosecutorial, and medical practices ignored or exacerbated the physical and emotional trauma that rape victims and other victims of sexual assault experienced. This prompted an increase in funding for rape crisis centers and services. Furthermore, the public became more sensitive to the lasting effects of sexual assault, especially on children, and more supportive of instituting educational programs about sexual abuse in schools and community organizations.[99]

But these measures had some significant negative consequences for the public discussion of crime and law and order. They were enacted in large part because feminists joined coalitions with law-and-order groups. If feminists had not allied themselves with these groups, the simmering backlash against the women's movement in the 1970s likely would have derailed rape reform legislation in many states.[100] The costs of this alliance were high. Women's groups entered into some unsavory coalitions and compromises that bolstered the law-and-order agenda and reduced their own capacity to serve as ideological bulwarks against the rising tide of conservatism. In Washington State, the women's lobby marketed a rape reform bill to the legislature as a law-and-order bill. The measure was eventually enacted in July 1975, in part by riding on the coattails of a new death penalty statute.[101] In California, the rape shield statute was named the Robbins Rape Evidence Law in honor of its co-sponsor, conservative Republican Sen. Alan Robbins. The name of liberal Sen. George Moscone, a co-author of the measure, is not associated with the law.[102] In pressing for limits on the cross-examination of rape victims and on bringing their sexual history into the courtroom, women's groups generally did not consider what effect such measures would have on a defendant's right to due process. At the time, this right was under assault from all sides as the war on crime was intensifying, and some legal aid societies and civil libertarians were expressing doubts about the constitutionality of rape shield laws and other legal reforms designed to protect sexual assault victims.[103]

While early anti-rape activists tended to eschew involvement with the state, and law enforcement in particular, some of them experimented with the vigilante tactics that we tend to associate more commonly with the victims' rights movement that emerged later on. Activists in Berkeley took matters into their own hands by visiting the home of an accused rapist en masse and waving signs that denounced him. Some rape crisis centers would independently publish the names of alleged sexual assailants who had been acquitted or were on parole or probation.[104] In 1973, members of a rape crisis center in East Lansing, Mich., reportedly scrawled "rapist" on a suspect's car, spray-painted the word across a front porch, and made warning telephone calls late at night.[105] In Los Angeles, women calling themselves the "anti-rape squad" vowed to pursue rapists, shave their heads, cover them with dye, and photograph them for posters that read: "THIS MAN RAPES WOMEN."[106] The feminist publication *Aegis* once featured on its cover the photograph of a poster that pictured a large gun with the warning: "YOU CAN'T RAPE A .38; WE WILL DEFEND OURSELVES." The brief article about the poster, which had been appearing mysteriously around Vancouver, B.C., had the headline: "You CAN Get A Man With A Gun" and concluded with the line, "WOW! I wish I had thought of it."[107]

As the victims' movement took shape, anti-rape activists mimicked some of its key tactics in order to secure funding and legislation from state officials. There was a great emphasis on women as victims. "In order to gain legitimacy and funding, anti-rape work had to focus on the plight of the victim. In many ways this focus is justified because violence brutalizes individual women," explained one feminist newsletter. But it also warned that an overemphasis on victimization might come at the cost of neglecting political analysis and organizing.[108] Members of the Southern California Rape Crisis Center (SCRCC) founded in 1974 were exhorted to "frame their actions as extensions of victims' needs or experiences."[109] Discursive politics was a centerpiece of their strategy. Activists used storytelling tactics that consisted of a "dramatic account of a victim's rape experience, the injustices of her experience, and the action that is called for from the audience and/or society." Staff members were encouraged to focus on the "horror stories" so as to create feelings of outrage among officials and the public.[110] In their detailed study of the SCRCC, Frederika E. Schmitt and Patricia Yancey Martin laud this approach as a prime example of Mary Fainsod Katzenstein's concept of the "unobtrusive mobilization inside institutions."[111] Feminists of this center avoided being openly confrontational or critical of mainstream organizations and individuals, yet were able to get what they wanted without being co-opted by the establishment, according to Schmitt and Martin.

If the rape issue is viewed narrowly, these groups were a success. They secured more resources, had greater access to the ears of state officials, and were able to persuade state legislatures to enact much of their legislative agenda. But looked at through another lens, these groups were profoundly co-opted. They abdicated the earlier commitment to functioning as independent sites for an oppositional ideology that broadly critiqued the state and society. And by framing the rape issue around "horror stories," they fed into the victims' movement's compelling image of a society held hostage to a growing number of depraved, marauding criminals. Thus, it is not that surprising that the mainstream tolerated and, in some cases, actively valued the efforts of groups like the SCRCC.[112]

The Anti-Rape Movement in Britain

In Britain, by contrast, violence against women did not become a central law-and-order issue. The anti-rape movement remained largely outside the mainstream even though British rape crisis centers consciously patterned themselves after groups first established in the United States. They were largely unsuccessful in drawing attention to how the British police and courts mistreated women who had been raped. The centers tended to remain marginalized because they had no national structure and hence no collective voice. Moreover, the "extreme feminist views" that dominated in most British centers were "unpalatable to those with political power and even to some raped women."[113] The victim support schemes associated with the National Association of Victims Support Schemes (NAVSS), with their emphasis on providing services to rape victims and other victims of crime rather than on remaking the criminal justice system or society, were more acceptable to the police and other parts of the state apparatus, notably the Home Office.[114] Over time these schemes secured a central place in government policy, pushing other victims' groups, such as the rape crisis centers, further to the margins.[115] Discussions of victims in Britain were remarkably gender-free. Issues related to women as victims were "bleached out . . . losing their distinctive connection with gender."[116] This was the result of the "historical failure of special interest groups" to penetrate the state and "the relative success of victim support."[117]

The British state also remained comparatively unresponsive to the anti-rape movement due to deep institutional factors. The Home Office had developed over the centuries into a highly autonomous institution largely insulated from the public.[118] By contrast, many of the top law enforcement officials in the United States are elected officials, including many judges, district attorneys, and even heads of police departments. This made them potentially more responsive under certain conditions to public pressures, be those from the right or the left. Civil servants in the Home Office generally looked askance at people with causes to prosecute, such as victims' rights or feminism. The Home Office maintained its distance from women's groups because they were not "house-trained," to use its words.[119]

British groups like Women Against Rape (WAR), Women Against Violence Against Women, and the London Rape Counselling and Research Project were founded in the 1970s on explicitly feminist – that is, radical feminist – principles. They embraced confrontational political methods, like taking to the streets to subject the home secretary to a mock trial and keeping the "staid and respectable political world at bay."[120] Unlike NAVSS, the women's movement did not emphasize the need to work closely with the police and the Home Office. The rape crisis centers and the refuges for battered women did not attempt to make overtures to the Home Office for money and, not surprisingly, the Home Office did not court what it viewed as distasteful evangelical pressure groups.

Unlike feminists in the United States, WAR explicitly reached out to the radical prison reform movement in Britain. It carried on a "difficult but productive dialogue" with groups like the Sex Offenses Working Group of Radical Alternatives to Prison (RAP), one of Britain's major radical prison groups.[121] WAR's report "Ask Any Woman" appeared in the *Abolitionist*, a publication of the radical prison movement. In that report, WAR walked a delicate line between opposing the relative leniency of rape sentences in Britain and calls to increase the absolute severity of sentences. WAR explicitly acknowledged that sentencing serves ideological purposes and that sharply reducing the sentences for most offenses would resolve the issue of the relative leniency of rape sentences. This would thwart attempts by conservative forces to use law-and-order campaigns to divert attention from the deeper social and structural causes of crime.[122] The link between WAR and RAP reflects the important influence feminists in Britain had on the development of the subfield of critical criminology, which had more established roots in Britain than on the continent or in the United States.[123]

Locked out or marginalized by the Home Office and Britain's other major criminal justice institutions, the women's movement did not seek political allies and political respectability by forging strategic political alliances with the rising conservative movement that chastised the Home Office and others for being too soft on crime and criminals. Women's groups in Britain generally resisted the temptation to make stiffer penalties for offenders a centerpiece of their activities. Hailing from a more radical tradition and comprised primarily of a local, grassroots membership, they were more suspicious of state-led, top-down solutions to the problem of violence against women to begin with. British women's groups mobilizing against rape were more driven by explicitly feminist concerns and did not conceive of or describe their actions in punitive criminal justice terms. Instead they persisted in seeing a strong relationship between sexual assault and wider power structures and did not seek closer cooperation with the police.[124] They consciously eschewed the word "victim" and any association with emerging victim support schemes like NAVSS.[125]

British rape crisis centers and refuges for battered women were less in need of and desirous of state money because of the more established voluntary tradition in victims' services, a less entrenched therapeutic state, and a more developed welfare state. As discussed in Chapter 4, the early victims' programs in Britain were based on a strong voluntary tradition and eschewed any broader political aims. Their primary goal was to act as a "good neighbor" or "good Samaritan" to crime victims. Services for victims were viewed as significant expressions of community concern that were considered as important as any practical help rendered.[126] Not surprisingly, then, the rape crisis centers and refuges for battered women heralded voluntary help, even though they maintained a distant relationship with the NAVSS, and did not consider professional help for victims as essential. The medical profession in Britain, which paid scant attention to the effects of rape, reinforced this view.[127] Voluntary services to aid rape victims were considered to be of a high quality and beneficial to victims. Few women ever saw a professional counselor or psychiatrist to deal with the emotional aftermath of rape.[128] British rape crisis centers and refuges tended to be staffed by volunteers and nonprofessionals animated by feminist principles rather than by apolitical professionals. They were under less pressure to conform because they never attracted large-scale funding.[129] The majority of British centers continued to operate as autonomous women's groups, unlike their counterparts in the United States. This started to change somewhat only in the mid-1990s, with the establishment of the Federation of Rape Crisis Centers in Manchester. It was designed to coordinate the activities of the rape crisis centers and make them more professional. Many of the centers changed their names and adopted a more social service, therapeutic approach.[130]

The strikingly different operating procedures between the Crown Prosecution Service in Britain and public prosecutors in the United States were another institutional factor that reinforced the gap between women's groups and law enforcement. In Britain, prosecutors are banned from consulting with witnesses prior to trial. This ban is intended to prevent prosecutors from briefing witnesses. One consequence of the ban is that when a rape victim's reputation comes under attack during the trial, as it often does, she has no one prepared to defend her. Whereas a rape victim in the United States might work closely with prosecutors for several months preparing the case for trial, in Britain she might not even know which barrister is prosecuting her case until she is called to appear at the trial.[131] This may help explain why the conviction rate for rape and attempted rape dropped significantly – from 24 percent of all reported cases in 1985 to 10 percent in 1996 – in the aftermath of the creation of the Crown Prosecution Service in 1986 in England and Wales.[132] In a number of other countries sexual assault victims are entitled to their own legal representation from the moment they report the attack.[133] In the United States, the LEAA and other government authorities generally did not advocate establishing independent legal representation for victims of sexual assault. They did devise numerous programs, however, to encourage closer cooperation between prosecutors and sexual assault victims by establishing ties with rape crisis centers, and by providing special counseling for victims and better training in sex crimes for law enforcement. This increased the permeability of the state, providing another site that was generally not available in Britain for the concerns of the anti-rape movement and the conservative law-and-order movement to intersect.

Differences in the political and institutional development of the police also help explain why women's groups and law enforcement remained further apart in Britain than in the United States.[134] Despite the sharp criticisms of the police made by the Wickersham Commission in the early 1930s, the enormous efforts to rationalize and professionalize U.S. police forces were not wildly successful.[135] Professionalism came to be equated with administrative efficiency. Police departments in the United States created new centralized bureaucracies that were "both resistant to further change but also isolated from the public."[136] This presented significant problems, as evidenced by the urban riots of 1943 and the upheavals of the 1960s, which focused public attention once again squarely on the inadequacies of the police, in particular their poor relationship with blacks and other groups in the community.[137] In creating the LEAA, the Johnson administration and Congress provided the police with enormous new resources. But in doing so, they exposed the performance of the police to greater public scrutiny in what has become a familiar pattern in U.S. history. This provided an opening for feminist critics of how the police handled rape and domestic abuse cases to get a serious hearing.

Public scrutiny of the police in Britain was more belated and less intense. Major disturbances in Britain's inner cities involving young blacks and other minorities beginning in the mid-1970s and intensifying in the 1980s did put pressure on a reluctant Home Office to introduce some police reforms.[138] But these reforms generally did not involve how law enforcement handled violence against women.[139] Despite intense public criticism and condemnation, the British police proved quite capable of maintaining their operational independence with the help of the Home Office and successive Conservative governments.[140] As such, unlike in the U.S. case, police reform did not serve as a convenient platform to launch a victim-centered view of law and order that favored more punitive, retributive policies.

To sum up, the British Home Office, police, and prosecutors did not turn a completely deaf ear to the anti-rape movement. But the changes in law enforcement procedures and laws dealing with sexual assault were minimal compared to the United States. The women's movement in Britain and elsewhere was comparatively less successful in pressuring the government and general public to address the problem of violence against women and in achieving public acceptance of other movement goals.[141] But some of the very institutional, historical, and ideological factors that stymied the women's movement in countries like Britain, Germany, and Sweden helped to ensure that these movements did not significantly bolster penal conservatives. Elsewhere feminists and their concerns remained relatively isolated from the formal political structures or were channeled into party and union structures. This reduced the likelihood that concerns about rape (and later domestic violence) would be seen primarily through law-and-order lenses. In the United States, by contrast, the women's movement, despite some of its radical origins and tendencies, ended up being far more mainstream than marginal, which had important consequences for penal policy. The U.S. women's movement contributed to the creation of a powerful and very particular kind of victims' rights movement, one that had a "distinct conservative bias" and an "unmistakably punitive retributive bent."[142]

Conclusion

The women's movement in the United States was among the first to draw widespread attention to the issue of rape in the early 1970s. At one level, the anti-rape movement in the United States was remarkably successful. Nearly every state enacted legislation designed to make it easier to convict and punish men accused of sexual assault (though the legal reforms varied greatly).[143] These rape law reforms had significant effects on public attitudes.[144] On the positive side, more services became available for victims of sexual assault, and the public and law enforcement officials were sensitized to the issue in ways they had not been before.[145] On the negative side, the mobilization against rape, with its emphasis on taking a tougher stance against men accused of sexual assault, helped to bolster a more punitive climate. The character of the rape crisis centers changed significantly as they began to work more closely with law enforcement agencies and professional social service agencies and organizations. And the rape reform legislation came at the cost of entering into coalitions with archly conservative law-and-order forces.

Although mainstream women's organizations are credited with putting rape, and later domestic violence, on the national agenda, the original rape crisis centers and shelters for battered women in the United States had a strong feminist, grassroots, radical orientation. Over the years, many of these centers and shelters were dramatically transformed, as was their relationship with the state. They developed formal and informal contacts with police, hospitals, and mental health and other social service agencies and became more dependent on government money and more supportive of law enforcement solutions. They also were increasingly staffed and administered by professionals, not volunteers. In contrast to what happened elsewhere, women's groups in the United States had much more interaction with state officials and government agencies at the local, state, and national levels at a time when the voice of penal conservatives was growing stronger in local and national politics. As a consequence, they were not well positioned to challenge the new conservatism in penal policy. Indeed, they ended up supporting policies that emboldened it.

Several factors explain why the anti-rape movement was more susceptible to being co-opted by the state and by penal conservatives. These include the different origins, timing, and development of the victims' movement, which were discussed in Chapter 4. Other factors were the greater ideological diversity of the U.S. women's movement; the prominence of elite-led, hierarchical women's organizations in the U.S. case; and important differences in key state structures, notably the courts and law enforcement. The U.S. women's movement was far more ideologically and institutionally diverse. It had an elite segment predisposed to working with a relatively porous state that was likewise predisposed to working with segments of the women's movement. The main vehicle for greater state involvement in the cause of violence against women was the LEAA, which served as an important conduit of money, expertise, and philosophy to the emerging movement of violence against women. By way of contrast, the Home Office and other law enforcement authorities in Britain, notably the police, maintained their distance from the women's groups mobilized around the issue of violence against women. Few leading politicians or female civil servants in Britain saw courting the women's vote or promoting the interests of women as part of their role, which affected the development of penal policy.

In Britain, the victims' movement and the women's movement remained largely at arm's length from one another. In the United States, they increasingly converged, which helped to embolden the law-and-order forces pressing on penal policy. Many contemporary feminists found themselves allied with law-and-order conservatives when violence against women reemerged as a central national issue. By the time the women's movement in Britain sought to politicize the issues of rape and domestic violence in the early-to-mid-1970s, the needs of victims had been an ongoing, though not leading, concern in elite British politics for nearly two decades, as shown in Chapter 4. The British movements against rape and domestic violence emerged and developed in a political environment in the 1970s and 1980s in which the politics of victims was already on a relatively more settled course. By contrast, the U.S. women's movement sought to make rape and domestic violence a cause at a moment when the politics of victimhood was still very embryonic, fluid, and volatile. Attention on the needs and rights of victims of rape and domestic violence (as discussed in the next chapter) helped to ignite and politicize a broader interest in victims that was emerging at about the same time in the United States.

6 THE BATTERED-WOMEN'S MOVEMENT AND THE DEVELOPMENT OF PENAL POLICY

L IKE THE ANTI-RAPE MOVEMENT, the mobilization against domestic violence in the United States racked up some extraordinary achievements in a relatively short period of time. By the early 1980s, over 500 shelters for battered women had been established. Hundreds of localities had reformed their legal and social services for abused women. Almost every state had created a coalition against domestic violence. In just a few years, the cause of battered women had captured the imagination of the nation, according to Susan Schechter, a veteran activist of the movement.[1] But the battered-women's movement turned out to be even more vulnerable to being co-opted by the state and conservative penal forces than the anti-rape movement that emerged before it. This was so, even though many activists against domestic violence were acutely aware of what they regarded as some of the regrettable compromises the anti-rape movement had made in order to secure funding and legitimacy and to expand its base of support.[2] The mobilization against domestic violence in the United States converged with the state in ways not seen in other countries. It increasingly reflected rather than challenged the growing state interest in taking a hard line against crime and criminals. In Britain, Sweden, Germany, and elsewhere, the issue of domestic violence did not propel a conservative law-and-order movement premised on the needs and rights of victims.

The U.S. battered-women's movement was more vulnerable to co-optation and compromise for several reasons. First, it had a more diverse base than the anti-rape movement from the outset. Segments of it were less critical of the state and more willing to accept government money with significant strings attached. Second, it was under greater pressure to secure state money than battered-women's movements elsewhere because the U.S. welfare state is less developed. Finally, it took shape later than the anti-rape movement. As such, it blossomed when the victims' movement was coming into its own and becoming more of a force to be reckoned with in American politics. With the growing interest in victim and witness programs, an explosion of state and federal funding became available to combat domestic violence before grassroots groups had firmly established themselves.

Diverse Origins of U.S. Battered-Women's Movement

From its inception, the U.S. battered-women's movement was divided over whether it was primarily service-oriented, or part of the feminist movement, or both.[3] An extremely diverse movement from the start, it had more difficulty building a national unified organization based on a coherent set of founding ideals and principles. The U.S. battered-women's movement was inspired by and modeled after the anti-rape movement in the United States and the refuge movement in Britain. The first refuge for battered women to receive widespread recognition opened in Chiswick, England, in 1972 and became a model for shelters in the United States.[4] The National Women's Aid Federation (NWAF) was the main organization for the battered-women's movement in Britain. Soon after its founding in 1975, the NWAF was able to overcome some significant rifts to become a coherent organization with a strong commitment to feminist principles.[5] Its counterpart in the United States, the National Coalition Against Domestic Violence (NCADV), remained far more divided. Founded in 1978, members of the NCADV differed over how radical its principles could be without impeding the organizing efforts of women in more conservative parts of the United States. They also disagreed over whether the NCADV should be composed primarily of independent, grassroots groups or include professional and governmental groups.[6]

Unlike the anti-rape movement, which traced its lineage directly to the radical wing of American feminism, the battered-women's movement had more varied roots. Alcoholics Anonymous, self-help groups, YWCA's, Junior Chambers of Commerce, churches, professional women's groups, and women's service clubs established or sponsored the first shelters, some as early as the mid-1960s, well before there was talk of a "battered-women's movement."[7] The first feminist shelter in the United States is believed to be the Women's House in St. Paul, Minn., which opened in 1974. The following year, the National Organization for Women (NOW) formed a task force on battered women at its annual convention. At that point, there were only about a dozen shelters or other programs for battered women in the United States.[8] Over the next five years, the battered-women's movement took off as national and local feminist groups embraced the cause. By June 1980, one national survey identified 175 shelters.[9] But fewer than half of the shelters had a feminist orientation or feminist origins.[10] By contrast, refuges in Britain were overwhelmingly affiliated with the NWAF, which was guided by explicitly feminist principles.[11]

Women, the Welfare State, and the Carceral State

Differences in the development of the welfare state in the United States and Britain also help explain why the battered-women's movement developed distinctively in each country. Activists in the United States faced greater pressures to secure state funding for shelters because the U.S. welfare state is comparatively less developed. From the outset, feminists in Britain were more focused than American feminists on achieving permanent housing for battered women. They had the liberty of concentrating on finding permanent solutions, partly because they did not have to worry as much about securing money to purchase and staff facilities to provide temporary shelter to abused women. Shelters in Britain could fund themselves primarily by charging rent to their residents, many of whom received some kind of social security support from the state. While public housing has been an integral feature of the British welfare state for some time, in the United States the government has provided welfare and public housing support for only the poorest of women.[12] The National Assistance Act (1948) served as an important platform for efforts to expand public housing in Britain. It gave welfare departments the discretionary authority to provide temporary accommodation for emergency cases of homelessness.[13] The act reversed the historic tendency to view homelessness as an individual rather than social problem.[14] In 1977, Parliament enacted the Housing (Homeless Persons) Act, which designated battered women a priority for rehousing if they had to leave home because of violence. Provision of public housing to battered women did vary across localities in Britain depending on the amount of housing available and on how state officials interpreted the act.[15] That said, public housing was generally more widely available at reasonable cost for battered women in Britain than in the United States.[16]

Feminists in Britain came to view social policy, not penal policy, as the most promising avenue to enable battered women "to escape from violence by achieving a certain economic independence through state provision of housing, social and health services and welfare benefits."[17] Just as the presence of a more developed welfare state in Britain predisposed feminists there to instinctively view social policy as a promising arena for a solution, it did the same for state authorities. In Britain, the state was responsive to calls from women's groups for practical social programs to assist victims of domestic violence, as evidenced by the relatively swift passage of the Housing (Homeless Persons) Act and other measures, and the 1981 publication of a government-commissioned report that emphasized how the absence of alternative housing was the chief obstacle for women seeking help to escape violence.[18] It was far less receptive than the American state, however, to criticisms of policing and other law enforcement practices in dealing with domestic violence and rape. The irony here is that by not legitimizing feminists' criticisms of law enforcement's unresponsiveness to violence against women, the British government reduced the likelihood that feminists would become accomplices in the brewing law-and-order movement in Britain. In essence, it neutralized the salience of violence against women as a law-and-order rallying point.

Two other factors help explain why the United States was less willing to expand the welfare state to combat domestic violence but was more ready to embrace policing and other law enforcement reforms to address this problem. First, creation of professional police forces committed to the abstract notion of serving the public rather than serving narrow parochial or partisan concerns was a more protracted political process fraught with controversy in the U.S. case, as shown in Chapter 3. Law enforcement authorities in the United States have a history of being more accessible to the public and more influenced by shifting political winds. The second factor is a related and contemporary development: the more distant, antagonistic relationship that existed between British law enforcement and women's groups in the 1970s and 1980s, which was discussed in Chapter 5.

In both countries, law enforcement authorities generally rejected demands for radical changes in how they responded to the problem of domestic violence. However, in the United States they were more willing to acknowledge the problem and the need for some new remedies in a way that the British authorities, especially the police and the Home Office, were not.[19] By conceding that law enforcement was partly to blame, criminal justice and other state authorities in the United States helped direct attention toward penal solutions and away from other alternatives, like an expansion of the welfare state or deeper societal changes. In doing so, they also secured a place for themselves to shape those penal solutions alongside women's groups. The British police and the Home Office, by contrast, kept feminists and other community groups at a distance. Despite numerous studies drawing attention to the shortcomings of the British police in the area of domestic violence, it was not until 1990 that the United Kingdom promulgated new national policies for the police to deal with this issue.[20] These deep historical and institutional factors coupled with contemporary developments help explain why the police in the United States and Britain responded so differently to the problem of domestic violence.

National Hearings on Battered Women

These differences were sharply evident in the striking contrast between national hearings on domestic violence in Britain in 1975 and in the United States three years later that catapulted the issue into the national limelight in each country. Under pressure from the NWAF, Parliament formed the Select Committee on Violence in Marriage in 1974. The committee held hearings on battered women during the first half of 1975.[21] In accordance with the norms of parliamentary hearings, witnesses called before the committee were neither asked nor permitted to make a presentation, but instead answered questions posed by the committee members. As a consequence, members of Parliament were well positioned to shape the discussion. The committee did not embrace feminists' arguments about the social rather than the individual causes of domestic violence. The committee also deflected calls for changes in police practices. It was extremely supportive, however, of witnesses' emphasis on the material needs of abused women and their children and of their calls to expand the welfare state to assist victims of domestic violence.

Shortly thereafter, Parliament passed several pieces of legislation to give practical help to women, such as the Housing (Homeless Persons) Act and the Domestic Violence and Matrimonial Proceedings Act (1976), which, among other things, gave abused women the right to remain in their homes and provided for exclusion orders. Though a number of witnesses criticized law enforcement's response to incidents of domestic violence, the committee made only modest recommendations in this area.[22] Significantly, neither witnesses nor committee members stressed the need for more criminal prosecutions of men accused of battering. In short, these hearings served to define the problem as largely a welfare state issue. The greater development of the welfare state in Britain, the historic insulation of the police from the public, and the institutional design of the parliamentary hearings help explain why domestic violence continued to be viewed primarily as a social issue, not a penal one.

These hearings stand in sharp contrast to the 1978 hearings on battered women sponsored by the U.S. Commission on Civil Rights, the first major effort by a national governmental body in the United States to address this issue. The commission was established by Congress in 1957 as a temporary, independent, bipartisan agency charged with gathering information and making recommendations to legislators and the president regarding the denial of equal protection of the laws. Britain had no comparable governmental body to examine the civil rights protections of various groups in society. The commission's "jurisdictional basis for studying the problem meant a strong focus on the law and law enforcement."[23] Witnesses who appeared before the commission presented prepared statements and submitted papers in addition to answering questions from its members. This allowed the witnesses more leeway to shape the discussion.

Given the commission's mandate, it is not surprising that its members encouraged witnesses to focus on the role of law enforcement, in contrast to members of the parliamentary select committee, who emphasized the inadequacies of the welfare state. In his opening remarks at the start of the commission's two-day hearings in January 1978, Chairman Arthur

S. Flemming stressed the importance of the issue of battered women to the field of civil rights.[24] Marjory D. Fields, an attorney for Brooklyn Legal Services who appeared before the commission, echoed what became a familiar theme during the hearings. She characterized wife beating as "a civil rights problem of enormous magnitude" and went on to say, "As a class, battered women are denied the protection afforded to other victims of crime. They are discriminated against by police, prosecutors, and judges." Fields suggested that "family violence be treated as a crime" and charged that the most serious problem was the failure of the police to respond adequately to calls for help from battered women.[25]

The civil rights commission hearings starkly revealed the patchwork, incoherent character of the means-tested U.S. welfare state and its limited capacity to provide abused women with sufficient resources to leave or get respite from violent relationships. An administrator of the Department of Health, Education and Welfare acknowledged in her testimony that her department did not have any programs designed specifically to assist abused women. She noted that middle- and upper-middle-class women could technically qualify to receive financial support from Aid to Families With Dependent Children (AFDC) if they were cut off from their family resources, but they had experienced difficulties in getting any actual help from the country's main public assistance program.[26] An administrator from the Department of Housing and Urban Development (HUD) testified that community development funds, one of the major federal resources for local communities, typically had not been available for battered women's shelters.[27] HUD's general counsel stated that women who left their homes because of domestic violence and are in need of long-term housing generally did not qualify for the country's major public housing programs.[28] A representative of the Labor Department testified that the only avenue of direct support for shelters came from funds the department administered under the Comprehensive Employment and Training Act (CETA), which paid for public service jobs in shelters.[29]

The LEAA and Domestic Violence

Some of the strongest critics of the government's response to domestic violence were officials in the Department of Justice who testified at the hearings. Jeannie Niedermeyer legitimized complaints from women's groups about the failure of law enforcement and other agencies to protect battered women from further abuse. She also faulted state agencies for their "general lack of responsiveness to the overall problem." Niedermeyer underscored the LEAA's long-standing interest in the problem of family disturbances, dating back to 1969 when a major effort was made to improve crisis intervention programs for police. Since then, she testified, the LEAA had spent $15 million on programs related to battered women and other forms of family violence, about a quarter of which went to police crisis intervention. She noted that the LEAA had recently established a program specifically designed to help battered women and other victims of family violence, the first federal agency to do so. While acknowledging that the criminal justice system could not be solely responsible for the domestic abuse problem, Justice Department officials portrayed the LEAA as the pioneer state agency in addressing this issue.[30]

And in many ways, it was. The LEAA and CETA were the two most significant government funding sources for shelters in the late 1970s and early 1980s. Before CETA was abolished under the Reagan administration in 1982, it was training and funding about half of all the paid workers in shelters.[31] Securing a CETA slot is what ultimately enabled many communities to open a shelter.[32] It is hard to get a handle on the total amount of LEAA money that was spent for battering and anti-rape programs, partly because the amount that states allocated from their LEAA block grants for such programs is unknown.[33] What is known is that by 1980 (its final year of funding), the LEAA was granting nearly $3 million to projects under the Family Violence Program – the biggest sum allocated by any federal agency for a domestic abuse program. The Family Violence Program, which was established in 1977, was an outgrowth of the LEAA's Victim and Witness Protection Program and Neighborhood Justice Program. It was the first federal program targeted specifically at battered women and other victims of violence in the home. On the eve of its demise, the LEAA was funding a total of twenty-five projects across the country under the Family Violence Program, including grassroots programs and grants directly to prosecutors' offices.[34]

LEAA and CETA money came with significant strings attached, which helped to transform the character of the shelters and the battered-women's movement. All LEAA projects provided services. As a condition of their grants, LEAA also required these projects to improve the criminal justice system and involve the community, that is, criminal justice, medical, and social service agencies. The main objective of these grants was "to improve the treatment given to these particular crime victims and thereby increase the number of crime reports and number of successful prosecutions," Niedermeyer of the Justice Department told the civil rights commission.[35] The criteria for qualifying for LEAA money were complicated and often involved creating direct linkages between the shelters and the criminal justice system. Shelters that received LEAA support were required to work closely with the police.[36] To encourage prosecution, district attorneys' offices created programs to encourage advocacy groups to act as liaisons with abused women. These groups were responsible for apprising battered women of court procedures and, in some cases, advising district attorneys on how to proceed with prosecution so as to increase the conviction rate.[37] The LEAA mandated that shelters add representatives from all the local criminal justice institutions, including police, courts, probation offices, jails, prisons, and district attorneys' offices, to their boards of directors.[38] The emphasis on boards was antithetical to the collective, nonhierarchical ethos of many feminist shelters.

While many shelters and women's groups eschewed LEAA money, over 10 percent of them accepted it.[39] Support from LEAA's Family Violence Program was critical in the establishment of the National Coalition Against Domestic Violence in 1978. The NCADV was a loose, broad-based coalition comprised of hundreds of groups and dozens of state coalitions that served as a network for sharing information, providing mutual support, and lobbying.[40] It accepted LEAA funding despite concerns about the federal government's approach to domestic violence.[41]

One of the most significant LEAA allocations was the approximately $1 million it gave between 1977 and 1980 to the Center for Women's Policy Studies, a Washington-based group founded in 1972. The LEAA funding helped the CWPS establish itself as a leading national voice on violence against women, to the dismay of some feminists. The CWPS used the money to provide technical assistance to LEAA's Family Violence Program and to develop a clearinghouse for information on domestic violence for government agencies and other groups. The CWPS also published *Response*, a monthly newsletter about domestic violence that featured the activities of the LEAA and other government agencies but also included more general information about research findings and programs. The CWPS came under fire from some feminists for seeing no daylight between the interests of the battered-women's movement and the criminal justice system. Some feminists castigated the CWPS for ignoring, belittling, or undermining the contributions of the grassroots battered-women's movement and feminist rape crisis centers and for papering over differences and contradictions among groups mobilized around the issue of violence against women.[42]

As shelters and other programs became more dependent on the LEAA and other government money, such as CETA funding, they were forced to be more accountable to outside authorities. These authorities generally viewed professional, apolitical, and nonideological staffs as more legitimate and worthy of support (as was the case with the rape crisis centers).[43] Pressure was also comparatively greater in the United States to create costly hierarchically organized shelters and programs staffed by salaried professionals because of the country's stronger therapeutic tradition.[44] Nonprofessional staff members and volunteers, many of whom were formerly battered women, felt marginalized. The shelters became more service-oriented as they focused on providing assistance to individual women and their families rather than on how to transform broader structures in society.[45] Their main priority was to provide basic emergency services, including temporary shelter, transportation, and counseling, rather than longer-term needs, like employment training and permanent new housing.[46]

When the LEAA was dismantled in 1980, the cause of domestic violence did not recede. The Reagan administration was initially conflicted about what if any role family violence should play in its war on crime. In its first year in office, it closed the Office of Domestic Violence, which President Jimmy Carter had created in 1979.[47] The final report of Reagan's Task Force on Victims of Crime called for creating a special task force on family violence.[48] Three years later, the Attorney General's Task Force on Family Violence recommended that violence in the family "be recognized and responded to as a criminal activity." It faulted the criminal justice system for its inconsistent, lenient, forgiving approach to domestic abuse and vowed: "The law should not stop at the front door of the family home." The task force characterized assaults against family members as "not only crimes against the individual but also crimes against the state." It rejected mediation and crisis intervention and endorsed "arrest as the preferred response in cases of family violence." While the report made some modest recommendations for additional social services to assist victims of domestic violence, its primary focus was on changes in law enforcement practices and relevant state statutes. Most of the recommendations for social services dealt with temporary emergency assistance, not expansions of the welfare state to provide women with the means to create lives independent of their abusers. The report concluded that prevention was the best strategy for dealing with domestic violence, and that effective prevention depended first and foremost on convincing potential victims and abusers that domestic violence "comprises criminal offenses that will be vigorously prosecuted."[49]

For years after the 1978 civil rights commission hearings, massive national efforts to pass federal legislation to fund shelters and provide other social services for battered women were repeatedly turned back. The steep drop in federal funding for domestic violence at the start of the Reagan administration was partially reversed in 1984.[50] Congress finally enacted the Family Violence and Prevention Act that year as an amendment to the Child Abuse Prevention and Treatment Act. This measure appropriated about $8 million annually, primarily for shelter services. That same year, the Victims of Crime Act (VOCA) was also enacted.[51] It authorized that federal fines paid by criminal offenders be used to fund state victim-compensation programs. Under VOCA, these programs gave priority to victims of sexual assault and of spousal and child abuse.[52] Funding was eventually secured because of the coalescence of a vibrant and influential victims' movement that brought the issue of domestic violence under its protective umbrella and made it a powerful symbol of the war on crime.

The Courts, the Police, and Domestic Violence

In the U.S. case, law enforcement solutions filled a vacuum created by an underdeveloped welfare state. These solutions were propelled along by a criminal justice state that, as we have seen, was more porous because of the distinct historical development of U.S. police forces, the more diverse nature of the women's movement (and the battered-women's movement in particular), the unique mandate of the U.S. Commission on Civil Rights, and the creation of the LEAA. There was one additional institutional factor: the courts. The opportunity to file class action and other lawsuits against the police and other criminal justice agencies provided an additional means to subject the response of the state, especially law enforcement, to public scrutiny in domestic violence cases.

The success of the U.S. civil rights movement opened up an opportunity to use the courts to address a broad range of civil rights violations in a way not available in many other countries. A series of lawsuits brought on behalf of battered women in the United States focused public attention on how law enforcement officials responded to domestic violence incidents. In 1976, separate class action suits were filed against the Oakland, Calif., police department and against the New York City police and its probation and family clerks for failing to protect abused women from further harm. In the Oakland case, a comprehensive settlement decree was finalized in November 1979. Under its terms, police were obligated to treat domestic violence like any other criminal behavior. Among other things, the settlement limited their discretion to not arrest accused abusers. It also included a provision to monitor the behavior of the police in domestic abuse incidents.[53]

The New York City case, *Bruno v. Codd*, resulted in a consent decree in 1978 that forced substantial changes in how New York City police handled domestic violence, and it became a model for other jurisdictions.[54] Another milestone legal decision was *Thurman v. City of Torrington*, in which a Connecticut woman was awarded over $2 million in damages in 1984 after a finding that the Torrington police had violated her civil rights by not adequately protecting her from her husband's repeated abuse.[55] This was the first reported federal case to conclude that the police's failure to arrest an abusive husband amounted to a constitutional violation.[56] In addition to forcing police to change their practices, these and similar lawsuits provided a mechanism for Americans to pry information about the performance of law enforcement agencies out of their government, which was already comparatively more transparent.

This stood in marked contrast to Britain and elsewhere. The British state "has been especially reluctant to create methods for implementing, monitoring and enforcing their rather meagre [sic] civil rights legislation."[57] While lawsuits may be brought to redress police action in Britain, even if they succeed, they usually do not result in major policy changes because they apply only to individual, specific cases.[58] This reduced the likelihood that the issue of domestic violence would be used to fuel the law-and-order movement in Britain but also reduced the pressure on the police to mend their ways. Furthermore, women's rights organizations in Britain, unlike their U.S. counterparts, had "virtually no capacity to mount strategic litigation campaigns" because they were so "highly decentralized and informally organized."[59] Because class action suits were not an option for aggrieved women, and the activities of the police and other government institutions are less subject to public scrutiny in Britain, the responsiveness of British law enforcement to instances of violence against women remained comparatively veiled. The content of Home Office directives on domestic abuse and police policies to deal with it generally were not available to the public, which made it more difficult to monitor law enforcement activities.[60]

The landmark Oakland, New York City, and *Thurman* cases sparked a flurry of other suits and legislation regarding the treatment of battered women in the United States. The country went through a mini-revolution beginning in the 1970s as states toughened their statutes and police departments were pressed to alter their practices.[61] While both Britain and the United States attempted to strengthen their civil remedies for domestic violence, there was a greater emphasis on law enforcement solutions in the latter. Here again the LEAA played a pivotal role. The LEAA pioneered the federal response to battered women. It drew national attention to the enormity of the problem of violence against women and underscored a woman's right to safety. But in doing so, it identified law enforcement as the primary arena for addressing the problem. Through its grants and research programs, the LEAA provided an important link between law enforcement, the battered-women's movement, and the burgeoning victims' rights movement that outlasted the life of the agency. LEAA-sponsored research and demonstration projects in law enforcement and police training in the 1970s and early 1980s provided models for many of the legal reforms related to domestic violence that were subsequently enacted.[62] While the LEAA initially backed noninterventional and therapeutic approaches, it soon shifted toward relying more on criminal justice remedies for domestic violence.[63] The National Institute of Justice, LEAA's successor, also produced important policy research directed at the police that emphasized how to improve their response to domestic violence.[64]

Presumptive arrest and mandatory arrest policies became the central pillars of criminal justice remedies for domestic violence. Before the 1970s, all but fourteen states mandated that police officers could not legally make a warrantless arrest unless they had witnessed the occurrence of the misdemeanor. By 1987, only eleven states did not provide some sort of warrantless arrest powers to the police for misdemeanors. By the early 1990s, forty-eight states had enacted some version of a statute authorizing warrantless arrests for misdemeanors related to domestic violence.[65] Another popular reform were no-drop policies, which prohibited battered women from dropping charges once they were filed, except under exceptional circumstances.[66]

The push to require the police to arrest accused batterers took off partly because of the lawsuits discussed earlier. In the aftermath of the *Thurman* case, the number of police departments requiring mandatory arrests in instances of domestic violence jumped significantly as insurance companies indicated they might not provide coverage to police departments that appeared unresponsive to intervening in domestic violence cases.[67] The results of the Minneapolis Domestic Violence Experiment, which found that mandatory arrests appeared to reduce the incidence of subsequent violence, also fueled enthusiasm for these policies.[68] While the Minneapolis study had some potentially serious problems, and the authors themselves were cautious about their conclusions, its results were aggressively promoted nonetheless.[69] The study "fed into an existing ideological framework of activist feminism on this issue."[70] The 1984 Attorney General's Task Force on Family Violence backed its conclusions, and a number of training guides for police departments began advocating mandatory arrest, even though this policy appeared to raise some significant constitutional issues.[71] The findings from the Minneapolis experiment were suggestive, not conclusive. Nonetheless, by the mid-1980s, a pro-arrest stance had become the consensus opinion among domestic violence activists in the United States, according to NCADV executive director Marcia Neimann.[72]

Other researchers, led by Lawrence W. Sherman who participated in the initial Minneapolis study, subsequently replicated that experiment in five other cities. They discovered that the deterrent effects of arrest varied widely depending on other variables, like the race of the abused women and their partners and whether the abusive men were employed or not.[73] Yet this did not prompt a wholesale retreat from mandatory arrest policies. Virtually any approach not supportive of mandatory arrest was dismissed as "reactionary."[74] Little attention was paid to the negative effects of arrest. Feminist activists and academics, who in other contexts often exhibited a deep mistrust of the police, generally did not see a problem with using the powers of the police in this manner.[75]

The Violence Against Women Act (VAWA)

As the battered-women's movement developed and became more entwined with the criminal justice system, the incidence of domestic violence did not recede significantly.[76] Thus, some activists and analysts began to question more vigorously whether new law enforcement strategies, like mandatory arrest and no-drop policies, empowered women and protected them from further harm.[77] As in the case of the anti-rape movement, some began to warn that a "feminist law-and-order stance" could spill over into more punitive treatment of female defendants and of men who belong to racial or ethnic minorities.[78] Questions arose about whether legal remedies that might be suitable for white women, such as greater dependence on the police to intervene, were appropriate for women of color. The latter tend to be more suspicious of involving the police and are under greater pressure not to politicize or publicize the issue of domestic violence for fear of dividing their communities or attracting additional negative attention to communities already under siege.[79]

By the early 1990s, deep divisions emerged about the intersection of gender, violence, race, and the state in ongoing debates about domestic violence.[80] Some conceded that, while the movement may have succeeded in making domestic violence a public issue, it was at the cost of defining the issue as a form of criminal deviance best dealt with by bolstering the law enforcement arm, and thus the social control capacity, of the state.[81] This, in turn, reinforced the view of women as vulnerable and in need of special protection, thus strengthening gender inequality.[82] Some feminists began to take a more nuanced view of the state and the law as the tough battles to secure legal reforms resulted in measures that in their view did not significantly improve the situation of battered women.[83] Some activists and scholars of feminism and the law began increasingly to question the utility of legal remedies. Others remained committed to them, even if this necessitated participating in unsavory coalitions with conservative political forces propelling the ascendant Republican majority.[84] The most striking example of this is the steadfast support for the 1994 Violence Against Women Act, the first major federal legislation targeted at this issue and the culmination of the efforts of a remarkable coalition of women and civil rights groups over several years.[85]

After Sen. Joe Biden (D-Del.) first introduced the VAWA in the Senate in 1990, it languished for several years.[86] In March 1994 it was incorporated into the massive crime bill then under consideration. In September 1994, President Bill Clinton signed the $30 billion Violent Crime Control and Law Enforcement Act. The crime bill allocated $1.6 billion to fund a variety of measures to reduce violence against women, including shelters, a national hotline for domestic abuse, and programs for rape education and prevention. Most of the money was earmarked for programs aimed at prevention, punishment, or provision of temporary services to abused women, not an expansion of the welfare state to give women the means to leave abusive situations. The measure contained several milestone protections. For example, it permitted some undocumented immigrants to petition for legal-resident status and suspended the deportation of battered immigrant women under certain circumstances. The centerpiece of the legislation was a controversial civil rights provision that established freedom from gender-motivated violence as a federally protected civil right. If a woman believed the violent act committed against her was motivated by gender bias, she could sue her attacker under federal civil rights law.[87] The U.S. Supreme Court eventually declared this provision of VAWA unconstitutional in 2000.[88]

VAWA was a considerable achievement in many ways. It heightened public awareness of violence against women, promoted greater cooperation between agencies with vastly different perspectives on the issue, and provided states with new resources to tackle this problem.[89] But VAWA also strongly emphasized law enforcement remedies. Most significantly, VAWA was part of the landmark crime bill, which allocated nearly $10 billion for new prison construction, expanded the death penalty to cover more than fifty federal crimes, and added a "three-strikes-and-you're-out" provision mandating life imprisonment for federal offenders convicted of three violent offenses. In the name of protecting women and children, it contained several measures that challenged established privacy protections, including a mandate that all states establish a registry for sex offenders or risk losing federal money.[90] The crime bill also permitted prosecutors in federal cases to introduce a defendant's previous history of sexual offenses into court proceedings.[91]

The consolidation of VAWA into the crime bill solidified the understanding of domestic violence and other violence against women as primarily criminal matters. VAWA "became a war flag for Congressional leaders who wanted to show they are tough on crime."[92] This was the culmination of a process that had been under way for more than two decades, ever since the women's movement successfully pricked the conscience of the nation about rape and domestic violence. While women's groups had some concerns about VAWA as it wound its way through Congress and became attached to the crime bill, they nonetheless spearheaded the effort to pass it. To secure passage, VAWA's supporters ended up aligning themselves with some of the conservative political forces that had been prosecuting the war on crime so zealously. They also distanced themselves from progressive groups and minorities fighting for measures like inclusion of the Racial Justice Act in the crime bill, which would have allowed people on death row to appeal their sentences on the basis of racial discrimination.[93] Around this time, the Clinton administration, a big champion of the crime bill, also was reinforcing the association between domestic violence and criminalization. On a number of occasions, Clinton and Attorney General Janet Reno stressed criminal measures when they talked about remedies for domestic violence, while ignoring the economic constraints that prevent many women from leaving abusive relationships.[94]

Some supporters of VAWA acknowledged that the legislation included some regrettable but necessary compromises to secure passage. They conceded there was a danger in submerging domestic violence into the anti-crime agenda.[95] Other proponents were highly unreflective. In a piece published in *Ms.* magazine, Linda Hirschman attacked the American Civil Liberties Union for the concerns it raised in connection with VAWA. She caricatured opposition to the legislation as just another example of the reflexive anti-statism that drives conservative politics in the United States. Despite more than two decades of mixed experience with relying on the legal system to alleviate domestic violence, and the enormous expansion of the prison system in the intervening years, she expressed strident confidence in criminal justice remedies to resolve social problems like domestic violence. "Though the VAWA is only a first step, it will go a long way toward bringing the rule of law to the home – a world that has been too long in a state of nature and thus in a state of war," Hirschman concluded.[96]

The activism on behalf of VAWA stands in sharp contrast to feminist groups' relative passivity in the concurrent debate over welfare reform. They did not become deeply involved in the legislative battles that culminated in passage of the Personal Responsibility and Work Opportunity Reconciliation Act of 1996, which dismantled AFDC, the country's main welfare program for the poor since the New Deal and an important source of economic support for some abused women.[97] Given the historical, institutional, and political factors discussed earlier, it is less surprising that feminists did not fix their gaze on the welfare state, even though research has shown that domestic violence is a major impediment to getting a job and becoming economically self-sufficient.[98] Feminists did not totally absent themselves from the welfare debate, but their involvement was relatively modest compared to their intense commitment to some version of VAWA.

Violence Against Women, Comparatively Speaking

While Britain faced a comparable backlash against the welfare state under Margaret Thatcher, this did not automatically result in a greater reliance on legal remedies to address domestic violence. British authorities were slow to reform their criminal statutes and law enforcement practices to address growing concerns about domestic abuse. British authorities generally rejected calls to tackle domestic violence by increasing penalties. The Home Office in Britain, which has jurisdiction over police departments, remained markedly reluctant to push the police to institute new practices to deal with domestic violence.[99] This is in sharp contrast to the United States, where the LEAA and the Justice Department served as a critical bridge between community groups and state law enforcement that had no parallel elsewhere.

Blessed with an extensive welfare state that was designed to be more than just a safety net for the very destitute, British government agencies already provided more social services to a wider range of the community. When confronted with a new issue like domestic violence, Britain's welfare state was more nimble. Critical social services and government programs like public housing and health care could "more easily become a part of the state response to a new issue simply because they already provide a service to the wider community."[100] The strong voluntary tradition in Britain and the presence of a more autonomous feminist movement put pressure on the state to respond somewhat to the subject of violence against women. But state officials, once they responded, chose to emphasize social welfare remedies over law enforcement ones, denying the issue of violence against women the law-and-order salience it enjoyed in the United States.

The formal and informal links that developed in the United States between law enforcement and women's groups mobilized against rape and domestic violence were rare in Britain, partly because the radical strand of feminism dominated from the start in Britain and because of the relative autonomy of the Home Office. The British women's movement was less ideologically diverse, relatively more autonomous, and more grassroots-oriented due to Britain's stronger socialist and radical traditions.[101] In short, British feminism "had no 'mainstream voice.'" In its early years, British feminism was a fragmented, localized movement that exhibited little interest in focusing on issues like the advancement of women in politics and business that were key for NOW in the United States.[102] In the U.S. case, the political weaknesses of parties and unions prompted women to organize separate gender-based groups, such as NOW. These groups tended to include a wide range of views that forced accommodation between radical and reformist wings.[103] When the women's movement in Britain finally sought to exert broader national influence, it attempted to do so through an existing structure with a class-based orientation, namely unions and the Labor Party, rather than by establishing a new mass-membership organization like NOW.[104] Women remained separate and unequal partners in British unions and the Labor Party and were not integrated into party and government structures the way they were in, say, Sweden. Thus, even when the Labor Party was in power, the concerns of women were secondary.[105] Women's concerns about domestic violence and sexual assault also held less sway in Britain because the criminal justice system was staffed almost exclusively by men, whereas in the United States women were entering law enforcement in significantly greater numbers.[106]

Coming out of this stronger radical tradition, many British shelters continued to be organized as nonhierarchical collectives run by volunteers, activists, and nonprofessional staffs.[107] Beginning in the 1980s, the British refuge movement faced greater pressure to compromise its founding feminist principles because of broader political changes. Heightened central control over local government expenditures under Thatcherism and changes in the regulations for the "cost of care" provided to women in refuges put the shelters under greater financial pressure. The professional, political, and academic backlash against feminism put them under greater ideological pressure. Furthermore, the Home Office strategically supported the expansion of victim support services to include victims of domestic violence and sexual assault as a way to undercut the work of the feminist-inspired groups.[108] The British shelters were better able to resist these pressures to compromise because of the existence of the Women's Aid Federation, the national organization that gave them clout and cohesion that the battered-women's groups in the United States lacked.[109] All this helps explain why the British women's movement was less vulnerable to compromising with conservative law-and-order forces, whose strength began growing in the 1970s.[110]

The subject of violence against women was not entirely depoliticized in Britain. For example, the Criminal Justice Act of 1991, in the works for more than a decade and widely considered an enlightened milestone designed to reduce Britain's prison population, established a proportionality principle for sentencing, but made exceptions for sexual and violent offenders.[111] Still, for much of the 1970s and 1980s, the focus in Britain was on "public" crime, not sexual or violent crime committed in private.[112]

Likewise in Germany, violence against women did not provide ammunition for the mobilization of a conservative law-and-order movement. Feminists in Germany hailed from a country with a strong socialist tradition and a relatively weak liberal one. Furthermore, they had not been directly exposed to and inspired by a civil rights movement mobilized around the issue of race, whose achievements seemed to suggest that the lowly status of other groups, such as women, might be improved by focusing on seeking equal rights and sameness of treatment. German feminists were not only more radical, but also more isolated. The hostility and indifference of both major political parties and the New Left to efforts to abolish a restrictive abortion law in West Germany in the 1970s resulted in the emergence of a deeply grassroots movement that made a virtue of its autonomy.[113] Shelters for battered women in Germany tended to be run by autonomous feminist groups who organized them as collectives. German feminists viewed these shelters as protective spaces where women could take charge of all aspects of their lives and could critique broader structures in society.[114] In Germany, the issue of violence against women had mixed results. While it did not provide fuel for a conservative law-and-order movement, neither did it serve as a potent issue to mobilize a wide swath of German women and acquaint them more broadly with feminism. Indeed, German women were left "almost untouched" by the feminist movement.[115]

In the Netherlands, the subject of violence against women also did not have the political salience it did in the United States. When the issue emerged in the early 1980s, the police, other members of the criminal justice system, and feminists themselves continued to view penal law as a last resort. The Dutch "culture of tolerance" does not entirely explain why.[116] The country's more developed welfare state and the presence of a police force that traditionally has emphasized the use of social skills rather than coercive power prompted the state to respond to domestic violence by emphasizing the need for adequate social services rather than more punitive policies. The revised constitution of 1983 might also have been a factor because it made it more difficult to arrest someone without a criminal charge.[117] While police in the United States were rewriting their training manuals to reflect new mandatory arrest and no-drop procedures, Dutch law enforcement officials remained "strikingly unanimous in avoiding the use of coercive power" to address domestic abuse.[118] The Dutch police and judiciary persisted in the belief that battered women were not victims of crime. Domestic violence did not become a bloody shirt to galvanize the growing interest in the plight of victims and to fuel penal conservatism in the Netherlands.

That said, the Dutch women's movement did edge closer to conservative and punitive forces beginning in the mid-1980s. Feminists protesting against what they characterized as the liberalization of pornography laws ended up finding themselves working side-by-side with conservatives engaged in a moral crusade to cleanse all aspects of Dutch society.[119] It took a particularly grievous case, the January 1984 release of a man suspected of six sexual assaults on the grounds of a shortage of prison cells, to trigger a public debate on the weak position of the victim in the Dutch criminal justice system. Dutch feminists were pivotal in forcing a confrontation with the authorities over this and similar cases. But even then the criminal justice authorities were able to reassert control quickly over the terms of the debate. Developments like these provided an important opening for penal conservatives like Dato Steenhuis, a prosecutor who held top posts in the Ministry of Justice in the 1980s, to launch an assault on the liberal humanitarianism that has long characterized Dutch penal policy.[120] The original issue – the neglect of the emotional and other needs of victims, especially women – was "distorted into a plea for more prison cells."[121]

The persistent inattention to the needs of victims began to undermine the credibility of the Dutch legal system, making it more vulnerable to pressures from penal conservatives and a growing victims' movement centered around women's issues.[122] The number of programs for crime victims at the local level increased rapidly in the 1980s in the Netherlands. But the Ministry of Justice generally kept some distance from these largely volunteer efforts, and prosecutors strongly resisted any substantial expansion of victims' rights.[123] Nonetheless, the Dutch prison population became one of the fastest growing in the world, threatening the country's cherished place as one of the least punitive countries in Europe.[124]

At the other extreme from the United States on the issue of punishment and violence against women is Sweden. Despite its progressive reputation and the fact that women held over 41 percent of all parliamentary seats by the early 1990s, Sweden has been surprisingly diffident about violence against women.[125] Because of the special way that feminist and women's groups are intertwined with the state, Sweden was slow to implement comprehensive reforms to address domestic violence and rape.[126] It has been difficult for a strong, independent, grassroots women's movement to coalesce in the long shadow cast by the highly centralized, corporatist Swedish state.[127] Swedish feminists generally are linked to the state either directly as government bureaucrats or indirectly through the women's sections of the country's political parties. As such, they have been highly dependent on ministerial bureaucrats to address the issue of violence against women. Government officials in Sweden have tended to be less knowledgeable about the problems that battered women face. Unlike in the United States, a vibrant coterie of lawyers, researchers, and others not affiliated with the state did not exist to explore this new terrain and press this issue. Tied to the state, feminists and feminist bureaucrats in Sweden have had a vested interest in defending the government against criticism. Indeed, the political establishment branded feminist critics as "sex racists."[128]

Sweden's more extensive welfare state also biased government ministers and civil servants toward remedies that emphasized the role of professionals and downplayed political analyses of the causes of and remedies for violence against women. Furthermore, the highly centralized Swedish state was not fertile ground for the development of the local initiatives and innovations that were so vital to the anti-rape and battered women's movements in the United States. The government maintained tight central control over any initiatives by, for example, closely monitoring the operations of the first shelters for battered women and the country's first rape crisis center, established in Stockholm in 1977.

Swedish diffidence is stunning when compared to the sea change in the public discussion of violence against women taking place in the United States at about the same time. As late as 1976, the government-backed Committee on Sexual Crimes appointed by Social Democratic Minister of Justice Lennart Geijer released a final report calling for a "modern perspective" on sexual assault, in which rape should be considered a "minor crime" because a woman's behavior is contributory. The committee also insisted that the penalties for sexual assault be reduced and that the existing provisions on incest be abolished.[129] In a rare display of dissent, the women's sections of the political parties denounced the Geijer report. The following year the Social Democrats were ousted from power, replaced by the first nonsocialist government since the early 1930s. The new government released a report in 1982 that explicitly rejected the analysis and proposals of the Geijer committee. It suggested a set of reforms for the criminal justice system and medical facilities to better meet the needs of women and children who were sexually abused.[130]

When the Social Democrats returned to power that same year, they did not embrace these reforms. Instead they focused on providing more resources for programs aimed at rehabilitating men convicted of sexual assault. No autonomous rape crisis centers emerged to pressure the government to do otherwise. Likewise, the National Organization for Emergency Shelters for Battered Women in Sweden (ROKS) was totally dependent on state money and the continued political support of the parties.[131] Because suing the state for negligence or civil rights violations was not an option, Swedish courts did not provide an alternative venue to hold the state accountable and change the public debate on sexual assault and domestic violence.[132]

As the Swedish government came under intensified pressure from abused women and their supporters in the 1990s, the state relented somewhat. In 1994 it increased expenditures to combat domestic violence and instituted some legal reforms that by then had become commonplace in the United States. Police officers did not as readily dismiss complaints of domestic violence, and prosecutors were more likely to suggest criminal law remedies. Professional social workers employed by the state remained remarkably indifferent to the issue, however. Overall, the Swedish state's response tended to be more symbolic than substantive.[133]

In short, the highly centralized and corporatist Swedish state was able to dominate the public debate on violence against women. It did not embrace feminist analyses popular elsewhere that linked rape and domestic violence to the persistent inequality and social subjugation of women. The state was so effective in controlling the public discussion of violence against women that it was not uncommon to hear Swedish women remark caustically that "in Sweden, women can't be raped because we are equal," according to R. Amy Elman.[134] By not legitimizing the issue of violence against women as a serious criminal matter and by not acknowledging any culpability on the part of law enforcement, the Swedish state helped to rob this issue of its potency. This occurred at a time when conservative parties were beginning to experiment with exploiting the law-and-order issue, and the Social Democrats and other leftist parties were following along with some reluctance.[135]

Over time, the Swedish state's apparent intransigence on rape and domestic violence did feed into a broader sense that it was failing to stem or take seriously the general rise in reported crime and expansion of drug use. By the mid-1990s this contributed to a more repressive penal environment, one in which victims were pitted against offenders in a quest to make tougher policies more palatable. While the prison population did not experience a rapid takeoff, a number of harsher policies were implemented, including longer sentences, tougher drug policies, electronic tagging, and greater restrictions on privileges and liberties for incarcerated people.[136]

To sum up, in the U.S. case, a porous state and a diverse, politicized women's movement assured that violence against women would become a contributing factor to the growing law-and-order movement and more conservative penal policies. In Britain, feminists faced off against a relatively more autonomous state that was not all that transparent and that was reasonably capable of keeping them at the political margins. The small core of politically neutral civil servants drawn from a narrow band of the elite presented a significant barrier to reform-oriented politics in Britain.[137] The British women's movement, which was more coherent, radical, and autonomous than its counterpart in the United States, eventually had some success in making the state address the subject of violence against women. The government responded by enhancing what Britain's welfare state had to offer to battered women. British feminists were less successful in forcing law enforcement to acknowledge its shortcomings in dealing with rape and domestic violence and instituting legal reforms. As a consequence, the subject of violence against women did not become the poster child for tough penal policies the way it did in the United States. Sexual assault and other violence against women were largely absent from Britain's law-and-order debate in the 1970s and much of the 1980s.[138] At the other extreme from the United States was Sweden, which had the most coherent state structures and the least autonomous women's movement. As a result, the state took a relatively blithe attitude toward domestic violence and sexual assault. The seriousness of the issue of violence against women and the need for legal reforms were minimized in Sweden. At the same time, the possibility that this issue could be used to embolden penal conservatives was neutralized.

Feminism, the State, and the Future of Penal Reform

Feminist scholars and activists made exceptional strides in addressing the issue of violence against women. They forced not only the U.S. state and society but also the field of criminology to acknowledge the severity of the problem. This was a significant shift. For the longest time, the field of criminology either neglected the study of women and crime altogether or treated women in a stereotypical, offhand fashion.[139] While feminists' initial criticisms of criminology focused on its neglect of women as offenders, some of their main achievements were in developing new theories and policies for women and children as victims.[140] Yet except for when feminists were advocating increased criminalization for certain offenses like sexual assault and domestic violence, penal policies and practices and the field of criminology remained largely untouched by other developments in feminism. "[T]he inching of feminist thought from margin towards centre has so far tamed feminism more than it has transformed the centre," according to Dorie Klein.[141] The 1994 crime bill and VAWA epitomized that process, for much of this legislation was "completely antithetical to anything that would be advocated by feminist criminology."[142]

The campaigns against domestic violence, rape, and pornography, which was not discussed here, forced a wider debate in feminism about whether to view the state and the law as primarily assets or liabilities for women.[143] However, few feminists considered at the time that by enlisting the state to combat violence against women, women's groups might be contributing to the construction of the carceral state. American feminists prosecuting the war on rape and domestic violence were remarkably unaware of or untouched by developments in the field of critical criminology, which rejects a view of the state as a neutral arbiter of social and economic disputes and understands crime primarily in terms of power relations.[144] This disconnect between feminism and critical criminology is not entirely surprising. Some feminists recoiled from critical criminology out of a belief that it underestimated or ignored the extent of violence against women. They also were troubled by what they saw as critical criminology's tendency to excuse criminals and place the blame for crime on wider structures like capitalism.[145]

In the decade since passage of VAWA, the chorus of doubts about relying on legal remedies to address violence against women has grown louder across a broad range of feminists, crime experts, academics, and social workers.[146] For example, as Nancy Hirschmann shows, complex economic and structural factors, not just the legal system, constrain the choices of battered women.[147] Concerns have been growing about mandatory arrest, presumptive arrest, no-drop policies, and tougher sentencing, because these legal remedies do not necessarily reduce violence against women and have contributed to greater state control of women, especially poor women.[148] Evidence is accumulating that battered women themselves are at greater risk of being arrested for domestic violence under mandatory arrest policies.[149] These policies also increase the chance that state protection agencies will remove the children of abused women from their homes because of reports of violence.[150] Furthermore, they appear to raise the probability that women involved even peripherally in the criminal activities of their abusive partners will be arrested and incarcerated for relatively minor infractions.[151] Critics also contend that mandatory arrest and no-drop policies disempower women, because they force women to press charges or leave abusive partners – or else face humiliation and shame from the authorities should they choose to stay.[152]

As the state's penal dragnet scoops up more women, and as the domestic violence rate appears to be declining recently, feminist scholars and activists are once again focusing on the plight of the female offender.[153] Since 1995, women have been the fastest growing segment of the U.S. prison population.[154] The rising number of women behind bars for minor drug violations or for being the unwitting or reluctant accomplices to abusive partners has highlighted the persistent problems with the drug war. The growing number of imprisoned mothers who have young children on the outside has underscored the largely ignored question of what effect prison has on the children of incarcerated parents.[155]

It is not obvious, however, that as feminists and activists reconnect with the female offender they will form bonds with some of the broader political forces attempting to roll back the carceral state. For example, many feminists continue to support ratcheting up criminal prosecutions for men who have physically or sexually assaulted women or children. At the same time, they have called upon the legal system to be more empathetic and caring toward women facing criminal charges for conduct like drug abuse, killing their abusers, or child neglect and abuse. Some feminists argue forcefully for compassionate approaches for women charged with crimes who themselves have been victims of abuse. "Yet, strikingly, feminists are not among those advocating forgiving, restorative approaches toward offenders who commit violence against women, or other kinds of violent crimes,"[156] argues Martha Minow. She contends that a highly retributive stance by women is counterproductive for many reasons. Most notably, with more than two million people behind bars, the overwhelming majority of them men, millions of women are the mothers, daughters, wives, and sisters of men entombed in the carceral state.[157]

A handful of feminists advocate experimenting with alternative schemes for dealing with violence against women and other crimes, such as restorative justice schemes.[158] Restorative justice emphasizes the humanity of both the offender and the victim and elevates repairing relationships between offenders and victims and within the community above retribution and law enforcement.[159] Its central aims are forgiveness and reconciliation, not punishment. Restorative justice is premised on minimizing the role of the state in meting out punishment and strengthening the role of the community, including victims and offenders, in dealing with crime.[160] John Braithwaite and Kathleen Daly, two leading advocates of restorative justice, contend that the criminal justice system can and should be reformed so as to "empower communities of concern" as well as victims. But they also emphasize how reformed "criminal justice institutions are no substitute for a stronger women's movement as the keystone to controlling violence against women."[161]

It is questionable whether alternative programs to address violence against women that deemphasize law enforcement – such as restorative justice – will take root in the United States. First, the law enforcement approach to domestic violence appears to be gaining ground elsewhere. For example, criminal justice strategies comprised more than half of a United Nations manual on domestic violence published in 1993. With its focus on individual criminality, the manual slighted the need for collective action separate from law enforcement to reduce domestic violence.[162] Furthermore, many feminists resist mediation, family conferences, and other restorative justice schemes. They see unwelcome parallels with the family courts created in the early twentieth century in the United States and with the crisis mediation strategies used by the police in the 1960s and early 1970s. In their view, these efforts diverted domestic violence out of formal legal channels and ended up sweeping the whole problem out of public view.[163] They criticize some prison reformers for their "insufficient appreciation of violent crime" and their uncritical acceptance of "an almost romantic notion of community as an ideal solution."[164]

Some feminists have tried to stake out a middle ground. Liv Finstad argues that sexual assault and other violence against women should not be taken out of formal legal channels such as the courts because these state institutions play an important symbolic role as the "executor of collective sorrow."[165] She suggests that the ritual of the courts to proclaim guilt or innocence be retained, but that alternatives to prison be established to compensate victims, make retribution to them, and possibly punish offenders. In attempting to plot an escape from the carceral state, Daly takes a more nuanced view of the victims' movements – that is *movements*, not movement. Whereas Braithwaite expresses significant doubts that crime-victim movements can ever be in keeping with the premises of restorative justice, and Stuart Scheingold and others view victim advocacy as inherently regressive, Daly sees the possibility for a new type of victims' movement that is "positive and progressive."[166] She imagines a "just response to crime that has both victims and victimizers in view."[167] The particular historical, political, and institutional context out of which the women's movement and the victims' rights movement emerged in the United States does raise the question of whether the United States is particularly ill-suited to nurture the kind of victim advocacy Daly has in mind. For a variety of reasons, the United States appears to be more prone to degenerating into regressive victim-centered politics and less capable of pursuing a more progressive approach to victims.

A number of critics suggest that the women's movement needs to address the problem of violence against women not by strengthening its ties with law enforcement and victims' groups, but by connecting up with other progressive reform movements calling for social justice, an expanded welfare state, and a retreat of the carceral state.[168] To do that, they argue, feminists need to develop and reaffirm a feminist vision of justice that incorporates some of the key insights of critical criminology, with its deep skepticism of expanding the law enforcement powers of the state to deal with social problems.[169] Claire Reinelt and others suggest that the state needs to be "viewed as a terrain of political struggles," which then makes "some form of political engagement likely." Yet engagement entails risks. Funding depends on economic and political forces not under one's control, and engaging with the state can entail many contradictions.[170]

To sum up, the terms "women's movement" and "battered-women's movement" encompass political forces that have strikingly distinct ideological and organizational expressions in different national settings, which had important implications for the development of penal policies.[171] Differences in state structures and the relative cohesion and independence of the women's movement were critical in shaping the cause of violence against women in the United States and elsewhere. The U.S. battered-women's movement was less skeptical of the state from the start than was the anti-rape movement. Some U.S. feminists active in the early battered women's movement did raise serious concerns about engaging with the state. They questioned whether domestic violence could be reduced while leaving "the fundamental social, political, and economic relations" associated with it unaddressed.[172] Nonetheless, they generally saw an enhanced criminal justice response to battering as a promising interim solution while they battled for a long-term remedy premised on the total restructuring of society.[173] Fixated on the ultimate need for a wholesale transformation of society where patriarchy, racism, and even capitalism would capitulate, they initially did not take a nuanced view of the state and the particular historical and institutional context in which it was situated.

On the historical side, they demonstrated a surprising amnesia about women's reform movements in U.S. history. Many of them treated domestic violence as largely "a problem in isolation, with neither history nor social context."[174] Feminists generally ignored how U.S. history is littered with punitive efforts to address violence against women and children that ended up idealizing the nuclear family and motherhood and emboldening political conservatives.[175]

On the institutional side, feminists slighted other possibilities to use the state instrumentally to help battered women that were not premised on punishing more men. They focused on how to reform the law enforcement arm of the state rather than on how to make the underdeveloped U.S. welfare state more capable of meeting the needs of battered women. This was not an act of total political free will. Their commitment to certain transformative ideals was certainly their own choice. But a combination of historical, institutional, and political factors conspired to fix their gaze on criminal justice remedies rather than on other solutions, like enhancing the welfare state. Moreover, to focus on the failures of the U.S. welfare state would have put them in the unenviable position of criticizing the welfare state at a time when it was already under siege with the ascendancy of Reaganomics.[176]

It is not possible to accurately assess the risks of engaging with the state on a specific issue like violence against women without fully appreciating the larger processes that created this particular state and the particular social movements swirling around it. In short, the state and social movements need to be institutionally and historically demystified. Failure to do so means that feminists and others will misjudge what the costs of engaging with the state are for women in particular, and society more broadly, in the shadow of the carceral state.

7   FROM RIGHTS TO REVOLUTION

Prison Activism and the Carceral State

> "The ultimate expression of law is not order – it's prison. There are hundreds upon hundreds of prisons, and thousands upon thousands of laws, yet there is no social order, no social peace."
>
> – George Jackson[1]

THE EXPLOSION OF PRISON UNREST in many Western countries from the 1960s to the 1980s belies just how distinctive the U.S. prisoners' rights movement was. The movement's roots, leadership, relationship with state institutions, and the broader political environment it operated in distinguished it from prison activism in other countries. Most importantly, race was the crucible for the contemporary prisoners' rights movement in the United States but not elsewhere. The most significant race-related factors that shaped the U.S. movement of course included the deep and long-standing racial cleavages in the United States. Beyond this social characteristic of the United States were specific race-related political and institutional factors: the origins and development of the black nationalist, civil rights, and black power movements; and the central role of the courts and a discourse on rights in American political development. These factors help explain an ironic outcome. The United States gave birth to a prisoners' rights movement that was initially more powerful and significant than prison reform movements that emerged elsewhere at roughly the same time. But the U.S. movement developed in ways that helped create conditions conducive to launching the "race to incarcerate."[2] As a result, the United States, a forerunner in the rights revolution, ended up being a forerunner in the construction of the carceral state.

The term "prisoners' rights movement" refers to much more than the flurry of court decisions affecting prisoners, defendants, and suspects beginning with some of the landmark cases of the 1960s. It encompasses the broader effort by a variety of groups and organizations from roughly the 1950s to the early 1980s to redefine the moral, political, economic, and legal status of defendants and offenders in democratic societies through a range of activities, including lawsuits, legislation, demonstrations, strikes, riots, and calls for revolution.[3] Analyses of this movement in the United States have centered primarily on two questions: Has all the litigation and mobilization around prisoners' rights and other penal reform issues resulted in a significantly higher quality of life behind bars? And, were judges and the courts the primary catalysts for this movement, or was their contribution, in the words of Gerald N. Rosenberg, more akin to "cutting the ribbon on a new project"?[4]

Scholars and others have identified some implications that these questions have for the rising incarceration rate in the United States. But few have delved deeply into the relationship between the U.S. prisoners' rights movement and the growing practice of relying on mass imprisonment as the penalty of choice in the United States. Some contend that the courts and society became more willing to send offenders to prison and impose longer sentences once prisons were perceived to be cleaner, safer, and better administered.[5] Another common view is that the prisoners' movement, with its emphasis on getting the courts to recognize prisoners' rights, prompted a backlash from conservatives and the public, who were alarmed that the rights pendulum had swung too far in the direction of suspects, defendants, and prisoners. This, in turn, reinforced the view of a zero-sum game between offenders on the one hand and victims and society on the other, which strengthened the public's resolve to be more punitive.[6] These explanations do not satisfactorily explain why the conservative backlash against offenders became so potent, however. The U.S. prisoners' movement and the rights discourse concerning prisoners need to be situated within a wider political context. The dense network of interest groups and organizations that initially gave the prisoners' rights issue such political traction developed in complicated ways that ultimately hastened the rise of the carceral state.

The U.S. prisoners' movement was exceptional because of the exceptional racial context in which it took root and developed. The presence of a growing and disproportionate number of blacks in U.S. prisons at a time of rising political mobilization and tension around racial issues focused government and public attention on prisons in a way not seen elsewhere. For a time, prisons became an important part of the political fabric and the touchstone for debates about fundamental political questions involving race, justice, and oppression. The world behind bars became a site for political struggle and action in ways it had not been before.

Other Western countries experienced revolutionary upsurges in the 1960s and 1970s, but they ran their course without resulting in a wholesale lockdown on prison activism and without reasserting such a divide between prisoners and the rest of society, especially victims of crime. The issue of prisoners never became a central feature of these revolutionary upsurges or of national politics. Because racial issues were such a defining

feature of the politics of the United States during this period, it is not surprising that prisons also became a central national issue. For a time, the
United States experienced a considerably more open and public debate
about penal policy. But that public debate was eventually more vulnerable to being captured by law-and-order conservatives proclaiming victims'
rights because of the distinctive way the prisoners' movement developed in
the United States. This chapter focuses on four factors specifically related
to race that explain the exceptional development of the U.S. prisoners'
rights movement and why this once formidable movement ultimately did
not pose a major obstacle to the construction of the carceral state: the
rapid racial transformation of the prison population beginning in the
1930s; the efforts by the Federal Bureau of Prisons to desegregate federal
penitentiaries from the 1940s onward; the mobilization of Black Muslims
and the Nation of Islam behind bars that started in earnest in the 1950s;
and the growth of the civil rights and black power movements.

Scholarship on Prison Reform

The contemporary prisoners' rights movement in the United States blossomed in the 1970s at about the same time that a number of scholars,
many of them social historians, began questioning the long-standing view
that earlier waves of prison reform in the eighteenth, nineteenth, and early
twentieth centuries were largely benevolent, humanitarian, and progressive. Some challenged the motivations of these earlier reformers, some
challenged their claims about the salutary consequences of their efforts,
and some challenged both.[7] These new works on the origins of the penitentiary and prison reform were part of a growing body of scholarship at
the time on the institutional history of the welfare state. The pioneering
study in this field was David Rothman's *The Discovery of the Asylum*,
which traces the rise of the penitentiary and other related institutions in
the United States.[8] It is a tale of how humanitarian intentions went awry
as prisons, intended to be sites of uplift and rehabilitation, became cold,
cruel warehouses. Rothman's successors attributed more varied motivations to the early penal reformers, including naked economic interests, the
need to assert control over restive, potentially disruptive groups in society,
and efforts to demonstrate and legitimize the exercise of state power.[9]

Given this backdrop, it is not surprising that studies of the contemporary prisoners' rights movement centered on whether all the litigation
and mobilization around prisoners' rights and other penal issues in the
1960s and 1970s resulted in more humane, livable prisons.[10] Some argue
that the prisoners' rights movement, despite some important shortcomings, had a powerful positive impact.[11] Egregious practices that had once
been commonplace, such as starvation, corporal punishment, the infamous Tucker telephone, and exposure to freezing temperatures, were

eliminated.[12] Censorship of reading materials and correspondence was reduced, and significant restrictions on the exercise of religion behind bars were relaxed.[13] James B. Jacobs and others credit the movement with creating enormous pressures for management reforms in prisons and jails. In their view, it produced a new generation of competent prison administrators beholden to operating according to written, rational rules and procedures.[14] Judicial intervention also compelled many states to spend more money on improving living conditions in prisons.[15]

Others contend that the U.S. prisoners' rights movement had far more limited effects on the living conditions and administrative practices in prisons and has to be measured against some considerable negative consequences.[16] Some argue that the lawsuits, court decrees, politicization of prisoners, and unpredictability and upheavals associated with the legal process created an authority vacuum and significant employee morale problems in many prisons. This resulted in more dangerous, violent conditions, at least in the short run.[17] Whereas Jacobs claims that these landmark legal decisions "spelled the end of the authoritarian regime in American penology," others contend they ushered in a more rational, less capricious, but nonetheless highly repressive system of control in prisons.[18] For example, Ben M. Crouch and James W. Marquart show how the courts, at the prodding of the prisoners' rights movement, compelled prison administrators in Texas to create formal bureaucratic apparatuses to govern prisons that turned out to be just as repressive as the earlier informal ones, but without the same degree of physical brutality.[19] While court interventions succeeded in bringing about "very significant improvements in prison conditions, even when actively resisted by prison officials," these improvements, in their view, fell "short of some ideal notion of 'justice.'"[20] Alvin J. Bronstein, the longtime director of the American Civil Liberties Union's National Prison Project, a leading prisoners' rights organization, characterizes the movement's achievements as significant but relatively modest.[21] Likewise, Susan Sturm argues that judicial intervention "can alleviate the most immediate and profound suffering" in prisons but is incapable of eradicating "deeper, more fundamental problems."[22]

The other main and related concern of much of the literature on the prisoners' rights movement centers more squarely on the relative influence of judges and the courts. Specifically, were judges the pivotal political actors in the transformation of the prison? And, if so, was their activism a desirable turn toward judicial policy making?[23] These questions are an extension of a long-standing debate in legal, scholarly, and political circles about whether the courts have the will and the way to initiate major social reforms and whether such judicial activism is an abuse of power.[24] Perhaps the crudest, most succinct political expression of this issue is the slogan Gov. George Wallace (D-Ala.) wielded in 1976: "Vote for George Wallace and give a barbed wire enema to a federal judge."[25] Many of those who argue that the courts had a significant and positive effect on penal reform maintain that it is not enough to examine just the individual legal decisions and how they were implemented in specific prisons. Rather, the "changing legal status of prisoners needs to be put in a larger sociopolitical context."[26]

As the prisoners' rights movement petered out in the 1980s, so did this interest in analyzing it in a broader sociopolitical perspective. Some important studies appeared about the role of the courts in penal policy and about the rise and fall of the prisoners' movement in specific locales.[27] But few examined the movement within a wider social, political, and historical context. Two notable exceptions are Eric Cummins's *The Rise and Fall of California's Radical Prison Movement*, to be discussed later, and Charles Epp's *The Rights Revolution: Lawyers, Activists, and Supreme Courts in Comparative Perspective*. Epp claims that the United States was a pioneer in the rights revolution for prisoners and other historically marginalized groups in society (such as women and blacks) not because of judicial independence, or the existence of a constitution that stresses rights, or the presence of a political culture infused with a rights consciousness. Rather, he credits the precocious creation of a dense, well-established support structure of rights-based groups that had the knowledge, expertise, organization, networks, and resources to bring about the revolution. Epp traces the origins of the rights revolution in the United States back to the 1910s and 1920s with the birth of organized advocacy groups like the American Civil Liberties Union (ACLU) and the National Association for the Advancement of Colored People (NAACP). These groups, together with important changes in the legal profession that he outlines, laid the basis for the explosion of the rights revolution in the 1960s.[28] To his credit, Epp situates the U.S. rights movement within a wider context. Still he views the rights revolution as largely an established fact to be celebrated. He does not consider, for example, whether the prisoners' rights movement had any negative long-term consequences on penal policy, in particular the country's readiness to incarcerate. To comprehend why the prisoners' rights movement ultimately did not stand in the way of the carceral state, it is important to consider some other political and institutional developments specifically related to race.

Transformation of U.S. Prisons and Early Penal Unrest

The first important development is the dramatic change in the U.S. prison population and the nature of prison protests between the 1930s and 1970s. During this period the prison population in the United States was transformed, even though the overall incarceration rate remained reasonably constant, despite some oscillations (see Figure 2, page 5). Prior to the 1930s, the overwhelming majority of prisoners were white, though blacks comprised significant minorities or even near majorities in some institutions, especially in the South. In the 1920s, blacks constituted just under a third of the total prison population.[29] The number and proportion of black prisoners began to grow substantially from the early 1930s onward.[30] In 1960, nearly 40 percent of people incarcerated in state prisons were nonwhite. By 1974, blacks and other nonwhites comprised just over half of the state prison population.[31] The federal prison system experienced similar changes. Blacks made up just 11 percent of the federal prison population in 1931. Two decades later they comprised nearly a quarter.[32] In 1989, for the first time in U.S. history, the majority of the prison population was black.[33]

These transformations of the prison population coincided with fundamental changes in the nature of prison unrest. U.S. prisons have a long history of being more violent and restive than prisons elsewhere. Going at least as far back as the 1850s, American prisons periodically have been gripped by waves of riots and other disturbances, some of which dominated national headlines for days. In the early twentieth century there were several periods of major unrest immediately before and after World War I, and then again in the late 1920s and at the onset of the Great Depression.[34] These disturbances prompted President Herbert Hoover and other public officials to push for major increases in federal spending on prisons and for a series of changes in the penal system to relieve overcrowding and other problems.[35] Major prison unrest in the late 1920s in upstate New York prompted the state to build the "ultimate prison." In 1931, New York officials opened the world's most expensive prison to date in Attica, which was billed as "paradise for convicts."[36]

Aside from Hoover's federal initiative and some individual state efforts, these earlier waves of prison riots and protests did not insinuate themselves into the political fabric and public consciousness. Prisons remained largely a world apart. People who were imprisoned lacked significant internal organizations to sustain their mobilizations. Furthermore, they did not have a message – or the means to deliver a message – that would resonate politically with a wider audience beyond the prison gates. During these early periods of rioting and unrest, prisoners' demands largely were related to calls for improvements in their day-to-day living conditions. Their organizations were fluid and ad hoc, out of which leaders would emerge.[37] The leadership was white, for the most part, though blacks and other minority groups participated in the unrest.[38] People on the inside generally had little organized support on the outside for their activities.

That began to change in the 1950s due to several important political developments specific to the United States. From 1950 to 1953, the country experienced more than fifty major prison disturbances, most of them in the North and West.[39] Few riots were reported in the South, where prison administrators relied on a cadre of select and privileged prisoners to maintain order.[40] Until the upheavals of the 1970s, this period was considered the worst ever by prison administrators. The common view of the 1950s riots is that they were primarily spontaneous uprisings directed at the horrendous living conditions.[41]

Desmond King complicates the standard accounts about prison unrest in the 1950s and the role of the state during this period.[42] First, he demonstrates that the riots in the early 1950s were not purely over "housekeeping demands" but had significant racial overtones with wider political implications than previously assumed.[43] Second, he shows how the courts were not the first major state actors to politicize the prisons and make them visible. Throughout the 1940s and 1950s, federal prison administrators were extremely conscious of racial issues as they attempted to desegregate federal penitentiaries. Third, King makes us rethink how we understand the origins of the prisoners' rights movement. Standard accounts generally begin with the mobilization of the Black Muslims in the 1950s and 1960s, which resulted in some path-breaking court decisions that opened the way for other prisoners and groups to challenge prison administrators and penal conditions in the courts. If King's account is correct, the Nation of Islam began organizing in an atmosphere that was already quite racially charged and in which the state played a more complex role than just standing in the way of Black Muslims pushing for greater religious freedom and other rights behind bars. Indeed, the state helped to politicize prisoners, especially around the issue of race.

King shows how World War II had a transformative effect on U.S. prisons, as it did on many other institutions in the United States.[44] The war brought an influx of new kinds of prisoners into federal penitentiaries for violations of the 1940 Selective Service Act. Between 1943 and 1947, violators of the conscription law comprised a significant minority of the new prison population, and the Bureau of Prisons characterized many of these prisoners as "very troublesome."[45] Elijah Muhammad, the founder of the Nation of Islam, which played such a pivotal role in prison activism in the 1950s and 1960s, was sent to a federal facility in Minnesota after refusing to be drafted in 1942.[46] These conscientious objectors, many of them sentenced to lengthy terms, tended to be more educated, politically active, and ready to challenge prison authorities on a number of fronts, especially race relations.[47] Militant conscientious objectors fought back in prisons using nonviolent resistance. Through prison work strikes and walkouts from penal camps run by the National Service Board for Religious Objectors, they helped to establish the idea of using nonviolent direct action to challenge the power of the state.[48]

World War II focused national and international attention on segregation in the U.S. armed forces, which spurred a wider debate about segregation in other government institutions. King brings to light the hitherto little-known story of just how troubled wardens and top administrators of the federal prison system were as early as the 1930s about the issue of segregation in penal facilities.[49] The leadership of the U.S. Bureau of Prisons set out to challenge the deeply entrenched segregationist practices in federal penitentiaries. From the establishment of the Federal Bureau of Prisons in 1930, the treatment of blacks had been "informed by the ethos and principle of segregation."[50] Blacks disproportionately received the worst jobs in prisons. Most penal institutions had separate living and work facilities for black and white prisoners. In many institutions, whites enjoyed wider privileges, including more relaxed supervision and greater access to reading rooms and other amusements.[51] Beginning in the 1940s, the Bureau of Prisons exploited its "autonomy to desegregate," which meant challenging entrenched local practices and customs. The bureau did not make a formal declaration of its intention to ban segregation in prisons until 1964, nearly a decade after the *Brown v. Board of Education* decision declaring the segregation of public schools unconstitutional. But as early as 1944, the bureau's director was pushing for an end to discrimination based on race or religion in federal penitentiaries and said that blacks should have "the same opportunities for training, work, and recreation as well as other privileges" that white prisoners enjoyed.[52] Wardens in the federal system interpreted the *Brown* decision as a vindication of the desegregation strategy they had been pursuing over the previous decade.[53]

Federal prison administrators, wittingly or unwittingly, put race at the center of prison life with their commitment to desegregate. The Bureau of Prisons sought to end segregation, but in its own time and in its own way. It stridently resisted efforts by prisoners themselves to lay claim to the race issue, be they politicized conscientious objectors who challenged the color line or, later, Black Muslims who organized their own tightly knit groups. That said, it did seek to dismantle the color line in federal facilities, often over the strenuous objections of prison staff members, many of whom hailed from local communities that were segregated.

Government authorities laid the groundwork in other ways for the establishment of a highly politicized prisoners' rights movement that had deep roots behind bars and significant ties and political notoriety outside. The growing confidence in the 1940s about the constructive role that government and education could play in remaking society infused penal policy in many states.[54] Belief was widespread that people in prison could be remade into constructive citizens through education and closer contact with the world beyond the prison gates. The contributions that prisoners and prison industries made to the military effort during World War II, and the lower level of prison unrest during the war years, fueled optimism among penal reformers that the United States was finally ready to embrace prison reform premised on the rehabilitative model.[55]

California took the rehabilitative ideal most to heart in the postwar years. After winning the governor's race in 1942, Republican Earl Warren emphatically stressed his commitment to creating a new penal system. He and others began portraying San Quentin and other California prisons as places to reform minds rather than punish bodies.[56] "The gates opened up, and the experts poured in," according to Cummins in his detailed study of the radical prison movement in California.[57] Group counseling, family picnics, greater access to reading materials through "bibliotherapy," and more contact with the outside world were cornerstones of this new approach.[58] By making prisons less closed institutions, state authorities provided an opening for people in prison to begin developing and retaining identities imported from outside. Their primary identity was no longer just their status as a prisoner.[59]

As it became apparent that group counseling was more difficult and expensive to provide than anticipated, prison authorities in California and other states began promoting libraries as an alternative or supplement to counseling. They became committed, to varying degrees, to surrounding those in prison with a richer intellectual atmosphere. This created considerable tensions. Libraries were supposed to enrich the education of prisoners and spur their rehabilitation. At the same time, libraries and the censorship of the mails and prison writings were supposed to keep certain ideas outside of prisons. Despite the best efforts of prison authorities to confiscate and destroy prisoners' writings and control what they read, the amount of contraband writing and reading materials exploded behind bars.[60]

California's zeal for rehabilitation helped to create the first in a long line of U.S. prisoners who became national and even international celebrities. Caryl Chessman, sentenced to death in 1948 after being found guilty of sexually assaulting and kidnapping two women on local lovers' lanes in California, became a prolific and best-selling author beginning with the 1954 publication of *Cell 2455 Death Row*. His supporters used this and his later prison writings as evidence that the "violent, menacing 'sex fiend'" portrayed by the media and prosecutors during his trial had been reformed.[61] For penal reformers, Chessman was Exhibit A in defense of the rehabilitative ideal, as he challenged his death sentence on the basis of his contributions as a legendary jailhouse lawyer and his therapeutic rehabilitation.[62]

Chessman became a national and international cause célèbre.[63] He was a model of how a prisoner could be empowered through writing and could subvert San Quentin's controls on reading and writing.[64] He inspired a worldwide movement opposed to his execution and to capital punishment.[65] His May 1960 death in the gas chamber after eight stays of execution and nearly a dozen years on death row spurred crowds in Rio de Janeiro to denounce the United States as a "miserable country." In

Lisbon, angry students smashed the U.S. embassy library, and throughout Western Europe expressions of support for Chessman rang out.[66] His
execution had major repercussions closer to home, particularly on how
the prisoners' rights movement subsequently developed. With his death,
prisoners and their supporters became increasingly disaffected from the
promised land of rehabilitation. His execution exposed the apparent hol-
lowness of the promise that rehabilitation would bring, if not release, at
least reprieve.[67]

Emergence of the Nation of Islam Behind Bars

This disaffection coincided with but did not cause the emergence of the
Nation of Islam as a powerful force within prisons and beyond by the early
1960s. It did help bolster the Black Muslims' compelling challenge to the
conventional understanding of who was sent to prison and why. The Black
Muslims set in motion a radical transformation in how prisoners viewed
themselves and how society viewed them. This had major consequences
for the carceral state that lasted long after the Nation of Islam ceased to
be a significant factor in penal politics by the mid-to-late 1960s.

As the Bureau of Prisons attempted to eliminate the most blatant
forms of discrimination in federal facilities, Black Muslims were qui-
etly organizing themselves in U.S. prisons. In the 1950s, they worked
"underground" educating new recruits and building up their organization. Their central task at this stage was organizing other blacks, primarily
through personal contact. Writing to prisoners to educate them about the
Muslim philosophy was a central activity of Black Muslims on the outside.
People in prison were encouraged to write to Elijah Muhammad. They
always received personal replies to their letters, along with some literature
about the Black Muslims, and sometimes even cash. Such correspondence
prompted many prisoners, most notably Malcolm X, to convert while in
prison.[68] Other leading black prison activists, notably Eldridge Cleaver
and George Jackson, underscored in their prison writings the significance
of the Black Muslims and noted how they themselves had been politicized
through their contacts with the Nation of Islam while in prison.[69] Well
disciplined and highly organized, the Black Muslims eventually were able
to reach a large number of blacks within and beyond the prison walls. By
1960, when they began pushing their demands more publicly, the Nation
of Islam had between 65,000 and 100,000 members, many of them in
prison.[70] It had the "allegiance or sympathy of most black prisoners" at
a time when the black prison population was growing significantly and
enthusiasm for the rehabilitative ideal was waning.[71]

In the early 1960s, the Black Muslims turned to the courts. Across
the country they filed lawsuits claiming that they had been discriminated
against on the basis of race and religion. They pushed in the courts for the

right to hold religious gatherings, purchase Korans, build mosques, and receive visits from Muslims outside prison.[72] Between 1961 and 1978, there were sixty-six reported federal decisions involving Black Muslims, by one count.[73] Mosques in all major cities gave important financial, organizational, and other support to efforts to secure prisoners' right to practice the Muslim religion.[74] Their demands set in motion a string of legal decisions that ended the courts' long-standing "hands-off" stance toward prisoners.

Prior to the 1960s, prisoners had few legal channels available for redress and, as a consequence, conditions of confinement remained severe. The 1871 Virginia case *Ruffin v. Commonwealth*, which affirmed the previous policy of declaring that "prisoners are slaves of the state," remained largely intact.[75] A couple of prison court cases decided in the 1940s seemed to suggest important limitations to this posture. But judges generally remained unwilling to intervene in prison affairs until the Muslims pressed the issue.[76] The Black Muslims were the catalyst for a string of court decisions that gave prisoners important and unprecedented protections and rights behind bars. Previously most prisoner complaints were brought by individual prisoners with a grievance. The Nation of Islam cases "were the first to be brought by an organized group as part of a consistent strategy."[77] The courts granted prisoners standing in federal courts to challenge prison conditions, rules, and regulations. They relaxed restrictions on prisoners providing legal aid to one another, on mail censorship, and on religious freedom. They enhanced due process protections for prisoners and held that denying them adequate medical care could constitute cruel and unusual punishment under the Eighth Amendment to the Constitution.[78] By 1974, few were surprised when the Supreme Court declared: "There is no iron curtain drawn between the Constitution and the prisons of this country."[79]

By the mid-1960s, the strength of the Nation of Islam began to decline precipitously. Internal organizational feuding, the Nation of Islam's rejection of more explicitly political activities, its strident separatist stance, its disinterest in changing fundamental power relations in prison, and its failure to deliver the support it had promised to prisoners debilitated the organization. The final critical blow was the 1965 assassination of Malcolm X, a hero to many black prisoners, who was distancing himself at the time of his death from the Nation of Islam's apolitical separatist stance.[80]

Despite its demise, the Nation of Islam left a powerful imprint on prison activism and on the long trajectory of penal politics. First, the Black Muslims established a collective and disciplined organization that was unprecedented in prison politics.[81] In doing so, they provided a model for other groups to organize in prison. By introducing a new ethos of group solidarity into prison life, they upended the prison norm of "do your own time" that had defined prison subculture.[82] Furthermore, once they went aboveground with their strikes and lawsuits, Black Muslims became an important window through which the prison was made more visible to the wider public. The barrage of litigation they instigated prompted the media and the public to focus intently for the first time on the inhumane conditions in many prisons. This litigation "forced the prison authorities and state officials into the open to defend themselves against the charges of prisoners."[83] The Black Muslims also engineered a dramatic shift in how prisoners viewed themselves and how society viewed them. With their emphasis on group identity and collective oppression, they laid claim to "the notion that blacks as a group were victims in society, that the miseries they faced were not the result of their own personal deficiencies."[84]

Finally, their activities provided a bridge to engage activists from the civil rights movement, and later a springboard to involve members of the New Left and the black power movement in prison issues. This had enormous long-term consequences for penal policy. The Nation of Islam demonstrated how outside support could be cultivated and could spell the difference between success and failure in prison activism. Prisons became the centerpiece of streams of activism in the United States and a high-profile political issue. The Nation of Islam emerged partly as a reaction against the civil rights movement. In the process, it provided an avenue for the civil rights movement, which initially paid little attention to penal issues, to embrace prison activism. The Black Muslims' emphasis on victimhood and rights was compatible with some of the main thrusts of the civil rights movement. Once the Nation of Islam made the courts a central battleground for prison issues, the legal profession and other prison reform groups streamed in, thus ushering the civil rights movement through the gates of the prison.

Prison Reform and the Civil Rights Movement

The civil rights movement was critical to the exceptional development of the prisoners' rights movement in the United States. By focusing so intently on stark segregationist practices in Southern schools, restaurants, and other public places, it underscored that the South was indeed a world apart. When the civil rights movement began to set its sights on prisons, the presence of so many penal farms in the South modeled on the old slave plantation system provided a ready target. As discussed in Chapter 3, many Southern states had created self-sufficient, state-run penal farms after the demise of the region's convict-lease system in the late nineteenth and early twentieth centuries. Conditions on these farms were savage and cruel. Prisoners typically toiled in the fields six days per week, ten hours per day, without adequate equipment or clothing – sometimes even without shoes. They were guarded by other convicts, known as "trusties," who relied on whips, guns, and a range of creative barbarities to keep prisoners in line. Warehoused in unventilated, overcrowded, and dilapidated barracks, people confined to penal farms were poorly fed and denied even basic medical care. For the first half of the twentieth century, this system went largely unchanged and unchallenged. Despite occasional scandals and periodic outcries and complaints from the public and the national corrections profession, the penal farms generally remained invisible.[85]

Conditions on these penal farms became a central concern of the civil rights movement and the prisoners' rights movement. Of the first six major prison reform cases decided by federal judges, "five, and arguably six, involved systems in the South."[86] Ultimately federal judges issued comprehensive orders calling for overhauls of the entire prison system or key pieces of the penal system in all eleven Southern states. By contrast, only four of the thirty-nine states outside of the South were "subject to comprehensive orders against their entire system."[87]

The civil rights movement helped make prisons visible, first in the South and later in the rest of the country. It provided the political context and resources for judges and the public to perceive and accept that one set of prisoners – those in the South – were subject to a "particularly objectionable form of punishment." This, in turn, provided an opening "to identify a more general problem that was applicable to state prisons throughout the nation."[88] The South served as a critical though not exclusive incubator for litigated prison reform. It was where the Legal Defense and Educational Fund of the NAACP had the most cooperating attorneys interested in prison reform issues. The LDF, which represented blacks in many of the landmark civil rights cases, was the first national organization to become deeply involved in efforts to reform prisons through litigation. The LDF viewed prison litigation as part of a broader effort to expand its activities in the mid-1960s beyond explicitly racial issues.[89] The South also had the largest concentration of segregated prisons, which gave courts, attorneys, and the Civil Rights Division of the U.S. Department of Justice an opening to challenge Southern prisons and expose their atrocious conditions.[90]

Not so surprisingly, interest in civil rights merged with prisoners' rights issues. Many lawyers followed a similar path. They started out focused on civil rights litigation. Then they moved on to challenging prison segregation and then on to contesting the constitutionality of many other prison practices and penal conditions. Lawyers involved in the core issues of the civil rights movement, including school desegregation, voting rights, and the defense of civil rights demonstrators, turned to "prison litigation issues after in a sense 'following their clients into jail.'"[91]

Major foundations began generously funding prisoners' rights projects and organizations.[92] The mainstream legal community also became a critical supporter of prisoners' rights. In 1970, the American Bar Association created the Commission on Correctional Facilities and Services to support prison reform. At least seven sections of the ABA eventually formed prisoners' rights committees. By 1974 nearly half of the states had established special prison reform committees.[93] Through the Office of Economic Opportunity (OEO) Legal Services and other programs, the federal government provided critical support for the establishment and development of hundreds of state and local legal aid groups that pursued prisoners' rights issues.[94] State and local governments also provided important support.[95]

The federal government supplied crucial help to the movement in other ways. The Civil Rights Act of 1964 gave the Department of Justice authority to sue for integration of public institutions. The Justice Department filed its first correctional desegregation lawsuit in 1969. For more than a decade after that it was seriously involved in prison and jail desegregation. It initiated its own desegregation investigations and intervened in many desegregation lawsuits initiated by private parties. The Civil Rights Division often used the desegregation lawsuits as an opening to challenge more general conditions in prisons and jails, even though its authority to do so rested on shakier legal ground. By 1980, the Department of Justice had been a key player in more than ten of the largest and most comprehensive prison cases and in many jail cases.[96]

From Rights to Revolution

The prison reform movement encompassed much more than the legal activism surrounding prisoners' rights. It included the wider effort by a variety of groups and organizations to redefine the status of prisoners through a span of activities ranging from lawsuits to strikes to riots. In the U.S. case, the prisoners' rights movement was deeply rooted in broader political currents involving first race – with the Nation of Islam and the civil rights movement – and then race and revolution. By the late 1960s, prison activism was enmeshed in revolutionary causes in a way not seen elsewhere. The U.S. prisoners' movement came to be seen at home and abroad as a vanguard of a worldwide liberation movement for oppressed people, especially people of color. The radical prisoners' movement that emerged in the late 1960s provided a bridge between the New Left, which was largely white, and the revolutionary black power movement, which was associated with groups like the Black Panthers.

Beginning in the late 1960s, the activities of the more radical strands of the prison movement began to overshadow the efforts of civil rights lawyers and other legal groups working on behalf of prisoners. U.S. prisons exploded, paralleling wider political unrest and rioting in many American cities.[97] In 1967, there were five prison riots. The following year the number tripled. In 1970 and 1971, there were twenty-seven and thirty-seven riots, respectively. In 1972, there were forty-eight, more than in any other year in U.S. history.[98] The number of organizations involved in reforming or eliminating prisons also exploded. Prison issues became a major public concern as prisons were gripped with these unprecedented waves of unrest.[99]

Once again, race and the actions of state authorities were critical factors in this development. With the fitful abolition of formal segregation in prisons in the 1960s and the barrage of legal challenges to prison administration and penal conditions, a void in prison structures and authority opened up. For much of the decade, relations between blacks and whites in prison were highly antagonistic.[100] The January 1967 massive race riot in San Quentin, in which about half of the 4,000 prisoners participated, exemplified this antagonism and was a major turning point for the prison movement.[101] Many prisoners acknowledged the self-defeating nature of the riot. Following the San Quentin upheaval, underground prison publications and radical ones on the outside began to emphasize the need for cross-racial struggles centered on issues of class. They also began to challenge the basic legitimacy of prisons, portraying them as an extension of an oppressive racial and class structure. This was a direct rebuke to the Nation of Islam, which emphasized strict racial segregation.[102] It also was a rebuke to the civil rights movement, which was ready to attack institutions like the courts and Congress, and explicitly racist practices like Jim Crow laws, but appeared unable or unwilling to indict larger social structures like race and class as oppressive.[103] Furthermore, while the civil rights movement did not reject interracial political activities in prisons, it did not go out of its way to encourage them or to develop a deeper analysis that could sustain broader political coalitions among prisoners.[104]

At the time of the San Quentin riot, notable blacks who had been or were imprisoned, such as George Jackson and Eldridge Cleaver, were gravitating toward Marxism. They started contending that lawbreaking should be viewed primarily as a political act aimed at an oppressive political and economic system. For example, in one of his most controversial claims, Cleaver initially argues in *Soul on Ice* that rape of a white woman by a black man could be characterized as an "insurrectionary act" by a victim against his oppressor.[105] Imprisoned blacks began to eschew the separatist stance of the Nation of Islam and started forging direct ties with the white radicals associated with the New Left in California and elsewhere.[106] The Chessman case had spurred Bay Area activists to take an interest in prisons in the late 1950s.[107] But the link between the New Left, which was primarily white, and black prison leaders did not solidify until the late 1960s.

In large part because of the charismatic leadership of Cleaver, Jackson, Huey Newton, Martín Sostre, and other imprisoned black and Latino leaders, the New Left began to view penal issues as central to its struggles against political and economic oppression.[108] Some members of the New Left became obsessed with the place of the prison in larger political struggles, according to Cummins.[109] The New Left began to idealize prisoners and started "thinking convicts, all convicts, were their soulmates and could be their leaders."[110] Cummins contends that the radical left was guilty of uncritical crime fetishism as it embraced the "deviant convict hero," seeing him as a new model for the revolution.[111]

The unity strikes in San Quentin in 1968 and the 1970 rebellion at California's Folsom prison, in which nearly 2,400 prisoners refused to leave their cells or contribute to the running of the prison for nineteen days, were dramatic expressions of the new interracial and political foundations of the emerging prison movement. The prisoners at Folsom issued thirty-one demands, many of them explicitly political but not necessarily radical.[112] The Folsom manifesto became a model for prisoner uprisings across the country.[113] Studies suggest, however, that even at the height of the movement "only a very small minority of prisoners were committed to radical political activities."[114] An examination of the manifestos issued by prisoners at Folsom, Attica, and elsewhere bolster this point, as does a 1971–73 survey of prisoners in maximum-security institutions in New York.[115] The Folsom demands were primarily concerned with practical political, economic, and legal issues – like the right to due process at parole and other hearings; better health and medical services; adequate facilities and opportunities to receive visitors; an end to tear-gassing prisoners locked in their cells; the abolition of indeterminate sentences; and the establishment of workers' compensation for prisoners injured on the job. The Attica manifesto begins with a denunciation of the prison system as the "authoritative fangs of cowards in power." But the twenty-seven demands that follow, which are modeled on the Folsom manifesto, are far from revolutionary.[116]

The San Quentin and Folsom uprisings had significant outside support and depended on interracial coalitions within. In their wake, prisoners across the country "began redefining their legal and social status, adopting political ideologies, and becoming involved in various forms of political activities."[117] The California uprisings reverberated so powerfully throughout the country's prison system because of additional factors, including the transfer of prisoners between correctional facilities, established contacts with outside organizers, and intense coverage in the popular media and the underground prison press.[118] These uprisings and the prison writings of people like George Jackson, sentenced in 1960 to an indeterminate term of one-year-to-life after pleading guilty to stealing $70 from a gasoline station, helped to awaken the political consciousness of black, Latino, and even white prisoners.[119] Prisoners set up their own elaborate alternative education systems (complete with a formal "education department" that issued educational guidelines) and underground reading groups. Left-leaning political books loaned free of charge became the main reading matter of many prisoners who could not afford the standard rental fee of one pack of cigarettes for other types of books from private lending libraries.[120] Many black and Latino prisoners began to regard their imprisonment as primarily an expression of racial, ethnic, and economic oppression on the part of the powerful.[121]

The public's perception of the prisoners' movement at the time was forged by the actions and writings of a "few committed convict revolutionaries," such as Cleaver, Jackson, and Angela Davis.[122] The legal trials and tribulations of Davis, charged with crimes relating to an attempt to free three San Quentin prisoners, and of Jackson and the other "Soledad Brothers" accused of killing a prison guard in 1970, became national and international sensations. Jackson's death under disputed circumstances in August 1971 during an alleged escape attempt further galvanized prisoners across the country. It helped spur the infamous September 1971 uprising at New York's Attica prison, in which ten hostages and twenty-nine prisoners were killed when the state retook the prison in a massive show of force.[123]

Even in the aftermath of the Attica bloodshed, public sympathy for prisoners was considerable. The Attica uprising prompted an outpouring of public and scholarly interest in how to make prisons more humane and in how to reduce the prison population.[124] Several major conferences on the criminal justice system called for reducing the prison population in their final reports.[125] Norman Carlson, director of the Federal Bureau of Prisons, declared at the time: "I am even more convinced that the long-run effect of Attica will be a positive step forward for prison reform."[126] The N.Y. State Special Commission on Attica, better known as the McKay Commission, noted the enormous problems associated with racism in the criminal justice system and concluded: "The problem of Attica will never be solved if we focus only on prisons themselves and ignore what the prisoners have gone through before they arrive at Attica."[127] In the wake of the Attica uprising, the ACLU's National Prison Project was formed.[128] Public opinion seemed to be on the side of prisoners, not the authorities.[129] A number of national advisory commissions called for a moratorium on prison construction, including the National Council on Crime and Delinquency and the National Advisory Commission on Criminal Justice Standards and Goals. The Unitarian Universalist Service Committee created the National Moratorium on Prison Construction at the instigation of the American Friends Service Committee.[130] These demands for a moratorium were largely ignored.[131] Despite this outpouring of public sympathy, just two years after Attica the national incarceration rate began its long march upwards, a march that has continued unabated for more than three decades now.

Cummins blames the revolutionary public image of the prisoners' movement for its rapid demise in the 1970s. He and others argue that the
left's romantic vision of prisoners and their revolutionary potential was
costly. It divided the prisoners' movement irreparably between reformers
and revolutionaries.[132] This romantic revolutionary vision became closely
identified in the public's mind with the urban terrorism and political
gangsterism of groups like the Weathermen, the Black Panthers, and the
Symbionese Liberation Army. The public responded to this "loco terrorism" by recoiling from prisoners and the left by the mid-1970s, thus creating an important vacuum that the right successfully filled with its law-and-
order campaign.[133] This gave prison administrators great leeway to crush
prisoners' political activity by terminating education programs, by placing greater restrictions on reading materials (even "disappearing" whole
prison libraries), by intensifying the surveillance of prisoners (including
developing clandestine counterintelligence operations in prisons), by creating more maximum-security prisons and special housing units to seg-
regate, isolate, and discipline prisoners, and by abolishing most prison
organizations.[134]

Cummins convincingly demonstrates how the demise of the prisoners'
movement created an important vacuum for the law-and-order movement to step into. He attributes much of the blame for this outcome to
the excesses of the New Left and its revolutionary romanticism. But it is
important to consider other features of the political and institutional context that allowed a revolutionary prison movement to emerge in the United
States that was unlike leftist upsurges elsewhere on behalf of prisoners
and that permitted the state and prison administrators to crush prison
activism behind bars and beyond the prison gates so decisively. This is an
exceptional outcome that had important implications for the subsequent
emergence of the carceral state.

Prisoners, Victims, and the Carceral State

The politics of prisons became an integral feature of national politics for
two intertwined reasons peculiar to the United States: race and the state.
First, for all the talk of a weak state, the U.S. state has a long and deep
history centered around reengineering the prison. Pockets of the prison
system were strongly committed to the rehabilitative ideal. As a consequence, experts and new ideas streamed into prisons, courtesy of the state,
helping to politicize life behind bars and pulling aside the iron curtain that
had shrouded prisons from the public up until that time. In the postwar
years, the government was actively involved in desegregating prisons. This
contributed to politicizing prisoners around race and other issues, setting
the stage for the emergence of the tightly knit, highly disciplined Nation of
Islam. The Black Muslims challenged the prison culture of "do your own

time." They also introduced the idea of prisoners as victims of the system rather than as transgressors of the system. Once the Black Muslims sought some salvation through court challenges, they were aided and abetted by the existence of a potent civil rights movement that had established important precedents for using the courts to push the state to enter policy areas that had previously been off limits.

Prisons in the United States became more transparent and "known" to the public because the court cases forced the iron curtain to part, at least for a time. Prior to the mid-1960s, prison officials were able to keep their operations hidden behind bars. People in prison who tried to inform the public were harshly punished or discredited.[135] The civil rights movement, with its focus initially on the racial transgressions in the South, primed the public to take a hard (and sympathetic) look first at penal farms in the South, and then at correctional facilities elsewhere. The movement also provided important legal and other resources for the prisoners' rights movement that emboldened it. The racially polarized and charged atmosphere in which these developments took place in the United States was a potent one for creating national and international figures identified with racial struggles, like Martin Luther King, Malcolm X, Eldridge Cleaver, Bobby Seale, Angela Davis, and Huey Newton. Prominent imprisoned blacks embraced the association between race and prison. As Etheridge Knight said in his preface to a collection of writings by black prisoners: "[T]he whole experience of the black man in America can be summed up in one word: prison."[136] Victimhood was a central theme of *The Autobiography of Malcolm X* and other prison writings that became best-sellers. This view of offender-as-victim in popular prison writings was reinforced by new developments in criminological theory, in particular the contributions of the then-emerging field of critical criminology. A central premise of critical criminology is that deviance is not necessarily a quality inherent in any particular behavior or person, but rather depends on how society chooses to define its rules and rule-breaking.[137]

This helps explain why the notion of victimhood became such a politically charged issue in the U.S. case. Elsewhere, a movement for victims could develop without first needing to wrest control of the idea of being a victim back from prisoners, many of whom were black, and their advocates. Because race was such a defining feature of the politics of this period in the United States, certain prisoners and former prisoners became towering public figures unlike anywhere else. They became national and international heroes or outlaws, depending on one's point of view, who staked an important part of their identity on a claim of victimhood, as exemplified by their time in prison. This greatly reduced the maneuverability of the state to engineer a quiet accommodation with the emerging victims-of-crime movement, as happened in Britain, that would not result in pitting victims of crime against offenders.[138]

The Prisoners' Movement in Britain

While Britain had its own sizable share of penal unrest from the 1960s onward, prisons impinged on the public and political psyches in different ways. The state was better situated to maintain control over both the prisons and the public debate surrounding the disturbances and the new prison activism. Compared to the prisoners' rights movement in the United States, the British movement was far more tentative and isolated. It had shallower roots inside prisons and within the wider public. Because the movement was weaker in Britain, and the British state was more coherent in important respects, the latter did not lose control of the public debate over penal policy and therefore did not have to reclaim it.

The prisoners' movement in Britain succeeded in exposing and publicizing some of the dire, abusive conditions in British prisons. But it did not dramatically alter the public's view of the relationship between prisons, offenders, and victims. As such, the prisoners' movement in Britain did not help to drive a wedge between victims of crime and offenders that a nascent conservative law-and-order movement could exploit. It also did not rupture the relatively cohesive set of state and other political elites who had long guided prison policy and kept it relatively insulated from the public. In short, it did not create highly favorable preconditions for policies of mass imprisonment.

Several fundamental political and institutional differences explain this outcome: the relative insignificance of race and ethnicity, until recently, as factors in British penal affairs or national politics; the presence of more established and entrenched prison reform groups with close ties to the government, notably the Howard League and the National Association for the Care and Rehabilitation of Offenders (NACRO); the presence of a nationally centralized prison system organized along paramilitary lines and staffed by highly organized and militant union members; the inaccessibility and unresponsiveness of the British courts to rights claims; and, related to that, the notorious secrecy surrounding what goes on in British prisons.

Since the 1960s, British prisons have had less unrest and less violent unrest than prisons in the United States.[139] Nonetheless, the unrest in British prisons has been considerable, especially when compared to other Western countries. Except for the Parkhurst riot in 1969, disturbances in British prisons were relatively infrequent until 1972, when a major wave of rooftop demonstrations struck the prison system. Subsequently, Hull (1976), Gartree (1978), and Albany (1983) erupted in large-scale riots. From the mid-1980s to early 1990s, Britain had more prison riots than any other European country. In April 1990, Strangeways prison in Manchester exploded. The Strangeways riot, which lasted twenty-five days and destroyed the prison, was the longest and most serious riot in

British history. It sparked major demonstrations elsewhere in the British prison system.[140]

The British disturbances began at roughly the same time that American prisons exploded in the late 1960s, but they occurred and unfolded in a markedly different political context. U.S. prisons had been impinging on the public consciousness for nearly a decade before San Quentin, Folsom, and Attica became household names. State efforts to desegregate prisons in the 1940s and 1950s, the execution of Caryl Chessman, the rise of the Black Muslims, the string of court cases expanding the rights of prisoners, and the activities of the civil rights movement had intensely focused national attention on prisons for more than a decade before U.S. prisons were rocked by the radical prison movement. The string of disturbances that began in San Quentin in 1967–68 and spread around the country over the next few years riveted national attention on prisons in a country that had become accustomed to viewing what happened in prisons as integral to the larger political fabric, and not as a world apart.

While the prisoners' movement in Britain raised public awareness about prisons in pockets of Britain, it did not spur the type of wide-scale public discussion of penal issues that occurred in the United States. Prisons entered the public mind in a starkly different context in Britain. The prisoners who became household names were not political figures like Malcolm X, George Jackson, and Eldridge Cleaver, but notorious criminals who had engineered dramatic escapes from prison. In 1964, Charles Wilson, serving a thirty-year sentence for his part in the Great Train Robbery, was freed by a break-in. The following year, Ronald Biggs, another veteran of the infamous mail train heist, escaped from an exercise yard in a carefully planned operation. Shortly thereafter, the master spy George Blake, who was serving a forty-year sentence, escaped, as did Frank Mitchell, dubbed the "mad axeman of Dartmoor." This slew of escapes by such high-profile criminals riveted national attention on prison security issues. The government responded by appointing Earl Montbatten, the Queen's cousin, to head a commission to investigate penal security problems.[141]

Mike Fitzgerald credits the Montbatten Commission with halting the treatment trend in Britain and with fostering "an obsession with physical security and overt control."[142] The main recommendation of the 1966 Montbatten report was to build one high-security fortress for the riskiest prisoners. That recommendation was not implemented. A second commission, established in February 1967 and headed by Leon Radzinowicz, a professor of criminology at Cambridge University, proposed dispersing high-risk prisoners in a number of specially constructed, high-tech institutions. In the wake of these two commissions, security was intensified throughout the British prison system. The number of maximum-security places dramatically increased, as did the number of prison officers. Enforcement of rules – even petty ones – tightened up as a regime of "electronic coffins" settled over the British penal system.[143]

This security clampdown prompted the 1969 Parkhurst riot and the string of disturbances in 1972. Prisoners protested, but they did so without having first been primed for organized politics. In the United States, the state's efforts to desegregate prisons and the subsequent activities of the Black Muslims, civil rights movement, and radical prison movement had fostered a wider political consciousness among U.S. prisoners that was largely absent among British prisoners. In Britain, prisoners' explanations for the unrest "focused on the alienation and brutality engendered by the unaccountable regime."[144] But British prisoners were poorly situated to press this charge because they did not have a larger compelling political context in which to insert this claim. Furthermore, conditions in British prisons generally remained hidden behind the iron curtain, and organized support within and without was minimal. As a consequence, while these disturbances eventually provoked a sense of crisis about prisons in Britain by the 1980s, the state was able to define the terms of the debate about penal policy. Its counterclaim that the unrest was largely the result of a few "bad apples" and malcontents who had subverted the prison population, rather than a symptom of more fundamental problems within the penal system, or of society more broadly, was quite persuasive for a considerable time.[145] The protests did not fundamentally disrupt the elite consensus regarding penal policy. The streams of prison activism remained politically isolated and were not associated with, and buoyed by, other powerful political currents and movements.

While two new organizations sprung up in the early 1970s to challenge the established penal reform lobby, they had relatively shallow political and organizational roots. Radical Alternatives to Prison (RAP) was founded in 1970. Two years later, Preservation of the Rights of Prisoners (PROP) was formed. These two groups, which differed significantly from one another, provided important support to protesting prisoners for a time. RAP challenged the legitimacy of criminal law, denouncing it as a tool of the socially and economically powerful. In the early 1970s it evolved from being a highly heterogeneous group to a smaller, more radical group that sought to abolish prisons and establish viable alternatives like community service.[146] In 1972, PROP "was instrumental in coordinating the 130 demonstrations that took place in over 40 British prisons" and in organizing a national strike in August that involved thousands of prisoners in dozens of institutions.[147] This wave of British protests was more akin to the U.S. prison protests of the late 1920s and early 1930s, which were aimed almost exclusively at existing prison conditions. The British protesters and their outside supporters did not challenge the wider understandings and legitimacy of prisons or connect their struggles to the struggles of other oppressed groups on the outside.[148]

There are several reasons why. First, the U.S. prisoners' movement had a political architecture that was without parallel in Britain because of the prior activities of the conscientious objectors, the Nation of Islam, the civil rights movement, and the radical organizations associated with the New Left and the black power movement. Over the years the activities of these groups helped destroy some of the barriers to political consciousness and organized political activity among U.S. prisoners. Moreover, their emphasis on the common situation of people in prison and on the importance of collective action helped neutralize the "treatment ideology" and notions about individual pathology that permeated U.S. prisons.[149] These groups demonstrated the importance of collective action inside, supported by organized groups outside. Furthermore, race was an important bridge that connected prisoners on the inside to politics on the outside in the U.S. case.

By contrast, the radical prisoners' movement in Britain did not garner wider public involvement. While PROP was able to pull off some important demonstrations within prisons, it did not have deep, sustained support on the outside. In contrast to the enormous public support for protests at San Quentin and Folsom, PROP had trouble mustering even a couple of dozen people to hold simultaneous demonstrations on the outside, according to Mike Fitzgerald, who was closely associated with the formation and development of PROP.[150] Few people on the outside made a firm commitment to PROP. While many radical criminologists backed the idea of PROP, only a handful became personally involved.[151]

RAP viewed PROP as more of a reformist organization, while the Home Office "was inclined in the early days at least to tar both groups with the same radical and disruptive brush."[152] The Home Office could do so without appearing completely intransigent (and thus enhancing the legitimacy of these groups and their complaints) because of the existence of the Howard League for Penal Reform, the long-established elite penal reform organization with close ties to the government. The Howard League had emerged as the preeminent force in penal reform by the 1930s. Over the decades it played a pivotal role in major penal reforms, like efforts to abolish the death penalty. While technically a voluntary group, it counted among its ranks magistrates, probation officers, social workers, and other middle-class professionals.[153] A tight organization with an established history of being led by elite reformers like Margery Fry with high-level social and political connections, the Howard League nonetheless successfully cultivated the impression that it was the voice of the public on penal matters.[154] The Howard League came under intense criticism in the late 1960s and 1970s for its "old methods of Establishment diplomacy."[155] It also was criticized for other shortcomings, like its failure to anticipate new trends in alternatives to imprisonment and its reluctance to oppose laws criminalizing victimless crimes like homosexuality.[156] Nonetheless, the Howard League still succeeded in positioning itself as the voice of reasonable reform and the voice of the public.

The Howard League provided the Home Office with a progressive veneer that made it appear responsive to demands for reform. This helped to marginalize RAP and PROP and make their demands appear more extreme.[157] For example, the Howard League criticized RAP for opposing all prison reforms, arguing that even if the main long-term goal was to abolish all prisons, it was important to alleviate the suffering of those currently incarcerated.[158] The government's close relationship with NACRO, which was discussed in Chapter 4, furthered bolstered the Home Office's reformist credentials and insulated it from charges that it was being intransigent on pressing penal issues. NACRO could be highly critical of the government, but within significant limits.[159]

Prisoners were not highly organized and politicized in Britain, but guards were. The Prison Officers' Association was notable for its tightly knit, quasi-military culture.[160] The POA engineered a crackdown on PROP in short order through its "Get Tough" campaign in August 1972 and other retaliatory actions over the years.[161] During the 1976 unrest at Hull, there were really two riots – one by the prisoners and another by retaliating guards, which PROP played an important part in documenting and exposing. While protesting prisoners in the United States certainly had to contend with serious violence from retaliating guards, this violence was not organized on the scale seen in Britain. Militant prison guards were quite successful at wresting the initiative from PROP.[162] The POA's high degree of solidarity acted as a significant check on any wider political ambitions PROP might aspire to. The prisoner group had enough trouble just maintaining a skeletal organization behind bars and documenting the escalating violence and brutality that prisoners were being subjected to by disgruntled guards. By the mid-to-late-1970s, the prison staff had become a central issue, perhaps *the* central issue, for the Home Office. Indeed, "open hostilities, or even anarchy" characterized the relationship between prison administrators and prison staff.[163] The Home Office was constantly battling the POA over staffing levels, pay, work conditions, and overtime.[164]

At the time of the prison uprisings in Britain, prisons remained a largely unknown quantity. The public, the press, and the courts had not been prying them open bit by bit for years, and the British state remained solidly committed to maintaining the iron curtain on what happened in prisons. In the U.S. case, the courts helped to pry open prisons and subject them to public and media scrutiny. This set an important context for the disturbances of the late 1960s and early 1970s. In the British case, inmates who attempted to use the courts to challenge prison conditions were routinely rebuffed.[165] Civil liberties groups in Britain lamented the absence of positive rights for prisoners, especially their limited options to challenge abysmal prison conditions, like damp and overcrowded cells and the absence of minimally acceptable standards of confinement.[166]

Prisons in England and Wales are primarily governed by the Prison Act of 1952.[167] Neither the 1952 act nor the rules it spawned contains a comprehensive statement on rights. While these measures elaborate some basic rules, for example regarding letters and visits, they do not create rights that are readily enforceable through the legal system.[168] British prisoners did not have anything comparable to the Eighth Amendment to the U.S. Constitution, which bans cruel and unusual punishment, or the Fourteenth Amendment's guarantee of due process, on which to mount challenges to the conditions of their confinement. British prisoners did not even have a right to see the Prison Rules. The Home Office gave them a "summary of those parts thought to be applicable to them."[169]

For a long time, the Prison Rules did not even permit prisoners to consult with a lawyer, much less initiate proceedings, without authorization from the home secretary, even if the Home Office was the target of the complaint.[170] In effect, prisoners had no right of access to a lawyer. The home secretary did not modify this practice until the early 1980s, two decades after prisoners in the United States had begun using the courts successfully to establish certain rights. The Home Office retreated somewhat because it was roundly condemned in a series of judgments by the European Court of Human Rights (ECHR) in Strasbourg, beginning with the *Golder* decision in 1975, and because of a couple of subsequent domestic court decisions.[171] The European Court also condemned the practice of blanket censorship as inconsistent with the European Convention on Human Rights.[172]

The convention was drafted in 1949–50 and came into force in September 1953. It was modeled on the Universal Declaration of Human Rights proclaimed by the United Nations in 1948, but it had one important difference – it included some means of enforcement. Britain played a major role in drawing up the convention, but it had resisted granting British citizens and organizations the individual right to petition the European Commission of Human Rights for redress of grievances under the convention. Furthermore, it opposed the creation of the European Court of Human Rights in 1959. Over the years it also resisted incorporation of the convention into domestic law, which would make its provisions directly enforceable in the British courts.[173] Under pressure from the Foreign Office and some members of Parliament, Britain indicated its willingness in 1966 to accept on a trial, three-year basis the right of individual petition and the compulsory jurisdiction of the European Court of Human Rights.[174] In the late 1960s, civil rights groups began to turn increasingly to the European Commission and the European Court for redress after their efforts at home were rebuffed.[175] Because appealing to the Commission and the Court was a relatively new and cumbersome process, the shift in British policy did not immediately open the floodgates to petitions on behalf of British prisoners and offenders, though it did result in some landmark decisions regarding prisoners' rights in Britain, which the Home Office honored in letter but not always in spirit.[176]

Prisons were also a lesser-known quantity in Britain because of the extreme centralization and extreme culture of secrecy of the prison system.[177] As one prisoner put it, borrowing from Oscar Wilde, "prison walls are built not to keep prisoners in but prying eyes out."[178] The Prison Act of 1877, which was strongly opposed by local governments, put every prison under the auspices of the central government and made the English prison service the second most centralized of all public services after the armed services.[179] When prisons were still under the control of local justices prior to the 1877 act, government inspectors compiled extensive reports documenting how prisons were maladministered. When control of all prisons was transferred to the central government, such criticism diminished.[180]

The central government in Britain maintained tight control over information about the day-to-day operations of the prison system.[181] It was aided by an obliging Official Secrets Act. Until passage of Britain's landmark Freedom of Information Act, which took effect on January 1, 2005, there was "no public right to knowledge about the affairs of government," and civil servants were "bound by law to silence about their activities."[182] The Official Secrets Act effectively prevented past and present employees from publicly discussing prison matters by putting them at risk of being criminally charged.[183] For those working in the prison service, it was an "express condition of employment" that they not talk to the press.[184] Until the 1970s, the Home Office largely ignored or denied the existence of prison riots and neglected to mention the upheavals in its annual reports and other official publications.[185] When British officials did begin to acknowledge riots in the early 1970s, they attempted to explain them away by focusing on the alleged pathology of the participating prisoners. In keeping with its entrenched habit of official reticence, the government also virtually denied the existence of PROP.[186] The British Home Office was not only unresponsive to requests for information on riots, but also for other basic information. For example, until the mid-1980s it was difficult to obtain basic data from the government, such as the number of blacks in British prisons.[187]

While British prisons were widely perceived to be in crisis in the late 1970s and 1980s, the state still maintained tight control over the public debate about prisons. The elite consensus regarding penal policy came under stress but did not rupture, even in the face of escalating prison unrest and the urban riots that convulsed Brixton, Liverpool, Birmingham, and other British cities in the mid-1980s and that predominantly involved black youths. These riots sparked a debate about the relationship between race and crime but did not rupture the elite consensus on criminal justice policy so as to create an opening for a conservative penal backlash.[188]

The May Commission set up by the Home Office acknowledged in its 1979 report that prison should be used as little as possible and that reducing the prison population should be a major goal of penal policy. At the same time, it gave credence to the reports of abhorrent prison conditions that PROP and others had documented. It called for a massive prison-building program to rocket British prisons from the Middle Ages to the modern age by ending practices like enforced cell sharing in centuries-old facilities that lacked modern plumbing and that relied on the daily "slopping out" of body wastes by prisoners.[189] Three years later, Britain embarked on what was billed as its biggest prison-building boom in about a century. It sought to construct about two dozen new facilities and yet engineer a reduction in the prison population. When the hoped-for drop in the prison population did not occur, elites redoubled their efforts to lower the incarceration rates, as discussed in Chapter 4, which resulted in some significant decreases in the prison population for a time.

Rioting by prisoners did not provoke powerful and widespread calls for a more punitive regime. Indeed, the riots sparked considerable public sympathy. In response to the 1986 prison riots, the hawkish *Daily Mail* published an article calling for sending fewer people to prison and for improvements in prison conditions.[190] After the 1990 Strangeways disturbances, *The Times* of London declared: "There is no bigger disgrace to Britain than its prisons."[191] The Strangeways riot prompted an unprecedented independent inquiry led by Lord Justice Woolf that "expanded to include a review of the prison system as a whole."[192] The report provided voluntary organizations, whose independence and basic role in Britain had been under attack, a much-needed boost to their legitimacy and to their campaign to reduce the prison population.[193] The Woolf report was generally sympathetic to many of the complaints prisoners had been raising. In a radical departure from previous reports, it rejected superficial, cosmetic changes, and it was sensitive to the broader social context in which prisons are located.[194] It insisted on national accreditation standards for all aspects of the prison regime and a decreased reliance on prisons to punish.[195] The Woolf report was an important impetus for the 1991 White Paper that resulted in the Criminal Justice Act of 1991.[196] While the White Paper and the 1991 act diluted some of the Woolf recommendations, they can hardly be read as blueprints for the creation of a carceral state in Britain.[197]

The nascent law-and-order movement in Britain was poorly situated to exploit the crisis in prisons and shift penal policy in a more punitive direction. This was partly due to how the victims issue had developed and also to certain institutional factors that helped to maintain an insulated elite consensus. The prisoners' movement was one additional and related factor. It did not bequeath to Britain national and international political celebrities who had served time and who could make powerful claims of victimhood rooted in charges of racial, ethnic, and economic oppression that would make it difficult for the state to broker and maintain a détente between offenders and crime victims. Furthermore, prisons entered the public mind first and foremost as a security issue in the late 1960s and early 1970s and not as a lightning rod for other political causes. A number of critical criminologists in Britain were pressing the point about the highly political nature of lawbreaking, but their arguments did not resonate the way they did in the United States. In the U.S. case, Jackson, Cleaver, and others were popularizing such ideas through their best-selling prison writings, through the lives they led, and by their imprisonment. For all these reasons, the prisoners' movement in Britain did not open up political space for a conservative backlash of a particular cast. While Britain responded to the penal unrest with a prison-building binge, this boom took place in the context of sustained elite anxiety about the escalating prison population, especially its contribution to the fiscal crisis of the state, which was discussed in Chapter 4. It resulted in various efforts to reduce the prison population in Britain, most notably passage of the Criminal Justice Act of 1991, the high point of the efforts to contain the carceral state in Britain.[198] In this process, civil servants engaged the public, but selectively, through voluntary pressure groups with close ties to the state.

In short, the radical prison movement in Britain was far more peripheral to popular politics than was the prisoners' movement in the United States.[199] While the movement established some key political connections, notably with radical feminists (see Chapters 5 and 6), prisons and penal unrest never became a defining issue for national politics in Britain. As a consequence, the British movement was more at liberty to develop and adapt to changed circumstances. Over time the prison movement insinuated itself into penal discussions at the elite level. In particular, it seriously engaged the Labor Party in the need to adopt a platform that reflected the growing consensus among the penal lobby's radicals and liberals.[200] That consensus was premised on the belief that expanding the prison system was not the solution for violence and that prisons needed to be held more accountable through reforms like legally enforceable minimal standards, the relaxation of censorship, and the creation of fairer internal procedures. The prison movement was instrumental in creating that new consensus, which outlasted organizations like RAP.[201]

Scandinavia and Prison Activism

The Scandinavian countries also faced an upsurge of prison unrest beginning in the mid-1960s. But, as in the British case, this unrest did not provide a significant opening for a conservative backlash for several reasons. First, Scandinavian prisons did not experience the same degree of violent unrest as did U.S. facilities. Offenders in Sweden are housed in relatively small prisons that hold a couple of hundred people at most, and that enjoy a high staff-to-prisoner ratio. The huge fortresses warehousing thousands of people that are so commonplace in the United States are unknown in Sweden.[202] Race was also a nonissue in the development of the prisoners' movement in Sweden. Because of the homogeneity of Swedish society, and thus of the prison staff and prison population, Swedish penal policy could develop without having to contend with the legacy of violence, oppression, and dissent that has characterized race relations in the United States.[203] Furthermore, Sweden did not make wide use of indeterminate sentences, which were an incendiary issue for U.S. prisoners.[204] Swedish offenders generally were eligible for parole after serving two-thirds of their sentence (if their sentence was longer than six months), and they took for granted that they had a definite release date.[205]

In 1966, KRUM, a national organization of prisoners, former prisoners, and professionals, many of them involved in corrections, was established in Sweden.[206] In keeping with Sweden's strong corporatist tradition, the authorities gave KRUM significant official recognition. It became an important forum for the development of penal policy but it also orchestrated penal protests, notably sitdown strikes. Members of KRUM could focus on broad questions of penal policy – such as how to resist the expansion of the prison system – because of considerable differences in the conditions of confinement in Sweden. Prisoners in Sweden did not need to mobilize to secure basic rights, for they retain all civil rights while incarcerated, including the right to vote. They were not subject to tight censorship of their mail and were able to maintain wide contacts with the outside through extensive use of furloughs and unsupervised visits in prison.[207]

Swedish offenders also had rights to redress from the government that have deep institutional and historical roots. Established in 1809 when the constitution was adopted, the Office of the Parliamentary Ombudsman gives Parliament authority to appoint a judicial ombudsman. This position has been an important avenue for addressing complaints lodged against the police, prosecutors, or corrections officials. Furthermore, Swedish prisoners have had more success establishing unions to represent their interests because of the greater power and wider acceptance of organized labor in Sweden.[208]

Over time KRUM's emphasis shifted from "criminal policy narrowly defined to a greater stress on political principles of a general kind."[209] For example, fighting "class society" was eventually added as an independent goal and placed ahead of goals related more directly to criminal justice policy. That said, penal policy and prisons never took center stage in the broader political life of Sweden the way they did for a time in the United States. Absent the racial issue, the rights issue, and the elevation of individual prisoners to national and international celebrities, prisons did not become an explosive national issue in Sweden. The country's corporatist tradition and the existence of a highly nationalized and centralized justice system in which all corrections operations are integrated into a central office (the National Prison and Probation Association) effectively channeled discussions about penal policy.[210] Unlike in the U.S. case, Sweden never experienced a significant rupture in the insulated elite consensus about prisons. In 1974, the Swedish Parliament approved the Correctional Treatment in Institutions Act. This act repudiated rehabilitation without providing an opening to crack down on offenders. The act called for interfering as little as possible with offenders and essentially acknowledged that confinement in a maximum-security facility was unlikely to bring about rehabilitation. It also acknowledged the enormous expense of maximum-security prisons and called for making the greatest use possible of cheaper alternatives like probation and local prisons for short-term confinement.[211] That act ushered in a significant but temporary drop in Sweden's prison population. In the 1980s, Sweden embraced more repressive penal policies, including tougher sentencing and a harsher regime behind bars. In the early 1990s, a center-right government was elected that had campaigned on tougher criminal justice policies.[212] While the overall system became more repressive, in the early 1990s the prison population was nearly identical to that of the early 1970s and remained one of the lowest in per capita terms in Europe.[213]

For some of the same reasons discussed in the Swedish case, penal policy did not become an explosive issue in Norway either. Norway's KROM never received the degree of official recognition that its Swedish counterpart KRUM did.[214] While pressures mounted to pursue more hard-line law-and-order policies, they did not result in a massive increase in incarceration, partly because of the particular political vitality of the prisoners' movement in Norway.[215]

Conclusion

In the U.S. case, the initial response to the unprecedented prison unrest of the late 1960s and early 1970s was a combination of repression and reform. Over time, reform yielded to repression. The U.S. prisoners' rights movement developed so as to facilitate a cleavage between victims and offenders that law-and-order conservatives were well poised to exploit. The reasons why are complex. This outcome is not simply the result of a public backlash prompted by a perception that the rights pendulum had swung too far in the direction of offenders and by growing fears of urban and prison unrest in the 1960s and 1970s. It also cannot be explained by simply pointing out that this is another instance of American exceptionalism rooted in the fact that the United States has an exceptional racial component to its political development that spawned a civil rights movement unlike any other, and then spawned urban and prison unrest and a conservative backlash unlike any other.

The U.S. prisoners' rights movement was distinctive on several accounts. It emerged earlier and had deeper roots inside prisons and in the wider society because of several important developments, including the rising proportion of blacks behind bars, the state's initial efforts to desegregate federal penal facilities, and the emergence of the Black Muslims as a formidable organization. The Nation of Islam and the civil rights movement pried open the courts, rendering them important arenas for prison activism. In the process, prisons were subjected to intense public scrutiny. The racially charged political atmosphere in which the prisoners' rights movement emerged provided an opportunity for race and imprisonment to become tightly connected issues. Imprisoned blacks and other minorities became national and international celebrities with large bases of support on the outside. With the help of the New Left, they made powerful and highly publicized claims that they were the true victims. They also promoted the idea that lawbreaking should be seen primarily as a political act aimed at a racially, economically, and politically repressive system.

The high-profile nature of the prisoners' rights issue and the claims of these activists helped foreclose any role for the state in brokering a détente between offenders, their sympathizers, and the emerging victims' movement. Indeed, these claims served to push the U.S. victims' movement in a more punitive direction, as women and other victims of violent crime sought to wrest the status of victim away from the black power movement and its allies in the New Left and elsewhere. This helps make comprehensible why the backlash against prison activism was so strident in the United States and why the state was so effective at decimating the movement once it sought to impose a lockdown on political activism behind bars. It also helps explain why the emerging conservative law-and-order movement was so well situated to shift the terms of the debate over penal policy in such a punitive direction.

Building more prisons in reaction to the disturbances of the 1960s only looks like a foreordained outcome now, decades after the fact. There could have been many different responses to the racial and other political unrest of the 1960s, like expanding the welfare state rather than expanding the carceral state. Political unrest by marginalized populations or radical groups does not necessarily result in the construction of a more authoritarian state heavily reliant on prisons, or to some other form of increased social control. The German case is a good example. West Germany enacted draconian emergency legislation in the early 1970s to tackle the real and perceived threat of political armed struggle posed by the Baader Meinhof Gang and other radical guerilla groups. Germany was widely criticized for vastly extending the state's policing and carceral powers to deal with political dissent and violent political unrest. Paradoxically, over the course of the next decade Germany was heralded for enacting model legislation designed to protect the rights of prisoners (the Prison Act of 1977) and for undertaking a major decarceration that drastically reduced its prison population.[216] The prison riots in Germany and France in the late 1960s and early 1970s had starkly different consequences than in the United States. While both countries introduced some harsher sanctions, the general thrust of prison reform was toward milder punishments and better treatment of prisoners.[217]

Singling out the racial and other political unrest of the 1960s and 1970s and the backlash they engendered to explain the emergence of the carceral state paints this era with too broad a brush. It is important to look more closely at the early origins and development of prison activism to explain why political elites and segments of the state have been so successful at creating, imposing, and legitimating a new racial and ethnic ordering premised on a vast expansion of the carceral state in the U.S. case. While the existence of a racial hierarchy may be a constant in American political development, the way it is manifested and sustained can vary significantly over time, as can the negative consequences of such a hierarchy.[218] To begin to undo the carceral state, it is necessary to understand the complex political architecture that created it in the first place, of which prison activism was one important component. Another major piece of that architecture is the movement to abolish the death penalty, to which we now turn.

8 CAPITAL PUNISHMENT, THE COURTS, AND THE EARLY ORIGINS OF THE CARCERAL STATE, 1920S–1960S

> "Gentlemen, I wish you all good luck. I believe I am going to a good place, and I am ready to go. I want only to say that a great deal has been said about me that is untrue. I am bad enough. It is cruel to make me out worse."
>
> – William Francis Kemmler[1]

B EGINNING with the 1966 gubernatorial races of Ronald Reagan in California and Claude Kirk, Jr., in Florida, the death penalty reemerged over the next two decades to become a central issue in key electoral contests.[2] By the 1990s, leading candidates for national or statewide office rarely opposed capital punishment. Politicians regularly boasted about their willingness and indeed eagerness to carry out executions.[3] In his 1990 reelection bid, Governor Bob Martinez (R-Fla.) proclaimed in his television ads: "I have now signed some 90 death warrants in the state of Florida." His commercials ended with a picture of a smiling Ted Bundy, the serial killer whose January 1989 execution after a decade on death row was memorialized by cheering crowds and printed T-shirts with a recipe for "Fried Bundy."[4] During the 1992 presidential primaries, Governor Bill Clinton made a point of flying back to Arkansas to sign the death warrant of Rickey Ray Rector, who had turned a gun on himself after killing a police officer in a robbery gone awry and ended up severely mentally handicapped.[5] Running for governor of California in 1998, Democrat Gray Davis cited repressive Singapore as a model for capital punishment. "You can't punish people enough as far as I'm concerned," he declared.[6] In that same spirit, Attorney General Bob Butterworth warned after a series of botched executions in Florida's electric chair, most notoriously the macabre 1997 death of Pedro Medina, whose head burst into flames: "People who wish to commit murder better not do it in the state of Florida, because we may have a problem with our electric chair."[7]

The central place capital punishment once again assumed in American politics and the enthusiasm politicians and public officials displayed for the ultimate penalty was a marked change from the 1950s and much of the 1960s. At that time, elected officials and their political rivals generally did not view opposition to the death penalty as a major political liability. Indeed, some of them became outspoken foes of capital punishment. Executions were resumed, first hesitantly in the 1970s after a decade-long moratorium, and then with matter-of-fact regularity, as politicians and public officials began to express openly their enthusiasm for executing their own citizens, including young offenders under the age of eighteen (something done almost nowhere else in the world) and the mentally retarded.[8]

This chapter and the next examine the contentious politics surrounding efforts to abolish and reinstate the death penalty in the United States. They trace how the United States went from being one of the world's leading executioners, to imposing a de facto moratorium on capital punishment in 1967, to resuming executions a decade later and becoming the last outpost for capital punishment in the West.[9] My analysis focuses on the political and legal framing of capital punishment – specifically, why and how it got framed in ways that facilitated the construction of the carceral state in the United States but not elsewhere.

The battle against capital punishment had enormous spillover effects. The death penalty became more than just a convenient symbol of one's commitment to hard-line penal policies. Rather, it developed so as to make the passions of the public a central and legitimate issue in the making of penal policy. This drew public attention away from extensive research showing that the death penalty has no significant deterrent effect, and it bolstered the more general contention that harsher penalties serve as a meaningful deterrent for all types of crime. It also deflected attention away from the broader question of what the limits are, if any, on the state's power to punish and kill, which was central to discussions of capital punishment and penal policy in Europe.

The legal disputes over capital punishment helped solidify a zero-sum view of victims and offenders in capital and noncapital cases that bolstered the consolidation of the conservative victims' rights movement. This is an exceptional outcome. As shown in the next chapter, Canada and Western Europe abolished the death penalty in the face of opinion polls showing strong, often massive, public support for it. Nonetheless, the end of capital punishment in Europe and Canada did not ignite a powerful countermovement that succeeded in bringing back executions in the name of defending victims and law and order.[10]

This exceptional outcome is only partially explained by the country's Southern inheritance. Because the South has consistently performed more executions than the rest of the nation as a whole, it is tempting to view the persistence of the death penalty and the ways it distorts penal policy as first and foremost a Southern – not a national – phenomenon, and as another example of how Southern exceptionalism is at the root of American exceptionalism. After all, the South was responsible for three out of every five executions between 1930 (the first year the federal government began collecting state-by-state data on executions) and 1964 (around the start of the major constitutional campaigns against capital punishment that led to the de facto moratorium on executions from 1967 to 1977).[11] Since the resumption of executions nearly three decades ago, the figures have become even more lopsided. Of the fifty-nine executions in 2004, fifty (or about 85 percent) were in the South or in border states.[12] Harris County, Tex., which includes the city of Houston, has carried out more executions and sentenced more people to death than all but one of the other forty-nine states.[13]

The preponderance of executions in the South bolsters the view that the region's brutal legacy of slavery, Jim Crow, and lynchings and its distinctive "culture of vengeance" explain why the death penalty lives on in the United States, defying the march toward abolition in other Western countries and much of the rest of the world.[14] Franklin Zimring suggests that capital punishment has tended to persist in those parts of the United States, generally in the South and Southwest, that have a long and established history of public lynchings.[15] In his view, lynchings were simultaneously an expression of the desire to maintain community control and intense local mistrust of state power. The death penalty, today carried out in the name of the victims of crime, not the state, serves a similar function, according to Zimring. In short, capital punishment as currently practiced in the United States is an updated expression of this deeply entrenched vigilante tradition.[16] This helps explain why the process of abolition could be "essentially uneventful" in Europe and the Commonwealth, while removal of the death penalty in the United States risks "leaving a hole in the culture" and thus is so fiercely resisted.[17]

Zimring may be correct about the broad cultural tendencies he identifies that are sustaining the death penalty in the South and that are in tension with other deep-seated traditions, most notably the tradition of due process. But as Barrington Moore suggests, cultural traditions do not persist on their own, but have to be recreated from one generation to the next, often at great cost.[18] While the overall tendency has been to hold fast to executions in the South as capital punishment loses its grip around much of the world, the death penalty has not remained a stagnant institution in the United States. Furthermore, much of the rest of the country has held on to capital punishment, despite a reluctance to actually carry out even a small number of the promised executions. Today the death penalty is legal in thirty-eight states and the other dozen are not immune to pressures to bring it back.[19] Under federal statutes, dozens of crimes are punishable by death. Public support for the death penalty, as measured by opinion polls, has been fairly comparable across regions, though the South tends to be the region *least* likely to support capital punishment.[20]

Certainly the South's legacy of slavery, Jim Crow, and lynchings set an important context for the resurrection and transformation of capital punishment in contemporary American politics. But the country's apartheid history is only the starting point for explaining how race mattered in the political development of capital punishment. This chapter and the next identify other important political and institutional factors that helped render the death penalty a key weapon in facilitating the politics of punitiveness and the expansion of the carceral state. They show how race got refracted through certain institutions at specific points in time – in particular, the courts and rights-based organizations. Most accounts of the courts and capital punishment focus on the legal strategies and landmark court decisions involving capital punishment in the 1960s and 1970s that brought about and then ended the decade-long moratorium on executions. But capital punishment was deeply lodged in the judicial process long before it became a national issue with the 1972 *Furman* decision and the 1976 *Gregg* decision that, respectively, suspended and reinstated the death penalty, and long before it became a cause célèbre among conservatives.

My analysis highlights some significant earlier developments, in particular the importance of the muted rights revolution that began in the United States in the late 1920s and set an important context for the subsequent development of capital punishment. The landmark decisions of the Warren Court expanding the rights of defendants and prisoners in the 1950s and 1960s have overshadowed this earlier revolution, which was pivotal to the political development of capital punishment and, ultimately, to the construction of the carceral state. It set important parameters and precedents for the public debate over the death penalty that opened up some major avenues to challenge capital punishment while foreclosing others. In short, capital punishment helped launch U.S. penal policy on a starkly different trajectory long before law-and-order politicians discovered the electoral votes to be harvested by promising to pull the switch early and often.

This chapter begins with a brief sketch of the early history of capital punishment in the United States. It then examines the institutional and political factors that account for the waning of executions from the 1930s to the early 1960s, prior to the emergence of the contemporary anti-death penalty movement. In particular, it focuses on the role of the courts and legal process in framing the political debate over capital punishment during these years. The chapter then examines the emergence and development of the anti-death penalty movement in the 1960s. Specifically, it looks at the strategies of the public interest groups that decided to challenge the constitutionality of capital punishment, and the response of the courts, politicians, public officials, and the proponents of capital punishment to that challenge. It shows how this struggle played out in ways that ultimately facilitated the expansion of the carceral state as capital punishment was resurrected and transformed.

Early Opposition to the Death Penalty

The death penalty has been a major undercurrent of American political development and has had an intimate connection with the prison for centuries. Capital punishment was intertwined with the invention of the penitentiary in the late eighteenth and early nineteenth centuries and with subsequent "penal reforms."[21] Periodically it has catapulted to the center of American politics and been "the subject of some of our most bitter debates," often during periods of wider political unrest.[22] Capital punishment was central to debates about state power and the establishment of the penitentiary during the founding (see Chapter 3). At that time, growing opposition to the death penalty fueled rising interest in building prisons, which were viewed as humanitarian, utilitarian alternatives to the gallows.[23] By the late eighteenth century, many of the states had overhauled their criminal codes so as to reduce the number of crimes punishable by death compared to the English penal code, which had greatly expanded the number of capital crimes under the Black Act and other measures in the eighteenth century.[24] This contraction of the death penalty "became a point of pride for Americans of the late eighteenth century."[25] That said, the colonies also created a huge number of capital statutes in the eighteenth century that only applied to blacks.[26] With the growth of slavery and the large plantation economy in the early decades of the new republic, the South further increased its number of capital crimes. Southern states created numerous capital statutes for offenses directly connected to slavery (for example, stealing and concealing slaves), and differentiated capital offenses based on the race of the offender and the race of the victim.[27]

Capital punishment became a central political issue once again beginning in the 1830s and 1840s as locally organized anti-gallows societies proliferated in the United States. These groups had close ties to the temperance and anti-slavery movements, and prominent opponents of slavery like Wendell Phillips and William Lloyd Garrison were outspoken foes of capital punishment. For a generation prior to the Civil War, the movement to abolish the death penalty "aroused violent debate over the ultimate source of justice."[28] During this period anti-death penalty sentiment was so pronounced that "European visitors were astonished by what the English novelist and naval officer Frederick Marryat called 'this aversion to capital punishment.'"[29] While the majority of the Northern states retained capital punishment, by 1860 all of them had reformed their penal codes so as to restrict the death penalty to murder and treason. Following the example set by Pennsylvania, many states also established various degrees for murder, which reduced the number of capital cases.[30] The high point of the anti-gallows movement in the antebellum years was 1846, when Michigan became the first English-speaking jurisdiction to abolish the death penalty for all crimes except treason, almost two decades before Portugal became the first European country to do so.[31] In the early 1850s, Rhode Island and Wisconsin eliminated the death penalty for all offenses, after which the anti-gallows movement began to wane with the distractions of the Mexican War, the intensifying struggle over slavery, and the coming of the Civil War.[32]

Anti-death penalty activism and sentiment lurched forward once again during the Progressive era, as the United States "retained its position in the forefront of the abolitionist movement."[33] In 1897, the U.S. Congress enacted legislation to reduce the number of federal crimes punishable by death. Over the next two decades, a record ten state legislatures abolished capital punishment. For every state that abolished the death penalty during the first two decades of the twentieth century, another two came close.[34] World War I stopped the anti-death-penalty movement in its tracks, much as the Civil War had done decades earlier. Concerns about maintaining political stability in the face of growing economic distress and fears that abolition had triggered a new spate of lynchings prompted eight states to reinstate the death penalty by the end of the 1930s.[35]

The Decline in Executions from the 1930s to the Early 1960s

After the bloodletting of the 1930s and 1940s, when the number of legally sanctioned executions reached record highs, the death penalty appeared to be dying out on its own without much political fanfare.[36] The annual number of executions fell from a high of 199 in 1935 to just 47 in 1962 and 21 in 1963.[37] This enormous drop occurred even though there was no widespread movement against the death penalty to speak of during this period. The one national organization dedicated to ending the death penalty, the American League to Abolish Capital Punishment founded in 1925, "barely survived the 1940s."[38] While public protests periodically erupted over specific cases, notably the 1953 executions of Julius and Ethel Rosenberg, these outbursts tended to focus on issues related to the relative guilt or innocence of particular offenders and did not challenge the fundamental constitutionality or morality of the death penalty.[39]

This precipitous drop in executions and the execution rate was a national phenomenon, though the pace and timing differed somewhat by region. It began in several populous North Central states in the mid-to-late-1930s and spread to the rest of the North by the early 1940s. Between the late 1940s and the early 1950s, the South experienced a massive drop in both the number of executions and the execution rate. For much of the next decade, the South continued to lead the nation in the annual number of executions, but its execution rate often was either lower than or reasonably comparable to much of the rest of the country.⁴⁰ Indeed, throughout the 1950s, the execution rates of the Northeast and the West exceeded those of the South. The rate in the North Central states consistently remained the nation's lowest.⁴¹

These figures arguably understate the South's dubious distinction as the nation's top executioner. They obviously are calculated based on the forty-plus states that had capital punishment on their books for at least some period between the 1930s and the 1960s. Notably, all of the states that were abolitionist for at least some time during this period were outside the South.⁴² Of the some two dozen jurisdictions that have abolished or partially abolished capital punishment (in many cases, only to have it reinstated) since Michigan led the way in 1846, only one, Tennessee, is in the South.⁴³ That said, it is important to keep in mind that the trend toward declining executions did reach belatedly deep into the South. Furthermore, some of the major death penalty states lay outside the South. Four of the top ten states that led the country in executions from the 1930s to the early 1960s were not in the South. In fact, New York State, today so identified with strong abolitionist sentiments, was a close second to Georgia in the total number of annual executions between the 1930s and the early 1960s.⁴⁴

This decline in the number of executions came about in the absence of a pronounced nationwide abolition movement and is not attributable to a significant increase in the number of abolitionist states.⁴⁵ Rather, it was primarily the consequence of broader changes in the political and institutional development of the legal system, which had important consequences for the subsequent political development of capital punishment. Notably, state and federal authorities assumed a larger role in governing the judicial system. This opened capital punishment up to greater legal and public scrutiny as local officials ceded control of the death penalty to state authorities.

Several specific developments were important in the evolution of capital punishment from being primarily a local, community responsibility to being a state one. The first was the move to end public executions (which typically were loud, unruly, festive spectacles that attracted thousands of spectators) and replace them with executions carried out in the relative privacy of jail yards. In the early 1830s, several states ended the practice of public executions.⁴⁶ By the start of the Civil War, every Northern state had done the same. State officials were prompted by concerns that the disruptive public executions were not having the desired deterrent effect, and that they posed serious challenges to government authority, especially when mobs of spectators became "outraged at bungled hangings and last minute reprieves."⁴⁷ Furthermore, the emerging middle class had begun to view these "spectacles of suffering" as an affront to their "genteel sensibility."[48] In the nineteenth century the tabloid press covered public executions in great detail, especially grisly mishaps on the gallows.[49] These accounts focused on the condemned and seldom discussed the plight of the victim and his or her family members in any great detail.[50] Government officials considered press coverage of executions to be such a threat to their authority that some of them moved to impose "gag" laws on journalists.[51]

By the turn of the twentieth century, several Southern states had ended public executions as well. In 1938, Kentucky became the last state to ban them.[52] As executions increasingly took place in the jail yard rather than in the public square, public participation in capital punishment did not end. It merely shifted from the execution phase to the trial phase. As discussed in Chapter 9, once executions moved inside the prison gates, audience attention shifted to the courtroom, which became the main site for public participation in capital punishment and eventually provided a stage to air victims' grievances and grief.

The move to private executions was followed by a related development. Starting in earnest in the 1890s, states "began to require that executions be performed under state rather than local authority, usually at a state facility."[53] From the 1890s to the 1920s, the total number of executions remained reasonably constant, but the proportion of state-imposed executions rose steeply as capital punishment was "delocalized," or converted from local to state authority.[54] The trend started in the North and spread to the West and the South, where there was a concerted move toward state-imposed capital punishment in the 1910s and 1920s.[55]

As new, more sophisticated technologies replaced the hangman and the public gallows, executions were transferred to designated central facilities, usually state-run penitentiaries. After introduction of the electric chair in New York State in 1890, the number of executions in the United States doubled over the next three decades.[56] Ironically, electrocutions carried out in state prisons became the preferred way of death during the Progressive era, a time of renewed interest in the rehabilitative promise of incarceration and in new kinds of penalties, like indeterminate sentences, probation, and parole.[57] This irony was not lost on the stewards of the penitentiary. In 1923, the Texas legislature moved to centralize its electrocutions at Huntsville prison after a spate of brutal lynchings the year before in central Texas. Captain R. F. Coleman, the prison's warden, submitted his letter of resignation, effective January 15, 1924, one day before Huntsville's first scheduled electrocution. He told reporters: "It just couldn't be done, boys. A warden can't be a warden and a killer too. The penitentiary is a place to reform a man, not to kill him."[58] Penitentiaries, long heralded as sites of reform and progress, became the primary institution for legitimizing a penal sanction whose very essence challenged the whole idea of rehabilitation and redemption on which the penitentiary and many subsequent penal reforms were justified.

As states took control of executions from local communities, capital punishment became more accountable to the wider legal process at a time when state and federal courts were developing the institutional capacity, expertise, and will to intervene more in criminal law matters. Capital punishment cases provided a springboard for greater federal supervision of criminal procedures at the state and local levels as the courts got more involved in delineating the rights of the accused and convicted. A series of landmark legal decisions gave capital defendants and people on death row additional legal avenues and resources to defend themselves and challenge their convictions. This contributed to the decline in executions prior to the early 1960s.

Juries also were factors in the precipitous drop in executions during this period. In 1838 Tennessee became the first state to permit jurors in murder cases to choose between death and a lesser sentence like life imprisonment. Concerned that jurors were failing to convict when death was the only option, other states began moving from mandatory to discretionary capital punishment. By the turn of the twentieth century, nearly two dozen states had done so. By World War I, another fourteen had. Only four states and the District of Columbia still had some form of mandatory capital punishment statutes as of 1949.[59] From the late 1930s onward, more juries began choosing life over death. This trend started in the North and moved to the South. During the 1930s, 145 people were sentenced to death on average each year.[60] By the early 1960s, this figure had dropped to 111.[61] Although the murder rate fell during this period, that alone does not explain the significant decline in death sentences.[62]

This drop in the number of death sentences and executions occurred in the absence of a recognizable death penalty movement – either for or against. Lawyers at the forefront of the battle against capital punishment at this time "were impressed" that this decline "had taken place despite a general belief that the rate of violent crime had increased and a clamor for measures to reduce it."[63] As the anti-communism hysteria of the 1940s and 1950s sputtered, elite opinion began moving away from the death penalty, and public opinion belatedly began to follow.[64] In 1956 the Methodists became the first mainline Protestant denomination to go on record opposing capital punishment. Other mainstream religious groups followed the Methodists, prompted partly by the controversy surrounding the execution of Caryl Chessman in 1960.[65] Official church statements opposing the death penalty began appearing regularly in the mainstream press.[66]

Except for the final few months of Chessman's battle to avoid execution, capital punishment remained largely a "collateral issue" that did not attract that much attention.[67] As such, elected officials and their political opponents did not view opposition to the death penalty as a political liability. An April 1960 poll by the *New York Herald Tribune* found that sitting governors in states outside the South opposed capital punishment by a 6-to-1 ratio.[68] Some governors did not merely oppose capital punishment, but forcefully challenged it. To demonstrate his faith in rehabilitation, Michael Disalle, the governor of Ohio from 1959 to 1963, made it a point to hire convicted murderers to serve on his household staff. Governor Terry Sanford's numerous statements against capital punishment were so well known that prisoners on North Carolina's death row pointedly referred to his opposition in their clemency appeals.[69] As one of his first acts as governor of Massachusetts, Democrat Chub Peabody, who squeaked into office in the 1962 election, introduced legislation in January 1963 to end capital punishment in his state. In presenting his bill, Peabody promised to commute all death sentences, including offenders convicted of killing police officers. He even vowed he would not sign the death warrant for the "Boston Strangler," if and when he was ever caught and convicted.[70]

Around this time, public opinion began to shift decisively against the death penalty for the first time in the history of modern scientific opinion polls. From 1953 on, Gallup polls showed a continued erosion in public support for capital punishment. Those in favor of capital punishment fell from 70 percent in 1953 to just 42 percent in 1966, the lowest point ever recorded.[71]

These shifts in elite and public opinion began well before the coalescence of a new national movement dedicated to abolishing the death penalty. As of the early 1960s, the two organizations that subsequently became so identified with the epic court battles challenging the constitutionality of capital punishment – the Legal Defense and Educational Fund (LDF) of the National Association for the Advancement of Colored People (NAACP) and the American Civil Liberties Union (ACLU) – had yet to take any official public stand against capital punishment, though they defended individuals in capital cases. As late as February 1967, when the final report of Lyndon Johnson's President's Commission on Law Enforcement and Administration of Justice was released, the death penalty still appeared incidental to percolating debates about law and order. Discussion of the death penalty merited just one page in the commission's *The Challenge of Crime*, which ran to more than a third of a million words and included more than 200 recommendations covering all aspects of crime and criminal justice.[72]

The Courts and Capital Punishment

In the mid-1960s an elite-led anti-death penalty movement began to take shape. The conventional understanding of the history of anti-death penalty activism is that the earlier waves of reform in the antebellum period and the Progressive era were premised primarily on moral and legislative strategies for challenging capital punishment. That changed decisively around the mid-1960s, so the argument goes, as public interest groups, notably the LDF and the ACLU, made a key decision, some would say a fateful decision – to launch an all-out assault on capital punishment through the courts by challenging its fundamental constitutionality rather than by attempting to abolish it through legislative means. As a consequence, the main arena to battle the death penalty shifted from state legislatures to the courts.[73]

Yet capital punishment was already lodged in the judicial process, which set it on a particular developmental path, long before the LDF and the ACLU brought about a de facto moratorium on capital punishment in 1967 and prodded the Supreme Court to address its fundamental constitutionality. Prior to the emergence of the contemporary anti-death penalty movement, capital punishment was already entangled with the development of the courts, criminal law procedures, and juries in ways not seen in other Western countries. From the 1930s to the mid-1960s, it was anchored almost exclusively in the judicial process. This set important parameters for its subsequent development and, consequently, for the way it could be challenged and defended not just in the courts but in the wider political arena once it became a high-profile political issue again. In the decades since the *Furman* and *Gregg* decisions, capital punishment cases have comprised the most frequent business of the Supreme Court.[74] In the century prior to the *Furman* decision, the Supreme Court rarely reviewed death penalty cases. However, the Court did make several important decisions in the decades immediately prior to *Furman* that were critical to the development of capital punishment and to shaping the politics of crime and punishment more broadly.

Prior to the Progressive era, the only organized litigants who regularly got the Supreme Court to hear their claims were those with economic or property disputes.[75] During the Progressive era a number of new rights organizations were founded. In the 1920s, a rights-advocacy network centered on the ACLU, the NAACP, and the American Jewish Congress was consolidated. It had the resources, expertise, and political savvy to eventually compel the Supreme Court to take up more rights-based claims.[76] As a result, criminal procedures became a new arena of Supreme Court action from the 1930s onward and thus were critical to the development of the national state and ultimately the carceral state.

Largely unknown and unappreciated "is the fact that the most complex and time-consuming litigation the NAACP undertook in its early years was not concerned with the constitutional right of equality as such but rather with criminal procedure requirements."[77] The most striking victories for civil rights in the interwar years involved Southern criminal cases tainted by Jim Crow.[78] Thanks to the efforts of the NAACP in the late 1920s and 1930s, the national government, through several landmark

Supreme Court decisions, put federal restrictions on capital punishment for the first time since the ratification of the Constitution a century and a half earlier. The Court established important procedural safeguards for capital defendants under the Fourteenth Amendment's due process clause. In *Moore v. Dempsey*, a capital murder case stemming from the Elaine, Ark., race riot of October 1919, the Court ruled in 1923 that state trials dominated by mob pressures violated the due process protections of the Fourteenth Amendment.[79] Prior to *Moore*, virtually no precedent existed for the intervention of federal courts in state criminal proceedings.[80] In *Powell v. Alabama*, the Court ordered a retrial in 1932 for the "Scottsboro boys," who had been convicted of raping a white woman and sentenced to die, on the grounds that poor defendants in capital cases were entitled to adequate legal counsel. The 1936 ruling in *Brown v. Mississippi* vacated the conviction and death sentences of three black tenant farmers accused of murdering a white planter and whose confessions were extracted under torture by deputy sheriffs.[81] Other decisions prohibited discrimination in jury selection and "generally clarified the procedural rights of criminal defendants."[82] The expansion of the federal habeas corpus writ in the early 1960s opened up additional new vistas for people on death row to challenge their sentences.[83] Taken together, these decisions gave defendants in capital cases and prisoners on death row new means and opportunities to begin whittling away at capital punishment on a case-by-case basis. These decisions help explain the steep drop in executions between the 1930s and the early 1960s.[84]

The United States was distinctive because of this early development of a comparatively expansive network of advocacy organizations that succeeded in prevailing on the Supreme Court to address rights-based claims.[85] This was one main reason why capital punishment was destined to be battled out on judicial rather than legislative terrain. The considerable success these groups had beginning in the 1930s in extending the rights of defendants appeared to confirm the wisdom of this strategy. Unlike in Britain and elsewhere, important parameters for a national debate over capital punishment were forged in the courts in the decades prior to the emergence in the 1960s and 1970s of a pronounced death penalty movement (either for or against) in the United States.

The NAACP was a central player in the emerging network of rights-advocacy groups that litigated these landmark capital cases. In 1939 it created a new corporation officially known as its Legal and Educational Defense Fund. The LDF's primary goal, in the words of longtime staff attorney Michael Meltsner, was "to pursue equality for blacks by bringing test cases in the courts challenging the laws and customs on which racial segregation rested."[86] In 1940, its full-time staff consisted of just one young lawyer, Thurgood Marshall. Over the next two decades, the LDF mushroomed. By 1961, it had a staff of seven lawyers and a budget of more than half a million dollars.[87] The LDF was at the forefront of the major civil rights cases of the 1940s and 1950s, including equal access to higher education, challenges to restrictive covenants and white primaries, and, of course, the 1954 *Brown v. Board of Education* decision calling for desegregation in public schools. The LDF was also at the forefront of some of the major capital punishment cases during this time. As Jack Greenberg, a longtime staff member and Marshall's successor as director-counsel of the LDF, explained: "Any organization that concerns itself with America's racial problems and their relationship to the law soon confronts the grim fact of capital punishment."[88]

Capital punishment was in many ways a natural issue for the LDF because it appeared so starkly discriminatory. Blacks were executed in disproportionate numbers.[89] It was virtually unheard of to execute a white for crimes committed against a black person.[90] South Carolina had not done so since 1880.[91] Blacks convicted of killing whites ran the greatest risk of being killed by the state. Whites convicted of rape were seldom executed, while blacks risked death for this offense, especially in the South.[92] Sophisticated statistical analyses of racial disparities in the exercise of capital punishment that were developed in earnest beginning in the late 1960s merely confirmed and quantified patterns that had been readily apparent for decades to anyone involved in the exercise of the death penalty.[93]

Even though blacks bore a disproportionate burden of the death penalty, the LDF and other rights groups were slow to launch a broad challenge to the constitutionality of capital punishment. Instead, until the early 1960s, the LDF fought capital punishment primarily on procedural grounds on a case-by-case basis. Most of these cases involved black men charged with raping white women.[94] Occasionally the LDF raised questions about the validity of capital punishment based on patterns of racial discrimination, but time and again the courts rejected such challenges.[95]

As the number of capital cases accumulated, the LDF considered attacking the death penalty on more sweeping constitutional grounds. But LDF lawyers did not begin to map out such a campaign until Supreme Court Justice Arthur J. Goldberg issued a dissenting opinion in an obscure Alabama rape case that the Court refused to hear in 1963. Goldberg's dissent from the Court's denial of certiorari in *Rudolph v. Alabama* was joined by Justices William O. Douglas and William J. Brennan. In his dissent, Goldberg urged the Court to take up the case and address three questions regarding the constitutionality of the death penalty that had not been raised by the defendant's lawyers, who had focused on procedural issues in this interracial capital rape case. First, Goldberg questioned whether imposition of the death penalty for rape violated "evolving standards of decency that mark the progress of [our] maturing society," or "standards of decency more or less universally accepted." He then asked whether "the taking of a human life to protect a value other than human life" was an excessive punishment. And finally, he questioned whether punishing rape with death constituted "unnecessary cruelty."[96]

This was a highly calculated and premeditated dissent.[97] Coming as it did and when it did, Goldberg's dissent laid down certain parameters for the debate over capital punishment that opponents of the death penalty in other countries did not have to contend with. Ironically, it helped to channel the national debate over capital punishment in ways that ultimately helped build the carceral state on the back of capital punishment. First, the Goldberg dissent provided a tantalizing opening to pursue the end of capital punishment through the courts. This helped to solidify the legal arena, not the political arena, as the main stage of action to abolish the death penalty. Second, the dissent did not cite racial discrimination "as relevant and, apparently, worthy of argument," even though "petitioner Rudolph was black and even though 90% of the persons executed for this crime since 1930 had been black."[98] Ironically the dissent served to spur the LDF, a group whose *raison d'être* was race-based claims, into taking greater action against capital punishment in the face of a Supreme Court that still appeared to be denying that racial concerns were relevant to the exercise of the death penalty.[99] Thus, capital punishment was further lodged in the civil rights movement even though the courts appeared unreceptive to claims that race mattered in the imposition of the death penalty. Furthermore, Goldberg's dissent made explicit reference to the Court's decision in *Trop v. Dulles*. In that 1958 case, the Court determined that the government could not strip Albert Trop of his citizenship as punishment for deserting the U.S. Army because this constituted "cruel and unusual punishment" under the Eighth Amendment, which must derive its meaning from society's "evolving standards of decency."[100] In this way, Goldberg inserted public opinion considerations into the national debate over capital punishment. Whether public sentiment for the death penalty was waxing or waning became a relevant factor in the debate over abolition in the United States. In other countries, notably Britain, this was not a central issue, as discussed in the next chapter.

The Broader Campaign Against Capital Punishment

Goldberg's dissent "jolted Fund lawyers into action."[101] Roughly around 1965, the Fund embarked on a wider legal campaign aimed primarily at abolishing the death penalty for rape. Capital punishment and race were to be explicitly linked for the first time in a national campaign. The LDF sought to postpone all capital rape cases on appeal as Marvin Wolfgang, from the sociology department at the University of Pennsylvania, collected the statistical data necessary to prove racial discrimination in rape sentencing. LDF attorneys used Wolfgang's research to argue for outright abolition of the death penalty in capital rape cases or creation of new procedural safeguards to prevent racial discrimination in sentencing.[102]

Propelled along by the logic of its legal arguments, the LDF soon decided to expand its campaign to cover all capital punishment defendants, not just blacks charged with rape. After all, other capital murder cases lacked many of the same procedural safeguards found wanting in capital rape cases and were vexed with discriminatory sentencing patterns (though they were not as stark as in capital rape cases). The LDF also decided to launch a broader assault because the courts appeared unreceptive to Wolfgang's sophisticated statistical analyses that demonstrated widespread racial discrimination in capital rape cases. A major turning point for the LDF was *Maxwell v. Bishop*, in which a U.S. District Court in 1966 was unpersuaded by the statistical evidence and refused to vacate the death sentence of William L. Maxwell, a young black man convicted of raping a white woman in Alabama. Two years later the U.S. Court of Appeals for the Eighth Circuit also rejected Maxwell's appeal based on the statistical evidence.[103]

The Fund had a political as well as a legal rationale for expanding its legal campaign against the death penalty. It hoped to make capital punishment a high-profile political issue by creating a huge backlog of cases in the courts and risking a "blood bath" should executions resume again. "A successful moratorium strategy would create a death-row logjam," explained LDF strategist Michael Meltsner.[104] Under its new strategy, the Fund sought to block all executions; "it would defend murderers as well as rapists, whites as well as blacks, Northerners as well as Southerners."[105] This was a massive undertaking without precedent. It required the LDF to be involved with potentially hundreds of cases nationwide. Soon after the moratorium strategy was announced, dozens of criminal lawyers and overburdened public defender agencies from around the country began inviting the LDF to assist in their capital cases and the number kept rising.[106]

The LDF was constrained to take full legal and political advantage of the opening that Goldberg's dissent appeared to present. While the Fund's resources had expanded significantly since its inception in 1939, so had its broad litigation responsibilities. Its staff was "still small, spread dangerously thin, and plagued by almost daily civil rights movement crises that required immediate action."[107] The fortuitous arrival of a $1 million grant from the Ford Foundation in 1967 to create the National Office for the Rights of the Indigent was critical to the Fund's new capital punishment project.[108] Still, the LDF's capital campaign "drained the Fund's budget, but was not itself appealing enough to excite potential contributors."[109]

On the political side, the LDF was constrained for several reasons. First, it was primarily a law office, not a political organization. Its tax-exempt status precluded political lobbying. Also, unlike the ACLU and the NAACP, it did not have local branches that could put pressure on and educate the public and state legislators.[110] Furthermore, two decades of major civil rights triumphs in the courts had biased the LDF toward legal solutions.[111] Once it expanded its campaign to challenge all death sentences, this civil rights organization found itself in the awkward position of defending numerous marginal, violent members of society, many of whom were "drawn from the most racist segment of white society."[112] As the Fund sought stays of execution for all rapists and murderers, it also drew national attention to heinous crimes that reinforced white stereotypes about black criminality.[113] Furthermore, the Fund sought to make capital punishment a high-profile political issue, yet it eschewed the public relations and public education aspects of its advocacy.[114] While the LDF had a larger political rationale for its legal strategy, it concentrated primarily on its legal campaign.

The ACLU was tagged with the responsibility of educating the wider public and legislators about capital punishment. But at a time when popular support for the death penalty was falling to record lows in the mid-1960s, the ACLU was poorly positioned to take advantage of the public's change of heart or the political opening presented by the Goldberg dissent and the LDF's new strategy. Before the ACLU could establish a national policy, it had to have the backing of its affiliates. Internal dissent about whether the death penalty constituted a civil liberties violation, regardless of how it was administered by the criminal justice system, prohibited the ACLU from officially taking a stance against capital punishment until 1965.[115] Even after the rights organization formally repudiated the death penalty, some disgruntled affiliates were unreliable allies.[116] Moreover, from the mid-1960s to the mid-1970s the ACLU was preoccupied with other civil liberties issues stemming from the civil rights movement, the Vietnam War, and Watergate.[117] And from the early-to-mid-1970s, the ACLU was gripped by a financial crisis and organizational disarray that threatened the effectiveness of the national organization and many of its affiliates.[118] While lawyers active in the ACLU played critical legal roles in certain capital cases, the ACLU did not enter the battle against the death penalty in a politically significant way until much later.[119] For example, it did not appoint a coordinator of state legislative efforts until 1974. Aryeh Neier, the director of the New York branch of the ACLU at the time, faults the civil rights organization for failing to invest more in a legislative campaign as early as the mid-1960s, when the climate was more favorable for abolition.[120] Likewise, he faults the NAACP, which was permitted to engage in lobbying (unlike the LDF), for not committing itself more strongly to the abolitionist cause.[121]

While the LDF and the ACLU succeeded in raising the political profile of capital punishment, they were less successful in reframing the issue in a politically desirable direction at a time when public sentiment on capital punishment was still fluid. The absence of an organized pro-death penalty movement or organized public sentiment in favor of capital punishment reduced pressure on these two organizations to develop a politically significant abolitionist movement that stretched beyond the courtroom. While a number of public officials and politicians certainly favored capital punishment, their support was muted. They did not utter bloodthirsty statements advocating more executions, nor did they promote capital punishment as a panacea for society's ills.[122] The ardent pro-death penalty stances of Reagan in California and Kirk in Florida have overshadowed the fact that views on the death penalty had not yet calcified, even on the right, as late as the mid-to-late 1960s.

Indeed, at the time there were some notable retreats among leading penal conservatives and proponents of the death penalty, and in some surprising parts of the country. J. Edgar Hoover, the longtime director of the FBI and for years one of the most forceful supporters of capital punishment, appeared to be abandoning the deterrence argument for the first time. In the FBI's annual report in 1968 Hoover conceded that murder is basically a "social problem" that is not affected by punishment. He no longer claimed that capital punishment served to deter the "bestial criminals" and "bestial killers" and conceded that the evidence about its deterrent value was "completely inconclusive."[123] Lester Maddox, Georgia's segregationist governor, went through semantic contortions to justify commuting the death sentence of William Patrick Clark, a 29-year-old man scheduled to be executed in April 1967 for the rape of a teenage girl after she left a Sunday church service.[124] In 1965, Governor Frank G. Clement (D-Tenn.) commuted all the death sentences in his state after the legislature defeated an abolition bill by a single vote.[125] In California, Jim Park, the warden of San Quentin, was cooperating with LDF and ACLU lawyers, making sure they were kept abreast of the latest status of various capital cases and whether execution dates had been set.[126]

If measured by the number of executions, the legal campaign appeared to be having great success. This further reduced pressure on the Fund and the ACLU to develop an effective political campaign. The number of executions dwindled from twenty-one in 1963 to seven in 1965 to just two in 1967.[127] In 1968, for the first time in U.S. history, not a single person was executed. For nearly a decade thereafter, no more executions took place as the constitutionality of capital punishment was tested in the courts and hundreds of prisoners piled up on death row. In 1968, abolitionists won what appeared at the time to be a significant victory when the Supreme Court ruled in *Witherspoon v. Illinois* that death-qualified juries were unconstitutional.[128]

Governors and other state officials became increasingly reluctant to carry out executions, even in the South and in capital punishment strongholds like Pennsylvania. In December 1970, Governor Winthrop Rockefeller, who had been defeated for reelection, commuted to life imprisonment the sentences of all fifteen prisoners on death row in Arkansas.[129] In Alabama, the Court of Appeals ruled that no executions could be carried out because an old state statute had stipulated that Kilby Prison near Montgomery be the site of executions, and Kilby had been razed in 1967.[130] In Pennsylvania, outgoing Attorney General Fred Speaker had the electric chair removed from Rockview Correctional Institution in January 1971 and had the "Death Room" converted into an office. The incoming governor, Milton Shapp, challenged Speaker's authority to dismantle the electric chair, but promised no one would be executed while he was governor.[131] Ronald Reagan ran on a pro-death penalty platform in 1966. And true to his promise, shortly after taking office as governor of California he unflinchingly supported the April 1967 execution of Aaron Mitchell, the state's first execution in four years.[132] Yet after the LDF and other abolitionists suffered a major legal setback in May 1971 with the Supreme Court's decisions in *McGautha v. California* and *Crampton v. Ohio*, Reagan followed the lead of other governors and vowed to take a wait-and-see approach to resuming executions in California as the constitutionality of the death penalty continued to hang in the balance.[133] No one else was executed in California during Reagan's tenure as governor. Even the Nixon administration initially appeared hesitant to jump into the fray about capital punishment. Nixon's first solicitor general, Erwin Griswold, defended the constitutionality of the death penalty in oral arguments as an amicus curiae in *McGautha* and *Crampton*, but only after being invited to participate by the Court.[134]

The *McGautha* and *Crampton* decisions were major defeats for the LDF and other abolitionists. The Court was unpersuaded by claims that capital punishment violated the Fourteenth Amendment's due process protections. It ruled that juries and judges should have absolute discretion to impose the death penalty in capital cases and could be trusted to act responsibly when "confronted with the truly awesome responsibility of decreeing death for a fellow human."[135] It also determined that juries were not required to decide the punishment at a separate proceeding after the trial that had determined guilt or innocence, thus giving its blessing to so-called unitary trials.[136] A month after the *McGautha* and *Crampton* decisions, the Supreme Court announced it would review several cases involving the constitutionality of capital punishment. But in agreeing in June 1971 to hear the group of cases collectively known as *Furman v. Georgia*, the Supreme Court signaled that the Constitution's ban on cruel and unusual punishment would be the primary entry point to decide the constitutionality of capital punishment.[137]

After the *McGautha* and *Crampton* setbacks, the LDF, the ACLU, and other abolitionists reaffirmed their legal strategy of blocking all executions. They also supported a bill in Congress imposing a two-year moratorium on executions and agreed to step up pressure on state executives to grant more commutations.[138] But these organizations were either unwilling or unable to put major resources into the political leg of this strategy, for the reasons discussed above.

To sum up, as late as 1971 capital punishment was not a signature issue for law-and-order conservatives. Thus the political arena offered abolitionists some leeway to frame the issue. But accustomed to fighting and winning in the courts and bereft of the resources necessary to wage a wider political campaign, the abolitionists focused, as they had for decades, on the legal arena instead. And here, while they did not face intense organized opposition, they were constrained by how the courts had framed issues related to the death penalty and crime and punishment in the past. The courts had indicated time and again that they were not receptive to arguments about how the death penalty was imposed in a racially discriminatory manner. They also were unpersuaded by data challenging the reported deterrent value of capital punishment.

The Supreme Court set important parameters for attacking and defending capital punishment in these earlier years that would subsequently help to lock in the carceral state, as elaborated in the next chapter. The fact that capital punishment was already so firmly lodged in the judicial process set severe constraints on the anti-death penalty movement that began to take shape in the mid-1960s. As shown in the next chapter, this helped to foreclose legislative strategies that proved to be so successful in abolishing capital punishment elsewhere, notably in Western Europe. It also contributed to a more punitive environment that hastened the rise of the carceral state.

9 THE POWER TO PUNISH AND EXECUTE

The Political Development of Capital Punishment, 1972 to Today

> "At a time in our history when the streets of the nation's cities inspire fear and despair, rather than pride and hope, it is difficult to maintain objectivity and concern for our fellow citizens. But, the measure of a country's greatness is its ability to retain compassion in time of crisis."
>
> – Justice Thurgood Marshall[1]

In the 1970s, the death penalty catapulted to the center of debates over crime and punishment in the United States and remained stubbornly lodged there, deforming U.S. penal policies and disfiguring U.S. society in ways not seen in other Western countries.[2] Specifically, capital punishment was critical to reframing the politics of punishment so as to bolster the emergence and consolidation of a conservative victims' movement premised on calls for victims' rights that marginalized questions about limits to the state's power to punish. The death penalty became such a potent contributor to the punitive law-and-order environment not merely because select politicians and public officials decided beginning in the 1960s to exploit this issue for electoral or ideological reasons. It is important to appreciate the nuances of the institutional and political context in which they did this. They made their moves at a time when capital punishment was already firmly anchored in the judicial process, as shown in Chapter 8. Groups and organizations likely to oppose the death penalty remained focused on the legal arena. This impeded the development of a wider political movement against the death penalty that could effectively exploit the mid-1960s trough in public support for capital punishment. But it did more than that.

The legal debate over the death penalty developed in ways that bolstered the construction of the carceral state. It helped conservative forces to capture the debate over the death penalty and penal policy, unimpeded by popular political resistance. It was not just that the Supreme Court did not close the door once and for all on capital punishment with its *Furman* decision in 1972 or that it cleared the way for the resumption of executions with the *Gregg* decision in 1976. A whole host of other legal decisions related to capital punishment bolstered the carceral state in subtle but profound ways. They fostered a public debate around capital punishment that reinforced wider punitive tendencies that were then surfacing in the United States and helped them take root. Specifically, the battle over capital punishment, initially confined to the courts, helped to enshrine in society a view that popular sentiments and passions are paramount in the formulation of penal policy. Furthermore, the judicial decisions and legal arguments involving capital punishment over the past three decades or so helped transform the death penalty into "the ultimate form of public victim recognition," something it had never been before in U.S. history.[3] As a result, the role of the state in capital punishment receded further to the margins of public scrutiny and challenge, contributing to a collapse of state and society in the making of penal policy and deflecting attention away from the question of what are the legitimate limits to the state's power to imprison and kill.

It is not my purpose here to provide an exhaustive analysis of the major recent Supreme Court cases relating to capital punishment or a blow-by-blow account of the strategies of the contemporary anti-death penalty movement. A number of analysts and key participants in the movement have already done that ably.[4] Instead, what follows is a stylized account that highlights how the legal debate over the death penalty and the evolving strategies of opponents and proponents helped to lock in the carceral state. In their analysis of why the law, as articulated by the Supreme Court, abruptly changes, Lee Epstein and Joseph F. Kobylka persuasively show how "the law, as legal actors frame it, matters, and matters dearly."[5] While Epstein and Kobylka demonstrate how the legal framing of capital punishment affected the fate of the death penalty in the courts, I focus on how it affected the broader debate over penal policy.

The chapter begins by analyzing the wider and enduring implications of *Furman v. Georgia* for penal policy, in particular how it enshrined public sentiment in the making of penal policy. It then looks at *Gregg v. Georgia* and how the deterrence argument, which was widely discredited elsewhere, propelled the debate over the reinstatement of the death penalty because of the strikingly different political, institutional, and social environment in which it was raised here in the United States. This helped neutralize one of the most powerful arguments against capital punishment – and, by extension, the carceral state – that is, that harsher penalties do not significantly deter people from committing crimes. The refinement of judicial regulation of capital punishment after *Gregg* had some unforeseen consequences. By initially according defendants in capital cases a wide berth to present mitigating evidence, the courts contributed to a political backlash. The constitutional politics of the death penalty and the politics of penal policy more broadly were transformed into "a contest to claim the status of victim."[6] The courtroom in capital cases was no longer just a site to determine guilt or innocence in a particular case. Rather, it provided a dramatic stage to magnify the suffering of all victims, the immorality that taints all offenders, and the fundamental antagonism between victims and offenders. This was a unique outcome unparalleled in other Western countries.

Furman v. Georgia and Public Sentiment

The *Furman* decision in June 1972 was a critical juncture in the political development of capital punishment and the construction of the carceral state. It occurred at a time when no organized pro-death penalty movement existed and when capital punishment was not yet a signature issue of the up-and-coming conservative movement. It served to legitimize "what the public wants" as a central factor in determining the fate of capital punishment and other penal issues.

From an immediate legal and legislative perspective, the most noteworthy aspects of *Furman* were how it vacated more than 600 death sentences and spurred a mad dash by dozens of state legislatures to rewrite their capital punishment statutes to meet the objections the Court had raised to standardless sentencing. From a political point of view, the ruling is significant because of how the fiercest opponents and proponents of capital punishment reframed the issue in strikingly similar terms. The dissenting justices denied that the American public had repudiated the death penalty. The LDF and other abolitionists contended that it had. In doing so, both proponents and opponents ended up legitimizing popular sentiment as an important factor in the making of penal policy. The battle then began to hinge on how to measure, shape, and interpret public sentiment on capital punishment and other penal matters.

This was a dramatic reframing of the issue of capital punishment that had wider political repercussions. It essentially legitimized public sentiment as the main political terrain on which the death penalty would be contested and on which the carceral state would be constructed and legitimized over the coming decades. It contributed to a collapse between the state and society in the making of penal policy not experienced elsewhere. This helped to legitimate a Roman Colosseum view of how to make penal policy. If the Romans wanted the Christians thrown to the lions, so be it. Furthermore, by failing to close the door once and for all on the death penalty by declaring it unconstitutional under all circumstances, the Supreme Court ensured that the legal arena would remain an important battleground for capital punishment. Judicial decisions involving the death penalty would continue to have wider repercussions for the development of penal policy and the politics of punishment. Even though *Furman* was a muddled decision, it was pivotal in steering the debate in this direction because the fiercest opponents and proponents did agree on one thing: public sentiment was critical.

This view of the primacy of public opinion was bolstered by events unfolding in California in the months leading up to the *Furman* decision. These events set an important context for how this landmark decision would be interpreted. A month after oral arguments in *Furman*, the California Supreme Court ruled in a decisive and surprising 6–1 verdict in February 1972 that capital punishment violated the state constitution's ban on "cruel or unusual punishment." The California court then vacated the death sentences of the 107 people on the state's death row. In *People v. Anderson*, Chief Justice Donald R. Wright, a Reagan appointee, argued for the majority that "evolving standards of decency" were the yardstick by which to measure cruel or unusual punishment under the California Constitution. He singled out the infrequency of executions as evidence that an informed public, when confronted with the reality of capital punishment, repudiates it.[7] Governor Reagan, who had promised previously to take a wait-and-see attitude following the 1971 *McGautha* decision while *Furman* remained unresolved, described himself as "deeply shocked and disappointed" by Wright's decision. He characterized it as "one more step toward totally disarming society in its fight against violence and crime."[8]

The California decision likely did not change any minds on the Supreme Court, but it did change the context in which *Furman* would be received and interpreted four months later.[9] The peculiarities of California's initiative and referendum process assured that the death penalty would not die with the California Supreme Court. In May 1972, the California State Senate rejected a proposal by Republican Senator George Deukmejian for legislation authorizing a referendum on a constitutional amendment to reinstate the death penalty. After this defeat, Attorney General Evelle Younger, backed by the state's Correctional Officers Association and other law enforcement groups, set out with the blessing of Governor Reagan to collect the necessary 500,000-plus signatures to put the issue of a constitutional amendment on the November 1972 ballot. Under Younger's leadership, police stations, sheriffs' offices, fire stations, correctional facilities, and even city halls were turned into headquarters for the massive petition drive in a remarkable use of public resources for political ends.[10] Proponents of the measure collected nearly twice the necessary signatures to put it on the ballot. That November voters approved by a 2-to-1 margin the proposal to amend the state constitution to restore to the California legislature the power to reinstate the death penalty.[11]

California's institutional environment, with its initiative and referendum option, gave the death penalty new life and set an important context for the political and popular interpretations of *Furman*. This institutional context, together with the specific way capital punishment had developed largely in the courts over the years, provided combustible fuel for penal populism. As a result, pro-death penalty sentiment ignited among political elites soon after the *Furman* decision was pronounced, and President Nixon was a key national instigator of it. Up until then, Nixon had run hot and cold on capital punishment. He pushed successfully in 1970 for a federal death penalty statute in cases of bombings that resulted in death, and in March 1972 made a speech in which he advocated death for drug pushers.[12] Yet he absented his administration from some of the key death penalty cases to come before the Supreme Court. Remarkably, the Nixon administration was not involved in litigating *Furman*.[13]

Even after the Supreme Court announced its intentions in June 1971 to rule on the constitutionality of capital punishment in *Furman*, pro-death penalty sentiment remained muted. No organized groups filed amicus curiae briefs in favor of retention. Of the twelve amicus briefs submitted during the litigation of the group of cases consolidated under *Furman v. Georgia*, all were in support of abolition.[14] The few organizations that were outspoken proponents of the death penalty were marginal groups whose national stature paled compared with abolitionist organizations like the LDF and the ACLU.[15] The main organized support for the death penalty consisted of state attorneys from California, Texas, and Georgia, the jurisdictions at the forefront of litigating these cases.

The 5–4 *Furman* decision has been described as "precarious, vague, and temporizing."[16] Comprised of nine separate opinions totaling 243 pages, it was the longest decision in the history of the Supreme Court.[17] While two of the justices viewed the death penalty as unconstitutional under all circumstances, the three others who comprised the majority only agreed that capital punishment as then imposed violated the Constitution. In an apparent reversal of *McGautha* and *Crampton*, they suggested that the unbounded discretion that juries exercised in capital trials was unconstitutional. In their view, standardless juries violated the Eighth Amendment prohibition on cruel and unusual punishment. In the famous words of Justice Potter Stewart, death sentences are "cruel and unusual" because they are "wantonly and freakishly" imposed in a way that is no more meaningful or rational than the random striking of lightning.[18]

The four dissenters were more united in their views. They argued that the Court's decision severely encroached on legislative prerogatives. Chief Justice Warren Burger suggested that state legislators might successfully write new statutes to satisfy the Court's objections, but in private conceded later that "[t]here will never be another execution in this country."[19] Taking direct aim at the central argument of the LDF, the lead counsel in the case, the dissenting justices denied that the American public had repudiated capital punishment. They disputed the LDF's claim that the death penalty "is a cruel and unusual punishment because it affronts the basic standards of decency of contemporary society."[20] In presenting its case, the Fund had harkened back to the *Trop* decision and the Goldberg dissent, and argued that the death penalty was at odds with "enlightened public opinion."[21] As evidence, the LDF pointed to a number of "objective indicators" that the death penalty was out of step with "the progress of a maturing society," including how rarely executions were carried out in the United States and abroad.[22]

The day after the *Furman* verdict was handed down, Nixon took the lead in denouncing it. Reiterating what Burger suggested in his dissent, Nixon declared at a press conference that "the holding of the Court must not be taken...to rule out capital punishment."[23] Nixon did not provide any details on what types of new state or federal death penalty statutes might satisfy the objections the Court had raised in *Furman*. His comments were significant nonetheless because he was the first major public figure to claim publicly that *Furman* had not abolished capital punishment.[24]

The political and legislative response to *Furman* was "fast, furious," and "bordered on hysteria."[25] Lester Maddox, by then Georgia's lieutenant governor, characterized the decision as "a license for anarchy, rape, murder."[26] Governor Nelson Rockefeller (R-N.Y.), who in 1965 signed legislation repealing capital punishment for most offenses in New York State, announced in 1973 to hundreds of cheering labor leaders that he was seriously considering bringing back the death penalty for major dealers of illicit drugs.[27] Some ten states quickly enacted mandatory death penalty statutes, and twenty-five others adopted some form of "guided discretion" death penalty legislation.[28]

The *Furman* decision galvanized such a powerful political backlash not merely because the Supreme Court had ruled that the death penalty (as then practiced) was unconstitutional. Nor because the abolitionists were ill-prepared to battle a backlash they did not see coming. Rather, over the years, capital punishment got lodged in the judicial process, as shown in Chapter 8, and got framed in a way that made public sentiment a central issue. California's *People v. Anderson* seared public sentiment into the capital punishment debate in the months prior to the *Furman* decision. Reagan, Nixon, and other hard-liners who chose to seize this moment to make an issue of capital punishment were so successful because abolitionists in the United States ended up having to tread a slippery slope of public opinion that their counterparts elsewhere did not have to contend with. Capital punishment was abolished in Canada and Western Europe in spite of public opinion, not because of public opinion. In the U.S. case, abolitionists had to prove that public sentiment had turned decisively against capital punishment, a very tall order.

The post-*Furman* strategy of the abolitionists consisted of three parts: a lobbying campaign led by the ACLU; LDF challenges to the new death penalty statutes in the courts; and the incorporation of new social scientific data on deterrence, racial discrimination, and public opinion into

their legal briefs.[29] This was treacherous terrain to battle capital punishment. The ACLU was ill-equipped to lead the campaign. The LDF risked
becoming overloaded by the number of new cases. The Supreme Court had
a history of being unreceptive to racial discrimination claims regarding the
death penalty. The sophisticated social science studies demonstrating that
public opinion polls on capital punishment masked much more nuanced
popular sentiment on the death penalty were overshadowed by blunter
evidence of the public's pro-death sentiments. As state legislatures briskly
passed dozens of new death penalty statutes, as the number of defendants
receiving the death penalty increased to record levels, and as public opinion polls showed that support for capital punishment was the highest in
two decades, it was hard to make a convincing case that the public had
rejected the death penalty.[30]

Gregg, Deterrence, and Public Opinion

Opponents of the death penalty were also handicapped because they were
unable to neutralize the deterrence argument, that is, the claim that executions significantly deter crime. Capital punishment, after simmering as an
issue for decades, became a national concern in the early 1970s at just the
moment when the U.S. homicide rate was escalating. Thus it became easy
for supporters of capital punishment to blame the de facto moratorium
on executions for the rising homicide rate that was a source of growing
public angst. The day after the *Furman* decision, Nixon claimed that the
death penalty served as a "necessary deterrent for capital crimes of certain
types."[31] This view held great sway, despite enormous social scientific evidence to the contrary. U.S. Senate hearings in 1973 on a bill to reintroduce
the federal death penalty were dominated by witnesses contending that
Furman had to be neutralized or else the country risked sinking deeper
into a morass of violent crime.[32] Studies showing the death penalty had
no significant deterrent effect on murder or other serious offenses did
not take center stage the way they had during the earlier debates over
abolition in Britain, Canada, and elsewhere for several reasons.

In the U.S. case, significant public funding was not made available to
study capital punishment's deterrence effect. While some individual states
established special commissions to investigate the death penalty, there was
no independent national effort to examine it. LBJ's crime commission
virtually ignored capital punishment. The LDF and private foundations,
notably the Russell Sage Foundation, funded some of the early research
on deterrence but their resources were quite limited.[33]

Most expert opinion agreed that the death penalty was not a deterrent,
but major scholarly and academic organizations in the United States generally did not mount any real effort to oppose capital punishment. Other
professional organizations involved in corrections, notably the National

Council on Crime and Delinquency and the American Correctional Association, took stances against capital punishment, but did not invest major resources in fighting it.[34] By contrast, nearly every criminologist in Britain joined the abolitionist campaign and put his or her expert credentials in the service of liberal reform.[35]

In the United States, private studies showing that the death penalty had no significant deterrent value had to compete with the cacophony created by other arguments about the death penalty and also with shifting public sentiment. For the first time in many decades, the anti-death penalty movement had to contend with growing elite and organized public support in favor of capital punishment. *Furman* did not ignite conservative groups to fight for the death penalty with the same intensity they mobilized against abortion after *Roe v. Wade*. But in 1972–73 we begin to see the emergence of organized support for capital punishment.

Law enforcement organizations were on the front lines of California's ballot referendum in 1972. Late that same year, the National Association of Attorneys General voted 32 to 1 in support of federal capital punishment legislation to address the defects identified in the *Furman* decision so that executions could resume.[36] The death penalty was also becoming a central issue for some victims' rights advocates. Frank G. Carrington, a leading spokesperson for the victims' movement, charged abolitionists with having "an utter disregard for the victims of crime."[37] New York City Mayor Ed Koch declared: "When the killer lives, the victim dies twice."[38]

While some organized support for the death penalty was emerging, there was still no "grand mobilization" by interest groups "to change the context of litigation on this issue."[39] The most significant shift toward active support of capital punishment in the years immediately after *Furman* came from political elites, in particular the White House, as the new death penalty statutes were challenged in the courts. Attorney General-designate Edward Levi extolled the deterrent value of the death penalty in January 1975.[40] Two months later, Robert H. Bork, solicitor general under Nixon and then President Gerald Ford, filed a lengthy amicus curiae brief supportive of capital punishment. In a sharp reversal, the federal government was now asserting that it had a "federal" interest in capital punishment, whereas previously it had viewed the death penalty as largely a state concern.[41]

In January 1976 the Supreme Court issued an order to review five capital punishment cases based on the new death penalty statutes enacted by state legislatures. As in 1972, the main legal proponents of the new statutes were state attorneys, but this time the White House aggressively sided with them. Instead of refuting the LDF point by point as they had in the past, the state attorneys went on the offensive and took various approaches in each of the cases, with little overlap between them. One exception was that they all joined Bork in denying that "evolving standards of decency" had turned against the death penalty. They presented evidence that in their view proved that public sentiment resoundingly approved of capital punishment.[42] In his brief, Bork affirmed the deterrent value of the death penalty, relying on an unpublished study that since has been widely discredited.[43] The deterrence issue appeared to have great sway with some of the justices. After presenting statistics from a 1973 FBI report documenting the escalating murder rate in the United States, Justice Lewis Powell suggested during oral arguments for *Gregg* in March 1976, "It is perfectly obvious from these figures that we need some way to deter the slaughter of Americans." Powell then awarded Bork five extra minutes to make his points about the deterrent value of the death penalty.[44]

On July 2, 1976, in a 7–2 decision in the three cases grouped together as *Gregg v. Georgia*, the Supreme Court essentially reinstated capital punishment. The *Gregg* decision affirmed that the new "guided discretion" statutes enacted by the states in the wake of *Furman* were constitutional.[45] The majority ruled that imposition of the death penalty under these new statutes did not constitute cruel and unusual punishment and was not an affront to evolving standards of decency.[46] It also took the controversial position that the death penalty served a legitimate government function of deterrence and retribution. That same day, in 5–4 decisions in two other cases, the Court struck down "mandatory" death penalty statutes in *Woodson v. North Carolina* and *Roberts v. Louisiana*.

The *Gregg* case reaffirmed the centrality of public opinion in the making of penal policy. It also drew public attention to the deterrence issue at an inauspicious moment – when escalating homicide rates coincided with the nation's de facto moratorium on executions. Sophisticated statistical studies proving the absence of any significant deterrent effect had great difficulty competing with these compelling facts on the ground and, as a result, were less effective in restraining penal populism. As in a number of capital punishment cases before and since, the justices demonstrated in *Gregg* that they paid close attention to public opinion polls, to the dismay of Justice Thurgood Marshall. In his dissent in *Gregg*, Marshall argued that the proper yardstick should be "the opinions of an *informed* citizenry."[47]

Life, Death, Victims, and Offenders After *Gregg*

The *Gregg* decision spurred abolitionist groups to mobilize. Several new organizations dedicated to battling the death penalty were born in its wake, including the National Coalition Against the Death Penalty. The human rights organization Amnesty International launched a major initiative against capital punishment in the United States beginning in the mid-1970s, and the Death Penalty Information Center (DPIC) was established in 1990 as a clearinghouse of information on capital punishment with generous initial funding from the J. Roderick MacArthur Foundation.[48]

By the early-to-mid-1980s, the ACLU had recovered somewhat and was on its way to becoming a leading foe of capital punishment and the new punitive politics. In 1984, it was the only organization opposing a package of anti-civil-libertarian crime bills. Four years later, the ACLU was the only major organization fighting several hundred bills introduced in Congress as part of the war on drugs. In 1986 it tried to influence public opinion on crime with a national conference sponsored jointly with the NAACP and the city of Atlanta, but the meeting had "little noticeable effect."[49] While the ACLU was bouncing back as an organization, the NAACP was experiencing organizational and financial disarray.[50] In addition, the NAACP and the LDF were consumed by a debilitating lawsuit over the LDF's use of the NAACP's initials. This strife depleted their resources and opened up a major rift between two of the country's leading civil rights organizations, rendering them of little use as the ACLU mounted a new push against capital punishment and the more punitive environment.[51]

As executions resumed with the killing of Gary Gilmore in 1977, the growing backlog of prisoners on death row "created a serious crisis in legal representation, overwhelming the resources of the ACLU and the LDF, the only two organizations providing any regular assistance."[52] But the *Gregg* decision did not prompt the expected "blood bath." Executions resumed with a trickle, not a gush. Over the next half-dozen years the Supreme Court upheld death sentences in just two cases while vacating capital punishment sentences in fourteen others as it put some important restrictions on the exercise of capital punishment. For example, it forbade the imposition of the death penalty in cases of rape of an adult and of kidnapping, and refused to permit the execution of fifteen-year-old murderers or of minor participants in felony murder cases. It also rendered a series of decisions involving procedural questions that were generally favorable to capital defendants.[53]

From around 1983 onward, the Supreme Court began a hasty retreat from involvement in many of the procedural details of the administration of the death penalty. The number of executions began rapidly to escalate, going from two in 1979 to five in 1983 to nearly a hundred in 1999, after which the annual number began to fall.[54] In the mid-1980s Chief Justice Warren Burger began publicly complaining that the appeals process in capital cases was too protracted, making it virtually impossible to execute anyone. This prompted other justices and prominent public officials to comment publicly on capital punishment and drew public attention to the growing backlog of people on death row and the big increase in the average time from sentencing to execution.[55] This fueled public concern that the courts were bending over backwards for capital defendants while denying victims and their families justice. It reinforced the unfounded belief that imposition of the death penalty would bring about "closure" and thus provide considerable psychological comfort to victims' families.[56]

This view was bolstered by a series of decisions involving victim impact statements. In the immediate aftermath of *Gregg*, the courts accorded defendants in capital cases expansive rights to present mitigating evidence. As a consequence, enormous attention focused in the courtroom on portraying the defendant as a sympathetic and tragic figure, which had the effect of overshadowing the grief and grievances of victims' families.[57] The 1976 *Woodson* decision was particularly important for this reframing of capital punishment. In vacating North Carolina's mandatory death penalty statute, the justices had affirmed that capital punishment proceedings must be "individualized" so as to permit capital defendants to present mitigating evidence. This provided a platform for *Lockett v. Ohio* two years later in which the Court insisted that capital defendants be permitted to present as mitigating factors almost "any aspect" of their "character or record and any circumstances of the offense" that might serve as a "basis for a sentence less than death."[58]

In response, prosecutors and other state officials pushed to permit the introduction of victim impact evidence in capital sentencing hearings. In *Booth v. Maryland* (1987) and *South Carolina v. Gathers* (1989) the Supreme Court ruled that such evidence was inadmissible. But in 1991 it reversed itself in *Payne v. Tennessee* and provided an opening for a dramatic reframing of capital punishment.[59] In the *Payne* decision, the Court tried to put victims and defendants on a more equal footing. This served to reinforce the zero-sum view of victims and offenders that is such powerful fuel for penal populism and that undergirded the ascendant victim rights' movement.[60] Since *Payne*, at least twelve states have authorized victim impact statements in capital cases. This created the opportunity for the capital courtroom to be turned into a morality play that pits the good and virtuous victim against the evil, morally bankrupt criminal – or tragically flawed defendant – depending on whether you represented the prosecution or the defense.[61] The grief and grievances of the victims' families then became central to the capital punishment process.

As a consequence, the death penalty was repersonalized. This was "a stark departure from the efforts begun with the privatization of executions in the 1830s to depersonalize the execution and to purify it from the polluting influences of individual emotion and desires."[62] All of this helped to solidify a view of capital punishment and punishment more broadly as primarily a contest between victims and offenders in which the state's power to punish was an incidental issue, as were questions about how the penal system discriminated against the poor and people of color. In such an atmosphere, it is not so surprising that the courts and legislators dismissed sophisticated studies demonstrating the racially discriminatory manner in which the death penalty is imposed and the absence of any significant deterrence effect. In the 1987 *McCleskey v. Kemp* decision, the Supreme Court once again rejected arguments based on statistical and other evidence showing how capital punishment is imposed in a racially discriminatory manner. This was a major defeat for the abolitionists. Seven years later, the Racial Justice Act, which proposed that defendants in capital cases be allowed to use statistical evidence to demonstrate whether race was a factor in the decision to invoke capital punishment, made little headway in the U.S. Congress.[63]

The Comparative Politics of Capital Punishment

Over the past few decades the death penalty has undergone a transformation not only in the United States but in Europe and Canada as well. In the United States it has become tightly tethered to national politics and the criminal justice process. In Europe it has been transformed from a national issue into an international human rights issue and has emerged as a penetrating symbol of the limits of state power. During the immediate postwar decades, abolition of the death penalty in many Western European countries and Canada was largely a matter of the internal politics of individual countries. International or bilateral pressure was largely nonexistent.[64] Over the past twenty-five years or so, however, capital punishment has become a fundamental human rights issue in Europe, which now considers the death penalty to be an affront to international human rights standards.[65] This great change obscures a startling and revealing fact about the successful wave of abolition that lapped across Western Europe after World War II: Leading European countries abolished the death penalty in the face of strong, sometimes overwhelming, public support for its retention.

When the constitution of the Federal Republic of Germany, with its ban on capital punishment, was promulgated in 1949, about three-quarters of the German public favored retention of the death penalty.[66] Yet the campaigns in the 1950s to reintroduce capital punishment in West Germany made little headway. By the 1960s, public support for the death penalty began to slide downward and remained there. A 1992 survey found that barely a quarter of those polled in the former West Germany favored capital punishment.[67] In France, the public strongly backed the death penalty in the 1960s and 1970s, but did not clamor for its widespread use. During the first year of the Mitterrand government in 1981, the National Assembly formally abolished capital punishment, four years after the guillotine was last used in what ended up being the final state execution in Western Europe to date.[68] Canada also abolished the death penalty despite public opinion polls favoring retention.[69] Public support for the death penalty remains considerable in a number of European countries and Canada today, ranging from bare majorities to more than two-thirds of those surveyed.[70] Yet none of these countries is likely to reinstate capital punishment in the foreseeable future.

The different institutional and political contexts help explain why Europe and Canada were able to abolish the death penalty despite strong public support for it, while the United States retained the death penalty and transformed it into a key building block of the carceral state. By the early 1960s, capital punishment was on a different trajectory in the United States than elsewhere. On the surface, the United States appeared to be swimming toward abolition, along with Britain and other Western European countries, as the number of executions fell and U.S. politicians did not perceive a substantial political risk to opposing capital punishment. But in the U.S. case, the main assault on capital punishment came as an outgrowth of the civil rights movement. The LDF initially got involved in battling capital punishment because blacks were disproportionately sentenced to death and executed by the state. Opponents of capital punishment thus naturally focused on the fairness of the criminal justice system to administer capital cases and, secondarily, on the apparent patterns of racial discrimination in its use. As U.S. courts became more receptive to rights-based claims, they appeared to be the most promising venue to challenge the death penalty.

Britain was developing and reckoning with a starkly different debate on capital punishment at this time. The British courts did not emerge as a promising arena to challenge the death penalty. Differences in the British legal system and the absence of a highly developed network of rights-based groups (or a significant civil rights movement) help explain why. Higher courts in Britain and elsewhere did not have to contend with a comparable rights revolution during the interwar years and after. In Britain, the appeal system continued to manifest "a marked reluctance to make itself too available" to criminal defendants.[71] Britain did belatedly experience a limited rights revolution in the late 1970s and early 1980s as its higher courts expanded some of the rights of prisoners, but not defendants' rights.[72] As Epp effectively shows, differences in the basic governing structures between the United States and Britain, notably a constitutionally guaranteed Bill of Rights and a Supreme Court with the power of judicial review, do not fully explain this outcome.[73] The U.S. Supreme Court was compelled to address civil rights and civil liberties early on because of the precocious development of a vibrant and powerful public interest sector centered on questions of rights, according to Epp.[74]

In Britain, the parameters for the brewing debate over capital punishment were set outside the courts. The final report of the Royal Commission on Capital Punishment in 1953 was pivotal.[75] Arguably the most systematic study of capital punishment up to that point, the 500-plus-page report did not directly recommend abolition. However, it marshaled an impressive array of evidence against the death penalty. Significant doubts about the deterrent value of the death penalty were a major theme of the report.[76] With its emphasis on deterrence, the report set up the terms of the debate over capital punishment in Britain for the next decade-and-a-half until formal abolition in 1969. It drew public attention to the deterrence evidence at a fortuitous time in Britain in the early 1950s when public alarm about crime was not at a high pitch.[77] The report analyzed capital punishment primarily from the vantage point of its utility in public policy, thus anchoring it in the political rather than the judicial realm. As such, capital punishment was defined as an issue that public servants other than judges were to be the final arbiters.

Canada underwent a similar experience with the death penalty. About the same time that *Furman* was being decided, Canada's Solicitor General's Office published a special report, *A Study of the Deterrent Effect of Capital Punishment With Special Reference to Canada.* It dismissed claims that the suspension of the death penalty in Canada in 1967 caused any increase in the homicide rate. This study was a successor to a mid-1950s study by a special parliamentary commission to investigate the death penalty that initiated some of the best research on capital punishment.[78]

In contrast to the United States, the national governments in Canada and Britain made considerable investments in publicly financed empirical research centering on disputed areas of fact in the administration of capital punishment. A central focus was the question of whether the death penalty deters homicide. Britain and Canada were more at liberty to focus singlemindedly on the deterrence issue and make that a central feature of the national debate because they did not have to contend with claims about how the death penalty was imposed in a racially discriminatory manner. Furthermore, concerns about crime were not yet on the rise in Britain at the time that the deterrence issue became prominent. So the deterrence question took center stage in a more dispassionate context.

When Britain formally abolished capital punishment for murder in 1969 toward the end of a five-year moratorium imposed in 1965, the public strongly disapproved of Parliament's actions.[79] Subsequently, public support for the death penalty did not diminish and may have hardened in the 1980s.[80] While members of the Conservative Party, notably Margaret Thatcher, proclaimed their support for capital punishment, they did not expend much energy or political capital to get it restored, even though the public strongly favored reinstatement and the Police Federation also pushed for it.[81] By the early 1990s, the House of Commons had debated and voted on reinstatement more than a dozen times since capital punishment was suspended twenty-five years earlier. Time and again, members of Parliament rejected the resumption of capital punishment by substantial majorities after "unavoidable set-piece debate[s]" whose outcome was readily apparent from the start.[82] This sharply contrasts with the stampede by U.S. politicians and public officials in the 1980s and early 1990s to make even more crimes punishable by death. As Senator Joseph Biden (D-Del.) grimly joked, the Democratic Party's get-tough proposals did "everything but hang people for jaywalking."[83]

Opposition to the Death Penalty in the Late 1990s and Beyond

As more and more legal avenues were closed in the 1980s and 1990s, U.S. opponents of the death penalty were forced to pursue other strategies. This brought about a resurgence of "political abolitionism" and the beginnings of yet another reframing of the death penalty debate. This may result in a significant retreat for capital punishment but perhaps at the cost of bolstering the carceral state.

In the late 1990s, the political and legal terrain surrounding capital punishment began to shift markedly. At the cusp of the twenty-first century, public support for the death penalty as measured by public opinion polls was at its lowest point in nearly two decades.[84] In 2005, the number of executions was about 60 percent of what it was in 1999, the high point since reinstatment in 1976.[85] The number of people sentenced to death each year plummeted to its lowest levels since the early 1970s.[86]

After numerous setbacks, abolitionists arguably got the upper hand in the debate for the first time in a generation.[87] In 1997, the American Bar Association, which has a history of fence-straddling on the issue of capital punishment, finally called for a moratorium on executions.[88] Over a dozen states considered moratorium legislation.[89] In 2000, Illinois became the first state to impose a moratorium, prompted by fears of executing the innocent. Two years later Maryland followed suit.[90] In June 2002, the Supreme Court surprised many foes of the death penalty by declaring that execution of mentally handicapped offenders was unconstitutional, reversing the stance it took in 1989.[91] That same month, the Court ruled that juries rather than judges must make the critical determination of facts that subjected convicted murderers to the death penalty.[92] Another huge milestone was Republican Governor George Ryan's January 2003 decision to spare the lives of all 167 men and women on death row in Illinois. Ryan acted in the wake of a steady stream of exonerations of innocent prisoners who had been wrongly sentenced to death that drew intense national and international attention to the fallibility and unfairness of the death penalty.[93] Two other milestones were the January 2005 Supreme Court decision declaring execution of juvenile offenders under age eighteen unconstitutional, and the recent decision by a St. Louis, Mo., prosecutor to investigate the 1995 state execution of Larry Griffin, who may become the first officially confirmed case of a person executed in the United States for a crime he did not commit.[94]

By focusing so intently recently on the injustice of sending innocent people to death, abolitionists have illuminated just how fallible and unfair the criminal justice system is more generally. In this respect, the latest wave of abolitionism may be complementary to brewing efforts to roll back the carceral state. But a word of caution is in order. Just because the death penalty helped build the carceral state, we should not assume that the recent surge in abolitionism will help raze it. Some abolitionist strategies aimed at undermining the death penalty may end up doing so at the cost of strengthening the carceral state. Carolyn S. Steiker and Jordan M. Steiker warn that recent legislative reforms, such as mandatory DNA preservation and testing and improved legal representation for capital offenders, could help legitimize the death penalty. These reforms offer "the appearance of much greater procedural regularity than they actually produce, thus inducing a false or exaggerated belief in the fairness of the entire system of capital punishment."[95] By extension, this could help bolster public confidence in the carceral state.

The current "obsessive focus" on the innocent, estimated to comprise anywhere from one percent to a third of the death row population, has overshadowed the wider question of what constitutes justice for the guilty housed on death row and elsewhere in the carceral state.[96] Public opinion polls and other research indicate that support for the death penalty tends to drop markedly when respondents are given a choice of life in prison without the possibility of parole (LWOP) as an alternative to a death sentence.[97] To nurture this sentiment, some opponents of the death penalty have promoted LWOP not as a compassionate alternative to death but as an equally tough – or even tougher – retributive moral sanction.[98] When he was governor of New York, Democrat Mario Cuomo began calling for wider use of LWOP and offered to sign away his clemency powers in an effort to neutralize public opposition to his firm anti-death penalty stance in the early 1990s.[99] In promoting LWOP, abolitionists risk legitimizing a sanction that, like the death penalty, is way out of line with human rights and sentencing norms in other Western countries.[100] Many European countries do not permit LWOP. Those that do use it sparingly.[101] Moreover, the emphasis on LWOP as an alternative to the death penalty appears to be legitimating the greater use of this sanction for non-capital cases. All of which emboldens the retributive tendencies that have contributed to the construction of the carceral state.

Historically LWOP was not a popular practice in the United States. Prior to 1974, it was used sparingly.[102] The prevalence of LWOP as an alternative sanction has increased markedly since the mid-1990s, when it was available in only sixteen death-penalty jurisdictions. By 2003, thirty-five of the thirty-eight capital punishment states, as well as the federal government and U.S. military, had some form of LWOP.[103] From 1992 to 2003, the total number of offenders serving a life sentence in state and federal prisons increased by 83 percent. As of 2003, one in eleven prisoners was serving a life sentence. Of the imprisoned lifers, one in four was serving a sentence of life without parole, compared with one in six in 1992. In the state of Michigan alone, there are at least 146 people serving LWOP sentences for offenses committed when they were fourteen-to-sixteen years old.[104] At the same time that the use of life sentences and LWOP sentences are on the rise, the use of discretionary releases, such as commutations by governors and the president, have been curtailed substantially.[105]

The Supreme Court has been extremely supportive of life sentences. In *Schick v. Reed* (1974) it dismissed any notion that LWOP was unconstitutional.[106] In *Harmelin v. Michigan* (1991), it ruled that LWOP sentences do not require the same "super due process" procedures mandated in capital punishment cases.[107] Thus, LWOP has become cheaper and easier to mete out.[108] Not surprisingly, the number of people serving life sentences without the possibility of parole has skyrocketed. This has become an acceptable sentence not only for murder, but also for a wide variety of other crimes, some of them quite trivial, as evidenced by the popularity of "three-strikes" legislation.[109] In *Lockyer v. Andrade* (2003), the Court affirmed a life sentence for a man whose third strike was the theft of $153 worth of videotapes intended as Christmas gifts for his nieces.[110]

LWOP has been a contentious issue for the abolitionist movement. Some leading abolitionists, most notably Sister Helen Prejean, author of *Dead Man Walking*, are strong defenders of LWOP.[111] Others have tried to finesse the issue by referring to the broad public support for LWOP without necessarily endorsing it outright.[112] In their recent book on capital punishment, the Reverend Jesse Jackson, Sr., and his son acknowledge that LWOP may be a means to end the death penalty but perhaps at the cost of emboldening the carceral state.[113] Some leading abolitionist groups, notably the American Friends Service Committee, Amnesty International, and the ACLU, have denounced LWOP or expressed deep reservations about it.[114] So has The Sentencing Project, one of the leading foes of the carceral state. A recent Sentencing Project study of offenders sentenced to life suggests that "the broadscale imposition of such penalties has resulted in the use of life imprisonment in ways that too often represent both ineffective and inhumane public policy."[115]

Over the past few years, opponents of the death penalty have been more successful then previously in neutralizing or winning debates over "deterrence, incapacitation, cost, fairness, and the inevitability of executing the innocent," according to public opinion research.[116] The downside of this is that retribution has become the most common justification given by supporters of capital punishment.[117] Advocates of the death penalty increasingly make the case for executions in the name of the families of homicide victims. Family members are portrayed as "needing" or somehow benefiting from the "retributive satisfaction" that the death penalty appears to promise.[118] The existing research on what short- and long-term effects the execution of a capital offender has on a homicide victim's family (or on the family of the condemned, for that matter) is scant. As a consequence, anecdotal evidence of how executions deliver closure, justice, and emotional solace to family members has had great sway in the debate over capital punishment recently.

One promising development is that victims' families opposed to the death penalty are becoming more outspoken. They have begun to organize themselves into advocacy groups and to speak out about the ways in which they are marginalized and denied support by victims services providers, prosecutors, and other public officials.[119] Some, most notably Bud Welch, whose only child, Julie, was killed in the 1995 Oklahoma City bombing, and the parents of Matthew Shepard, the gay college student tortured and murdered in Laramie, Wy., in 1998, have become outspoken foes of capital punishment. They have challenged the whole premise that the taking of another life will bring relief to victims' families.[120] This represents a potentially potent challenge to the girders of the carceral state.

Here, too, a note of caution is warranted. The United States may be approaching the point where the survivors of homicide victims can decisively affect whether the guilty will be sentenced to death or not. Yet "mercy as closure" is "as subjective a route to closure as vengeance." Both in their own way reinforce a "victim-centered jurisprudence."[121] The judicial system is judged primarily by its capacity to serve as a vehicle for the expression of private rage, grief, compassion, or mercy, rather than by alternative measures that consider the needs of victims, offenders, and society more broadly.

The Power to Punish

A number of analysts emphasize the symbolic value of capital punishment in American politics. They stress how U.S. society had used the death penalty "to express both its fear of crime and its revulsion of criminals."[122] But this begs the question of why capital punishment became such a powerful symbol in the United States but not elsewhere. The institution of capital punishment in the United States has been stubbornly impervious to rational or scientific arguments that have been its undoing elsewhere. In the U.S. case alone, attempts to abolish capital punishment sparked a powerful countermovement that succeeded in bringing back executions in the name of defending law and order that contributed to the construction of the carceral state.

Looking back on the 1960s from the vantage point of more than three decades of massive, nearly continuous, growth in the carceral state, it is tempting to single out the actions of key politicians as decisive turning points that set the United States firmly on its punitive path. Yet what is remarkable about the 1960s, for all the political and violent unrest, is that views on crime and punishment were still in great flux. This was particularly so in the case of capital punishment. For much of the decade, capital punishment was not a central issue. Politicians and public officials perceived the political costs of opposing the death penalty as low, or ones they were willing to pay. Even some public officials who became notorious law-and-order advocates, for example Richard Nixon and Georgia's Lester Maddox, did not immediately embrace death as the answer. Until the mid-1970s, one would be hard-pressed to talk about the existence of a pro-death penalty movement.

This chapter and the preceding one examined the wider political context in which capital punishment developed and was transformed as an institution. Through an exceptional set of circumstances, capital punishment got lodged in the judicial process long before the contemporary anti-death penalty movement congealed and well before the death penalty became a cause célèbre among conservative leaders and their followers. Lodged in the courts, its fiercest opponents became public interest lawyers and civil rights organizations bereft of a wider political movement to press the case for abolishing capital punishment. Initially these lawyers and groups did not have to contend with any organized movement dedicated to preserving the death penalty. As a consequence, the debate over the death penalty was channeled in certain directions that ironically helped to preserve capital punishment and lock in the carceral state.

The battle over the death penalty that erupted in the early 1970s contributed to the construction of the carceral state in complex ways. Because capital punishment had been anchored for decades in the judicial system, the legal debate surrounding the death penalty set up important parameters that helped lock in the carceral state. The legal arguments to which the abolitionists appealed were ambiguous and thus could be "infused with different meanings." Conservatives appropriated these arguments, most notably about the legitimacy of public sentiment in formulating penal policy. They also recognized that the death penalty had enormous potential for framing and directing how the public felt about broader social and political changes over the last three or four decades.[123]

When the decade-long moratorium on executions ended with Gary Gilmore's 1977 death by firing squad in Utah, capital punishment was on its way to becoming a central governing political institution in the United States. The number of executions since its reinstatement has yet to become a stampede, though the number of prisoners on death row today – about 3,400 – nearly equals the total number executed between 1930 and 1967.[124] Nonetheless, the death penalty has cast a long, dark shadow over the U.S. penal system and the politics of punishment.

By the late twentieth century, capital punishment and the carceral state had become firmly entrenched political institutions that were mutually reinforcing. Capital punishment insinuated itself in complex ways into the national debate on crime and punishment. To abolish capital punishment today risks delegitimizing other pieces of the carceral state. Steiker and Steiker argue that constitutional regulation of capital punishment played a significant role in entrenching the death penalty over the past three decades.[125] I go a step further to argue that the regulation of capital punishment in the courts had powerful spill-over effects. It shaped how proponents and opponents of the death penalty organized themselves. But it also helped to legitimize the conservative, zero-sum view of victims and offenders. It contributed to an erosion of the separation between state and society in the making of penal policy, allowing blunt measures of public passions, such as opinion polls, to be accorded a central role. This contributed to a reframing of the debate over crime and punishment in ways that facilitated the construction of the carceral state. Most significantly, it deflected attention away from the central question of what are the limits, if any, to the state's power to punish and kill.

10 CONCLUSION

Whither the Carceral State?

"The way prisons are run and their inmates treated gives a faithful picture of a society, especially of the ideas and methods of those who dominate that society. Prisons indicate the distance to which government and social conscience have come in their concern and respect for the human being."

– Milovan Djilas[1]

T HE EMERGENCE AND CONSOLIDATION of the U.S. carceral state was a major milestone in American political development that arguably rivals in significance the expansion and contraction of the welfare state in the postwar period. What we have witnessed is a "durable shift in governing authority," to use Karen Orren and Stephen Skowronek's elegant definition of what constitutes political development.[2] The state began to exercise vast new controls over millions of people, resulting in a remarkable change in the distribution of authority in favor of law enforcement and corrections at the local, state, and particularly the federal level.

This book takes the carceral state as a central object of historical study whose construction was an important chapter in American state-building and not just the manifestation of a successful political whim by strategic conservative politicians. This political development had multiple and "dispersed causes" that pre-date the 1960s.[3] The central focus has been on the political development of penal policy. But my account touches on some other important and recurrent themes and debates in American political development. First, it challenges the common understanding of the U.S. state as weak. Over the past three decades, the U.S. state has developed awesome powers and an extensive apparatus to monitor, incarcerate, and execute its citizens that is unprecedented in modern U.S. history and among other Western countries. This development raises deeply troubling questions about the health of democratic institutions in the United States.

Second, my analysis stresses the complex ways that the country's racial divide both thwarted and facilitated the establishment of the carceral state. For much of U.S. history, racial, ethnic, and regional divisions periodically acted as a check on the development of criminal justice institutions, especially at the national level, even as they fueled popular passions to criminalize certain behaviors and certain groups. The moral crusades over issues like "white slavery," Prohibition, and juvenile delinquency that regularly convulsed the country were a backhanded way of building the criminal justice apparatus by fits and starts. Once Jim Crow came tumbling down in the postwar decades, the path was clearer for the rapid development of these institutions, especially at the federal level.

This is an ironic outcome that underscores King and Smith's point about how a "white supremacist" order and a "transformative egalitarian" one have been and continue to be central features, if not mainsprings, of American political development.[4] My analysis bolsters their contention that these two orders remained powerfully linked to one another and are constantly evolving, not stagnant. Chapters 5 and 6, for example, showed how a commitment to greater gender equality by reducing rape and domestic violence got funnelled through a specific political and institutional context and got transformed in the process. The result was a more punitive environment that contributed to the construction of the carceral state that warehouses a disproportionate number of blacks and other minorities. Chapter 7 demonstrated how a powerful prisoners' movement premised on, among other things, calls for greater racial equality, helped propel a powerful law-and-order backlash whose wrath came down hardest on people of color.

My account problematizes the conventional periodization of the past four decades as the "law-and-order" era in at least three ways. First, it shows how law and order was a recurrent and major theme in American politics long before the 1960s. Second, it identifies a number of historically embedded institutional developments that laid the foundation for the construction of the carceral state. These include, to list but a few, the historical underdevelopment of the U.S. welfare state; the early establishment of an extensive network of rights-based and other public interest groups stretching back to the 1920s that helped lodge capital punishment in the courts, not the legislature; the exceptional nature of the origins and development of the public prosecutor in the United States; and the country's long history of morally charged crusades that helped build the law enforcement apparatus by fits and starts.

Finally, my analysis presents the contemporary law-and-order era as more fluid and contingent than is commonly assumed. Politicians so readily identified today as penal hard-liners, like Nixon, Reagan, and even segregationist Lester Maddox, did not immediately march in lockstep toward more punitive public policies after Barry Goldwater denounced the "growing menace" to personal safety in his electrifying speech before the Republican convention in 1964.[5] Nor did these public officials single-handedly impose the carceral state. Political leaders and government officials are not incidental in my account. But as Skowronek reminded us more than two decades ago, "states change (or fail to change) through political struggles rooted in and mediated by preestablished institutional arrangements."[6] My account singles out certain institutional arrangements as well as particular interest groups and social movements not usually associated with penal conservatism to explain why the creation of the carceral state did not face more political opposition. It highlights how engagement with the state over penal policy had unanticipated consequences for these groups and movements. For example, the risks of co-optation were high for some of them, especially the women's movement. To borrow from Theodore Lowi and Orren and Skowronek, "new government policies create[ed] new politics."[7]

Like other historically rooted accounts of the development of social policy and governing institutions, this one seeks to provide a means "to distinguish deeply rooted phenomena from new ones." But it also attempts to demonstrate "that what is was not always so, and thus not always must be so."[8] Sometimes scholars of American political development are guilty of overemphasizing how entrenched policy paths are.[9] As a consequence, they neglect critical junctures when politics no longer "proceeds according to existing political arrangements and ideological commitments" and instead veers off in a new direction that fundamentally changes the governing rules.[10] It is beyond the scope of this book to outline in its concluding chapter a laundry list of policy proposals to roll back the carceral state and a road map for how to achieve them.[11] Instead, extrapolating from the analysis of the preceding chapters, this final chapter focuses on the political prospects for reform, in particular the potential building blocks for a successful penal reform coalition.

Before doing so, I want to spell out what my vision of reform is. As in any discussion of public policy reform, we should not just assume that "reform" means progressive movement toward some social, economic, or political outcome that is widely recognized as necessary and desirable. Like other historically based accounts of the origins and development of social policy, this one underscores how measures heralded as "reforms" often have negative, unanticipated consequences. In the case of penal policy, many so-called reforms of the past resulted in a further consolidation of carceral power and the legitimization of continued abuses.

My vision of penal reform is premised on not just halting the expansion of the carceral state, but on dismantling it. This means slashing the U.S. incarceration rate to a level comparable to other advanced industrialized countries. A good goal to start with would be to reduce the state and federal prison population to its historic average of about 110 prisoners per 100,000. To reach that goal, the United States would have to cut its combined imprisonment rate for the states and the federal government by more than 75 percent.[12] Reform also means reducing the vast and growing racial and ethnic disparities in the incarcerated population. Furthermore, it entails infusing the U.S. penal system with an ethos of respect and dignity for its millions of prisoners, parolees, probationers, and former prisoners that is sorely lacking. In practical terms, this means restoring civil and other basic rights to prisoners and former prisoners in recognition of what Alexander Paterson, the famous English prison commissioner of the early twentieth century, once said: "Men come to prison as a punishment, not for punishment. It is the sentence of imprisonment, and not the treatment accorded in prison, that constitutes the punishment."[13] This means recognizing our "solidarity with the expelled of society" and making life behind bars as humane as possible, even if we cannot prove it reduces the recidivism rate.[14] As the Swedish Minister of Justice Herman Kling once said: "We must practice humanity without expecting anything in return."[15] Finally, reform means abolishing capital punishment in the United States. The death penalty, which virtually every other industrialized democracy has abandoned, props up the U.S. carceral state in complicated and troubling ways, as shown in Chapters 8 and 9.

Criminal justice reform is a highly fragile project.[16] Without some broader vision and movement for change, the U.S. carceral state, trimmed down a little by a few modest sentencing and drug law reforms, will be here to stay. That broader vision has to be premised on presenting the carceral state as first and foremost a pressing civil and human rights issue. To do that, opponents of the prison have to look at home and abroad. At home, they need to make the argument against the carceral state in terms of race, civil rights, and, yes, family values. But they also need to look abroad and link the movement to changes in international human rights norms and laws.

Elisabeth Clemens and Orren and Skowronek make the provocative suggestion that those who are excluded or repressed by the current governing and institutional arrangements may be the ones best poised to redirect policy toward a new path. These marginalized groups "will have a hard time getting a hearing from those in power." Nonetheless they are much more likely to challenge the legitimacy of the current system and to throw their support to those who call for fundamental institutional changes.[17] Certainly, the key building blocks of any successful penal reform coalition are likely to be marginalized groups, including African Americans and other minority groups disproportionately hurt by the carceral state, current and former prisoners and their families, and civil rights and human rights organizations. But it is hard to imagine these groups dismantling the carceral state without some support from more mainstream groups and organizations, like the legal profession, the judiciary, and academic experts on crime and punishment.

After first addressing the issue of the mounting economic pressures on the carceral state, this chapter discusses the potential contribution of each

of these groups to a reform coalition. It also identifies some of the risks of
engaging with the state over specific penal issues. The chapter concludes
with a discussion of the growing gulf between the federal government and
the states over penal policy and how the September 11 attacks and "war
on terror" may affect the future course of the carceral state.

Dollars, Sense, and Mass Incarceration

Some contend that growing public dismay over the crushing economic
costs of incarcerating more than two million people on any given day and
monitoring millions more on parole and probation heralds the beginning
of the end of the prison boom.[18] As evidence, they point to recent penal
developments in the states. In the face of the most serious economic down-
turn in more than a decade, many states began to reconsider some of their
penal policies and their overall approach to crime several years ago. As the
fastest growing item in most state budgets, corrections became a target for
budget cutters. Severe budget deficits forced some states to close prisons
and lay off guards. Deficits also prompted states to experiment with new
sentencing formulas, mostly directed at nonviolent offenders.[19] In 2001
and 2002, thirteen states enacted changes that softened some of their sentencing and drug policies.[20] During the 2003 legislative sessions, more
than two dozen did so. States repealed mandatory minimums for some
nonviolent offenses; relaxed truth-in-sentencing requirements; expanded
the number of people in prison eligible for early release; enhanced treatment options for nonviolent drug offenders; granted judges greater discretion in sentencing certain felony offenders; and expanded the use of
drug courts, the specialized courts first introduced in the late 1980s to
better process drug cases.[21]

Fiscally conservative Republicans previously known for being penal
hard-liners championed some of these recent relaxations in penal policy.
This prompted speculation that law-and-order Republicans, troubled by
mounting costs, are well poised to roll back the carceral state, much as
red-baiter Richard Nixon was well situated to breach the great political wall with China.[22] For example, former Senator Barry Goldwater
(R-Ariz.) was a key supporter of a 1996 ballot initiative passed in Arizona
that called for diverting drug offenders into treatment rather than sending them to prison. The Arizona measure inspired similar ballot initiatives in other states, including California, Michigan, and Ohio. Another
example is former Governor William G. Milliken, who recently characterized his signing of Michigan's mandatory minimum sentencing law
in 1978 as "the worst mistake of my career."[23] The longtime governor
supported a set of reforms enacted in late 2002 that eliminated most of
Michigan's mandatory minimum sentences, which were the harshest in the
nation.

We should be cautious about assuming that the fiscal crisis of the states and the softening of public opinion with the sustained drop in the crime rate over the past decade will automatically forge a durable and meaningful consensus on penal policy between penal reformers and fiscal and penal conservatives.[24] It was mistakenly assumed three decades ago that shared disillusionment on the right and the left with the rehabilitative ideal would shrink the prison population. Instead, it exploded. The foregoing analysis demonstrates that criminal justice policies often confound conventional distinctions between left and right, particularly on issues related to crime victims. The relationship between political leaders, social movements, interest groups, and governing institutions is highly contingent and volatile in the case of penal policy because the left–right divide is more blurred and because of certain institutional features of the U.S. criminal justice system and welfare state discussed in earlier chapters.

It is important to keep in mind that the race to incarcerate began in the 1970s at a time when states faced comparably dire financial straits. It was sustained despite wide fluctuations in the crime rate and in public opinion over the next two decades, as discussed in Chapter 2. The economic burden of the burgeoning carceral state was a glaring omission in public policy debates at the time.[25] In the 1980s, many foes of the prison buildup mistakenly took comfort in the belief that fiscal constraints would curb the number of people sent to prison. Yet as Norval Morris warned in his closing address to a conference on prison overcrowding more than two decades ago, fiscal concerns are "an extraordinarily weak reed to rely on" because "states and the federal government are capable of the most extraordinary absorption of increased numbers."[26] For instance, in 1994 the Harris County Commissioners in Texas attempted to increase taxes to cover the huge costs of capital punishment trials. Harris County includes the city of Houston, which has the dubious distinction of leading the country in capital cases. The county's voters rejected the tax hike. As a consequence, fire and ambulance services had to be cut to free up money to pay the enormous cost of prosecuting death penalty cases.[27]

The seemingly compelling economic rationale to shrink the carceral state is likely to be offset by several other factors. First, the sentencing laws of the 1990s remain quite rigid, despite some modest reforms.[28] While states have relaxed some drug laws, the penalties still remain very stiff. For instance, in 2001 the Louisiana legislature eliminated mandatory sentences for certain nonviolent offenses and cut many drug sentences in half. Defendants convicted of possessing 28 grams of cocaine now face sentences of five to thirty years, down from ten to sixty years.[29] Second, the "war on terror" may propel states to toughen up. In 2003, Oregon State Senator John Minnis, chairman of the Senate Judiciary Committee, proposed legislation that would make the crime of "terrorism" punishable by life imprisonment.[30] Finally, while the prison-industrial complex was not a central factor in constructing the carceral state, it has become a significant factor in sustaining it today as prison guards' unions, private prison companies, and the suppliers of everything from telephone services to Taser stun guns press on local communities, states, and the federal government to maintain the carceral state.[31]

The November 2004 defeat of Proposition 66 in California should add a note of caution to the budding optimism that economic pressures at the state level are bringing the carceral state to a halt.[32] Proposition 66, placed on the ballot by prisoners' families, called for relaxing California's "three-strikes" law, which is the harshest in the nation. The ballot initiative required that the "third strike" be for a "serious" or "violent" felony and not just for a minor infraction like petty theft, possession of small amounts of drugs, burglary of an unoccupied home, or failure to re-register on time as a sex offender. This ballot measure was designed to permit 4,500 people already sentenced to twenty-five-years-to-life terms under the existing three-strikes law whose third strike was a minor offense to be re-sentenced. This could save potentially billions of dollars in long-term incarceration costs. To neutralize charges that the initiative was soft on crime, Proposition 66 markedly stiffened the punishments for many sex crimes, most notably by making first-time sex offenders who were guilty of molesting a child under the age of ten eligible for a sentence of twenty-five years to life.

Proposition 66 enjoyed widespread support from about two-thirds of the public right up until the week before the election, according to opinion polls. Yet the measure ended up garnering only 46 percent on Election Day, due to a well-heeled last-minute advertising blitz financed by $2 million raised by Governor Arnold Schwarzenegger, $3.5 million from billionaire Henry Nicholas III, and at least $700,000 from the state's powerful prison guards' union. Opponents of the measure saturated the airwaves with commercials that stoked the public's fear of crime. One commercial featured Schwarzenegger misleadingly warning that, if Proposition 66 passed, "26,000 murderers, rapists and child molesters would be released to your neighborhood." The ad concluded with a scene of a cell door slamming shut on three prisoners.[33]

To make the economic arguments more persuasive, opponents of national and state trends in incarceration need to enlist the support of sectors of the criminal justice system other than corrections.[34] The criminal justice system has competing constituencies. Police chiefs, prosecutors, and other law enforcement officials have concerns about how escalating corrections costs are leaving less money available for services like policing and crime prevention.[35] Opponents of the carceral state also need to seek the support of state and nonstate actors involved in providing other essential services, like health care and education. They need to underscore which school does not get built, which hospital closes, and which public health program is curtailed because some prison had to be built and maintained. Some foes of the carceral state have been particularly effective at demonstrating how the costly race to incarcerate has been run on the backs of higher education, leaving many public colleges and universities strapped for cash. Others are successfully pressing the point that prisons do not necessarily bring economic prosperity to the local communities in which they are built.[36]

Some policy makers and legislators are now more sensitive to the connection between penal policy and long-term fiscal health. But others are not. A model example is North Carolina, which revolutionized its sentencing structure in 1994 based on the recommendations of the Sentencing and Policy Advisory Commission established by the state legislature in 1990. North Carolina created a new sentencing structure that was tougher on violent and habitual offenders and that established a variety of lesser, intermediate community punishments for nonviolent offenders. The linchpin of this transformation was the legislature's requirement that the commission develop a sophisticated computer model to forecast the resources needed to implement various recommended changes in penal policy. By law, the commission is required to make annual projections about the state's prison population over the coming decade. The simulation model developed by the commission has been extremely accurate. In 1980, North Carolina had the highest incarceration rate in the country. Two decades later it ranked thirty-first in the nation and had the second lowest rate in the South.[37]

In forcing economic considerations to be a central factor in determining prison policy, North Carolina may be more the exception than the rule. A number of other states now require fiscal impact statements whose effects on actual penal policy can vary enormously.[38] In many states, policy makers continue to pursue ad hoc solutions that may save money over the short run but may be extremely expensive over the long term. Budget cutters have targeted "nonessential" prison programs. These primarily include educational, substance abuse, and vocational programs. For example, in 2001 Illinois eliminated its $5.4 million budget for higher education in state prisons, a cutback that affected nearly 60 percent of its prisoners.[39] States are more receptive now to diverting first-time drug offenders into treatment rather than sending them to prison. But many of them also are reducing in-prison and community-based treatment programs.[40] While such cuts certainly save money over the short term, they may increase the recidivism rate over the long run and thus contribute to the maintenance of the carceral state.

Most prison costs are fixed ones, not amenable to significant budget cutting. Still, penal authorities and policy makers are under pressure to do something about escalating corrections budgets. So they are making cuts that do not save much money but are highly symbolic. Many of these cutbacks have a significant negative impact on the quality of life behind bars and on offenders' prospects for successful reentry after prison.[41] State authorities are responding to the crisis in corrections costs much as they and the private sector have responded to the periodic crisis of skyrocketing health-care costs over the past two decades – by reducing services and engaging in cost shifting. States have been doubling and even quadrupling the fees they charge offenders for items like monthly probation and parole supervision and electronic monitoring.[42] They have increased co-pays and fees for medical services, and some are even charging prisoners for their daily board. Furthermore, states have been restricting medical treatment and health-care screening and privatizing or contracting out services, notably health care, often with disastrous results.[43] One of the most mean-spirited budget moves has been reducing the amount and quality of food served to people in prison.[44]

As state budgets come under increased pressure, the risk is great that U.S. prisons will become even leaner and meaner. Rosa Davis, the chief assistant attorney general in Alabama, acknowledges that her state has slashed spending on corrections so much "that our prison system now looks like a third world country."[45] Alabama spends less per prisoner than any other state – about $10,000 per year. Its 28,000 prisoners are housed in prisons built for 12,000. Recently the state has been subject to two court orders to alleviate its overcrowded facilities, as well as additional litigation involving charges of grossly inadequate health care for people in prison.[46]

In short, the construction of the carceral state was the result of a complex set of historical, institutional, and political developments. No single factor explains its rise, and no single factor will bring about its demise. This should prompt us to be skeptical of claims that any single new development, such as mounting economic pressures, will undo the carceral state. As Samuel Gidley Howe, the nineteenth-century American philanthropist and prison reformer, soberly reminds us, "Institutions...so strongly built, so richly endowed...cannot be got rid of so easily."[47]

The latest data on incarceration trends are a sobering reminder of this. The recent spurt of sentencing and drug law reforms has yet to make any real dent in the overall size of the incarcerated population. The number of people in prison or jail has continued to grow, but at a slower rate, as shown in Table 1. The most significant slowdown has been in the rate of increase for state prisons. In the 1990s they were growing at an average annual rate of 6 percent. Since the mid-1990s, the rate has averaged less than half that. However, the incarceration rate for local jails has not experienced a comparable slowdown and actually accelerated significantly in 2002 and 2003. The growth of the federal prison population continues nearly unabated. In the 1990s, the federal prison system grew by an average of almost 9 percent annually. Since the mid-1990s, it has been growing

TABLE 1. *Percentage Change in Number of Prisoners Held in State or Federal Prisons or in Local Jails, 1999–2003*

Year	Total in custody	Federal[1]	State[1]	Local jails[2]	Incarceration rate[3]
1999	2.9	13.4	2.1	2.3	691
2000	2.1	6.6	1.5	2.5	684
2001	1.3	7.0	0.4	1.6	685
2002	3.7	5.8	2.5	5.4	701
2003	2.6	6.6	1.4	3.9	714
Average Annual Increase, 1995–2003					
	3.5	7.7	2.7	4.0	
Average Annual Increase, 1990–1999					
	5.7	8.8	6	4.6	

Sources: Bureau of Justice Statistics Bulletin, "Prisoners in 1999," August 2000, p. 2, Table 1; "Prisoners in 2000," August 2001, p. 2, Table 1; "Prisoners in 2001," July 2002, p. 2, Table 1; "Prisoners in 2002," July 2003, p. 2, Table 1; and "Prisoners in 2003," November 2004, p. 2, Table 1.

[1] Based on prisoners in state or federal prison on December 31.
[2] Based on inmates held in jail as of June 30.
[3] Number of prison and jail inmates per 100,000 U.S. residents at year end.

at an average of 7.7 percent per year, or more than two-and-a-half times the rate for the state prison population.

Civil Rights and the Carceral State

In making the case against the carceral state, opponents need to resist the temptation to reduce this mainly to a question of dollars and cents. Just as slavery was not defeated by economic arguments, the carceral state is fundamentally a social and political question, not an economic one.[48] To mount a sustained assault on it means knitting together a broad political coalition and movement that does not depend on the vagaries of the economy and is held together by more than just arguments about what is good for the bottom line.

Elite politicians did not single-handedly create the carceral state. Thus, a change of heart by some of them now may be a necessary but not sufficient condition for its dismantling. The recent focus on the softening of some Republican hard-liners has overshadowed the burgeoning movement of a wide range of other groups at the local, state, and national level now pushing politicians and policy makers to rethink the carceral state. For example, the organization Families Against Mandatory Minimums was critical in spearheading the enormous grassroots effort in Michigan that rolled back the state's harsh mandatory minimum statutes. FAMM eventually enlisted many organizations in its cause, including the NAACP, the

Michigan Catholic Conference, and prosecutors' and defense attorneys' associations.[49] The activities of national organizations like The Sentencing Project, the ACLU (which in 1994 called for the decriminalization of all drugs), and the Campaign for New Drug Policies (funded by billionaire George Soros and others) have been vital in mobilizing public support in favor of treatment over prison for substance abuse.[50]

Opponents of the carceral state should not automatically reject strategies based on asserting legal or other rights just because rights-based discourses have bolstered the carceral state in the past, most notably in the case of the consolidation of the conservative victims' rights movement discussed in Chapter 4. Rights discourses can make people more passive and dependent on the state and more vulnerable to co-optation. But they can also be "part of the larger process of political struggle."[51] As Kimberlé Crenshaw argues, "Most efforts to change an oppressive situation are bound to adopt the dominant discourse to some degree." Powerless people have few other options. "There are risks and dangers involved both in engaging in the dominant discourse *and* in failing to do so."[52] What the analysis of the preceding chapters should help do is to identify some of those potential risks and pitfalls and perhaps how to navigate around them.

Deteriorating prison conditions around the country and the disproportionate impact the carceral state has had on African Americans and other racial and ethnic minorities raise some serious civil rights questions. African Americans and other minority groups need to be central pillars of any reform coalition. But African Americans have been slow to enlist in the battle against the carceral state. Historically, black leaders have had a persistent unease about focusing on criminal justice issues. In the late nineteenth and early twentieth centuries, leading blacks like Booker T. Washington, W. E. B. DuBois, and Mary Church Terrell called for the abolition of convict leasing. But at the time, "many middle-class black leaders remained defensive about black criminality." They "often tempered their criticism of the legal system with calls for the moral reform of black people and the provision of juvenile facilities for young black offenders."[53] DuBois complained that blacks "continually and systematically neglect Negroes who have been arrested, or who are accused of crime, or who have been convicted and incarcerated."[54]

One can speculate that some of the same factors that prompted African Americans to distance themselves from the AIDS crisis in the black community in the 1980s and 1990s, as shown by Cathy Cohen, may be causing them to turn a blind eye to the crisis of blacks and the carceral state today.[55] The reluctance to embrace and publicize the plight of the disproportionate number of incarcerated African Americans may reflect fears that this will reflect unfavorably on blacks as a whole and impede black leaders' efforts to identify with what they perceive to be the middle-class moral values of the mainstream. Many black legislators and other black leaders initially were enthusiastic recruits in the war on drugs and even supported the enormous sentencing disparity between crack and powder cocaine, which disproportionately hurts African Americans.[56] Some civil rights groups have been reluctant to use the federal Voting Rights Act to challenge felon disenfranchisement laws "for fear of a backlash that might jeopardize the rights of the more privileged members of the black community."[57]

Some African-American leaders and groups have begun to speak out and mobilize more forcefully against the war on drugs and the carceral state. Calls are increasing to develop a principled framework for African Americans to engage selectively in jury nullification as an intermediate solution to challenge the carceral state.[58] The Rev. Jesse Jackson, Sr., and Colin Powell were the only national political figures to make mass imprisonment, particularly of black Americans, a central theme of their speeches to the Democratic and Republican conventions in 2000.[59] In 1993–94, the Congressional Black Caucus was a major factor in getting crime prevention programs included in the federal crime bill. The CBC also waged a valiant but ultimately losing battle to enact the Racial Justice Act, which would have permitted introducing into death penalty cases statistical evidence of racial discrimination in the administration of capital punishment. Their campaign for the Racial Justice Act made explicit links between civil rights issues and fair crime control policies. Shrewd political maneuvering by President Clinton helped defeat the act.[60]

The Legal Defense Fund of the NAACP and some other civil rights groups have begun to take up the cause of sentencing reform and other incarceration issues. Elaine R. Jones, the outgoing leader of the Fund, acknowledged that middle-class blacks were not initially aware of the huge negative repercussions of measures like the mandatory minimum drug laws.[61] The Fund has been at the forefront of challenging felon disenfranchisement laws in the courts.[62] The voting irregularities of the 2000 and 2004 presidential elections drew enormous public attention to the plight of the estimated five million Americans who are barred from voting by a maze of state laws that deny former felons the right to vote, sometimes temporarily, sometimes permanently. Florida's felon disenfranchisement law bans an estimated 600,000 former prisoners from voting for life.[63] The ban disproportionately affects African-American men, denying a quarter of Florida's black males access to the ballot. Nationwide, an estimated 13 percent of black males are disenfranchised by these bans.[64] Many other countries permit former felons and even current prisoners to vote, while others deny the right to vote to only certain categories of prisoners.[65] Civil rights activists "predict that voting rights for prisoners and ex-prisoners will be the next suffrage movement."[66] The American Correctional Association has called on states to end felon disenfranchisement, and Democrats in the House and Senate periodically have introduced legislation to restore voting rights to ex-offenders.[67] In 2005 Governor Tom Vilsack (D-Iowa) signed an order to restore the voting rights of all felons in his state who have completed their sentences, overturning one of the strictest disenfranchisement laws in the country.[68]

Despite the increase in activism by African Americans and others around incarceration issues, the idea that the vast and growing racial disparities in U.S. prisons is a cause for public alarm has yet to take hold with the wider public.[69] Opponents of the carceral state need to press policy makers and the public to take more account of how certain penal policies exacerbate racial disparities in incarceration. But they also need to present the construction of the carceral state as an unprecedented civil rights issue. Many of today's crime control policies fundamentally impede the economic, political, and social advancement of the most disadvantaged blacks and members of other minority groups in the United States.[70] Prison leaves them less likely to find gainful employment, vote, participate in other civic activities, and maintain ties with their families and communities.[71]

One of the best ways to underscore this point is to focus on the family. As Susan Phillips and Barbara Bloom suggest, by getting tough on crime, the United States has also gotten tough on the millions of children who will have a parent in prison at some point during their lifetimes.[72] In his speech before the 2000 Republican convention, Colin Powell stressed that "it's time to stop building jails in America and get back to the task of building our children."[73] Today more than 1.5 million children, or 2 percent of the nation's minors, have a parent in prison. More than half of all children with imprisoned parents are black. As of 2000, an astonishing 7.5 percent of black children had a parent in prison, as did one out of every forty Hispanic children.[74] The organization Mothers Reclaiming Our Children, founded in California in the early 1990s, battles the carceral state by emphasizing how each prisoner is someone's child. It "critically deploys the ideological power of motherhood to challenge the legitimacy" of the carceral state.[75] Another pioneering group emphasizing the link between families, children, and incarceration is Legal Services for Prisoners With Children, founded by Ellen Barry in San Francisco in 1978.[76] Groups like these still have an uphill battle to defend the rights of prisoners who are parents and children who have incarcerated parents. For instance, in early 2005 a bill was introduced in California to deny any person incarcerated for a violent offense an overnight family visit. The bill did not pass.

Strategies to unhinge the carceral state by highlighting rights issues, particularly the stark racial and ethnic disparities that permeate U.S. jails, prisons, and death row, are not risk free. They could perversely result in an increase in the number of people incarcerated and in those sentenced to death. There is a risk that penal conservatives, confronted with the growing racial and ethnic disparities of the U.S. carceral state, will respond with another wave of "leveling down" in penal policy. Instead of lessening the punishments for blacks and other minorities, they may attempt to raise the ante for whites by subjecting them to tougher sentences and invoking the death penalty more often for whites in another expression of brute liberal egalitarianism.

As James Q. Whitman argues, the much heralded "liberal" features of American political culture have ironically contributed to making the U.S. penal system harsher, more degrading, and less forgiving. In the absence or rejection of an aristocratic political culture and society, prison reform in the United States has historically been based on extending a brute egalitarianism, on giving all prisoners, regardless of their social or political status, the same "low-status" treatment. By contrast, Germany and France have deeply entrenched histories of making sharp distinctions between the treatment of "low-status" prisoners, that is common criminals, and "high-status" ones, such as political prisoners or members of the aristocracy. Prison reform in the modern era in France and Germany has meant extending the privileges traditionally accorded to "high-status" prisoners to more and more categories of offenders. This "leveling up" has been so extensive that by now prisoners "are not to be thought of as persons of a different and lower status than everybody else."[77]

In the United States, "leveling down" remains a real risk. In their dissent from a favorable report on the Racial Justice Act by the House Judiciary Committee, Representative Henry Hyde (R-Ill.) and others argued that, if the purpose of the legislation was really to remedy race-of-victim discrimination in capital punishment cases, there was a better solution: seek the death penalty in more instances in which blacks murdered blacks.[78] After the Minnesota Supreme Court invalidated the state's crack–powder cocaine penalty distinction, state legislators responded by raising the penalty for powder cocaine. President Clinton and members of Congress suggested a similar solution when confronted with evidence of stark racial disparities in sentencing for crack and powder cocaine offenses.[79]

The Carceral State and International Human Rights

The development of international human rights laws and norms related to criminal justice is another promising frontier for penal reform.[80] International and regional human rights laws and national constitutions and statutes currently grant vast procedural protections to criminal defendants in most Western countries and place limits on such practices as corporal punishment and torture. While pretrial custody and criminal trials are subject to strict regulation, the problem of unnecessarily long and disproportionate sentences has not been a central human rights issue. "It is time for legal philosophers and reformers to plug this 'human rights gap,'" according to Richard S. Frase. "Proportionality limitations on sentencing severity are closely related to human rights principles."[81] While the United States remains far outside the movement to develop international norms of sentencing and proportionality, Europe has begun to plug this gap.

For more than a century, "a great deal of pioneering zeal and faith has been invested" in the idea of creating international rules and standards for imprisonment.[82] Until recently, that promise has remained largely unfulfilled. The accelerated political and economic integration of Europe over the past couple of decades has increased pressure on European countries to be more aware of how their penal policies and prison conditions stack up against those of their neighbors. This has helped neutralize some of the growing internal political pressures to be more punitive in countries like Britain. The obstacles to establishing specific, stringent, and enforceable international prison and penal standards are considerable. Nonetheless, the Prison Rules promulgated by the Council of Europe demonstrate that international standards and principles – even if they fall short of some detailed and enforceable ideal – can exert a significant "moral and political influence."[83]

The trauma of World War II sensitized Europe to the urgent need for international standards for the protection of human rights and the treatment of prisoners. This resulted in the Universal Declaration of Human Rights in 1948 and the United Nations Standard Minimum Rules for the Treatment of Prisoners (SMRTP) in 1955, followed by the enactment of similar declarations by the Council of Europe in 1953 and 1973. Efforts to integrate Europe accelerated the push to establish penal norms for Europe. In 1981, the European Committee for Cooperation in Prison Affairs (CCPA) was given wide leeway to apply the SMRTP in Europe. In February 1987 the Council of Europe's Committee of Ministers adopted a set of prison rules drawn up under the auspices of the European Committee on Crime Problems.[84] Three guiding beliefs shaped these rules: that deprivation of liberty should be the sole instrument of punishment for those sent to prison; that reeducation and resocialization of offenders should be the main aim of treatment; and that prisons must respect the basic rights of individuals and foster a humane, dignified environment.[85] While the rules are not binding in international law, they have been influential because "they impose political obligations and exercise a moral sanction on national authorities."[86] The CCPA has broad powers to monitor and publicize information about prison conditions and penal policies in the member states. The information it disseminates through the Council of Europe's *Prison Information Bulletin* is vital for following comparative penal developments in Europe and identifying policies and practices that appear out of line. The CCPA has significant power and authority to ensure conformity with the rules.[87]

Efforts like these by the Council of Europe have contributed to the considerable self-consciousness in Britain about its relatively high incarceration rate (by European – but not American – standards). Britain's imprisonment rate has prompted unflattering comparisons and jibes, even by top British officials.[88] The United States is likewise highly vulnerable to unfavorable cross-national comparisons. Through their detailed reports on subjects like capital punishment, the widespread use of life sentences, supermax prisons, abuse of female prisoners, prison rape, and other disturbing conditions in U.S. prisons, human rights organizations like Amnesty International and Human Rights Watch and leading penal reform groups like The Sentencing Project have been drawing increased national and international attention to how U.S. penal practices are out of line with those of other Western countries.

Increased globalization and regional integration promise to whittle away at the vast sovereignty that the United States and other countries have enjoyed in the area of sentencing and penal policy.[89] But this will not necessarily result in lower incarceration rates. Pressure to adopt "fortress Europe" policies in the face of mounting concerns about immigration, organized crime, and drug trafficking have been exerting an upward push on incarceration rates in Europe for at least a decade.[90] A majority of European countries have experienced significant increases in their prison populations, and foreigners and second-generation immigrants are disproportionately incarcerated in European prisons. The French Parliament recently enacted a new criminal code that provides for life imprisonment without parole. In England and Wales, life imprisonment has received new attention in the context of drug trafficking and violent and sexual offenses.[91] While Germany's sentencing practices remain moderate compared to other countries, its courts and legislature have demonstrated a new willingness to respond to the growing public fear of crime by imposing lengthy sentences and other get-tough measures.[92]

Nonetheless, Europe is not moving overall in a more punitive direction. The extent of the U.S. carceral state continues to dwarf the imprisoned population of Europe, and European penal policy is still strikingly at odds with that of the United States.[93] The Dutch penal climate remains relatively mild. The Netherlands offers a range of alternatives to avoid imprisonment or shorten sentences, and Dutch prisons continue to be some of the most caring in the world. The Netherlands recently revised its prison policies to make its facilities more humane and to limit further the damaging effects of incarceration.[94] Norway and Portugal have abolished life imprisonment. The German Constitutional Court has ruled that life imprisonment must include the possibility of release (except for dangerous offenders). This prompted German legislators to amend the criminal code to allow parole in cases of life imprisonment after fifteen years for prisoners who do not present an ongoing threat to society.[95]

Other Western countries still have few legislatively imposed mandatory minimums. Judges and parole boards elsewhere retain broad discretion. European countries have resisted adopting legally binding sentencing guidelines like those widely used in the United States. They put greater restrictions on imposing consecutive sentences, offer more avenues to appeal unwarranted lengthy sentences, and have decisively abandoned the death penalty.[96]

Reform, the Legal Profession, and the Judiciary

Established professional organizations like the American Bar Association cannot be counted on to be the vanguard to roll back the carceral state.[97] That said, by weighing in or absenting itself at critical junctures, the ABA has affected the development of the carceral state over the years. In the 1950s and 1960s, the ABA was extremely active in developing model sentencing, arraignment, and bail standards.[98] In the 1970s, it was critical in bestowing "the imprimatur of the established legal community" on the prisoners' movement, as discussed in Chapter 7.[99] By the 1980s, the ABA had fallen largely silent on the issue of sentencing reform as its attention shifted to victims' rights.

In 1993, the American Bar Association reentered the fray over sentencing reform with its newly revised *Criminal Justice Standards for Sentencing*, which endorsed state-level sentencing commissions found in places like Minnesota, Oregon, and Washington State. More than four years in the making, this was the first national law project devoted to the problems of sentencing law and policy to appear in fifteen years.[100] In October 2003, ABA President Dennis W. Archer announced the formation of a commission to address injustices and inadequacies in prisons and corrections. Less than a year later, the ABA endorsed the commission's proposals for a return to more discretion in sentencing and for alternatives to long prison terms for less serious crimes.[101] The ABA commission was dubbed the "Kennedy Commission" because it was formed in the aftermath of a speech by Anthony M. Kennedy at the ABA's annual meeting that August in which the U.S. Supreme Court justice criticized the nation's imprisonment policies and called for a repeal of mandatory minimum sentencing laws.[102] During a hearing on the Supreme Court's budget several months earlier, Kennedy told Congress, "Two million people in prison is just unacceptable." Even U.S. Supreme Court Justice Clarence Thomas apparently nodded in agreement when Kennedy criticized mandatory minimums.[103]

Kennedy's actions are evidence of growing judicial activism with respect to the politics of sentencing and other penal issues. For decades the U.S. judiciary has been largely a bystander in some of the major overhauls of the criminal justice system. The Judicial Conference of the United States, the governing organization of the federal judiciary, is a "cumbersome body" that has little lawmaking authority and is not suited for policy innovation or political lobbying. In 1984 federal judges were "passive witnesses" to the legislation creating the U.S. Sentencing Commission. They were not even able to persuade legislators to assign judges the leading role in developing the sentencing guidelines.[104] Recently, more judges have been speaking out against the federal sentencing guidelines and policies like mandatory minimums. However, a majority of the judges now serving on the federal bench were appointed after the guidelines became effective in November 1987. It remains an open question whether they are prepared to jettison a system that many of them have invested so many years in learning.[105]

The Supreme Court's decision in January 2005 declaring the federal sentencing guidelines advisory rather than mandatory is likely to inflame the struggle between penal conservatives and the judiciary over whether Congress or the judiciary controls criminal sentencing. While the judiciary may have won the battle in the two-part Supreme Court decision, it may lose the war. The risk is great that congressional Republicans, the Justice Department, and the Bush administration, persistently unnerved by what they perceive as excessive judicial discretion, will seize on this decision to reassert a central role for the legislature in setting punishment policy and to reiterate their commitment to a hard line. Given that the Republican Party controls both houses of Congress and the White House, and that the Supreme Court has been closely divided over the guidelines question and other signature law-and-order issues (like the death penalty for juvenile offenders under the age of eighteen, which it declared unconstitutional by a 5-to-4 vote in early 2005), penal conservatives are well positioned to impose a new and even tougher sentencing regime that would pass judicial muster and serve to burnish their law-and-order credentials.[106] Congress appears to be moving in that direction. Republicans introduced several draconian crime measures in spring 2005 as the House moved to institute tougher mandatory minimum sentences. Representative James Sensenbrenner (R-Wis.), chairman of the House Judiciary Committee, introduced a bill that would increase the penalties for all drug offenses and included a mandatory two-year prison term for the crime of refusing to report quickly to the police anyone selling marijuana on a campus.[107] In May 2005 the House passed a sweeping bill to fight street gangs that would greatly increase the penalty for gang-related crimes and make more gang members eligible for the death penalty.[108]

Expertise and Politics

The reform agenda presented here lays down a challenge to both scholars of orthodox criminology and political science. The links between crime, criminal justice, and politics need to be more central to the fields of

criminology and political science.[109] Crime control and penal policy are
not just technical, administrative endeavors devoid of politics. Criminologists need to stop thinking of the political aspects of crime and punishment "as both too simple and too elusive to warrant their attention."[110]
As for political scientists, they need to accord the study of penal policy
and crime control a central place in the study of American politics. David
Bazelon, the chief judge of the U.S. Court of Appeals in Washington, D.C.,
reminded the American Society of Criminology in 1977, "[P]olitics is at
the heart of American criminology."[111] We need to recognize that crime
control strategies are profoundly political because they both reflect and
direct the distribution of power in society.[112] "[T]he relationship between
forms of penalty and forms of citizenship is of the first importance for
an understanding of the nature of political relations," according to David
Garland and Peter Young.[113] Experts need to overcome their squeamish-
ness about taking politics seriously. They also need to view engaging the
public in discussions about the future of the carceral state as part of their
professional responsibility. To that end, the need is great for more and better research presented in ways that are readily accessible to policy makers
and the general public.

Several critical areas remain largely unexplored, including comparative and historical scholarship on criminal justice; the implementation of
specific penal policies; and the collateral consequences of incarceration.
Policy makers, scholars, and activists need to pay more attention to documenting and explaining variations in sentencing and other penal practices
across borders. To do so, they must begin by closing the comparative data
gap. Cross-national statistics on crime rates, sentencing, and other aspects
of criminal justice can be incomplete or misleading, and thus vulnerable
to charges of comparing apples with oranges.[114]

Experts and activists also need to look more closely at the comparative history of various penal systems. Historical studies can serve several
purposes. First, studying a system over time helps illuminate the relative
significance or insignificance of political culture in explaining certain penal
developments. Taking the long historical view also sensitizes us to broad
similarities in the evolution of penal systems. It reminds us that the policies
of mass imprisonment that the United States has pursued over the past
three decades may be harbingers of penal developments elsewhere. Historical studies, like cross-national ones, can also be an important source
of new ideas. Furthermore, they are a potent reminder that "old ideas"
have "a way of coming back periodically, even when we do not recognize
them as 'reruns.'"[115]

While the fate of the welfare state has been a central concern of scholars
of American political development, the carceral state has not.[116] Yet the
subfield of American political development is particularly well situated
to take up some of the analytical and political challenges of the carceral

state because of its emphasis on historical and comparative approaches to understanding public policy; its sensitivity to how institutions, social movements, political coalitions, and ideological communities develop over time, often in unanticipated ways with unanticipated consequences; and its growing appreciation of how cross-national and international developments affect public policy.[117] In short, historical-institutional approaches "focus attention on the key features of how politics actually works."[118]

Another conspicuous research gap is the lack of detailed studies of how specific penal policies and programs are actually implemented. Ann Chih Lin's *Reform in the Making* and Zimring, Hawkins, and Kamin's *Punishment and Democracy* are important exceptions.[119] *Reform in the Making* examines the fate of rehabilitative programs in five medium-security prisons. Lin argues that the rehabilitative ideal was discredited and discarded without ever getting a fair hearing. She shows how identical programs will have vastly different effects on the ground depending on how prisons vary in their institutional need for order and the institutional values that govern their different strategies for maintaining order.

If the terms of the debate about prisons and crime are to change in the United States, we need a better understanding of implementation issues, but also of just how extensive the reach of correctional institutions is. Prisons mark not just the person who serves time, but his or her family, community, and the broader society.[120] For all the billions spent on prisons, so far there has been relatively little systematic attention to what John Hagan and Ronit Dinovitzer call the "collateral consequences" of prisons.[121] Alison Liebling, an expert on prison suicide, suggests that the "pains of imprisonment are basically underestimated," perhaps because they are awkward challenges to the belief that "prison works."[122] Many important questions go largely unaddressed. Why do former prisoners have such reduced incomes and employment rates?[123] What effect does having a mother or father in prison have on the children of incarcerated parents? Why are the homicide and suicide rates in U.S. correctional facilities so high?[124] As prisons warehouse more and more people with substance abuse problems, mental illnesses, and serious infectious diseases like HIV/AIDS, TB, and hepatitis C, and as more people grow old behind bars, what will happen to the distribution of health-care resources in prisons and the wider society?[125]

Experts and activists need to figure out how to make prisons, jails, and the lives they mark more visible to the wider society. In the nineteenth century, prisons opened their doors to the public and were a popular destination for gawking domestic and foreign tourists. In the 1960s and early 1970s, prison memoirs and accounts of life behind bars turned up on best-seller lists. Today, prisons are a mystery. One way to make prisons less a world apart is to reclaim the rehabilitative ideal, if for no other reason than that it is a recognition that the wider community has some connection to and responsibility for those it banishes behind bars.[126]

More and better research on prisons and making prisons visible again to the broader society are important first steps toward reversing the race to incarcerate. Zimring, Hawkins, and Kamin go further and argue that the experts may hold the key to changing the politics of crime and punishment in the United States. They contend that the country needs to figure out how to return criminal policy once again to the experts by creating criminal justice institutions that are more insulated from the politicians and the public. Their model is the U.S. Federal Reserve. "The lesson here for criminal justice reform is the importance of a commitment and respect for expertise, which is itself a justifying ideology for the insulated delegation of punishment power."[127] They suggest that sentencing commissions, if properly constructed, might serve as a model of insulated, delegated power for criminal justice policy analogous to what the Federal Reserve does for monetary policy.[128]

Zimring, Hawkins, and Kamin do not specify the political preconditions that would be required to create such insulated criminal justice institutions. They do concede that the conditions necessary to establish institutions insulated from democratic review and those necessary to maintain such institutions once they are up and running are not the same. Their analysis appears to suggest that they do not expect the public, with its anti-offender sentiments, to play a constructive role here. Leaving aside the question of whether the Fed is really apolitical, *Punishment and Democracy* may be guilty of expecting too much from the experts and too little from the public. In stressing the potentially constructive role that experts can play in penal policy, one has to keep in mind that the so-called experts have had a checkered history in penal reform. They have subjected people in prison to therapies ranging from the relatively harmless, like bibliotherapy, to the bizarre and dangerous, like testicular implantation.[129]

Zimring, Hawkins, and Kamin may also be taking too harsh and skeptical a view of the public. As discussed in Chapter 2, polls consistently indicate that U.S. public opinion on criminal justice is fickle and highly malleable in the face of specific events and political manipulation. Moreover, there is some evidence that penal populism may be peaking. A record number of measures to soften drug laws are pending or have been passed by state legislatures in recent years. National debates over high-profile death penalty cases, like the execution of Timothy McVeigh for the Oklahoma City bombing, and over the execution of juveniles, the mentally retarded, and the innocent indicate some softening of public sentiment on capital punishment.

If the comparative history of incarceration teaches us anything, it is that political leadership, not expertise alone, has been responsible for major decarcerations elsewhere. But politicians have to be pushed. In short, the public has to be mobilized and organized to undo the carceral state.[130] In Finland, the small group of experts involved in criminal justice in the 1960s and 1970s became convinced that Finland's high incarceration rate was a disgrace. They provided the data to demonstrate that Finland's rate was way out of line with that of other European countries and unrelated to the level of crime. They reached out to politicians, civil servants, and the public by arguing that criminal justice policy had to be seen in a wider societal context that stressed not only the costs of criminality but also the costs in monetary and human terms of controlling crime. That view was captured by their slogan: "Criminal policy is an inseparable part of social development policy."[131]

In rare instances, politicians are moved to act by strong personal beliefs about right and wrong. Early in the twentieth century, England underwent a major decarceration, prompted in large part by Winston Churchill. During his brief tenure as home secretary, Churchill expressed deep skepticism about what could be achieved through incarceration and quickly came to believe that the prison system was overused.[132] Churchill once said, "The mood and temper of the public in regard to the treatment of crime and criminals is one of the most unfailing tests of the civilization of any country."[133] The really interesting and pressing question today is not whether the experts, the politicians, or members of the public are going to lead the United States out of the crisis of the carceral state. But rather, how do you fashion an effective coalition from elements of all three groups to empty the country's prisons and to abolish capital punishment?

Co-optation, Compromise, and the State

While co-optation is always a possibility, opponents of the carceral state do not have the luxury of eschewing any involvement with the state. As discussed in Chapter 6, some feminists battling violence against women now recognize that they need an approach that neither relies upon nor rejects the state. This has led to some promising experimentation to address domestic violence and other crimes through restorative justice and alternative community programs that seek some type of reconciliation between victim and offender.[134] Another potentially promising development is the creation of "neighborhood district attorneys" that permit citizens to have more input into the role of the prosecutor.[135]

As opponents of the carceral state attempt to knit together broader coalitions, they need to be vigilant about striking compromises that leave the carceral state slightly leaner and less mean but more entrenched. Chapter 9 discussed some of the risks associated with seeking an end to capital punishment by supporting the alternative sentence of life in prison without the possibility of parole and by focusing primarily on the plight of the innocent on death row. Hate crimes legislation, recent campaigns against prison rape and human trafficking, and the spate of ballot initiatives related to drug and sentencing policies are other examples of measures that are fraught with potential risks for foes of the carceral state.

While the drug and sentencing ballot initiatives vary greatly, they share some common features. They risk reinforcing a disturbing distinction between deserving and undeserving offenders. Many of these initiatives sanction throwing the book at drug dealers, recidivists, and violent offenders, thus reinforcing powerful stereotypes about crime and criminals that may help bolster the fundamental legitimacy of the carceral state.[136] For example, Arizona's Proposition 200 called for placing drug abusers on probation and requiring them to undergo substance abuse treatment under court supervision. But it also explicitly excluded drug sellers and defendants with a violent criminal history or two prior convictions for personal drug possession or use. Furthermore it stiffened sanctions and denied parole to people convicted of committing a violent crime while under the influence of a controlled substance. California's Proposition 36, passed in 2000, does not permit defendants guilty of selling or manufacturing illegal drugs to be diverted into treatment. Defendants with prior violent felonies or some other specified nondrug offenses are not eligible for diversion either (with some exceptions). These ballot initiatives open up the possibility for wide disparities in sentencing, thus preserving "incarceration as a possible sentence for everyone but the safest of bets."[137] In many states, defendants who do not qualify for diversion to drug treatment are subject to most of the old sentencing laws, including in some cases very high mandatory minimums.[138]

Some of the new drug law reforms may exacerbate the already enormous racial disparities in prison. Poor and minority defendants are more likely to rely on crimes like burglary or street-level dealing to support their drug habits and to have a disqualifying criminal history due to racial profiling or previous criminal activity to support their drug use. Middle-class substance abusers qualify more often for diversion programs because they tend to face only a possession charge and to have no disqualifying criminal history.[139] Very few states have attempted to lessen the penalties for people who sell drugs or traffic in significant amounts of drugs.[140]

While the emphasis on drug law reform is welcome, we need to keep in mind that the war on drugs did not single-handedly create the carceral state, as discussed in Chapter 2. The carceral buildup began in the 1970s long before the war on drugs was launched in earnest. In the 1980s, about two-thirds of the growth in incarceration was attributed to locking up more nonviolent offenders, notably substance abusers. But by the 1990s, almost half of all growth in state prisons was the result of tougher sentences for violent criminals.[141]

Hate crimes legislation presents another potential bridge between left and right that could end up bolstering the carceral state. Some advocates of hate crimes legislation argue that these measures are an excellent way for the state to reaffirm its central and exclusive authority in inflicting punishment, and for conservatives and Republicans to reassert the primacy of crime as an issue for them. Some conservative opponents of hate crimes bills counter that the best way to decrease hate crimes is to double the penalties for all assaults.[142] What both stances have in common is a commitment to the carceral state.

Another dicey area for opponents of the carceral state is how much they should focus on improving day-to-day conditions behind bars. As Thomas Mathiesen argues, it is necessary to distinguish between positive reforms, which do not prop up the carceral state, and negative ones that do.[143] Yet it is not always so easy to draw a sharp line between negative and positive reforms. The Prison Rape Elimination Act signed into law in 2003 is a good case in point. The first-ever federal law to address rape in prison, it established the new National Prison Rape Reduction Commission to implement the act. This legislation was the result of a remarkable coalition of advocacy groups ranging from conservative organizations, like Focus on the Family, the Christian Coalition, and the Hudson Institute, to civil and human rights groups, including Stop Prisoner Rape, the NAACP, the ACLU, and Human Rights Watch.[144] To make this a major political issue meant drawing public attention to the horrors and prevalence of prison rape and to many of the devastating public health consequences associated with it. This strategy ran the risk of reinforcing the view of prisons as a Hobbesian world so unlike life on the outside. Such a portrait can be used to press for more protections for prisoners, but it also can nurture the view that prisoners are a fundamentally different segment of society; more violent, amoral, and dangerous, they are less deserving of basic human and civil rights and more deserving of being locked up for a very long time.

Growing opposition to human trafficking is another example of a popular cause that has broader implications for the carceral state. The campaign against human trafficking has been transformed into a crusade against all forms of prostitution and commercial sex. Conservative evangelical groups view this issue as one of their top foreign policy priorities.[145] They have used faith-based nongovernmental organizations, moral preaching, hyperbole about the extent of the problem, and calls for stepping up punishment and law enforcement tactics to press their cause. Recent guidelines issued by the U.S. Agency for International Development seek to deny funding to any group that does not take a strict abolitionist approach to prostitution, including ones that offer outreach services like HIV/AIDS counseling and birth control to sex workers. This has sparked tensions between the coalition of left, right, and nonpartisan groups working together since 1998 to stem human trafficking.[146] The Bush administration's crusade against human trafficking is reminiscent of the highly moralistic campaign against "white slavery" at the turn of the twentieth century that was so pivotal in building up the criminal justice apparatus of the United States, as discussed in Chapter 3.

The Federal Government and the Carceral State

The Bush administration's campaign against human trafficking is just part and parcel of the federal government's steadfast commitment to the carceral state. While the enthusiasm of state and local governments for the carceral state may be easing, the federal government's is not. The federal prison system is now the nation's largest, having surpassed the prison systems of Texas and California in 2002. As mentioned earlier, the federal system continues to grow at a rapid rate. In 2003, it increased by 6.6 percent, or nearly five times the rate of increase for state prisons (see Table 1). The average federal sentence is now fifty months, about double what it was in 1984. Racial disparities in the federal prison system have grown phenomenally since the imposition of the federal sentencing guidelines two decades ago.[147]

What we may be witnessing is the emergence of a growing gap between the states and Washington over penal policy and the maintenance of the law-and-order state. One of the most significant developments in law enforcement over the past thirty years has been the vast expansion of federal statutes to cover infractions previously considered solely state matters, such as carjacking.[148] Currently the country lacks a principled understanding of what the borders are between federal and state law enforcement in what purports to be a limited national system of criminal justice.[149] In reports issued in the late 1990s, two prominent groups – one created by the ABA and the other by Congress – challenged the expansion of the scope and power of federal law enforcement. They charged that this expansion "is largely wasteful and ineffective against violent crime" and "threatens both the appropriate federal-state-local balance and the public's confidence in our justice system."[150] The congressional group recommended a law requiring that every federal crime statute justify any overlap with state statutes and be subject to a sunset provision.

These developments in federal law enforcement long predate the Bush administration. In his waning days in office, President Clinton denounced the "unconscionable" sentencing distinction between crack and powder cocaine and called for "a re-examination of our entire policy on imprisonment."[151] Yet his administration did not fight to undo the cocaine sentencing differential. Indeed, it imaginatively pursued hard-line penal policies that dramatically expanded the federal government's role in law enforcement and allowed Clinton to capture successfully the law-and-order constituency.[152]

The Bush administration appears even more firmly committed to the war on drugs, capital punishment, an enhanced federal role in law enforcement, and other pillars of the carceral state. John Ashcroft, Bush's first attorney general, promised to "escalate the war on drugs." Bush selected two committed drug warriors to fill the two top drug policy positions in his administration: Asa Hutchinson as head of the Drug Enforcement Administration and John P. Waters as the nation's "drug czar."[153] Congress and the White House took on the judiciary by inserting a provision in the 2003 PROTECT Act, also know as the Amber Alert Bill, that puts strict limits on judges' ability to hand down sentences more lenient than the federal guidelines.[154] In 2004, Republicans on the House Judiciary Committee led a successful effort to force the United States Sentencing Commission to provide Congress with the names of federal judges who departed from the sentencing guidelines.[155] In August 2003 the Justice Department announced it would begin compiling data on judges who mete out lighter sentences than the federal guidelines prescribe, a move some critics likened to the creation of a "blacklist" of judges.[156] Ashcroft also issued new rules to limit plea bargaining. He told federal prosecutors to charge defendants with the most serious crime possible; to seek, almost without exception, the maximum sentence permitted; and to pursue the death penalty in a number of cases in which prosecutors had recommended against or did not seek capital punishment.[157]

At the start of the second term of the Bush administration, its position on the drug war softened slightly. The proposed 2006 federal budget eliminated more than $1 billion in federal law enforcement grants, including the Byrne grant program that helped subsidize the massive prison expansion. The proposed budget also doubled, even tripled in some cases, the funds for drug treatment programs.[158] Waters told Congress that the federal government needs to stop focusing so many resources on low-level drug offenders. "Don't break generation after generation . . . of young men, especially poor, minority young men in our cities, and [put] them in jail," he testified.[159] While these are potentially promising developments in the area of drug policy, the overall thrust of the Bush administration has been toward more punishment, not less.

The September 11 attacks and the resulting "war on terror" handed the White House a warrant to expand further the federal government's authority in domestic crime control and law enforcement in ways that are likely to prop up the carceral state. These include enlarging the role of the military, intelligence services, and the FBI in domestic law enforcement and domestic intelligence and clamping down on dissent through measures like the USA Patriot Act.[160] The Bush administration has begun using the far-reaching powers of the Patriot Act, supposedly intended to combat terrorism, to pursue criminal investigations that have no real connection to terrorist activities, like drug trafficking, white-collar crime, and child pornography.[161]

Since 9/11, the United States has also been instrumental in creating an archipelago of secret prisons scattered around the globe that raise vexing human rights and constitutional issues.[162] Ostensibly established to fight the "war on terror," these prisons will likely have deleterious "blowback" consequences at home and exert greater pressures on other countries to develop carceral states of their own.[163] Even prior to the September 11 attacks, the United States was actively involved in exporting its model of tough justice abroad through programs like the International Criminal Investigative Training Program. Created in 1986, based in the Justice Department, and funded with help from the State Department, this program has propped up police and prison systems in a number of countries with poor human rights records, including Haiti, Indonesia, the states of the former Soviet Union, and now Iraq.[164] For at least a decade now, U.S. think tanks and policy makers have aggressively worked to spread the American law-and-order model and have made some significant inroads with policy makers in Europe, especially Britain.[165] The September 11 attacks and the heightened national security concerns brought on by the "war on terror" may further fortify the carceral state at home and abroad.

Should the "war on terror" and U.S. wars in Iraq and Afghanistan continue without any end in sight, the mounting recruiting pressures on the military may shape the course of penal policy and the prospects for reform. During World War II, intense pressure for new military recruits and greater industrial and agricultural production to fight the war spurred a momentary shift in the public's perception of prisoners and prisons. Prison officials expanded vocational training for people in prison during the war and heralded the patriotic contributions of prisoners who donated blood, worked in prison industries (often at camps with minimal supervision), and accepted shortened sentences in exchange for agreeing to enlist in the military.[166] While the military has yet to embrace the carceral state as the next frontier in its recruitment efforts, it already has relaxed some of its recruiting standards to permit men and women who committed minor crimes to enlist.[167] Should U.S. prisons become a major new source of military recruits, as they did in World War II, it is unlikely that this will result in an unraveling of the carceral state. However, if the military sets its sights on people in prison to solve its current recruitment problems, this may provide important opportunities and potential dangers for reframing the wider debate over penal policy.

Conclusion

The daily incarceration of more than two million people, many of them poor blacks, Hispanics, and other members of ethnic or racial minorities, and the supervision of millions more on parole and probation, is a vast and tragic social experiment without precedent in the modern history of the United States or indeed any other Western country. While one can reach back in time to find some parallels with slavery in the United States, the creation of the carceral state was more subtle and complex than just drawing a straight line from the plantation to Jim Crow to the ghetto to the prison-industrial complex today.[168]

The United States presents a fundamental challenge to Durkheim's claim that punishment will grow milder as societies modernize. While continental Europe has been moving in a milder direction by fits and starts, the United States certainly has not. David Garland likens the infliction of punishment by the state on its citizens to "a civil war in miniature."[169] If this is so, then the United States is currently engaged in a massive war with itself.

With so many millions somehow enmeshed in the criminal justice system, the penal policies of the United States have a certain taken-for-granted quality. Just as it seemed unimaginable thirty years ago that the United States would be imprisoning its people at such unprecedented rates, today it seems almost unimaginable that the country will veer off in a new direction and begin to empty and board up its prisons. Yet as Mathiesen reminds us, "major repressive systems have succeeded in looking extremely stable almost until the day they have collapsed."[170]

NOTES

CHAPTER 1. THE PRISON AND THE GALLOWS: THE CONSTRUCTION
OF THE CARCERAL STATE IN AMERICA

1. Nathaniel Hawthorne, *The Scarlet Letter*, ed. Sculley Bradley, Richmond Croom Beatty, and E. Hudson Long (New York: W. W. Norton & Company, Inc., 1962), p. 38.

2. Michael Tonry, "Symbol, Substance, and Severity in Western Penal Policies," *Punishment & Society* 3, no. 4 (October 2001): 517–36.

3. Calculated from Theodore Caplow and Jonathan Simon, "Understanding Prison Policy and Population Trends," in *Crime and Justice – A Review of Research*, vol. 26, *Prisons*, ed. Michael Tonry and Joan Petersilia (Chicago and London: University of Chicago Press, 1999), p. 63; and Paige M. Harrison and Allen J. Beck, "Prisoners in 2003," *Bureau of Justice Statistics Bulletin*, November 2004, p. 2, Table 1. Over the past three decades the total number of incarcerated people increased ten-fold. Joel Dyer, *The Perpetual Prisoner Machine: How America Profits from Crime* (Boulder, CO: Westview Press, 2000).

4. Russia, which used to lead the United States by a hair, is now a distant third at 548 per 100,000 after several recent large-scale amnesties to relieve prison overcrowding in disease-infested facilities. Belarus is a distant second at 554 per 100,000. International Centre for Prison Studies, "Entire World – Prison Population Rates per 100,000 of the National Population," http://www.kcl.ac.uk/depsta/rel/icps/worldbrief/highest_to_lowest_rates.php (accessed November 30, 2004); Dan Gardner, "Jailbreak: After 70 Years, Russia Is Ready To Concede Its Tough-on-Crime Experiment Is a Costly, Merciless Failure," *The Ottawa Citizen*, March 12, 2002, p. C-3; and Fred Weir, "Mercy Rule: Russia Plans Mass Release of Inmates from Abusive Prisons," *In These Times*, February 19, 2001, pp. 5–6.

5. Calculated from International Centre for Prison Studies, "Entire World – Prison Population Totals," http://www.kcl.ac.uk/depsta/rel/icps/worldbrief/highest_to_lowest_rates.php (accessed November 30, 2004).

6. These figures include both people serving time in local jails as well as those incarcerated in state and federal prisons. Calculated from Dyer, *The Perpetual Prisoner Machine*, p. 1; and International Centre for Prison Studies, "Entire World – Prison Population Rates per 100,000 of the National Population."

7. For a good discussion of how studies of comparative prison use are fraught with possibilities for misinterpretation, see Ken Pease, "Cross-National Imprisonment

Rates," *British Journal of Criminology* 34 (1994): 116–30; and Warren Young and Mark Brown, "Cross-National Comparisons of Imprisonment," in *Crime and Justice: A Review of Research*, vol. 17, ed. Michael Tonry (Chicago: University of Chicago Press, 1993): 1–49.

8. Lauren E. Glaze and Seri Palla, "Probation and Parole in the United States, 2003," *Bureau of Justice Statistics Bulletin*, July 2004, p. 3.

9. Michael Tonry and Joan Petersilia, "American Prisons at the Beginning of the Twenty-First Century," in *Crime and Justice – A Review of Research*, vol. 26: *Prisons*, p. vii.

10. David Cole, *No Equal Justice: Race and Class in the Criminal Justice System* (New York: The New Press, 1999).

11. Michael Tonry, *Malign Neglect: Race, Crime and Punishment in America* (New York: Oxford University Press, 1995), p. 29; and Gerald David Jaynes and Robin W. Williams, Jr., eds., *A Common Destiny: Blacks and American Society* (Washington, DC: National Academy Press, 1989), p. 461, as cited in Lawrence M. Friedman, *Crime and Punishment in American History* (New York: Basic Books, 1993), p. 378. These figures may overstate the size of the white prison population because state prison data often failed in the past to distinguish between Hispanics and whites, lumping all of them together. "NCIA Report Finds Prison Race Statistics Distorted," *Prison Legal News*, March 2002, p. 26.

12. In 1980 three black men were enrolled in college or university for each black man in prison or jail, according to the Justice Policy Institute. Fox Butterfield, "Study Finds Big Increase in Black Men as Inmates Since 1980," *The New York Times*, August 28, 2002, p. A-14.

13. David Garland, *Punishment and Modern Society: A Study in Social Theory* (Chicago: University of Chicago Press, 1990), p. 125; and David Garland, *Punishment and Welfare: A History of Penal Strategies* (Aldershot, UK: Gower, 1985).

14. The current figure for the state and federal prison population (which excludes people in local jails) is 482 per 100,000. Prisons generally are state or federal facilities that house long-term offenders convicted of felonies. Jails are county or city facilities that hold pre-trial defendants, offenders convicted of misdemeanors, and felons serving short sentences. Harrison and Beck, "Prisoners in 2003," p. 4, Table 4; Alfred Blumstein and Allen J. Beck, "Population Growth in U.S. Prisons, 1980–1996," in *Crime and Justice – A Review of Research*, vol. 26, *Prisons*, p. 17. See also Margaret Cahalan, "Trends in Incarceration in the United States since 1880: A Summary of Reported Rates and the Distribution of Offenses," *Crime & Delinquency* 25 (1979): 9–41.

15. This is a paraphrase from Scott Christianson, *With Liberty for Some: 500 Years of Imprisonment in America* (Boston: Northeastern University Press, 1998), p. ix.

16. For a good review of revisionist works on the historiography of the prison, see Michael Ignatieff, "State, Civil Society, and Total Institutions: A Critique of Recent Social Histories of Punishment," in *Crime and Justice: An Annual Review of Research*, vol. 3, ed. Norval Morris and Michael Tonry (Chicago: University of Chicago Press, 1981): 153–92.

17. Norval Morris and David J. Rothman, "Introduction," in *The Oxford History of the Prison: The Practice of Punishment in Western Society*, ed. Norval Morris and David J. Rothman (New York: Oxford University Press, 1995), p. vii.

18. David Downes and Rod Morgan, "'Hostages to Fortune'? The Politics of Law and Order in Post-War Britain," in *The Oxford Handbook of Criminology*,

ed. Mike Maguire, Rod Morgan, and Robert Reiner (Oxford: Clarendon Press, 1994), p. 183. See also Andrew von Hirsch and Andrew Ashworth, "Law and Order," in *Principled Sentencing: Readings on Theory and Policy*, 2nd ed., ed. Andrew von Hirsch and Andrew Ashworth (Oxford: Hart Publishing, 1998).

19. Downes and Morgan, "'Hostages to Fortune'?" p. 184.
20. This is a slight twist on David Garland's argument that penal movements are forged by particular social movements within the constrains of larger social structures. Garland, *Punishment and Modern Society*, pp. 126–27; and Garland, *Punishment and Welfare*.
21. As E. P. Thompson shows in his detailed study of the Black Act of early eighteenth-century England, the ruling class made use of the law to further its own interests but never had an entirely free hand to do so. E. P. Thompson, *Whigs and Hunters: The Origins of the Black Act* (New York: Pantheon, 1975). See also David Philips, "A Just Measure of Crime, Authority, Hunters, and Blue Locusts: The 'Revisionist' Social History of Crime and the Law in Britain, 1780–1950," in *Social Control and the State*, ed. Stanley Cohen and Andrew Scull (New York: St. Martin's Press, 1983).
22. Charles Tilly, *From Mobilization to Revolution* (Reading, MA: Addison-Wesley, 1978).
23. For an example of this ruling-elite model by a leading social control theorist, see Richard Quinney, *Critique of Legal Order: Crime Control in Capitalist Society* (Boston: Little, Brown, 1973). For a challenge to that view, see Ernest Kahlar Alix, *Ransom Kidnapping in America, 1874–1974: The Creation of a Capital Crime* (Carbondale and Edwardsville: Southern Illinois University Press, 1978), pp. 187–88.
24. Common crime was "immensely disturbing" to President Lyndon Johnson. Negative and alarming images of crime were a consistent theme of his written and oral communications from 1964 to 1968. James D. Calder, "Presidents and Crime Control: Kennedy, Johnson and Nixon and the Influences of Ideology," *Presidential Studies Quarterly* 12, no. 4 (Fall 1982), pp. 578–79. In 1973, liberal Republican Governor Nelson Rockefeller of New York promoted what were then the toughest drug laws in the country. In 1976, Democratic Governor Jerry Brown of California endorsed and signed into law a provision that ended indeterminate sentencing and amended the state's penal code to read that the ultimate goal of imprisonment was no longer "rehabilitation" but "punishment." Democrat Mario Cuomo, through the creative use of his state's Urban Development Corporation, which was supposed to fund housing for the poor, "added more prison beds in New York than all the previous governors in the state's history combined." Eric Schlosser, "The Prison-Industrial Complex," *The Atlantic Monthly*, December 1998. President Clinton ardently promoted several draconian crime bills. Ann Chih Lin, "The Troubled Success of Crime Policy," in *The Social Divide: Political Parties and the Future of Activist Government*, ed. Margaret Weir (Washington, DC, and New York: The Brookings Institution and Russell Sage Foundation, 1998): 312–57. See also Evelyn Nieves, "California's Governor Plays Tough on Crime," *The New York Times*, May 23, 2000, p. A-16.
25. Marc Mauer, *Race to Incarcerate* (New York: The New Press, 1999), pp. 10 and 15–16. In the conclusion of his classic study of the birth of the penitentiary, originally published in 1971, David J. Rothman predicted, "[W]e have been gradually escaping from institutional responses, and one can foresee the period when incarceration will be used still more rarely than it is today." Rothman, *The*

Discovery of the Asylum: Social Order and Disorder in the New Republic, rev. ed. (Boston: Little, Brown and Company, 1990), p. 295.

26. The commission concluded, "The prison, reformatory and the jail have achieved only a shocking rate of failure." National Advisory Commission on Criminal Justice Standards and Goals, *Task Force on Corrections* (Washington, DC: Government Printing Office, 1973), p. 597, cited in Franklin E. Zimring and Gordon Hawkins, *The Scale of Imprisonment* (Chicago and London: University of Chicago Press, 1991), pp. 65–66.

27. Jonathan Simon, "From the Big House to the Warehouse: Rethinking Prisons and State Government in the 20th Century," *Punishment & Society* 2, no. 2 (April 2000), p. 217; and Stuart A. Scheingold, "Constructing the New Political Criminology: Power, Authority, and the Post-Liberal State," *Law and Social Inquiry* 23, no. 4 (Autumn 1998), p. 860.

28. For an excellent discussion of how identity politics as expressed through hate crimes legislation has distorted the public debate about crime in the United States, see James B. Jacobs and Kimberly Potter, *Hate Crimes: Criminal Law and Identity Politics* (New York: Oxford University Press, 1998).

29. Caplow and Simon, "Understanding Prison Policy," p. 84.

30. Franklin E. Zimring, Gordon Hawkins, and Sam Kamin, *Punishment and Democracy: Three Strikes and You're Out in California* (Oxford: Oxford University Press, 2001), p. 223.

31. The rate per 100,000 is 801 for Louisiana; 702 for Texas; 155 for Minnesota; and 141 for Maine. Harrison and Beck, "Prisoners in 2003," p. 4, Table 4.

32. See, for example, Zimring et al.'s discussion of why California's "three-strikes" law is much more punitive than "three-strikes" laws elsewhere. Zimring et al., *Punishment and Democracy*. See also Davey's excellent discussion of why similarly situated pairs of adjacent states sometimes have sharply different penal policies, in Joseph Dillon Davey, *The Politics of Prison Expansion: Winning Elections by Waging War on Crime* (Westport, CT: Praeger, 1998); David F. Greenberg and Valerie West, "State Prison Populations and Their Growth, 1971–1991," *Criminology* 39, no. 3 (August 2001): 615–53; Vanessa Barker, "The Politics of Punishing: Building a State Governance Theory of American Imprisonment Variation," *Punishment & Society* 8, no. 1 (January 2006): 5–32; and Bruce Western, *Punishment and Inequality in America* (New York: Russell Sage Foundation, forthcoming 2006), Chapter 3. Western's book manuscript came to my attention just as my book was going to press, so I was unable to fully engage its central arguments.

33. Among the factors singled out as significant include: differences in unemployment; racial inequality; economic inequality; welfare benefits; out-of-wedlock births; and the proportion of African Americans residing in the state. David Jacobs and Ronald D. Helms, "Toward a Political Model of Incarceration: A Time-Series Examination of Multiple Explanations for Prison Admission Rates," *American Journal of Sociology* 102, no. 6 (September 1996): 322–57; Jack Nagel, "The Relationship Between Crime and Incarceration Among the American States," *Policy Studies Review* 2 (1982): 193–202; Darnell F. Hawkins and Kenneth A. Hardy, "Black-White Imprisonment Rates: A State-by-State Analysis," *Social Justice* 16, no. 4 (Winter 1989): 75–94; and Katherine Beckett and Bruce Western, "Governing Social Marginality: Welfare, Incarceration, and the Transformation of State Policy," *Punishment & Society* 3, no. 1 (January 2001): 43–59.

34. For a good overview of state trends, see Zimring and Hawkins, *The Scale of Imprisonment*, Chapter 6.
35. The average rate of change dropped 2.1 percent in Massachusetts and 0.6 percent in New York State. Harrison and Beck, "Prisoners in 2003," p. 4, Table 4. More recent data indicate that New Jersey experienced a notable 14 percent drop between 1999 and mid-2005. Robert Moran, "N.J. Stands Out As Its Prison Population Falls," *Philadelphia Inquirer*, May 11, 2005, p. B-9.
36. Theodore Sasson, "William Horton's Long Shadow: 'Punitiveness' and 'Managerialism' in the Penal Politics of Massachusetts, 1988–99," in *Crime, Risk and Insecurity: Law and Order in Everyday Life and Political Discourse*, ed. Tim Hope and Richard Sparks (London and New York: Routledge, 2000): 238–51.
37. Harrison and Beck, "Prisoners in 2003," p. 4, Table 4, and n. 5.
38. John J. DiIulio, Jr., Steven K. Smith, and Aaron J. Saiger, "The Federal Role in Crime Control," in *Crime*, ed. James Q. Wilson and Joan Petersilia (San Francisco: Institute for Contemporary Studies Press, 1995), pp. 447–49; and Peter B. Kraska, ed., *Militarizing the American Criminal Justice System: The Changing Roles of the Armed Forces and the Police* (Boston: Northeastern University Press, 2001).
39. Franklin E. Zimring, "Imprisonment Rates and the New Politics of Criminal Punishment," paper presented at "The Causes and Consequences of Mass Imprisonment in the USA," New York University School of Law, February 26, 2000.
40. On the "culture of honor" and "culture of vengeance" in the South, see Richard E. Nisbett and Dov Cohen, *Culture of Honor: The Psychology of Violence in the South* (Boulder, CO: Westview Press, 1996); and Edward L. Ayers, *Vengeance and Justice: Crime and Punishment in the 19th-Century American South* (New York: Oxford University Press, 1984).
41. For a social control argument that stresses the continuities between slavery and mass imprisonment today, see Loïc Wacquant, "Deadly Symbiosis: When Ghetto and Prison Meet and Mesh," in *Mass Imprisonment: Social Causes and Consequences*, ed. David Garland (London: Sage Publications, 2001). Some other social control explanations of the incarceration boom are more sensitive to the specific historical context at a given moment. See, for example, Diana R. Gordon, *The Return of the Dangerous Classes: Drug Prohibition and Policy Politics* (New York: W. W. Norton & Co., 1994). For an overview of social control theories and some critical evaluations of them, see Stanley Cohen, *Visions of Social Control: Crime, Punishment and Classification* (Cambridge: Polity Press, 1985); Stanley Cohen, "The Critical Discourse on 'Social Control': Notes on the Concept as a Hammer," *International Journal of the Sociology of Law* 17 (1989): 347–57; Dorothy E. Chunn and Shelley A. M. Gavigan, "Social Control: Analytical Tool or Analytical Quagmire?" *Contemporary Crises* 12 (1988): 102–24; and David J. Rothman, "Social Control and the State," in *Social Control and the State*, ed. Stanley Cohen and Andrew Scull (New York: St. Martin's Press, 1983): 106–17.
42. In 1890, the incarceration rate in Southern prisons was 284 per 100,000 blacks and in Northern prisons it was 773 per 100,000 blacks. Monroe N. Work, "Negro Criminality in the South," *The Annals* 49 (September 1913), p. 75. The convict-lease population of Southern states ranged in the late nineteenth and early twentieth centuries between 1,000 and 2,000 convicts per state. Matthew J. Mancini, *One Dies, Get Another: Convict Leasing in the American South, 1866–1928* (Columbia: University of South Carolina Press, 1996).

By the 1880s, county prisoners began to greatly outnumber black convicts under the control of state authorities in the South. If one generously multiplies the 284 figure by 10 to take into account county convicts, the combined state and county incarceration rate is still less than one-half of what the nationwide incarceration rate is for black males today. On the county imprisonment rate in the South in the late nineteenth century and the logic behind multiplying the state figure by 10 to get an estimate of the county rate, see Mary Ellen Curtin, *Black Prisoners and Their World, Alabama, 1865–1900* (Charlottesville: University of Virginia Press, 2000), p. 148 and p. 232, n. 22.

43. Michael C. Dawson and Cathy Cohen, "Problems in the Study of Race," in *Political Science: State of the Discipline*, ed. Ira Katznelson and Helen V. Milner (New York: W. W. Norton & Co., 2002): 488–510.

44. Desmond S. King and Rogers M. Smith, "Racial Orders in American Political Development," *American Political Science Review* 99, no. 1 (February 2005): 75–92. For more on this point, see Chapter 10.

45. James Q. Whitman, *Harsh Justice: Criminal Punishment and the Widening Divide Between America and Europe* (Oxford: Oxford University Press, 2003), p. 207.

46. For more on this point, see Andrew J. Polsky, "The New 'Dismal Science'? The Lessons of American Political Development for Today," *Polity* 32, no. 3 (Spring 2000): 303–8.

47. Raymond Aron, *Main Currents in Sociological Thought*, vol. 1 (New Brunswick, NJ: Transaction Books, 1998), p. 313, quoted in David Garland, *The Culture of Control: Crime and Social Order in Contemporary Society* (Chicago: University of Chicago Press, 2001), p. 63.

CHAPTER 2. LAW, ORDER, AND ALTERNATIVE EXPLANATIONS

1. Quoted in Todd Gitlin, "We're All Authorities," *The New York Times Book Review*, May 23, 1999, p. 32.

2. Michael Hindus, *Prison and Plantation: Crime, Justice, and Authority in Massachusetts and South Carolina, 1767–1978* (Chapel Hill: The University of North Carolina Press, 1980), p. 101.

3. Negley K. Teeters and John D. Shearer, *The Prison at Philadelphia, Cherry Hill: The Separate System of Penal Discipline: 1829–1913* (New York: Columbia University Press, 1957), p. 114.

4. Georg Rusche and Otto Kirchheimer, *Punishment and Social Structure* (New York: Columbia University Press, 1939), p. 5, cited in Franklin E. Zimring and Gordon Hawkins, *Incapacitation: Penal Confinement and the Restraint of Crime* (New York: Oxford University Press, 1995), p. 13.

5. For a critical overview of the demographic, economic, and other deterministic explanations for the expansion of imprisonment, see Franklin E. Zimring and Gordon Hawkins, *The Scale of Imprisonment* (Chicago and London: University of Chicago Press, 1991), pp. 130–34; Theodore G. Chiricos and Miriam A. DeLone, "Labor Surplus and Punishment: A Review and Assessment of Theory and Evidence," *Social Problems* 39, no. 4 (1992): 421–46; and Warren Young, "Influences Upon the Use of Imprisonment: A Review of the Literature," *The Howard Journal* 25, no. 2 (May 1986): 125–36. For a sophisticated, nuanced political explanation rooted in the restructuring of the labor market away from industrial employment, see Jonathan Simon, *Poor Discipline: Parole and the Social Control of the Underclass* (Chicago: University of Chicago Press, 1993).

6. Bruce Western, Mary Pattillo, and David Weiman, "Introduction," in *Imprisoning America: The Social Effects of Mass Incarceration*, ed. Mary Pattillo, David Weiman, and Bruce Western (New York: Russell Sage Foundation, 2004), p. 3.

7. Kevin R. Reitz, "The Disassembly and Reassembly of U.S. Sentencing Practices," in *Sentencing and Sanctions in Western Countries*, ed. Michael Tonry and Richard S. Frase (Oxford: Oxford University Press, 2001), p. 244.

8. Michael Tonry, "Racial Disparities Getting Worse in U.S. Prisons and Jails," in *Sentencing Reform in Overcrowded Times: A Comparative Perspective*, ed. Michael Tonry and Kathleen Hatlestad (New York: Oxford University Press, 1997), p. 221.

9. Ann L. Pastore and Kathleen Maguire, eds., *Bureau of Justice Statistics Sourcebook of Criminal Justice Statistics – 2001* (Washington, DC: GPO, 2002), p. 486, Table 6.13.

10. Steven R. Donziger, ed., *The Real War on Crime: The Report of the National Criminal Justice Commission* (New York: Harper Perennial, 1996), p. 103. Blacks and Hispanics comprise 62 percent of the incarcerated population, but just one-quarter of the national population. Human Rights Watch, "Race and Incarceration in the United States: Human Rights Watch Press Backgrounder," February 27, 2002, http://hrw.org/background/usa/race (accessed March 7, 2002).

11. In 2002 the U.S. imprisonment rate for black males (not including those in jail) was 3,437 per 100,000. Kathleen Maguire and Ann L. Pastore, eds., *Sourcebook of Criminal Justice Statistics 2002* [online], http://www.albany.edu/sourcebook/, Table 6.27 (accessed December 3, 2004). The rate in South Africa in the early 1990s was 681 per 100,000. Fox Butterfield, "U.S. Expands Its Lead in the Rate of Imprisonment," *The New York Times*, February 11, 1992, p. A-16. A 1995 study by The Sentencing Project found that on any given day one in three black males in the 20-to-29 age group was in either prison or jail or was on probation or parole. Marc Mauer, *Race to Incarcerate* (New York: The New Press, 1999), pp. 124–25. See also Jerome G. Miller, *Search and Destroy: African-American Males in the Criminal Justice System* (New York: Cambridge University Press, 1996).

12. White males face a one in seventeen lifetime chance. Thomas P. Bonczar, "Prevalence of Imprisonment in the U.S. Population, 1972–2001," *Bureau of Justice Statistics Special Report*, August 2003, p. 1.

13. Western, *Punishment and Inequality in America* (manuscript on file with author, June 2005), p. 7.

14. The number of women in state and federal prisons jumped from 12,000 in 1980 to about 101,000 in 2003. Meda Chesney-Lind, "Women in Prison: From Partial Justice to Vengeful Equity," *Corrections Today* 60, n. 7 (December 1988), p. 66; Paige M. Harrison and Allen J. Beck, "Prisoners in 2003," *Bureau of Justice Statistics Bulletin*, November 2004, p. 4. See also Silja J. A. Talvi, "Women Behind Bars," *Prison Legal News*, June 2001, p. 1.

15. Harrison and Beck, "Prisoners in 2003," p. 4.

16. Mississippi and Oklahoma, the two states with the highest incarceration rates for females, are now incarcerating women at a rate comparable to the combined male and female rate of the United Kingdom, which is at the high end for Western Europe. Harrison and Beck, "Prisoners in 2003," p. 5; International Centre for Prison Studies, "Entire World – Prison Population Rates per 100,000", http://www.kcl.ac.uk/depsta/rel/icps/worldbrief/highest_to_lowest_rates.php (accessed November 30, 2004); and Talvi, "Women Behind Bars."

17. Christopher J. Mumola, *Incarcerated Parents and Their Children* (Washington, DC: U.S. Department of Justice, Bureau of Justice Statistics, August 2000), p. 2.

18. Western et al., "Introduction," p. 9; and Pattillo et al., ed., *Imprisoning America*, Chapters 2–5.

19. Denise Johnston and Michael Carlin, "When Incarcerated Parents Lost Contact with Their Children," *Prison Legal News*, February 2004, pp. 16–17; Tom Lowenstein, "Collateral Damage: The Children of Prisoners," *Prison Legal News*, June 2002, pp. 1–5; and Adrian Nicole LeBlanc, "Prison Is a Member of Their Family," *The New York Times Magazine*, January 12, 2003.

20. Lynn Bauer and Steven D. Owens, "Justice Expenditure and Employment in the United States, 2001," *Bureau of Justice Statistics Bulletin*, May 2004, p. 1. Figure for the 1970s calculated from U.S. Department of Justice, "Trends in Expenditure and Employment Data for the Criminal Justice System, 1971–1975" (Washington, DC: Government Printing Office, 1977), cited in Tony Platt and Paul Takagi, "Intellectuals for Law and Order: A Critique of the New Realists," *Crime and Social Justice* 8 (Fall-Winter 1977), p. 2; and the Bureau of Labor Statistics Web site, Consumer Price Index for All Urban Consumers (CPI-U), ftp://ftp.bls.gov/pub/special.requests/cpi/cpia/txt (accessed December 2, 2004).

21. Bauer and Owens, "Justice Expenditure and Employment in the United States, 2001," p. 1.

22. Henry Ruth and Kevin R. Reitz, *The Challenge of Crime: Rethinking Our Response* (Cambridge, MA: Harvard University Press, 2003), p. 92.

23. Jennifer Gonnerman, "Million-Dollar Blocks," *Village Voice*, November 16, 2004, p. 28.

24. From 1987 to 1998, state spending on corrections increased by 30 percent, while spending on higher education decreased by 18 percent. Tara-Jen Ambrosio and Vincent Schiraldi, *From Classrooms to Cellblocks: A National Perspective* (Washington, DC: The Justice Policy Institute, 1997), p. 5, Table 2.

25. Ambrosio and Schiraldi, *From Classrooms to Cellblocks*, pp. 7–9; Marc L. Miller, "Cells vs. Cops vs. Classrooms," in *The Crime Conundrum: Essays on Criminal Justice*, ed. Lawrence Friedman and George Fisher (Boulder, CO: Westview Press, 1997), pp. 139–42; and Eric Schlosser, "The Prison-Industrial Complex," *The Atlantic Monthly*, December 1998.

26. Human Rights Watch, *No Escape: Male Rape in U.S. Prisons* (New York: Human Rights Watch, April 2001).

27. An estimated 20 to 40 percent of U.S. prisoners are infected with hepatitis C. AIDS is the second leading cause of death in state prisons. The incidence of AIDS among people in prison is five times that of the population at large. David Rohde, "A Health Danger from a Needle Becomes a Scourge Behind Bars," *The New York Times*, August 6, 2001, p. A-1; Wil S. Hylton, "Sick on the Inside: Correctional HMOs and the Coming Prison Plague," *Harper's*, August 2003, pp. 43–54; "The Dark Side of America," editorial, *The New York Times*, May 17, 2004, p. A-20; Mark Wilson, "America's Prisons Turn a Blind Eye to HCV Epidemic," *Prison Legal News*, August 2003, pp. 1–4; Elisa Ludwig, "HIV/AIDS: 'A Public Health Disaster'," *Philadelphia Weekly*, July 25, 2001, p. 18; Matthew T. Clarke, "Deadly Drug-Resistant Staph in Prisons Throughout USA," *Prison Legal News*, December 2003, pp. 10–11; and Sasha Abramsky, "The Shame of Prison Health," *Prison Legal News*, June 2003, pp. 10–13.

28. James Q. Whitman, *Harsh Justice: Criminal Punishment and the Widening Divide Between America and Europe* (Oxford: Oxford University Press, 2003), p. 19.

29. "[E]ven when the Europeans decide to ball their fists and strike, they do not strike with the ferocity of Americans." Whitman, *Harsh Justice*, p. 71. See also Michael Tonry, "Rethinking Unthinkable Punishment Policies in America," *UCLA Law Review* 46, no. 6 (August 1999): 1751–91.

30. For more on the recent hard turn in Britain, see pp. 109–14; and Michael Tonry, *Punishment and Politics: Evidence and Emulation in the Making of Crime Control Policy* (Devon, UK: Willan Publishing, 2004).

31. Bob Dart, "Cops Can Cuff Any, All Suspects; Court Upholds Arrests for Minor Offenses," *The Atlanta Constitution*, April 25, 2001, p. A-1.

32. About 53 percent of state prisoners, 74 percent of people in jail, and 87 percent of federal prisoners were incarcerated for offenses that involved neither harm nor threat of harm to a victim. John Irwin, Vincent Schiraldi, and Jason Ziedenberg, *America's One Million Nonviolent Prisoners* (Washington, DC: The Justice Policy Institute, March 1999), p. 3, n. 6.

33. U.S. statistics are not directly comparable because many nonviolent offenders who serve no time in France are regularly incarcerated in the United States. Whitman, *Harsh Justice*, pp. 70–71.

34. Whitman, *Harsh Justice*, p. 71. For more comparisons of sentence lengths, see André Kuhn, "Incarceration Rates Around the World," in *Penal Reform in Overcrowded Times*, ed. Michael Tonry (Oxford: Oxford University Press, 2001), p. 113; and Michael Tonry and Kathleen Hatlestad, "Sentencing Reform," in *Sentencing Reform in Overcrowded Times*, pp. 9–10.

35. Irwin et al., *America's One Million Nonviolent Prisoners*, p. 3.

36. Fox Butterfield, "Mistreatment of Prisoners Is Called Routine in U.S.," *The New York Times*, May 8, 2004, p. A-11; Elif Kaban, "The United Nations Rebukes the U.S. Over Brutality in Prisons," *Reuters*, May 15, 2000; Anne-Marie Cusac, "Abu Ghraib, USA," *Prison Legal News*, July 2004, p. 1; and Todd Matthews, "Business as Usual: America's Long-Term Domestic and Foreign Policies Toward Prison Abuse," *Prison Legal News*, December 2004, pp. 1–5.

37. Alan Elsner, "Many U.S. Prisons Worse Than Guantánamo Bay," *Reuters*, January 30, 2002.

38. Alex Lichtenstein, "Chain Gang Blues," *Dissent* 43, no. 3 (Fall 1996): 6–10; and Michael Welch, *Punishment in America: Social Control and the Ironies of Imprisonment* (Thousand Oaks, CA: Sage, 1999), pp. 194–99.

39. Dan Pens, "Oppression on Rise in Arizona," in *The Celling of America: An Inside Look at the U.S. Prison Industry*, ed. Daniel Burton-Rose with Dan Pens and Paul Wright (Monroe, ME: Common Courage Press, 1998), p. 64.

40. Joseph Hallinan, *Going Up the River: Travels in a Prison Nation* (New York: Random House, 2001), pp. 4 and 13.

41. Gina Holland, "Alabama Punishment Declared Unconstitutional," *Associated Press*, June 27, 2002; and Hallinan, *Going Up the River*, p. 102. In 2002 the U.S. Supreme Court upheld a 1998 ruling that Alabama's practice of handcuffing prisoners to a metal pole for hours in the summer heat was unconstitutional.

42. Hallinan, *Going Up the River*, pp. 187 and 197.

43. For example, supermax prisoners lucky enough to receive counseling must speak to their therapists through a slit less than an inch wide that runs the length of each cell door. In this cell-front counseling, what a prisoner says to his or her therapist is open to anyone within earshot, including guards and other prisoners. Hallinan, *Going Up the River*, p. 208. For more on supermax prisons, see Robert Perkinson, "Shackled Justice: Florence Federal Penitentiary and the New Politics of Punishment," *Social Justice* 21, no. 3 (Fall 1994): 117–32; Roy D. King, "The

Rise and Rise of Supermax: An American Solution in Search of a Problem," *Punishment & Society* 1, no. 2 (October 1999): 163–86; Human Rights Watch, *Red Onion State Prison: Super-Maximum Security Confinement in the United States* (New York: Human Rights Watch, April 1999); and Human Rights Watch, *Out of Sight: Super-Maximum Security Confinement in the United States* (New York: Human Rights Watch, February 2000).

44. Mary Fainsod Katzenstein, "Rights Without Citizenship: Prison Activism in the U.S.," in *Routing the Opposition: Social Movements, Public Policy, and Democracy*, ed. David S. Meyer, Valerie Jenness, and Helen Ingram (Minneapolis: University of Minnesota Press, 2005); Margaret Colgate Love and Susan M. Kuzman, *Civil Disabilities of Convicted Felons: A State-By-State Survey* (Washington, DC: U.S. Department of Justice, Office of the Pardon Attorney, October 1996); Kathleen M. Olivares, Velmer S. Burton, Jr., and Francis T. Cullen, "The Collateral Consequences of a Felony Conviction: A National Study of State Legal Codes 10 Years Later," *Federal Probation* 60, no. 3 (September 1996): 10–17; Christopher Uggen and Jeff Manza, "Democratic Contraction? Political Consequences of Felon Disenfranchisement in the United States," *The American Sociological Review* 67, no. 6 (December 2002): 777–803; Christopher Uggen and Jeff Manza, "Lost Voices: The Civic and Political Views of Disenfranchised Felons," *Imprisoning America*: 165–204; Robert R. Preuhs, "State Felon Disenfranchisement Policy," *Social Science Quarterly* 82, no. 2 (December 2001): 733–48; and Jamie Fellner and Marc Mauer, *Losing the Vote: The Impact of Felony Disenfranchisement Laws in the United States* (Washington, DC and New York: The Sentencing Project and Human Rights Watch, October 1998).

45. Legal Action Center, *After Prison: Roadblocks to Reentry; A Report on State Legal Barriers Facing People With Criminal Records* (New York: Legal Action Center, 2004); Fox Butterfield, "Freed from Prison, but Still Paying a Penalty," *The New York Times*, December 20, 2002, sec. 1, p. 18; Stephen Burd, "Seeking Redemption for a Drug Law," *The Chronicle of Higher Education*, April 5, 2002, pp. A-17–19; Cynthia Godsoe, "The Ban on Welfare for Felony Drug Offenders: Giving a New Meaning to 'Life Sentence'," *Berkeley Women's Law Journal* 13 (1998): 257–67; and Patricia Allard, *Life Sentences: Denying Welfare Benefits to Women Convicted of Drug Offenses* (Washington, DC: The Sentencing Project, February 2002).

46. Andrew von Hirsch, "The Project of Sentencing Reform," in *Sentencing and Sanctions in Western Countries*, p. 406.

47. Marc Ancel, *Social Defense: The Future of Penal Reform* (Littleton, CO: Fred B. Rothman and Co., 1987), p. 213.

48. Whitman, *Harsh Justice*, p. 8.

49. Whitman, *Harsh Justice*, pp. 64 and 87.

50. Whitman, *Harsh Justice*, p. 84.

51. David Johnson, "Where the State Kills in Secret: Capital Punishment in Japan," paper presented at the Law & Society Association, Las Vegas, NV, June 2–5, 2005.

52. Stephen B. Bright and Patrick J. Keenan, "Judges and the Politics of Death: Deciding Between the Bill of Rights and the Next Election in Capital Cases," *Boston University Law Review* 75 (May 1995): 759–835. This practice was successfully challenged in 2002. In *Ring v. Arizona*, the U.S. Supreme Court ruled that juries rather than judges "must make the crucial factual determinations that subject a convicted murderer to the death penalty," thus invalidating the death penalty

statutes of five states and casting doubt on four others. Linda Greenhouse, "The Supreme Court: Capital Punishment; Justices Say Death Penalty Is Up to Juries, Not Judges," *The New York Times*, June 25, 2002, p. A-1.

53. Larry W. Koch and John F. Galliher, "Michigan's Continuing Abolition of the Death Penalty and the Conceptual Components of Symbolic Legislation," *Social and Legal Studies* 2, no. 3 (September 1993), p. 335. Many analysts contend that the Dukakis campaign was stopped in its tracks when CNN correspondent Bernard Shaw opened the second presidential debate by asking the Democratic candidate: "Governor, if Kitty Dukakis were raped and murdered, would you favor an irrevocable death penalty for the killer?" to which Dukakis calmly replied, "No, I don't, Bernard." Jack W. Germond and Jules Witcover, *Whose Broad Stripes and Bright Stars? The Trivial Pursuit of the Presidency* (New York: Warner Books, 1988), p. 5.

54. This figure of 50 includes countries that have completely abolished the death penalty and those that, having previously abolished it for ordinary crimes, went on to abolish it for all crimes. The 118 figure includes countries and territories that have abolished capital punishment in law or in practice. Of the 4 that reintroduced it, Nepal subsequently abolished it again. Amnesty International, "Facts and Figures on the Death Penalty," http://web.amnesty.org/pages/deathpenalty-facts-eng (accessed July 2, 2004).

55. These figures only include cases known to Amnesty International. The actual tally is certainly higher, especially for China, where newspapers and legislators have referred to thousands of executions per year, most of which are not specifically documented by credible outside organizations like Amnesty International. Amnesty International, "Facts and Figures on the Death Penalty."

56. Tonry and Hatlestad, "Sentencing Reform," p. 4; and Samuel H. Pillsbury, "Why Are We Ignored? The Peculiar Place of Experts in the Current Debate About Crime and Justice," *Criminal Law Bulletin* 31 (July/August 1995): 305–36.

57. Ruth and Reitz, *The Challenge of Crime*, p. 248.

58. Alfred Blumstein and Joan Petersilia, "Investigating in Criminal Justice Research," in *Crime*, ed. James Q. Wilson and Joan Petersilia (San Francisco: ICS Press, 1995), p. 468, in Ruth and Reitz, *The Challenge of Crime*, p. 49. By way of comparison, the National Institutes of Health budget is almost a thousand times as large as that for the National Institute of Justice. Furthermore, the NIH is relatively more independent than the government's primary research institution for criminal justice matters and far less obligated to be politically accountable to the party in power in the executive branch. Ruth and Reitz, *The Challenge of Crime*, p. 288.

59. Michael Tonry and Joan Petersilia, "American Prisons at the Beginning of the Twenty-First Century," in *Crime and Justice: A Review of Research*, vol. 26, p. 4.

60. Franklin E. Zimring, Gordon Hawkins, and Sam Kamin, *Punishment and Democracy: Three Strikes and You're Out in California* (Oxford: Oxford University Press, 2001), pp. 146 and 221.

61. For example, the FBI and U.S. Department of Justice were key in popularizing the term "serial murder" in the 1980s and inflating the prevalence of "serial killers" so as to attract maximum publicity and resources. They fostered the mistaken view that the United States faced an unprecedented and unparalleled threat from serial killers. Philip Jenkins, *Using Murder: The Social Construction of Serial Homicide* (New York: Aldine de Gruyter, 1994).

62. For a good discussion of the shortcomings of the UCR, see William J. Chambliss, *Power, Politics, and Crime* (Boulder, CO: Westview Press, 1999), pp. 35–42, on which this paragraph is based. See also William Spelman, "What Recent Studies Do (and Don't) Tell Us About Imprisonment and Crime," in *Crime and Justice: A Review of Research*, vol. 27, ed. Michael Tonry (Chicago: University of Chicago Press, 2000), pp. 433–35; Joseph Dillon Davey, *The New Social Contract: America's Journey from Welfare State to Police State* (Westport, CT: Praeger, 1995), Chapter 5; Victor E. Kappeler, Mark Blumberg, and Gary W. Potter, *The Mythology of Crime and Criminal Justice*, 3rd ed. (Prospect Heights, IL: Waveland Press, 2000), pp. 30–36; Ruth and Reitz, *The Challenge of Crime*, pp. 40–43; and Lawrence W. Sherman, "Needed: Better Ways to Count Crooks," *The Wall Street Journal*, December 3, 1998, p. A-22.

63. Chambliss, *Power, Politics, and Crime*, p. 37. Emphasis in the original. By that accounting method, the recorded homicide rate in the United States for 1996 would be cut nearly in half. It would equal about three times Sweden's rate. Federal Bureau of Investigation, *Uniform Crime Reports for the United States, 1996*, p. 13, http://www.fbi.gov/ucr/96cius.htm (accessed March 19, 2002).

64. Philip Jenkins, *Moral Panic: Changing Concepts of the Child Molester in Modern America* (New Haven: Yale University Press, 1998), p. 66.

65. The official National Crime Victimization Survey uses a random sample of U.S. households to determine how many people have been victims of specific crimes. Chambliss, *Power, Politics, and Crime*, p. 52; and Davey, *The New Social Contract*, pp. 76–77.

66. André Kuhn, "Prison Populations in Western Europe," in *Sentencing Reform in Overcrowded Times*, pp. 124–25. See also David Garland, *Punishment and Modern Society: A Study in Social Theory* (Chicago: Chicago University Press, 1990), p. 20; Stuart A. Scheingold, *The Politics of Law and Order: Street Crime and Public Policy* (New York and London: Longman, 1984); Matthew Yglesias, "The Research Wars," *The American Prospect*, December 2003, pp. 39–41; American Bar Foundation, "Reducing Crime by Increasing Incarceration," *Researching Law: An ABF Update* 6, no. 1 (Winter 1995): 1 and 4; and Zimring and Hawkins, *Incapacitation*.

67. Zimring and Hawkins, *The Scale of Imprisonment*, p. 122; and Mauer, *Race to Incarcerate*, p. 82.

68. Joseph Dillon Davey, *The Politics of Prison Expansion: Winning Elections By Waging War on Crime* (Westport, CT: Praeger, 1998), p. 27. See also James Austin and John Irwin, *Who Goes to Prison?* (San Francisco: National Council on Crime and Delinquency, 1991); and Zimring and Hawkins, *The Scale of Imprisonment*.

69. Allen J. Beck and Paige M. Harrison, "Prisoners in 2000," *Bureau of Justice Statistics Bulletin*, August 2001, p. 3, Table 3; and Donziger, ed., *The Real War on Crime*, p. 42.

70. Reitz, "The Disassembly and Reassembly of U.S. Sentencing Practices," p. 238; Elliot Currie, *Confronting Crime: An American Challenge* (New York: Pantheon Books, 1985), Chapter 3; and Warren Young and Mark Brown, "Cross-National Comparisons of Imprisonment," in *Crime and Justice: A Review of Research*, vol. 17, ed. Michael Tonry (Chicago: University of Chicago Press, 1993), p. 33. Even James Q. Wilson concedes that very large increases in the prison population produce only modest reductions in the crime rate. James Q. Wilson, "Prison in a Free Society," *Public Interest* 117 (1994), p. 38.

71. Michael Tonry, *Malign Neglect: Race, Crime and Punishment in America* (New York: Oxford University Press, 1995), p. 17.

72. William Spelman, "The Limited Importance of Prison Expansion," in *The Crime Drop in America*, ed. Alfred Blumstein and Joel Wallman (Cambridge: Cambridge University Press, 2000).

73. Western, *Punishment and Inequality in America* (manuscript on file with author, June 2005) Chapter 4, p. 26, and Chapter 7, p. 2.

74. Tonry and Petersilia, "American Prisons at the Beginning of the Twenty-First Century," p. 3; and Roger Lane, "Murder in America: A Historian's Perspective," in *Crime and Justice: An Annual Review of Research*, vol. 25, ed. Michael Tonry and Norval Morris (Chicago: University of Chicago Press, 1999). Gurr notes that these historical trends obscure some sharp deviations upward in violence, especially homicides, which he suggests are associated with periods of wartime that appear to legitimize violence. Ted Robert Gurr, "Historical Trends in Violent Crime: A Critical Review of the Evidence," in *Crime and Justice*, vol. 3, ed. Michael Tonry and Norval Morris (Chicago: University of Chicago Press, 1981), p. 345.

75. This point is more fully developed in later chapters.

76. Only one in ten arrests in the United States is for violent crime and only three arrests out of every hundred are for a violent crime that results in injury. Donziger, *The Real War on Crime*, p. 9.

77. The percentage of people sentenced to U.S. prisons for violent crimes is relatively low. It was 29.5 percent in 1996 and has not increased since 1991. Bureau of Justice Statistics, *Correctional Populations in the United States, 1996* (Washington, DC: U.S. Department of Justice, 1999), Table 1.23, cited in Michael Tonry, "Punishment Policies and Patterns in Western Countries," in *Sentencing and Sanctions in Western Countries*, p. 14.

78. Rosemary Gartner, "Age and Homicide in Different National Contexts," in *The Crime Conundrum: Essays in Criminal Justice*, ed. Lawrence M. Friedman and George Fisher (Boulder, CO: Westview, 1997); and James Lynch, "Crime in International Perspective," in *Crime*, ed. James Q. Wilson and Joan Petersilia (San Francisco: ICS Press, 1995), p. 11.

79. One study concluded that, excluding homicide, the United States had the highest crime rate in only one of fourteen categories of crime: attempted burglary. Donziger, *The Real War on Crime*, pp. 9–11.

80. Franklin E. Zimring and Gordon Hawkins, *Crime Is Not the Problem: Lethal Violence Is* (New York: Oxford University Press, 1997), p. xi. This fear of lethal violence gets translated into a general campaign against crime in which most of the extra resources end up being directed at nonviolent behavior because serious crimes of violence already are being seriously punished. See pp. 13 and 17.

81. Ray Surette, *Media, Crime, and Criminal Justice: Images and Realities* (Pacific Grove, CA: Brooks/Cole, 1992), Chapter 4; Katherine Beckett and Theodore Sasson, *The Politics of Injustice: Crime and Punishment in America* (Thousand Oaks, CA: Pine Forge Press, 2000), Chapter 5; Richard V. Ericson, Patricia M. Baranek, and Janet B. L. Chan, *Representing Order: Crime, Law, and Justice in the News Media* (Toronto: University of Toronto Press, 1991); and Robert Reiner, "Media Made Criminality: The Representation of Crime in the Mass Media," in *The Oxford Handbook of Criminology*, 2nd ed., ed. Mike Maguire, Rod Morgan, and Robert Reiner (Oxford: Clarendon Press, 1997): 189–231.

82. The regular editorials and editorial comments by Brent Staples in *The New York Times* on the imprisonment boom and its consequences are one laudable exception.

83. Julian V. Roberts, Loretta Stalans, David Indermauer, and Mike Hough, *Penal Populism and Public Opinion: Lessons from Five Countries* (Oxford: Oxford University Press, 2003), Chapter 5; and Ester Pollack, "A Study of Media and Crime," http://www.jmk.su.se/sidor/summaryPollack.htm (accessed January 21, 2005).

84. Sonja Snacken, Kristel Beyens, and Hilde Tubex, "Changing Prison Populations in Western Countries: Fate or Policy?" *European Journal of Crime, Criminal Law and Criminal Justice* 3 no. 1 (1995), p. 23.

85. John J. DiIulio, Jr., "Are Voters Fools? Crime, Public Opinion, and Representative Democracy," *Corrections Management Quarterly* 1, no. 3 (1997): 1–5; and William J. Bennett, John J. DiIulio, Jr., and John P. Walters, *Body Count: Moral Poverty . . . and How To Win America's War Against Crime and Drugs* (New York: Simon & Schuster, 1996). DiIulio's position on incarceration has since softened. See DiIulio, "Two Million Prisoners Are Enough," *The Wall Street Journal*, March 12, 1999, p. A-19.

86. Kathlyn Taylor Gaubatz, *Crime in the Public Mind* (Ann Arbor: University of Michigan Press, 1995).

87. On fluctuations in public support for capital punishment, see Chapters 8 and 9.

88. Elaine B. Sharp, *The Sometime Connection: Public Opinion and Social Policy* (Albany: SUNY Press, 1999), p. 52, Figure 2–3, and p. 53.

89. Richard S. Frase, "Comparative Perspectives on Sentencing Policy and Research," in *Sentencing and Sanctions in Western Countries*, p. 268.

90. A review of Gallup polls from 1930 to 1997 reveals that it was not until 1994 that a majority of respondents listed crime and violence as "the most important problem" facing the United States. Even then it had to share top billing with health care. Chambliss, *Power, Politics, and Crime*, p. 20, Table 1.1. See also Katherine Beckett, *Making Crime Pay: Law and Order in Contemporary American Politics* (New York: Oxford University Press, 1997), pp. 23–25.

91. From 1994 to 1997, crime and violence were listed as leading problems, sharing the top billing with health care (1994), unemployment/jobs (1995), and drugs (1996 and 1997). Chambliss, *Power, Politics, and Crime*, p. 20, Table 1.1.

92. Francis T. Cullen, Bonnie S. Fisher, and Brandon K. Applegate, "Public Opinion about Punishment and Corrections," in *Crime and Justice: A Review of Research*, vol. 27, ed. Michael Tonry (Chicago: University of Chicago Press, 2000), p. 1.

93. On the mushiness of public opinion, see Cullen et al., "Public Opinion about Punishment and Corrections"; on public ignorance, see Julian V. Roberts and Loretta J. Stalans, "Crime, Criminal Justice, and Public Opinion," in *The Handbook of Crime and Punishment*, ed. Michael Tonry (New York: Oxford University Press, 1998), pp. 37–38.

94. For example, public opinion surveys show that many Americans believe that more than half of all serious crime is violent, when the actual figure is less than 15 percent, and that juveniles are responsible for a much higher proportion of violent crime than they are. Ted Gest, *Crime & Politics: Big Government's Erratic Campaign for Law and Order* (Oxford: Oxford University Press, 2001), p. 267.

95. Julian V. Roberts, "American Attitudes About Punishment: Myth and Reality," in *Sentencing Reform in Overcrowded Times*, pp. 250–55; Roberts and Stalans,

"Crime, Criminal Justice, and Public Opinion," p. 50; and Roberts et al., *Penal Populism and Public Opinion*, pp. 21–27, and Chapter 6.

96. Lawrence Bobo and Devon Johnson, "A Taste for Punishment: Black and White Americans' Views on the Death Penalty and the War on Drugs," *Du Bois Review* 1, no. 1 (Spring 2004), p. 153.

97. Stephen D. Gottfredson and Ralph B. Taylor, "Attitudes of Correctional Policymakers and the Public," in *America's Correctional Crisis: Prison Populations and Public Policy*, ed. Stephen D. Gottfredson and Sean McConville (New York: Greenwood Press, 1987): 57–75.

98. When surveyors pose questions about sentencing preferences after first providing information about alternatives to prison, such as community-based sanctions, support for prison erodes. This holds for a range of crimes, including violent ones. Roberts, "American Attitudes About Punishment," pp. 250–51.

99. Roberts, "American Attitudes About Punishment," pp. 253–54; Roberts and Stalans, "Crime, Criminal Justice, and Public Opinion," p. 50; and Anthony N. Doob, "The United States Sentencing Commission Guidelines: If You Don't Know Where You Are Going, You Might Not Get There," in *The Politics of Sentencing Reform*, ed. Chris Clarkson and Rod Morgan (Oxford: Clarendon-Oxford University Press, 1995), p. 210, fn. 23.

100. Roberts, "American Attitudes About Punishment," pp. 253–54; and Cullen et al., "Public Opinion About Punishment," pp. 28–33. On waning public support for incarceration, see Peter D. Hart Research Associates, *Changing Public Attitudes Toward the Criminal Justice System* (New York: The Open Society Institute, February 2002); and Justice Policy Institute, *Cutting Correctly: New Prison Policies for Times of Fiscal Crisis* (Washington, DC: Justice Policy Institute, February 2001).

101. For example, this was the stance taken by many participants in the conference "Critical Resistance East: Beyond the Prison Industrial Complex," Critical Northeast Regional Organizing Committee, Columbia University Law School, March 9–11, 2001.

102. L. Randall Wray, "A New Economic Reality: Penal Keynesianism," *Challenge* 43, no. 5 (September–October 2000): 31–59; Mike Davis, *Ecology of Fear* (New York: Metropolitan Books, 1998), p. 416; and Peter T. Kilborn, "Rural Towns Turn to Prisons to Reignite Their Economies," *The New York Times*, August 1, 2001, p. A-1.

103. Hallinan, *Going Up the River*. The phrase "race to incarcerate" comes from Mauer, *Race to Incarcerate*.

104. Joel Dyer, *The Perpetual Prisoner Machine: How America Profits from Crime* (Boulder, CO: Westview, 2000); Welch, *Punishment in America*, Chapter 13; Brigette Sarabi and Edwin Bender, *The Prison Payoff: The Role of Politics and Private Prisons in the Incarceration Boom* (Portland, OR: Western States Center and Western Prison Project, November 2000); Bryan Gruley, "Wanted: Criminals: Why Did Mississippi Agree to Pay for Cells for 'Ghost Inmates'?" *The Wall Street Journal*, September 6, 2001, p. A-1; Joseph T. Hallinan, "Bailed Out: Shaky Private Prisons Find Vital Customers in Federal Government," *The Wall Street Journal*, November 6, 2001, p. A-1; Burton-Rose et al., eds., *The Celling of America*; Nils Christie, *Crime Control as Industry: Toward GULAGS, Western Style*, 2nd ed. (London and New York: Routledge, 1994); Scott Christianson, *With Liberty for Some: 500 Years of Imprisonment in America*

(Boston: Northeastern University Press, 1998), pp. 290–95; and Anne L. Schneider, "Public-Private Partnerships in the U.S. Prison System," *American Behavioral Scientist* 43, no. 1 (September 1999): 192–208.

105. Hallinan, *Going Up the River*, pp. xiv–xv, xvi, and 125. CCA's stock subsequently plummeted. See p. 184.

106. Hallinan, *Going Up the River*, p. 204.

107. Steven Donziger, "The Prison-Industrial Complex: What's Driving the Rush to Lock 'em Up," *The Washington Post*, March 17, 1996, p. 24, in Welch, *Punishment in America*, p. 277.

108. Hallinan, *Going Up the River*, p. 156.

109. At a minimum, this revolving door has created potential conflicts of interest. Michael Quinlan, the former head of the Federal Bureau of Prisons, retired in 1992 and became chief executive of a spinoff company of the CCA. Edwin Meese, III, Reagan's attorney general, is chairman of the Enterprise Prison Institute, a group pushing to make inmate labor more accessible to private industry. Hallinan, *Going Up the River*, pp. 173–74. See also Sarabi and Bender, *The Prison Payoff*; and American Federation of State, County and Municipal Employees, *The Evidence Is Clear: Crime Shouldn't Pay* (Washington, DC: AFSCME, n.d.).

110. Christianson, *With Liberty for Some*, p. 294.

111. For more on the growing movement to challenge the carceral state, see Chapter 10.

112. Ruth Wilson Gilmore, remarks at the workshop "Prisons in Rural America: Overview for Social Change Activists," at "Critical Resistance East" conference.

113. Craig Gilmore, remarks at the workshop "Prisons in Rural America: Overview for Social Change Activists," at "Critical Resistance East" conference. Grace Defina of the Concerned Citizens of Wayne County, Penn., which battled the construction of a prison in her community, made similar points at the workshop. Hallinan's account of Youngstown, Ohio's deep disillusionment after the CCA built a brand new prison there bolsters this view. "Knowing what I know now," said the mayor of Youngstown, "I would never have allowed CCA to build a prison here." Hallinan, *Going Up the River*, p. 185. See also Barry Yeoman, "Steeltown Lockdown," *Mother Jones*, May/June 2000, pp. 38–47.

114. These figures include jails, prisons, and detention centers for undocumented immigrants. Douglas McDonald et al., *Private Prisons in the United States: An Assessment of Current Practice* (Cambridge, MA: Abt Associates, Inc., July 16, 1998), p. iii.

115. Theodore Caplow and Jonathan Simon, "Understanding Prison Policy and Population Trends," in *Crime and Justice – A Review of Research*, vol. 26, p. 93.

116. Alfred Blumstein and Allen J. Beck, "Population Growth in U.S. Prisons, 1980–1996," in *Crime and Justice – A Review of Research*, vol. 26, pp. 20–21.

117. FBI, *Crime in the United States, 2000* (Washington, DC: GPO, 2001), p. 220, Table 32, cited in Ruth and Reitz, *The Challenge of Crime*, p. 211.

118. Diana R. Gordon, *The Return of the Dangerous Classes: Drug Prohibition and Policy Politics* (New York: W. W. Norton & Co., 1994); and Staughton and Alice Lynd, "Prison Advocacy in a Time of Capital Disaccumulation," *Monthly Review* 53, no. 3 (July/August 2001): 128–41.

119. Michael Tonry, "Racial Politics, Racial Disparities, and the War on Crime," *Crime and Delinquency* 40, no. 4 (October 1994), p. 480; and Michael Tonry,

"Drug Policies Increasing Racial Disparities in U.S. Prisons," in *Sentencing Reform in Overcrowded Times*.

120. Tonry, "Racial Politics, Racial Disparities," p. 483.

121. Federal sentencing guidelines mandate the same five-year minimum prison term for possessing or selling 5 grams of cocaine, an amount equal to the weight of a nickel, as for 500 grams of powder cocaine. Stuart Taylor, Jr., "It's Time to Stop Packing Prisons With Two-Bit Crack Users," Atlantic Online, http://www.theatlantic.com/politics/nj/taylor2002-05-07.htm (accessed January 15, 2005); and Tonry, "Racial Politics, Racial Disparities," p. 488.

122. John C. McWilliams, "Through the Past Darkly: The Politics and Policies of America's Drug War," *Journal of Policy History* 3, no. 4 (1991): 356–414.

123. Zimring and Hawkins, *The Scale of Imprisonment*, p. 135, Figure 5.7.

124. Sebastian Scheerer, "The New Dutch and German Drug Laws: Social and Political Conditions for Criminalization and Decriminalization," *Law & Society Review* 12, no. 4 (Summer 1978): 585–606. For a concise summary of evolving drug policies in Western Europe in recent years, see Robert J. MacCoun and Peter Reuter, "Drug Control," in *The Handbook of Crime and Punishment*: 207–38. For the longer historical and comparative view, see Robert J. MacCoun and Peter Reuter, *Drug War Heresies: Learning from Other Vices, Times and Places* (Cambridge: Cambridge University Press, 2001); and Robert J. MacCoun and Peter Reuter, eds., "Cross-National Drug Policy," special issue, *The Annals of the American Academy of Political and Social Science* 582 (July 2002).

125. J. F. Galliher and L. Basilick, "Utah's Liberal Drug Laws: Structural Foundations and Triggering Events," *Social Problems* 26 no. 3 (February 1979): 284–97.

126. Kai T. Erikson, *Wayward Puritans: A Study in the Sociology of Deviance* (New York: John Wiley & Sons, Inc., 1966), p. 6. Emphasis in the original.

127. Erikson, *Wayward Puritans*, p. 69.

128. Ruth and Reitz, *The Challenge of Crime*, p. 211.

129. For more on the U.S. Congress and drug policy in the early years of the Nixon administration, see Ruth D. Peterson, "Discriminatory Decision Making at the Legislative Level: An Analysis of the Comprehensive Drug Abuse Prevention and Control Act of 1970," *Law and Human Behavior* 9, no. 3 (1985): 243–69.

130. On Rockefeller, Nixon, and the war on drugs, see Michael Massing, *The Fix* (New York: Simon & Schuster, 1998), pp. 126–29; Edward Jay Epstein, *Agency of Fear: Opiates and Political Power in America* (New York: G. P. Putnam's Sons, 1977), Chapter 2; and Eva Bertram, Morris Blachman, Kenneth Sharpe, and Peter Andreas, *Drug War Politics: The Price of Denial* (Berkeley: University of California Press, 1996), pp. 105–09.

131. Epstein, *Agency of Fear*, p. 53; and McWilliams, "Through the Past Darkly," pp. 371–75.

132. Massing, *The Fix*, p. 137; and McWilliams, "Through the Past Darkly," p. 375.

133. The results of the University of Michigan annual survey of high school drug use released in January 1994 showed the first increase in marijuana use in fourteen years. This up-tick prompted the Clinton administration to stake out a more hard-line position on drugs, even though marijuana use was still less than half what it had been in the late 1970s, and consumption of hard drugs remained negligible. Massing, *The Fix*, pp. 213–19. See also McWilliams, "Through the Past Darkly," pp. 375–80; and Tonry, *Malign Neglect*, pp. 83–104.

134. Massing, *The Fix*, Chapter 11.

135. "Drug War Urged After Bias Death," *Chicago Tribune*, June 26, 1986, p. 2, quoted in Hallinan, *Going Up the River*, p. 44. In another instance, Rev. Jackson appeared to sanction the war on drugs and the law-and-order crusade when he made the controversial remark: "There is nothing more painful to me at this stage in my life than to walk down the street and hear footsteps and start thinking about robbery – then look around and see somebody white and feel relieved." "Perspectives," *Newsweek*, December 13, 1993, p. 17.

136. Beckett, *Making Crime Pay*, p. 25.

137. That year it shared top billing in the Gallup poll with the budget deficit. Chambliss, *Power, Politics, and Crime*, p. 20, Table 1.1. For an excellent nuanced analysis of U.S. public opinion on drugs, see Roberts et al., *Penal Populism and Public Opinion*, Chapter 9.

138. See, for example, Nancy E. Marion, *A History of Federal Crime Control Initiatives, 1960–1993* (Westport, CT: Praeger, 1994); and Gerald Caplan, "Reflections on the Nationalization of Crime, 1964–1968," *Law and the Social Order* 3 (1973): 583–635.

139. Beckett, *Making Crime Pay*, p. 106.

140. Davey, *The Politics of Prison Expansion*. For a variation of this argument that focuses on California, see Sasha Abramsky, *Hard Time Blues* (New York: St. Martin's Press, 2002).

141. Caplow and Simon, "Understanding Prison Policy"; Scheingold, *The Politics of Law and Order*, Chapter 2; and Beckett, *Making Crime Pay*.

142. Thomas Byrne Edsall with Mary D. Edsall, *Chain Reaction: The Impact of Race, Rights, and Taxes on American Politics* (New York: Norton, 1991); and Tali Mendelberg, "Executing Hortons: Racial Crime in the 1988 Presidential Campaign," *Public Opinion Quarterly* 61, no. 1 (Spring 1997): 134–57. For an overview of the role of law and order in presidential campaigns from the 1960s onward, see James O. Finekenauer, "Crime as a National Political Issue, 1964–76: From Law and Order to Domestic Tranquility," *Crime and Delinquency* 24, no. 1 (January 1978): 13–27. On how Clinton's get-tough record is "virtually indistinguishable" from that of his Republican predecessors, see Ronald Kramer and Raymond Michalowski, "The Iron Fist and the Velvet Tongue: Crime Control Policies in the Clinton Administration," *Crime and Justice* 22, no. 2 (1995), p. 95. See also Tony G. Poveda, "Clinton, Crime, and the Justice Department," *Social Justice* 21, no. 3 (1994): 73–84; Anthony M. Platt, "The Politics of Law and Order," *Social Justice* 21, no. 3 (1994): 3–13; and David Burnham and Susan Long, "The Clinton Era by the Numbers," *The Nation*, January 29, 2001, pp. 20–22.

143. Beckett, *Making Crime Pay*, pp. 83–88; Beckett and Sasson, *The Politics of Injustice*, p. 74; and Christian Parenti, *Lockdown America: Police and Prisons in the Age of Crisis* (London and New York: Verso, 1999), p. 169.

144. Caplow and Simon, "Understanding Prison Policy," pp. 70–71 and 79–80; and Zimring et al., *Punishment and Democracy*, pp. 174–75.

145. David Garland, *The Culture of Control: Crime and Social Order in Contemporary Society* (Chicago: University of Chicago Press, 2001), pp. 38–39.

146. Garland, *The Culture of Control*, p. 20; and David Garland, "The Limits of the Sovereign State: Strategies of Crime Control in Contemporary Society," *The British Journal of Criminology* 36, no. 4 (Autumn 1996): 445–71.

147. Garland, *The Culture of Control*, p. 53. See also Diana R. Gordon, *The Justice Juggernaut: Fighting Street Crime, Controlling Citizens* (New Brunswick, NJ:

Rutgers University Press, 1990). For a complementary view that examines the "culture of control" in California, see Tom R. Tyler and Robert J. Boeckmann, "Three Strikes and You Are Out, but Why? The Psychology of Public Support for Punishing Rule Breakers," *Law & Society Review* 31, no. 2 (1997): 237–65. For a challenge to the "culture of control" view using survey research, see Bert Useem, Raymond V. Liedka, and Anne Morrison Piehl, "Popular Support for the Prison Build-up," *Punishment & Society* 5, no. 1 (January 2003): 5–32.

148. Beckett makes these points about Garland in Katherine Beckett, "Crime and Control in the Culture of Late Modernity," *Law & Society Review* 35, no. 4 (2001), pp. 900 and 922.

149. Garland, *The Culture of Control*, p. 75.

150. William Lyons and Stuart A. Scheingold, "The Politics of Crime and Punishment," in *The Nature of Crime: Continuity and Change*, vol. 1 (Washington, DC: National Institute of Justice, 2000), p. 124.

151. Lyons and Scheingold, "The Politics of Crime and Punishment," p. 124; and Tim Hope and Richard Sparks, "Risk, Insecurity, and the Politics of Law and Order," in *Crime, Risk and Insecurity: Law and Order in Everyday Life and Political Discourse*, ed. Tim Hope and Richard Sparks (London and New York: Routledge, 2000): 1–10.

152. For analyses that look closely at important cultural differences at the local level, see Uwe Ewald, "Criminal Victimization and Social Adaptation in Modernity: Fear of Crime and Risk Perception in the New Germany," in *Crime, Risk and Insecurity*; and Lucia Zedner, "The Pursuit of Security," in *Crime, Risk and Insecurity*. For an emphasis on national cultural differences rather than the cultural consequences of the rise of late modernity, see Michael Tonry, "Symbol, Substance, and Severity in Western Penal Policies," *Punishment & Society* 3, no. 4 (October 2001): 517–36.

153. On the NRA, see Paul Wright, "Citizen Anti-Crime Initiatives? How the Gun Lobby Bankrolls the War on Crime," in *The Celling of America*; and Dyer, *The Perpetual Prisoner Machine*, p. 145. On the American Legislative Exchange Council, see Sarabi and Bender, *The Prison Payoff*; and Brigette Sarabi, "ALEC in the House: Corporate Bias in Criminal Justice Legislation," *Prison Legal News*, January 2002, pp. 1–4.

154. On the role of conservative intellectuals in pushing penal policy to the right, see Platt and Takagi, "Intellectuals for Law and Order"; Ruth and Reitz, *The Challenge of Crime*, pp. 80–91; and Andrew Rutherford, *Transforming Criminal Policy: Spheres of Influence in the United States, The Netherlands and England and Wales* (Winchester, UK: Wayside Press, 1996), Chapter 2.

155. Francis A. Allen, *The Decline of the Rehabilitative Ideal: Penal Policy and Social Purpose* (New Haven: Yale University Press, 1981), p. 2; and David J. Rothman, *Conscience and Convenience: The Asylum and Its Alternatives in Progressive America* (Boston: Little, Brown and Co., 1980), Chapter 2.

156. Indeterminate sentences had several other purposes. They served as carrots to maintain social control in prisons and as a means to alleviate overcrowding when prison capacity remained fixed. Jonathan D. Casper, David Brereton, David Neal et al., *The Implementation of the California Determinate Sentencing Law* (Washington, DC: U.S. Department of Justice, National Institute of Justice, May 1982), pp. 233–35. For the early history of federal sentencing reform, see Kate Stith and Jośe Cabranes, *Fear of Judging: Sentencing Guidelines in the Federal Courts* (Chicago: University of Chicago Press, 1998), Chapter 1.

157. American Friends Service Committee, *Struggle for Justice: A Report on Crime and Punishment in America* (New York: Hill and Wang, 1971), p. 8.

158. American Friends Service Committee, *Struggle for Justice*, pp. 46–47.

159. For other examples of criticism of the rehabilitative model and the vast discretionary powers reportedly associated with it, much of it written by sympathetic liberals, see Erik Olin Wright, ed., *The Politics of Punishment* (New York: Harper and Row, 1973); Alvin J. Bronstein, "Reform Without Change: The Future of Prisoners' Rights," *The Civil Liberties Review* 4, no. 3 (September/October 1977), p. 30; Kenneth Culp Davis, *Discretionary Justice: A Preliminary Inquiry* (Baton Rouge: Louisiana State University, 1969); Marvin E. Frankel, *Criminal Sentences: Law Without Order* (New York: Hill and Wang, 1973); Andrew von Hirsch, *Doing Justice: The Choice of Punishments; Report of the Committee for the Study of Incarceration* (New York: Hill and Wang, 1975); and Twentieth Century Fund, *Fair and Certain Punishment: Report of the Twentieth Century Fund Task Force on Criminal Sentencing* (New York: McGraw-Hill, 1976).

160. "Sentencing in America is a national scandal," Kennedy charged. "Every day our system of sentencing breeds massive injustice. Judges are free to roam at will, dispensing ad hoc justice in ways that defy both reason and fairness." Edward M. Kennedy, "Introduction to Symposium on Sentencing," *Hofstra Law Review* 7, no. 1–9 at 1–3 (1978), cited in Leon Radzinowicz and Roger Hood, "The American Volte-Face in Sentencing Thought and Practice," in *Crime, Proof, and Punishment: Essays in Memory of Sir Rupert Cross*, ed. C. F. H. Tapper (London: Butterworths, 1981), p. 139. Senator Kennedy co-sponsored with Senator Strom Thurmond (R-S.C.) a series of federal sentencing reform bills that led to the establishment of the federal sentencing commission under the 1984 Sentencing Reform Act. The commission's guidelines, which went into effect in 1987, carried "a heavy presumption of imprisonment for most offenders" and gave "little regard for any mitigating circumstances involved in an offense." See Mauer, *Race to Incarcerate*, pp. 58–59. See also Kate Stith and Steve Y. Koh, "The Politics of Sentencing Reform: The Legislative History of the Federal Sentencing Guidelines," *Wake Forest Law Review* 28 (1993): 223–90; and Stith and Cabranes, *Fear of Judging*.

161. "With the acknowledged failure of rehabilitation by the very people who had pushed it so ardently, punishment began to resurface as an appropriate justification for the criminal justice system." Ronald Bayer, "Crime, Punishment, and the Decline of Liberal Optimism," *Crime and Delinquency* 27, no. 2 (April 1981), p. 187. For other accounts that stress the significance of the convergence of right and left around sentencing reform with the decline of liberal optimism in rehabilitation, see Stith and Koh, "The Politics of Sentencing Reform," p. 285; Lynne Goodstein and John Hepburn, *Determinate Sentencing and Imprisonment: A Failure of Reform* (Cincinnati: Anderson Publishing Co., 1985), pp. 24–26; Lawrence F. Travis, III, "The Politics of Sentencing Reform," in *Sentencing Reform: Experiments in Reducing Disparity*, ed. Martin L. Forst (Newbury Park, CA: Sage, 1982), p. 59; Casper et al., *The Implementation of the California Determinate Sentencing Law*, p. 17; Francis T. Cullen and Karen E. Gilbert, *Reaffirming Rehabilitation* (Cincinnati: Anderson Publishing Co., 1982), pp. 13–17; Marc Mauer, "Why Are Tough on Crime Policies So Popular?," *Stanford Law and Policy Review* 11 (1999), p. 14; Alfred Blumstein, "Prison Populations: A

System Out of Control," in *Crime and Justice: An Annual Review of Research*, vol. 10, ed. Michael Tonry and Norval Morris (Chicago: University of Chicago Press, 1988), pp. 237–41; and Eric Schlosser, "The Prison-Industrial Complex," *The Atlantic Monthly*, December 1998.

162. Blumstein, "Prison Populations: A System Out of Control," pp. 238–39; and David J. Rothman, "The Crime of Punishment," *The New York Review of Books*, February 17, 1994, p. 36.

163. Rothman, "The Crime of Punishment, p. 36. On Minnesota and Washington State, see Debra Dailey, "Minnesota's Sentencing Guidelines – Past and Future," in *Sentencing Reform in Overcrowded Times*, pp. 35–49; and William C. Collins, "Discussion on Colloquium, 'The Prison Overcrowding Crisis'," *New York University Review of Law and Social Change* 12, no. 1 (1983–84), pp. 343–44.

164. Garland, *Culture of Control*, p. 64.

165. Robert Martinson, "What Works? Questions and Answers About Prison Reform," *The Public Interest* 35 (1974): 22–54.

166. Robert Martinson, "New Findings, New Views: A Note of Caution Regarding Sentencing Reform," *Hofstra Law Review* (Winter 1979): 243–58.

167. Andrew von Hirsch, "The Future of the Proportionate Sentence," in *Punishment and Social Control: Essays in Honor of Sheldon L. Messinger*, ed. Thomas G. Blomberg and Stanley Cohen (New York: Aldine de Gruyter, 1995), p. 133.

168. Jonathan D. Casper, "Determinate Sentencing and Prison Crowding in Illinois," *University of Illinois Review* 2 (1984), p. 240.

169. Roberts et al., *Penal Populism and Public Opinion*, pp. 35–36.

170. Reitz, "Sentencing," in *The Handbook of Crime and Punishment*: 542–62.

171. On the Canadian backlash against reform, see Herbert Gamberg and Anthony Thomson, *The Illusion of Prison Reform* (New York: Peter Lang, 1984), pp. 117–131. For Britain, see David Downes and Rod Morgan, "'Hostages to Fortune'? The Politics of Law and Order in Post-War Britain," in *The Oxford Handbook of Criminology*; for Australia, see Arie Freiberg, "Sentencing and Punishment in Australia in the 1990s," in *Sentencing Reform in Overcrowded Times*: 35–49; for Sweden, see Andrew von Hirsch, "Sentencing Reform in Sweden," in *Sentencing Reform in Overcrowded Times*; and Andrew von Hirsch, "The Swedish Sentencing Law," in *Principled Sentencing: Readings in Theory and Policy*, ed. Andrew von Hirsch and Andrew Ashworth (Oxford: Hart Publishing, 1998).

172. Whitman, *Harsh Justice*, pp. 72–73.

173. Ann Chih Lin, *Reform in the Making: The Implementation of Social Policy in Prison* (Princeton: Princeton University Press, 2000), pp. 10–11.

174. Stith and Koh, "The Politics of Sentencing Reform," p. 287 and p. 228, n. 23.

175. Norval Morris, *The Future of Imprisonment* (Chicago: University of Chicago Press, 1974); and Nigel Walker, *Treatment and Justice in Penology and Psychiatry: The 1976 Sandoz Lecture* (Edinburgh: Edinburgh University Press, 1976), in Garland, *The Culture of Control*, p. 65.

176. Garland, *The Culture of Control*, p. 34.

177. Albert P. Melone and Robert Slagter, "Interest Group Politics and the Reform of the Federal Criminal Code," in *The Political Science of Criminal Justice*, ed. Stuart Nagel, Erika Fairchild, and Anthony Champagne (Springfield, IL: Charles C. Thomas, 1983): 41–55; Erika Fairchild, "Interest Groups in the Criminal

Justice Process," *Journal of Criminal Justice* 9, no. 2 (1981): 181–94; Richard A. Berk and Peter H. Rossi, *Prison Reform and State Elites* (Cambridge, MA: Ballinger, 1977); and John P. Heinz, Robert W. Gettleman, and Morris Seeskin, "Legislative Politics and the Criminal Law," *Northwestern Law Review* 64, no. 3 (July–August 1969): 277–358.

CHAPTER 3. UNLOCKING THE PAST: THE NATIONALIZATION
AND POLITICIZATION OF LAW AND ORDER

1. Quoted in Mark Green, "The Evil of Access," *The Nation*, December 30, 2002, p. 19.
2. Charles Tilly, "Reflections on the History of European State-Making," in *The Formation of National States in Western Europe*, ed. Charles Tilly (Princeton: Princeton University Press, 1975), p. 49. See also David H. Bayley, "The Police and Political Development in Europe," in *The Formation of National States in Western Europe*: 328–79.
3. Lawrence M. Friedman, *Crime and Punishment in American History* (New York: Basic Books, 1993), p. 27.
4. Even sixty years after the creation of the office of the attorney general, the staff consisted of just two clerks and a messenger. Paul W. Keve, *Prisons and the American Conscience: A History of U.S. Federal Corrections* (Carbondale and Edwardsville: Southern Illinois University Press, 1991), p. 9. See also Homer Cummings and Carl McFarland, *Federal Justice: Chapters in the History of Justice and the Federal Executive* (New York: The Macmillan Company, 1937), pp. v and 79.
5. The legislation creating the Department of Justice gave it sweeping powers. Embroiled in the political passions of Reconstruction and charged with enforcing the controversial Enforcement Acts, the new department was crippled by charges of corruption and abuse of power. Cummings and McFarland, *Federal Justice*, pp. 226 and 230–48.
6. Cummings and McFarland, *Federal Justice*, pp. 374–81.
7. Texas created the Texas Rangers, while the brief experiment with a state police force did not last in Massachusetts. David R. Johnson, *American Law Enforcement: A History* (St. Louis, MO: Forum Press, 1981), pp. 156–57.
8. Until then, the federal government contracted out its prisoners to local jails and state prisons and then poorly tracked what happened to offenders serving sentences for federal crimes. Keve, *Prisons and the American Conscience*, p. 25; and Clifford E. Simonsen, "Federal Bureau of Prisons," in *Encyclopedia of American Prisons*, ed. Marilyn D. McShane and Frank P. Williams, III (New York and London: Garland Publishing, 1996).
9. James Morone demonstrates in great detail how the roaring moral fervor at the soul of American politics complements and at times is in tension with liberalism in American political development and makes a similar argument about state-building in *Hellfire Nation: The Politics of Sin in American History* (New Haven: Yale University Press, 2003).
10. "To the extent that American history is the story of immigration, then American colonial history is largely the story of the immigration of prisoners," according to Scott Christianson. *With Liberty for Some: 500 Years of Imprisonment in America* (Boston: Northeastern University Press, 1998), p. 13.
11. Christianson, *With Liberty for Some*, p. 13.

12. A. Roger Ekirch, *Bound for America: The Transportation of British Convicts to the Colonies, 1718–1775* (Oxford: Clarendon – Oxford University Press, 1987), p. 27, cited in Christianson, *With Liberty for Some*, p. 25. This figure may be low, according to Christianson, because it underestimates the number sent before 1718, it ignores debtors, and it does not include convicts transported by France, Spain, and Holland.

13. Benjamin Franklin, a victim of burglary, denounced England's unloading of felons as "an insult and contempt, the cruellest [sic], that ever one people offered to another." He suggested the colonies retaliate by shipping some of their indigenous rattlesnakes to England, where they could be released into the finest parks. In *Pennsylvania Gazette*, May 9, 1751, cited in Christianson, *With Liberty for Some*, pp. 50–51. On impressment, see pp. 64–65.

14. This paragraph is based primarily on Christianson, *With Liberty for Some*, pp. 3, 13, 60, 64–65, and 82–83.

15. Adam Hirsch, *The Rise of the Penitentiary: Prisons and Punishment in Early America* (New Haven: Yale University Press, 1992), pp. 47 and 54; and Paul Takagi, "The Walnut Street Jail: A Penal Reform to Centralize the Powers of the State," in *Punishment and Penal Discipline: Essays on the Prison and the Prisoners' Movement*, ed. Tony Platt and Paul Takagi (San Francisco: Crime and Social Justice Associates, 1980): 48–56.

16. Ronald J. Pestritto, *Founding the Criminal Law: Punishment and Political Thought in the Origins of America* (DeKalb: Northern Illinois University Press, 2000), p. 3. See also David J. Rothman, *The Discovery of the Asylum: Social Order and Disorder in the New Republic*, rev. ed. (Boston: Little, Brown and Company, 1990), pp. 60–61.

17. Lawrence Friedman, "The Development of American Criminal Law," in *Law and Order in American History*, ed. Joseph M. Hawes (Port Washington, NY: Kennicut Press, 1979), p. 6.

18. See Chapter 7.

19. Hirsch, *The Rise of the Penitentiary*, p. 47.

20. For accounts that stress to varying degrees the importance or primacy of Enlightenment ideas and religious humanism in the creation of the penitentiary in the late eighteenth and early nineteenth centuries, see Blake McKelvey, *American Prisons: A History of Good Intentions* (Montclair, NJ: Patterson Smith, 1977); W. David Lewis, *From Newgate to Dannemora: The Rise of the Penitentiary in New York, 1796–1848* (Ithaca, NY: Cornell University Press, 1965); John Bender, *Imagining the Penitentiary: Fiction and Architecture of Mind in Eighteenth-Century England* (Chicago: University of Chicago Press, 1987), Chapter 1; Negley Teeters, *The Cradle of the Penitentiary: The Walnut Street Jail at Philadelphia, 1773–1835* (Philadelphia: Lippincott, 1935); and Orlando F. Lewis, *The Development of American Prisons and Prison Customs* (Montclair, NJ: Patterson Smith, 1967; originally published in 1922). Michael Ignatieff acknowledges the importance of Enlightenment ideas and religious humanitarianism, but takes a more jaded view of their influence and situates his analysis of the origins of the penitentiary within a broader context of changes in the political economy and class relations at the time. Ignatieff, *A Just Measure of Pain: The Penitentiary in the Industrial Revolution, 1750–1850* (New York: Columbia University Press, 1978).

21. Beccaria's *On Crimes and Punishment* first appeared in 1764 and was quickly translated into English. As early as 1770, John Adams was already quoting it. See Rothman, *The Discovery of the Asylum*, p. 59.

22. For an overview of Enlightenment ideas about crime and punishment, see Lewis, *From Newgate to Dannemora*, pp. 16 and 20; and Pestritto, *Founding the Criminal Law*, pp. 6 and 65.

23. See, for example, Christopher L. Tomlins and Bruce H. Mann, eds., *The Many Legalities of Early America* (Chapel Hill: University of North Carolina Press, 2001).

24. Hirsch, *The Rise of the Penitentiary*; Thomas L. Dumm, *Democracy and Punishment: Disciplinary Origins of the United States* (Madison: University of Wisconsin Press, 1987); Louis P. Masur, *Rites of Execution: Capital Punishment and the Transformation of American Culture, 1776–1865* (New York: Oxford University Press, 1989); and Michael Meranze, *Laboratories of Virtue: Punishment, Revolution, and Authority in Philadelphia, 1760–1835* (Chapel Hill: University of North Carolina Press, 1996).

25. Masur, *Rites of Execution*, p. 4. For example, the question of whether capital punishment was lawful and whether criminal law in the country was too harsh were subjects of debate among graduating students at Yale and other elite institutions during this period. Masur, *Rites of Execution*, pp. 52 and 85. For more on the early history of capital punishment, see Chapter 8 in this volume.

26. "Benefit of clergy" derived from a privilege originally enjoyed by clerics who were tried by the royal courts of the Middle Ages. By the eighteenth century, offenders convicted of minor crimes punishable by capital punishment could save themselves from the gallows by claiming they were "clergy." Ignatieff, *A Just Measure of Pain*, p. 19; and Lewis, *From Newgate to Dannemora*, pp. 7–8.

27. Pestritto, *Founding the Criminal Law*, p. 46.

28. Pestritto, *Founding the Criminal Law*, pp. 140–41.

29. Pestritto, *Founding the Criminal Law*, p. 46.

30. Friedman, *Crime and Punishment in American History*, pp. 74 and 63; and Masur, *Rites of Execution*, p. 65.

31. Stuart Banner, *The Death Penalty: An American History* (Cambridge, MA: Harvard University Press, 2002), Chapter 4.

32. George Washington Smith, "Description of the Eastern State Penitentiary of Pennsylvania" (Philadelphia, 1829), p. 7, cited in Meranze, *Laboratories of Virtue*, p. 1.

33. Meranze, *Laboratories of Virtue*, pp. 14–16. In a similar vein, Dumm argues that the "emergence of the penitentiary in the United States was a project *constitutive* of liberal democracy." *Democracy and Punishment*, p. 6. Emphasis in the original.

34. The authorities initially sought to control executions in a manner that heightened the terror and spectacle of public hangings. Often neither the prisoner nor the audience would be told of a pardon ahead of time. "The criminals were taken to the edge of death – accompanied by coffins, paraded through the streets to the scaffold, the rope prepared, their confessions taken – and then, at the last minute, the hand of the state brought them back to life." Meranze, *Laboratories of Virtue*, p. 42.

35. Rush said of the prison: "Let the avenue to this house be rendered difficult and gloomy by mountains or morasses. Let its doors be of iron; and let the grating, occasioned by opening and shutting them, be encreased [sic] by an echo from a neighboring mountain, that shall extend and continue a sound that shall deeply pierce the soul." Quoted in Meranze, *Laboratories of Virtue*, p. 133.

36. Pestritto, *Founding the Criminal Law*, pp. 6–8; Masur, *Rites of Execution*, pp. 41–43 and 54; and Lewis, *From Newgate to Dannemora*, p. 6.

37. Friedman, *Crime and Punishment in American History*, p. 32. The early criminal code of the Puritans, "The Laws and Liberties of Massachusetts" (1648), included a list of capital crimes, each accompanied by specific citations from the Bible. Friedman, p. 34. See also Rothman, *The Discovery of the Asylum*, pp. 17–18; and Morone, *Hellfire Nation*, Chapters 1–3.

38. Lewis, *From Newgate to Dannemora*, p. 3; and Takagi, "The Walnut Street Jail," p. 51.

39. Lewis, *From Newgate to Dannemora*, pp. 3–4 and 21. For a good overview of the early ideological origins of the penitentiary, see Ignatieff, *A Just Measure of Pain*, Chapters 3 and 8.

40. Shelley Bookspan, *A Germ of Goodness: The California State Prison System, 1851–1944* (Lincoln: University of Nebraska Press, 1991), p. xix.

41. Pestritto, *Founding the Criminal Law*, pp. 9, 112, 132–33, and 135; and James Madison, Alexander Hamilton, and John Jay, *The Federalist Papers,* ed. Isaac Kramnick (London: Penguin Books, 1987), pp. 279–86.

42. Pestritto, *Founding the Criminal Law*, p. 119.

43. Pestritto, *Founding the Criminal Law*, pp. 119–20.

44. In 1796, the Virginia legislature did eliminate the death penalty for all crimes except murder and certain crimes committed by slaves, but did not enact Jefferson's other proposals for bodily punishments. Friedman, *Crime and Punishment in American History*, p. 73.

45. For more on the early origins of the anti-death penalty movement, see Chapter 8.

46. Hirsch, *The Rise of the Penitentiary*, p. 107. See also pp. 106 and 108–09.

47. Michael Hindus, *Prison and Plantation: Crime, Justice, and Authority in Massachusetts and South Carolina, 1767–1978* (Chapel Hill: The University of North Carolina Press, 1980).

48. Hindus, *Prison and Plantation*, p. xix.

49. Hindus, *Prison and Plantation*, p. xxvii.

50. Edward L. Ayers, *Vengeance and Justice: Crime and Punishment in the 19th-Century American South* (New York: Oxford University Press, 1984), p. 52

51. Ayers, *Vengeance and Justice*, p. 35.

52. For example, in 1850, Georgia, with a population of 900,000, had 43 prisoners; Massachusetts, with a comparable population, had 1,236 convicts. Alex Lichtenstein, *Twice the Work of Free Labor: The Political Economy of Convict Labor in the New South* (London: Verso, 1996), p. 23.

53. Ayers, *Vengeance and Justice*, p. 71. See also Hindus, *Prison and Plantation*.

54. Two notable exceptions were North and South Carolina, which persisted in building state penitentiaries during Reconstruction. Matthew J. Mancini, *One Dies, Get Another: Convict Leasing in the American South, 1866–1928* (Columbia: University of South Carolina Press, 1996), p. 199.

55. Mark T. Carleton, *Politics and Punishment: The History of the Louisiana Penal System* (Baton Rouge: Louisiana State University Press, 1971); Lichtenstein, *Twice the Work of Free Labor*; Ayers, *Vengeance and Justice*, esp. Chapter 6; Donald R. Walker, *Penology for Profit: A History of the Texas Prison System, 1867–1912* (College Station: Texas A&M University Press, 1988); Christianson, *With Liberty for Some*, pp. 181–83; Martha A. Myers, *Race, Labor and Punishment in the New South* (Columbus: Ohio State University Press, 1998); Mary Ellen Curtin, *Black Prisoners and Their World: Alabama, 1865–1900* (Charlottesville: University of Virginia Press, 2000); Mancini, *One Dies, Get Another*; Mildred C. Fierce, *Slavery Revisited: Blacks and the Southern Convict Lease System, 1865–1933* (New York: Africana Studies Research Center,

Brooklyn College, CUNY, 1994); David M. Oshinsky, *"Worse Than Slavery":
Parchman Farm and the Ordeal of Jim Crow Justice* (New York: The Free
Press, 1996); and Christopher R. Adamson, "Punishment After Slavery: Southern State Penal Systems, 1865–1890," *Social Problems* 30, no. 5 (June 1983):
555–68.

56. Northern states generally favored the prison-contract-labor system, whereby
companies contracted with the state for the labor of a certain number of convicts.
The state remained responsible for the care of the prisoners, while the contractor
provided the materials necessary for the specific contracted work.

57. In 1880, a warden in the South advertised three grades of prisoners for sale using
well-known terms from the slavery era: "full-hands" for $5 per month, "medium-
hands" for $2.50 per month, and "dead-hands" for just keep. McKelvey,
American Prisons: A History of Good Intentions, p. 203.

58. Christianson, *With Liberty for Some*, p. 181.

59. For more on the work and living conditions of the leased convicts, see Karen A.
Shapiro, *A New South Rebellion: The Battle Against Convict Labor in the Ten-
nessee Coalfields, 1871–1896* (Chapel Hill: The University of North Carolina
Press, 1998), Chapter 3; Lichtenstein, *Twice the Work of Free Labor*; and
Mancini, *One Dies, Get Another*, Chapter 3.

60. McKelvey, *American Prisons: A History of Good Intentions*, p. 202; Mancini,
One Dies, Get Another, Chapter 11; and Fierce, *Slavery Revisited*, p. 117.

61. The official death rate in Southern prisons was at least three times higher than
in Northern ones. The actual rate was likely much higher. Christianson, *With
Liberty for Some*, p. 182. In the state of Mississippi in the 1880s, the proportion
of convicts who died was estimated to be nine times that of a typical Northern
prison. Ayers, *Vengeance and Justice*, p. 201. See also Friedman, *Crime and
Punishment in American History*, p. 95; Carleton, *Politics and Punishment*, p. 43;
and Oshinsky, *"Worse Than Slavery"*, Chapter 9.

62. Curtin, *Black Prisoners and Their World*; Ayers, *Vengeance and Justice*, p. 191;
and Lichtenstein, *Twice the Work of Free Labor*.

63. At a detailed presentation to the National Prison Association in 1897, T. J. Hill,
a prison official from Tennessee, credited convict labor with developing natural
resources that were "impossible of development by free labor" and also lauded
this labor system for proletarianizing black labor. Lichtenstein, *Twice the Work
of Free Labor*, p. 75.

64. Shapiro, *A New South Rebellion*.

65. Between 1880 and 1940, 10 percent of Alabama's annual state budget came from
convict leasing. Ronald L. Lewis, *Black Coal Miners in America: Race, Class,
and Community Conflict, 1780–1980* (Lexington: University Press of Kentucky,
1987), cited in Myers, *Race, Labor and Punishment*, p. 10.

66. This paragraph is based primarily on Shapiro, *A New South Rebellion*, pp. 211–
17; and Fierce, *Slavery Revisited*.

67. For example, James Kimble Vardaman, the Populist champion of white
supremacy, campaigned for governor of Mississippi on a platform promising
to end convict leasing because it enriched white planters and railroad barons at
the expense of poor whites. Mancini, *One Dies, Get Another*, Chapter 8; and
Oshinsky, *'Worse Than Slavery'*, Chapters 4 and 5.

68. Carleton, *Politics and Punishment*, p. 58.

69. C. Vann Woodward, *Origins of the New South, 1877–1913* (Baton Rouge:
Louisiana State University Press, 1951), p. 215.

70. Ayers, *Vengeance and Justice*, p. 219. Northern prison administrators and reformers initially saw the convict-lease system as a symbol of all that was wrong with the backward South. Their views changed after the National Prison Association held its first meeting in the South in 1886 in Atlanta. After touring a nearby convict-labor camp, Northern delegates concluded that because the Southern prison population consisted primarily of blacks, "prison discipline had to be harsher and the work more demanding" than in the North. Their acceptance of convict leasing was also predicated on a "strong desire for sectional reconciliation between North and South." Curtin, *Black Prisoners and Their World*, pp. 170 and 173.

71. Walker, *Penology for Profit*, p. 77; and Mancini, *One Dies, Get Another*, Chapter 10.

72. Walker, *Penology for Profit*, p. 181.

73. Jane Zimmerman, "The Penal Reform Movement in the South during the Progressive Era, 1890–1917," *The Journal of Southern History* 17, no. 4 (1951), p. 475.

74. Zimmerman, "The Penal Reform Movement in the South," pp. 475–76.

75. Douglas A. Blackmon, "Hard Time: From Alabama's Past, Capitalism and Racism in Cruel Partnership," *The Wall Street Journal*, July 16, 2001, p. A-1.

76. Matthew J. Mancini, "Race, Economics, and the Abandonment of Convict Leasing," *Journal of Negro History* 63, no. 4 (October 1978): 339–52.

77. In 1904, not even 3 percent of Georgia's 57,000 miles of roads were surfaced. A decade later, Georgia had 13,000 miles of surfaced roads, surpassing all the other states in the South and ranking fifth in the United States. Lichtenstein, *Twice the Work of Free Labor*, p. 177.

78. Lichtenstein, *Twice the Work of Free Labor*, p. 181.

79. Lichtenstein, *Twice the Work of Free Labor*, Chapter 7.

80. Lichtenstein, *Twice the Work of Free Labor*, p. 168.

81. "The chain gangs which built the roads of the twentieth-century South became an enduring symbol of southern backwardness, brutality, and racism; in fact, they were the embodiment of the Progressive ideals of southern modernization, penal reform, and racial moderation," Lichtenstein concludes in his detailed study of convict labor in Georgia. Lichtenstein, *Twice the Work of Free Labor*, p. 16. See also Fierce, *Slavery Revisited*, Chapter 4.

82. Lichtenstein, *Twice the Work of Free Labor*, pp. 160 and 190–91; and Myers, *Race, Labor and Punishment*, pp. 25–26. For more on the federal role in convict leasing, see Desmond King, "A Strong or Weak State? Race and the U.S. Federal Government in the 1920s," *Ethnic and Racial Studies* 21, no. 1 (January 1998): 21–47.

83. Lichtenstein, *Twice the Work of Free Labor*, pp. 190–91; Myers, *Race, Labor and Punishment*, pp. 25–26; and Alex Lichtenstein, "Chain Gang Blues," *Dissent* 43, no. 3 (Fall 1996): 6–10.

84. Rothman, *The Discovery of the Asylum*, p. 3.

85. Rothman, *The Discovery of the Asylum*, p. 62.

86. Roger Lane, "Urban Police and Crime in Nineteenth-Century America," in *Crime and Justice: A Review of Research*, vol. 15, ed. Michael Tonry and Norval Morris (Chicago: University of Chicago Press, 1992), p. 26.

87. Samuel Walker, *A Critical History of Police Reform* (Lexington, MA: Lexington Books, 1977), p. 4.

88. Walker, *A Critical History of Police Reform*, p. 4.

89. Abraham Lincoln, "Address Before the Young Men's Lyceum of Springfield, Illinois," January 27, 1938, in *The Collected Works of Abraham Lincoln*, vol. 1, ed. Roy P. Basler, Marion Dolores Pratt, and Lloyd A. Dunlap (New Brunswick, NJ: Rutgers University Press, 1953), pp. 109–10.

90. Lane, "Urban Police and Crime"; David R. Johnson, *Policing the Urban Underworld: The Impact of Crime on the Development of the American Police, 1800–1887* (Philadelphia: Temple University Press, 1979); Bruce C. Johnson, "Taking Care of Labor: The Police in American Politics," *Theory and Society* 3, no. 1 (1976): 89–117; and Walker, *A Critical History of Police Reform*.

91. Walker, *A Critical History of Police Reform*, p. 4. Much of this violence was instigated and orchestrated by prominent leaders of the community who nonetheless talked about the need to preserve "law and order." W. Eugene Hollon, *Frontier Violence: Another Look* (New York: Oxford University Press, 1974), pp. 27–28.

92. Paul Boyer, *Urban Masses and Moral Order in America, 1820–1920* (Cambridge, MA: Harvard University Press, 1978), p. 69.

93. Representative of the tenor of the times, in 1840 the *Philadelphia Public Ledger* warned: "Almost every day furnishes some new and melancholy exhibition of that spirit which sets law at defiance. . . . Today a citizen is tied to a tree and scourged, tomorrow another is hoisted upon a tree and hanged, on the next a dozen are hanged all together, on a fourth an editor is shot, on a fifth a man is burned alive." October 29, 1840, cited in Philip D. Jordon, *Frontier Law and Order: Ten Essays* (Lincoln: University of Nebraska Press, 1971), p. 66.

94. Richard Altick, *Victorian Studies in Scarlet* (New York: Norton, 1970), p. 10, quoted in Carolyn Strange, "Murder and Meanings in U.S. Historiography," *Feminist Studies* 25, no. 3 (Fall 1999), p. 679.

95. Rothman, *The Discovery of the Asylum*, p. xxx.

96. Anne-Marie Szymanski, "Horse Thieves, Vigilantes, and the Reduction of Crime Rates in Nineteenth Century America," Policy History Conference of the *Journal of Policy History*, Clayton, MO, May 30–June 2, 2002.

97. Boyer, *Urban Masses and Moral Order in America*, pp. 19–29 and 77–79.

98. Lane, "Urban Police and Crime," p. 18; Johnson, "Taking Care of Labor," pp. 91–92; and Johnson, *American Law Enforcement*, Chapter 2.

99. This is not to deny that the police were fiercely resisted at the local level, as evidenced by antipolice riots by the poor, by industrial workers, and by others. Phil Scraton, "Unreasonable Force: Policing, Punishment and Marginalization," in *Law, Order and the Authoritarian State: Readings in Critical Criminology*, ed. Phil Scraton (Milton Keynes, UK: Open University Press, 1987), pp. 148–49.

100. Lane, "Urban Police and Crime," p. 18. See also Walker, *A Critical History of Police Reform*, p. 14.

101. Walker, *A Critical History of Police Reform*, p. 7.

102. Johnson, "Taking Care of Labor," pp. 92–93.

103. Lane, "Urban Police and Crime," p. 20.

104. Lane, "Urban Police and Crime," p. 12; and Johnson, *Policing the Urban Underworld*, pp. 96–99.

105. Johnson, "Taking Care of Labor," p. 93.

106. Lane, "Urban Police and Crime," p. 9.

107. Robert M. Fogelson, *Big-City Police* (Cambridge, MA: Harvard University Press, 1977), cited in Lane, "Urban Police and Crime," p. 12. See also Johnson, *Policing the Urban Underworld*, p. 117; and Johnson, *American Law Enforcement*, pp. 26–27.

108. Johnson, *Policing the Urban Underworld*, pp. 184–85.

109. Johnson, "Taking Care of Labor," p. 92.
110. Johnson, *American Law Enforcement*, Chapter 4.
111. Murray Kempton, "Son of Pinkerton," *The New York Review of Books*, May 20, 1971, pp. 22–25.
112. Frank Morn, *"The Eye that Never Sleeps": A History of the Pinkerton National Detective Agency* (Bloomington: Indiana University Press, 1982), esp. Chapter 4 and pp. 100 and 163; and Johnson, "Taking Care of Labor."
113. Morn, *"The Eye that Never Sleeps"*, p. 100.
114. "Governments are organized to protect life and property. These functions should not be transferred to private individuals and hired detectives until we are ready to acknowledge government a failure. Let public order be preserved by public authority," Bryan said. Quoted in Morn, *"The Eye that Never Sleeps"*, p. 102.
115. Morn, *"The Eye that Never Sleeps"*, pp. 102–05.
116. Cited in Morn, *"The Eye that Never Sleeps"*, p. 107. The House and Senate reports concluded that the states, not the federal government, should be responsible for regulating the private police forces. Subsequently, a number of states enacted bills to tighten up control of private police. Morn, *"The Eye that Never Sleeps"*, pp. 107–108. The ignominious role of private police forces received renewed attention during the New Deal as the LaFollette Committee launched an unprecedented investigation into the relationship between civil liberties, labor organizations, and the violent, illegal conduct of private police forces. Jerald S. Auerbach, *Labor and Liberty: The LaFollette Committee and the New Deal* (Indianapolis: Bobbs-Merrill, 1966).
117. For more on the early history of campaigns against family violence, see pp. 118–21.
118. Roy Lubove, "The Progressives and the Prostitute," *The Historian* 24 (May 1962), pp. 308–09.
119. See, for example, Barbara Meil Hobson, *Uneasy Virtue: The Politics of Prostitution and the American Reform Tradition* (New York: Basic Books, 1987); and Mara L. Keire, "The Vice Trust: A Reinterpretation of the White Slavery Scare in the United States, 1907–1917," *Journal of Social History* 35, no. 1 (2001): 5–41.
120. David J. Rothman, *Conscience and Convenience: The Asylum and Its Alternatives in Progressive America* (Boston: Little, Brown and Co., 1980), p. 60.
121. Eric C. Schneider, "Review of Mary E. Odem, *Delinquent Daughters: Protecting and Policing Adolescent Female Sexuality in the United States, 1885–1920*," *Journal of Social History* 30 (Summer 1997): 987–88.
122. Nicole Hahn Rafter, *Partial Justice: Women in State Prisons, 1800–1935* (Boston: Northeastern University Press, 1985), p. 59.
123. Theodore Roosevelt, *Autobiography* (1913), p. 237, cited in Mark Thomas Connelly, *The Response to Prostitution in the Progressive Era* (Chapel Hill: The University of North Carolina Press, 1980), p. 83; and Hobson, *Uneasy Virtue*, pp. 153–54.
124. Connelly, *The Response to Prostitution*, p. 20.
125. Lubove, "The Progressives and the Prostitute," p. 313; and Connelly, *The Response to Prostitution*, p. 55.
126. Connelly, *The Response to Prostitution*, pp. 49–60.
127. Connelly, *The Response to Prostitution*, p. 56.
128. For a brief legislative history of the Mann Act, see Edward H. Levi, *An Introduction to Legal Reasoning* (Chicago: University of Chicago Press, 1948), pp. 33–40.
129. "The white-slave traffic, while not so extensive, is much more horrible than any black-slave traffic ever was in the history of the world," argued Mann. 45

Congressional Record 548 (1910), cited in David J. Langum, *Crossing Over the Line: Legislating Morality and the Mann Act* (Chicago: University of Chicago Press, 1994), p. 43.

130. Marlene D. Beckman, "The White Slave Traffic Act: Historical Impact of a Federal Crime Policy on Women," in *Criminal Justice Politics and Women: The Aftermath of Legally Mandated Change*, ed. Claudine SchWeber and Clarice Feinman (New York: Haworth Press, 1985).

131. Calculated from Langum, *Crossing Over the Line*, pp. 61 and 150.

132. Hobson, *Uneasy Virtue*, p. 165.

133. Connelly, *The Response to Prostitution*, p. 139.

134. Ruth Rosen, *The Lost Sisterhood: Prostitution in America, 1900–1918* (Baltimore: The Johns Hopkins University Press, 1982), p. 35.

135. With the help of federal funding, thirty states had constructed facilities to detain women with a venereal disease by 1919. Connelly, *The Response to Prostitution*, p. 143.

136. Connelly, *The Response to Prostitution*, p. 149.

137. Hobson, *Uneasy Virtue*, p. 176; and Connelly, *The Response to Prostitution*, p. 144.

138. Walker, *A Critical History of Police Reform*, pp. 102–03; and Allen F. Davis, "Welfare, Reform and World War I," *American Quarterly* 19, no. 3 (Fall 1967), pp. 530–31.

139. Beginning in the late 1920s, prosecutors focused more on commercial violations of the Mann Act rather than on prosecuting adulterers and others engaging in noncommercial sexual relations, the main targets of federal prosecutors during the law's first decade and a half. From the late 1920s onward, the Mann Act was also selectively used to punish gangsters, blacks who dared to have white girlfriends, people who espoused political views unacceptable to the authorities, and other "undesirables." See Langum, *Crossing the Line*, Chapter 8.

140. Rosen, *The Lost Sisterhood*, p. 37.

141. Estelle B. Freedman, *Their Sisters' Keepers: Women's Prison Reform in America, 1830–1930* (Ann Arbor: University of Michigan Press, 1981), p. 130.

142. Gene E. Carte and Elaine H. Carte, *Police Reform in the United States: The Era of August Vollmer* (Berkeley: University of California Press, 1975), p. 103.

143. Cummings and McFarland, *Federal Justice*, p. 480.

144. Langum, *Crossing the Line*, p. 49.

145. For a discussion of court decisions involving the Mann Act, see Langum, *Crossing the Line*, esp. Chapters 3, 5, and 6; and Levi, *An Introduction to Legal Reasoning*, pp. 40–57.

146. Hobson, *Uneasy Virtue*, pp. 166 and 170.

147. Morn, *"The Eye that Never Sleeps"*, p. 72.

148. Theodore Roosevelt, "The Law Must Be Enforced," "The Enforcement of Law," and "A Year of Reform," in *The Works of Theodore Roosevelt*, vol. 14, ed. Herman Hagedorn (New York: Charles Scribners, 1926), pp. 181–238.

149. Jay Berman, "Theodore Roosevelt as Police Commissioner of New York: The Birth of Modern American Police Administration," in *Theodore Roosevelt: Many-Sided American*, ed. Natalie A. Naylor, Douglas Brinkley, and John Allen Gable (Interlaken, NY: Heart of the Lakes Publishing, 1992), pp. 171–85.

150. The 1901 assassination furthered the cause of police reform and was instrumental in the establishment of the International Association of Police Chiefs in the United States. Carte and Carte, *Police Reform in the United States*, p. 13.

151. Walker, *A Critical History of Police Reform*, pp. 77–78.

152. Theodore Roosevelt, "Speech Before the National Convention of the Progressive Party, Chicago, Illinois," August 6, 1912, in *The Essential Theodore Roosevelt*, ed. John Gabriel Hunt (New York: Gramercy Books, 1994), p. 306.

153. Virgil W. Peterson, *Crime Commissions in the United States* (Chicago: Chicago Crime Commission, 1945), p. 10. According to Homer Cummings, FDR's attorney general, "widespread lawlessness forced itself upon popular attention" after World War I. Cummings and McFarland, *Federal Justice*, p. 475.

154. David E. Ruth, *Inventing the Public Enemy: The Gangster in American Culture, 1918–1934* (Chicago: University of Chicago Press, 1996), p. 1.

155. Charles Frederick Carter, "The Carnival of Crime in the United States," *Current History* 15 (February 1922), p. 756, cited in Ruth, *Inventing the Public Enemy*, p. 11.

156. Kenneth O'Reilly, "A New Deal for the FBI: The Roosevelt Administration, Crime Control, and National Security," *The Journal of American History* 69, no. 3 (December 1982), p. 641.

157. Ruth, *Inventing the Public Enemy*, pp. 144–45.

158. Michael Woodiwiss, *Crime, Crusades and Corruption: Prohibition in the United States, 1900–1987* (Totowa, NJ: Barnes and Noble, 1988), pp. 14–15; and Ernest Gordon, *The Wrecking of the Eighteenth Amendment* (Francetown, NH: The Alcohol Information Press, 1943), Chapter 2.

159. Walter Lippmann, "The Underworld: A Stultified Conscience," *The Forum* (February 1931), p. 69, quoted in William Howard Moore, *The Kefauver Committee and the Politics of Crime, 1950–1952* (Columbia: University of Missouri Press, 1974), p. 10.

160. Woodiwiss, *Crime, Crusades and Corruption*, p. 15.

161. By 1929, an estimated 1,360 people nationwide had been killed in incidents related to Prohibition; at least 1,000 had been wounded. Woodiwiss, *Crime, Crusades and Corruption*, pp. 18–19.

162. James D. Calder, *The Origins and Development of Federal Crime Control Policy* (Westport, CT: Praeger, 1993), pp. 29 and 31. Passed shortly after Hoover was elected, the Jones Act leveled $10,000 fines or sentences of up to five years for first-time offenders of the Volstead Act, the enforcement arm of Prohibition. Morone, *Hellfire Nation*, p. 330.

163. Calder, *The Origins and Development of Federal Crime Control*, p. 5. Willard M. Oliver makes a similar point about Hoover. Oliver, *The Law and Order Presidency* (Upper Saddle River, NJ: Prentice Hall, 2003), p. 65.

164. Calder, *The Origins and Development of Federal Crime Control*, p. 33.

165. Calder, *The Origins and Development of Federal Crime Control*, p. 78.

166. These included cigarette smoking, the negative influence of immigrants, the breakdown of the nuclear family, and the decay of traditional religious and moral values. John Vernon, "The Wickersham Commission and William Monroe Trotter," *Negro History Bulletin* 1 (January–March 1999).

167. Earnest J. Hopkins, *Our Lawless Police: A Study of the Unlawful Enforcement of the Law* (New York: The Viking Press, 1931), p. 13. See also Walker, *A Critical History of Police Reform*, pp. 132–33.

168. Samuel Walker, *Popular Justice: A History of American Criminal Justice*, 2nd. ed. (New York: Oxford University Press, 1998), p. 155; and Fabian Franklin, *Nuggets from the Wickersham Report* (New York: Riverside Press, 1931); and Hopkins, *Our Lawless Police*.

169. Woodiwiss, *Crime, Crusades and Corruption*, p. 29; and Deok-Ho Kim, "A House Divided: The Wickersham Commission and National Prohibition," PhD dissertation, State University of New York at Stony Brook, August 1992.

170. Calder, *The Origins and Development of Federal Crime Control*, pp. 117–18 and 124–28.

171. As late as 1926, Justice Department officials conceded that Prohibition agents were appointed on the basis of political endorsements. Gordon, *The Wrecking of the Eighteenth Amendment*, p. 11.

172. Calder, *The Origins and Development of Federal Crime Control*, Chapter 7; and Keve, *Prisons and the American Conscience*, Chapter 6.

173. Ness of the Prohibition Bureau became a national figure as he courted publicity by keeping the press informed of his exploits and making sure that cameras were on hand when he raided the brewery or warehouse of some notorious gangster like Al Capone. Woodiwiss, *Crime, Crusades and Corruption*, p. 25.

174. Morone, *Hellfire Nation*, pp. 329–30.

175. Calder, *The Origins and Development of Federal Crime Control*, pp. 166–67.

176. O'Reilly, "A New Deal for the FBI," p. 641.

177. Jacquelyn Dowd Hall, *Revolt Against Chivalry: Jessie Daniel Ames and the Women's Campaign Against Lynching* (New York: Columbia University Press, 1979), p. 137; and Hugh Davis Graham and Ted Robert Gurr, eds., "Editors' Introduction," in *The History of Violence in America: Historical and Comparative Perspectives* (New York: Praeger, 1969).

178. George C. Rable, "The South and the Politics of Antilynching Legislation," in *Lynching, Racial Violence, and Law*, ed. Paul Finkelman (New York: Garland Publishing, 1992), pp. 204–05. On state-level antilynching legislation, David A. Gerber, "Lynching and Law and Order: Origin and Passage of the Ohio Anti-Lynching Law of 1896," in *Lynching, Racial Violence, and Law*.

179. The association contended that "lynching tends inevitably to destroy all respect for law and order." "Resolutions," Conference of Southern White Women, Atlanta, Ga., November 1, 1930; Pronouncement, Tennessee Association of Southern Women for the Prevention of Lynching, ASWPL Papers, quoted in Hall, *Revolt Against Chivalry*, p. 197.

180. Mary Jane Brown, *Eradicating This Evil: Women in the American Anti-Lynching Movement, 1892–1940* (New York: Garland, 2000).

181. In many instances, police officers, other law enforcement officials, and prominent members of the community were central figures in carrying out the lynchings. Hall, *Revolt Against Chivalry*, p. 140.

182. In a letter sent to a congressional opponent of antilynching legislation, Ames said: "I am keenly conscious that agitation for a Federal law is focusing Southern attention on the crime of lynching, which is desirable. [But] a lynching is not to me a political argument for a Federal law." Quoted in Hall, *Revolt Against Chivalry*, p. 247. Ames was ultimately at odds with the wishes of many members of the ASWPL, who had concluded by the mid-1930s that local solutions were not working. Brown, *Eradicating This Evil*, p. 14.

183. For example, in 1911 *The New York Times* reported that mothers and fathers in New York City's Little Italy were "almost in a state of panic," living in dread that "at any hour their child might be snatched up and carried off" by the ethnic criminal societies known as the Black Hand. *The New York Times*, August 30, 1911, p. 4, cited in Ernest Kahlar Alix, *Ransom Kidnapping in America, 1874–1974: The Creation of a Capital Crime* (Carbondale and Edwardsville: Southern Illinois University Press, 1978), pp. 32–33.

184. *The New York Times*, June 12, 1917, p. 5, cited in Alix, *Ransom Kidnapping*, p. 35.

185. Alix, *Ransom Kidnapping*, p. 137.

186. Cummings and McFarland, *Federal Justice*, pp. 478–79.

187. Mitchell emphasized that the federal government was under severe constitutional restrictions and could only supplement, not supplant, the local authorities. Alix, *Ransom Kidnapping*, pp. 70–77.

188. Arthur C. Millspaugh, *Crime Control by the National Government* (Washington, DC: The Brookings Institution, 1937), p. 51; and O'Reilly, "A New Deal for the FBI," pp. 641–42.

189. Woodiwiss, *Crime, Crusades and Corruption*, p. 27.

190. Woodiwiss, *Crime, Crusades and Corruption*, pp. 20–21.

191. Anslinger instigated the "Reefer Madness" scares of the 1930s and 1940s, which portrayed users of marijuana as psychotic killers. Michael Massing, *The Fix* (New York: Simon & Schuster, 1998), p. 86. See also Edward Jay Epstein, *Agency of Fear: Opiates and Political Power in America* (New York: G. P. Putnam's Sons, 1977), p. 33.

192. William E. Leuchtenburg, *Franklin D. Roosevelt and the New Deal, 1932–1940* (New York: Harper & Row, 1963), p. 333.

193. O'Reilly, "A New Deal for the FBI," p. 642; and Alix, *Ransom Kidnapping*, p. 118.

194. Alix, *Ransom Kidnapping*, p. 90

195. Franklin D. Roosevelt, "Annual Message to the Congress," January 3, 1934, in *The Public Papers and Addresses of Franklin D. Roosevelt*, vol. 3, ed. Samuel Rosenman (New York: Random House, 1938), pp. 12–13.

196. See his remarks to the 1934 Attorney General's Conference on Crime in Walker, *A Critical History of Police Reform*, pp. 154–55.

197. "Kidnapping epidemic" was a widely used phrase at the time. Alix, *Ransom Kidnapping*, p. 78. On fear of local impotence, see Leuchtenburg, *Franklin D. Roosevelt and the New Deal*, pp. 13–16.

198. Walker, *A Critical History of Police Reform*, p. 151.

199. "San Jose Vigilantes Lynch 2 Hart Killers," *The Post Enquirer*, November 27, 1933, p. 1, reprinted in Harry Farrell, *Swift Justice: Murder and Vengeance in a California Town* (New York: St. Martin's Press, 1992), p. xiii.

200. Alix, *Ransom Kidnapping*, p. 95.

201. Franklin D. Roosevelt, "Address Before the Federal Council of Churches of Christ in America – 'The Right to a More Abundant Life,' December 6, 1933," in Rosenman, ed., *Public Papers and Addresses*, p. 519.

202. Farrell, *Swift Justice*, pp. 277–78.

203. Dominic J. Capeci, "The Lynching of Cleo Wright: Federal Protection of Constitutional Rights During World War II," in *Lynching, Racial Violence, and Law*; Amii Barnard, "The Application of Critical Race Feminism to the Anti-Lynching Movement: Black Women's Fight Against Race and Gender Ideology, 1892–1920," *UCLA Women's Law Journal* 3, no. 7 (1993): 1–38; and National Association for the Advancement of Colored People, *Thirty Years of Lynching in the United States, 1889–1918* (New York: NAACP, April 1919).

204. Alix, *Ransom Kidnapping*, pp. 90–91.

205. Homer Cummings, "Progress Toward a Modern Administration of Criminal Justice," *American Bar Association Journal* 22, no. 5 (May 1936), p. 346.

206. O'Reilly, "A New Deal for the FBI," p. 642.

207. Cummings and McFarland, *Federal Justice*, p. 482.

208. The package included the Fugitive Felon Law, the Stolen Property Act, the Anti-Racketeering Act, the National Firearms Act, amendments to the federal bank robbery statute and the Lindbergh Act, and a measure that gave bureau agents full authority to make arrests and carry guns. O'Reilly, "A New Deal for the FBI," p. 643.

209. Sanford Ungar, *FBI* (New York: Atlantic, Little & Brown, 1975), pp. 74–77, cited in O'Reilly, "A New Deal for the FBI," p. 642.

210. "Roosevelt Opens Attack on Crime, Signing Six Bills as 'Challenge'," *The New York Times*, May 19, 1934, p. A-1.

211. Keve, *Prisons and the American Conscience*, pp. 174–79.

212. Cummings, "Progress Toward a Modern Administration," p. 349.

213. Keve, *Prisons and the American Conscience*, pp. 155–63 and 170; and McKelvey, *American Prisons*, p. 307.

214. O'Reilly, "A New Deal for the FBI," p. 639. The name was officially changed to the Federal Bureau of Investigation in 1935.

215. Ironically, the American Civil Liberties Union saw Hoover as a vast improvement over his predecessors and supported his appointment. Walker, *A Critical History of Police Reform*, p. 78.

216. Woodiwiss, *Crime, Crusades and Corruption*, p. 35.

217. Leuchtenburg, *Franklin D. Roosevelt and the New Deal*, p. 334.

218. Woodiwiss, *Crime, Crusades and Corruption*, p. 36. In 1934, Hollywood adopted a binding production code requiring movies to show that crime did not pay and prohibiting unflattering portrayals of law enforcement officials. Walker, *Popular Justice*, p. 161.

219. Cummings, "Progress Toward a Modern Administration," p. 347.

220. The G-men were so revered at the time that companies began to market G-men pajamas. O'Reilly, "A New Deal for the FBI," p. 645.

221. Alix, *Ransom Kidnapping*, p. 102.

222. For example, in June 1938 *The New York Times* carried four-column aerial photos of 2,000 people participating in the "greatest manhunt ever seen in Florida" to find a five-year-old boy, James Bailey Cash, kidnapped from his bed. Alix, *Ransom Kidnapping*, p. 121.

223. William J. Chambliss, *Power, Politics, and Crime* (Boulder, CO: Westview Press, 1999), p. 34.

224. Calder, *The Origins and Development of Federal Crime Control*, pp. 89–92.

225. For more on the manipulation of crime statistics, see p. 24.

226. John D. Rockefeller appeared in a photograph on the front page of *The New York Times* having his fingerprints taken, and FDR submitted a copy of his prints to the FBI. Walker, *A Critical History of Police Reform*, pp. 157–58.

227. Walker, *A Critical History of Police Reform*, pp. 158–61.

228. O'Reilly, "A New Deal for the FBI," p. 645.

229. Johnson, *American Law Enforcement*, p. 175.

230. O'Reilly, "A New Deal for the FBI," p. 640.

231. Estelle B. Freedman, "'Uncontrolled Desires': The Response to the Sexual Psychopath, 1920–1960," *The Journal of American History* 74, no. 1 (January 1987), pp. 91–92 and 94; and Philip Jenkins, *Moral Panic: Changing Concepts of the Child Molester in Modern America* (New Haven: Yale University Press, 1998), Chapter 3.

232. Jenkins, *Moral Panic*, p. 93.

233. Jenkins, *Moral Panic*, p. 103. For example, leading researchers expressed doubts about the potentially harmful effects of incest. Wardell Pomeroy, one of the

original members of the Alfred Kinsey team, argued that incest between adults and children could be "a satisfying and enriching experience." Pomeroy quoted in Diana E. H. Russell, *The Secret Trauma* (New York: Basic Books, 1986), pp. 3 and 8, cited in Jenkins, *Moral Panic*, p. 104. See also Linda Gordon, *Heroes of Their Own Lives: The Politics and History of Family Violence, Boston 1880–1960* (New York: Viking, 1988), pp. 207–08 and 221–22.

234. Jenkins, *Moral Panic*, p. 115.

235. 1946 Roundtable on Post-War Juvenile Delinquency in "Who's to Blame for Juvenile Delinquency," *Rotarian* 68 (April 1946), pp. 20–24, cited in James Gilbert, *A Cycle of Outrage: America's Reaction to the Juvenile Delinquent in the 1950s* (New York: Oxford University Press, 1986), p. 28.

236. Gilbert, *A Cycle of Outrage*, pp. 35–39 and Chapter 3.

237. Gilbert, *A Cycle of Outrage*, p. 64.

238. Gilbert, *A Cycle of Outrage*, p. 66.

239. Gilbert, *A Cycle of Outrage*, p. 80.

240. This discussion of the campaign against comic books is based on Gilbert, *A Cycle of Outrage*, especially pp. 80–81 and 101.

241. Daniel Bell, "Crime as an American Way of Life," in *The End of Ideology: On the Exhaustion of Political Ideas in the Fifties* (Glencoe, IL: Free Press, 1960).

242. Addressing a conference on delinquency in 1954, Senator Robert Hendrickson (R-N. J.) said: "Not even the Communist conspiracy could devise a more effective way to demoralize, disrupt, confuse, and destroy our future citizens than apathy on the part of adult Americans to the scourge known as Juvenile Delinquency." Quoted in Gilbert, *A Cycle of Outrage*, p. 75.

243. Woodiwiss, *Crime, Crusades and Corruption*, p. 17.

244. *Daily Mirror*, June 8, 1936, quoted in Woodiwiss, *Crime, Crusades and Corruption*, p. 51.

245. Woodiwiss, *Crime, Crusades and Corruption*, pp. 55–71.

246. For more on the Chessman case and capital punishment, see pp. 173–74, 179, 185, and 205.

247. Moore, *The Kefauver Committee*, pp. 41–43.

248. Woodiwiss, *Crime, Crusades and Corruption*, p. 100.

249. Theodore Wilson, "The Kefauver Committee 1950," in *Congress Investigates, 1792–1974*, ed. Arthur M. Schlesinger, Jr. (New York: Chelsea House Publishers, 1975), pp. 360–62; Woodiwiss, *Crime, Crusades and Corruption*, pp. 98–101.

250. Wilson, "The Kefauver Committee 1950," p. 354.

251. Wilson, "The Kefauver Committee 1950," p. 362.

252. Moore, *The Kefauver Committee*, pp. 184–85.

253. Wilson, "The Kefauver Committee 1950," p. 373.

254. James D. Calder, "Presidents and Crime Control: Kennedy, Johnson and Nixon and the Influences of Ideology," *Presidential Studies Quarterly* 12, no. 4 (Fall 1982), pp. 578–79.

255. Moore, *The Kefauver Committee*, p. 237.

256. Moore, *The Kefauver Committee*, pp. 235–37.

257. On Tocqueville's commission, see the introduction by Thorsten Sellin to Gustave de Beaumont and Alexis de Tocqueville, *On the Penitentiary System in the United States and Its Application in France* (Carbondale: Southern Illinois University Press, 1979).

258. Beaumont and Tocqueville, *On the Penitentiary System*, p. 79.

259. Other analysts make a similar point with respect to Britain. See Paul Gilroy and Joe Sim, "Law, Order and the State of the Left," in *Law, Order and the Authoritarian State*, pp. 73–76; and David Dixon and Elaine Fishwick, "The Law and Order Debate in Historical Perspective," in *Law and Order in British Politics*, ed. Philip Norton (Aldershot, UK: Gower, 1984), p. 22.

CHAPTER 4: THE CARCERAL STATE AND THE WELFARE STATE:
THE COMPARATIVE POLITICS OF VICTIMS

1. Jan van Dijk, "Ideological Trends Within the Victims Movement: An International Perspective," in *Victims of Crime: A New Deal?*, ed. Mike Maguire and John Pointing (Buckingham, UK: Open University Press, 1988), p. 117.
2. The summary that follows of these various ideological currents is based on van Dijk, "Ideological Trends," pp. 116–18.
3. For more on the "care ideology," see LeRoy G. Schultz, "The Violated: A Proposal To Compensate Victims of Violent Crime," in *Considering the Victim: Readings in Restitution and Victim Compensation*, ed. Joe Hudson and Burt Galaway (Springfield, IL: Charles C. Thomas, 1975).
4. Nils Christie, "Conflicts as Property," *The British Journal of Criminology* 17, no. 1 (January 1977): 1–15.
5. See, for example, Katherine Beckett, *Making Crime Pay: Law and Order in Contemporary American Politics* (New York: Oxford University Press, 1997); Lynne N. Henderson, "The Wrongs of Victim's Rights," *Stanford Law Review* 37, no. 4 (April 1985): 937–1021; Robert Elias, "Which Victim Movement? The Politics of Victim Policy," in *Victims of Crime: Problems, Policies, and Programs*, ed. Arthur J. Lurigio, Wesley G. Skogan, and Robert C. Davis (Newbury Park, CA: Sage Publications, 1980); and Samuel Walker, *Sense and Nonsense About Crime and Drugs: A Policy Guide* (Belmont, CA: Wadsworth Publishing Co., 1994).
6. Richard Nixon, "Transcripts of Acceptance Speeches by Nixon and Agnew to the GOP Convention," *The New York Times*, August 9, 1968, p. A-20, cited in Valerie Jenness and Ryken Grattet, *Making Hate a Crime: From Social Movement to Law Enforcement* (New York: Russell Sage Foundation, 2001), p. 26. As president, Nixon made law and order a central part of his platform but did not put the issue of crime victims high up on his agenda.
7. Gerald R. Ford, "Special Message to the Congress on Crime," June 19, 1975, in *Public Papers of the Presidents of the United States: Containing the Public Messages, Speeches, and Statements of the President, 1975*, vol. 1 (Washington, DC: GPO, 1977), p. 840.
8. Quoted in Steven Rathgeb Smith and Susan Freinkel, *Adjusting the Balance: Federal Policy and Victim Services* (Westport, CT: Greenwood, 1988), p. 1.
9. Clinton then threw his support behind a proposal introduced by Senator Dianne Feinstein (D-Calif.) to create the Victims Bill of Rights. Bruce Shapiro, "Victims & Vengeance: Why the Victims' Rights Amendment Is a Bad Idea," *The Nation*, February 10, 1997, p. 12.
10. Mike Maguire and Joanna Shapland, "Provision for Victims in an International Context," in *Victims of Crime*, 2nd ed., ed. Robert C. Davis, Arthur J. Lurigio, and Wesley G. Skogan (Thousand Oaks, CA: Sage, 1997), p. 212.
11. Maguire and Shapland, "Provision for Victims," p. 223.
12. A similar dynamic took place in Canada, where political elites pushed for abolition of the death penalty against the wishes of most of the public. As a concession,

the Canadian Parliament enacted in 1976 key pieces of the hurriedly prepared "Peace and Security Package," which, among other things, established that victims were now a central topic and problem for the central government in Canada. Paul A. Rock, *A View from the Shadows: The Minister of the Solicitor General of Canada and the Making of the Justice for Victims of Crime Initiative* (Oxford: Clarendon Press, 1986), pp. 53 and 129–39.

13. For more on Britain and abolition of the death penalty, see pp. 228–30.
14. For more on Fry, see R. I. Mawby and M. L. Gill, *Crime Victims: Needs, Services and the Voluntary Sector* (London: Tavistock, 1987), pp. 39–40; Robert D. Childres, "Compensation for Criminally Inflicted Personal Injury," in *Considering the Victim*, pp. 368–70; Paul Rock, *Helping Victims of Crime: The Home Office and the Rise of Victim Support in England and Wales* (Oxford: Clarendon Press, 1990), pp. 48–53; and Margery Fry et al., "Compensation for Victims of Criminal Violence: A Round Table," *Journal of Public Law* 8 (1959): 191–253.
15. Canada and Australia established victim compensation schemes in 1967, followed by Northern Ireland in 1968 and Sweden in 1971. Robert Elias, *Victims of the System* (New Brunswick, NJ: Transaction Books, 1983), p. 26.
16. Kent M. Weeks, "The New Zealand Criminal Injuries Compensation Scheme," *Southern California Law Review* 43 (1970), p. 109.
17. Owen Woodhouse, "Personal Injury Legislation in New Zealand," *International Labour Review* 119, no. 3 (May–June 1980): 321–34; and Weeks, "The New Zealand Criminal Injuries Compensation Scheme," pp. 116–18.
18. Woodhouse, "Personal Injury Legislation in New Zealand," p. 326.
19. Ernest Mastromatteo, "New Zealand's Universal Disability System," *Occupational Health & Safety Canada,* September/October 1993. In the intervening decades since it was first established, the Accident Compensation scheme has undergone some significant and controversial changes. See Ross Wilson, "ACC 1997: A Fairer Scheme or a Breach of the Social Contract?" *New Zealand Journal of Industrial Relations* 22/23, no. 3/1 (December 1997/February 1998): 301–10; Sandra Coney, "New Zealand: Changes in Accident Compensation," *The Lancet* 339 (April 4, 1992): 862–63; and Sandra Coney, "New Zealand: Accident Compensation Changes," *The Lancet* 338 (December 21–28, 1991): 1583–84.
20. Margery Fry, "Justice for Victims," in *Considering the Victim*, p. 54.
21. Rock, *Helping Victims of Crime*, pp. 53–75.
22. Maguire and Shapland, "Provision for Victims in an International Context," p. 217.
23. Home Office, *Compensation for Victims of Crimes of Violence* (London: HMSO, 1964), p. 4, cited in Mawby and Gill, *Crime Victims*, p. 43. See also R. I. Mawby, "Victims' Needs or Victims' Rights: Alternative Approaches to Policy-Making," in *Victims of Crime: A New Deal?*, p. 128.
24. Rock, *Helping Victims of Crime*, p. 75.
25. Mike Maguire and John Pointing, "Introduction: The Rediscovery of the Crime Victim," in *Victims of Crime: A New Deal?*.
26. Tim Newburn, *Crime and Criminal Justice Policy* (London and New York: Longman, 1995), pp. 153–54.
27. Lord Windlesham, *Responses to Crime*, vol. 1 (Oxford: Clarendon Press, 1987), p. 38. See also Peter T. Burns, "A Comparative Overview of the Criminal Injuries Compensation Schemes," *Victimology: An International Journal* 8, no. 3–4 (1983): 102–10.

28. Childres, "Compensation for Criminally Inflicted Personal Injury."

29. James E. Starrs, "A Modest Proposal to Insure Justice for Victims of Crime," *Minnesota Law Review* 50 (1965), p. 291.

30. In 1967 and 1969 he reintroduced similar legislation but without success. Stephen Schafer, *Compensation and Restitution to Victims of Crime*, 2nd ed. (Montclair, NJ: Patterson Smith, 1970), p. 157.

31. In introducing the legislation, Senator Mansfield said: "The point has been reached where we must give consideration to the victim of crime.... For him, society has failed miserably.... When the protection of society is not sufficient to prevent a person from being victimized, society then has the obligation to compensate the victim for that failure of protection." "Public Pay for Crime Victims: An Idea That Is Spreading," *U.S. News and World Report*, April 5, 1971, p. 40.

32. In addition to California, New York (1966), Hawaii (1967), Massachusetts (1968), Maryland (1968), New Jersey (1971), and Alaska (1972) had established compensation schemes by the early 1970s. Joe Hudson and Burt Galaway, "Conclusion," in *Considering the Victim*, p. 438.

33. Schafer, *Compensation and Restitution to Victims of Crime*, pp. 132–33.

34. Mawby and Gill, *Crime Victims*, pp. 47–48. This was not true of all state-level programs for victims. New Jersey enacted a program based on entitlement, rather than needs, in which one's economic status was irrelevant. Surveys found that victims in New Jersey tended to be more satisfied with the state program than victims in New York, which enacted a needs-based compensation scheme. Elias, *Victims of the System*, pp. 244–45.

35. Elias, *Victims of the System*, pp. 28–29.

36. The State Board of Control is an administrative body responsible for carrying out audits for the legislature in cases of claims against the state. Boyd Wright, "What About the Victims? Compensation for the Victims of Crime," in *Considering the Victim*, p. 403; and Schafer, *Compensation and Restitution to Victims of Crime*, pp. 132–33.

37. Elizabeth A. Stanko, "Victims R US: The Life History of 'Fear of Crime' and the Politicisation of Violence," in *Crime, Risk and Insecurity: Law and Order in Everyday Life and Political Discourse*, ed. Tim Hope and Richard Sparks (London and New York: Routledge, 2000), p. 23.

38. Richard F. Sparks, *Research on Victims of Crime: Accomplishments, Issues and New Directions* (Rockville, MD: National Institute of Mental Health, Center for Studies of Crime and Delinquency, 1982), p. 41.

39. Maguire and Pointing, "Introduction: The Rediscovery of the Crime Victim," pp. 7–8.

40. Lucia Zedner, "Victims," in *The Oxford Handbook of Criminology*, ed. Mike Maguire, Rod Morgan, and Robert Reiner (Oxford: Clarendon Press, 1994), p. 1210.

41. Alan Phipps, "Radical Criminology and Criminal Victimization: Proposals for the Development of Theory and Intervention," in *Confronting Crime*, ed. Roger Matthews and Jock Young (London: Sage, 1986), p. 106. See also pp. 99–102.

42. Sparks, *Research on Victims of Crime*, pp. 43–47.

43. For more on the Uniform Crime Reports, see p. 24.

44. Mawby and Gill, *Crime Victims*, pp. 115 and 118; Zedner, "Victims," pp. 1208–10; and Elias, *Victims of the System*, p. 3.

45. Sparks, *Research on Victims of Crime*, pp. 54–57.

46. Maguire and Pointing, "Introduction," pp. 7–8.

47. Helen Reeves, "Afterward," in *Victims of Crime: A New Deal?*, p. 204.

48. Annika Snare and Ulla Bondeson, "Criminological Research in Scandinavia," in *Crime and Justice: An Annual Review of Research*, vol. 6, ed. Michael Tonry and Norval Morris (Chicago: University of Chicago Press, 1985); and Sparks, *Research on Victims of Crime*, pp. 51–52.

49. Ezzat A. Fattah, "Victims and Victimology: The Facts and the Rhetoric," in *Towards a Critical Victimology*, ed. Ezzat A. Fattah (New York: St. Martin's Press, 1992), pp. 48–49; and Ezzat A. Fattah, "The Need for a Critical Victimology," in *Towards a Critical Victimology*, p. 12.

50. van Dijk, "Ideological Trends Within the Victims Movement," p. 125.

51. Henderson, "The Wrongs of Victim's Rights," p. 1020.

52. Josephine Gittler, "Expanding the Role of the Victim in a Criminal Action: An Overview of Issues and Problems," *Pepperdine Law Review* 11 (1984), p. 146.

53. Gittler, "Expanding the Role of the Victim," pp. 146–49.

54. Henderson, "The Wrongs of Victim's Rights," p. 965. According to psychiatrist Frank Ochberg, a victim advocate and expert on post-traumatic stress disorder, "Survivors often do less hating than one might expect.... The co-victims, the next of kin of the injured and dead, are more often the ones moved to rage and vengeance, if not hatred." Shapiro, "Victims & Vengeance," p. 18. See also Joanna Shapland, "The Victim, the Criminal Justice System, and Compensation," *British Journal of Criminology* 24, no. 2 (April 1984), p. 135.

55. Joanna Shapland, "Victims and the Criminal Justice System," in *From Crime Policy to Victim Policy: Reorienting the Justice System*, ed. Ezzat A. Fattah (New York: St. Martin's Press, 1986). For an overview of advances in research over the past two decades on the psychological consequences of victimization and the needs of crime victims, see Fran H. Norris, Krzysztof Kaniasty, and Martie P. Thompson, "The Psychological Consequences of Crime: Findings From a Longitudinal Population-Based Study," in *Victims of Crime*, 2nd. ed.; and Heather Strang, *Repair or Revenge: Victims and Restorative Justice* (Oxford: Clarendon Press, 2002), pp. 11–23.

56. Katherine Beckett and Theodore Sasson, *The Politics of Injustice: Crime and Punishment in America* (Thousand Oaks, CA: Pine Forge Press, 2000), p. 156.

57. Malcolm M. Feeley and Austin Sarat, *The Policy Dilemma: Federal Crime Policy and the Law Enforcement Assistance Administration, 1968–1978* (Minneapolis: University of Minnesota Press, 1980), p. 4.

58. Mawby and Gill, *Crime Victims*, p. 118.

59. Feeley and Sarat, *The Policy Dilemma*, p. 4. On the origins of the Safe Streets Act, see pp. 40–49; and Richard Harris, *The Fear of Crime* (New York: Praeger, 1969).

60. Feeley and Sarat, *The Policy Dilemma*, p. 58.

61. Feeley and Sarat, *The Policy Dilemma*, p. 47.

62. Congress voted to disband the LEAA in 1979 and phase out its projects over the next eighteen months. Frank J. Weed, *Certainty of Justice: Reform in the Crime Victim Movement* (New York: Walter de Gruyter, 1995), p. 61.

63. Peter B. Kraska, ed., *Militarizing the American Criminal Justice System: The Changing Roles of the Armed Forces and the Police* (Boston: Northeastern University Press, 2001).

64. Weed, *Certainty of Justice*, p. 8; Edward Jay Epstein, *Agency of Fear: Opiates and Political Power in America* (New York: G. P. Putnam's Sons, 1977), p. 260;

and Twentieth Century Fund Task Force on the Law Enforcement Assistance Administration, *Law Enforcement: The Federal Role* (New York: McGraw-Hill, 1976), pp. vii–viii.

65. Feeley and Sarat, *The Policy Dilemma*, pp. 5–6.
66. Epstein, *Agency of Fear*, pp. 75–76; Feeley and Sarat, *The Policy Dilemma*, pp. 5–6; and Weed, *Certainty of Justice*, p. 8.
67. Robert E. Taylor, "Shutting Down the LEAA," *The Wall Street Journal*, December 1, 1980, p. 34.
68. John P. J. Dussich, "Evolving Services for Crime Victims," in *Perspectives on Crime Victims*, ed. Burt Galaway and Joe Hudson (St. Louis, MO: C.V. Mosby, 1981): 27–32; and Twentieth Century Fund Task Force, *Law Enforcement: The Federal Role*, pp. 61–66.
69. Weed, *Certainty of Justice*, pp. 8–11. See also R. Emerson Dobash and Russell P. Dobash, *Women, Violence and Social Change* (London and New York: Routledge, 1992), p. 176.
70. Beckett and Sasson, *The Politics of Injustice*, p. 161.
71. On the entrenched therapeutic tradition in the United States, see Andrew J. Polsky, *The Rise of the Therapeutic State* (Princeton: Princeton University Press, 1991); Nancy A. Matthews, *Confronting Rape: The Feminist Anti-Rape Movement and the State* (New York and London: Routledge, 1994), pp. xiv and 7; and Dobash and Dobash, *Women, Violence, and Social Change*, p. 214.
72. Weed, *Certainty of Justice*, pp. 8–12; and Marlene A. Young, "The '80s: NOVA's Decade of Success; The '90s: Planning for Future Achievement," *The NOVA Newsletter* 14, no. 2 (1990): 1–4.
73. This ABA committee produced important publications on victim-related issues, and its members regularly appeared before Congress to support certain legislation. Frank Carrington and George Nicholson, "The Victims' Movement: An Idea Whose Time Has Come," *Pepperdine Law Review* 11 (1984), pp. 10–11.
74. Weed, *Certainty of Justice*, p. 60.
75. Weed, *Certainty of Justice*, p. 61.
76. Weed, *Certainty of Justice*, p. 61. See also Carrington and Nicholson, "The Victims' Movement: An Idea Whose Time Has Come."
77. Mawby and Gill, *Crime Victims*, p. 131.
78. Edward Stout and John H. Stein, "Victim Justice: A New Balance," *The NOVA Newsletter* 14, no. 8–12 (1990), p. 23.
79. William P. Barr, "Bringing Criminals to Justice; Bringing Justice to the Victim," *The NOVA Newsletter* 16, no. 11 (1992), p. 2. Emphasis in the original. See also the laudatory front-page obituary for Frank Carrington in "Victims' Movement Mourns Carrington Death," *The NOVA Newsletter* 15, no. 9 (1991); and the remarks by President George H. W. Bush at the 1991 "Crime Summit" featured in "President Bush: 'Take Back the Streets,'" *The NOVA Newsletter* 15, no. 3 (1991): 1–2.
80. For a good summary of the legislation passed at the local, state, and national level, see Robert Elias, *Politics of Victimization: Victims, Victimology, and Human Rights* (New York: Oxford University Press, 1986), Chapter 3; and Deborah P. Kelly and Edna Erez, "Victim Participation in the Criminal Justice System," in *Victims of Crime*, 2nd ed.
81. See, for example, the role that victim advocacy groups played in the passage of Washington State's controversial Community Protection Act, which included some stringent measures for sexual offenders, including a provision that permits

preventive detention for "sexual predators." Stuart A. Scheingold, Toska Olson, and Jana Pershing, "Sexual Violence, Victim Advocacy, and Republican Criminology: Washington State's Community Protection Act," *Law & Society Review* 28, no. 4 (1994): 729–63.

82. Curtis J. Sitomer, "New Civil Rights Thrust: Aid for Victims," *Christian Science Monitor*, April 5, 1983, p. 1, cited in Shirley S. Abrahamson, "Redefining Roles: The Victims' Rights Movement," *Utah Law Review* 517, no. 3 (1985), p. 525.

83. Frank Carrington and George Nicholson, "Victims' Rights: An Idea Whose Time Has Come – Five Years Later: The Maturing of an Idea," *Pepperdine Law Review*, 17, no. 1 (1989), p. 5, n. 21.

84. Carrington and Nicholson, "Victims' Rights: Five Years Later," p. 5.

85. Money for the fund comes from fines collected in federal criminal cases and other penalties assessed on offenders. Carrington and Nicholson, "Victims' Rights: Five Years Later," p. 3.

86. David L. Roland, "Progress in the Victim Reform Movement: No Longer the 'Forgotten Victim'," *Pepperdine Law Review* 17, no. 1 (1989), pp. 38–42.

87. Abrahamson, "Redefining Roles," p. 530. For an overview of these rights, see pp. 543–59.

88. This summary of major pieces of federal legislation involving victims is based primarily on Robert C. Davis, Nicole J. Henderson, and Caitlin Rabbitt, "Executive Summary," in *Effects of State Victim Rights Legislation on Local Criminal Justice Systems* (New York: Vera Institute of Justice, April 2002).

89. Elias, *Politics of Victimization*, p. 239; Robert Elias, "Community Control, Criminal Justice and Victim Services," in *Towards a Critical Victimology*; Robert Elias, "The Symbolic Politics of Victim Compensation," *Victimology: An International Journal* 8, no. 1–2 (1983): 213–24; and Davis, Henderson, and Rabbitt, *Effects of State Victim Rights Legislation*.

90. Weed, *Certainty of Justice*, p. 18.

91. National Organization for Victim Assistance, *Directory of Victim Assistance Programs and Resources* (Dubuque, IA: Kendall/Hunt Publishing Company, 1994).

92. Wendy J. Hamilton, "Mothers Against Drunk Driving – MADD in the USA," *Injury Prevention* 6 (2000): 90–91. See also Frank J. Weed, "Organizational Mortality in the Anti-Drunk-Driving Movement: Failure Among Local MADD Chapters," *Social Forces* 69, no. 3 (March 1991): 851–68; and John D. McCarthy, "Activists, Authorities, and Media Framing of Drunk Driving," in *New Social Movements: From Ideology to Identity*, ed. Enrique Laraña, Hank Johnston, and Joseph R. Gusfield (Philadelphia: Temple University Press, 1994).

93. For more on this survey, see Weed, *Certainty of Justice*, pp. 102–17.

94. Beckett and Sasson, *The Politics of Injustice*, p. 161.

95. Beckett and Sasson, *The Politics of Injustice*, p. 161, n. 71.

96. Weed, *Certainty of Justice*, pp. 93–97.

97. This discussion of the von Bulow Center is based primarily on Weed, *Certainty of Justice*, pp. 67–94.

98. Carrington and Nicholson, "Victims' Rights: Five Years Later." The U.S. Department of Justice provided other critical support for victims. For example, the Commission on Victim Witness Assistance was established in 1974 by the National District Attorneys Association with funding from the Justice Department. Mawby and Gill, *Crime Victims*, p. 118.

99. Joan E. Jacoby, *The American Prosecutor: A Search for Identity* (Lexington, MA: Lexington Books, 1980), p. xv.

100. Jacoby, *The American Prosecutor*, p. 3.
101. Jacoby, *The American Prosecutor*, pp. xvi and 29.
102. Henderson, "The Wrongs of Victim's Rights," p. 940.
103. Marvin E. Wolfgang, "Victim Compensation in Crimes of Personal Violence," in *Considering the Victim*.
104. Jacoby, *The American Prosecutor*, p. 36.
105. Jacoby, *The American Prosecutor*, p. 10.
106. Jacoby, *The American Prosecutor*, p. 10.
107. Henderson, "The Wrongs of Victim's Rights," p. 938.
108. Henderson, "The Wrongs of Victim's Rights," p. 939.
109. This discussion of the early history of blood feuds and victim restitution is based primarily on Henderson, "The Wrongs of Victim's Rights," esp. pp. 938–40; Jack Kress, "Progress and Prosecution," *The Annals of the American Academy of Political and Social Science* 423 (January 1976): 99–116; and Paul Rock, "Victims, Prosecutors and the State in Nineteenth Century England and Wales," *Criminal Justice* 4, no. 4 (2004): 331–54.
110. Some analysts trace the origins of the expansive powers of the public prosecutor in the United States back to the writ of *nolle prosequi*, which originated in England and was transplanted to the United States. By filing a writ of *nolle prosequi*, the attorney general indicated the crown's intention not to prosecute and in effect gave the state the power to dismiss the prosecution. Under the common-law system the writ of *nolle prosequi* became "vested exclusively in the prosecutor without any judicial restraint." Aynes, "Constitutional Considerations," p. 106; Abraham S. Goldstein, "Prosecution: History of the Public Prosecutor," in *Encyclopedia of Criminal Justice*, vol. 3, ed. Sanford H. Kadish (New York: New Press, 1983), p. 1242; and Jacoby, *The American Prosecutor*, pp. 30–32.
111. The following discussion of the development of the public prosecutor during the colonial and founding eras in the United States is based on Goldstein, "Prosecution," pp. 1242–46; Gittler, "Expanding the Role of the Victim," pp. 125–32; and Jacoby, *The American Prosecutor*, Chapter 1.
112. Abrahamson, "Redefining Roles," p. 521.
113. Jacoby, *The American Prosecutor*, p. 18.
114. Goldstein, "Prosecution," p. 1243.
115. This occurred primarily in parts of Connecticut, New York, New Jersey, Pennsylvania, and Delaware, perhaps because the Dutch who settled these areas brought with them to the New Netherlands the concept of the *schout*, a public official who combined the duties of prosecutor and sheriff. Goldstein, "Prosecution," p. 1243; and Gittler, "Expanding the Role of the Victim," pp. 128–29.
116. Gittler, "Expanding the Role of the Victim," pp. 130–32.
117. Stephen Skowronek, *Building a New American State: The Expansion of National Administrative Capacities, 1877–1920* (Cambridge: Cambridge University Press, 1982); and Mary E. Vogel, "The Social Origins of Plea Bargaining: Conflict and the Law in the Process of State Formation, 1830–1860," *Law & Society Review* 33, no. 1 (1999), pp. 161–64.
118. Thomas Weigend, "Prosecution: Comparative Aspects," in *Encyclopedia of Criminal Justice*, vol. 3, p. 1296.
119. Earl H. DeLong and Newman Baker, "The Prosecuting Attorney – Provisions of Law Organizing the Office," *Journal of Criminal Law and Criminology* 23, no. 6 (March 1933), quoted in Jacoby, *The American Prosecutor*, p. 33.

120. Gittler, "Expanding the Role of the Victim," p. 131.
121. By the time of the Civil War, twenty-four of the thirty-four states had established elected judiciaries. Larry Berkson, Scott Beller, and Michele Grimaldi, *Judicial Selection in the United States: A Compendium of Provisions* (Chicago: American Judicature Society, 1980), p. 4. As new states joined the Union, all adopted popular elections for some or all judges until the admission of Alaska in 1959. Stephen B. Bright and Patrick J. Keenan, "Judges and the Politics of Death: Deciding Between the Bill of Rights and the Next Election in Capital Cases," *Boston University Law Review* 75 (May 1995), n. 302 and pp. 818–20. See also John Cornyn, "Ruminations on the Nature of Texas Judging," *St. Mary's Law Review* 25, no. 1 (1993): 367–84.
122. Jacoby, *The American Prosecutor*, pp. 25–26.
123. Goldstein, "Prosecution," p. 1243.
124. Goldstein, "Prosecution," p. 1244.
125. This paragraph is based on Weigend, "Prosecution: Comparative Aspects," p. 1297.
126. Goldstein, "Prosecution," p. 1244. See also James Vorenberg, "Decent Restraint of Prosecutorial Power," *Harvard Law Journal* 94, no. 7 (May 1981), p. 1525.
127. Aynes, "Constitutional Considerations," p. 99.
128. Gittler, "Expanding the Role of the Victim," p. 131.
129. For a review of court cases challenging the prerogative of prosecutors to bring charges in a case, see Aynes, "Constitutional Considerations," pp. 99–103; and Abraham S. Goldstein, "Defining the Role of the Victim in Criminal Prosecution," *Mississippi Law Review* 52 (1982), pp. 550–58.
130. Goldstein, "Prosecution," p. 1245.
131. Aynes, "Constitutional Considerations," p. 99. See also Vorenberg, "Decent Restraint of Prosecutorial Power," p. 1546.
132. Kenneth Culp Davis, *Discretionary Justice: A Preliminary Inquiry* (Baton Rouge: Louisiana State University, 1969), Chapter 7.
133. Zedner, "Victims," p. 1232; and Matti Joutsen, "Listening to the Victim: The Victim's Role in European Criminal Justice Systems," *Wayne Law Review* 34 (1987–88): 95–124.
134. Weigend, "Prosecution: Comparative Aspects," p. 1303.
135. Aynes, "Constitutional Considerations," p. 104; and Gittler, "Expanding the Role of the Victim," p. 179.
136. Richard Frase and Thomas Weigend, "German Criminal Justice as a Guide to American Law Reform: Similar Problems, Better Solutions?" *Boston College International and Comparative Law Review* 18, no. 2 (Summer 1995), p. 350.
137. Frase and Weigend, "German Criminal Justice," p. 350.
138. Frase and Weigend, "German Criminal Justice," p. 351.
139. Davis, *Discretionary Justice*, Chapter 7; and Weigend, "Prosecution: Comparative Aspects," p. 1303.
140. See Gittler, "Expanding the Role of the Victim," pp. 179–80; and Aynes, "Constitutional Considerations," p. 104.
141. On Michigan, see Aynes, "Constitutional Considerations," p. 105. On provisions in Utah and Wisconsin to curb prosecutorial discretion, see Abrahamson, "Redefining Roles," pp. 540–41.
142. Gittler, "Expanding the Role of the Victim," pp. 168–69.
143. Shapiro, "Victims & Vengeance," p. 18.

144. Leslie Sebba, "The Victim's Role in the Penal Process: A Theoretical Orientation," *American Journal of Comparative Law* 30, no. 1 (1982): 217–40.

145. David Downes, *Contrasts in Tolerance: Post-War Penal Policy in the Netherlands and England and Wales* (Oxford: Clarendon Press, 1988), p. 19.

146. Peter J. van Koppen, "The Dutch Supreme Court and Parliament: Political Decisionmaking Versus Nonpolitical Appointments," *Law & Society Review* 24, no. 3 (1990), p. 753.

147. Van Koppen, "The Dutch Supreme Court and Parliament," p. 755.

148. This discussion of the German case is based primarily on Thomas Weigend, *Assisting the Victim: A Report on Efforts to Strengthen the Position of the Victim in the American System of Criminal Justice* (Freiburg: Max Planck Institute for Foreign and International Criminal Law, 1981), esp. pp. 65–67. This is not to gloss over some important differences among the inquisitorial systems on the continent. Frase and Weigend, for example, contend that the French judicial system is far more inquisitorial in practice than the German one, which in their view shares some important features with the U.S. system. Frase and Weigend, "German Criminal Justice," p. 359.

149. Mawby and Gill, *Crime Victims*, p. 115.

150. Weigend, *Assisting the Victim*, p. 67.

151. Dieter Eppenstein, "Weisser Ring: Lobby for Victims of Crime," in *Particular Groups of Victims*, Pt. 1, ed. Günther Kaiser, H. Kury, and H. J. Albrecht (Freiburg: Max Planck Institute, 1991), pp. 137–49.

152. James Q. Whitman, *Harsh Justice: Criminal Punishment and the Widening Divide Between America and Europe* (Oxford: Oxford University Press, 2003), p. 70.

153. Almost every state has since required that prosecutors have a law degree to hold office. Many small towns and rural counties still depend on the services of part-time prosecutors who continue their private law practices. Jacoby, *The American Prosecutor*, pp. 34–35.

154. Weigend, "Prosecution: Comparative Aspects," p. 1297.

155. Frase and Weigend, "German Criminal Justice," p. 320.

156. John Graham, "Decarceration in the Federal Republic of Germany: How Practitioners Are Succeeding Where Policy-Makers Failed," *British Journal of Criminology* 30, no. 3 (Spring 1990), pp. 154–55; and Johannes Feest, "Reducing the Prison Population: Lessons from the West German Experience?," in *Imprisonment: European Perspectives*, ed. John Muncie and Richard Sparks (New York: St. Martin's Press, 1991), pp. 136–37.

157. Hans-Jörg Albrecht, "Sentencing and Punishment in Germany," in *Sentencing Reform in Overcrowded Times: A Comparative Perspective*, ed. Michael Tonry and Kathleen Hatlestad (New York: Oxford University Press, 1997), pp. 141–43.

158. "Sociological perspectives in the study of the law have a long history of German scholarship," according to Rueschemeyer. They have their origins in the seminal contributions of Max Weber and other founding fathers of modern sociology, who provided "the nucleus of the sociology of law as an emergent discipline." Dietrich Rueschemeyer, "Sociology of Law in Germany," *Law & Society Review* 5, no. 2 (November 1970), pp. 225–26 and 228–29.

159. Christian Pfeiffer, "Crisis in American Criminal Policy? A Letter to Mrs. J. Reno, Attorney General of the United States of America," *European Journal on Criminal Policy and Research* 4, no. 2 (1996).

160. Graham, "Decarceration," p. 167.

161. Joachim J. Savelsberg, "Knowledge, Domination, and Criminal Punishment," *American Journal of Sociology* 99, no. 4 (January 1994), pp. 931–32 and 934–35.

162. Ronald Akers, "Linking Sociology and Its Specialties: The Case of Criminology," *Social Forces* 71 (1995): 1–16, cited in Joachim J. Savelsberg, Ryan King, and Lara Cleveland, "Politicized Scholarship? Science on Crime and the State," *Social Problems* 49, no. 3 (2002), p. 329.

163. Savelsberg et al., "Politicized Scholarship?," p. 329; and Joan Petersilia, "Policy Relevance and the Future of Criminology," *Criminology* 29, no. 1 (1991): 1–13.

164. Savelsberg, "Knowledge, Domination, and Criminal Punishment."

165. Savelsberg, "Knowledge, Domination, and Criminal Punishment," p. 931. Chief Justice William H. Rehnquist warned in 2002 that the low salaries and difficult confirmation process in the United States were discouraging many lawyers in private practice from seeking federal judgeships. As a consequence, the U.S. judicial system is drawing more of its judges from people already in public service. This puts the U.S. system at risk of becoming more like the European system of career judges that "simply do not command the respect and enjoy the independence of ours," according to Rehnquist. Linda Greenhouse, "Rehnquist Sees a Loss of Prospective Judges," *The New York Times*, January 1, 2002, p. A-16.

166. Michael Tonry, "Punishment Policies and Patterns in Western Countries," in *Sentencing and Sanctions in Western Countries*, ed. Michael Tonry and Richard S. Frase (Oxford: Oxford University Press, 2001), p. 9, Table 1.1.

167. From early 1983 to early 1988, the increase in the incarcerated population for all countries included in the Council of Europe's *Prison Information Bulletin* averaged 3 percent per year. In West Germany the incarcerated population declined by 3.5 percent annually over the same period. Graham, "Decarceration," p. 150.

168. J. J. M. van Dijk quoted in Downes, *Contrasts in Tolerance*, p. 13.

169. Jacquelien Soetenhorst-de Savornin Lohman, "The Victim Issue in the Political Agenda of the Netherlands," *Victimology: An International Journal* 10, no. 1–4 (1985), p. 692.

170. This reversed "the previous position which insisted on prosecution *unless* the public interest demanded it be waived." Emphasis in the original. Downes, *Contrasts in Tolerance*, p. 13.

171. Van Koppen, "The Dutch Supreme Court and Parliament," p. 745.

172. Downes, *Contrasts in Tolerance*; and David Downes, "The Origins and Consequences of Dutch Penal Policy Since 1945," in *Imprisonment: European Perspectives*.

173. Downes, "The Origins and Consequences of Dutch Penal Policy," p. 118.

174. Peter J. Tak, "Sentencing and Punishment in the Netherlands," in *Sentencing and Sanctions in Western Countries*, p. 172.

175. Downes, *Contrasts in Tolerance*, p. 101; and Downes, "The Origins and Consequences of Dutch Penal Policy," p. 121.

176. Andrew Rutherford, *Transforming Criminal Policy: Spheres of Influence in the United States, the Netherlands and England and Wales* (Winchester, UK: Wayside Press, 1996), p. 60.

177. See pp. 156–57 for a discussion of the women's movement in the Netherlands and its shifting position on crime and punishment.

178. For a good discussion of why a punitive victims' movement centered on rights did not emerge in Canberra, Australia, see Strang, *Repair or Revenge*, Chapter 2.

179. Mawby and Gill, *Crime Victims*, Chapter 5. On the relatively undeveloped voluntary sector in Germany, see Lucia Zedner, "In Pursuit of the Vernacular: Comparing Law and Order Discourse in Britain and Germany," *Social and Legal Studies* 4 (1995), p. 525. On the role of *nolle prosequi*, see n. 110 above.
180. Van Dijk, "Ideological Trends," p. 123.
181. Weigend, "Prosecution: Comparative Aspects," 1298–99.
182. Rock, "Victims, Prosecutors and the State."
183. Gittler, "Expanding the Role of the Victim," pp. 178–79.
184. Gittler, "Expanding the Role of the Victim," p. 179.
185. Lord Windlesham, *Responses to Crime: Penal Policy in the Making*, vol. 2 (Oxford: Clarendon Press, 1993), p. 24. For more on how the British prosecution system works, see Michael Zander, *Cases and Materials on the English Legal System*, 5th ed. (London: Weidenfeld and Nicolson, 1988), pp. 204–37.
186. Zedner, "Victims," p. 1233.
187. On the early history of NACRO and the NVA, see Rock, *Helping Victims of Crime*, Chapter 3, esp. pp. 98–114.
188. Quoted in Rock, *Helping Victims of Crime*, p. 113.
189. Rock, *Helping Victims of Crime*, p. 138.
190. Mike Maguire and Claire Corbett, *The Effects of Crime and the Work of Victims Support Schemes* (Aldershot, UK: Gower, 1987), p. 2. According to the *First Annual Report* of the National Association of Victims Support Services, "The use of volunteers as visitors was not just a money-saving device but a very positive aspect of the scheme – a clear message that fellow-citizens *do* care." Emphasis in the original. NAVSS, *First Annual Report* (London: NAVSS, 1981), p. 15, cited in Mawby and Gill, *Crime Victims*, p. 91. See also Christopher Holton and Peter Raynor, "Origins of Victims Support Philosophy and Practice," in *Victims of Crime: A New Deal?*.
191. Rock, *Helping Victims of Crime*, p. 163.
192. On the erosion of the political consensus, see Windlesham, *Responses to Crime*, vol. 2, Chapter 4; Newburn, *Crime and Criminal Justice Policy*, p. 172; and David Downes and Rod Morgan, "'Hostages to Fortune'?" The Politics of Law and Order in Post-War Britain," in *The Oxford Handbook of Criminology*, p. 187.
193. John Croft, "Criminological Research in Great Britain, With a Note on the Council of Europe," in *Crime and Justice: An Annual Review of Research*, vol. 5, ed. Michael Tonry and Norval Morris (Chicago: University of Chicago Press, 1983).
194. Windlesham, *Responses to Crime*, vol. 2, p. 13.
195. Rock, *Helping Victims of Crime*, p. 26. See also Anthony Sampson, *The Changing Anatomy of Britain* (New York: Random House, 1982), p. 173.
196. Rock, *Helping Victims of Crime*, p. 25.
197. Rock, *Helping Victims of Crime*, p. 414.
198. Rock, "Victims, Prosecutors and the State," pp. 345–46.
199. Rock, *Helping Victims of Crime*, p. 366.
200. Rock, *Helping Victims of Crime*, p. 250.
201. Rock, *Helping Victims of Crime*, p. 173. See also Mawby and Gill, *Crime Victims*, p. 104.
202. For example, NAVSS withdrew from the World Society of Victimology after it began campaigning for a United Nations charter of victims' rights. Rock, *Helping Victims of Crime*, pp. 173 and 192–93. See also Reeves, "Afterward," p. 24.

203. Mawby and Gill, *Crime Victims*, pp. 102–03; Holton and Raynor, "Origins of Victims Support."

204. Rock, *Helping Victims of Crime*, p. 191.

205. Paul Rock, "Governments, Victims and Policies in Two Countries," *British Journal of Criminology* 28, no. 1 (Winter 1988), p. 60; and Newburn, *Crime and Criminal Justice Policy*, p. 165. By contrast, NOVA's 1985 *Campaign for Victims Rights: A Practical Guide* offers advice on how best to reach the media and suggests that victims could be used effectively at press conferences to show the negative impact that crime has had on their lives. Mawby and Gill, *Crime Victims*, p. 130.

206. Windlesham, *Responses to Crime*, vol. 1, pp. 56–59.

207. Rock, *Helping Victims of Crime*, p. 411.

208. Alan Phipps, "Ideologies, Political Parties, and Victims of Crime," in *Victims of Crime: A New Deal?*, pp. 177–78; and Rock, *Helping Victims of Crime*, pp. 184–85.

209. Rock, *Helping Victims of Crime*, pp. 393–95.

210. For an interesting contrast between the approach of the British and Canadian governments to victim-related issues, see Rock, "Governments, Victims and Policies in Two Countries."

211. Paul D. Pierson, *Dismantling the Welfare State? Reagan, Thatcher, and the Politics of Retrenchment* (New York: Cambridge University Press, 1994).

212. Paul Gilroy and Joe Sim, "Law, Order and the State of the Left," in *Law, Order and the Authoritarian State: Readings in Critical Criminology*, ed. Phil Scraton (Milton Keynes, UK: Open University Press, 1987), p. 73.

213. Richard Sparks, "State Punishment in Advanced Capitalist Countries," in *Punishment and Social Control*, 2nd. ed., ed. Thomas G. Blomberg and Stanley Cohen (New York: Aldine de Gruyter, 2003), p. 33.

214. Mike Nash and Stephen P. Savage, "A Criminal Record? Law, Order, and Conservative Policy," in *Public Policy in Britain*, ed. Stephen P. Savage, Rob Atkinson, and Lynton Robins (Basingstoke, UK: Macmillan, 1994), p. 137. While there were significant heated disagreements about some penal issues in the 1950s and 1960s, notably capital punishment and corporal punishment, the proponents and opponents cut across party lines, and these issues generally were treated as matters of individual conscience, not partisan politics. Windlesham, *Responses to Crime*, vol. 2, p. 105–06. It was not until 1970 that a party manifesto suggested that the level or type of crime could be attributed to the politics of the party in power. Downes and Morgan, "'Hostages to Fortune'?" pp. 185–87.

215. Quoted in Nash and Savage, "A Criminal Record?" p. 137.

216. Michael Brake and Chris Hale, "Law and Order," in *Beyond Thatcherism*, ed. Richard Sparks and Phillip Brown (Milton Keynes, UK: University Press, 1989), quoted in Chris Hale, "Economy, Punishment and Imprisonment," *Contemporary Crises: Law, Crime and Social Policy* 13 (1989), p. 346.

217. Richard Sparks, "State Punishments in Advanced Capitalist Countries," p. 33.

218. John Pratt, "Law and Order Politics in New Zealand 1986: A Comparison With the United Kingdom," *International Journal of the Sociology of Law* 16 (1988), p. 107.

219. Between 1979 and 1984, public expenditures for the police doubled. Expenditures on criminal justice and law enforcement increased by almost 40 percent in real terms between 1979 and 1985. Newburn, *Crime and Criminal Justice Policy*, p. 62; I. Taylor, "Law and Order/Moral Order: The Changing Rhetoric of the

Thatcher Government," *Socialist Register*, 1987, in press, cited in Pratt, "Law and Order Politics in New Zealand 1986," p. 109; and Nash and Savage, "A Criminal Record?" p. 137.

220. Nash and Savage, "A Criminal Record?," p. 137; and Michael Cavadino and James Dignan, *The Penal System: An Introduction* (London: Sage, 1992), Chapter 8.

221. Cavadino and Dignan, *The Penal System*, p. 122.

222. Nash and Savage, "A Criminal Record?" p. 143.

223. Nash and Savage, "A Criminal Record?," p. 143. See also Andrew von Hirsch and Andrew Ashworth, "Law and Order," in *Principled Sentencing: Readings in Theory and Policy*, ed. Andrew von Hirsch and Andrew Ashworth (Oxford: Hart Publishing, 1998).

224. Windlesham, *Responses to Crime*, vol. 2, pp. 30 and 297–98.

225. Newburn, *Crime and Criminal Justice Policy*, pp. 172–77.

226. Windlesham, *Responses to Crime*, vol. 2, pp. 28–29.

227. This discussion of Faulkner is based largely on Rutherford, *Transforming Criminal Policy*, Chapter 4.

228. M. J. Moriarty, "The Policy-Making Process: How It Is Seen From the Home Office," in *Penal Policy-Making in England*, ed. N. Walker (Cambridge: University of Cambridge Institute of Criminology, 1977), p. 133, cited in Windlesham, *Responses to Crime*, vol. 2, p. 106.

229. Windlesham, *Responses to Crime*, vol. 2, p. 245.

230. Home Office, *Crime, Justice and Protecting the Public. The Government's Proposals for Legislation* (London: HMSO, 1990), p. 6, quoted in Rutherford, *Transforming Criminal Policy*, p. 104.

231. For more on the riots, see Chapter 7.

232. On the 1991 act, see Windlesham, *Responses to Crime*, vol. 2, Chapter 9; Newburn, *Crime and Criminal Justice Policy*, pp. 172–78; Cavadino and Dignan, *The Penal System*, Chapter 4; Andrew Ashworth, "The Decline of English Sentencing and Other Stories," in *Sentencing and Sanctions in Western Countries*; Nash and Savage, "A Criminal Record?" pp. 149–51; and Rod Morgan, "Punitive Policies and Politics Crowding English Prisons," in *Sentencing Reform in Overcrowded Times*, pp. 143–46.

233. Rutherford, *Transforming Criminal Policy*, p. 127.

234. The prison population in Britain fell from 54,000 in 1988 to less than 45,000 in 1990. After the introduction of the Criminal Justice Act of 1991, it fell even more sharply. By early 1993, the prison population had dwindled to 40,000, its lowest point since the late 1970s. Newburn, *Crime and Criminal Justice Policy*, p. 36; Hale, "Economy, Punishment and Imprisonment," p. 334; and Andrew Ashworth, "English Sentencing: From Enlightenment to Darkness in a Decade," in *Penal Reform in Overcrowded Times*, ed. Michael Tonry (Oxford: Oxford University Press, 2001), p. 257.

235. Faulkner quoted in Rutherford, *Transforming Criminal Policy*, p. 128.

236. This was another example of what Don C. Gibbons describes as the "galvanizing role of 'fatal anecdotes.'" "Review Essay: Crime, Criminologists, and Public Policy," *Crime & Delinquency* 45, no. 3 (1999), p. 403.

237. Downes and Morgan, "'Hostages to Fortune'?" p. 198; and Estella Baker, "From 'Making Bad People Worse' to 'Prison Works': Sentencing Policy in England and Wales in the 1990s," *Criminal Law Forum* 7, no. 3 (1996): 639–71.

238. Downes and Morgan, "'Hostages to Fortune'?" pp. 187–98.

239. Thatcher's new government eliminated the ACPS and a number of other nondepartmental bodies like it because the Conservatives viewed them as distasteful sources of patronage and government bloat, and perhaps because they had no taste for independent advice. Windlesham, *Responses to Crime*, vol. 2, pp. 148–51; and Ashworth, "The Decline of English Sentencing," pp. 85–86.

240. For a novel interpretation somewhat at odds with mine that stresses how the radical criminologists of the 1970s, with their emphasis on individualism and with their deep misgivings about all aspects of state power, critically prepared the ideological foundation for the new hard line in penal policy that crystallized two decades later in legislation like the Criminal Justice Act of 1993, see Robert R. Sullivan, *Liberalism and Crime: The British Experience* (Lanham, MD: Lexington Books, 2000).

241. Nash and Savage, "A Criminal Record?," p. 159.

242. Nash and Savage, "A Criminal Record?" p. 159. See also Morgan, "Punitive Policies and Politics."

243. Quoted in Nash and Savage, "A Criminal Record?" p. 159.

244. Marc Mauer, *Race to Incarcerate* (New York: The New Press, 1999), p. 13.

245. This discussion of the law Lords and the House of Lords is based primarily on Windlesham, *Responses to Crime*, vol. 2, pp. 6–7 and 427–32.

246. Windlesham, *Responses to Crime*, vol. 2, p. 427.

247. Windlesham, *Responses to Crime*, vol. 2, pp. 6–7 and 427.

248. Ashworth, "The Decline of English Sentencing," p. 76.

249. Ashworth, "The Decline of English Sentencing."

250. Cavadino and Dignan, *The Penal System*, pp. 92–98.

251. This discussion of magistrates and judges is based primarily on Cavadino and Dignan, *The Penal System*, pp. 79–91.

252. For more on British magistrates, see Sampson, *The Changing Anatomy of Britain*, pp. 154–56.

253. Cavadino and Dignan, *The Penal System*, pp. 90–91.

254. Sampson, *The Changing Anatomy of Britain*, p. 149.

255. Ashworth, "The Decline of English Sentencing."

256. Rutherford, *Transforming Criminal Policy*, pp. 127–28.

257. A. Ashworth and J. Gardner et al., "Neighboring on the Oppressive," *Criminal Justice*, vol. 16 (1998), cited in von Hirsch and Ashworth, "Law and Order," p. 420, n. 2 and p. 421, n. 19.

258. Ashworth, "The Decline of English Sentencing."

259. Ashworth, "The Decline of English Sentencing," pp. 80–81.

260. Ashworth, "The Decline of English Sentencing," p. 82.

261. For example, Derek Lewis, the Director of the Prison Service in England and Wales from 1992 to 1995, raises this concern in his memoir. Derek Lewis, *Hidden Agendas: Politics, Law and Disorder* (London: Hamish Hamilton, 1997). See also David Downes and Rod Morgan, "The British General Election 2001: The Centre-Right Consensus," *Punishment & Society* 4, no. 1 (2002): 81–96; and Michael Tonry, *Punishment and Politics: Evidence and Emulation in the Making of Crime Control Policy* (Devon, UK: Willan Publishing, 2004).

262. Rutherford, *Transforming Criminal Policy*, p. 132.

263. Nils Christie coined the term "joint moral community." Nils Christie, *Crime Control as Industry: Toward GULAGS, Western Style*, 2nd ed. (London and New York: Routledge, 1994).

264. Rutherford, *Transforming Criminal Policy*, p. 129.

265. Paul Rock, *Constructing Victims' Rights: The Home Office, New Labour, and Victims* (Oxford: Oxford University Press, 2004).
266. Rock, *Constructing Victims' Rights*, pp. 13 and 16.
267. Rock, *Constructing Victims' Rights*, p. 569.
268. Rock, *Constructing Victims' Rights*, pp. 173–85.
269. Rock, *Constructing Victims' Rights*, pp. 483 and 570.
270. Andrew L. Sonner charged at the end of his tenure as head of the Criminal Justice Section of the ABA in 1991–92 that the victims' rights movement was "emerging as another criminal justice sacred cow, immune from incisive critical observation and analysis." "Ex-ABA Leader Levels Contorted Charges Against NOVA," *The NOVA Newsletter* 16, no. 8 (1993), p. 5.

CHAPTER 5: NOT THE USUAL SUSPECTS: FEMINISTS, WOMEN'S GROUPS, AND THE ANTI-RAPE MOVEMENT

1. Elizabeth Cady Stanton, "There Will Be No Gallows When Mothers Make the Laws" (1868), in *Voices Against Death: American Opposition to Capital Punishment, 1787–1975*, ed. Philip English Mackey (New York: Burt Franklin & Co., 1976), p. 121.
2. On the relative success of the women's movement in the United States, see Joyce Gelb, "Social Movement 'Success': A Comparative Analysis of Feminism in the United States and United Kingdom," in *The Women's Movements of the United States and Western Europe*, ed. Mary Fainsod Katzenstein and Carol McClung Mueller (Philadelphia: Temple University Press, 1987).
3. Theda Skocpol, *Protecting Soldiers and Mothers: The Political Origins of Social Policy in the United States* (Cambridge, MA: Belknap Press of Harvard University Press, 1992).
4. Linda Gordon, review of *Women and Temperance: The Quest for Power and Liberty, 1873–1900*, by Ruth Bordin, and *Their Sisters' Keepers: Women's Prison Reform in America, 1830–1930*, by Estelle B. Freedman, *Signs* 7, no. 4 (1982): 886–89.
5. Nicole Hahn Rafter, *Partial Justice: Women in State Prisons, 1800–1935* (Boston: Northeastern University Press, 1985), preface.
6. Estelle B. Freedman, *Their Sisters' Keepers: Women's Prison Reform in America, 1830–1930* (Ann Arbor: University of Michigan Press, 1981), p. 25.
7. Rafter, *Partial Justice*, p. 13
8. Freedman, *Their Sisters' Keepers*, p. 15.
9. Francis Lieber, introduction to Gustave de Beaumont and Alexis de Tocqueville, *On the Penitentiary System in the United States, and Its Application in France* (Philadelphia, 1833), p. xv, cited in Barbara Meil Hobson, *Uneasy Virtue: The Politics of Prostitution and the American Reform Tradition* (New York: Basic Books, 1987), p. 110.
10. Freedman, *Their Sisters' Keepers*, p. 45.
11. Black women were generally excluded from the reformatories. If admitted, they were housed in small, segregated cottages. Rafter, *Partial Justice*, p. 37.
12. Rafter, *Partial Justice*, pp. xxvi and 39. See also Lucia Zedner, "Wayward Sisters: The Prison for Women," in *The Oxford History of the Prison: The Practice of Punishment in Western Society*, ed. Norval Morris and David J. Rothman (New York: Oxford University Press, 1995).
13. Rafter, *Partial Justice*, p. 25; and Freedman, *Their Sisters' Keepers*, p. 14.

14. Rafter, *Partial Justice*, p. 41.

15. Rafter, *Partial Justice*, p. 25.

16. For a detailed study of one of the leading women prison reformers, see Margaret Hope Bacon, *Abby Hopper Gibbons: Prison Reformer and Social Activist* (Albany: SUNY Press, 2000).

17. Rafter, *Partial Justice*, p. xxiii.

18. For more on the lasting consequences that the reformatory movement had for the treatment of black women, see Rafter, *Partial Justice*, esp. Chapter 6 and conclusion. For its lasting effects on the treatment of incarcerated women, see Freedman, *Their Sisters' Keepers*, Chapters 3 and 8. For an account that stresses the persistence of the maternalist tradition in prison reform despite waning enthusiasm for reformatories per se after the 1930s, see Estelle B. Freedman, *Maternal Justice: Miriam Van Waters and the Female Reform Tradition* (Chicago: University of Chicago Press, 1996).

19. For a detailed discussion of the differences in these two phases, see Rafter, *Partial Justice*; and Freedman, *Maternal Justice*.

20. Rafter, *Partial Justice*, p. 61. Here Rafter challenges Rothman's view that the Progressives were primarily concerned with finding noninstitutional solutions and alternatives to incarceration. David J. Rothman, *Conscience and Convenience: The Asylum and Its Alternatives in Progressive America* (Boston: Little, Brown and Co., 1980).

21. Elizabeth Pleck, "Criminal Approaches to Family Violence, 1640–1980," in *Crime and Justice: A Review of Research*, vol. 11, ed. Lloyd Ohlin and Michael Tonry (Chicago: University of Chicago, 1989), pp. 19–20, 36–37, and 39.

22. Linda Gordon, *Heroes of Their Own Lives: The Politics and History of Family Violence: Boston, 1880–1960* (New York: Viking, 1988), Chapter 2; and Anthony M. Platt, *The Child Savers*, 2nd ed. (Chicago: University of Chicago Press, 1977).

23. On journalistic accounts, see Philip Jenkins, *Moral Panic: Changing Concepts of the Child Molester in Modern America* (New Haven: Yale University Press, 1998), pp. 35–36.

24. Linda Gordon, "Family Violence, Feminism, and Social Control," *Feminist Studies* 12, no. 3 (Fall 1986), pp. 459–60.

25. Gordon, *Heroes of Their Own Lives*, Chapter 8; and William L. O'Neill, *Everyone Was Brave: The Rise and Fall of Feminism in America* (Chicago: Quadrangle, 1969), p. 352.

26. Pleck, "Criminal Approaches to Family Violence," pp. 41–42.

27. Pleck, "Criminal Approaches to Family Violence," p. 44.

28. Elizabeth Pleck, "Feminist Responses to 'Crimes Against Women,' 1868–1896," *Signs* 8, no. 3 (1983), p. 453.

29. Pleck, "Feminist Responses," p. 457.

30. Maryland (1882), Delaware (1901), and Oregon (1906) enacted laws to punish wife-beaters with the whipping post. Pleck, "Criminal Approaches to Family Violence," p. 40.

31. Pleck, "Feminist Responses," p. 461.

32. Elizabeth Pleck, *Domestic Tyranny: The Making of Social Policy Against Family Violence from Colonial Times to the Present* (New York: Oxford University Press, 1989), p. 65. Stanton's position was somewhat ambiguous because she could also be a forceful opponent of capital punishment. See Stanton, "There Will Be No Gallows When Mothers Make the Laws."

33. These black women reformers viewed this concern for the protection of women as excessive and a pretext for reinforcing racist and segregationist sentiments and policies. Mary Jane Brown, *Eradicating This Evil: Women in the American Anti-Lynching Movement, 1892–1940* (New York: Garland, 2000), Chapter 3.

34. Margaret May, "Violence in the Family: An Historical Perspective," in *Violence and the Family*, ed. J. P. Martin (Chichester, NY: John Wiley & Sons, 1978).

35. Pleck, "Feminist Responses," p. 469. See also May, "Violence in the Family," pp. 137–50.

36. May, "Violence in the Family," pp. 146–49.

37. Carol Bauer and Lawrence Ritt, "'A Husband Is a Beating Animal' – Frances Power Cobbe Confronts the Wife-Abuse Problem in Victorian England," *International Journal of Women's Studies* 6, no. 2 (March/April 1983), pp. 104 and 112–13; Carol Bauer and Lawrence Ritt, "Wife-Abuse, Late-Victorian English Feminists, and the Legacy of Frances Power Cobbe," *International Journal of Women's Studies* 6, no. 3 (May/June 1983): 195–207. See also Nancy Tomes, "A 'Torrent of Abuse': Crimes of Violence Between Working-Class Men and Women in London, 1840–1875," *Journal of Social History* 11, no. 3 (Spring 1978): 328–45.

38. Pleck, "Feminist Responses," p. 460.

39. Bauer and Ritt, "'A Husband Is a Beating Animal'," pp. 109–10 and 112–13.

40. Bauer and Ritt, "'A Husband Is a Beating Animal'," pp. 111–12.

41. Bauer and Ritt, "Wife-Abuse, Late-Victorian English Feminists," p. 198.

42. Martin Wiener, *Men of Blood: Violence, Manliness and Criminal Justice in Victorian England* (Cambridge: Cambridge University Press, 2004), pp. 3 and 289.

43. Pleck, "Feminist Responses," p. 469.

44. This is not to say they did not expose and denounce the lenient sentences that husbands who abused their wives received. Bauer and Ritt, "Wife-Abuse, Late-Victorian English Feminists." On the greater militancy of British feminists, see Gelb, "Social Movement 'Success'," pp. 269–70.

45. Prior to the emergence of the anti-rape movement, prosecutors largely ignored this crime. For example, in 1969 the New York City police made 1,085 arrests for rape, but only 18 men were convicted. Jeffrey Toobin, "The Consent Defense," *The New Yorker*, September 1, 2003, p. 41.

46. Susan Schechter, *Women and Male Violence: The Visions and Struggles of the Battered Women's Movement* (Boston: South End Press, 1982), p. 31. For more on these two strands, see Deborah L. Rhode, *Justice and Gender: Sex Discrimination and the Law* (Cambridge: Harvard University Press, 1989), pp. 59–60.

47. Myra Marx Ferree, "Equality and Autonomy: Feminist Politics in the United States and West Germany," in *The Women's Movements of the United States and Western Europe*. For more on the dominant influence of liberalism on American feminism, see Rhode, *Justice and Gender*, pp. 12 and 17; and Nancy Hirschmann, *Toward a Feminist Theory of Freedom* (Princeton: Princeton University Press, 2003).

48. Debra C. Minkoff, *Organizing for Equality: The Evolution of Women's and Racial-Ethnic Organizations in America, 1955–1985* (New Brunswick: Rutgers University Press, 1995), p. 121.

49. Nancy A. Matthews, *Confronting Rape: The Feminist Anti-Rape Movement and the State* (New York and London: Routledge, 1994), pp. xii–xiv.

50. Matthews, *Confronting Rape*, p. xv.

51. Ferree, "Equality and Autonomy," p. 183. See also R. Emerson Dobash and Russell P. Dobash, *Women, Violence and Social Change* (London and New York: Routledge, 1992), p. 23; and O'Neill, *Everyone Was Brave*.

52. Rhode, *Justice and Gender*, p. 57; and Jo Freeman, "The Origins of the Women's Liberation Movement," *American Journal of Sociology* 78 (1983), pp. 797–98.

53. Judith Hole and Ellen Levine, *Rebirth of Feminism* (New York: Quadrangle, 1971), pp. 82–83 and 87; and Freeman, "The Origins of the Women's Liberation Movement," pp. 798–99.

54. On tensions within the U.S. women's movement, see Anne N. Costain and W. Douglas Costain, "Strategy and Tactics of the Women's Movement in the United States: The Role of Political Parties," in *The Women's Movements of the United States and Western Europe*, pp. 197–98; Hole and Levine, *Rebirth of Feminism*, pp. 87–95; and Maryann Barakso, *Governing NOW: Grassroots Activism in the National Organization for Women* (Ithaca and London: Cornell University Press, 2004).

55. Matthews, *Confronting Rape*, p. xii.

56. Hole and Levine, *Rebirth of Feminism*, p. 157.

57. Matthews, *Confronting Rape*, p. xii.

58. June Burdy Csida and Joseph Csida, *Rape: How To Avoid It and What To Do About It If You Can't* (Chatsworth, CA: Books for Better Living, 1974), p. 149.

59. R. I. Mawby and M. L. Gill, *Crime Victims: Needs, Services and the Voluntary Sector* (London: Tavistock, 1987), p. 80. For more on the early history of the anti-rape movement, see R. Amy Elman, *Sexual Subordination and State Intervention: Comparing Sweden and the United States* (Providence: Berghahn Books, 1996), pp. 66–68.

60. Mary Ann Largen, "History of Women's Movement in Changing Attitudes, Laws, and Treatment Toward Rape Victims," in *Sexual Assault: The Victim and the Rapist*, ed. Marcia J. Walker and Stanley L. Brodsky (Lexington, MA: Heath Books, 1976), pp. 69–73.

61. Mary Ann Largen, "Grassroots Centers and National Task Forces: A Herstory of the Anti-Rape Movement," *Aegis* 32 (Autumn 1981): 46–52, cited in Frank J. Weed, *Certainty of Justice: Reform in the Crime Movement* (New York: Walter de Gruyter, 1995), p. 13.

62. Matthews, *Confronting Rape*, p. 15

63. This discussion of the Crusade is based on Lisa Brodyaga et al., *Rape and Its Victims: A Report for Citizens, Health Facilities and Criminal Justice Agencies* (Washington, DC: National Institute of Law Enforcement and Criminal Justice, 1975), pp. 138–39.

64. Matthews, *Confronting Rape*, pp. 7–8.

65. See, for example, Law Enforcement Assitance Administration, *LEAA Task Force on Women* (Washington, DC: LEAA, 1975).

66. For a brief discussion of the LEAA report, see Vicki McNickle Rose, "Rape as a Social Problem: A Byproduct of the Feminist Movement," *Social Problems* 25, no. 1 (October 1977), p. 77.

67. Brodyaga et al., *Rape and Its Victims*, p. 139.

68. Steven Rathgeb Smith and Susan Freinkel, *Adjusting the Balance: Federal Policy and Victim Services* (Westport, CT: Greenwood, 1988), pp. 81–82.

69. Smith and Freinkel, *Adjusting the Balance*, p. 81.

70. Janet Gornick, Martha R. Burt, and Karen J. Pittman, "Structure and Activities of Rape Crisis Centers in the Early 1980s," *Crime and Delinquency* 31, no. 2 (April 1985), p. 260.

71. Debra Whitcomb et al., *An Exemplary Project: Stop Rape Crisis Center, Baton Rouge, Louisiana* (Washington, DC: National Institute of Law Enforcement and Criminal Justice, 1979).

72. *Feminist Alliance Against Rape Newsletter*, September-October 1976, pp. 11–12, cited in Schechter, *Women and Male Violence*, p. 41.

73. For details on funding, see Smith and Freinkel, *Adjusting the Balance*, pp. 91–94.

74. Schechter, *Women and Male Violence*, p. 41.

75. This information on funding comes from Weed, *Certainty of Justice*, p. 14.

76. Gornick et al., "Structure and Activities of Rape Crisis Centers"; and Weed, *Certainty of Justice*, p. 14.

77. The discussion of rape crisis centers in California in the next few paragraphs is based primarily on Matthews, *Confronting Rape*, esp. pp. xii, 39, 73–74, 106–09, 116–26, and 135–38.

78. Brodyaga et al., *Rape and Its Victims*, pp. 125–27.

79. Several analysts caution that rape crisis centers did not fall neatly into two types – feminist, grassroots centers on the one hand and streamlined, hierarchical, apolitical social service agencies on the other. That said, the original feminist guiding principles increasingly yielded to or were in contention with a far more diverse set of concerns about how to combat violence against women. In the words of Nancy Matthews, they became "contested terrain." Matthews, *Confronting Rape*, p. xv. See also Amy Fried, "'It's Hard To Change What We Want To Change': Rape Crisis Centers as Organizations," *Gender & Society* 8, no. 4 (December 1994): 562–83; and Gornick et al., "Structure and Activities of Rape Crisis Centers."

80. Matthews, *Confronting Rape*, pp. 150–51.

81. Matthews, *Confronting Rape*, p. 126.

82. Matthews, *Confronting Rape*, p. 39.

83. Quoted in Matthews, *Confronting Rape*, p. 134.

84. Matthews, *Confronting Rape*, p. 142.

85. Nancy A. Matthews, "Surmounting a Legacy: The Expansion of Racial Diversity in a Local Anti-Rape Movement," *Gender & Society* 3, no. 4 (December 1989), p. 525.

86. Schechter, *Women and Male Violence*, p. 40. See also Kimberlé Crenshaw, "Mapping the Margins: Intersectionality, Identity Politics, and Violence Against Women of Color," *Stanford Law Review* 43, no. 6 (1991), pp. 1269, 1273, and 1277; Angela Y. Davis, *Women, Culture, and Politics* (New York: Random House, 1989), pp. 43–45; Angela Harris, "Race and Essentialism in Feminist Legal Theory," in *Feminist Legal Theory: Readings in Law and Gender*, ed. Katharine T. Bartlett and Rosanne Kennedy (Boulder, CO: Westview Press, 1991). On the early history of the anti-lynching movement and its challenge to white supremacist claims about rape, see Amii Barnard, "The Application of Critical Race Feminism to the Anti-Lynching Movement: Black Women's Fight Against Race and Gender Ideology, 1892–1920," *UCLA Women's Law Journal* 3, no. 7 (1993): 1–38.

87. Matthews, *Confronting Rape*, p. 151.

88. Aaronette M. White, "I Am Because We Are: Combined Race and Gender Political Consciousness Among African American Women and Men Anti-Rape Activists," *Women's Studies International Forum* 24, no. 1 (2001): 11–24.

89. Brodyaga et al., *Rape and Its Victims*, p. 126.

90. Matthews, *Confronting Rape*, p. 154.

91. Matthews, *Confronting Rape*, p. 159.

92. Esther I. Madriz, "Images of Criminals and Victims: A Study on Women's Fear and Social Control," *Gender & Society* 11, no. 3 (June 1997), pp. 352 and 342. On the genesis and impact of the Willie Horton case, see Tali Mendelberg, *The Race Card: Campaign Strategy, Implicit Messages, and the Norm of Equality* (Princeton: Princeton University Press, 2001), Chapters 5 and 6.

93. Laureen France and Nancy McDonald, "They Call It Rehabilitation," *Aegis*, Winter/Spring 1980, p. 27. See also Donna Whittlesey, "Feminist Models for Offender Treatment," *Aegis*, Winter/Spring 1980, pp. 33–36.

94. Aaronette M. White, "Talking Feminist, Talking Black: Micromobilization Processes in a Collective Protest Against Rape," *Gender & Society* 13, no. 1 (February 1999): 77–100.

95. Lawrence Herman, "What's Wrong With the Rape Reform Laws?" *The Civil Liberties Review*, 3, no. 5 (December 1976/January 1977), p. 73.

96. Leigh Bienen, "Rape Reform Legislation in the United States: A Look at Some Practical Effects," *Victimology: An International Journal* 8, nos. 1–2 (1983): 139–51; Leigh Bienen, "Rape III: National Developments in Rape Reform Legislation," *Women's Rights Law Reporter* 6, no. 3 (Spring 1980): 171–217; and Weed, *Certainty of Justice*, p. 15.

97. Bienen, "Rape III," pp. 173–75. As of 1974, death was still the maximum penalty for rape in at least ten states. "Revolt Against Rape," *Time*, July 22, 1974, p. 85, cited in Rose, "Rape as a Social Problem," p. 84. See also pp. 209–12 in this volume.

98. Rhode, *Justice and Gender*, pp. 251–52; Bienen, "Rape Reform Legislation in the United States"; Wallace D. Loh, "Q: What Has Reform of Rape Legislation Wrought? A: Truth in Criminal Labelling," *Journal of Social Issues* 37, no. 4 (Fall 1981): 28–51; Carol Bohmer, "Rape and the Law," in *Confronting Rape and Sexual Assault*, ed. Mary E. Odem and Jody Clay-Warner (Wilmington, DE: SR Books, 1998), p. 224; and Jeanne C. Marsh, Alison Geist, and Nathan Caplan, *Rape and the Limits of Law Reform* (Boston: Auburn House, 1982), p. 106.

99. Bienen, "Rape Reform Legislation" and "Rape III"; Rose, "Rape as a Social Problem"; Gerald D. Robin, "Forcible Rape: Institutionalized Sexism in the Criminal Justice System," *Crime and Delinquency* 23 (April 1977): 136–53; and Rhode, *Justice and Gender*, p. 252.

100. Bienen, "Rape III," p. 171.

101. Loh, "Q: What Has Reform of Rape Legislation Wrought?" pp. 34–35.

102. Lynne N. Henderson, "The Wrongs of Victim's Rights," *Stanford Law Review* 37, no. 4 (April 1985), p. 949, n. 70. See also Thomas E. McDermott, III, "California Rape Evidence Reform: An Analysis of Senate Bill 1678," *Hastings Law Journal* 26 (1975): 1551–73.

103. Rose, "Rape as a Social Problem," pp. 82–83; and Herman, "What's Wrong With the Rape Reform Laws?"

104. Loret Ulmschneider, "Dallas Rapists See Their Names Printed," *Feminist Alliance Against Rape News*, July–August 1977, pp. 2–5, cited in Smith and Freinkel, *Adjusting the Balance*, p. 77.

105. "Women Against Rape," *Time*, April 23, 1973, p. 104.

106. "The Rape Wave," *Newsweek*, January 29, 1973, p. 59.

107. *Aegis*, September/October 1979, p. 49.

108. *Feminist Alliance Against Rape News*, September-October 1976, pp. 11–12, cited in Schechter, *Women and Male Violence*, pp. 42–43.

109. Frederika E. Schmitt and Patricia Yancey Martin, "Unobtrusive Mobilization by an Institutionalized Rape Crisis Center: 'All We Do Comes from Victims'," *Gender & Society* 13, no. 3 (June 1999), p. 372.

110. Schmitt and Martin, "Unobtrusive Mobilization," p. 377.

111. Mary Fainsod Katzenstein, "Feminism Within American Institutions: Unobtrusive Mobilization in the 1980s," *Signs* 16, no. 1 (1990): 27–54; and Mary Fainsod Katzenstein, *Faithful and Fearless: Moving Feminist Protest Inside the Church and Military* (Princeton: Princeton University Press, 1998).

112. Schmitt and Martin suggest that such mainstream support is surprising. "Unobtrusive Mobilization," p. 365.

113. Claire Corbett and Kathy Hobdell, "Volunteer-Based Services to Rape Victims: Some Recent Developments," in *Victims of Crime: A New Deal?*, ed. Mike Maguire and John Pointing (Milton Keynes, UK: Open University Press, 1988), p. 48.

114. For more on NAVSS, see pp. 103–05, 113, 133, 134, and 135.

115. Adam Crawford, "Salient Themes Towards a Victim Perspective and the Limitations of Restorative Justice: Some Concluding Comments," in *Integrating a Victim Perspective Within Criminal Justice*, ed. Adam Crawford and Jo Goodey (Aldershot, UK: Ashgate, 2000); and Paul Rock, *Constructing Victims' Rights: The Home Office, New Labour, and Victims* (Oxford: Oxford University Press, 2004), p. 126.

116. Rock, *Constructing Victims' Rights*, p. 127.

117. Rock, *Constructing Victims' Rights*, p. 118.

118. For more on the Home Office, see Chapter 4.

119. Paul Rock, *Helping Victims of Crime: The Home Office and the Rise of Victim Support in England and Wales* (Oxford: Clarendon Press, 1990), p. 44.

120. Rock, *Helping Victims of Crime*, p. 183.

121. Mick Ryan and Tony Ward, "From Positivism to Postmodernism: Some Theoretical and Strategic Reflections on the Evolution of the Penal Lobby in Britain," *International Journal of the Sociology of the Law* 20 (1992), p. 326. For more about RAP, see pp. 186–87 and 192 in this volume.

122. "Ask Any Woman," *Abolitionist* 19 (1985), p. 6, cited in Tony Ward, "Symbols and Noble Lies: Abolitionism, 'Just Deserts,' and Crimes of the Powerful," in *Abolitionism: Towards a Non-Repressive Approach to Crime*, ed. Herman Bianchi and René van Swaaningen (Amsterdam: Free University Press, 1986), p. 81. For a similar view that questions the utility of relying on harsher sentences to address rape and warns feminists that such a stance could play into the hands of "generally oppressive and usually class-specific law and order policies," see Jill Box-Grainger, "Sentencing Rapists," in *Confronting Crime*, ed. Roger Matthews and Jock Young (London: Sage, 1986), p. 48. This was originally published in 1982 by Radical Alternatives to Prison, the British radical prison reform group.

123. René van Swaaningen, *Critical Criminology: Visions from Europe* (London: Sage Publications, 1997), pp. 75–76 and 81–82; and Jock Young, "Radical Criminology in Britain: The Emergence of a Competing Paradigm," *British Journal of Criminology* 28, no. 2 (Spring 1988): 289–313.

124. Anna T., "Feminist Responses to Sexual Abuse: The Work of the Birmingham Rape Crisis Centre," in *Victims of Crime: A New Deal?*, pp. 60–64. See also Mawby and Gill, *Crime Victims*, p. 84.

125. Rock, *Helping Victims of Crime*, pp. 178–82.
126. Mike Maguire and Claire Corbett, *The Effects of Crime and the Work of Victims Support Schemes* (Aldershot, UK: Gower, 1987), p. 2.
127. Maguire and Corbett, *The Effects of Crime*, p. 204.
128. Maguire and Corbett, *The Effects of Crime*, p. 173.
129. Marian Foley, "Professionalising the Response to Rape," in *Working With Violence*, ed. Carol Lupton and Terry Gillespie (Houndsmills, UK: Macmillan, 1994).
130. Jeanne Gregory and Susan Lees, *Policing Sexual Assault* (London and New York: Routledge, 1999), p. 178.
131. Susan Lees, "Judicial Rape," *Women's Studies International Forum* 16, no. 1 (1993), p. 14.
132. Gregory and Lees, *Policing Sexual Assault*, pp. 2–3.
133. This is so in Denmark, Norway, and Canada, for example. Lees, "Judicial Rape," p. 35, fn. 5.
134. For more on the historical-institutional roots of these differences, see pp. 52–55.
135. Bruce C. Johnson, "Taking Care of Labor: The Police in American Politics," *Theory and Society* 3, no. 1 (1976), p. 102. For more on the Wickersham Commission, see pp. 61–62, 69, and 136 in this volume.
136. Samuel Walker, *A Critical History of Police Reform* (Lexington, MA: Lexington Books, 1977), p. 55.
137. Walker, *A Critical History of Police Reform*, p. 169.
138. Phil Scraton, "Unreasonable Force: Policing, Punishment and Marginalization," in *Law, Order and the Authoritarian State: Readings in Critical Criminology*, ed. Phil Scraton (Milton Keynes, UK: Open University Press, 1987), pp. 145–89; and Paul Gordon, "Community Policing: Towards the Local Police State?" in *Law, Order and the Authoritarian State*: 121–44.
139. Mike Nash and Stephen P. Savage, "A Criminal Record? Law, Order, and Conservative Policy," in *Public Policy in Britain*, ed. Stephen P. Savage, Rob Atkinson, and Lynton Robins (Basingstoke, UK: Macmillan, 1994), pp. 140–41.
140. Scraton, "Unreasonable Force," p. 182.
141. Ferree, "Equality and Autonomy"; Gelb, "Social Movement 'Success'"; and Elman, *Sexual Subordination and State Intervention*.
142. Ezzat A. Fattah, "Preface," in *Towards a Critical Victimology*, ed. Ezzat A. Fattah (New York: St. Martin's Press, 1992), p. xi.
143. Cassia Spohn and Julie Horney, *Rape Law Reform: A Grassroots Revolution and Its Impact* (New York: Plenum Press, 1992), p. 35.
144. For a summary of the major studies of the impact of rape law reform, see Spohn and Horney, *Rape Law Reform*, pp. 29–32.
145. Spohn and Horney, *Rape Law Reform*, p. 175.

CHAPTER 6: THE BATTERED-WOMEN'S MOVEMENT AND THE DEVELOPMENT OF PENAL POLICY

1. Susan Schechter, *Women and Male Violence: The Visions and Struggles of the Battered Women's Movement* (Boston: South End Press, 1982), p. 320.
2. See, for example, the testimony of Yolanda Bako and Lisa Leghorn in U.S. Commission on Civil Rights, "Battered Women: Issues of Public Policy; Proceedings of a Consultation Sponsored by the U.S. Commission on Civil Rights," Washington, DC, January 30–31, 1978 (Washington, DC: U.S. Commission on Civil Rights, 1978), pp. 68 and 138–39; Schechter, *Women and Male Violence*, pp. 133–34;

Steven Rathgeb Smith and Susan Freinkel, *Adjusting the Balance, Federal Policy and Victim Services* (Westport, CT: Greenwood, 1988), pp. 140–41.

3. Schechter, *Women and Male Violence*, p. 241.

4. R. I. Mawby and M. L. Gill, *Crime Victims: Needs, Services and the Voluntary Sector* (London: Tavistock, 1987), p. 75.

5. On the early rifts in the NWAF, see Betsy Warrior, "Divided But Not Defeated: The Battered Women's Movement in Britain," *Aegis*, January–February 1979, pp. 4–6; and Jo Sutton, "The Growth of the British Movement for Battered Women," *Victimology: An International Journal* 2, no. 3–4 (1977–78): 576–84.

6. Cathy Avina, "Progress Report – The National Coalition Against Domestic Violence," *Aegis*, January–February 1979, pp. 4–6.

7. John M. Johnson, "Program Enterprise and Official Cooptation in the Battered Women's Shelter Movement," *American Behavioral Scientist* 24, no. 6 (1981), p. 831. For more on the diversity of the battered-women's movement, see Marlena Studer, "Wife Beating as a Social Problem," *International Journal of Women's Studies* 7, no. 5 (1984): 412–22.

8. Johnson, "Program Enterprise and Official Cooptation," p. 830.

9. Kathleen J. Ferraro, "Battered Women and the Shelter Movement," PhD dissertation, Arizona State University, 1981, cited in Johnson, "Program Enterprise and Official Cooptation," p. 830.

10. Ferraro, "Battered Women and the Shelter Movement"; and Colorado Association for Aid to Battered Women, *Monograph on Services to Battered Women* (Washington, DC: Department of HEW, Office of Domestic Violence, 1978), cited in Johnson, "Program Enterprise and Official Cooptation," p. 831. Another survey concluded that only about 15 percent of shelters had their origins in consciousness-raising groups, rape crisis groups, or the National Coalition Against Domestic Violence. U.S. Department of Health and Human Services, Office of Human Development Services, *A Monograph on Services to Battered Women* (Washington, DC: DHHS, 1980), p. 21, cited in R. Emerson Dobash and Russell P. Dobash, *Women, Violence and Social Change* (London and New York: Routledge, 1992), pp. 67–68.

11. V. Binney, G. Harkell, and J. Nixon, *Leaving Violent Men: A Study of Refuges and Housing for Battered Women* (Leeds: King's English Bookprinters Ltd., 1981), p. iii, cited in Dobash and Dobash, *Women, Violence and Social Change*, p. 68.

12. Dobash and Dobash, *Women, Violence and Social Change*, p. 67.

13. John Greve, *London's Homeless* (London: G. Bell & Sons, 1964), p. 43.

14. Dobash and Dobash, *Women, Violence and Social Change*, p. 95.

15. Sutton, "The Growth of the British Movement for Battered Women," p. 583.

16. This discussion of public housing is based primarily on Dobash and Dobash, *Women, Violence and Social Change*, esp. pp. 42, 95–96, and 124. As the British welfare state continued to come under attack in the 1980s and 1990s, it did make some significant retreats in the area of public housing that disadvantaged victims of domestic violence. Ellen Malos and Gill Hague, "Women, Housing, Homelessness and Domestic Violence," *Women's Studies International Forum*, 20, no. 3 (1997), pp. 398–99.

17. Dobash and Dobash, *Women, Violence and Social Change*, p. 75.

18. Binney et al., *Leaving Violent Men*, cited in Dobash and Dobash, *Women, Violence and Social Change*, p. 66.

19. Dobash and Dobash, *Women, Violence and Social Change*, p. 153.

20. Jeanne Gregory and Susan Lees, *Policing Sexual Assault* (London and New York: Routledge, 1999), p. 11.

21. This account of the British hearings is based primarily on Dobash and Dobash, *Women, Violence and Social Change*, pp. 112–28.

22. Dobash and Dobash, *Women, Violence and Social Change*, p. 125.

23. Dobash and Dobash, *Women, Violence and Social Change*, p. 130.

24. U.S. Commission on Civil Rights, "Battered Women," pp. 1–2.

25. Marjory Fields, testimony before the U.S. Commission on Civil Rights, "Battered Women," pp. 20–21 and 23.

26. Presentation of Connie Downey, U.S. Commission on Civil Rights, "Battered Women," pp. 172–73.

27. Presentation of Betty Kaufman, U.S. Commission on Civil Rights, "Battered Women," p. 174. Subsequently, HUD promulgated new regulations that made shelters eligible for community development funds. See Allene Joyce Skinner, director, Women's Policy and Programs Division, HUD, memo, June 1, 1978, U.S. Commission on Civil Rights, "Battered Women," p. 649.

28. Ruth T. Prokop, letter to Arthur S. Fleming (sic), February 24, 1978, submitted to U.S. Commission on Civil Rights, "Battered Women," p. 640.

29. Presentation of Mary Hilton, Department of Labor, U.S. Commission on Civil Rights, "Battered Women," pp. 178–80. For more on the fragmented nature of the federal programs and their limitations in addressing domestic violence, see Schechter, *Women and Male Violence*, pp. 196–99.

30. Testimony of Jeannie Niedermeyer, U.S. Commission on Civil Rights, "Battered Women," pp. 176–78; and Charles Benjamin Schudson, "The Criminal Justice System as Family: Trying the Impossible for Battered Women," prepared statement, U.S. Commission on Civil Rights, "Battered Women," pp. 365–70.

31. Elizabeth Felter, "A History of the State's Response to Domestic Violence," in *Feminists Negotiate the State: The Politics of Domestic Violence*, ed. Cynthia R. Daniels (Lantham, MD: University Press of America, 1997).

32. Smith and Freinkel, *Adjusting the Balance*, p. 139.

33. Schechter, *Women and Male Violence*, p. 186.

34. These figures on funding come primarily from Schechter, *Women and Male Violence*, p. 186. See also Kathleen J. Tierney, "The Battered Women Movement and the Creation of the Wife Beating Problem," *Social Problems* 29, no. 3 (February 1982): 207–20.

35. Testimony of Jeannie Niedermeyer, U.S. Commission on Civil Rights, "Battered Women," p. 191.

36. Kathleen J. Ferraro, "The Legal Response to Women Battering in the United States," in *Women, Policing, and Male Violence: International Perspectives*, ed. Jalna Hanmer, Jill Radford, and Elizabeth A. Stanko (London and New York: Routledge, 1989), p. 159.

37. See, for example, the discussion of the Domestic Abuse Intervention Project, which grew out of the battered-women's movement in Duluth, Minn., in Ellen Pence and Melanie Shepard, "Integrating Feminist Theory and Practice: The Challenge of the Battered Women's Movement," in *Feminist Perspectives on Wife Abuse*, ed. Kersti Yllö and Michele Bograd (Newbury Park, CA: Sage, 1988). On a similar program in San Francisco, see Elizabeth M. Schneider, "Legal Reform Efforts to Assist Battered Women: Past, Present, and Future," Report to the Ford Foundation, Brooklyn Law School, July 1990, cited in Demie Kurz, "Battering and the Criminal Justice System: A Feminist View," in *Domestic Violence: The*

Changing Criminal Justice Response, ed. Eve S. Buzawa and Carl G. Buzawa (Westport, CT: Auburn House, 1992), pp. 34–35.

38. Johnson, "Program Enterprise and Official Cooptation," p. 834.

39. Colorado Association for Aid to Battered Women, *Monograph on Services to Battered Women*, p. 42, cited in Johnson, "Program Enterprise and Official Cooptation," p. 834.

40. Joyce Gelb, "The Politics of Wife Abuse," in *Families, Politics, and Public Policy: A Feminist Dialogue on Women and the State*, ed. Irene Diamond (New York: Longman, 1983).

41. Robert Elias, "Which Victim Movement? The Politics of Victim Policy," in *Victims of Crime: Problems, Policies, and Programs*, ed. Arthur J. Lurigio, Wesley G. Skogan, and Robert C. Davis (Newbury Park, CA: Sage Publications, 1980), p. 234.

42. This discussion of the CWPS is drawn primarily from Schechter, *Women and Male Violence*, pp. 189–91.

43. Dobash and Dobash, *Women, Violence and Social Change*, pp. 29–30; Schechter, *Women and Male Violence*, Chapter 4; and Smith and Freinkel, *Adjusting the Balance*, Chapter 6.

44. On the stronger therapeutic tradition, see pp. 87, 105, 134, and 135 in this volume; and Schechter, *Women and Male Violence*, p. 246.

45. Lois Ahrens, "From Collective to Coopted," *Aegis*, September–October 1978, pp. 5–8; and Lois Ahrens, "Battered Women's Refuges: Feminist Cooperatives vs. Social Service Institutions," *Aegis*, Summer/Autumn 1980, pp. 9–15.

46. Liane V. Davis, Jan L. Hagen, and Theresa J. Early, "Social Services for Battered Women: Are They Adequate, Accessible, and Appropriate?" *Social Work: Journal of the National Association of Social Workers* 39, no. 6 (1994): 695–704.

47. Rachelle Brooks, *Feminists Negotiate the State: The Politics of Domestic Violence*, ed. Cynthia R. Daniels (Lanham, MD: University Press of America, 1997), p. 68.

48. David S. Davis, "State and Right-Wing Repression: The Production of Crime Policies," *Crime and Social Justice* 20 (1983), p. 127.

49. U.S. Department of Justice, *Attorney General's Task Force on Family Violence* (Washington, DC: GPO, 1984). For direct quotations, see pp. 10–12, 22, and 64.

50. Smith and Freinkel, *Adjusting the Balance*, p. 156.

51. For more on VOCA, see pp. 89, 126, and 147.

52. Ferraro, "The Legal Response to Women Battering in the United States," p. 159; and Dobash and Dobash, *Women, Violence and Social Change*, pp. 140–41.

53. For more on the Oakland case, see Pauline W. Gee, "Ensuring Police Protection for Battered Women: The Scott v. Hart Suit," *Signs* 8, no. 3 (Spring 1983): 554–67.

54. Laurie Woods, "Litigation on Behalf of Battered Women," *Women's Rights Law Reporter* 5 (1978): 7–33.

55. James B. Halsted, "Domestic Violence: Its Legal Definitions," in *Domestic Violence: The Changing Criminal Justice Response*, pp. 158–59.

56. Marvin Zalman, "The Courts' Response to Police Intervention in Domestic Violence," in *Domestic Violence: The Changing Criminal Justice Response*, p. 89.

57. Dobash and Dobash, *Women, Violence and Social Change*, p. 205.

58. Dobash and Dobash, *Women, Violence and Social Change*, pp. 204–05.

59. Charles R. Epp, *The Rights Revolution: Lawyers, Activists, and Supreme Courts in Comparative Perspective* (Chicago: University of Chicago Press, 1998), p. 149.

60. Dobash and Dobash, *Women, Violence and Social Change*, pp. 203–04. In one notable example, it took more than two years of negotiations before one researcher studying the prosecution of rape cases received permission to sit in the well of the court at jury trials in Old Bailey, the central criminal court in London. Susan Lees, "Judicial Rape," *Women's Studies International Forum* 16, no. 1 (1993), p. 12.

61. Lisa G. Lerman, "Protection of Battered Women: A Survey of State Legislation," *Women's Rights Law Reporter* 6, no. 4 (1980): 271–84.

62. Eve S. Buzawa and Carl G. Buzawa, *Domestic Violence: The Criminal Justice Response* (Newbury Park, CA: Sage, 1990), pp. 70–73.

63. Conflict resolution tactics involving mediation and other alternatives to formal arrest or prosecution to deal with domestic violence were first used in the 1970s by the New York City police and were later adopted by hundreds of police departments. Eve S. Buzawa and Carl G. Buzawa, "The Impact of Arrest on Domestic Violence: Introduction," *American Behavioral Scientist* 36, no. 5 (May 1993), p. 567. See also Buzawa and Buzawa, *Domestic Violence: The Criminal Justice Response*, pp. 78–79.

64. Dobash and Dobash, *Women, Violence and Social Change*, pp. 167 and 205.

65. Halsted, "Domestic Violence: Its Legal Definitions," p. 156. For more on presumptive and mandatory arrest policies, see Buzawa and Buzawa, *Domestic Violence: The Criminal Justice Response*, Chapters 8 and 9.

66. For a good overview of the history and the pros and cons of mandatory arrest and no-drop policies, see Elizabeth M. Schneider, *Battered Women and Feminist Lawmaking* (New Haven: Yale University Press, 2000), pp. 184–88.

67. Halsted, "Domestic Violence: Its Legal Definitions," p. 159; and Buzawa and Buzawa, *Domestic Violence: The Criminal Justice Response*, p. 75. By the 1980s, most large urban police departments had some kind of mandatory arrest policy in place. Lawrence W. Sherman, *Policing Domestic Violence: Experiments and Dilemmas* (New York: Free Press, 1992), p. 110.

68. Lawrence W. Sherman and Richard A. Berk, "The Specific Deterrent Effects of Arrest for Domestic Assault," *American Sociological Review* 49 (1984): 261–72.

69. On some of the problems with the study and growing doubts about mandatory arrest policies, see Arnold Binder and James Meeker, "Arrest as a Method to Control Spouse Abuse," in *Domestic Violence: The Changing Criminal Justice Response*, pp. 131–33; Dobash and Dobash, *Women, Violence and Social Change*, p. 201; Zalman, "The Courts' Response to Police Intervention in Domestic Violence," pp. 104–06; Buzawa and Buzawa, *Domestic Violence: The Criminal Justice Response*, pp. 98–102; Richard J. Gelles, "Constraints Against Domestic Violence: How Well Do They Work," *American Behavioral Scientist* 36, no. 5 (May 1993). See also the other contributions to "The Impact of Arrest on Domestic Violence," special edition, *American Behavioral Scientist* 36, no. 5 (May 1993).

70. Zalman, "The Courts' Response to Police Intervention in Domestic Violence," p. 84.

71. The Supreme Court concluded in 1959 in *Draper v. United States* that arrests for misdemeanors without warrants should be used only rarely and said that they raised concerns akin to the problem of warrantless searches. Binder and Meeker, "Arrest as a Method to Control Spouse Abuse," pp. 135–38.

72. Ferraro, "The Legal Response to Women Battering," pp. 162–63.

73. Janell D. Schmidt and Lawrence W. Sherman, "Does Arrest Deter Domestic Violence?" *American Behavioral Scientist* 36, no. 5 (May 1993): 601–09; and Sherman, *Policing Domestic Violence*. For a good overview of the evolution of Sherman's work on domestic violence, see Jo Dixon, "The Nexus of Sex, Spousal Violence, and the State," *Law & Society Review* 29, no. 2 (1995): 359–76.

74. Buzawa and Buzawa, "Introduction," in *Domestic Violence: The Changing Criminal Justice Response*, p. xiii.

75. Some did raise such concerns relatively early on. See, for example, Buzawa and Buzawa, *Domestic Violence: The Criminal Justice Response*, p. 568; Ferraro, "The Legal Response to Women Battering," p. 176; and Susan Schechter, "The Future of the Battered Women's Movement," *Aegis*, Summer/Autumn 1980, pp. 20–25.

76. A major study of violence found that the rate of violent victimization of males had decreased from 1973 to 1991 while remaining constant for women. Ronet Bachman, *Violence Against Women: A National Crime Victimization Survey Report* (Washington, DC: U.S. Department of Justice, January 1994).

77. See, for example, Daisy Quarm and Martin D. Schwartz, "Domestic Violence in Criminal Court: An Examination of New Legislation in Ohio," in *Criminal Justice Politics and Women: The Aftermath of Legally Mandated Change*, ed. Claudine SchWeber and Clarice Feinman (New York: The Haworth Press, 1985); and Nancy Hirschmann, *Toward a Feminist Theory of Freedom* (Princeton: Princeton University Press, 2003), pp. 115–16 and 133–34.

78. Kathleen Daly, "Criminal Justice Ideologies and Practices in Different Voices: Some Feminist Questions About Justice," *International Journal of the Sociology of Law* 17 (February 1989): 1–18.

79. Kimberlé W. Crenshaw, "Mapping the Margins: Intersectionality, Identity Politics, and Violence Against Women of Color," *Stanford Law Review* 43, no. 6 (1991), pp. 1245–57.

80. For an overview of these divisions, see Dixon, "The Nexus of Sex, Spousal Violence, and the State."

81. Tamar Pitch, "Critical Criminology, the Construction of Social Problems, and the Question of Rape," *The International Journal of the Sociology of Law* 13 (1985): 35–46.

82. Diane Mitsch Bush, "Women's Movements and State Policy Reform Aimed at Domestic Violence Against Women: A Comparison of the Consequences of Movement Mobilization in the U.S. and India," *Gender & Society* 6, no. 4 (December 1992), p. 599; and Hirschmann, *Toward a Feminist Theory of Freedom*, p. 131. The incipient women's self-defense movement directly challenged this view of women. Patricia Searles and Ronald J. Berger, "The Feminist Self-Defense Movement: A Case Study," *Gender & Society* 1, no. 1 (March 1987): 33–60.

83. See, for example, the contributions to Daniels, ed., *Feminists Negotiate the State*, especially Daniels, "Introduction: The Paradoxes of State Power"; and Anne Sparks, "Feminists Negotiate the Executive Branch: The Policing of Male Violence."

84. For examples of scholars who increasingly question legal, rights-based solutions, see Carol Smart, *Feminism and the Power of the Law* (London and New York: Routledge, 1989); and Katharine T. Bartlett and Rosanne Kennedy, eds., *Feminist Legal Theory: Readings in Law and Gender* (Boulder, CO: Westview Press, 1991),

especially the essay by Elizabeth M. Schneider, "The Dialectic of Rights and Politics: Perspectives from the Women's Movement."

85. The National Organization for Women Legal Defense and Education Fund directed a task force to push for the legislation which ultimately encompassed more than 1,000 organizations. Julie Goldscheid et al., "The Civil Rights Remedy of the Violence Against Women Act: Legislative History, Policy Implications and Litigation Strategy; A Panel Discussion Sponsored by the Bar of the City of New York," *Journal of Law and Policy* 4, no. 2 (1996), p. 395.

86. On the legislative history of the act, see Brooks, "Feminists Negotiate the Legislative Branch."

87. Schneider, *Battered Women and Feminist Lawmaking*, pp. 185–95. See also Julie Goldscheid et al., "The Civil Rights Remedy of the Violence Against Women Act."

88. John Leo, "Was It Law or Poetry? Supreme Court Strikes Down Part of the Violence Against Women Act," *U.S. News and World Report*, 128, no. 21 (May 29, 2000).

89. Marcia R. Chaiken et al., *State and Local Change and the Violence Against Women Act* (Washington, DC: National Institute of Justice, 2001).

90. Robert E. Freeman-Longo, "Reducing Sexual Abuse in America: Legislating Tougher Laws or Public Education and Prevention," *New England Journal on Criminal Abuse & Civil Confinement* 23, no. 2 (1997), p. 312.

91. Catherine S. Manegold, "Quiet Winners in House Fight on Crime: Women," *The New York Times*, August 25, 1994, p. A-19.

92. Manegold, "Quiet Winners in House Fight on Crime."

93. Ann Chih Lin, "The Troubled Success of Crime Policy," in *The Social Divide: Political Parties and the Future of Activist Government*, ed. Margaret Weir (Washington, DC, and New York: The Brookings Institution and Russell Sage Foundation, 1998). For more on the Racial Justice Act, see pp. 227, 247 and 249 of this volume.

94. Schneider, *Battered Women and Feminist Lawmaking*, p. 293–94, n. 65.

95. Schneider, *Battered Women and Feminist Lawmaking*, Chapter 10; and Cynthia R. Daniels et al., "Feminist Strategies: The Terms of Negotiation," in *Feminists Negotiate the State*.

96. Linda Hirschman, "Making Safety a Civil Right," *Ms.*, September/October 1994, p. 47.

97. Rinku Sen, "The First Time Was Tragedy, Will the Second Be Farce?" *Color Lines*, Fall 2000; and Katha Pollitt, "Subject to Debate: Dead Again?" *The Nation*, July 13, 1998, p. 10. One notable exception was NOW. See Maryann Barakso, *Governing NOW: Grassroots Activism in the National Organization for Women* (Ithaca, NY: Cornell University Press, 2004), p. 123.

98. Schneider, *Battered Women and Feminist Lawmaking*, p. 294, n. 66.

99. Sutton, "The Growth of the British Movement for Battered Women," p. 581. For more on the relative unresponsiveness of the British police to violence against women, see Tony Faragher, "The Police Response to Violence Against Women in the Home," in *Private Violence and Public Policy: The Needs of Battered Women and the Response of the Public Sector*, ed. Jan Pahl (London: Routledge & Kegan Paul, 1985), p. 121; and Gelb, "The Politics of Wife Abuse."

100. Dobash and Dobash, *Women, Violence and Social Change*, pp. 142–43.

101. From the 1970s onward, women in the British movement tended to identify themselves as "radical feminists," who emphasized separatism from men and established institutions like the government, and "socialist feminists," who stressed

the importance of class and of establishing linkages with the Labor Party and trade union movement. Anna Coote and Beatrix Campbell, *Sweet Freedom: The Struggle for Women's Liberation* (Oxford: Basil Blackwell, 1987), pp. 18–23.

102. Angela Weir and Elizabeth Wilson, "The British Women's Movement," *New Left Review* 148 (November/December 1984), p. 75.

103. Joyce Gelb, "Social Movement 'Success': A Comparative Analysis of Feminism in the United States and United Kingdom," in *The Women's Movements of the United States and Western Europe*, ed. Mary Fainsod Katzenstein and Carol McClung Mueller (Philadelphia: Temple University Press, 1987).

104. Weir and Wilson, "The British Women's Movement," p. 100.

105. Mary Ruggie, "Workers' Movements and Women's Interests: The Impact of Labor-State Relations in Britain and Sweden," in *The Women's Movements of the United States and Western Europe*, p. 255.

106. Dobash and Dobash, *Women, Violence and Social Change*, p. 209; and Clarice Feinman, *Women in the Criminal Justice System*, 3rd ed. (Westport, CT: Praeger, 1994), Chapters 4 and 6.

107. There were some tensions within the British refuge movement between radicals and reformers. Jan Pahl, "Refuges for Battered Women: Social Provision or Social Movement," *Journal of Voluntary Action Research* 8, no. 1–2 (1979): 25–35.

108. Terry Gillespie, "Under Pressure: Rape Crisis Centers, Multi-Agency Work, and Strategies for Survival," in *Working With Violence*, ed. Carol Lupton and Terry Gillespie (Houndsmills, UK: Macmillan, 1994).

109. Carol Lupton, "The British Refuge Movement: The Survival of an Ideal?" in *Working With Violence*, pp. 60–61, 69, and 71–73.

110. Mawby and Gill, *Crime Victims*, p. 62.

111. Michael Cavadino and James Dignan, *The Penal System: An Introduction* (London: Sage, 1992), p. 108. For more on the 1991 act, see pp. 108, 109, 112, 155, 191, and 192 of this volume.

112. John Pratt, "Law and Order Politics in New Zealand 1986: A Comparison With the United Kingdom," *International Journal of the Sociology of Law* 16 (1988): pp. 103–26.

113. This discussion of the German case is based primarily on Myra Marx Ferree, "Equality and Autonomy: Feminist Politics in the United States and West Germany," in *The Women's Movements of the United States and Western Europe*, pp. 176–77 and 185.

114. S. Plogstedt and C. Douglas, "German Feminism Discussed," *Off Our Backs*, November 1982, cited in Ferree, "Equality and Autonomy," p. 187.

115. Ferree, "Equality and Autonomy," p. 189.

116. On the "culture of tolerance" in the Netherlands, see David Downes, *Contrasts in Tolerance: Post-War Penal Policy in the Netherlands and England and Wales* (Oxford: Clarendon Press, 1988).

117. Olga J. Zoomer, "Policing Woman Beating in the Netherlands," in *Women, Policing, and Male Violence: International Perspectives*, ed., Jalna Hanmer, Jill Radford, and Elizabeth A. Stanko (London and New York: Routledge, 1989), pp. 153–54, n. 1.

118. Zoomer, "Policing Woman Beating in the Netherlands," p. 134.

119. Chrisje Brants and Erna Kok, "Penal Sanctions as a Feminist Strategy: A Contradiction in Terms? Pornography and Criminal Law in the Netherlands," *International Journal of the Sociology of Law* 14 (1986), p. 282; Jolande uit Beijerse and Renée Kool, "The Traitorous Temptation of Criminal Justice: Deceptive Appearances? The Dutch Women's Movement, Violence Against Women and

the Criminal Justice System," in *Gender, Sexuality, and Social Control*, ed. Bill Rolston and Mike Tomlinson (Bristol, UK: The European Group for the Study of Deviance and Social Control, 1990): 253–73; and René van Swaaningen, "Feminism, Criminology and Criminal Law: Troublesome Relationships," in *Gender, Sexuality, and Social Control*: 211–37.

120. Andrew Rutherford, *Transforming Criminal Policy: Spheres of Influence in the United States, The Netherlands and England and Wales* (Winchester, UK: Wayside Press, 1996), Chapter 3.

121. Jacquelien Soetenhorst-de Savornin Lohman, "The Victim Issue in the Political Agenda of The Netherlands," *Victimology: An International Journal* 10, no. 1–4 (1985), p. 687.

122. Lohman, "The Victim Issue in the Political Agenda of the Netherlands," p. 694.

123. Jacquelien Soetenhorst, "Victim Support Programs: Between Doing Good and Doing Justice," in *Crime and Its Victims: International Research and Public Policy Issues*, ed. Emilio C. Viano (New York: Hemisphere, 1989).

124. Between 1985 and 1997, the incarceration rate in the Netherlands increased by 123 percent compared to 116 percent in the United States. In the early 1970s, the incarceration rate in the Netherlands was 20 per 100,000 people. By 2000 it stood at 90 per 100,000. The 1970s figure may be somewhat misleading because at the time many offenders were on a waiting list to be incarcerated. Peter J. Tak, "Sentencing and Punishment in the Netherlands," in *Sentencing and Sanctions in Western Countries*, ed. Michael Tonry and Richard S. Frase (Oxford: Oxford University Press, 2001), p. 151; and Peter J. Tak and Anton M. van Kalmthout, "Prison Population Growing Faster in the Netherlands Than in the United States," in *Penal Reform in Overcrowded Times*, ed. Michael Tonry (Oxford: Oxford University Press, 2001), p. 162. See also Nils Christie, *Crime Control as Industry: Toward GULAGS, Western Style*, 2nd ed. (London and New York: Routledge, 1994), pp. 47–48; Josine Junger-Tas, "Dutch Penal Policies Changing Direction," in *Penal Reform in Overcrowded Times*; and René van Swaaningen and Gerard de Jonge, "The Dutch Prison System and Penal Policy in the 1990s: From Humanitarian Paternalism to Penal Business Management," in *Western European Penal Systems: A Critical Anatomy*, ed. Vincenzo Ruggiero, Mick Ryan, and Joe Sim (London: Sage, 1995).

125. R. Amy Elman, *Sexual Subordination and State Intervention: Comparing Sweden and the United States* (Providence, RI: Berghahn Books, 1996), p. 121; and Lizette Alvarez, "Sweden Boldly Exposes a Secret Side of Women's Lives," *The New York Times*, April 6, 2005, p. 4.

126. This discussion of the Swedish case is based primarily on Elman, *Sexual Subordination*.

127. Elman, *Sexual Subordination*, Chapter 2.

128. Maud Eduards, "The Women's Shelter Movement," in *Towards a New Democratic Order? Women's Organizing in Sweden in the 1990s*, ed. Gunnel Gustafsson, Maud Eduards, and Malin Rönnblom (Stockholm: Publica, 1997), in R. Amy Elman, "Unprotected by the Swedish Welfare State Revisited: Assessing a Decade of Reforms for Battered Women," *Women's Studies International Forum* 24, no. 1 (2001), p. 39.

129. Elman, *Sexual Subordination*, p. 71.

130. Elman, *Sexual Subordination*, p. 72.

131. Elman, *Sexual Subordination*, p. 117.

132. Elman, *Sexual Subordination*, p. 119.

133. Elman, "Unprotected by the Swedish Welfare State Revisited."

134. Elman, *Sexual Subordination*, p. 92.
135. On rising conservatism in Swedish penal politics, see Henrik Tham, "Law and Order as a Leftist Project? The Case of Sweden," *Punishment & Society* 3, no. 3 (July 2001): 409–26.
136. Karen Leander, "The Normalization of Swedish Prisons," in *Western European Penal Systems*, pp. 186 and 190–91.
137. Douglas Ashford, *Policy and Politics in Britain: The Limits of Consensus* (Philadelphia: Temple University Press, 1981); Anthony Sampson, *The Changing Anatomy of Britain* (New York: Random House, 1982), esp. Chapter 10; and Gelb, "Social Movement 'Success'."
138. Faragher, "The Police Response to Violence Against Women," p. 121.
139. Kathleen Daly and Meda Chesney-Lind, "Feminism and Criminology," *Justice Quarterly* 5, no. 4 (1988), p. 498; Meda Chesney-Lind, "Preface," in *International Feminist Perspectives in Criminology: Engendering a Discipline*, ed. Nicole Hahn Rafter and Frances Heidensohn (Buckingham, UK: Open University Press, 1995); Laureen Snider, "Female Punishment: From Patriarchy to Backlash?" in *The Blackwell Companion to Criminology*, ed. Colin Sumner (Oxford: Blackwell Publishers, 2003); and Loraine Gelsthorpe and Allison Morris, eds., *Feminist Perspectives in Criminology* (Milton Keynes, UK: Open University Press, 1990).
140. Nicole Hahn Rafter, "Introduction: The Development of Feminist Perspectives on Crime," in *International Feminist Perspectives in Criminology*, p. 7.
141. Dorie Klein, "Crime Through Gender's Prism: Feminist Criminology in the United States," in *International Feminist Perspectives in Criminology*, p. 219.
142. Klein, "Crime Through Gender's Prism," p. 216.
143. See, for example, Catharine A. MacKinnon, "Feminism, Marxism, Method and the State: Toward Feminist Jurisprudence," in *Feminist Legal Theory: Readings in Law and Gender*: 181–200; and Smart, *Feminism and the Power of the Law*. For a good overview of this debate, see Wendy Brown, *States of Injury: Power and Freedom in Late Modernity* (Princeton: Princeton University Press, 1995), esp. Chapter 7.
144. For representative early works in the field of critical criminology, see Richard Quinney, *The Social Reality of Crime* (Boston: Little, Brown, 1970); Stuart Hall, Chas Critcher, Tony Jefferson, John Clarke, and Brian Roberts, *Policing the Crisis: Mugging, the State, and Law and Order* (Houndsmills, UK: Macmillan, 1978); and Alan A. Block and William J. Chambliss, *Organizing Crime* (New York: Elsevier, 1981).
145. For example, Eileen Fairweather charged that "the far left continues to push its lunatic line: that all criminals no matter how vicious are in some way rebelling against capitalism." Eileen Fairweather, "The Law of the Jungle in King's Cross," *New Society* 2 (December 1982), pp. 375–77, cited in Susan Edwards, "Violence Against Women: Feminism and the Law," in *Feminist Perspectives in Criminology*, p. 148.
146. Deborah Sontag, "Fierce Entanglements," *The New York Times Magazine*, November 17, 2002; and Neil S. Websdale, "Predators: The Social Construction of Stranger-Danger in Washington State as a Form of Patriarchal Ideology," *Women and Criminal Justice* 7, no. 2 (1996).
147. Hirschmann, *Toward a Feminist Theory of Freedom*, p. 13.
148. Donna Coker, "Crime Control and Feminist Law Reform in Domestic Violence Law: A Critical Review," *Buffalo Criminal Law Review* 4, no. 2 (2001), p. 807.

149. Joan Zorza and Laurie Woods, *Analysis and Policy Implications of the New Domestic Violence Police Studies* (New York: National Organization for Women Legal Defense and Education Fund, 1994).

150. Chris Lombardi, "Justice for Battered Women," *The Nation*, July 15, 2002, pp. 24–27; Somini Sengupta, "Judge Assails City Agency on Abuse Cases," *The New York Times*, August 18, 2001, p. B-3; and William Glaberson, "New York to Settle With 3 Battered Women Over Removal of Children From Their Homes," *The New York Times*, September 15, 2002, p. 35.

151. Coker, "Crime Control and Feminist Law Reform," pp. 813–14.

152. Linda G. Mills goes so far as to argue that such policies "can themselves be forms of abuse" for battered women. "Killing Her Softly: Intimate Abuse and the Violence of State Intervention," *Harvard Law Journal* 113 (December 1999), p. 554; and Linda G. Mills, "Intuition and Insight: A New Job Description for the Battered Woman's Prosecutor and Other More Modest Proposals," *UCLA Women's Law Journal* 7, no. 2 (1997). See also Sontag, "Fierce Entanglements"; and Buzawa and Buzawa, *Domestic Violence: The Criminal Justice Response*, pp. 122–24.

153. The number of nonfatal crimes by intimate partners against women declined by nearly half between 1993 and 2001. Still, these crimes remain a serious problem, comprising 20 percent of all violent crime against women in 2001. Callie Marie Rennison, "Intimate Partner Violence, 1993–2001," *Bureau of Justice Statistics; Crime Data in Brief* (Washington, DC: U.S. Department of Justice, February 2003), p. 1.

154. Since 1995, the annual rate of growth in the number of female inmates has averaged 5.4 percent, compared to 3.6 percent for male inmates. U.S. Bureau of Justice Statistics, *Prison and Jail Inmates at Midyear 2002* (Washington, DC: U.S. Department of Justice, April 2003), p. 5.

155. John Hagan and Ronit Dinovitzer, "Collateral Consequences of Imprisonment for Children, Communities, and Prisoners," in *Crime and Justice: A Review of Research*, vol. 26, *Prisons*, ed. Michael Tonry and Joan Petersilia (Chicago: University of Chicago Press, 1999).

156. Martha Minow, "Between Vengeance and Forgiveness: Feminist Responses to Violent Injustice," *New England Law Review* 32, no. 4 (Summer 1998), p. 974.

157. Minow, "Between Vengeance and Forgiveness," p. 972.

158. John Braithwaite and Kathleen Daly, "Masculinities, Violence and Communitarian Control," in *Just Boys Doing Business? Men, Masculinity and Crime*, ed. Tim Newburn and Elizabeth B. Stanko (London: Routledge, 1994.) See also Freeman-Longo, "Reducing Sexual Abuse in America"; and Lois Presser and Emily Gaarder, "Can Restorative Justice Reduce Battering? Some Preliminary Considerations," *Social Justice* 27, no. 1 (Spring 2000): 175–95.

159. Minow, "Between Vengeance and Forgiveness," p. 969. See also Heather Strang, *Repair or Revenge: Victims and Restorative Justice* (Oxford: Clarendon Press, 2002), Chapter 3.

160. John Braithwaite and Philip Pettit, *Not Just Deserts: A Republican Theory of Criminal Justice* (Oxford: Oxford University Press, 1990); and John Braithwaite and Philip Pettit, "Comment – Republican Criminology and Victim Advocacy," *Law & Society Review* 28, no. 4 (1994): 765–76.

161. Braithwaite and Daly, "Masculinities, Violence and Communitarian Control," p. 209.

162. Margaret Hobart, "Review: Strategies for Confronting Domestic Violence: A Resource Manual by United Nations Center for Social Development and Humanitarian Affairs," *Women & Politics* 17, no. 1 (1997): 99–101.

163. Lisa G. Lerman, "Mediation of Wife Abuse Cases: The Adverse Impact of Informal Dispute Resolution on Women," *Harvard Women's Law Journal* 7, no. 1 (Spring 1984); Buzawa and Buzawa, *Domestic Violence: The Criminal Justice Response*, p. 80; and Janet Rifkin, "Mediation in the Justice System: A Paradox for Women," *Women & Criminal Justice* 1, no. 1 (1989): 41–54. On the history of the family courts, see Dobash and Dobash, *Women, Violence and Social Change*, pp. 158–60.

164. Howard Davidson, "Community Control Without State Control: Issues Surrounding a Feminist and Prison Abolitionist Approach to Violence Against Women," in *Abolitionism: Towards a Non-Repressive Approach to Crime*, ed. Herman Bianchi and René van Swaaningen (Amsterdam: Free University Press, 1986), p. 133.

165. Liv Finstad, "Sexual Offenders Out of Prison: Principles for a Realistic Utopia," *International Journal of the Sociology of Law* 18 (May 1990), p. 166.

166. Braithwaite and Pettit, "Comment," pp. 773–74; Stuart A. Scheingold, Toska Olson, and Jana Pershing, "Sexual Violence, Victim Advocacy, and Republican Criminology: Washington State's Community Protection Act," *Law & Society Review* 28, no. 4 (1994), p. 731; and Kathleen Daly, "Comment – Men's Violence, Victim Advocacy, and Feminist Redress," *Law & Society Review* 28, no. 4 (1994), p. 780.

167. Daly proposes an alternative that would "bring the suffering and injustice of victims to light, see victimization in social and relational terms, and work toward changing relations of power, privilege, and dependency." Daly, "Comment – Men's Violence," p. 780.

168. M. Kay Harris, "Moving Into the New Millennium: Toward a Feminist Vision of Justice," *Prison Journal* 67, no. 2 (Fall-Winter 1987): 27–38; and Laureen Snider, "Criminalization: Panacea for Men Who Assault Women but Anathema for Corporate Criminals," in *Social Inequality, Social Justice*, ed. Dawn H. Currie and Brian D. MacLean (Vancouver: Collective Press, 1994), p. 110.

169. Chesney-Lind, "Preface," p. xiii; and Pitch, "Critical Criminology, the Construction of Social Problems, and the Question of Rape." Laureen Snider suggests that while criminal laws and penal policies may be able to achieve important symbolic gains, the costs can be severe as they distract attention from more promising avenues of change. She faults feminists and other groups for being so "susceptible to 'agendas of criminalization'" and so uncritical of the social control function of the state. Snider, "Criminalization: Panacea for Men Who Assault Women," pp. 102 and 109; and Laureen Snider, "Towards Safer Societies: Punishment, Masculinities and Violence Against Women," *The British Journal of Criminology* 38, no. 1 (Winter 1998), p. 15.

170. Claire Reinelt, "Moving onto the Terrain of the State: The Battered Women's Movement and the Politics of Engagement," in *Feminist Organizations: Harvest of the New Women's Movement*, ed. Myra Marx Ferree and Patricia Yancey Martin (Philadelphia: Temple University Press, 1995), pp. 98 and 101. See also Schneider, *Battered Women and Feminist Lawmaking*, p. 198; and Brown, *States of Injury*, Chapter 7.

171. For a development of this point, see Mary Fainsod Katzenstein, "Comparing the Feminist Movements of the United States and Western Europe," in *The Women's Movements of the United States and Western Europe*, p. 5.

172. Gregg Barak, "Feminist Connections and the Movement Against Domestic Violence: Beyond Criminal Justice Reform," *Journal of Crime & Justice* 9 (1986), p. 151.
173. See, for example, Schechter, *Women and Male Violence.*
174. Schneider, *Battered Women and Feminist Lawmaking*, pp. 27–28. Wini Breines and Linda Gordon make a similar point in "The New Scholarship on Family Violence," *Signs* 8, no. 3 (Spring 1983): 490–531. There are some notable exceptions. See, for example, Elizabeth Pleck, *Domestic Tyranny: The Making of Social Policy Against Family Violence from Colonial Times to the Present* (New York: Oxford University Press, 1987); Linda Gordon, *Heroes of Their Own Lives: The Politics and History of Family Violence: Boston, 1880–1960* (New York: Viking, 1988); and the review essay by Judith R. Walkowitz, "The Politics of Prostitution," *Signs* 6, no. 1 (Autumn 1980): 123–35.
175. Ferraro does make this point about the U.S. case. Ferraro, "The Legal Response to Women Battering," p. 181.
176. For a development of this point, see Jean Bethke Elshtain, "Politics and the Battered Woman," *Dissent*, Winter 1985, p. 57.

CHAPTER 7: FROM RIGHTS TO REVOLUTION: PRISON ACTIVISM AND THE CARCERAL STATE

1. George Jackson, *Blood in My Eye* (New York: Random House, 1972), pp. 99–100.
2. Marc Mauer, *Race to Incarcerate* (New York: The New Press, 1999).
3. James B. Jacobs, "The Prisoners' Rights Movement and Its Impacts, 1960–80," in *Crime and Justice: An Annual Review of Research*, vol. 2, ed. Norval Morris and Michael Tonry (Chicago: University of Chicago Press, 1980), p. 431.
4. Gerald N. Rosenberg, *The Hollow Hope: Can Courts Bring About Social Change?* (Chicago: University of Chicago Press, 1991), p. 338.
5. Margo Schlanger suggests that by "promoting the comforting idea of the 'lawful prison,' the litigation movement may have smoothed the way for even harsher sentences and criminal policies." See, "Beyond the Hero Judge: Institutional Reform Litigation as Litigation," *Michigan Law Review* 97 (May 1999), n. 19. Malcolm M. Feeley and Edwin L. Rubin echo this view. See *Judicial Policy Making and the Modern State: How the Courts Reformed America's Prisons* (Cambridge: Cambridge University Press, 1998), p. 375.
6. For an account that stresses and laments the emphasis on the rights of victims at the expense of offenders, see Frank Carrington and George Nicholson, "The Victims' Movement: An Idea Whose Time Has Come," *Pepperdine Law Review* 11 (1984): 1–14. For one that identifies and laments a conservative backlash because of the expansion of prisoners' rights, see Katherine Beckett and Theodore Sasson, *The Politics of Injustice: Crime and Punishment in America* (Thousand Oaks, CA: Pine Forge Press, 2000), pp. 156–57.
7. For a good introduction to this literature, see Michael Ignatieff, "State, Civil Society, and Total Institutions: A Critique of Recent Social Histories of Punishment," in *Crime and Justice: An Annual Review of Research*, vol. 3, ed. Norval Morris and Michael Tonry (Chicago: University of Chicago Press, 1981), pp. 153–92.
8. David J. Rothman, *The Discovery of the Asylum: Social Order and Disorder in the New Republic*, rev. ed. (Boston: Little, Brown and Company, 1990). See also

David J. Rothman, *Conscience and Convenience: The Asylum and Its Alternatives in Progressive America* (Boston: Little, Brown and Co., 1980).

9. For an explanation that emphasizes a combination of economic and humanitarian motivations, see Michael Ignatieff, *A Just Measure of Pain: The Penitentiary in the Industrial Revolution, 1750–1850* (New York: Columbia University Press, 1978); and Alexander W. Pisciotta, *Benevolent Repression: Social Control and the American Reformatory Prison Movement* (New York: NYU Press, 1994). On the need to control restive populations, see Anthony M. Platt, *The Child Savers*, 2nd ed. (Chicago: University of Chicago Press, 1977). On prisons and the diffuse exercise of power, see Michel Foucault, *Discipline and Punishment: The Birth of the Prison* (New York: Vintage Books, 1979). On how prisons and the idea of the penitentiary were used self-consciously to bolster state power and legitimacy in the founding decades, see Thomas L. Dumm, *Democracy and Punishment: Disciplinary Origins of the United States* (Madison: University of Wisconsin Press, 1987).

10. For an excellent overview of the range of opinions on these issues, see the contributions to John J. DiIulio, Jr., ed., *Courts, Corrections, and the Constitution: The Impact of Judicial Intervention on Prisons and Jails* (New York: Oxford University Press, 1990).

11. Jacobs, "The Prisoners' Rights Movement," p. 460. See also James B. Jacobs, *Stateville: The Penitentiary in Mass Society* (Chicago: University of Chicago Press, 1977); Feeley and Rubin, *Judicial Policy Making and the Modern State*; Ben M. Crouch and James W. Marquart, *An Appeal to Justice: Litigated Reform of Texas Prisons* (Austin: University of Texas Press, 1989), p. 233; and Stuart A. Scheingold, *The Politics of Rights: Lawyers, Public Policy, and Political Change* (New Haven: Yale University Press, 1974), p. 131.

12. The Tucker telephone, used by the Tucker Reformatory in Arkansas, shot electric current through telephone wires attached to a prisoner's genitals. Alvin J. Bronstein, "Reform Without Change: The Future of Prisoners' Rights," *The Civil Liberties Review* 4, no. 3 (1977), p. 28.

13. Jacobs, "The Prisoners' Rights Movement," pp. 462 and 465.

14. Jacobs, "The Prisoners' Rights Movement," pp. 458–59; and Jacobs, *Stateville*, Chapters 5 and 6. On the positive effects of judicial intervention on jails, see Wayne N. Welsh, *Counties in Court: Jail Overcrowding and Court-Ordered Reform* (Philadelphia: Temple University Press, 1995).

15. See, for example, William A. Taggart, "Redefining the Power of the Federal Judiciary: The Impact of Court-Ordered Prison Reform on State Expenditures for Corrections," *Law & Society Review* 23, no. 2 (1989): 241–72.

16. On implementation issues, see Donald P. Baker, Randolph M. Blotky, Keith M. Clemens, and Michael L. Dillard, "Judicial Intervention in Corrections: The California Experience – An Empirical Study," *UCLA Law Review* 20 (1972–73): 452–580; and M. Kay Harris and Dudley P. Spiller, Jr., *After Decision: Implementation of Judicial Decrees in Correctional Settings* (Washington, DC: American Bar Association, 1976), pp. 25–26, cited in Rosenberg, *The Hollow Hope*, p. 306; and David F. Greenberg and Fay Stender, "The Prison as a Lawless Agency," *Buffalo Law Review* 21, no. 3 (Spring 1972): 799–838.

17. Jacobs, largely a champion of the positive effects of the prisoners' rights movement, also concedes some of these points. See *Stateville*, Chapters 5 and 6. See also John J. DiIulio, Jr., "Understanding Prisons: The New Old Penology," *Law and Social Inquiry* 16, no. 1 (Winter 1991): 65–99; John J. DiIulio, Jr., *Governing Prisons: A Comparative Study of Correctional Management* (New York: Free

Press, 1987); and Mark Colvin, "The 1980 New Mexico Prison Riot," *Social Problems* 29, no. 5 (June 1982), p. 459. For an overview of the prison violence literature, see Anthony E. Bottoms, "Interpersonal Violence and Social Order in Prisons," in *Crime and Justice – A Review of Research*, vol. 26, *Prisons*, ed. Michael Tonry and Joan Petersilia (Chicago and London: University of Chicago Press, 1999), pp. 205–81.

18. Jacobs, "The Prisoners' Rights Movement," p. 434.

19. Crouch and Marquart, *An Appeal to Justice*, pp. 230–31. For alternative views of the Texas case, see John J. DiIulio, Jr., "The Old Regime and the *Ruiz* Revolution: The Impact of Judicial Intervention on Texas Prisons," in *Courts, Corrections, and the Constitution*; and Sheldon Ekland-Olson and Steve J. Martin, "*Ruiz*: A Struggle Over Legitimacy," in *Courts, Corrections, and the Constitution*. Mark Colvin attributes the extreme violence and brutality of the 1980 riot at the Penitentiary of New Mexico in Santa Fe to an authority vacuum created as a new and incompetent prison administration tried to wrest control of the facility from prisoners, upending long-standing patterns of control and relationships that had kept the prison relatively calm. Colvin, "The 1980 New Mexico Prison Riot." See also Adolph Saenz, *Politics of a Prison Riot: The 1980 Prison Riot, Its Consequences and Aftermath* (Corrales, NM: Rhombus Publishing Co., 1986).

20. Crouch and Marquart, *An Appeal to Justice*, p. 236.

21. Bronstein concludes that "[m]ost prison systems are so diseased and bankrupt" that the achievements of the prisoners' rights movement "represent only the smallest and earliest steps of a very long journey." Bronstein, "Reform Without Change," p. 44. On the ACLU's involvement in prisoner issues from the mid-1960s to the mid-1970s, see Samuel Walker, *In Defense of American Liberties: A History of the ACLU*, 2nd. ed. (Carbondale: Southern Illinois University Press, 1999), pp. 310–12.

22. Susan P. Sturm, "Resolving the Remedial Dilemma: Strategies of Judicial Intervention in Prisons," *University of Pennsylvania Law Review* 138 (1990), pp. 910–11. Rosenberg makes a similar point when he concludes in *The Hollow Hope* that "[m]any of the worst conditions have been improved to at least minimal standards, but problems still abound." See p. 307.

23. For those who claim that the judiciary's role and significance are overstated, see Rosenberg, *The Hollow Hope*; Charles R. Epp, *The Rights Revolution: Lawyers, Activists, and Supreme Courts in Comparative Perspective* (Chicago: University of Chicago Press, 1998); Schlanger, "Beyond the Hero Judge"; Susan P. Sturm, "Lawyers at the Prison Gates: Organizational Structure and Prison Advocacy," *University of Michigan Journal of Law Reform* 27, no. 1 (1993). For those who accord judges a significant if not preeminent role, see Feeley and Rubin, *Judicial Policy Making and the Modern State*; and Jacobs, "The Prisoners' Rights Movement."

24. For a succinct overview of this debate, see Peter H. Schuck, "Public Law Litigation and Social Reform," *Yale Law Journal* 102, no. 2 (May 1993), pp. 1769–70.

25. *Birmingham Post-Herald*, January 15, 1976, p. 1., cited in Tinsley E. Yarbrough, "The Alabama Prison Litigation," *Justice System Journal* 9, no. 3 (1984), p. 287.

26. Jacobs, "The Prisoners' Rights Movement," p. 431. Scheingold, for example, contends that an emphasis on rights is a potentially powerful political tool that can prompt a realignment of political forces that is beneficial to disadvantaged groups in society like prisoners. Stuart A. Scheingold, *The Politics of Rights*, pp. 148 and 211.

27. See, for example, Ronald Berkman, *Opening the Gates: The Rise of the Prisoners' Movement* (Lexington, MA: Lexington Books, 1979); and Steve J. Martin and Sheldon Ekland-Olson, *Texas Prisons: The Walls Come Tumbling Down* (Austin: Texas Monthly Press, 1987).

28. Epp, *The Rights Revolution*, pp. 18–21 and Chapter 3. For more on how Epp's argument relates to my own, see pp. 228 in this volume.

29. Mary Frances Berry and John Blassingame, "American Archipelago: Blacks and Criminal Justice," in *Race, Class, and Gender: An Anthology*, ed. Margaret L. Andersen and Patricia Hill Collins (Belmont, CA: Wadsworth Publishing, 1992), p. 435.

30. Between 1930 and 1936, the black incarceration rate rose substantially to a level about three times greater than for whites, while the white incarceration rate actually decreased. Hans von Hentig, "The Criminality of the Negro," *Journal of the American Institute of Criminal Law and Criminology* 30 (March–April 1940), p. 663.

31. Scott Christianson, "Our Black Prisoners," *Crime & Delinquency* 27, no. 3 (July 1981): 364–75.

32. Calculated from Desmond King, *Separate and Unequal: Black Americans and the U.S. Federal Government* (Oxford: Clarendon Press, 1995), p. 147, Table 5.1. These figures mask some important differences between federal institutions, some of which had black-majority populations by the 1950s. King, *Separate and Unequal*, p. 164, Table 5.6.

33. Loïc Wacquant, "Suitable Enemies: Foreigners and Immigrants in the Prisons of Europe," *Punishment & Society* 1, no. 2 (October 1999): 215–32.

34. On the major periods of prison unrest in the United States, see Vernon Fox, *Violence Behind Bars: An Explosive Report on Prison Riots in the United States* (New York: Vantage Press, 1956), p. 13; Robert Adams and Jo Campling, *Prison Riots in Britain and the USA* (New York: St. Martin's Press, 1992), Chapter 3; G. David Garson, "The Disruption of Public Administration: An Investigation of Alternative Theories of the Relationship Among Administrators, Reformers, and Involuntary Social Service Clients," *Law & Society Review* 6, no. 4 (May 1972): 531–61; and Bert Useem and Peter Kimball, *States of Siege: U.S. Prison Riots, 1971–1986* (New York: Oxford University Press, 1989), p. 19.

35. Fox, *Violence Behind Bars*, pp. 22 and 45. For more on Hoover and penal policy, see p. 62 of this volume.

36. Useem and Kimball, *States of Siege*, p. 19.

37. Fox, *Violence Behind Bars*.

38. John Pallas and Robert Barber, "From Riot to Revolution," *Issues in Criminology* 7, no. 2 (Fall 1972), pp. 3–4.

39. Larry E. Sullivan, *The Prison Reform Movement: Forlorn Hope* (Boston: Twayne Publishers, 1990), p. 46; and Richard McCleary, "Correctional Administration and Political Change," in *Prison Within Society*, ed. Lawrence Hazelrigg (Garden City, NY: Doubleday, 1968), p. 130, cited in Pallas and Barber, "From Riot to Revolution," p. 3.

40. Fox, *Violence Behind Bars*, p. 311. Many of the riots took place in state-level institutions that underwent major transformations after World War II, as lax, convict-run prisons were replaced by reform-oriented institutions under tighter control of professional administrators. William D. Pederson, "Inmate Movements and Prison Uprisings: A Comparative Study," *Social Science Quarterly* 59, no. 3 (December 1978): 509–24.

41. See, for example, Austin H. MacCormick, "Behind the Prison Riots," *Annals* 293 (May 1954): 17–27.

42. King, *Separate and Unequal.*

43. The phrase "housekeeping demands" comes from Berkman, who says, "What was at stake in the riots of the 1950s was not the architecture of the house, but the way it was kept." Berkman, *Opening the Gates,* p. 39. Adams and Campling characterize the riots from the 1930s to early 1950s as primarily protests against prison conditions, but note that the number of riots involving collective consciousness and broader-based demands rose in the late 1950s. Adams and Campling, *Prison Riots in Britain and the USA,* p. 46.

44. On the effects of World War II on American political development, see, for example, Daniel Kryder, *Divided Arsenal: Race and the American State During World War II* (Cambridge: Cambridge University Press, 2000); and Bartholomew H. Sparrow, *From the Outside In: World War II and the American State* (Princeton: Princeton University Press, 1996).

45. United States Bureau of Prisons, Archives Division, Proceedings of the Federal Prison Wardens Conference 1944, p. 5, "Introductory Remarks," James V. Bennett, director of the Bureau of Prisons, cited in King, *Separate and Unequal,* p. 147.

46. K. Butler, "The Muslims Are No Longer an Unknown Quantity," *Corrections Magazine* 4, no. 2 (1978), pp. 55–57 and 60–63, cited in Adams and Campling, *Prison Riots in Britain and the USA,* p. 75.

47. King, *Separate and Unequal,* p. 144. See also King's discussion of the race riot that was narrowly averted in 1951 at the Mill Point Penitentiary in West Virginia, pp. 162–63.

48. Walker, *In Defense of American Liberties,* pp. 149–51.

49. Desmond King, "A Strong or Weak State? Race and the US Federal Government in the 1920s," *Ethnic and Racial Studies* 21, no. 1 (January 1998): 21–47.

50. King, *Separate and Unequal,* p. 170.

51. King, *Separate and Unequal,* p. 150; and James B. Jacobs, "Race Relations and the Prisoner Subculture," in *Crime and Punishment: An Annual Review of Research,* vol. 1, ed. Norval Morris and Michael Tonry (Chicago: Chicago University Press, 1979), pp. 4–5.

52. United States Bureau of Prisons, Archives Division, Prisoners' Welfare, Box 41, File segregation, letter from Director James Bennett to Jean Henry, Race Discrimination in the War Effort, August 5, 1943, cited in King, *Separate and Unequal,* pp. 163–64.

53. King, *Separate and Unequal,* p. 164.

54. Useem and Kimball, *States of Siege,* pp. 8–11.

55. "It literally took a war to blast our prisons out of stagnation and routine and set them once more on the road to reform and progress." Harry Elmer Barnes, *Report on the Progress of the State Prison War Program Under the Government Division of the War Production Board* (Washington, DC: War Production Board, 1944), p. 1. See also pp. 39 and 94; and Maury Maverick and William H. Burke, *Prisons in Wartime: Report on the Progress of State Prison Industries Under the Government Division of the War Production Board* (Washington, DC: War Production Board, November 1943).

56. Eric Cummins, *The Rise and Fall of California's Radical Prison Movement* (Stanford, CA: Stanford University Press, 1994), p. 9. See also Shelley Bookspan,

A Germ of Goodness: The California State Prison System, 1851–1944 (Lincoln: University of Nebraska Press, 1991), esp. Chapter 6.

57. Cummins, *The Rise and Fall of California's Radical Prison Movement*, p. 12.
58. Cummins, *The Rise and Fall of California's Radical Prison Movement*, p. 14.
59. Leo Carroll, *Hacks, Blacks, and Cons: Race Relations in a Maximum Security Prison* (Lexington, MA: Lexington Books, 1974).
60. This discussion of "bibliotherapy" is based primarily on Cummins, *The Rise and Fall of California's Radical Prison Movement*, Chapter 2.
61. Theodore Hamm, *Rebel and a Cause: Caryl Chessman and the Politics of the Death Penalty in Postwar California, 1948–1974* (Berkeley: University of California Press, 2001), p. 7.
62. According to Hamm, this put Chessman in somewhat of a bind because he had refused all along to admit his guilt. Hamm, *Rebel and a Cause*, Chapter 3.
63. For more on the Chessman case and the death penalty, see p. 205.
64. Chessman's notoriety provoked a backlash from prison authorities. Richard A. McGee, California's director of corrections, ordered all manuscripts written by prisoners on death row confiscated until after their executions. Cummins, *The Rise and Fall of California's Radical Prison Movement*, p. 41.
65. See Hamm, *Rebel and a Cause*, Chapter 3. See also Roger E. Schwed, *Abolition and Capital Punishment: The United States' Judicial, Political, and Moral Barometer* (New York: AMS Press, Inc., 1983), pp. 73–91.
66. Hamm, *Rebel and a Cause*, p. 135. For an anguished personal account of the Chessman execution written nearly four decades after the fact, see Edmund G. (Pat) Brown with Dick Adler, *Public Justice, Private Mercy: A Governor's Education on Death Row* (New York: Weidenfeld & Nicolson, 1989), esp. Chapter 2.
67. Hamm, *Rebel and a Cause*, p. 63.
68. Jacobs, "The Prisoners' Rights Movement," p. 431; Berkman, *Opening the Gates*, pp. 50–55; and John Irwin, *Prisons in Turmoil* (Boston: Little, Brown, 1980), pp. 68–69.
69. Jacobs, "Race Relations and the Prisoner Subculture," p. 8.
70. Cummins, *The Rise and Fall of California's Radical Prison Movement*, p. 65.
71. Pallas and Barber, "From Riot to Revolution," p. 7.
72. Pallas and Barber, "From Riot to Revolution," p. 7.
73. Jacobs, "The Prisoners' Rights Movement."
74. Berkman, *Opening the Gates*, p. 52.
75. Steve Fischer, "Due Process Rights of Prisoners," in *Encyclopedia of American Prisons*, ed. Marilyn D. McShane and Frank P. Williams, III (New York and London: Garland Publishing, 1996), p. 174; and Feeley and Rubin, *Judicial Policy Making and the Modern State*, pp. 30–34.
76. Scott Christianson, *With Liberty for Some: 500 Years of Imprisonment in America* (Boston: Northeastern University Press, 1998), pp. 252–53.
77. Feeley and Rubin, *Judicial Policy Making and the Modern State*, p. 37.
78. For concise summaries of these landmark legal cases, see Rosenberg, *Hollow Hope*; Gordon Hawkins, *The Prison: Policy and Practice* (Chicago: University of Chicago Press, 1976), Chapter 6; Schlanger, "Beyond the Hero Judge"; Feeley and Rubin, *Judicial Policy Making and the Modern State*, Chapter 2; Lawrence M. Friedman, *Crime and Punishment in American History* (New York: Basic Books, 1993), pp. 309–16; Jacobs, "The Prisoners' Rights Movement," pp. 434–36; Fischer, "Due Process Rights of Prisoners," pp. 174–76;

Christianson, *With Liberty for Some*, pp. 254–64; and Berkman, *Opening the Gates*, pp. 40–49.

79. *Wolff v. McDonnell* 418 U.S. 539 (1974), quoted in Useem and Kimball, *States of Siege*, p. 12.

80. Berkman, *Opening the Gates*, pp. 53–54; and Irwin, *Prisons in Turmoil*, p. 70.

81. Berkman, *Opening the Gates*, p. 55.

82. Jacobs, *Stateville*; Jacobs, "The Prisoners' Rights Movement," p. 435; and Juanita Díaz-Cotto, *Gender, Ethnicity and the State: Latina and Latino Prison Politics* (Albany: SUNY Press, 1996).

83. Berkman, *Opening the Gates*, p. 50.

84. Pallas and Barber, "From Riot to Revolution," p. 6.

85. On penal farm conditions, see Feeley and Rubin, *Judicial Policy Making and the Modern State*, pp. 52–54; and Mark T. Carleton, *Politics and Punishment: The History of the Louisiana Penal System* (Baton Rouge: Louisiana State University Press, 1971), esp. Chapters 5 and 6 on conditions at Louisiana's Angola prison, dubbed "America's worst prison."

86. The sixth was Oklahoma. Feeley and Rubin, *Judicial Policy Making and the Modern State*, p. 41.

87. While many of the remaining non-Southern states faced extensive litigation, most of this litigation involved individual penal facilities, not entire state systems. Feeley and Rubin, *Judicial Policy Making and the Modern State*, p. 42.

88. Feeley and Rubin, *Judicial Policy Making and the Modern State*, p. 150.

89. Schlanger, "Beyond the Hero Judge," n. 85; and Jack Greenberg, *Crusaders in the Courts: How a Dedicated Band of Lawyers Fought for the Civil Rights Revolution* (New York: Basic Books, 1994), Chapters 31 and 32.

90. It is important here not to overstate the significance of the South at the cost of underplaying important simultaneous developments involving prisons in the North. Prison-related litigation was certainly more prevalent in the South than elsewhere and attracted more national attention. But "the southern cases happened concurrent with, not earlier than, prison and jail cases all over the nation in which courts ordered remedies for unconstitutional conditions." Schlanger, "Beyond the Hero Judge," pp. 2028–30.

91. David J. Rothman, "Decarcerating Prisoners and Patients," *Civil Liberties Review* 1 (1973), pp. 8 and 14, cited in Schlanger, "Beyond the Hero Judge," n. 85.

92. Prisoners' rights groups received about $200 million from foundations in 1969, the first year any such grants were made. By 1975, they were receiving about $900 million a year from foundations. Over the next five years funding dropped but still averaged over $600 million annually. Data from Craig Jenkins, as cited in Useem and Kimball, *States of Siege*, p. 41 and p. 252, n. 41.

93. American Bar Association, Commission on Correctional Facilities and Services, *When Society Pronounces Judgment* (Washington, DC: American Bar Association, 1975), cited in Jacobs, "The Prisoners' Rights Movement," p. 438.

94. Jacobs, "The Prisoners' Rights Movement," pp. 437–38. In August 1971 the U.S. Department of Justice, with the written approval of John Mitchell, Nixon's attorney general, intervened on behalf of prisoners in Mississippi, the first time the federal government had done so in a prison reform suit. R. Welch, "Developing Prisoner Self-Help Techniques: The Early Mississippi Experience," *Prison Law Monitor* 2 (October 1979), p. 118.

95. Useem and Kimball, *States of Siege*, p. 41.

96. These resources dried up after the Reagan administration assumed office in 1981. The Justice Department halted initiation of new lawsuits for several years and even switched sides in a number of ongoing court cases. On the role of the U.S. Department of Justice, see Schlanger, "Beyond the Hero Judge," pp. 2024–26.

97. For an overview of this urban unrest, see Jerome H. Skolnick, *The Politics of Protest* (New York: Ballantine Books, 1969).

98. Useem and Kimball, *States of Siege*, p. 18. While analysts agree on this upward trend, their year-by-year numbers differ somewhat. Larry Sullivan counts thirty-nine prison riots in 1969 and fifty-nine in 1970. See *The Prison Reform Movement*, p. 94.

99. Irwin, *Prisons in Turmoil*, p. 87.

100. Berkman, *Opening the Gates*, p. 58; and Irwin, *Prisons in Turmoil*, pp. 72–76.

101. Pallas and Barber, "From Riot to Revolution," p. 11.

102. For more on the San Quentin riot, see Berkman, *Opening the Gates*, pp. 58–60.

103. Skolnick, *The Politics of Protest*, p. 129; and Berkman, *Opening the Gates*, p. 101.

104. Berkman, *Opening the Gates*, p. 101.

105. He later rejects this view. Eldridge Cleaver, *Soul on Ice* (New York: Dell Publishing, 1968), pp. 13–17.

106. Irwin, *Prisons in Turmoil*, p. 77; and Sullivan, *The Prison Reform Movement*, Chapter 6.

107. Cummins, *The Rise and Fall of California's Radical Prison Movement*, p. 61.

108. Sostre was an imprisoned Puerto Rican activist who became a cause célèbre in the United States and abroad. Amnesty International declared him a political prisoner and his case drew the support of renowned international figures, most notably the Soviet dissident Andrei Sakharov. Díaz-Cotto, *Gender, Ethnicity and the State*, pp. 31–34.

109. For example, a 1968 manifesto published in the *Berkeley Barb*, a leading publication of the New Left in the Bay Area, declared: "The future of our struggle is the future of crime in the streets." The position of the White Panthers in Ann Arbor was: "Free all prisoners everywhere – they are our brothers." Cummins, *The Rise and Fall of California's Radical Prison Movement*, pp. 125 and 127. See also p. 93 and Chapter 7 on George Jackson.

110. Cummins, *The Rise and Fall of California's Radical Prison Movement*, p. 126.

111. Cummins, *The Rise and Fall of California's Radical Prison Movement*, p. 94, and Chapter 6. For more on the radicals' romanticization of prisons and prisoners, see Irwin, *Prisons in Turmoil*, pp. 116–117; and Karen Wald, "The San Quentin Six Case: Perspective and Analysis," in *Punishment and Penal Discipline: Essays on the Prison and the Prisoners' Movement*, ed. Tony Platt and Paul Takagi (San Francisco: Crime and Social Justice Associates, 1980), pp. 165–75.

112. Irwin, *Prisons in Turmoil*, Appendix A, pp. 249–62.

113. Berkman, *Opening the Gates*, p. 79; and Irwin, *Prisons in Turmoil*, pp. 107–10. The California uprisings had a ripple effect even in out-of-the-way places like the prison in Walla Walla, Wash. See Charles Stastny and Gabrielle Tyrnauer, *Who Rules the Joint? The Changing Political Culture of Maximum-Security Prisons in America* (Lexington, MA: D.C. Heath, 1982), pp. 135–58.

114. Irwin, *Prisons in Turmoil*, p. 119.

115. The survey found that while a high proportion of the prisoners exhibited quasi-radical or militant views, virtually none exhibited full-blown ideologies similar to those espoused by George Jackson or Eldridge Cleaver. Robert Johnson and

Dennis D. Dorin, "Dysfunctional Ideology: The Black Revolutionary in Prison," in *Offenders and Corrections*, ed. Denis Szabo and Susan Katzenelson (New York: Praeger, 1978), p. 41.

116. According to Irwin, a careful reading of these manifestos "confirms the protesting prisoners' reasonableness, insight, and sophistication." Irwin, *Prisons in Turmoil*, p. 151. See also Hawkins, *The Prison: Policy and Practice*, pp. 76–77; and Irwin, *Prisons in Turmoil*, Appendix E, pp. 255–59.

117. Irwin, *Prisons in Turmoil*, p. 87.

118. Irwin, *Prisons in Turmoil*, p. 109.

119. See, for example, George L. Jackson, *Soledad Brother: The Prison Letters of George Jackson* (New York: Coward-McCann, 1970); and Jackson, *Blood in My Eye*, regarded as his political treatise. *Soledad Brother* initially sold more than 400,000 copies before it went out of print. It was reissued in 1994. *Soledad Brother: The Prison Letters of George Jackson*, foreword by Jonathan Jackson, Jr. (Chicago: Lawrence Hill Books, 1994), pp. ix and xi.

120. Cummins, *The Rise and Fall of California's Radical Prison Movement*, p. 139.

121. Díaz-Cotto, *Gender, Ethnicity and the State*, p. 45.

122. Irwin, *Prisons in Turmoil*, p. 120; and Wald, "The San Quentin Six Case: Perspective and Analysis."

123. Useem and Kimball, *States of Siege*, p. 27; and Irwin, *Prisons in Turmoil*, p. 144.

124. Blake McKelvey, *American Prisons: A History of Good Intentions* (Montclair, NJ: Patterson Smith, 1977), p. 373; Yitzhak Bakal, ed., *Closing Correctional Institutions: New Strategies for Youth* (Lexington, MA: Lexington Books, 1973); Jerome G. Miller, *Last One Over the Wall: The Massachusetts Experiment in Closing Reform Schools* (Columbus: Ohio State University Press, 1991); William G. Nagel, *The New Red Barn: A Critical Look at the Modern American Prison* (New York: Walker, 1973); Jessica Mitford, *Kind and Usual Punishment: The Prison Business* (New York: Alfred A. Knopf, 1973); Gordon Hawkins, *The Prison: Policy and Practice*, p. 43; and Lloyd E. Ohlin, ed., *Prisoners in America* (Englewood Cliffs, NJ: Prentice-Hall Inc., 1973).

125. See, for example, Annual Chief Justice Earl Warren Conference on Advocacy in the United States, *A Program for Prison Reform: The Final Report* (Cambridge, MA: The Roscoe Pound-American Trial Lawyers Foundation, 1972); and Twentieth Century Fund Task Force on Criminal Sentencing, *Fair and Certain Punishment* (New York: McGraw-Hill, 1976).

126. Quoted in Gerard Wagner and Fred Cohen, "Attica: A Look at the Causes and the Future," *Criminal Law Bulletin* 7 (1971), p. 832.

127. N.Y. State Special Commission, Attica, *The Official Report of the New York State Special Commission on Attica* (New York: Barton, 1972), p. xix, cited in Adams and Campling, *Prison Riots in Britain and the USA*, p. 85.

128. Thomas J. Hickey, "National Prison Project," in *Encyclopedia of American Prisons*, pp. 329–30; and Walker, *In Defense of American Liberties*, pp. 310–12.

129. Asked in 1972 whether laxness by prison authorities was the main cause of recent prison unrest, 58 percent of the respondents to a 1972 Louis Harris poll answered that "authorities don't understand inmates' needs," while just under a quarter responded that "authorities [are] too easy on inmates." Louis Harris column, *Chicago Tribune*, February 7, 1972, cited in Irwin, *Prisons in Turmoil*, p. 112.

130. Mauer, *Race to Incarcerate*, pp. 15–16. This was a particularly significant reversal for the National Council on Crime and Delinquency, which previously had been advising corrections personnel on how to build bigger and better prisons. Leslie

T. Wilkins, "Crime and Criminal Justice at the Turn of the Century," in *Readings in Criminal Justice*, ed. Richter H. Moore, Jr., Thomas C. Marks, Jr., and Robert V. Barrow (Indianapolis: The Bobbs-Merrill Company, Inc., 1976).

131. For example, the 1974 Master Plan of the Federal Bureau of Prisons called for adding nearly three dozen new correctional institutions. Hawkins, *The Prison*, p. 43.

132. See the discussion of California's Prisoners' Union in Cummins, *The Rise and Fall of California's Radical Prison Movement*, pp. 252–58; and also Irwin, *Prisons in Turmoil*, Chapter 4.

133. Cummins, *The Rise and Fall of California's Radical Prison Movement*, p. 229. Adams and Campling make a similar point. See *Prison Riots in Britain and the USA*, p. 78.

134. Cummins, *The Rise and Fall of California's Radical Prison Movement*, Chapters 9 and 10; and Irwin, *Prisons in Turmoil*, pp. 146–52.

135. Martin and Ekland-Olson, *Texas Prisons*, p. 25.

136. Etheridge Knight et al., *Black Voices From Prison* (New York: Pathfinder Press, 1970), p. 5.

137. Other basic premises of critical criminology are that the definitions of crime are politically and socially constructed by powerful groups and promulgated through ideology and coercion; that criminal acts can be rational and, under certain conditions, a form of resistance to oppressive structures; that official crime statistics reflect "particular definitions and decisions about the enforcement of the law"; and that the causes of crime must be examined from a structuralist point of view. Liz Kelly and Jill Radford, "The Problem of Men: Feminist Perspectives on Sexual Violence," in *Law, Order and the Authoritarian State: Readings in Critical Criminology*, ed. Phil Scraton (Milton Keynes, UK: Open University Press, 1987), pp. 237–38.

138. See Chapter 4 for more on the victims' movement in Britain and elsewhere.

139. Adams and Campling, *Prisons in Britain and the USA*, p. 172; and Herman Bianchi, Mario Simondi, and Ian Taylor, eds., *Deviance and Control in Europe: Papers from the European Group for the Study of Deviance and Social Control* (London: John Wiley, 1975).

140. Michael Cavadino and James Dignan, *The Penal System: An Introduction* (London: Sage, 1992), p. 18; Tim Newburn, *Crime and Criminal Justice Policy* (London and New York: Longman, 1995), pp. 24–25; Mick Ryan, "The Woolf Report: On the Treadmill of Prison Reform?" *The Political Quarterly* 63, no. 1 (January 1992): 50–56; and Joe Sim, "'We Are Not Animals, We Are Human Beings': Prisons, Protest, and Politics in England and Wales, 1969–1990," *Social Justice* 18, no. 3 (Fall 1991), p. 107; and Phil Scraton, Joe Sim, and Paula Skidmore, *Prisons Under Protest* (Buckingham, UK: Open University Press, 1991).

141. Mike Fitzgerald, *Prisoners in Revolt* (New York: Penguin, 1977), p. 49; Roy D. King, "Control in Prisons," in *Accountability and Prisons: Opening Up a Closed World*, ed. Mike Maguire, Jon Vagg, and Rod Morgan (London: Tavistock Publications, 1985); and Mick Ryan, *Politics of Penal Reform* (Harlow, UK: Longman, 1983), p. 35.

142. Fitzgerald, *Prisoners in Revolt*, p. 49.

143. The phrase "electronic coffins" comes from R. King and K. Elliott, *Albany: Birth of a Prison – End of an Era* (London: Routledge and Kegan Paul, 1977), p. 3, quoted in Sim, "'We Are Not Animals'," p. 111. See also pp. 109–10; and Newburn, *Crime and Criminal Justice Policy*, pp. 20–21.

144. Sim, "'We Are Not Animals'," p. 112.

145. Sim, "'We Are Not Animals'," p. 108. See also Elaine Player and Michael Jenkins, "Introduction," in *Prisons After Woolf: Reform Through Riot*, ed. Elaine Player and Michael Jenkins (London: Routledge, 1994).

146. Mick Ryan, *The Acceptable Pressure Group – Inequality in the Penal Lobby: A Case Study of the Howard Lobby and RAP* (Farnborough, UK: Saxon House, 1978), p. 4; and Mick Ryan and Tony Ward, "From Positivism to Postmodernism: Some Theoretical and Strategic Reflections on the Evolution of the Penal Lobby in Britain," *International Journal of the Sociology of the Law* 20 (1992), p. 322.

147. Andrew Rutherford, *Prisons and the Process of Justice: The Reductionist Challenge* (London: Heinemann, 1984), pp. 81–82; Fitzgerald, *Prisoners in Revolt*; and Ryan, *Politics of Penal Reform*, Chapter 3.

148. Fitzgerald, *Prisoners in Revolt*, p. 182.

149. Fitzgerald, *Prisoners in Revolt*, pp. 216–18.

150. Fitzgerald, *Prisoners in Revolt*, p. 181.

151. One exception was in London, where PROP did build some wider grassroots support among trade unions, trades councils, and colleges. Fitzgerald, *Prisoners in Revolt*, pp. 185–86 and 189.

152. Ryan, *The Acceptable Pressure Group*, p. 114.

153. Established in the 1860s and named after John Howard, the late eighteenth-century prison reformer who collected and publicized sensational information on prison conditions in England and Wales, the Howard Association merged with the more militant Penal Reform League in 1921 to become the Howard League for Penal Reform. Ryan, *The Acceptable Pressure Group*, pp. 2–3 and 35–42; and James B. Christoph, *Capital Punishment and British Politics: The British Movement to Abolish the Death Penalty, 1945–57* (Chicago: University of Chicago Press, 1962), pp. 27–29. On the early history of the Howard League, see Ryan, *The Acceptable Pressure Group*, Chapter 3; and Gordon Rose, *The Struggle for Penal Reform: The Howard League and Its Predecessors* (London: Stevens and Sons Limited, 1961).

154. Rose, *The Struggle for Penal Reform*, p. 281.

155. Terrence Morris, *The Observer*, August 27, 1972, quoted in Ryan, *The Acceptable Pressure Group*, p. 87.

156. Ryan, *The Acceptable Pressure Group*, pp. 87–92.

157. Ryan, *The Acceptable Pressure Group*, pp. 77–78 and 157.

158. Ryan and Ward, "From Positivism to Postmodernism," p. 324.

159. Ryan, *The Acceptable Pressure Group*, p. 114.

160. Adams and Campling, *Prison Riots in Britain and the USA*, p. 123.

161. Adams and Campling, *Prison Riots in Britain and the USA*, pp. 159–72; and Newburn, *Crime and Criminal Justice Policy*, p. 24.

162. Fitzgerald, *Prisoners in Revolt*, p. 161.

163. Michael Zander, professor of law at the London School of Economics, quoted in Lord Windlesham, *Responses to Crime*, vol. 1 (Oxford: Clarendon Press, 1987), p. 241.

164. Newburn, *Crime and Criminal Justice Policy*, p. 25; Peter Evans, *The Prison Crisis* (London: Allen and Unwin, 1980), pp. 1–2; Vivien Stern, *Bricks of Shame: Britain's Prisons*, 2nd ed. (London: Penguin Books, 1989), p. 63.

165. "There is a marked reluctance to recognize rights in prisoners in any form which would enhance the court's potential as an overseer of prison conditions." Genevra Richardson, "Judicial Intervention in Prison Life," in *Accountability and Prisons*, p. 52.

166. Larry Gostin and Marie Staunton, "The Case for Prison Standards: Conditions of Confinement, Segregation, and Medical Treatment," in *Accountability and Prisons*.

167. Mike Maguire, Jon Vagg, and Rod Morgan, "Introduction," in *Accountability and Prisons*, p. 6.

168. Genevra Richardson, "From Rights to Expectations," in *Prisons After Woolf*, pp. 80–82.

169. This summary did not even include basic information like the fact that prisoners' letters would be censored. David Leigh, *The Frontiers of Secrecy: Closed Government in Britain* (London: Junction Books, 1980), p. 96.

170. J. E. Thomas and Richard Pooley, *The Exploding Prison: Prison Riots and the Case of Hull* (London: Junction Books, 1980), p. 85.

171. James Fawcett, "Applications of the European Convention on Human Rights," in *Accountability and Prisons*, p. 74. Until the 1979 *St. Germain* decision by Britain's Court of Appeal, procedures of disciplinary hearings were not subject to judicial review. The 1984 *Tarrant* decision permitted but did not guarantee prisoners legal representation at those hearings. Edward Fitzgerald, "Prison Discipline and the Courts," in *Accountability and Prisons*, pp. 33–34 and 36–38. See also Stern, *Bricks of Shame*, pp. 99–101.

172. Leigh, *The Frontiers of Secrecy*, pp. 97–101; Ryan, *Politics of Prison Reform*, p. 84; and Fawcett, "Applications of the European Convention on Human Rights," pp. 74–75.

173. The European Convention on Human Rights has yet to be fully incorporated into British law. However, the Human Rights Act of 1998 does incorporate some specified rights. "Human Rights Act 1998," http://www.hmso.gov.uk/acts/acts1998/19980042.htm (accessed March 25, 2005).

174. By the 1960s, a number of other European countries had accepted the right of individual petition and the compulsory jurisdiction of the Court, making Britain's resistance more stark and vulnerable to outside criticism. The Foreign Office also feared that Britain's failure to accept these two principles was undermining its efforts to condemn the human rights record of the Soviet Union and other Eastern European countries. Lord Windlesham, *Responses to Crime: Penal Policy in the Making*, vol. 2 (Oxford: Clarendon Press, 1993), pp. 368–69.

175. Mick Ryan, "Liberalism and Civil Society: The Pressure Group Politics of Law and Order – Liberty: Networking Criminal Justice in Defense of Civil Liberties, 1979–1997," http://www.psa.ac.uk/cps/1998/ryan.pdf (accessed July 18, 2005).

176. This brief history of the European Commission of Human Rights and the European Court of Human Rights is based on Windlesham, *Responses to Crime*, vol. 2, pp. 368–69; Kenneth Neale, "The European Prison Rules: Contextual, Philosophical and Practical Aspects," in *Imprisonment: European Perspectives*, ed. John Muncie and Richard Sparks (New York: St. Martin's Press, 1991); and Fawcett, "Applications of the European Convention on Human Rights." For more on international developments in penal policy, see pp. 249–52 in this volume.

177. Stern, *Bricks of Shame*, p. 3.

178. Tony Ward, "Review Essay on *Prisons Under Protest*," *Social Justice* 18, no. 3 (1991), p. 227.

179. Adams and Campling, *Prison Riots in Britain and the USA*, p. 105; and Thomas and Pooley, *The Exploding Prison*, p. 21.

180. In the words of Sidney and Beatrice Webb, after 1878 British prisons became a "'silent world,' shrouded, so far as the public is concerned, in almost complete darkness." *English Prisons Under Local Government* (New York: Longmans, Green and Co., 1922), p. 236. See also Séan McConville, "The Victorian Prison: England, 1865–1965," in *The Oxford History of the Prison: The Practice of Punishment in Western Society*, ed. Norval Morris and David J. Rothman (New York: Oxford University Press, 1995).

181. Ryan, *Politics of Prison Reform*, p. 82.

182. Leigh, *The Frontiers of Secrecy*, p. 36; and "What Britain's Freedom of Information Act Means," *The Economist*, December 29, 2004.

183. Fitzgerald, *Prisoners in Revolt*, p. 120; Joe Sim, *Medical Power in Prisons: The Prison Medical Service in England, 1774–1989* (Milton Keynes, UK: Open University Press, 1990), p. 113. On the origins of the Official Secrets Act, see Leigh, *The Frontiers of Secrecy*, pp. 36–38.

184. Leigh, *The Frontiers of Secrecy*, p. 106.

185. Adams and Campling, *Prison Riots in Britain and the USA*, pp. 16 and 118; and Fitzgerald, *Prisoners in Revolt*, p. 136.

186. Adams and Campling, *Prison Riots in Britain and the USA*, p. 121.

187. Sim, *Medical Power in Prisons*, p. 125.

188. John Lea and Jock Young, *What Is To Be Done About Law and Order?* (London: Pluto Press, 1993), esp. Chapters 5 and 6.

189. Windlesham, *Responses to Crime*, vol. 1, pp. 212, 226, 229, and 241–42.

190. Peter Paterson, "Disgrace of the Men Who Run Our Prisons," *Daily Mail*, May 2, 1986, p. 6, from Stern, *Bricks of Shame*, p. 2.

191. *The Times*, July 28, 1990, quoted in Neale, "The European Prison Rules," p. 214.

192. Ryan, "The Woolf Report: On the Treadmill of Prison Reform?," p. 55.

193. Vivien Stern, "The Future of the Voluntary Sector and the Pressure Groups," in *Prisons After Woolf*, p. 245.

194. Player and Jenkins, "Introduction," in *Prisons After Woolf*, p. 10.

195. Adams and Campling, *Prison Riots in Britain and the USA*, p. 169; and Ryan, "The Woolf Report: On the Treadmill of Prison Reform?," pp. 52–53.

196. United Kingdom, Home Office, *Custody, Care and Justice: The Way Ahead for the Prison Service in England and Wales* (London: HMSO, 1991).

197. Ryan, "The Woolf Report: On the Treadmill of Prison Reform?," p. 56; and Mike Nash and Stephen P. Savage, "A Criminal Record? Law, Order, and Conservative Policy," in *Public Policy in Britain*, ed. Stephen P. Savage, Rob Atkinson, and Lynton Robins (Basingstoke, UK: Macmillan, 1994), p. 155.

198. David Downes and Rod Morgan, "'Hostages to Fortune'? The Politics of Law and Order in Post-War Britain," in *The Oxford Handbook of Criminology*, ed. Mike Maguire, Rod Morgan, and Robert Reiner (Oxford: Clarendon Press, 1994), pp. 206–15.

199. For a discussion of penal activism in Australia, see George Zdenkowski and David Brown, *The Prison Struggle: Changing Australia's Penal System* (Ringwood, Australia: Penguin Books, Australia, 1982).

200. Ryan and Ward, "From Positivism to Postmodernism," p. 327.

201. RAP's active membership and financial resources dwindled in the 1980s. By the time its journal the *Abolitionist* ceased publication in 1987, RAP was largely defunct. Established groups, like the National Association of Probation Officers, and newer groups became the torchbearers of RAP's radical tradition. Ryan and Ward, "From Positivism to Postmodernism," pp. 327–28.

202. David A. Ward, "Sweden: The Middle Way to Prison Reform?" in *Prisons: Present and Possible*, ed. Marvin E. Wolfgang (Lexington, MA: D.C. Heath, 1979), p. 126; Thomas Mathiesen and Wiggo Røine, "The Prison Movement in Scandinavia," in *Deviance and Control in Europe*, 85–95; and Ulla Bondeson, *Prisoners in Prison Societies* (New Brunswick, NJ: Transaction Publishers, 1989).

203. Ward, "Sweden: The Middle Way to Prison Reform?" p. 154.

204. On the explosiveness of indeterminate sentences in U.S. prisons, see Samuel Walker, *Taming the System: The Control of Discretion in Criminal Justice, 1950–1990* (New York and Oxford: Oxford University Press, 1993), Chapter 5; Cummins, *The Rise and Fall of California's Radical Prison Movement*, pp. 257–58; and Sheldon Messinger and Philip E. Johnson, "California's Determinate Sentencing Statute: History and Issues," in *The Criminal Justice System: Materials on the Administration and Reform of the Criminal Law*, ed. Franklin E. Zimring and Richard S. Frase (Boston: Little, Brown and Co., 1980): 950–97.

205. Ward, "Sweden: The Middle Way to Prison Reform?" p. 161.

206. KRUM stands for the National Swedish Association for Penal Reform. On the early history of KRUM, see Thomas Mathiesen, *The Politics of Abolition* (New York: John Wiley & Sons, 1974), Chapter 4.

207. Ward, "Sweden: The Middle Way to Prison Reform?" pp. 110–11 and 126. See also David A. Ward, "Inmate Rights and Prison Reform in Sweden and Denmark," *The Journal of Criminal Law, Criminology and Police Science* 63, no. 2 (1972): 240–55.

208. Mathiesen and Røine, "The Prison Movement in Scandinavia," p. 89. On the formidable resistance to prisoner unions in the United States, see Paul R. Comeau, "Labor Unions for Prison Inmates: An Analysis of a Recent Proposal for the Organization of Inmate Labor," *Buffalo Law Review* 21 (1972): 963–85.

209. Mathiesen, *The Politics of Abolition*, p. 42.

210. Ward, "Sweden: The Middle Way to Prison Reform?" p. 108.

211. Ward, "Sweden: The Middle Way to Prison Reform?" p. 136.

212. It wielded slogans like, "Keep them locked in so we can go out!" Karen Leander, "The Normalization of Swedish Prisons," in *Western European Penal Systems: A Critical Anatomy*, ed. Vincenzo Ruggiero, Mick Ryan, and Joe Sim (London: Sage, 1995), p. 169.

213. Leander, "The Normalization of Swedish Prisons," pp. 172–73.

214. KROM stands for Norwegian Association for Penal Reform. Mathiesen, *The Politics of Abolition*, p. 51.

215. Sweden's KRUM ceased to exist by the late 1970s, while Norway's KROM has remained an integral part of Norwegian penal politics and policy. Thomas Mathiesen, "About KROM–Past-Present-Future" (Oslo: Institute for Sociology of Law, 1995).

216. Claudius Messner and Vincenzo Ruggiero, "Germany: The Penal System Between Past and Future," in *Western European Penal Systems: A Critical Anatomy*, pp. 128–48. For a critical analysis of the Prison Act of 1977, see Renate M. Prowse, Hartmut-Michael Weber, and Charles R. M. Wilson, "Rights and Prisons in Germany: Blueprint for Britain?" *International Journal of the Sociology of Law* 10 (1992): 111–34.

217. James Q. Whitman, *Harsh Justice: Criminal Punishment and the Widening Divide Between America and Europe* (Oxford: Oxford University Press, 2003), pp. 193–94.

218. Thomas C. Holt, *The Problem of Race in the 21st Century* (Cambridge: Harvard University Press, 2000), pp. 18–24 and 113–14; and Desmond S. King and Rogers M. Smith, "Racial Orders in American Political Development," *American Political Science Review* 99, no. 1 (February 2005): 75–92.

CHAPTER 8: CAPITAL PUNISHMENT, THE COURTS, AND THE EARLY ORIGINS
OF THE CARCERAL STATE, 1920S–1960S

1. These are the final words of William Kemmler, the first person to die in the electric chair, executed on August 6, 1890, in New York State. Quoted in Richard Cohen, "Goodbye, William!" *The New York Review of Books*, August 14, 2003, p. 18.

2. During his campaign, Kirk visited the Florida state penitentiary at Raiford, shook hands with the men on death row, and told them with a smile, "If I'm elected, I may have to sign your death warrant." Michael Meltsner, *Cruel and Unusual: The Supreme Court and Capital Punishment* (New York: Random House, 1973), p. 127. On Reagan and the death penalty, see John H. Culver, "The Politics of Capital Punishment in California," in *The Political Science of Criminal Punishment*, ed. Stuart Nagel, Erika Fairchild, and Anthony Champagne (Springfield, IL: Charles C. Thomas, 1983), pp. 15–18.

3. Michael A. Mello, *Dead Wrong: A Death Row Lawyer Speaks Out Against Capital Punishment* (Madison: University of Wisconsin Press, 1997), pp. 21–22; and Stephen B. Bright, "The Politics of Capital Punishment: The Sacrifice of Fairness for Executions," in *America's Experiment with Capital Punishment: Reflections on the Past, Present, and Future of the Ultimate Penal Sanction*, 2nd ed., James R. Acker, Robert M. Bohm, and Charles S. Lanier (Durham, NC: Carolina Academic Press, 2003), p. 130.

4. During his 1979 trial, Bundy's statewide name recognition was second only to the governor's. David Von Drehle, *Among the Lowest of the Dead: Inside Death Row* (New York: Fawcett Crest, 1995), pp. 283 and 393; John Bessler, *Death in the Dark: Midnight Executions in America* (Boston: Northeastern University Press, 1997), p. 146; Mello, *Dead Wrong*, p. 32; and Glenn L. Pierce and Michael L. Radelet, "The Role and Consequences of the Death Penalty in American Politics," *New York University Review of Law and Social Change* 18 (1990–91), pp. 721–22. For a vivid, compelling, and disturbing portrait of the public spectacle surrounding the execution of Aileen Wuornos in October 2002 for the murders of seven men in Florida, see *Aileen: Life and Death of a Serial Killer*, 89 min., Lafayette Films, 2004.

5. Rector was so mentally incapacitated that he set aside his piece of pecan pie from his "last supper," mistakenly thinking he would be around to eat it later. Robert Jay Lifton and Greg Mitchell, *Who Owns Death? Capital Punishment, the American Conscience, and the End of Executions* (New York: Harper-Collins, 2000), pp. 100–01. In his reelection bid, Clinton's first set of television commercials focused on his enthusiasm for expanding use of the death penalty. Todd S. Purdum, "Clinton Gets Early Start on Ad Campaign Trail," *The New York Times*, June 27, 1995, p. A-14.

6. Lifton and Mitchell, *Who Owns Death?*, p. 135.

7. Lifton and Mitchell, *Who Owns Death?*, p. 56.

8. Since 1990 eight countries are known to have executed offenders who were under age eighteen at the time they committed their crimes. The United States has carried out the greatest number of known executions of juvenile offenders, nineteen of them since 1990. Amnesty International, "Facts and Figures on the Death Penalty," http://web.amnesty.org/pages/deathpenalty-facts-eng (accessed July 2, 2004). In January 2005, by a 5-to-4 decision in *Roper v. Simmons*, the U.S. Supreme Court ruled that it was unconstitutional to execute juvenile offenders for crimes committed before the age of eighteen. Linda Greenhouse, "Supreme Court, 5–4, Forbids Execution in Juvenile Crime," *The New York Times*, March 2, 2005, p. A-1.

   In 2002 the U.S. Supreme Court declared in *Atkins v. Virginia* that the execution of people who are mentally retarded is unconstitutional, but did not set up a standard for determining who is mentally retarded. Linda Greenhouse, "The Supreme Court: The Death Penalty; Citing 'National Consensus,' Justices Bar Death Penalty for Retarded Defendants," *The New York Times*, June 21, 2002, p. A-1. Kyrgyzstan was the only other country known to execute mentally handicapped people on a regular basis. Harold Hongju Koh, "A Dismal Record on Executing the Retarded," *The New York Times*, June 14, 2001, sec. 4, p. 33.

9. Of the 500 or so known executions reported on average annually worldwide from 1958 to 1962, half were carried out in just four of the eighty-nine countries where capital punishment was still legal. Despite more than two decades of decline in the number of executions, the United States, with its average of 49 executions annually, was among these top 4 – along with South Africa (100), Korea (68), and Nigeria (51). William J. Bowers, Glenn L. Pierce, and John F. McDevitt, *Legal Homicide: Death as Punishment in America, 1864–1982* (Boston: Northeastern University Press, 1984), pp. 147–48.

10. Roger Hood, *The Death Penalty: A World-Wide Perspective* (Oxford: Oxford University Press, 1996), p. 223; Lifton and Mitchell, *Who Owns Death?*, p. 247; and Carol S. Steiker, "Capital Punishment and American Exceptionalism," *Oregon Law Review* 81 (2002).

11. Bowers et al., *Legal Homicide: Death as Punishment in America*, pp. 28–29.

12. Death Penalty Information Center, "Facts about the Death Penalty," March 17, 2005, http://www.deathpenaltyinfo.org/Factsheet.pdf (accessed April 1, 2005).

13. Bryan Denson, "Death Penalty: Equal Justice?" *Houston Post*, October 16, 1994, p. A-1, in Stephen B. Bright, "Discrimination, Death, and Denial: Race and the Death Penalty," in *Machinery of Death: The Reality of America's Death Penalty Regime*, ed. David R. Dow and Mark Dow (New York: Routledge, 2002), p. 46. See also David Michael Smith, "The Death Penalty Capital of the Western World," *Peace Review* 13, no. 4 (December 2001): 495–501. Texas, widely considered to be the country's leading executioner, in fact sentences a smaller proportion of convicted murderers to death than the national average. That said, once sentenced, people on death row in Texas are more likely to be executed than in many other states. Adam Liptak, "Study Revises Texas's Standing as a Death Penalty Leader," *The New York Times*, February 14, 2004, p. A-10.

14. On the "culture of vengeance," see Edward L. Ayers, *Vengeance and Justice: Crime and Punishment in the 19th-Century American South* (New York: Oxford University Press, 1984); and Richard E. Nisbett and Dov Cohen, *Culture of Honor: The Psychology of Violence in the South* (Boulder, CO: Westview Press, 1996).

15. Franklin E. Zimring, *The Contradictions of American Capital Punishment* (Oxford: Oxford University Press, 2003). For a provocative challenge to Zimring's political culture argument, see David Garland, "Capital Punishment and American Culture," *Punishment & Society* 7, no. 4 (October, 2005): 347–65.

16. James W. Marquart, Sheldon Ekland-Olson, and Jonathan R. Sorensen make a similar point in their study of the death penalty in Texas, which emphasizes what they call the state's "cultural tradition of exclusion." *The Rope, the Chair, and the Needle: Capital Punishment in Texas, 1923–1990* (Austin: University of Texas Press, 1994), p. 4.

17. Zimring, *The Contradictions of American Capital Punishment*, p. 136.

18. Barrington Moore, Jr., *Social Origins of Dictatorship and Democracy: Lord and Peasant in the Making of the Modern World* (Boston: Beacon Press, 1966), pp. 486–87.

19. John H. Culver, "Capital Punishment Politics and Policies in the States, 1977–1997," *Crime, Law and Social Change* 32 (1999): 287–300. For a good blow-by-blow account of the efforts to reinstate the death penalty in Kansas, see James M. Galliher and John F. Galliher, "'Deja Vu All Over Again': The Recurring Life and Death of Capital Punishment Legislation in Kansas," *Social Problems* 44, no. 3 (August 1997): 369–85.

20. Bohm speculates that this may be because more blacks and more poor people live in the South, two demographic groups that are generally less supportive of capital punishment. Robert M. Bohm, "American Death Penalty Opinion, 1936–1986: A Critical Examination of the Gallup Polls," in *The Death Penalty in America: Current Research*, ed. Robert M. Bohm (Cincinnati, OH: Andersen Publishing Co., 1991), p. 127. In the 1970s, about a third of blacks polled supported capital punishment in cases of murder, which was about 30 percentage points lower than white support. That black-white gap began to narrow subsequently. A 1991 poll found that a majority of blacks (52 percent) for the first time approved of the death penalty for murder, compared with 75 percent of whites. Blacks in the South were least likely to support capital punishment (44 percent). Marquart et al., *The Rope, the Chair, and the Needle*, p. 191. That gap appeared to have widened substantially again by the late 1990s. A January 2000 poll by ABC News found that 69 percent of whites and just 38 percent of blacks supported the death penalty. Lifton and Mitchell, *Who Owns Death?*, p. 217.

    Zimring does present public opinion data suggesting that while the South may not be more supportive of capital punishment per se, it is more supportive of "vigilante values." Zimring, *The Contradictions of American Capital Punishment*, pp. 98–118.

21. This discussion of the early history of capital punishment in the United States is based primarily on David Brion Davis, "The Movement to Abolish Capital Punishment in America, 1787–1861," in *From Homicide to Slavery: Studies in American Culture*, ed. David Brion Davis (New York: Oxford University Press, 1986): 17–40; Louis Filler, "Movements to Abolish the Death Penalty in the United States," *The Annals of the American Academy of Political and Social Science* 284 (November 1952): 124–36; Michael Meranze, *Laboratories of Virtue: Punishment, Revolution, and Authority in Philadelphia, 1760–1835* (Chapel Hill: University of North Carolina Press, 1996); Ronald J. Pestritto, *Founding the Criminal Law: Punishment and Political Thought in the Origins of America* (DeKalb, IL: Northern Illinois University Press, 2000); Raymond Paternoster, *Capital Punishment in America* (New York: Lexington Books, 1991), pp. 4–9; Stuart Banner,

The Death Penalty: An American History (Cambridge, MA: Harvard University Press, 2002); Philip English Mackey, "Introduction: An Historical Perspective," in *Voices Against Death: American Opposition to Capital Punishment, 1787–1975,* ed. Philip English Mackey (New York: Burt Franklin & Co., 1976); and Louis P. Masur, *Rites of Execution: Capital Punishment and the Transformation of American Culture, 1776–1865* (New York: Oxford University Press, 1989).

22. Banner, *The Death Penalty,* p. 3.

23. One needs to be careful not to overstate how much the early penal reformers viewed the penitentiary as a humanitarian alternative to the death penalty. They emphasized both the reformative promise of the prison and its punitive potential. Benjamin Rush, an early champion of the penitentiary and opponent of capital punishment, proposed constructing prisons in remote locations "to which the road was 'difficult and gloomy,' where the clang of the iron gates would be 'encreased by an echo from a neighboring mountain, that should extend and continue a sound that shall deeply pierce the soul.'" Banner, *The Death Penalty,* p. 109.

   The influential Italian penal philosopher Cesare Beccaria advocated replacing capital punishment with what he characterized as the "perpetual slavery" of the penitentiary. Quoted in Scott Christianson, *With Liberty for Some: 500 Years of Imprisonment in America* (Boston: Northeastern University Press, 1998), p. 26.

24. Enacted in 1723, the Black Act created fifty new capital offenses, many of them for comparatively minor violations, like hunting and poaching. E. P. Thompson, *Whigs and Hunters: The Origins of the Black Act* (New York: Pantheon, 1975); and Douglas Hay, "Property, Authority, and the Criminal Law," in *Albion's Fatal Tree: Crime and Society in Eighteenth-Century England,* ed. Douglas Hay, Peter Linebaugh, John Rule, E. P. Thompson, and Cal Winslow (New York: Pantheon, 1975): 17–63.

25. Banner, *The Death Penalty,* p. 99.

26. Banner, *The Death Penalty,* pp. 8 and 99.

27. In 1816, Georgia made rape or attempted rape of a white woman by a black man punishable by death. It also reduced the minimum penalty from seven years to two and removed the "hard labor" requirement for white men convicted of raping white women. The punishment for white men convicted of raping slaves or free blacks was a fine or imprisonment at the discretion of the courts. Bowers et al., *Legal Homicide,* p. 140.

28. Davis, "The Movement to Abolish Capital Punishment," p. 17.

29. Quoted in Banner, *The Death Penalty,* p. 113.

30. Banner, *The Death Penalty,* p. 131; and Paternoster, *Capital Punishment in America,* p. 6.

31. Michigan's measure became effective in 1847. Franklin E. Zimring and Gordon Hawkins, *Capital Punishment and the American Agenda* (Cambridge: Cambridge University Press, 1986), p. 28.

32. Herbert H. Haines, *Against Capital Punishment: The Anti-Death Penalty Movement in America, 1972–1994* (New York: Oxford University Press, 1996), pp. 8–9.

33. Zimring and Hawkins, *Capital Punishment and the American Agenda,* p. 28.

34. Banner, *The Death Penalty,* p. 222.

35. John Galliher, Gregory Ray, and Brent Cook, "Abolition and Reinstatement of Capital Punishment During the Progressive Era and Early 20th Century," *Journal of Criminal Law and Criminology* 83 (Fall 1992): 538–76; and Haines, *Against*

Capital Punishment, pp. 9–11.

This picture would not be complete without mentioning lynchings, which had much in common with legally imposed executions. In the 1890s, almost three out of every five executions were lynchings conducted outside of any official local or state authority. In the early 1900s, the balance began to shift toward legally sanctioned executions as the number of lynchings began to fall. Bowers et al., *Legal Homicide*, pp. 55–56 and p. 54, Table 2–3. See also Charles David Phillips, "Exploring Relations Among Forms of Social Control: The Lynching and Execution of Blacks in North Carolina, 1889–1918," *Law & Society Review* 21, no. 3 (1987): 361–74; and E. M. Beck, James L. Massey, and Stewart E. Tolnay, "The Gallows, the Mob, and the Vote: Lethal Sanctioning of Blacks in North Carolina and Georgia, 1882–1930," *Law & Society Review* 23, no. 2 (1989): 317–31.

36. Official government statistics on executions only go back to 1930, when the Bureau of Prisons, a division of the Justice Department, began collecting them for the first time in the wake of the national furor over the executions of anarchists Nicola Sacco and Bartolomeo Vanzetti in 1927.

37. A more meaningful figure that takes into account fluctuations in the number of homicides is the number of annual executions per 100 homicides in death penalty states. This number dropped precipitously from a high of 2.01 in 1938 to just 0.58 and 0.24 in 1962 and 1963, respectively. All these figures come from Bowers et al., *Legal Homicide*, pp. 25–26, Table 1–4.

38. Haines, *Against Capital Punishment*, pp. 10–11.

39. Mackey, "Introduction: An Historical Perspective," p. xli.

40. The execution rate is the number of executions in a specified five-year interval divided by the number of homicides in death penalty jurisdictions for the five-year interval ending one year earlier in a particular region. Bowers et al., *Legal Homicide*, p. 26, Table 1–4, n. b.

41. The total number of executions in the South dropped from 420 between 1945 and 1949 to 244 from 1950 to 1954, and the execution rate fell from 1.82 to 1.09. Bowers et al., *Legal Homicide*, p. 29, Table 1–5.

42. The abolitionist states were: Alaska, Delaware, Hawaii, Maine, Michigan, North Dakota, Rhode Island, and Wisconsin. For a chart of when specific states abolished, partially abolished, and/or restored the death penalty, see Hugo Adam Bedau, "Background and Developments," in *The Death Penalty in America: Current Controversies*, ed. Hugo Adam Bedau (New York: Oxford University Press, 1997), p. 9, Table 1–2.

43. Tennessee partially abolished capital punishment in 1915, only to restore it four years later, largely out of a concern about a rise in lynchings. Galliher et al., "Abolition and Reinstatement of Capital Punishment," pp. 556–58.

44. Georgia had 366 to New York's 329. The other top ten states were: Texas (297), California (292), North Carolina (263), Ohio (172), Florida (170), South Carolina (162), Mississippi (154), and Pennsylvania (152). Paternoster, *Capital Punishment in America*, p. 13, Table 1–4.

45. Between 1930 and 1963, only two states, Alaska and Hawaii, permanently abolished the death penalty. Delaware abolished it in 1958, only to restore it three years later. Bedau, "Background and Developments," p. 9, Table 1–2.

46. Annulla Linders, "The Execution Spectacle and State Legitimacy: The Changing Nature of the American Execution Audience, 1833–1937," *Law & Society Review* 36, no. 3 (2002), p. 616, n. 7; and James R. Acker and Charles S. Lanier,

"Beyond Human Ability? The Rise and Fall of Death Penalty Legislation," in *America's Experiment with Capital Punishment*, 2nd. ed., p. 91.

47. Bowers et al., *Legal Homicide*, p. 44; and Banner, *The Death Penalty*, p. 146.

48. Pieter Spierenburg, *The Spectacle of Suffering: Executions and the Evolution of Repression* (Cambridge: Cambridge University Press, 1984); and Banner, *The Death Penalty*, p. 152.

49. "[D]etailed descriptions of the convict, the audience, the setting, and the death struggle, minute by minute, gasp by gasp" were a staple of the penny press. Linders, "The Execution Spectacle," p. 638.

50. Linders, "The Execution Spectacle," p. 647.

51. These "gag" laws usually ended up being "short-lived or ineffectual." Linders, "The Execution Spectacle," p. 638.

52. Banner, *The Death Penalty*, pp. 146–55. The last truly public execution took place in 1936 in Owensboro, Ky., as 20,000 people gathered to watch Rainey Bertha, a black man, go to the gallows for the rape and murder of a white woman. In 1937, 1,500 people were admitted by special passes into the stockade that enclosed the gallows for a semi-public execution in Galena, Mo. Acker and Lanier, "Beyond Human Ability?" p. 91. Mississippi reportedly held semi-public executions as late as the early 1940s. Craddock Goins, "The Traveling Executioner," *The American Mercury* 54 (1942), pp. 93–97, cited in Linders, "The Execution Spectacle," p. 616, n. 7.

53. After Vermont carried out the first execution under state authority in January 1864, the movement toward state-imposed executions stalled for more than two decades. Bowers et al., *Legal Homicide*, pp. 43 and 49–50.

54. Bowers et al., *Legal Homicide*, p. 52.

55. In the 1890s, locally imposed executions comprised about 87 percent of the total. By the 1920s, there was almost a complete reversal as state-imposed executions represented nearly 89 percent of the total. Bowers et al., *Legal Homicide*, pp. 54–55.

56. Bruce Shapiro, "Capital Offense," *The New York Times Magazine*, March 26, 2000, pp. 19–20. The electric chair has been replaced with lethal injection in all but one state, Nebraska. Cohen, "Goodbye, William!" p. 18.

57. Jonathan Simon, *Poor Discipline: Parole and the Social Control of the Underclass* (Chicago: University of Chicago Press, 1993); and David J. Rothman, *Conscience and Convenience: The Asylum and Its Alternatives in Progressive America* (Boston: Little, Brown and Co., 1980).

58. "Ex-Warden Sleeps as Five Negroes Die," *Dallas Morning News*, February 8, 1924, quoted in Marquart et al., *The Rope, the Chair, and the Needle*, p. 17. During this period, corrections professionals were at the forefront of opposition to capital punishment, most notably Lewis E. Lawes, the longtime warden of Sing Sing prison. Lewis E. Lawes, "Why I Changed My Mind," in *Voices Against Death*: 192–204.

59. Bowers et al., *Legal Homicide*, p. 11, Table 1–2; and Paternoster, *Capital Punishment in America*, pp. 16–17.

60. Bowers et al., *Legal Homicide*, p. 15.

61. Calculated from Margaret Werner Cahalan and Lee Anne Parsons, *Historical Corrections Statistics in the United States, 1850–1984* (Washington, DC: U.S. Department of Justice, Bureau of Justice Statistics, December 1986), p. 17 and p. 18, Table 2–7. Data for the 1930s and 1940s are incomplete and are estimated

to be 8 percent higher than the official numbers in this table. In computing the averages, I inflated the official figures by 8 percent.

62. Banner, *The Death Penalty*, p. 227.

63. Meltsner, *Cruel and Unusual*, p. 52.

64. During the anti-communist hysteria of the 1950s, Texas Governor Allan Shivers seriously proposed capital punishment as a penalty for membership in the Communist Party. Mackey, "Introduction: An Historical Perspective," p. xli.

65. For more on the Chessman case, see pp. 173–74.

66. James J. Megivern, *The Death Penalty: An Historical and Theological Survey* (New York: Paulist Press, 1997), p. 322; and Jesse L. Jackson, Sr., Jesse L. Jackson, Jr., and Bruce Shapiro, *Legal Lynching: The Death Penalty and America's Future* (New York: The New Press, 2001), Chapter 7.

67. Roger E. Schwed, *Abolition and Capital Punishment: The United States' Judicial, Political, and Moral Barometer* (New York: AMS Press, Inc., 1983), pp. 91–92.

68. U.S. House, Subcommittee No. 2 of the Committee on the Judiciary, "Abolition of Capital Punishment," 86th Congress, 2nd. Sess. (May 5, 1960), p. 27.

69. Banner, *The Death Penalty*, p. 240.

70. Alan Rogers, "'Success – At Long Last': The Abolition of the Death Penalty in Massachusetts, 1928–1984," *Boston College Third World Journal* 22, no. 2 (2002), p. 325.

71. After bottoming out in 1966, support for the death penalty began to rise substantially, reaching 75 percent in favor and just 17 percent against by 1985. By 1994, 80 percent of those polled favored capital punishment, the highest level ever recorded. Bohm, "American Death Penalty Opinion, 1936–1986," p. 116, Table 8.1; and Robert M. Bohm, "American Death Penalty Opinion: Past, Present, and Future," in *America's Experiment with Capital Punishment*, p. 27.

72. Hugo Adam Bedau, *The Courts, the Constitution, and Capital Punishment* (Lexington, MA: Lexington Books, 1977), p. 1. The commission ended up sidestepping the issue somewhat. It favored abolition of all death penalties but implied that capital punishment was ultimately an issue for individual states to resolve themselves. Hugo Adam Bedau, *Death Is Different: Studies in the Morality, Law, and Politics of Capital Punishment* (Boston: Northeastern University Press, 1987), p. 144.

73. See, for example, Haines, *Against Capital Punishment*, p. 11; Theodore Hamm, *Rebel and a Cause: Caryl Chessman and the Politics of the Death Penalty in Postwar California, 1948–1974* (Berkeley: University of California Press, 2001), p. 8; and Schwed, *Abolition and Capital Punishment*, p. 176.

74. Zimring, *The Contradictions of American Capital Punishment*, p. 9.

75. Charles R. Epp, *The Rights Revolution: Lawyers, Activists, and Supreme Courts in Comparative Perspective* (Chicago: University of Chicago Press, 1998), pp. 44–45.

76. Epp, *The Rights Revolution*, pp. 48–52.

77. Richard C. Cortner, *A Mob Intent on Death: The NAACP and the Arkansas Race Riot Cases* (Middletown, CT: Wesleyan University Press, 1988), p. 3.

78. Michael J. Klarman, *From Jim Crow to Civil Rights: The Supreme Court and the Struggle for Racial Equality* (New York: Oxford University Press, 2004), pp. 117–35.

79. Bedau, *Death Is Different*, p. 13; and Cortner, *A Mob Intent on Death*, pp. 154–55.

80. Klarman, *From Jim Crow to Civil Rights*, p. 117.

81. Sensitive to charges that Mississippi was becoming a lawless state beholden to lynch mobs, state law enforcement officials "arrested the suspects, kept the lynch mob at bay, and tortured the men themselves." Jerome H. Skolnick, "On Controlling Torture," in *Punishment and Social Control*, 2nd ed., ed. Thomas G. Blomberg and Stanley Cohen (New York: Aldine de Gruyter, 2003), p. 218. See also Haines, *Against Capital Punishment*, p. 24.

82. Bowers et al., *Legal Homicide*, pp. 63–64; and Zimring, *The Contradictions of American Capital Punishment*, p. 69.

83. Haines, *Against Capital Punishment*, p. 24.

84. Banner, *The Death Penalty*, p. 246.

85. Epp, *The Rights Revolution*.

86. The LDF was established as a separate entity so it could take advantage of tax-deductible contributions denied to organizations like the NAACP that spend a substantial amount of time and other resources on lobbying. Meltsner, *Cruel and Unusual*, pp. 5–6.

87. Jack Greenberg, *Crusaders in the Courts: How a Dedicated Band of Lawyers Fought for the Civil Rights Revolution* (New York: Basic Books, 1994), pp. 21 and 509.

88. Jack Greenberg and Jack Himmelstein, "Varieties of Attack on the Death Penalty," *Crime and Delinquency* 15, no. 1 (January 1969), p. 113.

89. On the 3,859 people executed under civil authority in the United States between 1930 and 1967, 54 percent were black. During that time, blacks comprised 10 to 12 percent of the population. U.S. Department of Justice, "Capital Punishment, 1981" (Washington, DC: GPO, 1982), in Michael L. Radelet and Margaret Vandiver, "Race and Capital Punishment: An Overview of the Issues," *Crime and Social Justice* 25 (1986), p. 98.

90. Walt Espy found only thirty instances of whites being executed for committing crimes against blacks among the nearly 16,000 legal executions in the United States since the seventeenth century that he has documented. Michael L. Radelet, "Executions of Whites for Crimes Against Blacks: Exceptions to the Rule?" *Sociological Quarterly* 30 (1989), p. 532.

91. The next instance in South Carolina occurred more than a century later. In 1991 Donald "Peewee" Gaskins, a white prisoner who had confessed to stabbing, shooting, and drowning thirteen people and was convicted of ten murders, was executed for killing fellow prisoner Rudolph Tyner, who was black. David Cole, *No Equal Justice: Race and Class in the Criminal Justice System* (New York: The New Press, 1999), p. 132.

92. Between 1930 and 1967, 455 men were executed for rape, 405 of whom (or 89 percent) were black. U.S. Department of Justice, "Capital Punishment, 1981," in Radelet and Vandiver, "Race and Capital Punishment," p. 98.

93. One of the path-breaking studies that was used as a basis for some of the early major legal challenges to the death penalty found that 13 percent of blacks convicted of rape in the South between 1945 and 1965 were sentenced to death compared to just 2 percent of whites. Marvin E. Wolfgang and Marc Reidel, "Race, Judicial Discretion, and the Death Penalty," *The Annals of the American Academy of Political and Social Science* 407 (1973), p. 129. Another famous study of murder and nonnegligent homicide cases in Georgia from 1973 to 1979 found, after controlling for other variables, that defendants whose victims were white were 4.3 times more likely to receive a death sentence. David C. Baldus, George Woodworth, and Charles Pulaski, Jr., *Equal Justice and the Death Penalty*

(Boston: Northeastern University Press, 1990). The results of this study were the basis for *McCleskey v. Kemp*, in which the LDF challenged Georgia's death penalty on the basis of intentional racial discrimination. The Supreme Court rejected this argument in a 5–4 decision in April 1987. Lee Epstein and Joseph F. Kobylka, *The Supreme Court and Legal Change: Abortion and the Death Penalty* (Chapel Hill: The University of North Carolina Press, 1992), pp. 121–28.

For a survey of some of the early statistical studies, see Radelet and Vandiver, "Race and Capital Punishment," pp. 101–06. For an overview of more recent statistical analyses of race and capital punishment, see David C. Baldus and George Woodworth, "Race Discrimination and the Death Penalty: An Empirical and Legal Overview," in *America's Experiment with Capital Punishment*: pp. 501–51.

94. For a brief overview of these cases, see Greenberg and Himmelstein, "Varieties of Attack on the Death Penalty," pp. 113–14; and Banner, *The Death Penalty*, pp. 247–48 and 363, n. 35. For a detailed insider account of the incredible Groveland, Fla., case of the early 1950s in which four black men were charged with raping a white women that Greenberg credits with being "the single most influential experience persuading me to launch the LDF capital punishment program in the late 1960s," see Greenberg, *Crusaders in the Courts*, pp. 93–106, 133–35, 140–49, and 258–59.

95. Greenberg and Himmelstein, "Varieties of Attack on the Death Penalty," p. 113.

96. *Rudolph v. Alabama*, 375 U.S. 889, 84 S.Ct. 155, 11 L.Ed.2d 119, quoted in Jack Greenberg, *Cases and Materials on Judicial Process and Social Change: Constitutional Litigation* (St. Paul, MN: West Publishing Co., 1977), pp. 429–30.

97. Alan Dershowitz, Goldberg's clerk, sent copies of the dissent "to every lawyer" he knew in the United States. Ian Gray and Moira Stanley, *A Punishment in Search of a Crime* (New York: Avon Books, 1989), p. 331.

98. Greenberg, *Cases and Materials on Judicial Process and Social Change*, p. 431.

99. In describing the overall mission of the LDF, director-counsel Jack Greenberg said: "Race was always the factor. There had to be a racial factor." Quoted in Eric L. Muller, "The Legal Defense Fund's Capital Punishment Campaign: The Distorting Influence of Death," *Yale Law and Policy Review* 4 (1985), p. 162.

100. *Trop v. Dulles*, 356 U.S. 86, 101, 78 S.Ct. 590, 2 L.Ed.2d. 630, quoted in *Rudolph. v. Alabama*, Greenberg, *Cases and Materials on Judicial Process and Social Change*, p. 430. In the decision, the Supreme Court affirmed that capital punishment was widely accepted and could not be considered cruel and unusual punishment.

101. Meltsner, *Cruel and Unusual*, p. 28.

102. Muller, "The Legal Defense Fund's Capital Punishment Campaign," pp. 165–66.

103. Eventually, the U.S. Supreme Court agreed to review *Maxwell*, but only on two other issues: standardless sentencing, or the unguided discretion juries had to choose death over life, and unitary trials in which juries determined guilt or innocence and also punishment in a single proceeding. In 1970 the Court vacated Maxwell's death sentence on other grounds without ruling on these two issues. For more on *Maxwell v. Bishop*, see Epstein and Kobylka, *The Supreme Court and Legal Change*, pp. 49–53 and 60–67; Meltsner, *Cruel and Unusual*, pp. 149–67; and Greenberg, *Cases and Materials on Judicial Process and Social Change*, pp. 433–44.

104. Meltsner, *Cruel and Unusual*, p. 107.

105. Meltsner, *Cruel and Unusual*, p. 106.

106. Meltsner, *Cruel and Unusual*, pp. 109–10.

107. Greenberg, *Crusaders in the Courts*, p. 284. See also the remarks by Anthony Amsterdam in Bertram H. Wolfe, *Pileup on Death Row* (Garden City, NY: Doubleday, 1973), pp. 244–45.

108. Meltsner, *Cruel and Unusual*, p. 109; Greenberg, *Crusaders in the Courts*, pp. 371–72.

109. Muller, "The Legal Defense Fund's Capital Punishment Campaign," p. 184. By the mid-1970s, the capital punishment campaign was consuming an estimated 10 to 20 percent of the organization's resources, and the Fund's board began raising questions about how its resources were being allocated. Greenberg, *Crusaders in the Courts*, p. 454; and Bedau, *Death Is Different*, p. 136.

110. Aryeh Neier, *Only Judgment: The Limits of Litigation in Social Change* (Middletown, CT: Wesleyan University Press, 1982), p. 197.

111. Muller, "The Legal Defense Fund's Capital Punishment Campaign," pp. 166–67.

112. Michael Meltsner, quoted in Muller, "The Legal Defense Fund's Capital Punishment Campaign," p. 181. Three weeks before he was executed in January 1977, Gary Gilmore published a vitriolic, racially charged letter directed against the NAACP in which he castigated "uncle tom [sic] blacks" for trying to stop his execution. Neier, *Only Judgment*, p. 209.

113. Muller, "The Legal Defense Fund's Capital Punishment Campaign," p. 178.

114. Muller, "The Legal Defense Fund's Capital Punishment Campaign," pp. 177–79.

115. The ACLU's board of directors asserted in 1965 that "capital punishment is so inconsistent with the underlying values of a democratic system that the imposition of the death penalty for any crime is a denial of civil liberties." Norman Dorsen, *Frontiers of Civil Liberties* (New York: Pantheon Books, 1968), p. 278. See also Schwed, *Abolition and Capital Punishment*, p 113.

116. Dorsen, *Frontiers of Civil Liberties*, pp. 270–78; and Schwed, *Abolition and Capital Punishment*, p. 113.

117. Samuel Walker, *In Defense of American Liberties: A History of the ACLU*, 2nd ed. (Carbondale: Southern Illinois University Press, 1999), Chapters 12, 13, and 14.

118. Walker, *In Defense of American Liberties*, pp. 327–40.

119. Haines, *Against Capital Punishment*, pp. 49–50.

120. Neier, *Only Judgment*, pp. 198 and 207.

121. Neier, *Only Judgment*, p. 212.

122. Meltsner, *Cruel and Unusual*, pp. 55–56.

123. Wolfe, *Pileup on Death Row*, pp. 67–68 and 301.

124. Supportive of an abolition bill under consideration in the legislature, Maddox was looking for a way out of being the first governor to resume executions in Georgia since 1964. Clark provided the excuse. Upon hearing that Clark said he wanted to be executed, Maddox declared: "He must be nuts. Even animals want to live. I don't believe any person who has any sense at all would want to die." Maddox then commuted Clark's sentence. Wolfe, *Pileup on Death Row*, pp. 29–30.

125. Wolfe, *Pileup on Death Row*, p. 48.

126. Wolfe, *Pileup on Death Row*, p. 310.

127. *National Prisoner Statistics Report: Capital Punishment, 1984* (Washington, DC: Bureau of Justice Statistics, n.d.), p. 12, in Haines, *Against Capital Punishment*, p. 12, Table 2.

128. State trial courts subsequently learned how to circumvent this decision that had initially appeared to prohibit excluding potential jurors who expressed any qualms about the death penalty. Bedau, *Death Is Different*, p. 147; and Epstein and Kobylka, *The Supreme Court and Legal Change*, pp. 56–58.

129. Bedau, *Death Is Different*, p. 140; Meltsner, *Cruel and Unusual*, pp. 233–36.

130. Alabama's State Supreme Court later set aside this decision. Meltsner, *Cruel and Unusual*, pp. 237–38.

131. Meltsner, *Cruel and Unusual*, pp. 236–37.

132. Wolfe, *Pileup on Death Row*, Part 1, pp. 3–62.

133. Meltsner, *Cruel and Unusual*, p. 245.

134. Epstein and Kobylka, *The Supreme Court and Legal Change*, pp. 67 and 131.

135. *McGautha v. California*, 602 U.S. 183 1971, p. 208, in James R. Acker, "The Death Penalty: A 25-Year Retrospective and a Perspective on the Future," *Criminal Justice Review* 21, no. 2 (Autumn 1996), p. 143. The *McGautha* and *Crampton* cases were all the more significant – and devastating – for the abolitionist cause because Justice Hugo Black declared in his concurring opinion that capital punishment did not violate the Eighth Amendment's prohibition on "cruel and unusual punishment" or the Fourteenth Amendment's guarantee of due process. Greenberg, *Cases and Materials on Judicial Process and Social Change*, pp. 457–64.

136. Acker, "The Death Penalty," pp. 142–44.

137. Epstein and Kobylka, *The Supreme Court and Legal Change*, p. 69.

138. The cases were *Furman v. Georgia, Branch v. Texas, Jackson v. Georgia*, and *Aikens v. California*. The first three were consolidated under *Furman*. The death sentence in *Aikens* was vacated when the California Supreme Court ruled in February 1972 in *People v. Anderson* that capital punishment was unconstitutional under the state's constitution. Wolfe, *Pileup on Death Row*, pp. 392–93.

CHAPTER 9: THE POWER TO PUNISH AND EXECUTE: THE POLITICAL DEVELOPMENT OF CAPITAL PUNISHMENT, 1972 TO TODAY

1. Thurgood Marshall, *Furman v. Georgia* 408 US 238 (1972), p. 371.

2. Michael A. Mello, *Dead Wrong: A Death Row Lawyer Speaks Out Against Capital Punishment* (Madison: University of Wisconsin Press, 1997), p. 12; and Franklin E. Zimring and Gordon Hawkins, *Capital Punishment and the American Agenda* (Cambridge: Cambridge University Press, 1986), p. 164.

3. Jonathan Simon, "Violence, Vengeance and Risk: Capital Punishment in the Near-Liberal State," unpublished mss., 1997, quoted in Austin Sarat, *When the State Kills: Capital Punishment and the American Condition* (Princeton: Princeton University Press, 2001), p. 19.

4. Stuart Banner, *The Death Penalty: An American History* (Cambridge: Harvard University Press, 2002), Chapters 9 and 10; Raymond Paternoster, *Capital Punishment in America* (New York: Lexington Books, 1991), Chapters 2 and 3; Herbert H. Haines, *Against Capital Punishment: The Anti-Death Penalty Movement in America, 1972–1994* (New York: Oxford University Press, 1996); Michael Meltsner, *Cruel and Unusual: The Supreme Court and Capital Punishment* (New York: Random House, 1973); Jack Greenberg, *Crusaders in the Courts: How a Dedicated Band of Lawyers Fought for the Civil Rights Revolution* (New York: Basic Books, 1994), Chapter 32; Lee Epstein and Joseph F. Kobylka, *The Supreme Court and Legal Change: Abortion and the Death Penalty*

(Chapel Hill: The University of North Carolina Press, 1992), Chapters 3 and 4; Jack Greenberg, *Cases and Materials on Judicial Process and Social Change: Constitutional Litigation* (St. Paul, MN: West Publishing Co., 1977), Chapter 5; Norman Dorsen, *Frontiers of Civil Liberties* (New York: Pantheon Books, 1968), Chapter 18; and Aryeh Neier, *Only Judgment: The Limits of Litigation in Social Change* (Middletown, CT: Wesleyan University Press, 1982), Chapter 12.

5. Epstein and Kobylka, *The Supreme Court and Legal Change*, p. xiv.

6. Austin Sarat, "Capital Punishment as a Legal, Political, and Cultural Fact: An Introduction," in *The Killing State: Capital Punishment in Law, Politics, and Culture*, ed. Austin Sarat (New York: Oxford University Press, 1999), p. 14. See also Sarat, *When the State Kills*, p. 52.

7. Meltsner, *Cruel and Unusual*, pp. 281–82.

8. Bertram H. Wolfe, *Pileup on Death Row* (Garden City, NY: Doubleday, 1973), p. 384.

9. Epstein and Kobylka, *The Supreme Court and Legal Change*, p. 77; and Banner, *The Death Penalty*, pp. 260–64.

10. Peter Petrakis, "The Death Penalty Initiative," *San Francisco Bay Guardian*, October 4, 1972, in Wolfe, *Pileup on Death Row*, p. 409.

11. Meltsner, *Cruel and Unusual*, pp. 281–87 and 306; Wolfe, *Pileup on Death Row*, pp. 390–92 and 408–09.

12. Wolfe, *Pileup on Death Row*, p. 392; Meltsner, *Cruel and Unusual*, p. 212.

13. Epstein and Kobylka, *The Supreme Court and Legal Change*, p. 131.

14. Hugo Adam Bedau, *Death Is Different: Studies in the Morality, Law, and Politics of Capital Punishment* (Boston: Northeastern University Press, 1987), p. 142.

15. They included the John Birch Society, the Liberty Lobby, and Americans for Effective Law Enforcement. Bedau, *Death Is Different*, p. 142.

16. Bedau, *Death Is Different*, p. 166.

17. Mark Costanzo, *Just Revenge: Costs and Consequences of the Death Penalty* (New York: St. Martin's Press, 1997), p. 20.

18. *Furman v. Georgia*, 408 U.S. 238 1972, pp. 309–10, in Paternoster, *Capital Punishment in America*, p. 55.

19. Bob Woodward and Scott Armstrong, *The Brethren* (New York: Simon and Schuster, 1979), p. 219, quoted in Epstein and Kobylka, *The Supreme Court and Legal Change*, p. 80.

20. Brief for Petitioner, *Aiken* [sic] v. *California* (1971), in Greenberg, *Cases and Materials on Judicial Process and Social Change*, p. 478.

21. For more on the *Trop* case and the Goldberg dissent, see p. 210.

22. Brief for Petitioner, *Aiken* [sic] *v. California* (1971), in Greenberg, *Cases and Materials on Judicial Process and Social Change*, pp. 480–81 and 478.

23. "Transcript of President's News Conference Emphasizing Foreign Affairs," June 30, 1972, quoted in Epstein and Kobylka, *The Supreme Court and Legal Change*, p. 84.

24. Epstein and Kobylka, *The Supreme Court and Legal Change*, p. 84.

25. James R. Acker, "The Death Penalty: A 25-Year Retrospective and a Perspective on the Future," *Criminal Justice Review* 21, no. 2 (Autumn 1996), p. 145; and Zimring and Hawkins, *Capital Punishment and the American Agenda*, p. 38.

26. Meltsner, *Cruel and Unusual*, p. 290.

27. Jerry M. Flint, "States on the Move," *The New York Times*, March 11, 1973, p. 1.

28. Acker, "The Death Penalty: A 25-Year Retrospective," p. 145.

29. Epstein and Kobylka, *The Supreme Court and Legal Change*, p. 91.

30. The number of defendants who received death sentences in 1974, two years after *Furman*, was 166, exceeding the previous record of 158 in 1935. In 1975, the number was 322, nearly twice the prior all-time high. Margaret Werner Cahalan and Lee Anne Parsons, *Historical Corrections Statistics in the United States, 1850–1984* (Washington, DC: U.S. Department of Justice, Bureau of Justice Statistics, December 1986), p. 18, Table 2–7. On public opinion trends, see Robert M. Bohm, "American Death Penalty Opinion, 1936–1986: A Critical Examination of the Gallup Polls," in *The Death Penalty in America: Current Research*, ed. Robert M. Bohm (Cincinnati, OH: Andersen Publishing Co., 1991), p. 116, Table 8.1.

31. "Transcript of President's News Conference Emphasizing Foreign Affairs," June 30, 1972, quoted in Hugo Adam Bedau, "The Nixon Administration and the Deterrent Effect of the Death Penalty," *University of Pittsburgh Law Review* 34 (1973), p. 557.

32. Hugo Adam Bedau, *The Courts, the Constitution, and Capital Punishment* (Lexington, MA: Lexington Books, 1977), p. 98.

33. Bedau, *Death Is Different*, p. 143.

34. Bedau, *Death Is Different*, pp. 141–42.

35. David Garland and Richard Sparks, "Criminology, Social Theory, and the Challenge of Our Times," in *Criminology and Social Theory*, ed. David Garland and Richard Sparks (Oxford: Oxford University Press, 2000), p. 11.

36. Meltsner, *Cruel and Unusual*, p. 308.

37. Frank G. Carrington, *The Victims* (New Rochelle, NY: Arlington House, 1975), p. 182.

38. Ian Gray and Moira Stanley, "Introduction," in *A Punishment in Search of a Crime: Americans Speak Out Against the Death Penalty*, ed. Ian Gray and Moira Stanley (New York: Avon Books, 1989), p. 16.

39. Epstein and Kobylka, *The Supreme Court and Legal Change*, p. 307.

40. Linda Charlton, "Attorney General Designate Asserts Death Penalty, If Enforced, Is Deterrent," *The New York Times*, January 28, 1975, in Epstein and Kobylka, *The Supreme Court and Legal Change*, p. 97.

41. Epstein and Kobylka, *The Supreme Court and Legal Change*, p. 97.

42. Epstein and Kobylka, *The Supreme Court and Legal Change*, pp. 104–06 and p. 341, n. 4.

43. For more on this study by Isaac Ehrlich and other research on the death penalty and the deterrence question, see Glenn L. Pierce and Michael L. Radelet, "The Role and Consequences of the Death Penalty in American Politics," *New York University Review of Law and Social Change* 18 (1990–91): 711–28.

44. The account of this exchange between Powell and Bork comes from Epstein and Kobylka, *The Supreme Court and Legal Change*, p. 109.

45. While these statutes were not identical, they generally shared some essential features, including standards narrowing the range of offenses punishable by death, creation of bifurcated guilt and penalty trials, and mandated review of capital convictions by appellate courts. Acker, "The Death Penalty: A 25-Year Retrospective," p. 145.

46. Epstein and Kobylka, *The Supreme Court and Legal Change*, p. 113.

47. Marshall dissent in *Gregg v. Georgia*, as excerpted in Greenberg, *Cases and Materials on Judicial Process and Social Change*, p. 628. Emphasis in the original.

48. On the reemergence of "political abolitionism," see Haines, *Against Capital Punishment*, Chapter 3.
49. Samuel Walker, *In Defense of American Liberties: A History of the ACLU*, 2nd ed. (Carbondale IL: Southern Illinois University Press, 1999), p. 358.
50. Greenberg, *Crusaders in the Courts*, p. 485.
51. Greenberg, *Crusaders in the Courts*, pp. 484–86.
52. Walker, *In Defense of American Liberties*, p. 359.
53. For a concise summary of these decisions, see Acker, "The Death Penalty: A 25-Year Retrospective," pp. 147–48; and J. Mark Lane, "'Is There Life Without Parole?' A Capital Defendant's Right to a Meaningful Alternative Sentence," *Loyola (Los Angeles) Law Review* 26 (1992–93), pp. 329–32.
54. Walker, *In Defense of American Liberties*, p. 359; Acker, "The Death Penalty: A 25-Year Retrospective," pp. 149–50; Jonathan Simon and Christine Spaulding, "Tokens of Our Esteem: Aggravating Factors in the Era of Deregulated Death Penalties," in *The Killing State*: 81–113; and http://www.deathpenaltyinfo.org/, "Facts About the Death Penalty," August 27, 2004 (accessed September 9, 2004).
55. Epstein and Kobylka, *The Supreme Court and Legal Change*, p. 122. For example, in 1991 President George H. W. Bush lamented the lack of "a workable death penalty – which is to say a real death penalty." George H. W. Bush, "Remarks at Attorney General's Crime Summit: President Bush: 'Take Back the Streets,'" *The NOVA Newsletter* 15, no. 3 (1991): 1–2.
56. Susan Bandes, "When Victims Seek Closure: Forgiveness, Vengeance, and the Role of Government," *Fordham Urban Law Journal* 27, no. 5 (June 2000): 1599–1606; and Margaret Vandiver, "The Impact of the Death Penalty on the Families of Homicide Victims and of Condemned Prisoners," in *America's Experiment with Capital Punishment: Reflections on the Past, Present, and Future of the Ultimate Penal Sanction*, 2nd ed., ed. James R. Acker, Robert M. Bohm, and Charles S. Lanier. (Durham, NC: Carolina Academic Press, 2003): 613–45.
57. Austin Sarat, "Narrative Strategy and Death Penalty Advocacy," *Harvard Civil Rights-Civil Liberties Law Review* 31 (1996): 353–81.
58. *Lockett v. Ohio* 438 U.S. 586 (1978), p. 606, quoted in Bedau, *Death Is Different*, p. 178. See also Paternoster, *Capital Punishment in America*, p. 76.
59. Vivian Berger, "*Payne* and Suffering – A Personal Reflection and a Victim-Centered Critique," *Florida State University Law Review* 20 (1992): 21–65; and Sharon English, "It's Time for a Cam*Payne*," *The NOVA Newsletter* 15, no. 9 (1991), p. 2.
60. In her concurring opinion, Justice Sandra Day O'Connor graphically captured this sentiment when she declared, "[Murder] transforms a living person with hopes, dreams and fears into a corpse, thereby taking away all that is special and unique about the person. The Constitution does not preclude a State from deciding to give some of that back." *Payne v. Tennessee*, p. 832, as quoted in Jennifer L. Culbert, "The Sacred Name of Pain: The Role of Victim Impact Evidence in Death Penalty Sentencing Decisions," in *Pain, Death, and the Law*, ed. Austin Sarat (Ann Arbor: University of Michigan Press, 2001), p. 107.
61. Charles F. Baird and Elizabeth E. McGinn, "Re-Victimizing the Victim: How Prosecutorial and Judicial Discretion Are Being Exercised to Silence Victims Who Oppose Capital Punishment," *Stanford Law and Policy Review* 15 (2004), p. 463. In 1980, only a few jurisdictions permitted consideration

of the impact of a crime on the victim in noncapital cases. By the late 1990s, nearly every state allowed victims to give their input at sentencing and in parole decisions, and many permitted written and oral victim impact statements in noncapital cases. National Organization for Victim Assistance, "NOVA's Mission, Purposes, Accomplishments, and Organizational Structure," http://www.trynova.org/victims/mission.html (accessed August 30, 2004).

62. Annulla Linders, "The Execution Spectacle and State Legitimacy: The Changing Nature of the American Execution Audience, 1833–1937," *Law & Society Review* 36, no. 3 (2002), p. 647.

63. Linda Faye Williams, "Race and the Politics of Social Policy," in *The Social Divide: Political Parties and the Future of Activist Government*, ed. Margaret Weir (Washington, DC, and New York: The Brookings Institution and Russell Sage Foundation, 1998), pp. 430–32.

64. Franklin E. Zimring, *The Contradictions of American Capital Punishment* (New York: Oxford University Press, 2003), p. 17.

65. Richard J. Wilson, "The Influence of International Law and Practice on the Death Penalty in the United States," in *America's Experiment with Capital Punishment*: 147–65; and William A. Schabas, "The Abolition of Capital Punishment from an International Law Perspective," paper presented at "Convergence of Criminal Justice Systems – Bridging the Gaps," International Society for the Reform of Criminal Law, The Hague, August 24–28, 2003.

66. In some parts of Germany support for capital punishment was overwhelming, as high as 86 percent in the state of Scheswig-Holstein. Richard J. Evans, *Rituals of Retribution: Capital Punishment in Germany, 1600–1987* (Oxford: Oxford University Press, 1996), pp. 797–98.

67. Evans, *Rituals of Retribution*, pp. 775–804; and M. Mohrenschlager, "The Abolition of Capital Punishment in the Federal Republic of Germany: German Experiences," *Revue Internationale de Droit Pénal* 58 (1987): 509–19.

68. Robert Jay Lifton and Greg Mitchell, *Who Owns Death? Capital Punishment, the American Conscience, and the End of Executions* (New York: Harper-Collins, 2000), p. 247; and Zimring, *The Contradictions of American Capital Punishment*, pp. 16–17.

69. David Chandler, *Capital Punishment in Canada: A Sociological Study of Repressive Law* (Toronto: McClelland and Stewart, 1976), Chapter 2. Canada conducted its last execution in 1962 and abolished capital punishment on a trial basis in 1967 except for the murder of prison guards and police officials. In 1976 Canada abolished the death penalty for ordinary crimes and in 1998 for all crimes. Paul A. Rock, *A View from the Shadows: The Ministry of the Solicitor General of Canada and the Making of the Justice for Victims of Crime Initiative* (Oxford: Clarendon Press, 1986), pp. 118–39; and David Garland, "Capital Punishment and American Culture," *Punishment & Society* 7, no. 4 (October, 2005): 347–65.

70. Joshua Micah Marshall, "Death in Venice: Europe's Death-Penalty Elitism," *The New Republic*, July 31, 2000, p. 14.

71. Michael Zander, *Cases and Materials of the English Legal System*, 5th ed. (London: Weidenfeld & Nicolson, 1988), p. 559, cited in Charles R. Epp, *The Rights Revolution: Lawyers, Activists, and Supreme Courts in Comparative Perspective* (Chicago: University of Chicago Press, 1998), p. 122.

72. Epp, *The Rights Revolution*, pp. 145–46.

73. Epp, *The Rights Revolution*, Chapter 3, esp. pp. 30–35.

74. Epp attributes the emergence and consolidation of this rights network to differences in the training, structure, and demographics of the U.S. legal profession; the greater availability of state-sponsored legal counsel for the indigent; more sources of outside funding for rights organizations (especially from wealthy individuals and foundations); and strong support for an activist rights agenda in the U.S. Justice Department from the 1930s onward. Epp, *The Rights Revolution*, Chapters 4, 7, and 8.

75. This was a successor to the inquiry made by the Select Committee of the House of Commons in 1929–30, which was the first serious investigation of capital punishment by any national government in the twentieth century. The committee's main recommendation was that the death penalty be abolished for an experimental period of five years. Ernest Gowers, *A Life for a Life? The Problem of Capital Punishment* (London: Chatto and Windus, 1956), p. 42; and Bedau, *The Courts, the Constitution, and Capital Punishment*, p. 101.

76. The report's section on deterrence concluded: "It is accordingly important to view this question in a just perspective and not to base a penal policy in relation to murder on exaggerated estimates of the uniquely deterrent force of the death penalty." Royal Commission on Capital Punishment, 1949–1953, *Report* (London: HMSO, September 1953), p. 24. See also James B. Christoph, *Capital Punishment and British Politics: The British Movement to Abolish the Death Penalty, 1945–57* (Chicago: University of Chicago Press, 1962); and Gowers, *A Life for a Life?*, Chapter 5. On the early history of abolition in Britain, see Randall McGowen, "History, Culture and the Death Penalty: The British Debates, 1840–70," *Historical Reflections/Reflexions Historiques* 29, no. 2 (Summer 2003): 229–49; and Randall McGowen, "Civilizing Punishment: The End of the Public Execution in England," *Journal of British Studies* 33 (July 1994): 257–82.

77. Likewise in Germany, the deterrence discussion surfaced at a time when concern about crime was low. Thus, it was harder to make a compelling argument that the death penalty was needed to stem violent crime. Indeed, the murder rate actually fell after promulgation of Germany's Basic Law, which abolished the death penalty. Evans, *Rituals of Retribution*, p. 798.

78. Chandler, *Capital Punishment in Canada*, pp. 21–22 and 26–29; and Bedau, *The Courts, the Constitution, and Capital Punishment*, p. 101.

79. Lord Windlesham, *Responses to Crime: Penal Policy in the Making*, vol. 2, (Oxford: Clarendon Press, 1993), pp. 53–64 and 82–90; and Christoph, *Capital Punishment and British Politics*. In 1998 Britain formally abolished capital punishment for all crimes.

80. Support ranged from two-thirds to three-quarters of the population in the 1980s. Windlesham, *Responses to Crime: Penal Policy in the Making*, vol. 2, pp. 417–18; and N. C. M. Elder, "Conclusion," in *Law and Order and British Politics*, ed. Philip Norton (Aldershot: Gower, 1984), p. 198.

81. Elder, "Conclusion," p. 198; Marshall, "Death in Venice"; and David Downes, *Contrasts in Tolerance: Post-War Penal Policy in The Netherlands and England and Wales* (Oxford: Clarendon Press, 1988), pp. 70–71.

82. Windlesham, *Responses to Crime: Penal Policy in the Making*, vol. 2, pp. 89–90 and 417–19.

83. Guy Gugliotta, "Crime Bill a Hostage of Politics," *Washington Post*, August 5, 1992, p. A-1.

84. An October 2005 Gallup poll found 64 percent favored the death penalty, the lowest level in more than a quarter-century. See Death Penalty Information Web site, http://deathpenaltyinfo.org/newsanddev.php?scid=23 (accessed February 22, 2006).

85. From 2000 to 2005, an average of 67 people were executed each year in the United States. Calculated from, "Facts About the Death Penalty," Death Penalty Information Center, www.deathpenaltyinfo.org (accessed December 10, 2005). See also Adam Liptak, "Fewer Death Sentences Being Imposed in U.S.," *The New York Times*, September 15, 2004, p. A-16.

86. From 2000 to 2003, the number of death sentences averaged 175 per year, compared with nearly 300 annually in the 1990s. Calculated from U.S. Bureau of Justice Statistics, "Capital Punishment Annual Reports, 1977–2003," as found in "Death Sentences By Year, 1977–2003," http://www.deathpenaltyinfo.org/article.php?scid=9&did=873 (accessed September 9, 2004).

87. Linda Lutton, "The End of Executions: The Anti-Death Penalty Movement Is Gathering Force," *In These Times*, October 30, 2000, p. 26.

88. The ABA adopted a resolution calling for a moratorium on the death penalty until capital punishment jurisdictions could "ensure that death penalty cases are administered fairly and impartially" and "minimize the risk that innocent persons may be executed." Jeffrey L. Kirchmeier, "Death Penalty Symposium: A Call to Action; A Moratorium on Executions Presented by the American Bar Association," *New York City Law Review* 4 (Spring 2002), p. 113.

89. Lutton, "The End of Executions," p. 26.

90. Dirk Johnson, "Illinois, Citing Faulty Verdicts, Bars Executions," *The New York Times*, February 1, 2000, p. A-1; Dirk Johnson, "Shoddy Defense by Lawyers Puts Innocents on Death Row," *The New York Times*, February 5, 2000, p. A-1; and Francis X. Clines, "Death Penalty Is Suspended in Maryland," *The New York Times*, May 10, 2002, p. A-20.

91. Margaret Talbot, "The Executioner's I. Q. Test," *The New York Times Magazine*, June 29, 2003, p. 30.

92. *Ring v. Arizona* invalidated the capital punishment laws of five states and put in doubt the laws of four others. Linda Greenhouse, "The Supreme Court: Capital Punishment; Justices Say Death Penalty Is Up to Juries, Not Judges," *The New York Times*, June 25, 2002, p. A-1.

93. Jodi Wilgoren, "Citing Issues of Fairness, Governor Clears Out Death Row in Illinois," *The New York Times*, January 12, 2003, p. A-1; David Goodman, "The Conversion of Gov. Ryan," *Amnesty Now*, Spring 2003, pp. 10–13; Jonathan Alter, "The Death Penalty on Trial," *Newsweek*, June 12, 2000, pp. 18–31; and *Deadline*, the documentary about Ryan's decision to issue a blanket clemency that was televised July 30, 2004 on NBC's *Dateline* show.

94. Linda Greenhouse, "Supreme Court, 5–4, Forbids Execution in Juvenile Crime," *The New York Times*, March 2, 2005, p. A-1; and Kate Zernike, "Man Executed in 1995 Could Be Cleared in Inquiry," *The New York Times*, July 19, 2005, p. A-15.

95. Carol S. Steiker and Jordan M. Steiker, "Should Abolitionists Support Legislative 'Reform' of the Death Penalty?" *Ohio State Law Journal* 63 (2002), p. 422. For examples of these reforms, see Jim Yardley, "Texas Retooling Criminal Justice in Wake of Furor," *The New York Times*, June 1, 2001, p. A-1; Jim Yardley, "Texas Steps Toward Death Penalty Referendum," *The New York Times*, April 12, 2001,

p. A-26; Jim Yardley, "Of All Places: Texas Wavering on Death Penalty," *The New York Times*, August 19, 2001, sec. 4, p. 4; JoAnn Wypijewski, "Death and Texas," *The Nation*, July 16, 2001, pp. 20–22; and Alan Berlow, "The Broken Machinery of Death," *The American Prospect*, July 30, 2001, pp. 16–17.

96. David Feige, "The Dark Side of Innocence," *The New York Times Magazine*, June 15, 2003, p. 15. The one percent figure comes from David R. Dow, "The Problem of 'Innocence,'" in *Machinery of Death: The Reality of America's Death Penalty Regime*, ed. David R. Dow and Mark Dow (New York: Routledge, 2002), p. 5. For higher estimates, see Gordon P. Waldo and Raymond Paternoster, "Tinkering With the Machinery of Death: The Failure of a Social Experiment," in *Punishment and Social Control*, 2nd ed., ed. Thomas G. Blomberg and Stanley Cohen (New York: Aldine de Gruyter, 2003), p. 312.

97. Phoebe C. Ellsworth and Samuel R. Gross, "Hardening of the Attitudes: Americans' Views of the Death Penalty," *Journal of Social Issues* 50, no. 2 (1994): 19–52; Lane, "'Is There Life Without Parole?'" pp. 364–65; William J. Bowers, Margaret Vandiver, and Patricia H. Dugan, "A New Look at Public Opinion on Capital Punishment: What Citizens and Legislators Prefer," in *Politics, Crime Control, and Culture*, ed. Stuart A. Scheingold (Aldershot: Ashgate/Dartmouth, 1997): 209–47; and Richard C. Dieter, "Sentencing for Life: Americans Embrace Alternatives to the Death Penalty," in *The Death Penalty in America: Current Controversies*, ed. Hugo Adam Bedau (New York: Oxford University Press, 1997): 116–34.

98. Haines, *Against Capital Punishment*, pp. 140 and 180; Julian H. Wright, Jr., "Life-without-parole: An Alternative to Death or Not Much of a Life at All?" *Vanderbilt Law Review* 43 (March 1990), p. 566; Paternoster, *Capital Punishment in America*, p. 287; Scott Turow, "To Kill or Not to Kill," *The New Yorker*, January 6, 2003, p. 47. These contemporary abolitionists remind one of Lewis E. Lawes, the warden of New York's Sing Sing prison in the 1920s and 1930s and an ardent opponent of the death penalty, who said: "Death fades into insignificance when compared with life imprisonment. To spend each night in jail, day after day, year after year, gazing at the bars and longing for freedom, is indeed expiation." Lewis E. Lawes, "Why I Changed My Mind," in *Voices Against Death: American Opposition to Capital Punishment, 1787–1975*, ed. Philip E. Mackey (New York: Burt Franklin & Co., 1976), p. 194. In a similar vein, Cesare Beccaria, the eighteenth-century Italian legal reformer, denounced executions as a "momentary spectacle" that is far less effective as a deterrent than "the continued example of a man deprived of his liberty." Quoted in Michael H. Reggio, "History of the Death Penalty," in *Society's Final Solution: A History and Discussion of the Death Penalty*, ed. Laura E. Randa (Lanham, MD: University Press of America, 1997), p. 5.

99. Haines, *Against Capital Punishment*, p. 179.

100. According to the Council of Europe, "A crime prevention policy which accepts keeping a prisoner for life even if he is no longer a danger to society would be compatible neither with modern principles on the treatment of prisoners during the execution of their sentence nor with the idea of reintegration of offenders into society." United Nations, "Life Imprisonment," 1995, p. 5, cited in Marc Mauer, Ryan S. King, and Malcolm C. Young, "The Meaning of 'Life': Long Prison Sentences in Context" (Washington, DC: The Sentencing Project, May 2004), p. 1. See also Estella Baker, "From 'Making Bad People Worse' to 'Prison Works': Sentencing Policy in England and Wales in the 1990s," *Criminal Law Forum* 7,

no. 3 (1996), pp. 66–69; and Dirk van Zyl Smit, *Taking Life Imprisonment Seriously in National and International Law* (The Hague and New York: Kluver Law International, 2002).

101. Mauer et al., "The Meaning of 'Life'," p. 28.

102. Wright, "Life-without-parole."

103. Robert M. Bohm, "The Economic Costs of Capital Punishment: Past, Present, and Future," in *America's Experiment with Capital Punishment*, p. 591.

104. All the figures in this paragraph come from Mauer et al., "The Meaning of 'Life'," pp. 3 and 17; and Fox Butterfield, "Almost 10% of All Prisoners Are Now Serving Life Terms," *The New York Times*, May 12, 2004, p. A-17.

105. Michael Rigby, "Number of Presidential Pardons Declining," *Prison Legal News*, December 2003, p. 39. Concerned about these trends, in an address to the ABA in 2003 Supreme Court Justice Anthony Kennedy called upon the legal group to help "reinvigorate the pardon process" which has been "drained of its moral force" now that commutations have become infrequent. Quoted in Mauer et al., "The Meaning of 'Life'," p. 29.

106. Wright, "Life-without-parole," pp. 535–37; and Paternoster, *Capital Punishment in America*, p. 279.

107. Lane, "'Is There Life Without Parole?'" pp. 351–53.

108. Bohm, "The Economic Costs of Capital Punishment," pp. 591–92. In Texas, each death penalty case costs taxpayers on average $2.3 million, about three times the lifetime cost of imprisoning someone at the highest level of security. Richard C. Dieter, "Millions Misspent: What Politicians Don't Say About the High Costs of the Death Penalty," in *The Death Penalty in America: Current Controversies*, p. 402.

109. Franklin E. Zimring, Gordon Hawkins, and Sam Kamin, *Punishment and Democracy: Three Strikes and You're Out in California* (Oxford: Oxford University Press, 2001).

110. Linda Greenhouse, "Justices Uphold Long Sentences in Repeat Cases," *The New York Times*, March 6, 2003, p. A-1; and Mauer et al., "The Meaning of 'Life'," p. 2.

111. See Hilary Mantel's review of Sister Helen Prejean's *The Death of Innocents: An Eyewitness Account of Wrongful Executions* (New York: Random House, 2004), in "The Right to Life," *The New York Review of Books*, May 12, 2005, pp. 4–8.

112. Haines, *Against Capital Punishment*, pp. 140–41.

113. Jesse L. Jackson, Sr., Jesse L. Jackson, Jr., and Bruce Shapiro, *Legal Lynching: The Death Penalty and America's Future* (New York: The New Press, 2001), pp. 125–27.

114. Laura Magnani, "Considering Life Without Possibility of Parole or Release," http://www.afsc.org/pwork/0499/049911.htm (accessed October 22, 2001); and Haines, *Against Capital Punishment*, pp. 140–41.

115. Mauer et al., "The Meaning of 'Life'," p. 33.

116. Michael L. Radelet and Marion J. Borg, "The Changing Nature of Death Penalty Debates," *Annual Review of Sociology* 26 (2000): 43–61.

117. The tenacity of this retributive streak is also apparent in the absence of public or official outrage over the increasingly harsh living conditions of prisoners on death row, conditions that are comparable to those at Abu Ghraib prison in Iraq that provoked a national and international uproar in spring 2004. It is also evident in public and state support for death by lethal injection even in the face of mounting

evidence that this so-called painless method of execution actually causes much pain and suffering for many of the condemned. Adam Liptak, "On Death Row, a Battle Over the Fatal Cocktail," *The New York Times*, September 16, 2004, p. A-16; Bob Williams, "Mississippi Death Row Conditions Unconstitutional; Sweeping Reforms Ordered," *Prison Legal News*, April 2004, pp. 26–27; Robert Johnson, "Life Under Sentence of Death: Historical and Contemporary Perspectives," in *America's Experiment with Capital Punishment*: 647–71; and Anne-Marie Cusac, "Abu Ghraib, USA," *Prison Legal News*, July 2004, pp. 1 and 3–4.

118. Radelet and Borg, "The Changing Nature of Death Penalty Debates."

119. One of the best known of these groups is Murder Victims' Families for Reconciliation. Rachel King, *Don't Kill in Our Names: Families of Murder Victims Speak Out Against the Death Penalty* (New Brunswick, NJ: Rutgers University Press, 2003); and Robert Renny Cushing and Susannah Sheffer, *Dignity Denied: The Experience of Murder Victims' Families Who Oppose the Death Penalty* (Cambridge, MA: Murder Victims' Families for Reconciliation, 2002).

120. Bud Welch, "Speaking Out Against the Execution of Timothy McVeigh," in *Machinery of Death*: 275–81.

121. Vik Kanwar, "Capital Punishment as 'Closure': The Limits of a Victim-Centered Jurisprudence," *New York University Review of Law and Social Change* 27 (2001/2002), pp. 247 and 255; and Jonathan Simon, "Fearless Speech in the Killing State: The Power of Capital Crime Victim Speech," *North Carolina Law Review* 82 (May 2004).

122. Paternoster, *Capital Punishment in America*, p. 286. See also Zimring and Hawkins, *Capital Punishment and the American Agenda*, p. 11; and Bedau, *Death Is Different*, p. 8.

123. Here I am drawing explicit parallels with McGowen's excellent analysis of the defeat of the British abolitionists in the nineteenth century. McGowen, "History, Culture and the Death Penalty," pp. 248–49.

124. Between 1930 and 1967, the United States carried out 3,859 executions. Calculated from Bowers et al., *Legal Homicide*, pp. 25–26, Table 1–4.

125. Steiker and Steiker, "Should Abolitionists Support Legislative 'Reform' of the Death Penalty?"; and Carol S. Steiker and Jordan M. Steiker, "Judicial Developments in Capital Punishment Law," in *America's Experiment with Capital Punishment*: 55–83.

CHAPTER 10: CONCLUSION: WHITHER THE CARCERAL STATE?

1. Milovan Djilas, *Of Prisons and Ideas* (San Diego, CA: Harcourt, Brace, Jovanovich, 1986), p. 139.

2. Karen Orren and Stephen Skowronek, *The Search for American Political Development* (Cambridge: Cambridge University Press, 2004), p. 123.

3. This phrase comes from Orren and Skowronek, *The Search for American Political Development*, p. 199.

4. Desmond S. King and Rogers M. Smith, "Racial Orders in American Political Development," *American Political Science Review* 99, no. 1 (February 2005): 75–92.

5. "Barry Goldwater's Acceptance Speech," 1964 Republican National Convention, http://www.nationalcenter.org/Goldwater.html (accessed September 21, 2004).

6. Stephen Skowronek, *Building a New American State: The Expansion of National Administrative Capacities, 1877–1920* (Cambridge: Cambridge University Press, 1982), p. ix.

7. Theodore Lowi, "American Business, Public Policy, Case Studies and Political Theory," *World Politics* 16, no. 4 (1964): 677–715, in Orren and Skowronek, *The Search for American Political Development*, p. 102.

8. Roger Lane, "Urban Police and Crime in Nineteenth-Century America," ed. Michael Tonry and Norval Morris, *Crime and Justice: A Review of Research*, vol. 15 (Chicago: University of Chicago Press, 1992), p. 3.

9. Andrew J. Polsky, "The New 'Dismal Science'? The Lessons of American Political Development for Today," *Polity* 32, no. 3 (Spring 2000): 303–8.

10. Orren and Skowronek, *The Search for American Political Development*, p. 102.

11. For some good lists of sensible recommendations, see Henry Ruth and Kevin R. Reitz, *The Challenge of Crime: Rethinking Our Response* (Cambridge, MA: Harvard University Press, 2003), pp. 106–16 and 240–48; Vincent Schiraldi and Judith Greene, "Reducing Correctional Costs in an Era of Tightening Budgets and Shifting Public Opinion," *Federal Sentencing Reporter* 14, no. 6 (May/June 2002): 332–36; and Kate Stith and Joŝe Cabranes, *Fear of Judging: Sentencing Guidelines in the Federal Courts* (Chicago: University of Chicago Press, 1998), Chapter 5.

12. And even then, its rate would still exceed the average incarceration rate of 100 per 100,000 for the major countries of Western Europe. Calculated from "Europe – Prison Population Rates per 100,000 of the National Population," International Centre for Prison Studies, http://www.kcl.ac.uk/depsta/rel/icps/worldbrief/highest_to_lowest_rates.php (accessed March 9, 2005).

13. Quoted in S. K. Ruck, ed., *Paterson on Prisons* (London: Frederick Muller, 1951), p. 3, in Vivien Stern, *A Sin Against the Future: Imprisonment in the World* (Boston: Northeastern University Press, 1998), p. 197.

14. John van Blad, Hans Mastrigt, and Niels Uildriks, "Hulsman's Abolitionist Perspective: The Criminal Justice System as a Social Problem," in *The Criminal Justice System as a Social Problem: An Abolitionist Perspective*, ed. John van Blad, Hans Mastrigt, and Niels Uildriks (Rotterdam: Erasmus Universiteit, 1987), p. 49.

15. Quoted in Francis T. Cullen and Karen E. Gilbert, *Reaffirming Rehabilitation* (Cincinnati, OH: Anderson Publishing Co., 1982), p. xxii.

16. Marc Mauer, "The Fragility of Criminal Justice Reform," *Social Justice* 21, no. 3 (Fall 1994), p. 27.

17. Orren and Skowronek, *The Search for American Political Development*, p. 106; and Elisabeth Stephanie Clemens, *The People's Lobby: Organizational Innovation and the Rise of Interest Group Politics in the United States, 1890–1925* (Chicago: University of Chicago Press, 1997).

18. Drake Bennett and Robert Kuttner, "Crime and Redemption," *The American Prospect*, December 2003, p. 36.

19. Fox Butterfield, "Inmates Go Free to Help States Reduce Deficits," *The New York Times*, December 19, 2002, p. A-1; and Fox Butterfield, "Tight Budgets Force States to Reconsider Crime and Penalties," *The New York Times*, January 21, 2002, p. A-1. In fiscal 2002, twenty-five states were forced to reduce their corrections budgets. The only government sector affected more often by budget cuts was higher education, which was slashed in twenty-nine states. Daniel F. Wilhelm

and Nicholas R. Turner, *Is the Budget Crisis Changing the Way We Look at Sentencing and Incarceration?* (New York: Vera Institute of Justice, June 2002), p. 2.

20. Wilhelm and Turner, *Is the Budget Crisis Changing the Way We Look at Sentencing and Incarceration?*, p. 5.

21. For details on these changes, see Jon Wool and Don Stemen, *Changing Fortunes or Changing Attitudes? Sentencing and Corrections Reforms in 2003* (New York: Vera Institute of Justice, March 2004); and Ryan S. King and Marc Mauer, *State Sentencing and Corrections Policy in an Era of Fiscal Restraint* (Washington, DC: The Sentencing Project, February 2002). On drug courts, see Douglas A. Berman, "The Start of the Next Revolution?: Recent State Reforms in the Sentencing of Drug Offenders," *Federal Sentencing Reporter* 14, no. 6 (May/June 2002), p. 329.

22. Butterfield, "With Cash Tight, States Reassess"; and Bennett and Kuttner, "Crime and Redemption."

23. Matthew Clarke, "Strapped States Threaten Prisoner Release to Extort Revenue," *Prison Legal News,* September 2003, p. 3.

24. On recent shifts in public opinion showing decreased concern about crime and growing doubts about the war on drugs and meting out harsh prison sentences for nonviolent offenders, see Peter D. Hart Research Associates, Inc., "The New Politics of Criminal Justice: Summary of Findings," January 2002, cited in Wilhelm and Turner, *Is the Budget Crisis Changing the Way We Look at Sentencing and Incarceration?*, p. 5; and Schiraldi and Greene, "Reducing Correctional Costs in an Era of Tightening Budgets," pp. 332–33.

25. Todd R. Clear and Patricia M. Harris, "The Costs of Incarceration," in *America's Correctional Crisis: Prison Populations and Public Policy*, ed. Stephen D. Gottfredson and Sean McConville (New York: Greenwood Press, 1987), pp. 37–38.

26. Norval Morris, "Closing Address," *New York University Review of Law and Social Change* 12, no. 1 (1983–84), p. 353.

27. Mark Costanzo, *Just Revenge: Costs and Consequences of the Death Penalty* (New York: St. Martin's Press, 1997), pp. 61–62.

28. Butterfield, "Tight Budgets Force States to Reconsider."

29. Wilhelm and Turner, *Is the Budget Crisis Changing the Way We Look at Sentencing and Incarceration?*, p. 5.

30. "Terrorism" was so broadly defined in this legislation that being present at a demonstration considered "disruptive" could result in a life sentence. Harry Esteve, "Inside the Capitol in This March, Protestors Could Get Hard Time," *The Oregonian*, March 24, 2003, p. C-1. See also Michelle Garcia, "N.Y. Using Terrorism Law to Prosecute Street Gang; Critics Say Post-9/11 Legislation Is Being Applied Too Broadly," *Washington Post*, February 1, 2005, p. A-3.

31. For a revealing glimpse of the wide range of companies and organizations that have a financial stake in the carceral state, see Silja J. A. Talvi, "Cashing in On Cons," *In These Times*, February 28, 2005, p. 16.

32. This account of Proposition 66 is based on "California Initiative to Soften '3-Strikes' Law Defeated; DNA Collection From Arrestees Approved," *Prison Legal News*, January 2005, pp. 18–19; and Louis Freedberg, "Reforming Three Strikes," *The Nation*, November 1, 2004, pp. 7–8.

33. Weeks earlier Sacramento Superior Court had ruled that similar claims be stricken from the campaign literature mailed to all voters because they were "patently false." "California Initiative to Soften '3-Strikes' Law Defeated," p. 18.

The results of the 2004 election were not entirely bleak for penal reformers in California. Voters in Los Angeles rejected a half-cent increase in the sales tax that would have raised $560 million per year to pay for 5,000 additional police officers. At the same time they approved a $500 million bond measure to improve the city's drainage system. John E. Dannenberg, "Los Angeles Voters Reject 5,000 More Cops; Invest in Clear Ocean Instead," *Prison Legal News*, January 2005, p. 23.

34. Marc L. Miller, "Cells vs. Cops vs. Classrooms," ed. Lawrence Friedman and George Fisher, *The Crime Conundrum: Essays on Criminal Justice* (Boulder, CO: Westview Press, 1997), p. 128.

35. Miller, "Cells vs. Cops vs. Classrooms," p. 152.

36. Bell Gale Chevigny, "Prison Activists Come of Age," *The Nation*, July 24/31, 2000, pp. 27–30; Annette Fuentes, "Unchained: From the Bay Area to the Big Apple, Youth Activists Target Juvenile Jails," *In These Times*, July 8, 2002, pp. 16–17; and Sasha Abramsky, "Incarceration, Inc.," *The Nation*, July 19/26, 2004, pp. 22–25.

37. Wilhelm and Turner, *Is the Budget Crisis Changing the Way We Look at Sentencing and Incarceration?*, pp. 7–8; Ronald F. Wright, "Flexibility in North Carolina Structured Sentencing, 1995–1997," in *Penal Reform in Overcrowded Times*, ed. Michael Tonry (Oxford: Oxford University Press, 2001); and Ronald F. Wright, "North Carolina Prepares for Guidelines Sentencing," in *Penal Reform in Overcrowded Times*.

38. Wilhelm and Turner, *Is the Budget Crisis Changing the Way We Look at Sentencing and Incarceration?*, p. 10.

39. Wilhelm and Turner, *Is the Budget Crisis Changing the Way We Look at Sentencing and Incarceration?*, p. 3.

40. Wool and Stemen, *Changing Fortunes or Changing Attitudes?*, p. 7.

41. Joan Petersilia, *When Prisoners Come Home: Parole and Prisoner Reentry* (New York: Oxford University Press, 2003); and Jeremy Travis and Christy Visher, eds., *Prisoner Reentry and Crime in America* (Cambridge: Cambridge University Press, 2005).

42. Wool and Stemen, *Changing Fortunes or Changing Attitudes?*, p. 4.

43. Lonnie Burton, "The Deadly Health Services of Naphcare in Alabama," *Prison Legal News*, October 2003, pp. 1–5; Ira P. Robbins, "Managed Health Care in Prisons as Cruel and Unusual Punishment," *Journal of Criminal Law and Criminology* 90, no. 1 (Fall 1999); and Paul von Zielbauer, "As Health Care in Jail Goes Private, 10 Days Can Be a Death Sentence," *The New York Times*, February 27, 2005, sec. 1, p. 1.

44. Prisons are serving fewer fresh vegetables and fruits and substituting cheaper processed meats, starches, and powdered milk. Some states have reduced the number of daily calories budgeted for each prisoner and have even cut back to two meals a day on weekends and holidays. Food is a very small budget item for prisons. About 80 percent of prison costs go for guards' salaries. Butterfield, "With Cash Tight, States Reassess Long Jail Terms"; and "Budget Cuts to Include Food Service Programs," *Correctional News*, 9 no. 5 (July/August 2003), p. 1.

45. Butterfield, "With Cash Tight, States Reassess."

46. Wool and Stemen, *Changing Fortunes or Changing Attitudes?*, p. 8; and Paul von Zielbauer, "Company's Troubled Answer for Fragile Alabama Inmates," *The New York Times*, August 1, 2005, p. A-1.

47. Quoted in Edgardo Rotman, "The Failure of Reform: United States, 1865–1965," in *The Oxford History of the Prison: The Practice of Punishment in Western Society*, ed. Norval Morris and David J. Rothman (New York: Oxford University Press, 1995), p. 194.

48. As Norval Morris contends, "Ultimately, the case for intermediate punishments rests not on utilitarian crime-prevention and cost-saving grounds, though both are relevant. It rests on principles of justice." Norval Morris, "The Contemporary Prison, 1965 – Present," in *The Oxford History of the Prison*, p. 257.

49. Clarke, "Strapped States Threaten Prisoner Release," p. 3.

50. Michael M. O'Hear, "When Voters Choose the Sentence: The Drug Policy Initiatives in Arizona, California, Ohio, and Michigan," *Federal Sentencing Reporter* 14, no. 6 (May/June 2002): 337–43. On the ACLU and decriminalization, see Samuel Walker, *In Defense of American Liberties: A History of the ACLU*, 2nd ed. (Carbondale, IL: Southern Illinois University Press, 1999), p. xvii.

51. Elizabeth M. Schneider, "The Dialectic of Rights and Politics: Perspectives from the Women's Movement," in *Feminist Legal Theory: Readings in Law and Gender*, ed. Katharine T. Bartlett and Rosanne Kennedy (Boulder, CO: Westview Press, 1991), p. 320.

52. Kimberlé Williams Crenshaw, "Race, Reform and Retrenchment: Transformation and Legitimation in Antidiscrimination Law," *Harvard Law Review* 101, no. 7 (May 1988), pp. 1368–69. Emphasis in the original.

53. Mary Ellen Curtin, *Black Prisoners and Their World, Alabama, 1865–1900* (Charlottesville, VA: University of Virginia Press, 2000), pp. 9–10 and Chapter 10.

54. He singled out the black middle class in particular for "join[ing] with the bloodhounds in anathematizing every Negro in jail." W. E. B. DuBois, "Courts and Jails," *The Crisis*, March 1932, in *The Selected Writings of W. E. B. DuBois*, ed. Walter Wilson (New York: Signet Classics, 1970), pp. 126–27.

55. Cathy J. Cohen, *The Boundaries of Blackness: AIDS and the Breakdown of Black Politics* (Chicago: University of Chicago Press, 1999).

56. See p. 33. See also Randall Kennedy, *Race, Crime, and the Law* (New York: Pantheon, 1997), pp. 370–72.

57. Dorian T. Warren, "The Intersection Between Voting Rights and Criminal Justice: The National Black Organizational Response to Felon Disenfranchisement," unpublished paper on file with author, June 2000.

58. Paul Butler, "Racially Based Jury Nullification: Black Power in the Criminal Justice System," *Yale Law Journal* 105, no. 3 (December 1995): 677–725. For a scorching criticism of jury nullification as a reform strategy, see Kennedy, *Race, Crime, and the Law*, pp. 295–310.

59. "Jesse Jackson Delivers Remarks at Democratic National Convention," http://www.cnn.com/ELECTION/2000/conventions/democratic/transcripts/u060815.html (accessed March 16, 2005); and "General Colin Powell (Ret.) Delivers Remarks at Republican Convention," http://www.cnn.com/ELECTION/2000/conventions/republican/transcripts/u000731.html (accessed March 16, 2005).

60. Mauer, "The Fragility of Criminal Justice Reform," p. 26; Linda Faye Williams, "Race and the Politics of Social Policy," in *The Social Divide: Political Parties and the Future of Activist Government*, ed. Margaret Weir (Washington, DC, and New York: The Brookings Institution and Russell Sage Foundation, 1998): 417–63; and Holly Idelson, "Racial Sentencing Provision Snarls Crime Legislation," *Congressional Quarterly*, June 25, 1994, p. 1713.

61. During her tenure, the Fund took up the case of Kemba Smith, a young black woman sentenced to twenty-four years in prison for her minor connection to a drug ring run by her boyfriend. To garner support for Smith, Jones rented a limousine and took the presidents of two leading black women's organizations to see her in prison. "I needed them to see their daughters and nieces, to identify with the issue," Jones explained. "They did, and they did not let that case go." Lynette Clemetson, "NAACP Legal Defense Fund Chief Retires," *The New York Times*, January 16, 2004, p. A-10.

62. Rebecca Perl, "The Last Disenfranchised Class," *The Nation*, November 24, 2003, p. 13.

63. Linda Greenhouse, "Supreme Court Declines to Hear 2 Cases Weighing the Right of Felons to Vote," *The New York Times*, November 9, 2004, p. A-19.

64. Fox Butterfield, "Freed From Prison, but Still Paying a Penalty," *The New York Times*, December 20, 2002, sec. 1, p. 18; and Jamie Fellner and Marc Mauer, *Losing the Vote: The Impact of Felony Disenfranchisement Laws in the United States* (Washington, DC, and New York: The Sentencing Project and Human Rights Watch, October 1998), p. 2.

65. Christopher Uggen and Jeff Manza, "Lost Voices: The Civic and Political Views of Disenfranchised Felons," in *Imprisoning America: The Social Effects of Mass Incarceration*, ed. Mary Pattillo, David Weiman, and Bruce Western (New York: Russell Sage Foundation, 2004), p. 166. Vermont and Maine are the only states that permit people in prison to vote. Pam Belluck, "When the Voting Bloc Lives Inside a Cellblock," *The New York Times*, November 1, 2004, p. A-12.

66. Perl, "The Last Disenfranchised Class," p. 11; Miles S. Rapoport, "Restoring the Vote," *The American Prospect*, August 13, 2001, pp. 13–14; and Mary Fainsod Katzenstein, "How Different? A Comparison of the Movement Challenging Ex-Felon Disenfranchisement with Suffrage Politics of an Earlier Time," paper presented at the American Political Science Association, Boston, August 29–September 1, 2002.

67. Eric Lichtblau, "Confusing Rules Deny Vote to Ex-Felons, Study Says," *The New York Times*, February 20, 2005, sec. 1, p. 24.

68. This order followed on the heels of a similar restoration of voting rights in Nebraska, which together with Iowa was one of the last two states outside of the South to end its ban. Kate Zernike, "Iowa Governor Will Give Felons the Right to Vote," *The New York Times*, June 18, 2005, p. A-8.

69. Michael Tonry, *Malign Neglect: Race, Crime and Punishment in America* (New York: Oxford University Press, 1995), p. 183.

70. Tonry, *Malign Neglect*, pp. 207–8.

71. Pattillo, Weiman, and Western, eds., *Imprisoning America*.

72. Susan Phillips and Barbara Bloom, "In Whose Best Interest? The Impact of Changing Public Policy on Relatives Caring for Children With Incarcerated Parents," *Child Welfare* 77 (1998), p. 539, cited in John Hagan and Ronit Dinovitzer, "Collateral Consequences of Imprisonment for Children, Communities, and Prisoners," *Crime and Justice: A Review of Research*, vol. 26, *Prisons*, ed. Michael Tonry and Joan Petersilia (Chicago: University of Chicago Press, 1999), p. 138.

73. "Colin Powell (Ret.) Delivers Remarks at Republican Convention."

74. Bruce Western, Mary Pattillo, and David Weiman, "Introduction," *Imprisoning America*, p. 9.

75. Ruth Wilson Gilmore, "You Have Dislodged a Boulder: Mothers and Prisoners in the Post Keynesian California Landscape," *Transforming Anthropology* 8, no. 1 & 2 (1999), p. 27.

76. Chevigny, "Prison Activists Come of Age," p. 28.

77. James Q. Whitman, *Harsh Justice: Criminal Punishment and the Widening Divide Between America and Europe* (Oxford: Oxford University Press, 2003), p. 8.

78. Kennedy, *Race, Crime, and the Law*, p. 347.

79. Kennedy, *Race, Crime, and the Law*, p. 385.

80. Michael Tonry, "Punishment Policies and Patterns in Western Countries," in *Sentencing and Sanctions in Western Countries*, ed. Michael Tonry and Richard S. Frase (Oxford: Oxford University Press, 2001), p. 25.

81. Richard S. Frase, "Comparative Perspectives on Sentencing Policy and Research," in *Sentencing and Sanctions in Western Countries*, p. 278.

82. Kenneth Neale, "The European Prison Rules: Contextual, Philosophical and Practical Aspects," in *Imprisonment: European Perspectives*, ed. John Muncie and Richard Sparks (New York: St. Martin's Press, 1991), p. 203. See also Leena Kurki, "International Standards for Sentencing and Punishment," in *Sentencing and Sanctions in Western Countries*.

83. Neale, "The European Prison Rules," p. 211.

84. Neale, "The European Prison Rules," p. 206. For a copy of those rules, see Council of Europe, "The European Prison Rules, 1987," in *Imprisonment: European Perspectives*.

85. Neale, "The European Prison Rules," p. 207.

86. Neale, "The European Prison Rules," p. 211.

87. Neale, "The European Prison Rules," p. 213.

88. In 1986, former Home Secretary Roy Jenkins acidly remarked at a party conference: "At least we lead Europe in the ... size of our prison population, the Turks having given that race up in despair." Quoted in Lord Windlesham, *Responses to Crime: Penal Policy in the Making*, vol. 2 (Oxford: Clarendon Press, 1993), p. 211.

89. Rod Morgan, "International Controls on Sentencing and Punishment," in *Sentencing and Sanctions in Western Countries*.

90. Morgan, "International Controls on Sentencing and Punishment"; Joe Sim, Vincenzo Ruggiero, and Mick Ryan, "Punishment in Europe: Perceptions and Commonalities," in *Western European Penal Systems: A Critical Anatomy*, ed. Vincenzo Ruggiero, Mick Ryan, and Joe Sim (London: Sage, 1995); Heike Jung, "Criminal Justice: A European Perspective," *Criminal Law Review*, April 1993: 237–45; Henrik Tham, "Law and Order as a Leftist Project? The Case of Sweden," *Punishment & Society* 3, no. 3 (July 2001): 409–26; and Keith B. Richburg, "A Breakthrough Fueled by Rising Fear; French Rightist Was Confident of Appeal of Views on Immigrants, Crime," *Washington Post*, April 23, 2002, p. A-13.

91. Hans-Jörg Albrecht, "Post-Adjudication Dispositions in Comparative Perspective," in *Sentencing and Sanctions in Western Countries*, p. 303.

92. Thomas Weigend, "Sentencing and Punishment in Germany," in *Sentencing and Sanctions in Western Countries*, p. 212.

93. On the proportion of foreigners in European prisons, see Loïc Wacquant, "Suitable Enemies: Foreigners and Immigrants in the Prisons of Europe," *Punishment & Society* 1, no. 2 (October 1999): 215–32.

94. Prisoners are no longer denied the right to vote, and each prisoner has some statutorily guaranteed activities, including open-air visits, visits by family and friends, recreation, and sports. Productive labor for twenty-six hours per week is also a central part of the new policy. Peter J. Tak, "Sentencing and Punishment in The Netherlands," in *Sentencing and Sanctions in Western Countries*, pp. 184–85.

95. Albrecht, "Post-Adjudication Dispositions in Comparative Perspective," p. 303.

96. Frase, "Comparative Perspectives on Sentencing Policy and Research," pp. 273–74.

97. Historically the legal profession and the ABA have not played central roles in progressive reforms. Walker, *In Defense of American Liberties*, pp. 88–89 and 201–02; and Albert P. Melone, *Lawyers, Public Policy and Interest Group Politics* (Washington, DC: University Press of America, 1977).

98. Walker, *In Defense of Civil Liberties*, p. 12 and Chapter 3.

99. James B. Jacobs, "The Prisoners' Rights Movement and Its Impacts, 1960–80," ed. Norval Morris and Michael Tonry, *Crime and Justice: An Annual Review of Research*, vol. 2 (Chicago: University of Chicago Press, 1980), p. 438.

100. Kevin R. Reitz and Curtis R. Reitz, "Building a Sentencing Reform Agenda: The ABA's New Sentencing Standards," *Judicature* 78, no. 4 (January–February 1995), p. 189.

101. American Bar Association, House of Delegates, *Daily Journal*, 2004 Annual Meeting, Atlanta, Ga., August 9–10, 2004, www.abanet.org/leadership/2004/annual/2004annualDailyJournal.doc (accessed March 15, 2005).

102. American Bar Association, news release, "ABA Forms New Commission to Review Mandatory Minimum Sentences, Prison Conditions and Pardons," October 6, 2003, http://www.abanet.org/media/oct03/100603_1.html (accessed March 20, 2005); and "Justice Kennedy Speaks Out," editorial, *The New York Times*, August 12, 2003, p. A-16.

103. Anne Gearan, Associated Press, "Supreme Court's Kennedy Says 2 Million Inmates Is Too Many," *Houston Chronicle*, April 10, 2003, p. A-2.

104. Kate Stith and Steve Y. Koh, "The Politics of Sentencing Reform: The Legislative History of the Federal Sentencing Guidelines," *Wake Forest Law Review* 28, no. 2 (1993), pp. 251–52.

105. Stith and Cabranes, *Fear of Judging*, Chapter 5.

106. Linda Greenhouse, "Supreme Court Transforms Use of Sentence Guidelines," *The New York Times*, January 13, 2005, p. A-1; and Carl Hulse and Adam Liptak, "New Fight Over Controlling Punishments Is Widely Seen," *The New York Times*, January 13, 2005, p. A-29.

107. Drug Policy Alliance, "Alliance Action Network," May 11, 2005.

108. The bill broadened the definition of a gang to include three people who have committed at least two crimes together, at least one of them violent. David D. Kirkpatrick, "Congress Rekindles Battle on Mandatory Sentences," *The New York Times*, May 11, 2005, p. A-14; and Erica Werner, Associated Press, "House OKs Measure to Get Tough," *The Philadelphia Inquirer*, May 12, 2005, p. A-13.

109. David Garland and Peter Young charge that orthodox criminology severed those links. David Garland and Peter Young, "Towards a Social Analysis of Penalty," in *The Power to Punish: Contemporary Penalty and Social Analysis*, ed. David Garland and Peter Young (London and Atlantic Highlands, NJ: Heinemann Educational Books and Humanities Press, 1983), p. 5.

110. Stuart A. Scheingold, "Constructing the New Political Criminology," *Law and Social Inquiry* 23, no. 4 (Autumn 1998), p. 860.

111. David L. Bazelon, "The Hidden Politics of Criminology," *Federal Probation* 42, no. 2 (June 1978), p. 3.

112. Scheingold, "Constructing the New Political Criminology," p. 857.

113. Garland and Young, "Towards a Social Analysis of Penalty," p. 22.

114. Frase, "Comparative Perspectives on Sentencing Policy and Research," p. 284.

115. Frase, "Comparative Perspectives on Sentencing Policy and Research," p. 285.

116. For example, see the work on American political development and the welfare state by Marie Gottschalk, Jacob Hacker, Chris Howard, Robert Lieberman, Cathie Jo Martin, Paul Pierson, Suzanne Mettler, Theda Skocpol, and others.

117. Richard Bensel, "The Tension between American Political Development as a Research Community and as a Disciplinary Subfield," *Studies in American Political Development* 17, no. 1 (Spring 2003): 103–06.

118. Rogers Smith, "Substance and Methods in APD Research," *Studies in American Political Development* 17, no. 1 (Spring 2003), p. 111.

119. Franklin E. Zimring, Gordon Hawkins, and Sam Kamin, *Punishment and Democracy: Three Strikes and You're Out in California* (Oxford: Oxford University Press, 2001); and Ann Chih Lin, *Reform in the Making: The Implementation of Social Policy in Prison* (Princeton: Princeton University Press, 2000).

120. For an excellent analysis of the effects of incarceration on inequality, wages, and family life, see Bruce Western, *Punishment and Inequality in America*, (New York: Russell Sage Foundation, forthcoming 2006), Chapters 5–7.

121. Hagan and Dinovitzer, "Collateral Consequences of Imprisonment": 121–62.

122. Alison Liebling, "Prison Suicide and Prisoner Coping," in *Crime and Justice – A Review of Research*, vol. 26, *Prisons*, Michael Tonry and Joan Petersilia (Chicago and London: University of Chicago Press, 1999): 283–359.

123. Some promising new work in this area includes Bruce Western and Sara McLanahan, "Fathers Behind Bars: The Impact of Incarceration on Family Formation," in *Contemporary Perspectives in Family Research* 2 (2000): 307–22; and Bruce Western and Becky Pettit, "Incarceration and Racial Inequality in Men's Employment," *Industrial and Labor Relations Review* 54, no. 1 (2000): 3–16.

124. Anthony E. Bottoms, "Interpersonal Violence and Social Order in Prisons," in *Crime and Justice – A Review of Research*, vol. 26: 205–81; and Liebling, "Prison Suicide and Prisoner Coping."

125. Douglas C. McDonald, "Medical Care in Prisons," in *Crime and Justice–A Review of Research*, vol. 26: 427–78.

126. Stephen D. Sowle, "A Regime of Social Death: Criminal Punishment in the Age of Prisons," *New York University Review of Law and Social Change* 21, no. 3 (1994–95), p. 565.

127. Zimring et al., *Punishment and Democracy*, p. 209.

128. Zimring et al., *Punishment and Democracy*, pp. 212–14.

129. In this procedure, physicians removed the testicles from men who had just been executed, ground them into a substance the consistency of toothpaste, and injected them with a syringe into the abdomens of other prisoners. Joseph Hallinan, *Going Up the River: Travels in a Prison Nation* (New York: Random House, 2001), p. 77.

130. David Garland makes a similar point. See Garland, *The Culture of Control: Crime and Social Order in Contemporary Society* (Chicago: University of Chicago Press, 2001), p. 205.

131. Tapio Lappi-Seppälä, "Sentencing and Punishment in Finland: The Decline of the Repressive Ideal," in *Sentencing and Sanctions in Western Countries*, p. 108. See also Patrik Tömudd, "Sentencing and Punishment in Finland," in *Sentencing Reform in Overcrowded Times: A Comparative Perspective*, ed. Michael Tonry and Kathleen Hatlestad (New York: Oxford University Press, 1997).

132. Andrew Rutherford, *Prisons and the Process of Justice: The Reductionist Challenge* (London: Heinemann, 1984), p. 124.

133. David Garland, *Punishment and Modern Society: A Study in Social Theory* (Chicago: University of Chicago Press, 1990), p. 215.

134. Chevigny, "Prison Activists Come of Age," p. 29.

135. Todd R. Clear, *The Community Justice Ideal: Preventing Crime and Achieving Justice* (Boulder, CO: Westview Press, 1999), p. 20.

136. O'Hear, "When Voters Choose the Sentence," p. 342.

137. O'Hear, "When Voters Choose the Sentence," p. 341.

138. O'Hear, "When Voters Choose the Sentence," p. 341.

139. O'Hear, "When Voters Choose the Sentence," p. 341.

140. One notable exception is Delaware, where some advocacy groups and legislators successfully made the case that people who possess or sell certain quantities of drugs do so primarily because they are addicts. Recently they were able to strike a compromise brokered by the state's sentencing commission that relaxed Delaware's long-standing three-year mandatory minimum for first-time felony traffickers. Other important exceptions include Michigan, which reduced the mandatory minimum for most drug offenses, including sale of illegal drugs, and Washington State, which implemented a new drug sentencing grid. Wool and Stemen, *Changing Fortunes or Changing Attitudes?*, pp. 10–11 and n. 29.

141. Allen J. Beck, "Understanding Growth in U.S. Prison and Parole Populations," paper presented at the Annual Conference on Criminal Justice Research and Evaluation: Enhancing Policy and Practice," Washington, DC, July 21, 1999, p. 5, Table 8, cited in Ruth and Reitz, *The Challenge of Crime*, p. 97. It remains uncertain whether these "violent criminals" targeted for longer sentences were truly dangerous offenders or a mixture of serious offenders and petty criminals. Ruth and Reitz, *The Challenge of Crime*, p. 98.

142. David Chang, "Beyond Uncompromising Positions: Hate Crimes Legislation and the Common Ground Between Republicans and Gay Rights Advocates," *Fordham Urban Law Journal* 21, no. 4 (Summer 1994): 1097–1105. For other views on how hate crimes laws might affect the broader debate over crime and punishment, see James B. Jacobs and Kimberly Potter, *Hate Crimes: Criminal Law and Identity Politics* (New York: Oxford University Press, 1998); Valerie Jenness and Kendal Broad, *Hate Crimes: New Social Movements and the Politics of Violence* (New York: Aldine de Gruyter, 1997); and Valerie Jenness and Ryken Grattet, *Making Hate a Crime: From Social Movement to Law Enforcement* (New York: Russell Sage Foundation, 2001).

143. Thomas Mathiesen, *The Politics of Abolition* (New York: John Wiley & Sons, 1974), pp. 174–76.

144. Paige Welch, "Prison Rape Elimination Act of 2003 Signed Into Law; Commission To Be Formed Soon," *Prison Legal News*, March 2004, p. 6; and Brent Staples, "The Federal Government Gets Real About Sex Behind Bars," *The New York Times*, November 27, 2004, p. A-14.

145. Attorney General John Ashcroft characterized human trafficking as "pure and unadulterated evil." "The Girls Next Door," letter to the editor, *The New York Times Magazine*, February 15, 2004, p. 6.

146. Tara McKelvey, "Of Human Bondage," *The American Prospect*, November 2004, pp. 17–20; Peter Landesman, "The Girls Next Door," *The New York Times Magazine*, January 25, 2004; and Eartha Melzer, "Trafficking in Politics," *In These Times*, March 28, 2005, pp. 20–21.

147. As of 2002, whites made up 35 percent of the federal prison population, down from nearly 60 percent in 1984. Hispanics imprisoned on immigration charges explain some of this dramatic shift. In 1984, blacks and whites received, on average, sentences of just over two years in the federal system. Two decades later, the figures were six years for blacks and four years for whites. Associated Press, "Sentencing Guideline Study Finds Continuing Disparities," *The New York Times*, November 27, 2004, p. A-11.

148. The U.S. Congress enacted about 59 percent of all existing federal criminal statutes in the first 180 years of the country's history. The remaining 41 percent were enacted in just the past thirty years. James Strazzella, Task Force Reporter, *The Federalization of Criminal Law* (Washington, DC: American Bar Association Criminal Justice Section, 1998), pp. 7–12, cited in Ruth and Reitz, *The Challenge of Crime*, p. 158.

149. Franklin E. Zimring and Gordon Hawkins, "Toward a Principled Basis for Federal Crime Legislation," *The Annals of the American Academy of Political and Social Science* 543 (January 1996): 15–26.

150. This summary of the findings of these two reports comes from Ruth and Reitz, *The Challenge of Crime*, pp. 159–60.

151. Jann S. Wenner, "Bill Clinton: The Rolling Stone Interview," *Rolling Stone*, December 28, 2000–January 4, 2001, p. 97.

152. David Burnham and Susan Long, "The Clinton Era by the Numbers," *The Nation*, January 29, 2001, pp. 20–22.

153. Peter Schrag, "A Quagmire for Our Time," *The American Prospect*, August 13, 2001, p. 29.

154. That insertion drew the ire of Chief Justice William Rehnquist. Linda Greenhouse, "Chief Justice Attacks Law Infringing on Judges," *The New York Times*, January 1, 2004, p. A-14.

155. Hulse and Liptak, "New Fight Over Controlling Punishments."

156. Eric Lichtblau, "Justice Department to Monitor Judges for Sentences Shorter Than Guidelines Suggest," *The New York Times*, August 9, 2003, p. A-12.

157. George Fisher, "A Practice as Old as Justice Itself," *The New York Times*, September 28, 2003, sec. 4, p. 11; Bennett and Kuttner, "Crime and Redemption," p. 37; and Benjamin Weiser and William Glaberson, "Ashcroft Pushes Executions in More Cases in New York," *The New York Times*, February 6, 2002, p. A-1.

158. While the budget called for eliminating some anti-drug programs in the schools, most notably DARE, the widely discredited school education program, it included some disturbing law-and-order thrusts, including a proposal to give states $25 million per year to carry out random drug testing in the schools. "Money Talks: A New Direction in the War on Drugs?" *Drug Policy News*, February 17, 2005, p. 1.

159. "Money Talks: A New Direction in the War on Drugs?"

160. Eric Schmitt, "Wider Military Role in U.S. Urged," *The New York Times*, July 16, 2002, sec. 1, p. 16; Adam Liptak, "Changing the Standard," *The New York Times*, May 31, 2002, p. A-1; Don Van Natta, Jr., "Government Will Ease Limits on Domestic Spying by F.B.I.," *The New York Times*, May 30, 2002, p. A-1; and Peter B. Kraska, ed. *Militarizing the American Criminal Justice System:*

The Changing Roles of the Armed Forces and the Police (Boston: Northeastern University Press, 2001).

161. Eric Lichtblau, "U.S. Uses Terror Law to Pursue Crimes From Drugs to Swindling," *The New York Times*, September 28, 2003, sec. 1, p. 1.

162. On the global network of secret prisons, see Andrew Buncombe and Kim Sengupta, "Secret U.S. Jails Hold 10,000," *New Zealand Herald*, http://www.nzhearld.co.nz/storydisplay.cfm?storyID=3566058&msg (accessed March 16, 2005); Lisa Hajjar, "In the Penal Colony," *The Nation*, February 7, 2005, pp. 23–30; and Jane Mayer, "Outsourcing Terror: The Battle Over 'Extraordinary Rendition,'" *The New Yorker*, February 14/21, 2005.

163. Chalmers Johnson, *Blowback: The Costs and Consequences of American Empire* (New York: Metropolitan Books, 2000).

164. Leah Caldwell, "Iraqi Dungeons and Torture Chambers Under New, American Trained Management," *Prison Legal News*, September 2004, pp. 1–5.

165. Loïc Wacquant, "The Advent of a Penal State Is Not a Destiny," *Social Justice* 28, no. 3 (2001): 11–87; and Loïc Wacquant, "US Exports Zero Tolerance," *Le Monde*, April 1999.

166. Harry Elmer Barnes, *Report on the Progress of the State Prison War Program Under the Government Division of the War Production Board* (Washington, DC: War Production Board, 1944).

167. Bob Herbert, "They Won't Go," *The New York Times*, June 13, 2005, p. A-17.

168. A more telling comparison may be with the legal system of Nazi Germany. As Whitman argues in his comparative historical analysis of the development of penal policy in the United States, France, and Germany, "the use of law-and-order politics as a way of mobilizing popular support is something we share, disturbingly enough, with the Nazis." Whitman, *Harsh Justice*, pp. 56 and 202–3.

169. Garland, *Punishment and Modern Society*, p. 292.

170. Thomas Mathiesen, *Prison on Trial: A Critical Assessment* (London: Sage Publications, 1990), p. 167.

SELECT BIBLIOGRAPHY

Abrahamson, Shirley S. "Redefining Roles: The Victims' Rights Movement." *Utah Law Review* 3 (1985): 517–67.

Abramsky, Sasha. *Hard Times Blues*. New York: St. Martin's Press, 2002.

———. "Incarceration, Inc." *The Nation*, July 19/24, 2004: 22–25.

Acker, James R. "The Death Penalty: A 25-Year Retrospective and a Perspective on the Future." *Criminal Justice Review* 21.2 (Autumn 1996): 139–60.

Acker, James R., and Charles S. Lanier. "Beyond Human Ability? The Rise and Fall of Death Penalty Legislation." In *America's Experiment with Capital Punishment: Reflections on the Past, Present, and Future of the Ultimate Penal Sanction*. 2nd ed. James R. Acker, Robert M. Bohm, and Charles S. Lanier, eds. Durham, NC: Carolina Academic Press, 2003: 85–125.

Adams, Robert, and Jo Campling. *Prison Riots in Britain and the USA*. New York: St. Martin's Press, 1992.

Adamson, Christopher R. "Punishment After Slavery: Southern State Penal Systems, 1865–1890." *Social Problems* 30.5 (June 1983): 555–68.

Ahrens, Lois. "From Collective to Coopted." *Aegis*, September–October 1978: 5–8.

———. "Battered Women's Refuges: Feminist Cooperatives vs. Social Service Institutions." *Aegis*, Summer/Autumn 1980: 9–15.

Aileen: Life and Death of a Serial Killer: 89 min. Lafayette Films, 2004.

Akers, Ronald. "Linking Sociology and Its Specialties: The Case of Criminology." *Social Forces* 71.1(1992): 1–16.

Albrecht, Hans-Jörg. "Sentencing and Punishment in Germany." In *Sentencing Reform in Overcrowded Times: A Comparative Perspective*. Michael Tonry and Kathleen Hatlestad, eds. New York: Oxford University Press, 1997: 188–221.

———. "Post-Adjudication Dispositions in Comparative Perspective." In *Sentencing and Sanctions in Western Countries*. Michael Tonry and Richard S. Frase, eds. Oxford: Oxford University Press, 2001: 293–330.

Alix, Ernest Kahlar. *Ransom Kidnapping in America, 1874–1974: The Creation of a Capital Crime*. Carbondale and Edwardsville, IL: Southern Illinois University Press, 1978.

Allard, Patricia. *Life Sentences: Denying Welfare Benefits to Women Convicted of Drug Offenses*. Washington, DC: The Sentencing Project, February 2002.

Allen, Francis A. *The Decline of the Rehabilitative Ideal: Penal Policy and Social Purpose*. New Haven: Yale University Press, 1981.

Ambrosio, Tara-Jen, and Vincent Schiraldi. *From Classrooms to Cellblocks: A National Perspective*. Washington, DC: The Justice Policy Institute, 1997.

American Bar Association, Commission on Correctional Facilities and Services. *When Society Pronounces Judgment*. Washington, DC: American Bar Association, 1975.

American Bar Foundation. "Reducing Crime by Increasing Incarceration." *Researching Law: An ABF Update*. 6.1 (Winter 1995): 1 and 4.

American Friends Service Committee. *Struggle for Justice: A Report on Crime and Punishment in America*. New York: Hill and Wang, 1971.

Ancel, Marc. *Social Defense: The Future of Penal Reform*. Littleton, CO: Fred B. Rothman and Co., 1987.

Andersen, Margaret L., and Patricia Hill Collins, eds. *Race, Class, and Gender: An Anthology*. Belmont, CA: Wadsworth Publishing, 1992.

Annual Chief Justice Earl Warren Conference on Advocacy in the United States. *A Program for Prison Reform: The Final Report*. Cambridge, MA: The Roscoe Pound-American Trial Lawyers Foundation, 1972.

Ashford, Douglas. *Policy and Politics in Britain: The Limits of Consensus*. Philadelphia: Temple University Press, 1981.

Ashworth, Andrew. "The Decline of English Sentencing and Other Stories." In *Sentencing and Sanctions in Western Countries*. Michael Tonry and Richard S. Frase, eds. Oxford: Oxford University Press, 2001: 62–91.

————. "English Sentencing: From Enlightenment to Darkness in a Decade." In *Penal Reform in Overcrowded Times*. Michael Tonry, ed. Oxford: Oxford University Press, 2001.

Auerbach, Jerald S. *Labor and Liberty: The LaFollette Committee and the New Deal*. Indianapolis: Bobbs-Merrill, 1966.

Austin, James, and John Irwin. *Who Goes to Prison?* San Francisco: National Council on Crime and Delinquency, 1991.

Avina, Cathy. "Progress Report – The National Coalition Against Domestic Violence." *Aegis*, January–February 1979: 4–6.

Ayers, Edward L. *Vengeance and Justice: Crime and Punishment in the 19th-Century American South*. New York: Oxford University Press, 1984.

Aynes, Richard L. "Constitutional Considerations: Government Responsibility and the Right Not to Be a Victim." *Pepperdine Law Review* 11 (1984): 63–116.

Bachman, Ronet. *Violence Against Women: A National Crime Victimization Survey Report*. Washington, DC: U.S. Department of Justice, January 1994.

Bacon, Margaret Hope. *Abby Hopper Gibbons: Prison Reformer and Social Activist*. Albany: SUNY Press, 2000.

Baird, Charles F., and Elizabeth E. McGinn. "Re-Victimizing the Victim: How Prosecutorial and Judicial Discretion Are Being Exercised to Silence Victims Who Oppose Capital Punishment." *Stanford Law and Policy Review* 15.2(2004): 447–69.

Bakal, Yitzhak, ed. *Closing Correctional Institutions: New Strategies for Youth*. Lexington, MA: Lexington Books, 1973.

Baker, Donald P., Randolph M. Blotky, Keith M. Clemens, and Michael L. Dillard. "Judicial Intervention in Corrections: The California Experience – An Empirical Study." *UCLA Law Review* 20 (1972–73): 452–580.

Baker, Estella. "From 'Making Bad People Worse' to 'Prison Works': Sentencing Policy in England and Wales in the 1990s." *Criminal Law Forum* 7.3 (1996): 639–71.

Baldus, David C., and George Woodworth. "Race Discrimination and the Death Penalty: An Empirical and Legal Overview." In *America's Experiment with Capital Punishment: Reflections on the Past, Present, and Future of the Ultimate Penal*

Sanction. 2nd ed. James R. Acker, Robert M. Bohm, and Charles S. Lanier, eds. Durham, NC: Carolina Academic Press, 2003: 501–51.

Baldus, David C., George Woodworth, and Charles Pulaski, Jr. *Equal Justice and the Death Penalty.* Boston: Northeastern University Press, 1990.

Bandes, Susan. "When Victims Seek Closure: Forgiveness, Vengeance, and the Role of Government." *Fordham Urban Law Journal* 27.5 (June 2000): 1599–1606.

Banner, Stuart. *The Death Penalty: An American History.* Cambridge, MA: Harvard University Press, 2002.

Barak, Gregg. "Feminist Connections and the Movement Against Domestic Violence: Beyond Criminal Justice Reform." *Journal of Crime & Justice* 9 (Winter 1986): 139–62.

Barakso, Maryann. *Governing NOW: Grassroots Activism in the National Organization for Women.* Ithaca, NY: Cornell University Press, 2004.

Barker, Vanessa. "The Politics of Punishing: Building a State Governance Theory of American Imprisonment Variation." *Punishment & Society* 8.1 (January 2006): 5–32.

Barnard, Amii. "The Application of Critical Race Feminism to the Anti-Lynching Movement: Black Women's Fight Against Race and Gender Ideology, 1892–1920." *UCLA Women's Law Journal* 3.7 (1993): 1–38.

Barnes, Harry Elmer. *Report on the Progress of the State Prison War Program Under the Government Division of the War Production Board.* Washington, DC: War Production Board, 1944.

Barr, William P. "Bringing Criminals to Justice; Bringing Justice to the Victim." *The NOVA Newsletter* 16.11 (1992).

Bartlett, Katharine T., and Rosanne Kennedy, eds. *Feminist Legal Theory: Readings in Law and Gender.* Boulder, CO: Westview Press, 1991.

Basler, Roy P., Marion Dolores Pratt, and Lloyd A. Dunlap, eds. *The Collected Works of Abraham Lincoln.* Vol. 1. New Brunswick, NJ: Rutgers University Press, 1953.

Bauer, Carol, and Lawrence Ritt. "'A Husband Is a Beating Animal' – Frances Power Cobbe Confronts the Wife-Abuse Problem in Victorian England." *International Journal of Women's Studies* 6.2 (March/April 1983): 99–118.

———. "Wife-Abuse, Late-Victorian English Feminists, and the Legacy of Frances Power Cobbe." *International Journal of Women's Studies* 6.3 (May/June 1983): 195–207.

Bauer, Lynn, and Steven D. Owens. "Justice Expenditure and Employment in the United States, 2001." *Bureau of Justice Statistics Bulletin,* May 2004.

Bayer, Ronald. "Crime, Punishment, and the Decline of Liberal Optimism." *Crime and Delinquency* 27.2 (April 1981): 169–90.

Bayley, David H. "The Police and Political Development in Europe." In *The Formation of National States in Western Europe.* Charles Tilly, ed. Princeton: Princeton University Press, 1975: 328–79.

Bazelon, David L. "The Hidden Politics of Criminology." *Federal Probation* 42.2 (June 1978): 3–9.

Beaumont, Gustave de, and Alexis de Tocqueville. *On the Penitentiary System in the United States and Its Application in France.* Intro. by Thorsten Sellin. Forward by Herman R. Lantz. Carbondale, IL: Southern Illinois University Press, 1979.

Beck, Allen J., and Paige M. Harrison. "Prisoners in 2000." *Bureau of Justice Statistics Bulletin.* August 2001.

Beck, E. M., James L. Massey, and Stewart E. Tolnay. "The Gallows, the Mob, and the Vote: Lethal Sanctioning of Blacks in North Carolina and Georgia, 1882–1930." *Law & Society Review* 23.2 (1989): 317–31.

Beckett, Katherine. *Making Crime Pay: Law and Order in Contemporary American Politics*. New York: Oxford University Press, 1997.

———. "Crime and Control in the Culture of Late Modernity." *Law & Society Review* 35.4 (2001): 899–929.

Beckett, Katherine, and Theodore Sasson. *The Politics of Injustice: Crime and Punishment in America*. Thousand Oaks, CA: Pine Forge Press, 2000.

Beckett, Katherine, and Bruce Western. "Governing Social Marginality: Welfare, Incarceration, and the Transformation of State Policy." *Punishment & Society* 3.1 (January 2001): 43–59.

Beckman, Marlene D. "The White Slave Traffic Act: Historical Impact of a Federal Crime Policy on Women." In *Criminal Justice Politics and Women: The Aftermath of Legally Mandated Change*. Claudine SchWeber and Clarice Feinman, eds. New York: Haworth Press, 1985: 85–101.

Bedau, Hugo Adam. "The Nixon Administration and the Deterrent Effect of the Death Penalty." *University of Pittsburgh Law Review* 34 (1973): 557–66.

———. *The Courts, the Constitution, and Capital Punishment*. Lexington, MA: Lexington Books, 1977.

———. *Death Is Different: Studies in the Morality, Law, and Politics of Capital Punishment*. Boston: Northeastern University Press, 1987.

———. "Background and Developments." In *The Death Penalty in America: Current Controversies*. Hugo Adam Bedau, ed. New York: Oxford University Press, 1997.

Bell, Daniel. "Crime as an American Way of Life." In *The End of Ideology: On the Exhaustion of Political Ideas in the Fifties*. Daniel Bell. Glencoe, IL: Free Press, 1960.

Bender, John. *Imagining the Penitentiary: Fiction and Architecture of Mind in Eighteenth-Century England*. Chicago: University of Chicago Press, 1987.

Bennett, Drake, and Robert Kuttner. "Crime and Redemption." *The American Prospect*, December 1, 2003: 36.

Bennett, William J., John J. DiIulio, Jr., and John P. Walters. *Body Count: Moral Poverty . . . and How To Win America's War Against Crime and Drugs*. New York: Simon & Schuster, 1996.

Bensel, Richard. "The Tension between American Political Development as a Research Community and as a Disciplinary Subfield." *Studies in American Political Development* 17.1 (Spring 2003): 103–6.

Berger, Vivian. "*Payne* and Suffering – A Personal Reflection and a Victim-Centered Critique." *Florida State University Law Review* 20 (1992): 21–65.

Berk, Richard A., and Peter H. Rossi. *Prison Reform and State Elites*. Cambridge, MA: Ballinger, 1977.

Berkman, Ronald. *Opening the Gates: The Rise of the Prisoners' Movement*. Lexington, MA: Lexington Books, 1979.

Berkson, Larry, Scott Beller, and Michele Grimaldi. *Judicial Selection in the United States: A Compendium of Provisions*. Chicago: American Judicature Society, 1980.

Berlow, Alan. "The Broken Machinery of Death." *The American Prospect*, July 30, 2001: 16–17.

Berman, Douglas A. "The Start of the Next Revolution?: Recent State Reforms in the Sentencing of Drug Offenders." *Federal Sentencing Reporter* 14.6 (May/June 2002): 327–31.

Berman, Jay. "Theodore Roosevelt as Police Commissioner of New York: The Birth of Modern American Police Administration." In *Theodore Roosevelt: Many-Sided American*. Natalie A. Naylor, Douglas Brinkley, and John Allen Gable, eds. Interlaken, NY: Heart of the Lakes Publishing, 1992: 171–85.

Berry, Mary Frances, and John Blassingame. "American Archipelago: Blacks and Criminal Justice." In *Race, Class, and Gender: An Anthology*. Margaret L. Andersen and Patricia Hill Collins, eds. Belmont, CA: Wadsworth Publishing, 1992: 429–42.

Bertram, Eva, Morris Blachman, Kenneth Sharpe, and Peter Andreas. *Drug War Politics: The Price of Denial*. Berkeley: University of California Press, 1996.

Bessler, John. *Death in the Dark: Midnight Executions in America*. Boston: Northeastern University Press, 1997.

Bianchi, Herman, Mario Simondi, and Ian Taylor, eds. *Deviance and Control in Europe: Papers from the European Group for the Study of Deviance and Social Control*. London: John Wiley, 1975.

Bianchi, Herman, and René van Swaaningen, eds. *Abolitionism: Towards a Non-Repressive Approach to Crime*. Amsterdam: Free University Press, 1986.

Bienen, Leigh. "Rape III: National Developments in Rape Reform Legislation." *Women's Rights Law Reporter* 6.3 (Spring 1980): 171–217.

———. "Rape Reform Legislation in the United States: A Look at Some Practical Effects." *Victimology: An International Journal* 8.1–2 (1983): 139–51.

Binder, Arnold, and James Meeker. "Arrest as a Method to Control Spouse Abuse." In *Domestic Violence: The Changing Criminal Justice Response*. Eve S. Buzawa and Carl G. Buzawa, eds. Westport, CT: Auburn House, 1992.

Block, Alan A., and William J. Chambliss. *Organizing Crime*. New York: Elsevier, 1981.

Blomberg, Thomas G., and Stanley Cohen, eds. *Punishment and Social Control: Essays in Honor of Sheldon L. Messinger*. New York: Aldine de Gruyter, 1995.

———, eds. *Punishment and Social Control*. 2nd ed. New York: Aldine de Gruyter, 2003.

Blumstein, Alfred. "Prison Populations: A System Out of Control." In *Crime and Justice: An Annual Review of Research*. Vol. 10. Michael Tonry and Norval Morris, eds. Chicago: University of Chicago Press, 1988: 231–67.

Blumstein, Alfred, and Allen J. Beck. "Population Growth in U.S. Prisons. 1980–1996." In *Crime and Justice – A Review of Research*. Vol. 26. *Prisons*. Michael Tonry and Joan Petersilia, eds. Chicago and London: The University of Chicago Press, 1999: 17–61.

Blumstein, Alfred, and Joan Petersilia. "Investigating in Criminal Justice Research." In *Crime*. James Q. Wilson and Joan Petersilia, eds. San Francisco: ICS Press, 1995.

Bobo, Lawrence, and Devon Johnson. "A Taste for Punishment: Black and White Americans' Views on the Death Penalty and the War on Drugs." *Du Bois Review* 1.1 (Spring 2004): 151–80.

Bohm, Robert M. "American Death Penalty Opinion, 1936–1986: A Critical Examination of the Gallup Polls." In *The Death Penalty in America: Current Research*. Robert M. Bohm, ed. Cincinnati, OH: Andersen Publishing Co., 1991: 113–44.

———. "American Death Penalty Opinion: Past, Present, and Future." In *America's Experiment with Capital Punishment: Reflections on the Past, Present, and Future of the Ultimate Penal Sanction*. James R. Acker, Robert M. Bohm, and Charles S. Lanier, eds. 2nd ed. Durham, NC: Carolina Academic Press, 2003: 27–54.

———. "The Economic Costs of Capital Punishment: Past, Present, and Future." In *America's Experiment with Capital Punishment: Reflections on the Past, Present, and Future of the Ultimate Penal Sanction*. 2nd ed. James R. Acker, Robert M. Bohm, and Charles S. Lanier, eds. Durham, NC: Carolina Academic Press, 2003: 573–94.

Bohmer, Carol. "Rape and the Law." In *Confronting Rape and Sexual Assault*. Mary E. Odem and Jody Clay-Warner, eds. Wilmington: SR Books, 1998: 247–62.

Bonczar, Thomas P. "Prevalence of Imprisonment in the U.S. Population, 1972–2001." *Bureau of Justice Statistics Special Report*, August 2003.

Bondeson, Ulla. *Prisoners in Prison Societies*. New Brunswick, NJ: Transaction Publishers, 1989.

Bookspan, Shelley. *A Germ of Goodness: The California State Prison System, 1851–1944*. Lincoln: University of Nebraska Press, 1991.

Bottoms, Anthony E. "Interpersonal Violence and Social Order in Prisons." In *Crime and Justice – A Review of Research*. Vol. 26. *Prisons*. Michael Tonry and Joan Petersilia, eds. Chicago and London: University of Chicago Press, 1999: 205–81.

Bowers, William J., Glenn L. Pierce, and John F. McDevitt. *Legal Homicide: Death as Punishment in America, 1864–1982*. Boston: Northeastern University Press, 1984.

———. "Capital Punishment and Contemporary Values: People's Misgivings and the Court's Misperceptions." *Law & Society Review* 27.1 (1993): 157–75.

Bowers, William J., Margaret Vandiver, and Patricia H. Dugan. "A New Look at Public Opinion on Capital Punishment: What Citizens and Legislators Prefer." In *Politics, Crime Control and Culture*. Stuart A. Scheingold, ed. Aldershot, UK: Ashgate, 1997: 243–316.

Box-Grainger, Jill. "Sentencing Rapists." In *Confronting Crime*. Roger Matthews and Jock Young, eds. London: Sage, 1986: 31–52.

Boyer, Paul. *Urban Masses and Moral Order in America, 1820–1920*. Cambridge, MA: Harvard University Press, 1978.

Braithwaite, John, and Kathleen Daly. "Masculinities, Violence and Communitarian Control." In *Just Boys Doing Business? Men, Masculinity and Crime*. Tim Newburn and Elizabeth B. Stanko, eds. London: Routledge, 1994.

Braithwaite, John, and Philip Pettit. *Not Just Deserts: A Republican Theory of Criminal Justice*. Oxford: Oxford University Press, 1990.

———. "Comment – Republican Criminology and Victim Advocacy." *Law & Society Review* 28.4 (1994): 765–76.

Brake, Michael, and Chris Hale. "Law and Order." In *Beyond Thatcherism*. Richard Sparks and Phillip Brown, eds. Milton Keynes, UK: Open University Press, 1989.

Brants, Chrisje, and Erna Kok. "Penal Sanctions as a Feminist Strategy: A Contradiction in Terms? Pornography and Criminal Law in the Netherlands." *International Journal of the Sociology of Law* 14 (1986): 269–86.

Breines, Wini, and Linda Gordon. "The New Scholarship on Family Violence." *Signs* 8.3 (Spring 1983): 490–531.

Bright, Charles. *The Powers That Punish: Prison and Politics in the Era of the 'Big House,' 1920–1955*. Ann Arbor: University of Michigan Press, 1994.

Bright, Stephen B. "Discrimination, Death, and Denial: Race and the Death Penalty." In *Machinery of Death: The Reality of America's Death Penalty Regime*. David R. Dow and Mark Dow, eds. New York: Routledge, 2002.

———. "The Politics of Capital Punishment: The Sacrifice of Fairness for Executions." In *America's Experiment with Capital Punishment: Reflections on the Past, Present, and Future of the Ultimate Penal Sanction*. 2nd ed. James R. Acker, Robert M. Bohm, and Charles S. Lanier, eds. Durham, NC: Carolina Academic Press, 2003: 127–46.

Bright, Stephen B., and Patrick J. Keenan. "Judges and the Politics of Death: Deciding Between the Bill of Rights and the Next Election in Capital Cases." *Boston University Law Review* 75 (May 1995): 759–835.

Brodyaga, Lisa, Margaret Gates, and Susan Singer. *Rape and Its Victims: A Report for Citizens, Health Facilities and Criminal Justice Agencies*. Washington, DC: National Institute of Law Enforcement and Criminal Justice, 1975.

Bronstein, Alvin J. "Reform Without Change: The Future of Prisoners' Rights." *The Civil Liberties Review* 4.3 (1977): 27–45.

Brooks, Rachelle. "Feminists Negotiate the Legislative Branch: The Violence Against Women Act." In *Feminists Negotiate the State: The Politics of Domestic Violence*. Cynthia R. Daniels, ed. Lanham, MD: University Press of America, 1997.

Brown, David, and Russell Hogg. "Essentialism, Radical Criminology and Left Realism." *Australian and New Zealand Journal of Criminology* 25 (December 1992): 195–230.

Brown, Edmund G. (Pat) with Dick Adler. *Public Justice, Private Mercy: A Governor's Education on Death Row*. New York: Weidenfeld & Nicolson, 1989.

Brown, Mary Jane. *Eradicating This Evil: Women in the American Anti-Lynching Movement, 1892–1940*. New York: Garland, 2000.

Brown, Wendy. *States of Injury: Power and Freedom in Late Modernity*. Princeton: Princeton University Press, 1995.

Burnham, David, and Susan Long. "The Clinton Era by the Numbers." *The Nation*, January 29, 2001: 20–22.

Burns, Peter T. "A Comparative Overview of the Criminal Injuries Compensation Schemes." *Victimology: An International Journal* 8.3–4 (1983): 102–10.

Burton, Lonnie. "The Deadly Health Services of Naphcare in Alabana." *Prison Legal News*, October 2003: 1–5.

Burton-Rose, Daniel, Dan Pens, and Paul Wright, eds. *The Celling of America: An Inside Look at the U.S. Prison Industry*. Monroe, ME: Common Courage Press, 1998.

Bush, Diane Mitsch. "Women's Movements and State Policy Reform Aimed at Domestic Violence Against Women: A Comparison of the Consequences of Movement Mobilization in the U.S. and India." *Gender & Society* 6.4 (December 1992): 587–608.

Bush, George. H. W. "Remarks at Attorney General's Crime Summit: President Bush: 'Take Back the Streets.'" *The NOVA Newsletter* 15.3 (1991): 1–2.

Butler, K. "The Muslims Are No Longer an Unknown Quantity." *Corrections Magazine* 4.2 (1978): 55–57, 60–63.

Butler, Paul. "Racially Based Jury Nullification: Black Power in the Criminal Justice System." *Yale Law Journal* 105.3 (December 1995): 677–725.

Buzawa, Eve S., and Carl G. Buzawa. *Domestic Violence: The Criminal Justice Response*. Newbury Park, CA: Sage, 1990.

———. "The Impact of Arrest on Domestic Violence: Introduction." *American Behavioral Scientist* 36.5 (May 1993): 558–74.

———, eds. *Domestic Violence: The Changing Criminal Justice Response*. Westport, CT: Auburn House, 1992.

Cahalan, Margaret. "Trends in Incarceration in the United States since 1880: A Summary of Reported Rates and the Distribution of Offenses." *Crime & Delinquency* 25 (1979): 9–41.

Cahalan, Margaret, and Lee Anne Parsons. *Historical Corrections Statistics in the United States, 1850–1984*. Washington, DC: U.S. Department of Justice, Bureau of Justice Statistics, December, 1986.

Calder, James D. "Presidents and Crime Control: Kennedy, Johnson and Nixon and the Influences of Ideology." *Presidential Studies Quarterly* 12.4 (Fall 1982): 574–89.

————. *The Origins and Development of Federal Crime Control Policy*. Westport, CT: Praeger, 1993.

Caldwell, Leah. "Iraqi Dungeon Torture Chambers Under New, American Trained Management." *Prison Legal News*, September 2004: 1–5.

Capeci, Dominic J. "The Lynching of Cleo Wright: Federal Protection of Constitutional Rights During World War II." In *Lynching, Racial Violence, and Law*. Paul Finkelman, ed. New York: Garland Publishing, 1992: 33–50.

Caplan, Gerald. "Reflections on the Nationalization of Crime, 1964–1968." *Law and the Social Order* 3 (1973): 583–635.

Caplow, Theodore, and Jonathan Simon. "Understanding Prison Policy and Population Trends." In *Crime and Justice–A Review of Research*. Vol. 26. *Prisons*. Michael Tonry and Joan Petersilia, eds. Chicago and London: University of Chicago Press, 1999: 63–120.

Carleton, Mark T. *Politics and Punishment: The History of the Louisiana Penal System*. Baton Rouge: Louisiana State University Press, 1971.

Carrington, Frank. *The Victims*. New Rochelle, NY: Arlington House, 1975.

Carrington, Frank, and George Nicholson. "The Victims' Movement: An Idea Whose Time Has Come." *Pepperdine Law Review* 11 (1984): 1–14.

————. "Victims' Rights: An Idea Whose Time Has Come – Five Years Later: The Maturing of an Idea." *Pepperdine Law Review* 17.1 (1989): 1–18.

Carroll, Leo. *Hacks, Blacks, and Cons: Race Relations in a Maximum Security Prison*. Lexington, MA: Lexington Books, 1974.

Carte, Gene E., and Elaine H. Carte. *Police Reform in the United States: The Era of August Vollmer*. Berkeley: University of California Press, 1975.

Carter, Charles Frederick. "The Carnival of Crime in the United States." *Current History* 15 (February 1922).

Casper, Jonathan D. "Determinate Sentencing and Prison Crowding in Illinois." *University of Illinois Review* 2 (1984): 231–52.

————, et al. *The Implementation of the California Determinate Sentencing Law*. Washington, DC: U.S. Department of Justice, National Institute of Justice, May 1982.

Cavadino, Michael, and James Dignan. *The Penal System: An Introduction*. London: Sage, 1992.

Chaiken, Marcia R., et al. *State and Local Change and the Violence Against Women Act*. Washington, DC: National Institute of Justice, 2001.

Chambliss, William J. *Power, Politics, and Crime*. Boulder, CO: Westview Press, 1999.

Chandler, David. *Capital Punishment in Canada: A Sociological Study of Repressive Law*. Toronto: McClelland and Stewart, 1976.

Chang, David. "Beyond Uncompromising Positions: Hate Crimes Legislation and the Common Ground Between Republicans and Gay Rights Advocates." *Fordham Urban Law Journal* 21.4 (Summer 1994): 1097–1105.

Chesney-Lind, Meda. "Preface." In *International Feminist Perspectives in Criminology: Engendering a Discipline*. Nicole Hahn Rafter and Frances Heidensohn, eds. Buckingham, UK: Open University Press, 1995.

Chevigny, Bell Gale. "Prison Activists Come of Age." *The Nation*, July 24/31, 2000: 27–30.

Childres, Robert D. "Compensation for Criminally Inflicted Personal Injury." In *Considering the Victim: Readings in Restitution and Victim Compensation*. Joe Hudson and Burt Galaway, eds. Springfield, IL: Charles C. Thomas, 1975: 363–92.

Chiricos, Theodore G., and Miriam A. DeLone. "Labor Surplus and Punishment: A Review and Assessment of Theory and Evidence." *Social Problems* 39.4 (1992): 421–46.

Christianson, Scott. "Our Black Prisoners." *Crime & Delinquency* 27.3 (July 1981): 364–75.

_____. *With Liberty for Some: 500 Years of Imprisonment in America*. Boston: Northeastern University Press, 1998.

Christie, Nils. "Conflicts as Property." *The British Journal of Criminology* 17.1 (January 1977): 1–15.

_____. *Crime Control as Industry: Toward GULAGS, Western Style*. 2nd ed. London and New York: Routledge, 1994.

Christoph, James B. *Capital Punishment and British Politics: The British Movement to Abolish the Death Penalty, 1945–57*. Chicago: University of Chicago Press, 1962.

Chunn, Dorothy E., and Shelly A. M. Gavigan. "Social Control: Analytical Tool or Analytical Quagmire?" *Contemporary Crises* 12 (1988): 102–124.

Clarke, Matthew. "Strapped States Threaten Prisoner Release to Extort Revenue." *Prison Legal News*, September 2003.

Clarkson, Chris, and Rod Morgan, eds. *The Politics of Sentencing Reform*. Oxford: Clarendon – Oxford University Press, 1995.

Clear, Todd R. *The Community Justice Ideal: Preventing Crime and Achieving Justice*. Boulder, CO: Westview Press, 1999.

Clear, Todd R., and Patricia M. Harris. "The Costs of Incarceration." In *America's Correctional Crisis: Prison Populations and Public Policy*. Stephen D. Gottfredson and Sean McConville, eds. New York: Greenwood Press, 1987: 37–55.

Cleaver, Eldridge. *Soul on Ice*. New York: Dell Publishing, 1968.

Clemens, Elisabeth S. *The People's Lobby: Organizational Innovation and the Rise of Interest Group Politics in the United States, 1890–1925*. Chicago: University of Chicago Press, 1997.

Cohen, Cathy J. *The Boundaries of Blackness: AIDS and the Breakdown of Black Politics*. Chicago: University of Chicago Press, 1999.

Cohen, Richard. "Goodbye, William!" *The New York Review of Books*, August 14, 2003: 18.

Cohen, Stanley. *Visions of Social Control: Crime, Punishment and Classification*. Cambridge: Polity Press, 1985.

_____. "The Critical Discourse on 'Social Control': Notes on the Concept as a Hammer." *International Journal of the Sociology of Law* 17 (1989): 347–57.

Coker, Donna. "Crime Control and Feminist Law Reform in Domestic Violence Law: A Critical Review." *Buffalo Criminal Law Review* 4.2 (2001): 801–60.

Cole, David. *No Equal Justice: Race and Class in the Criminal Justice System*. New York: The New Press, 1999.

Collins, William C. "Discussion on Colloquium, 'The Prison Overcrowding Crisis'". *New York University Review of Law and Social Change* 12.1 (1983–84).

Colvin, Mark. "The 1980 New Mexico Prison Riot." *Social Problems* 29.5 (June 1982): 449–62.

Comeau, Paul R. "Labor Unions for Prison Inmates: An Analysis of a Recent Proposal for the Organization of Inmate Labor." *Buffalo Law Review* 21 (1972): 963–85.

Coney, Sandra. "New Zealand: Accident Compensation Changes." *The Lancet* 338 (December 21–28, 1991): 1583–84.

Connelly, Mark Thomas. *The Response to Prostitution in the Progressive Era*. Chapel Hill: University of North Carolina Press, 1980.

Coote, Anna, and Beatrix Campbell. *Sweet Freedom: The Struggle for Women's Liberation*. Oxford: Basil Blackwell, 1987.

Corbett, Claire, and Kathy Hobdell. "Volunteer-Based Services to Rape Victims: Some Recent Developments." In *Victims of Crime: A New Deal?* Mike Maguire and John Pointing, eds. Milton Keynes, UK: Open University Press, 1988.

Cornyn, John. "Ruminations on the Nature of Texas Judging." *St. Mary's Law Review* 25.1 (1993): 367–84.

Cortner, Richard C. *A Mob Intent on Death: The NAACP and the Arkansas Race Riot Cases*. Middletown, CT: Wesleyan University Press, 1988.

Costain, Anne N., and W. Douglas Costain. "Strategy and Tactics of the Women's Movement in the United States: The Role of Political Parties." In *The Women's Movements of the United States and Western Europe*. Mary Fainsod Katzenstein and Carol McClung Mueller, eds. Philadelphia: Temple University Press, 1987.

Costanzo, Mark. *Just Revenge: Costs and Consequences of the Death Penalty*. New York: St. Martin's Press, 1997.

Council of Europe. "The European Prison Rules, 1987." In *Imprisonment: European Perspectives*. John Muncie and Richard Sparks, eds. New York: St. Martin's Press, 1991.

Crawford, Adam. "Salient Themes Towards a Victim Perspective and the Limitations of Restorative Justice: Some Concluding Comments." In *Integrating a Victim Perspective Within Criminal Justice*. Adam Crawford and Jo Goodey, eds. Aldershot UK: Ashgate, 2000.

Crenshaw, Kimberlé W. "Race, Reform and Retrenchment: Transformation and Legitimation in Antidiscrimination Law." *Harvard Law Review* 101.7 (May 1988): 1331–87.

———. "Mapping the Margins: Intersectionality, Identity Politics, and Violence Against Women of Color." *Stanford Law Review* 43.6 (1991): 1241–99.

Croft, John. "Criminological Research in Great Britain, With a Note on the Council of Europe." In *Crime and Justice: An Annual Review of Research*. Vol. 5. Michael Tonry and Norval Morris, eds. Chicago: University of Chicago Press, 1983.

Crouch, Ben M., and James W. Marquart. *An Appeal to Justice: Litigated Reform of Texas Prisons*. Austin: University of Texas Press, 1989.

Csida, June Burdy, and Joseph Csida. *Rape: How To Avoid It and What To Do About It If You Can't*. Chatsworth, CA: Books for Better Living, 1974.

Culbert, Jennifer L. "The Sacred Name of Pain: The Role of Victim Impact Evidence in Death Penalty Sentencing Decisions." In *Pain, Death, and the Law*. Austin Sarat, ed. Ann Arbor: University of Michigan Press, 2001: 103–35.

Cullen, Francis T., Bonnie S. Fisher, and Brandon K. Applegate. "Public Opinion about Punishment and Corrections." In *Crime and Justice: A Review of Research*. Vol. 27. Michael Tonry, ed. Chicago: University of Chicago Press, 2000.

Cullen, Francis T., and Karen E. Gilbert. *Reaffirming Rehabilitation*. Cincinnati: Anderson Publishing Co., 1982.

Culver, John H. "The Politics of Capital Punishment in California." In *The Political Science of Criminal Punishment*. Stuart Nagel, Erika Fairchild, and Anthony Champagne, eds. Springfield, IL: Charles C. Thomas, 1983: 14–26.

———. "Capital Punishment Politics and Policies in the States, 1977–1997." *Crime, Law and Social Change* 32 (1999): 287–300.

Cummings, Homer. "Progress Toward a Modern Administration of Criminal Justice." *American Bar Association Journal* 22.5 (May 1936): 345–49.

Cummings, Homer, and Carl McFarland. *Federal Justice: Chapters in the History of Justice and the Federal Executive*. New York: The Macmillan Company, 1937.

Cummins, Eric. *The Rise and Fall of California's Radical Prison Movement*. Stanford, CA: Stanford University Press, 1994.

Currie, Elliot. *Confronting Crime: An American Challenge*. New York: Pantheon Books, 1985.

Curtin, Mary Ellen. *Black Prisoners and Their World: Alabama, 1865–1900*. Charlottesville: University of Virginia Press, 2000.

Cusac, Ann-Marie. "Abu Ghraib, USA." *Prison Legal News*, July 2004: 1 and 3–4.

Cushing, Robert Renny, and Susannah Sheffer. *Dignity Denied: The Experience of Murder Victims' Families Who Oppose the Death Penalty*. Cambridge, MA: Murder Victims' Families for Reconciliation, 2002.

Dailey, Debra. "Minnesota's Sentencing Guidelines – Past and Future." In *Sentencing Reform in Overcrowded Times: A Comparative Perspective*. Michael Tonry and Kathleen Hatlestad, eds. New York: Oxford University Press, 1997: 35–49.

Daly, Kathleen. "Criminal Justice Ideologies and Practices in Different Voices: Some Feminist Questions About Justice." *International Journal of the Sociology of the Law* 17 (February 1989): 1–18.

_____. "Comment – Men's Violence, Victim Advocacy, and Feminist Redress." *Law & Society Review* 28.4 (1994): 777–86.

Daly, Kathleen, and Meda Chesney-Lind. "Feminism and Criminology." *Justice Quarterly* 5.4 (1988): 497–538.

Daniels, Cynthia R., ed. *Feminists Negotiate the State: Politics of Domestic Violence*. Lanham, MD: University Press of America, 1997.

_____. "Introduction: The Paradoxes of State Power." *Feminists Negotiate the State: Politics of Domestic Violence*. Cynthia Daniels, ed. Lanham, MD: University Press of America, 1997.

Daniels, Cynthia R., et al. "Feminist Strategies: The Terms of Negotiation." *Feminists Negotiate the State: Politics of Domestic Violence*. Cynthia Daniels, ed. Lanham, MD: University Press of America, 1997.

Dannenberg, John E. "Los Angeles Voters Reject 5,000 More Cops; Invest in Clear Ocean Instead." *Prison Legal News*, January 2005: 23.

Davey, Joseph Dillon. *The New Social Contract: America's Journey from Welfare State to Police State*. Westport, CT: Praeger, 1995.

_____. *The Politics of Prison Expansion: Winning Elections by Waging War on Crime*. Westport, CT: Praeger, 1998.

Davidson, Howard. "Community Control Without State Control: Issues Surrounding a Feminist and Prison Abolitionist Approach to Violence Against Women." In *Abolitionism: Towards a Non-Repressive Approach to Crime*. Herman Bianchi and René van Swaaningen, eds. Amsterdam: Free University Press, 1986.

Davis, Allen F. "Welfare, Reform and World War I." *American Quarterly* 19.3 (Fall 1967): 516–33.

Davis, Angela Y. *Women, Culture, and Politics*. New York: Random House, 1989.

Davis, David Brion. "The Movement to Abolish Capital Punishment in America, 1787–1861." In *From Homicide to Slavery: Studies in American Culture*. David Brion Davis, ed. New York: Oxford University Press, 1986: 17–40.

Davis, David S. "State and Right-Wing Repression: The Production of Crime Policies." *Crime and Social Justice* 20 (1983): 121–37.

Davis, Kenneth Culp. *Discretionary Justice: A Preliminary Inquiry*. Baton Rouge: Louisiana State University, 1969.

Davis, Liane. "Battered Women: The Transformation of a Social Problem." *Social Work* 32 (July–August 1987): 306–11.

Davis, Liane, Jan L. Hagen, and Theresa J. Early. "Social Services for Battered Women: Are They Adequate, Accessible, and Appropriate?" *Social Work: Journal of the National Association of Social Workers* 39.6 (1994): 695–704.

Davis, Mike. *Ecology of Fear.* New York: Metropolitan Books, 1998.

Davis, Robert C., Nicole J. Henderson, and Caitlin Rabbitt. *Effects of State Victim Rights Legislation on Local Criminal Justice Systems.* New York: Vera Institute of Justice, April 2002.

Dawson, Michael C., and Cathy Cohen. "Problems in the Study of Race." In *Political Science: State of the Discipline.* Ira Katznelson and Helen V. Milner, eds. New York: W. W. Norton & Co., 2002: 488–510.

Díaz-Cotto, Juanita. *Gender, Ethnicity, and the State: Latina and Latino Prison Politics.* Albany: SUNY Press, 1996.

Dieter, Richard C. "Millions Misspent: What Politicians Don't Say About the High Costs of the Death Penalty." In *The Death Penalty in America: Current Controversies.* Hugo Adam Bedau, ed. New York: Oxford University Press, 1997: 401–10.

———. "Sentencing for Life: Americans Embrace Alternatives to the Death Penalty." In *The Death Penalty in America: Current Controversies.* Hugo Adam Bedau, ed. New York: Oxford University Press, 1997: 116–34.

DiIulio, John J., Jr. *Governing Prisons: A Comparative Study of Correctional Management.* New York: Free Press, 1987.

———. "The Old Regime and the *Ruiz* Revolution: The Impact of Judicial Intervention on Texas Prisons." In *Courts, Corrections, and the Constitution: The Impact of Judicial Intervention on Prisons and Jails.* John DiIulio, Jr., ed. New York: Oxford University Press, 1990.

———. "Understanding Prisons: The New Old Penology." *Law and Social Inquiry* 16.1 (Winter 1991): 65–99.

———. "Are Voters Fools? Crime, Public Opinion, and Representative Democracy." *Corrections Management Quarterly* 1.3 (1997): 1–5.

———, ed. *Courts, Corrections, and the Constitution: The Impact of Judicial Intervention on Prisons and Jails.* New York: Oxford University Press, 1990.

DiIulio, John, Jr., Steven K. Smith, and Aaron J. Saiger. "The Federal Role in Crime Control." In *Crime.* James Q. Wilson and Joan Petersilia, eds. San Francisco: Institute for Contemporary Studies Press, 1995: 445–62.

Dixon, David, and Elaine Fishwick. "The Law and Order Debate in Historical Perspective." In *Law and Order in British Politics.* Philip Norton, ed. Aldershot, UK: Gower, 1984.

Dixon, Jo. "The Nexus of Sex, Spousal Violence, and the State." *Law & Society Review* 29.2 (1995): 359–76.

Dobash, R. Emerson, and Russell P. Dobash. *Women, Violence and Social Change.* London and New York: Routledge, 1992.

Donziger, Steven R., ed. *The Real War on Crime: The Report of the National Criminal Justice Commission.* New York: Harper Perennial, 1996.

Doob, Anthony N. "The United States Sentencing Commission Guidelines: If You Don't Know Where You Are Going, You Might Not Get There." In *The Politics of Sentencing Reform.* Chris Clarkson and Rod Morgan, eds. Oxford: Clarendon – Oxford University Press, 1995.

Dorsen, Norman. *Frontiers of Civil Liberties.* New York: Pantheon Books, 1968.

Dow, David R. "The Problem of 'Innocence.'" In *Machinery of Death: The Reality of America's Death Penalty Regime.* David R. Dow and Mark Dow, eds. New York: Routledge, 2002.

Downes, David. *Contrasts in Tolerance: Post-War Penal Policy in The Netherlands and England and Wales.* Oxford: Clarendon Press, 1988.

——. "The Origins and Consequences of Dutch Penal Policy Since 1945." In *Imprisonment: European Perspectives.* John Muncie and Richard Sparks, eds. New York: St. Martin's Press, 1991.

Downes, David, and Rod Morgan. "'Hostages to Fortune'? The Politics of Law and Order in Post-War Britain." In *The Oxford Handbook of Criminology.* Mike Maguire, Rod Morgan, and Robert Reiner, eds. Oxford: Clarendon Press, 1994: 183–232.

——. "The British General Election 2001: The Centre-Right Consensus." *Punishment & Society* 4.1 (2002): 81–96.

Dumm, Thomas L. *Democracy and Punishment: Disciplinary Origins of the United States.* Madison: University of Wisconsin Press, 1987.

Dussich, John P. J. "Evolving Services for Crime Victims." In *Perspectives on Crime Victims.* Burt Galaway and Joe Hudson, eds. St. Louis, MO: C. V. Mosby, 1981.

Dyer, Joel. *The Perpetual Prisoner Machine: How America Profits from Crime.* Boulder, CO: Westview, 2000.

Edsall, Thomas Byrne, with Mary D. Edsall. *Chain Reaction: The Impact of Race, Rights, and Taxes on American Politics.* New York: Norton, 1991.

Edwards, Susan. "Violence Against Women: Feminism and the Law." In *Feminist Perspectives in Criminology.* Loraine Gelsthorpe and Allison Morris, eds. Milton Keynes, UK: Open University Press, 1990.

Ekland-Olson, Sheldon, and Steve J. Martin. "*Ruiz*: A Struggle Over Legitimacy." In *Courts, Corrections, and the Constitution: The Impact of Judicial Intervention on Prisons and Jails.* John DiIulio, Jr., ed. New York: Oxford University Press, 1990.

Elder, N. C. M. "Conclusion." In *Law and Order and British Politics.* Philip Norton, ed. Aldershot, UK: Gower, 1984.

Elias, Robert. "Which Victim Movement? The Politics of Victim Policy." In *Victims of Crime: Problems, Policies, and Programs.* Arthur J. Lurigio, Wesley G. Skogan, and Robert C. Davis, eds. Newbury Park, CA: Sage Publications, 1980.

——. "The Symbolic Politics of Victim Compensation." *Victimology: An International Journal* 8.1–2 (1983): 213–24.

——. *Victims of the System.* New Brunswick, NJ: Transaction Books, 1983.

——. *Politics of Victimization: Victims, Victimology, and Human Rights.* New York: Oxford University Press, 1986.

——. "Community Control, Criminal Justice and Victim Services." *Towards a Critical Victimology.* Ezzat A. Fattah, ed. New York: St. Martin's Press, 1992.

——. *Victims Still: The Political Manipulation of Crime Victims.* Newbury Park, CA: Sage, 1993.

Ellsworth, Phoebe C., and Samuel R. Gross. "Hardening of the Attitudes: Americans' Views of the Death Penalty." *Journal of Social Issues* 50.2 (1994): 19–52.

Elman, R. Amy. *Sexual Subordination and State Intervention: Comparing Sweden and the United States.* Providence: Berghahn Books, 1996.

——. "Unprotected by the Swedish Welfare State Revisited: Assessing a Decade of Reforms for Battered Women." *Women's Studies International Forum* 24.1 (2001): 39–52.

Elshtain, Jean Bethke. "Politics and the Battered Woman." *Dissent,* Winter 1985: 62–69.

English, Sharon. "It's Time for a CamPayne." *The NOVA Newsletter* 15.9 (1991): 2.

Epp, Charles R. *The Rights Revolution: Lawyers, Activists, and Supreme Courts in Comparative Perspective.* Chicago: University of Chicago Press, 1998.

Eppenstein, Dieter. "Weisser Ring: Lobby for Victims of Crime." In *Particular Groups of Victims*, Pt. 1. Günther Kaiser, H. Kury, and H. J. Albrecht, eds. Freiburg: Max Planck Institute, 1991: 137–49.

Epstein, Edward Jay. *Agency of Fear: Opiates and Political Power in America*. New York: G. P. Putnam's Sons, 1977.

Epstein, Lee, and Joseph F. Kobylka. *The Supreme Court and Legal Change: Abortion and the Death Penalty*. Chapel Hill: University of North Carolina Press, 1992.

Ericson, Richard V., Patricia M. Baranek, and Janet B. L. Chan. *Representing Order: Crime, Law, and Justice in the News Media*. Toronto: University of Toronto Press, 1991.

Erikson, Kai T. *Wayward Puritans: A Study in the Sociology of Deviance*. New York: John Wiley & Sons, 1966.

Evans, Peter. *The Prison Crisis*. London: Allen and Unwin, 1980.

Evans, Richard J. *Rituals of Retribution: Capital Punishment in Germany, 1600–1987*. Oxford: Oxford University Press, 1996.

Ewald, Uwe. "Criminal Victimization and Social Adaptation in Modernity: Fear of Crime and Risk Perception in the New Germany." In *Crime, Risk and Insecurity: Law and Order in Everyday Life and Political Discourse*. Tim Hope and Richard Sparks, eds. London and New York: Routledge, 2000.

Fairchild, Erika. "Interest Groups in the Criminal Justice Process." *Journal of Criminal Justice* 9.2 (1981): 181–94.

Faragher, Tony. "The Police Response to Violence Against Women in the Home." In *Private Violence and Public Policy: The Needs of Battered Women and the Response of the Public Sector*. Jan Pahl, ed. London: Routledge & Kegan Paul, 1985.

Farrell, Harry. *Swift Justice: Murder and Vengeance in a California Town*. New York: St. Martin's Press, 1992.

Fattah, Ezzat A. "Victims and Victimology: The Facts and the Rhetoric." In *Towards a Critical Victimology*. Ezzat A. Fattah, ed. New York: St. Martin's Press, 1992: 29–56.

————. "The Need for a Critical Victimology." In *Towards a Critical Victimology*. Ezzat A. Fattah, ed. New York: St. Martin's Press, 1992: 3–26.

————. "Preface." In *Towards a Critical Victimology*. Ezzat A. Fattah, ed. New York: St. Martin's Press, 1992.

Fawcett, James. "Applications of the European Convention on Human Rights." In *Accountability and Prison*. Mike Maguire, Jon Vagg, and Rod Morgan, eds. London: Tavistock Publications, 1985: 60–78.

Feeley, Malcolm M., and Edwin L. Rubin. *Judicial Policy Making and the Modern State: How the Courts Reformed America's Prisons*. Cambridge: Cambridge University Press, 1998.

Feeley, Malcolm M., and Austin D. Sarat. *The Policy Dilemma: Federal Crime Policy and the Law Enforcement Assistance Administration, 1968–1978*. Minneapolis: University of Minnesota, 1980.

Feest, Johannes. "Reducing the Prison Population: Lessons from the West German Experience?" In *Imprisonment: European Perspectives*. John Muncie and Richard Sparks, eds. New York: St. Martin's Press, 1991: 131–45.

Feige, David. "The Dark Side of Innocence." *The New York Times Magazine*, June 15, 2003.

Feinman, Clarice. *Women in the Criminal Justice System*. 3rd ed. Westport, CT: Praeger, 1994.

Fellner, Jamie, and Marc Mauer. *Losing the Vote: The Impact of Felony Disenfranchisement Laws in the United States*. Washington, DC, and New York: The Sentencing Project and Human Rights Watch, October 1998.

Felter, Elizabeth. "A History of the State's Response to Domestic Violence." In *Feminists Negotiate the State: The Politics of Domestic Violence*. Cynthia R. Daniels, ed. Lantham, MD: University Press of America, 1997.

Ferraro, Kathleen J. "The Legal Response to Women Battering in the United States." In *Women, Policing, and Male Violence: International Perspectives*. Jalna Hanmer, Jill Radford, and Elizabeth A. Stanko, eds. London and New York: Routledge, 1989: 154–85.

Ferree, Myra Marx. "Equality and Autonomy: Feminist Politics in the United States and West Germany." In *The Women's Movements of the United States and Western Europe*. Mary Fainsod Katzenstein and Carol McClung Mueller, eds. Philadelphia: Temple University Press, 1987: 172–95.

Fierce, Mildred C. *Slavery Revisited: Blacks and the Southern Convict Lease System, 1865–1933*. New York: Africana Studies Research Center, Brooklyn College, CUNY, 1994.

Filler, Louis. "Movements to Abolish the Death Penalty in the United States." *The Annals of the American Academy of Political and Social Science* 284 (November 1952): 124–36.

Finekenauer, James O. "Crime as a National Political Issue, 1964–76: From Law and Order to Domestic Tranquility." *Crime and Delinquency* 24.1 (January 1978): 13–27.

Finkelman, Paul, ed. *Lynching, Racial Violence, and Law*. New York: Garland Publishing, 1992.

Finstad, Liv. "Sexual Offenders Out of Prison: Principles for a Realistic Utopia." *International Journal of the Sociology of Law* 18 (May 1990): 157–77.

Fischer, Steve. "Due Process Rights of Prisoners." In *Encyclopedia of American Prisons*. Marilyn D. McShane and Frank P. Williams, III, eds. New York and London: Garland Publishing, 1996: 174–76.

Fitzgerald, Edward. "Prison Discipline and the Courts." In *Accountability and Prisons: Opening Up a Closed World*. Mike Maguire, Jon Vagg, and Rod Morgan, eds. London: Tavistock Publications, 1985.

Fitzgerald, Mike. *Prisoners in Revolt*. New York: Penguin, 1977.

Fogelson, Robert M. *Big-City Police*. Cambridge, MA: Harvard University Press, 1977.

Foley, Marian. "Professionalising the Response to Rape." In *Working With Violence*. Carol and Terry Gillespie, eds. Houndsmills, UK: Macmillan, 1994.

Ford, Gerald R. "Special Message to the Congress on Crime," June 19, 1975. *Public Papers of the Presidents of the United States: Containing the Public Messages, Speeches and Statements of the President, 1975*. Vol. 1. Washington, DC: GPO, 1977.

Forst, Martin L., ed. *Sentencing Reform: Experiments in Reducing Disparity*. (Newbury Park, CA: Sage, 1982).

Foucault, Michel. *Discipline and Punishment: The Birth of the Prison*. New York: Vintage Books, 1979.

Fox, Vernon. *Violence Behind Bars: An Explosive Report on Prison Riots in the United States*. New York: Vantage Press, 1956.

France, Laureen, and Nancy McDonald. "They Call It Rehabilitation." *Aegis*, Winter/Spring, 1980.

Frankel, Marvin E. *Criminal Sentences: Law Without Order*. New York: Hill and Wang, 1973.

Franklin, Fabian. *Nuggets from the Wickersham Report*. New York: Riverside Press, 1931.

Frase, Richard S. "Comparative Perspectives on Sentencing Policy and Research." In *Sentencing and Sanctions in Western Countries*. Michael Tonry and Richard S. Frase, eds. Oxford: Oxford University Press, 2001: 259–92.

Frase, Richard S., and Thomas Weigend. "German Criminal Justice as a Guide to American Law Reform: Similar Problems, Better Solutions?" *Boston College International and Comparative Law Review* 18.2 (Summer 1995): 317–60.

Freedberg, Louis. "Reforming Three Strikes." *The Nation*, November 1, 2004: 7–8.

Freedman, Estelle B. *Their Sisters' Keepers: Women's Prison Reform in America, 1830–1930*. Ann Arbor: University of Michigan Press, 1981.

———. "'Uncontrolled Desires': The Response to the Sexual Psychopath, 1920–1960." *The Journal of American History* 74.1 (January 1987): 83–106.

———. *Maternal Justice: Miriam Van Waters and the Female Reform Tradition*. Chicago: University of Chicago Press, 1996.

Freeman, Jo. "The Origins of the Women's Liberation Movement." *American Journal of Sociology* 78.4 (1973): 792–811.

Freeman-Longo, Robert E. "Reducing Sexual Abuse in America: Legislating Tougher Laws or Public Education and Prevention." *New England Journal on Criminal Abuse & Civil Confinement* 23.2 (1997): 303–31.

Freiberg, Arie. "Sentencing and Punishment in Australia in the 1990s." In *Sentencing Reform in Overcrowded Times: A Comparative Perspective*. Michael Tonry and Kathleen Hatlestad, eds. New York: Oxford University Press, 1997: 35–49.

———. "Three Strikes and You're Out – It's Not Cricket: Colonization and Resistance in Australian Sentencing." In *Sentencing and Sanctions in Western Countries*. Michael Tonry and Richard S. Frase, eds. New York: Oxford University Press, 2001: 29–61.

Fried, Amy. "'It's Hard To Change What We Want To Change': Rape Crisis Centers as Organizations." *Gender & Society* 8.4 (December 1994): 562–83.

Friedman, Lawrence M. "The Development of American Criminal Law." In *Law and Order in American History*. Joseph M. Hawes, ed. Port Washington, NY: Kennicut Press, 1979.

———. *Crime and Punishment in American History*. New York: Basic Books, 1993.

Friedman, Lawrence, and George Fisher, eds. *The Crime Conundrum: Essays on Criminal Justice*. Boulder, CO: Westview Press, 1997.

Fry, Margery. "Justice for Victims." In *Considering the Victim: Readings in Restitution and Victim Compensation*. Joe Hudson and Burt Galaway, eds. Springfield, IL: Charles C. Thomas, 1975.

Fry, Margery, Glanville Williams, J. L. Montrose, Fred E. Imlau, Frank W. Miller et al. "Compensation for Victims of Criminal Violence: A Round Table." *Journal of Public Law* 8 (1959): 191–253.

Fuentes, Annette. "Unchained: From the Bay Area to the Big Apple, Youth Activists Target Juvenile Jails." *In These Times*, July 8, 2002: 16–17.

Galliher, James M., and John F. Galliher. "'Deja Vu All Over Again': The Recurring Life and Death of Capital Punishment Legislation in Kansas." *Social Problems* 44.3 (August 1997): 369–85.

Galliher, John F., and Linda Basilick. "Utah's Liberal Drug Laws: Structural Foundations and Triggering Events." *Social Problems* 26.3 (February 1979): 284–97.

Galliher, John, Gregory Ray, and Brent Cook. "Abolition and Reinstatement of Capital Punishment During the Progressive Era and Early 20th Century." *Journal of Criminal Law and Criminology* 83 (Fall 1992): 538–76.

Gamberg, Herbert, and Anthony Thomas. *The Illusion of Prison Reform*. New York: Peter Lang, 1984.

Garland, David. *Punishment and Welfare: A History of Penal Strategies*. Aldershot, UK: Gower, 1985.

_____. *Punishment and Modern Society: A Study in Social Theory*. Chicago: University of Chicago Press, 1990.

_____. "The Limits of the Sovereign State: Strategies of Crime Control in Contemporary Society." *The British Journal of Criminology* 36.4 (Autumn 1996): 445–71.

_____. *The Culture of Control: Crime and Social Order in Contemporary Society*. Chicago: University of Chicago Press, 2001.

_____. "Capital Punishment and American Culture." *Punishment & Society* 7.4 (October 2005): 347–65.

Garland, David, and Richard Sparks. "Criminology, Social Theory, and the Challenge of Our Times." In *Criminology and Social Theory*. David Garland and Richard Sparks, eds. Oxford: Oxford University Press, 2000: 1–22.

Garland, David, and Peter Young. "Towards a Social Analysis of Penalty." In *The Power to Punish: Contemporary Penalty and Social Analysis*. David Garland and Peter Young, eds. London and Atlantic Highlands, NJ: Heinemann Educational Books and Humanities Press, 1983: 1–36.

Garson, G. David. "The Disruption of Public Administration: An Investigation of Alternative Theories of the Relationship Among Administrators, Reformers, and Involuntary Social Service Clients." *Law & Society Review* 6.4 (May 1972): 531–62.

Gartner, Rosemary. "Age and Homicide in Different National Contexts." In *The Crime Conundrum: Essays in Criminal Justice*. Lawrence M. Friedman and George Fisher, eds. Boulder, CO: Westview, 1997.

Gaubatz, Kathlyn Taylor. *Crime in the Public Mind*. Ann Arbor: University of Michigan Press, 1995.

Gee, Pauline W. "Ensuring Police Protection for Battered Women: The Scott v. Hart Suit." *Signs* 8.3 (Spring 1983): 554–67.

Gelb, Joyce. "The Politics of Wife Abuse." In *Families, Politics, and Public Policy: A Feminist Dialogue on Women and the State*. Irene Diamond, ed. New York: Longman, 1983.

_____. "Social Movement 'Success': A Comparative Analysis of Feminism in the United States and United Kingdom." In *The Women's Movements of the United States and Western Europe*. Mary Fainsod Katzenstein and Carol McClung Mueller, eds. Philadelphia: Temple University Press, 1987.

Gelles, Richard J. "Constraints Against Domestic Violence: How Well Do They Work?" *American Behavioral Scientist* 36.5 (May 1993).

Gelsthorpe, Loraine, and Allison Morris, eds. *Feminist Perspectives in Criminology*. Milton Keynes, UK: Open University Press, 1990.

Gerber, David A. "Lynching and Law and Order: Origin and Passage of the Ohio Anti-Lynching Law of 1896." In *Lynching, Racial Violence, and Law*. Paul Finkelman, ed. New York: Garland Publishing, 1992.

Germond, Jack, and Jules Witcover. *Whose Broad Stripes and Bright Stars? The Trivial Pursuit of the Presidency*. New York: Warner Books, 1988.

Gest, Ted. *Crime & Politics: Big Government's Erratic Campaign for Law and Order*. Oxford: Oxford University Press, 2001.

Gibbons, Don C. "Review Essay: Crime, Criminologists, and Public Policy." *Crime & Delinquency* 45.3 (1999): 389–99.

Gilbert, James. *A Cycle of Outrage: America's Reaction to the Juvenile Delinquent in the 1950s.* New York: Oxford University Press, 1986.

Gillespie, Terry. "Under Pressure: Rape Crisis Centers, Multi-Agency Work, and Strategies for Survival." In *Working With Violence.* Carol Lupton and Terry Gillespie, eds. Houndsmills, UK: Macmillan, 1994.

Gilmore, Ruth Wilson. "You Have Dislodged a Boulder: Mothers and Prisoners in the Post Keynesian California Landscape." *Transforming Anthropology* 8.1-2 (1999): 12–38.

Gilroy, Paul, and Joe Sim. "Law, Order and the State of the Left." In *Law, Order and the Authoritarian State: Readings in Critical Criminology.* Phil Scraton, ed. Milton Keynes, UK: Open University Press, 1987.

Gittler, Josephine. "Expanding the Role of the Victim in a Criminal Action: An Overview of Issues and Problems." *Pepperdine Law Review* 11 (1984): 117–82.

Glaze, Lauren E., and Seri Palla. "Probation and Parole in the United States, 2003." *Bureau of Justice Statistics Bulletin,* July 2004.

Godsoe, Cynthia. "The Ban on Welfare for Felony Drug Offenders: Giving a New Meaning to 'Life Sentence'." *Berkeley Women's Law Journal* 13 (1998): 257–67.

Goldscheid, Julie, et al. "The Civil Rights Remedy of the Violence Against Women Act: Legislative History, Policy Implications and Litigation Strategy; A Panel Discussion Sponsored by the Bar of the City of New York." *Journal of Law and Policy* 4, no. 2 (1996): 383–434.

Goldstein, Abraham S. "Defining the Role of the Victim in Criminal Prosecution." *Mississippi Law Review* 52 (1982): 515–61.

———— "Prosecution: History of the Public Prosecutor." *Encyclopedia of Criminal Justice.* Sanford H. Kadish, ed. New York: New Press, 1983: 1242–1246.

Goodstein, Lynne, and John Hepburn. *Determinate Sentencing and Imprisonment: A Failure of Reform.* Cincinnati: Anderson Publishing Co., 1985

Gordon, Diana R. *The Justice Juggernaut: Fighting Street Crime, Controlling Citizens.* New Brunswick, NJ: Rutgers University Press, 1990.

————. *The Return of the Dangerous Classes: Drug Prohibition and Policy Politics.* New York: W. W. Norton & Co., 1994.

Gordon, Ernest. *The Wrecking of the Eighteenth Amendment.* Francetown, NH: The Alcohol Information Press, 1943.

Gordon, Linda. Review of Ruth Bordin, *Women and Temperance: The Quest for Power and Liberty 1873–1900* and Estelle B. Freedman, *Their Sisters' Keepers: Women's Prison Reform in America, 1830–1930. Signs* 7.4 (1982): 886–89.

————. "Family Violence, Feminism, and Social Control." *Feminist Studies* 12.3 (Fall 1986): 453–78.

————. *Heroes of Their Own Lives: The Politics and History of Family Violence, Boston, 1880–1960.* New York: Viking, 1988.

Gordon, Paul. "Community Policing: Towards the Local Police State?" In *Law, Order and the Authoritarian State: Readings in Critical Criminology.* Phil Scraton, ed. Milton Keynes, UK: Open University Press, 1987: 121–44.

Gornick, Janet, Martha R. Burt, and Karen J. Pittman. "Structure and Activities of Rape Crisis Centers in the Early 1980s." *Crime and Delinquency* 31.2 (April 1985): 247–68.

Gostin, Larry, and Marie Staunton. "The Case for Prison Standards: Conditions of Confinement, Segregation, and Medical Treatment." In *Accountability and Prisons:*

Opening Up a Closed World. Mike Maguire, Jon Vagg, and Rod Morgan, eds. London: Tavistock Publications, 1985.

Gottfredson, Stephen D., and Séan McConville eds. *America's Correctional Crisis: Prison Populations and Public Policy.* New York, Greenwood Press, 1987.

Gottschalk, Marie. *The Shadow Welfare State: Labor, Business, and the Politics of Health Care in the United States.* Ithaca, NY: Cornell University Press, 2000.

———. "Black Flower: Prisons and the Future of Incarceration." *The Annals of the American Academy of Political and Social Science* 582 (July 2002): 195–227.

Gowers, Ernest. *A Life for a Life? The Problem of Capital Punishment.* London: Chatto and Windus, 1956.

Graham, Hugh Davis, and Ted Robert Gurr, eds. *The History of Violence in America: Historical and Comparative Perspectives.* New York: Praeger, 1969.

Graham, John. "Decarceration in the Federal Republic of Germany: How Practitioners Are Succeeding Where Policy-Makers Failed." *British Journal of Criminology* 30.3 (Spring 1990): 150–70.

Gray, Ian, and Moira Stanley. *A Punishment in Search of a Crime: Americans Speak Out Against the Death Penalty.* New York: Avon Books, 1989.

Greenberg David F., and Fay Stender. "The Prison as a Lawless Agency." *Buffalo Law Review* 21.3 (Spring 1972): 799–838.

Greenberg, David F., and Valerie West. "State Prison Populations and Their Growth, 1971–1991." *Criminology* 39.3 (2001): 615–53.

Greenberg, Jack. *Cases and Materials on Judicial Process and Social Change: Constitutional Litigation.* St. Paul, MN: West Publishing Co., 1977.

———. *Crusaders in the Courts: How a Dedicated Band of Lawyers Fought for the Civil Rights Revolution.* New York: Basic Books, 1994.

Greenberg, Jack, and Jack Himmelstein. "Varieties of Attack on the Death Penalty." *Crime and Delinquency* 15.1 (January 1969): 112–20.

Gregory, Jeanne, and Susan Lees. *Policing Sexual Assault.* London and New York: Routledge, 1999.

Greve, John. *London's Homeless.* London: G. Bell & Sons, 1964.

Gurr, Ted Robert. "Historical Trends in Violent Crime: A Critical Review of the Evidence." In *Crime and Justice.* Vol. 3. Michael Tonry and Norval Morris, eds. Chicago: University of Chicago Press, 1981: 295–353.

Hagan, John, and Ronit Dinovitzer. "Collateral Consequences of Imprisonment for Children, Communities, and Prisoners." In *Crime and Justice – A Review of Research.* Vol. 26. *Prisons.* Michael Tonry and Joan Petersilia, eds. Chicago: University of Chicago Press, 1999.

Hagedorn, Herman, ed. *The Works of Theodore Roosevelt.* Vol. 14. New York: Charles Scribners, 1926.

Haines, Herbert H. *Against Capital Punishment: The Anti-Death Penalty Movement in America, 1972–1994.* New York: Oxford University Press, 1996.

Hajjar, Lisa. "In the Penal Colony." *The Nation*, February 7, 2005; 23–30.

Hale, Chris. "Economy, Punishment and Imprisonment." *Contemporary Crises: Law, Crime and Social Policy* 13 (1989): 327–49.

Hall, Jacquelyn Dowd. *Revolt Against Chivalry: Jessie Daniel Ames and the Women's Campaign Against Lynching.* New York: Columbia University Press, 1979.

Hall, Stuart, Chas Critcher, Tony Jefferson, John Clarke, and Brian Roberts. *Policing the Crisis: Mugging, the State, and Law and Order.* Houndsmills, UK: Macmillan, 1978.

Hallinan, Joseph. *Going Up the River: Travels in a Prison Nation.* New York: Random House, 2001.

Halsted, James B. "Domestic Violence: Its Legal Definitions." In *Domestic Violence: The Changing Criminal Justice Response.* Eve S. Buzawa and Carl G. Buzawa, eds. Westport, CT: Auburn House, 1992.

Hamilton, Wendy J. "Mothers Against Drunk Driving–MADD in the USA." *Injury Prevention* 6 (2000): 90–91.

Hamm, Theodore. *Rebel and a Cause: Caryl Chessman and the Politics of the Death Penalty in Postwar California, 1948–1974.* Berkeley: University of California Press, 2001.

Hanmer, Jalna. "Women and Policing in Britain." In *Women, Policing, and Male Violence: International Perspectives.* Jalna Hanmer, Jill Radford et al., eds. London and New York: Routledge, 1989.

Harris, Angela. "Race and Essentialism in Feminist Legal Theory." In *Feminist Legal Theory: Readings in Law and Gender.* Katharine T. Bartlett and Rosanne Kennedy, eds. Boulder, CO: Westview Press, 1991.

Harris, M. Kay. "Moving Into the New Millennium: Toward a Feminist Vision of Justice." *Prison Journal* 67.2 (Fall-Winter 1987): 27–38.

Harris, M. Kay, and Dudley P. Spiller, Jr. *After Decision: Implementation of Judicial Decrees in Correctional Settings.* Washington, DC: American Bar Association, 1976.

Harris, Richard. *The Fear of Crime.* New York: Praeger, 1969.

Harrison, Paige M., and Allen J. Beck. "Prisoners in 2003." *Bureau of Justice Statistics Bulletin,* November 2004.

Hawkins, Darnell F., and Kenneth A. Hardy. "Black-White Imprisonment Rates: A State-by-State Analysis." *Social Justice* 16.4 (Winter 1989): 75–94.

Hawkins, Gordon. *The Prison: Policy and Practice.* Chicago: University of Chicago Press, 1976.

Hay, Douglas. "Property, Authority, and the Criminal Law." In *Albion's Fatal Tree: Crime and Society in Eighteenth-Century England.* Douglas Hay, Peter Linebaugh, John Rule, E. P. Thompson, and Cal Winslow, eds. New York: Pantheon, 1975: 17–63.

Heinz, John P., Robert W. Gettleman, and Morris Seeskin. "Legislative Politics and the Criminal Law." *Northwestern Law Review* 64.3 (July-August 1969): 277–358.

Henderson, Lynne N. "The Wrongs of Victim's Rights." *Stanford Law Review* 37.4 (April 1985): 937–1021.

Herman, Lawrence. "What's Wrong With the Rape Reform Laws?" *The Civil Liberties Review* 3.5 (December 1976/January 1977): 60–73.

Hickey, Thomas J. "National Prison Project." In *Encyclopedia of American Prisons.* Marilyn D. McShane and Frank P. Williams, III, eds. New York and London: Garland Publishing, 1996: 329–30.

Hindus, Michael. *Prison and Plantation: Crime, Justice, and Authority in Massachusetts and South Carolina, 1767–1978.* Chapel Hill: University of North Carolina Press, 1980.

Hirsch, Adam. *The Rise of the Penitentiary: Prisons and Punishment in Early America.* New Haven: Yale University Press, 1992.

Hirschman, Linda. "Making Safety a Right." *Ms.,* September–October 1994.

Hirschmann, Nancy. *Toward a Feminist Theory of Freedom.* Princeton: Princeton University Press, 2003.

Hobart, Margaret. "Review: Strategies for Confronting Domestic Violence: A Resource Manual by United Nations Center for Social Development and Humanitarian Affairs." *Women & Politics* 17.1 (1997): 99–101.

Hobson, Barbara Meil. *Uneasy Virtue: The Politics of Prostitution and the American Reform Tradition.* New York: Basic Books, 1987.

Hole, Judith, and Ellen Levine. *Rebirth of Feminism.* New York: Quadrangle, 1971.

Hollon, W. Eugene. *Frontier Violence: Another Look.* New York: Oxford University Press, 1974.

Holt, Thomas C. *The Problem of Race in the 21st Century.* Cambridge, MA: Harvard University Press, 2000.

Holton, Christopher, and Peter Raynor. "Origins of Victims Support Philosophy and Practice." In *Victims of Crime: A New Deal?* Mike Maguire and John Pointing, eds. Buckingham, UK: Open University Press, 1988.

Hood, Roger. *The Death Penalty: A World-Wide Perspective.* Oxford: Oxford University Press, 1996.

Hope, Tim, and Richard Sparks, eds. *Crime, Risk and Insecurity: Law and Order in Everyday Life and Political Discourse.* London and New York: Routledge, 2000.

Hopkins, Earnest J. *Our Lawless Police: A Study of the Unlawful Enforcement of the Law.* New York: The Viking Press, 1931.

Horan, James David. *The Pinkertons: The Detective Dynasty that Made History.* New York: Crown, 1968.

Hudson, Joe, and Burt Galaway. "Conclusion." In *Considering the Victim: Readings in Restitution and Victim Compensation.* Joe Hudson and Burt Galaway, eds. Springfield, IL: Charles C. Thomas, 1975.

Human Rights Watch. *The Human Rights Watch Global Report on Prisons.* New York: Human Rights Watch, June 1993.

_____. *Red Onion State Prison: Super-Maximum Security Confinement in the United States.* New York: Human Rights Watch, April 1999.

_____. *Out of Sight: Super-Maximum Security Confinement in the United States.* New York: Human Rights Watch, February 2000.

_____. *No Escape: Male Rape in U.S. Prisons.* New York: Human Rights Watch, April 2001.

Hunt, John Gabriel, ed. *The Essential Theodore Roosevelt.* New York: Gramercy Books, 1994.

Ignatieff, Michael. *A Just Measure of Pain: The Penitentiary in the Industrial Revolution, 1750–1850.* New York: Columbia University Press, 1978.

_____. "State, Civil Society, and Total Institutions: A Critique of Recent Social Histories of Punishment." In *Crime and Justice: A Review of Research.* Vol. 3. Norval Morris and Michael Tonry, eds. Chicago: University of Chicago Press, 1981: 153–92.

Irwin, John. *Prisons in Turmoil.* Boston: Little, Brown, 1980.

Irwin, John, Vincent Schiraldi, and Jason Ziedenberg. *America's One Million Nonviolent Prisoners.* Washington, DC: The Justice Policy Institute, March 1999.

Jackson, George L. *Soledad Brother: The Prison Letters of George Jackson.* New York: Coward-McCann, 1970.

_____. *Blood in My Eye.* New York: Random House, 1972.

_____. *Soledad Brother: The Prison Letters of George Jackson.* Foreword by Jonathan Jackson, Jr. Chicago: Lawrence Hill Books, 1994.

Jackson, Jesse L., Sr., Jesse L. Jackson, Jr., and Bruce Shapiro. *Legal Lynching: The Death Penalty and America's Future.* New York: The New Press, 2001.

Jacobs, David, and Ronald D. Helms. "Toward a Political Model of Incarceration: A Time-Series Examination of Multiple Explanations for Prison Admission Rates." *American Journal of Sociology* 102.6 (September 1996): 322–57.

Jacobs, James B. *Stateville: The Penitentiary in Mass Society.* Chicago: University of Chicago Press, 1977.

———. "Race Relations and the Prisoner Subculture." In *Crime and Punishment: An Annual Review of Research*. Vol. 1. Norval Morris and Michael Tonry, eds. Chicago: Chicago University Press, 1979: 1–27.

———. "The Prisoners' Rights Movement and Its Impacts, 1960–80." In *Crime and Justice: An Annual Review of Research*. Vol. 2. Norval Morris and Michael Tonry, eds. Chicago: University of Chicago Press, 1980: 429–470.

Jacobs, James B., and Kimberly Potter. *Hate Crimes: Criminal Law and Identity Politics*. New York: Oxford University Press, 1998.

Jacoby, Joan E. *The American Prosecutor: A Search for Identity*. Lexington, MA: Lexington Books, 1980.

Jenkins, Philip. *Using Murder: The Social Construction of Serial Homicide*. New York: Aldine de Gruyter, 1994.

———. *Moral Panic: Changing Concepts of the Child Molester in Modern America*. New Haven: Yale University Press, 1998.

Jenness, Valerie, and Kendal Broad. *Hate Crimes: New Social Movements and the Politics of Violence*. New York: Aldine de Gruyter, 1997.

Jenness, Valerie, and Ryken Grattet. *Making Hate a Crime: From Social Movement to Law Enforcement*. New York: Russell Sage Foundation, 2001.

Johnson, Bruce C. "Taking Care of Labor: The Police in American Politics." *Theory and Society* 3.1 (1976): 89–117.

Johnson, Chalmers. *Blowback: The Costs and Consequences of American Empire*. New York: Metropolitan Books, 2000.

Johnson, David R.. *Policing the Urban Underworld: The Impact of Crime on the Development of the American Police, 1800–1887*. Philadelphia: Temple University Press, 1979.

———. *American Law Enforcement: A History*. St. Louis, MO: Forum Press, 1981.

———. *Illegal Tender: Counterfeiting and the Secret Service in the Nineteenth Century*. Washington, DC: Smithsonian Institution Press, 1991.

Johnson, David T. "Where the State Kills in Secret: Capital Punishment in Japan." Paper presented at the Law & Society Association, Las Vegas, NV, June 2–5, 2005.

Johnson, John M. "Program Enterprise and Official Cooptation in the Battered Women's Shelter Movement." *American Behavioral Scientist* 24.6 (1981): 827–42.

Johnson, Robert. "Life Under Sentence of Death: Historical and Contemporary Perspectives." In *America's Experiment with Capital Punishment: Reflections on the Past, Present, and Future of the Ultimate Penal Sanction*. 2nd ed. James R. Acker, Robert M. Bohm, and Charles S. Lanier, eds. Durham, NC: Carolina Academic Press, 2003.

Johnson, Robert, and Dennis D. Dorin. "Dysfunctional Ideology: The Black Revolutionary in Prison." In *Offenders and Corrections*. Denis Szabo and Susan Katzenelson, eds. New York: Praeger, 1978.

Jordon, Philip D. *Frontier Law and Order: Ten Essays*. Lincoln: University of Nebraska Press, 1971.

Joutsen, Matti. "Listening to the Victim: The Victim's Role in European Criminal Justice Systems." *Wayne Law Review* 34 (1987–88).

Jung, Heike. "Criminal Justice: A European Perspective." *Criminal Law Review* (April 1993): 237–45.

Junger-Tas, Josine. "Dutch Penal Policies Changing Direction." In *Penal Reform in Overcrowded Times*. Michael Tonry, ed. Oxford: Oxford University Press, 2001.

Kanwar, Vik. "Capital Punishment as 'Closure': The Limits of a Victim-Centered Jurisprudence." *New York University Review of Law and Social Change* 27 (2001/2002): 215–56.

Kappeler, Victor E., Mark Blumberg, and Gary W. Potter. *The Mythology of Crime and Criminal Justice.* 3rd ed. Prospect Heights, IL: Waveland Press, 2000.

Katzenstein, Mary Fainsod. "Comparing the Feminist Movements of the United States and Western Europe." In *The Women's Movements of the United States and Western Europe.* Mary Fainsod Katzenstein and Carolyn M. Mueller, eds. Philadelphia: Temple University Press 1987.

———. "Feminism Within American Institutions: Unobtrusive Mobilization in the 1980s." Signs 16.1 (1990): 27–54.

———. *Faithful and Fearless: Moving Feminist Protest Inside the Church and Military.* Princeton: Princeton University Press, 1998.

———. "Rights Without Citizenship: Prison Activism in the U.S." In *Routing the Opposition: Social Movements, Public Policy, and Democracy.* David S. Meyer, Valerie Jenness, and Helen Ingram, eds. Minneapolis: University of Minnesota Press, 2005.

Katzenstein, Mary Fainsod, and Rubin, Katherine Davison. "How Different? A Comparison of the Movement Challenging Ex-Felon Disenfranchisement with Suffrage Politics of an Earlier Time." Paper presented at the American Political Science Association, Boston, August 29-September 1, 2002.

Katznelson, Ira, and Helen V. Milner, eds. *Political Science: The State of the Discipline.* New York: Norton, 2002.

Katznelson, Ira, Kim Geiger, and Daniel Kryder. "Limiting Liberalism: The Southern Veto in Congress, 1933–1950." *Political Science Quarterly* 108.2 (Summer 1993): 283–306.

Keire, Mara L. "The Vice Trust: A Reinterpretation of the White Slavery Scare in the United States, 1907–1917." *Journal of Social History* 35.1 (2001): 5–41.

Kelly, Deborah P., and Edna Erez. "Victim Participation in the Criminal Justice System." In *Victims of Crime.* Robert C. Davis, Arthur J. Lurigio, and Wesley G. Skogan, eds. Thousand Oaks, CA: Sage, 1997.

Kelly, Liz, and Jill Radford. "The Problem of Men: Feminist Perspectives on Sexual Violence." In *Law, Order and the Authoritarian State: Readings in Critical Criminology.* Phil Scraton, ed. Milton Keynes, UK: Open University Press, 1987.

Kennedy, Randall. *Race, Crime, and the Law.* New York: Pantheon Books, 1997.

Keve, Paul W. *Prisons and the American Conscience: A History of U.S. Federal Corrections.* Carbondale and Edwardsville: Southern Illinois University Press, 1991.

King, Desmond S. *Separate and Unequal: Black Americans and the U.S. Federal Government.* Oxford: Clarendon Press, 1995.

———. "A Strong or Weak State? Race and the US Federal Government in the 1920s." *Ethnic and Racial Studies* 21.1 (January 1998): 21–47.

King, Desmond S., and Rogers M. Smith. "Racial Orders in American Political Development." *American Political Science Review* 99:1 (February 2005): 75–92.

King, Rachel. *Don't Kill in Our Names: Families of Murder Victims Speak Out Against the Death Penalty.* New Brunswick, NJ: Rutgers University Press, 2003.

King, Roy D. "Control in Prisons." In *Accountability and Prisons: Opening Up a Closed World.* Mike Maguire, Jon Vagg, and Rod Morgan, eds. London: Tavistock Publications, 1985.

King, Ryan S., and Marc Mauer. *State Sentencing and Corrections Policy in an Era of Fiscal Restraint.* Washington, DC: The Sentencing Project, February 2002.

Kirchmeier, Jeffrey L. "Death Penalty Symposium: A Call to Action: A Moratorium on Executions Presented by the American Bar Association." *New York City Law Review* 4 (Spring 2002).

Klarman, Michael J. *From Jim Crow to Civil Rights: The Supreme Court and the Struggle for Racial Equality.* New York: Oxford University Press, 2004.

Klein, Dorie. "Crime Through Gender's Prism: Feminist Criminology in the United States." In *International Feminist Perspectives in Criminology: Engendering a Discipline.* Nicole Hahn Rafter and Frances Heidensohn, eds. Buckingham, UK: Open University Press, 1995.

Knight, Etheridge, et al. *Black Voices From Prison.* New York: Pathfinder Press, 1970.

Koch, Larry W., and John F. Galliher. "Michigan's Continuing Abolition of the Death Penalty and the Conceptual Components of Symbolic Legislation." *Social and Legal Studies* 2.3 (September 1993): 323–46.

Koetting, Mark G., and Vincent Schiraldi. "Singapore West: The Incarceration of 200,000 Californians." *Social Justice* 24.1 (Spring 1997): 40–53.

Kramer, Ronald, and Raymond Michalowski. "The Iron Fist and the Velvet Tongue: Crime Control Policies in the Clinton Administration." *Crime and Justice* 22.2 (1995): 87–100.

Kraska, Peter B., ed. *Militarizing the American Criminal Justice System: The Changing Roles of the Armed Forces and the Police.* Boston: Northeastern University Press, 2001.

Kress, Jack. "Progress and Prosecution." *The Annals of the American Academy of Political and Social Science* 423 (1976): 99–116.

Kryder, Daniel. *Divided Arsenal: Race and the American State During World War II.* Cambridge: Cambridge University Press, 2000.

Kuhn André. "Prison Populations in Western Europe." In *Sentencing Reform in Overcrowded Times: A Comparative Perspective.* Michael Tonry and Kathleen Hatlestad, eds. New York: Oxford University Press, 1997: 124–33.

———. "Incarceration Rates Around the World." In *Penal Reform in Overcrowded Times.* Michael Tonry, ed. Oxford: Oxford University Press, 2001.

Kurki, Leena. "International Standards for Sentencing and Punishment." In *Sentencing and Sanctions in Western Countries.* Michael Tonry and Richard S. Frase, eds. Oxford: Oxford University Press, 2001: 331–78.

Kurz, Demie. "Battering and the Criminal Justice System: A Feminist View." In *Domestic Violence: The Changing Criminal Justice Response.* Eve S. Buzawa and Carl G. Buzawa, eds. Westport, CT: Auburn House, 1992: 21–38.

LaFree, Gary, et al. "Introduction to Volume 1: The Changing Nature of Crime in America." In *The Nature of Crime: Continuity and Change.* Vol. 1. Washington, DC: National Institute of Justice, 2000.

Landesman, Peter. "The Girls Next Door." *The New York Times Magazine,* January 25, 2004.

Lane, J. Mark. "'Is There Life Without Parole?' A Capital Defendant's Right to a Meaningful Alternative Sentence." *Loyola (Los Angeles) Law Review* 26 (1992–93): 327–93.

Lane, Roger. "Urban Police and Crime in Nineteenth-Century America." In *Crime and Justice: A Review of Research.* Vol. 15. Michael Tonry and Norval Morris, eds. Chicago: University of Chicago Press, 1992: 1–50.

———. "Murder in America: A Historian's Perspective." In *Crime and Justice: An Annual Review of Research.* Vol. 25. Michael Tonry and Norval Morris, eds. Chicago: University of Chicago Press, 1999.

Langum, David J. *Crossing Over the Line: Legislating Morality and the Mann Act.* Chicago: University of Chicago Press, 1994.

Laraña, Enrique, Hank Johnston, and Joseph R. Gusfield, eds. *New Social Movements: From Ideology to Identity.* Philadelphia: Temple University Press, 1994.

Largen, Mary Ann. "History of Women's Movement in Changing Attitudes, Laws, and Treatment Toward Rape Victims." In *Sexual Assault: The Victim and the Rapist.* Marcia J. Walker and Stanley L. Brodsky, eds. Lexington, MA: Heath Books, 1976: 69–73.

Law Enforcement Assistance Administration. *LEAA Task Force on Women.* Washington, DC: LEAA, 1975.

Lawes, Lewis E. "Why I Changed My Mind." In *Voices Against Death: American Opposition to Capital Punishment, 1787–1975.* Philip E. Mackey, ed. New York: Burt Franklin & Co., 1976: 192–204.

Lea, John, and Jock Young. *What Is To Be Done About Law and Order?* London: Pluto Press, 1993.

Leander, Karen. "The Normalization of Swedish Prisons." In *Western European Penal Systems: A Critical Anatomy.* Vincenzo Ruggiero, Mick Ryan, and Joe Sim, eds. London: Sage, 1995: 169–93.

Lees, Susan. "Judicial Rape." *Women's Studies International Forum* 16.1 (1993).

Legal Action Center. *After Prison: Roadblocks to Reentry: A Report on State Legal Barriers Facing People With Criminal Records.* New York: Legal Action Center, 2004.

Leigh, David. *The Frontiers of Secrecy: Closed Government in Britain.* London: Junction Books, 1980.

Lerman, Lisa G. "Protection of Battered Women: A Survey of State Legislation." *Women's Rights Law Reporter* 6.4 (1980): 271–84.

———. "Mediation of Wife Abuse Cases: The Adverse Impact of Informal Dispute Resolution on Women." *Harvard Women's Law Journal* 7.1 (Spring 1984).

Leuchtenburg, William E. *Franklin D. Roosevelt and the New Deal, 1932–1940.* New York: Harper & Row, 1963.

Levi, Edward H. *An Introduction to Legal Reasoning.* Chicago: University of Chicago Press, 1948.

Lewis, Derek. *Hidden Agendas: Politics, Law and Disorder.* London: Hamish Hamilton, 1997.

Lewis, Orlando F. *The Development of American Prisons and Prison Customs.* Montclair, NJ: Patterson Smith, 1967 [1922].

Lewis, Ronald L. *Black Coal Miners in America: Race, Class, and Community Conflict, 1780–1980.* Lexington: University Press of Kentucky, 1987.

Lewis, W. David. *From Newgate to Dannemora: The Rise of the Penitentiary in New York, 1796–1848.* Ithaca, NY: Cornell University Press, 1965.

Lichtenstein, Alex. *Twice the Work of Free Labor: The Political Economy of Convict Labor in the New South.* London: Verso, 1996.

———. "Chain Gang Blues." *Dissent* 43.3 (Fall 1996): 6–10.

Liebling, Alison. "Prison Suicide and Prisoner Coping." In *Crime and Justice – A Review of Research.* Vol. 26. *Prisons.* Michael Tonry and Joan Petersilia, eds. Chicago and London: University of Chicago Press, 1999: 283–359.

Lifton, Robert Jay, and Greg Mitchell. *Who Owns Death? Capital Punishment, the American Conscience, and the End of Executions.* New York: Harper-Collins, 2000.

Lin, Ann Chih. "The Troubled Success of Crime Policy." In *The Social Divide: Political Parties and the Future of Activist Government.* Margaret Weir, ed. Washington, DC, and New York: The Brookings Institution and Russell Sage Foundation, 1998: 312–57.

_____. *Reform in the Making: The Implementation of Social Policy in Prison.* Princeton: Princeton University Press, 2000.

Linders, Annulla. "The Execution Spectacle and State Legitimacy: The Changing Nature of the American Execution Audience, 1833–1937." *Law & Society Review* 36.3 (2002): 607–55.

Loh, Wallace D. "Q: What Has Reform of Rape Legislation Wrought? A: Truth in Criminal Labelling." *Journal of Social Issues* 37.4 (Fall 1981): 28–51.

Lohman, Jacquelien Soetenhorst-de Savornin. "The Victim Issue in the Political Agenda of The Netherlands." *Victimology: An International Journal* 10.1–4 (1985): 687–98.

Lombardi, Chris "Justice for Battered Women." *The Nation*, July 15, 2002.

Love, Margaret Colgate, and Susan M. Kuzman. *Civil Disabilities of Convicted Felons: A State-By-State Survey.* Washington, DC: U.S. Department of Justice, Office of the Pardon Attorney, October 1996.

Lubove, Roy. "The Progressives and the Prostitute." *The Historian* 24 (May 1962): 309–30.

Lupton, Carol. "The British Refuge Movement: The Survival of an Ideal?" In *Working With Violence.* Carol Lupton and Ted Gillespie, eds. Houndsmills, UK: Macmillan, 1994.

Lutton, Linda. "The End of Executions: The Anti-Death Penalty Movement is Gathering Force." *In These Times*, October 30, 2000: 26.

Lynd, Staughton, and Alice Lynd. "Prison Advocacy in a Time of Capital Disaccumulation." *Monthly Review* 53.3 (July/August 2001): 128–41.

Lynch, James. "Crime in International Perspective." In *Crime.* James Q. Wilson and Joan Petersilia, eds. San Francisco: ICS Press, 1995.

Lyons, Williams, and Stuart A. Scheingold. "The Politics of Crime and Punishment." In *The Nature of Crime: Continuity and Change.* Vol. 1. Washington, DC: National Institute of Justice, 2000.

MacCormick, Austin H. "Behind the Prison Riots." *The Annals of the American Academy of Political and Social Science* 293 (May 1954): 17–27.

MacCoun, Robert J., and Peter Reuter. "Drug Control." In *The Handbook of Crime and Punishment.* Michael J. Tonry, ed. Oxford: Oxford University Press, 1998: 207–38.

_____. *Drug War Heresies: Learning From Other Vices, Times, and Places.* Cambridge: Cambridge University Press, 2001.

_____, eds. "Cross-National Drug Policy." *The Annals of the American Academy of Political and Social Science* 582 (July 2002).

Mackey, Philip English. "Introduction: An Historical Perspective." In *Voices Against Death: American Opposition to Capital Punishment, 1787–1975.* Philip English Mackey, ed. New York: Burt Franklin & Co., 1976.

MacKinnon, Catharine A. "Feminism, Marxism, Method and the State: Toward Feminist Jurisprudence." In *Feminist Legal Theory: Readings in Law and Gender.* Katharine T. Bartlett and Rosanne Kennedy, eds. Boulder, CO: Westview Press, 1991: 181–200.

Madison, James, Alexander Hamilton, and John Jay. *The Federalist Papers.* Isaac Krammick, ed. London: Penguin Books, 1987.

Madriz, Esther I. "Images of Criminals and Victims: A Study on Women's Fear and Social Control." *Gender & Society* 11.3 (June 1997): 342–56.

Maguire, Mike, and Claire Corbett. *The Effects of Crime and the Work of Victims Support Schemes.* Aldershot: Gower, 1987.

Maguire, Mike, and John Pointing. "Introduction: The Rediscovery of the Crime Victim." In *Victims of Crime: A New Deal?.* Mike Maguire and Jon Pointing, eds. Milton Keynes, UK: Open University Press, 1988.

Maguire, Mike, and Joanna Shapland. "Provision for Victims in an International Context." In *Victims of Crime.* 2nd ed. Robert C. Davis, Arthur J. Lurigio, and Wesley G. Skogan, eds. Thousand Oaks, CA: Sage, 1997.

Maguire, Mike, Rod Morgan, and Robert Reiner, eds. *The Oxford Handbook of Criminology.* 1st ed. Oxford: Clarendon Press, 1994.

———, eds. *The Oxford Handbook of Criminology.* 2nd ed. Oxford: Clarendon Press, 1997.

Maguire, Mike, Jon Vagg, and Rod Morgan, eds. *Accountability and Prisons: Opening Up a Closed World.* London: Tavistock Publications, 1985.

Malos, Ellen, and Gill Hague. "Women, Housing, Homelessness and Domestic Violence." *Women's Studies International Forum* 20.3 (1997): 397–410.

Mancini, Matthew J. "Race, Economics, and the Abandonment of Convict Leasing." *Journal of Negro History* 63.4 (October 1978): 339–52.

———. *One Dies, Get Another: Convict Leasing in the American South, 1866–1928.* Columbia: University of South Carolina Press, 1996.

Mantel, Hilary. "The Right to Life." *The New York Review of Books,* May 12, 2005: 4–8.

Marion, Nancy E. *A History of Federal Crime Control Initiatives, 1960–1993.* Westport, CT: Praeger, 1994.

Marquart, James W., Sheldon Ekland-Olson, and Jonathan R. Sorensen. *The Rope, the Chair, and the Needle: Capital Punishment in Texas, 1923–1990.* Austin: University of Texas Press, 1994.

Marsh, Jeanne C., Alison Geist, and Nathan Caplan. *Rape and the Limits of Law Reform.* Boston: Auburn House, 1982.

Marshall, Micah. "Death in Venice: Europe's Death-Penalty Elitism." *The New Republic,* July 31, 2000: 14.

Martin, Steve J., and Sheldon Ekland-Olson. *Texas Prisons: The Walls Come Tumbling Down.* Austin: Texas Monthly Press, 1987.

Martinson, Robert. "What Works? Questions and Answers About Prison Reform." *The Public Interest* 35 (1974): 22–54.

———. "New Findings, New Views: A Note of Caution Regarding Sentencing Reform." *Hofstra Law Review* 7.2 (Winter 1979): 243–58.

Massing, Michael. *The Fix.* New York: Simon & Schuster, 1998.

Mastromatteo, Ernest. "New Zealand's Universal Disability System." *Occupational Health & Safety Canada,* September/October 1993: 124–27.

Masur, Louis P. *Rites of Execution: Capital Punishment and the Transformation of American Culture, 1776–1865.* New York: Oxford University Press, 1989.

Mathiesen, Thomas. *The Politics of Abolition.* New York: John Wiley & Sons, 1974.

———. *Prison on Trial: A Critical Assessment.* London: Sage Publications, 1990.

———. "About KROM–Past-Present-Future" Oslo: Institute for Sociology of Law, 1995.

Mathiesen, Thomas, and Wiggo Røine. "The Prison Movement in Scandinavia." In *Deviance and Control in Europe: Papers from the European Group for the Study of Deviance and Social Control.* Herman Bianchi, Mario Simondi, and Ian Taylor, eds. London: John Wiley, 1975: 85–95.

Matthews, Nancy A. "Surmounting a Legacy: The Expansion of Racial Diversity in a Local Anti-Rape Movement." *Gender & Society* 3.4 (December 1989): 518–32.

———. *Confronting Rape: The Feminist Anti-Rape Movement and the State*. New York and London: Routledge, 1994.

Matthews, Roger, and Jock Young, eds. *Confronting Crime*. London: Sage, 1986.

Mauer, Marc. "The Fragility of Criminal Justice Reform." *Social Justice* 21.3 (Fall 1994): 14–29.

———. "Why Are Tough on Crime Policies So Popular?" *Stanford Law and Policy Review* 11 (1999).

———. *Race to Incarcerate*. New York: The New Press, 1999.

Mauer, Marc, Ryan S. King, and Malcolm C. Young. "The Meaning of 'Life': Long Prison Sentences in Context." Washington, DC: The Sentencing Project, May 2004.

Maverick, Maury, and William H. Burke. *Prisons in Wartime: Report on the Progress of State Prison Industries Under the Government Division of the War Production Board*. Washington, DC: War Production Board, November 1943.

Mawby, R. I. "Victims' Needs or Victims' Rights: Alternative Approaches to Policy-Making." In *Victims of Crime: A New Deal?* Mike Maguire and John Pointing, eds. Buckingham, UK: Open University Press, 1988.

Mawby, R. I., and M. L. Gill. *Crime Victims: Needs, Services and the Voluntary Sector*. London: Tavistock, 1987.

May, Margaret. "Violence in the Family: An Historical Perspective." In *Violence and the Family*. J. P. Martin, ed. Chichester, UK: John Wiley & Sons, 1978.

Mayer, Jane. "Outsourcing Terror: The Battle Over 'Extraordinary Rendition'." *The New Yorker*, February 14/21, 2005.

McCarthy, John D. "Activists, Authorities, and Media Framing of Drunk Driving." In *New Social Movements: From Ideology to Identity*. Enrique Laraña, Hank Johnston, and Joseph R. Gusfield, eds. Philadelphia: Temple University Press, 1994.

McCleary, Richard. "Correctional Administration and Political Change." In *Prison Within Society*. Lawrence Hazelrigg, ed. Garden City, NY: Doubleday, 1968.

McConville, Séan. "The Victorian Prison: England, 1865–1965." In *The Oxford History of the Prison: The Practice of Punishment in Western Society*. Norval Morris and David J. Rothman, eds. New York: Oxford University Press, 1995.

McDermott, Thomas E., III. "California Rape Evidence Reform: An Analysis of Senate Bill 1678." *Hastings Law Journal* 26 (1975): 1551–73.

McDonald, Douglas C. "Medical Care in Prisons." In *Crime and Justice – A Review of Research*. Vol. 26. *Prisons*. Michael Tonry and Joan Petersilia, eds. Chicago and London: University of Chicago Press, 1999: 427–78.

McGowen, Randall. "Civilizing Punishment: The End of the Public Execution in England." *Journal of British Studies* 33 (July 1994): 257–82.

———. "History, Culture and the Death Penalty: The British Debates, 1840–70." *Historical Reflections/Reflexions Historiques* 29.2 (Summer 2003): 229–49.

McKelvey, Blake. *American Prisons: A History of Good Intentions*. Montclair, NJ: Patterson Smith, 1977.

McKelvey, Tara. "Of Human Bondage." *The American Prospect*, November 2, 2004: 17–20.

McWilliams, John C. "Through the Past Darkly: The Politics and Policies of America's Drug War." *Journal of Policy History* 3.4 (1991): 356–414.

Megivern, James J. *The Death Penalty: An Historical and Theological Survey*. New York: Paulist Press, 1997.

Mello, Michael A. *Dead Wrong: A Death Row Lawyer Speaks Out Against Capital Punishment*. Madison: University of Wisconsin Press, 1997.

Melone, Albert P. *Lawyers, Public Policy and Interest Group Politics*. Washington, DC: University Press of America, 1977.

Melone, Albert P., and Robert Slagter. "Interest Group Politics and the Reform of the Federal Criminal Code." In *The Political Science of Criminal Justice*. Stuart Nagel, Erika Fairchild, and Anthony Champagne, eds. Springfield, IL: Charles C. Thomas, 1983: 41–55.

Meltsner, Michael. *Cruel and Unusual: The Supreme Court and Capital Punishment*. New York: Random House, 1973.

Melzer, Eartha. "Trafficking in Politics." *In These Times*, March 28, 2005: 20–21.

Mendelberg, Tali. "Executing Hortons: Racial Crime in the 1988 Presidential Campaign." *Public Opinion Quarterly* 61.1 (Spring 1997): 134–57.

_____. *The Race Card: Campaign Strategy, Implicit Messages, and the Norm of Equality*. Princeton: Princeton University Press, 2001.

Meranze, Michael. *Laboratories of Virtue: Punishment, Revolution, and Authority in Philadelphia, 1760–1835*. Chapel Hill: University of North Carolina Press, 1996.

Messinger, Sheldon, and Philip E. Johnson. "California's Determinate Sentencing Statute: History and Issues." In *The Criminal Justice System: Materials on the Administration and Reform of the Criminal Law*. Franklin E. Zimring and Richard S. Frase, eds. Boston: Little, Brown and Co., 1980: 950–97.

Messner, Claudius, and Vincenzo Ruggiero. "Germany: The Penal System Between Past and Future." In *Western European Penal Systems: A Critical Anatomy*. Vincenzo Ruggiero, Mick Ryan, and Joe Sim, eds. London: Sage, 1995: 128–48.

Miller, Jerome G. *Last One Over the Wall: The Massachusetts Experiment in Closing Reform Schools*. Columbus: Ohio State University Press, 1991.

_____. *Search and Destroy: African-American Males in the Criminal Justice System*. New York: Cambridge University Press, 1996.

Miller, Marc L. "Cells vs. Cops vs. Classrooms." *The Crime Conundrum: Essays on Criminal Justice*. Lawrence Friedman and George Fisher, eds. Boulder, CO: Westview Press, 1997: 127–61.

Mills, Linda G. "Intuition and Insight: A New Job Description for the Battered Woman's Prosecutor and Other More Modest Proposals." *UCLA Women's Law Journal* 7.2 (1997): 183–99.

_____. "Killing Her Softly: Intimate Abuse and the Violence of State Intervention." *Harvard Law Journal* 113 (December 1999): 550–613.

Millspaugh, Arthur C. *Crime Control by the National Government*. Washington, DC: The Brookings Institution, 1937.

Minkoff, Debra C. *Organizing for Equality: The Evolution of Women's and Racial-Ethnic Organizations in America, 1955–1985*. New Brunswick, NJ: Rutgers University Press, 1995.

Minow, Martha. "Between Vengeance and Forgiveness: Feminist Responses to Violent Injustice." *New England Law Review* 32.4 (Summer 1998): 967–81.

Mitford, Jessica. *Kind and Usual Punishment: The Prison Business*. New York: Alfred A. Knopf, 1973.

Mohrenschlager, M. "The Abolition of Capital Punishment in the Federal Republic of Germany: German Experiences." *Revue Internationale de Droit Pénal* 58 (1987): 509–19.

Moore, Barrington, Jr. *Social Origins of Dictatorship and Democracy: Lord and Peasant in the Making of the Modern World*. Boston: Beacon Press, 1966.

Moore, Richter H., Jr., Thomas C. Marks, Jr., and Robert V. Barrow. *Readings in Criminal Justice*. Indianapolis: The Bobbs-Merrill Company, Inc., 1976.

Moore, William Howard. *The Kefauver Committee and the Politics of Crime, 1950–1952*. Columbia: University of Missouri Press, 1974.

Morgan, Rod. "Punitive Policies and Politics Crowding English Prisons." In *Sentencing Reform in Overcrowded Times: A Comparative Perspective*. Michael Tonry and Kathleen Hatlestad, eds. New York: Oxford University Press, 1997.

———. "International Controls on Sentencing and Punishment." In *Sentencing and Sanctions in Western Countries*. Michael Tonry and Richard S. Frase, eds. Oxford: Oxford University Press, 2001: 379–404.

Morn, Frank. *"The Eye that Never Sleeps": A History of the Pinkerton National Detective Agency*. Bloomington: Indiana University Press, 1982.

Morone, James. *Hellfire Nation: The Politics of Sin in American History*. New Haven: Yale University Press, 2003.

Morris, Norval. *The Future of Imprisonment*. Chicago: University of Chicago Press, 1974.

———. "Closing Address." *New York University Review of Law and Social Change* 12.1 (1983–84): 349–56.

Morris, Norval, and David J. Rothman. "Introduction." In *The Oxford History of the Prison: The Practice of Punishment in Western Society*. Norval Morris and David J. Rothman, eds. New York: Oxford University Press, 1995.

Moulden, John V., and Anne Russell. "'Is It MADD Trying to Rate the States?' – A Citizen Activist Approach to DWI Prevention." *Alcohol, Drugs and Driving* 10.3–4 (1994).

Muller, Eric L. "The Legal Defense Fund's Capital Punishment Campaign: The Distorting Influence of Death." *Yale Law and Policy Review* 4 (1985): 158–87.

Mumola, Christopher J. *Incarcerated Parents and Their Children*. Washington, DC: U.S. Department of Justice, Bureau of Justice Statistics, August 2000.

Muncie, John, and Richard Sparks, eds. *Imprisonment: European Perspectives*. New York: St. Martin's Press, 1991.

Myers, Martha A. *Race, Labor and Punishment in the New South*. Columbus: Ohio State University Press, 1998.

Nagel, Jack. "The Relationship Between Crime and Incarceration Among the American States." *Policy Studies Review* 2 (1982): 193–202.

Nagel, Stuart, Erika Fairchild, and Anthony Champagne. *The Political Science of Criminal Justice*. Springfield, IL: Charles C. Thomas, 1983.

Nagel, William G. *The New Red Barn: A Critical Look at the Modern American Prison*. New York: Walker, 1973.

Nash, Mike, and Stephen P. Savage. "A Criminal Record? Law, Order, and Conservative Policy." In *Public Policy in Britain*. Stephen P. Savage, Rob Atkinson, and Lynton Robins, eds. Basingstoke: Macmillan, 1994: 137–55.

National Advisory Commission on Criminal Justice Standards and Goals. *Task Force on Corrections*. Washington, DC: GPO, 1973.

National Association for the Advancement of Colored People. *Thirty Years of Lynching in the United States, 1889–1918*. New York: NAACP, April 1919.

National Organization for Victim Assistance. *Directory of Victim Assistance Programs and Resources*. Dubuque, IA: Kendall/Hunt Publishing Company, 1994.

Neale, Kenneth. "The European Prison Rules: Contextual, Philosophical and Practical Aspects." In *Imprisonment: European Perspectives*. John Muncie and Richard Sparks, eds. New York: St. Martin's Press, 1991: 203–17.

Neier, Aryeh. *Only Judgment: The Limits of Litigation in Social Change.* Middletown, CT: Wesleyan University Press, 1982.

Newburn, Tim. *Crime and Criminal Justice Policy.* London and New York: Longman, 1995.

Nisbett, Richard E., and Dov Cohen. *Culture of Honor: The Psychology of Violence in the South.* Boulder, CO: Westview, 1996.

Norris, Fran H., Krzysztof Kaniasty, and Martie P. Thompson. "The Psychological Consequences of Crime: Findings From a Longitudinal Population-Based Study." In *Victims of Crime.* 2nd ed. Robert C. Davis, Arthur J. Lurigio, and Wesley G. Skogan, eds. Thousand Oaks, CA: Sage, 1997.

Norton, Philip, ed. *Law and Order in British Politics.* Aldershot, UK: Gower, 1984.

O'Hear, Michael M. "When Voters Choose the Sentence: The Drug Policy Initiatives in Arizona, California, Ohio, and Michigan." *Federal Sentencing Reporter* 14.6 (May/June 2002): 337–43.

Ohlin, Lloyd E., ed. *Prisoners in America.* Englewood Cliffs, NJ: Prentice-Hall Inc., 1973.

Olivares, Kathleen M., Velmer S. Burton, Jr., and Francis T. Cullen. "The Collateral Consequences of a Felony Conviction: A National Study of State Legal Codes 10 Years Later." *Federal Probation* 60.3 (September 1996): 10–17.

Oliver, Willard M. *The Law and Order Presidency.* Upper Saddle River, NJ: Prentice Hall, 2003.

O'Neill, William L. *Everyone Was Brave: The Rise and Fall of Feminism in America.* Chicago: Quadrangle, 1969.

O'Reilly, Kenneth. "A New Deal for the FBI: The Roosevelt Administration, Crime Control, and National Security." *The Journal of American History* 69.3 (December 1982).

Orren, Karen, and Stephen Skowronek. *The Search for American Political Development.* Cambridge: Cambridge University Press, 2004.

Oshinsky, David M. *"Worse Than Slavery": Parchman Farm and the Ordeal of Jim Crow Justice.* New York: The Free Press, 1996.

Pahl, Jan. "Refuges for Battered Women: Social Provision or Social Movement." *Journal of Voluntary Action Research* 8.1–2 (1979): 25–35.

————, ed. *Private Violence and Public Policy: The Needs of Battered Women and the Response of the Public Sector.* London: Routledge & Kegan Paul, 1985.

Pallas, John, and Robert Barber. "From Riot to Revolution." *Issues in Criminology* 7.2 (Fall 1972): 1–19.

Parenti, Christian. *Lockdown America: Police and Prisons in the Age of Crisis.* London and New York: Verso, 1999.

Pastore, Ann L., and Kathleen Maguire, eds. *Bureau of Justice Statistics Sourcebook of Criminal Justice Statistics–2001.* Washington, DC: GPO, 2002.

Paternoster, Raymond. *Capital Punishment in America.* New York: Lexington Books, 1991.

Pattillo, Mary, David Weiman, and Bruce Western, eds. *Imprisoning America: The Social Effects of Mass Incarceration.* New York: Russell Sage Foundation, 2004.

Pease, Ken. "Cross-National Imprisonment Rates." *British Journal of Criminology* 34 (1994): 116–30.

Pederson, William D. "Inmate Movements and Prison Uprisings: A Comparative Study." *Social Science Quarterly* 59.3 (December 1978): 509–24.

Pence, Ellen, and Melanie Shepard. "Integrating Feminist Theory and Practice: The Challenge of the Battered Women's Movement." In *Feminist Perspectives on Wife Abuse.* Kersti Yllö and Michele Bograd, eds. Newbury Park, CA: Sage, 1988.

Perkinson, Robert. "Shackled Justice: Florence Federal Penitentiary and the New Politics of Punishment." *Social Justice* 21.3 (Fall 1994): 117–32.

——. "Between the Worst of the Past and the Worst of the Future." *Radical History Review* 71 (1998): 207–16.

Perl, Rebecca. "The Last Disenfranchised Class." *The Nation*, November 24, 2003: 11–14.

Pestritto, Ronald J. *Founding the Criminal Law: Punishment and Political Thought in the Origins of America.* DeKalb: Northern Illinois University Press, 2000.

Petersilia, Joan. "Policy Relevance and the Future of Criminology." *Criminology* 29.1 (1991): 1–13.

——. *When Prisoners Come Home: Parole and Prisoner Reentry.* New York: Oxford University Press, 2003.

Peterson, Ruth D. "Discriminatory Decision Making at the Legislative Level: An Analysis of the Comprehensive Drug Abuse Prevention and Control Act of 1970." *Law and Human Behavior* 9.3 (1985): 243–69.

Peterson, Virgil W. *Crime Commissions in the United States.* Chicago: Chicago Crime Commission, 1945.

Pfeiffer, Christian. "Crisis in American Criminal Policy? A Letter to Mrs. J. Reno, Attorney General of the United States of America." *European Journal on Criminal Policy and Research* 4.2 (1996).

Philips, David. "A Just Measure of Crime, Authority, Hunters, and Blue Locusts: The 'Revisionist' Social History of Crime and the Law in Britain, 1780–1950." In *Social Control and the State.* Stanley Cohen and Andrew Scull, eds. New York: St. Martin's Press, 1983.

Phillips, Charles David. "Exploring Relations Among Forms of Social Control: The Lynching and Execution of Blacks in North Carolina, 1889–1918." *Law & Society Review* 21.3 (1987): 361–74.

Phipps, Alan. "Radical Criminology and Criminal Victimization: Proposals for the Development of Theory and Intervention." In *Confronting Crime.* Roger Matthews and Jock Young, eds. London: Sage, 1986.

——. "Ideologies, Political Parties, and Victims of Crime." In *Victims of Crime: A New Deal?* Mike Maguire and John Pointing, eds. Buckingham, UK: Open University Press, 1988.

Pierce, Glenn L., and Michael L. Radelet. "The Role and Consequences of the Death Penalty in American Politics." *New York University Review of Law and Social Change* 18 (1990–91): 711–28.

Pierson, Paul D. *Dismantling the Welfare State? Reagan, Thatcher, and the Politics of Retrenchment.* New York: Cambridge University Press, 1994.

Pillsbury, Samuel H. "Why Are We Ignored? The Peculiar Place of Experts in the Current Debate about Crime and Justice." *Criminal Law Bulletin* 31 (July/August 1995): 305–36.

Pisciotta, Alexander W. *Benevolent Repression: Social Control and the American Reformatory Prison Movement.* New York: NYU Press, 1994.

Pitch, Tamar. "Critical Criminology, the Construction of Social Problems, and the Question of Rape." *The International Journal of the Sociology of Law* 13 (1985): 35–46.

Platt, Anthony M. *The Child Savers.* 2nd ed. Chicago: University of Chicago Press, 1977.

——. "The Politics of Law and Order." *Social Justice* 21.3 (1994): 3–13.

Platt, Tony, and Paul Takagi. "Intellectuals for Law and Order: A Critique of the New Realists." *Crime and Social Justice* 8 (Fall/Winter 1977): 1–16.

_____, eds. *Punishment and Penal Discipline: Essays on the Prison and the Prisoners' Movement*. San Francisco: Crime and Social Justice Associates, 1980.

Player, Elaine, and Michael Jenkins. "Introduction." In *Prisons After Woolf: Reform Through Riot*. Elaine Player and Michael Jenkins, eds. London: Routledge, 1994.

Pleck, Elizabeth. "Feminist Responses to 'Crimes Against Women,' 1868–1896." *Signs* 8.3 (1983): 451–70.

_____. *Domestic Tyranny: The Making of Social Policy Against Family Violence from Colonial Times to the Present*. New York: Oxford University Press, 1987.

_____. "Criminal Approaches to Family Violence, 1640–1980." In *Crime and Justice: A Review of Research*, vol. 11. Lloyd Ohlin and Michael Tonry, eds. Chicago: University of Chicago, 1989: 19–57.

Pollitt, Katha. "Subject to Debate: Dead Again?" *The Nation*, July 13, 1998: 10.

Pollock-Byrne, Jocelyn M. *Women, Prison, and Crime*. Pacific Grove, CA: Brooks/Cole Publishing Company, 1990.

Polsky, Andrew J. *The Rise of the Therapeutic State*. Princeton: Princeton University Press, 1991.

_____. "The New 'Dismal Science'? The Lessons of American Political Development for Today." *Polity* 32.3 (Spring 2000): 303–08.

Poveda, Tony G. "Clinton, Crime, and the Justice Department." *Social Justice* 21.3 (1994): 73–84.

Pratt, John. "Law and Order Politics in New Zealand 1986: A Comparison With the United Kingdom." *International Journal of the Sociology of Law* 16 (1988): 103–26.

Prejean, Sister Helen. *The Death of Innocents: An Eyewitness Account of Wrongful Executions*. New York: Random House, 2004.

Presser, Lois, and Emily Gaarder. "Can Restorative Justice Reduce Battering? Some Preliminary Considerations." *Social Justice* 27.1 (Spring 2000): 175–95.

Preuhs, Robert R. "State Felon Disenfranchisement Policy." *Social Science Quarterly* 82.2 (December 2001): 733–48.

Prowse, Renate M., Hartmut-Michael Weber, and Charles R. M. Wilson. "Rights and Prisons in Germany: Blueprint for Britain?" *International Journal of the Sociology of the Law* 10 (1992): 111–34.

Quarm, Daisy, and Martin D. Schwartz. "Domestic Violence in Criminal Court: An Examination of New Legislation in Ohio." In *Criminal Justice Politics and Women: The Aftermath of Legally Mandated Change*. Claudine SchWeber and Clarice Feinman, eds. New York: The Haworth Press, 1985.

Quinney, Richard. *The Social Reality of Crime*. Boston: Little, Brown, 1970.

_____. *Critique of Legal Order: Crime Control in Capitalist Society*. Boston: Little, Brown, 1973.

Rable, George C. "The South and the Politics of Antilynching Legislation." In *Lynching, Racial Violence, and Law*. Paul Finkelman, ed. New York: Garland Publishing, 1992.

Radelet, Michael L. "Executions of Whites for Crimes Against Blacks: Exceptions to the Rule?" *Sociological Quarterly* 30 (1989): 529–44.

Radelet, Michael L., and Marion J. Borg. "The Changing Nature of Death Penalty Debates." *Annual Review of Sociology* 26 (2000): 43–61.

Radelet, Michael L., and Margaret Vandiver. "Race and Capital Punishment: An Overview of the Issues." *Crime and Social Justice* 25 (1986): 94–113.

Radford, Jill. "Women and Policing: Contradictions Old and New." In *Women, Policing, and Male Violence: International Perspectives*. Jalna Hanmer, Jill Radford, and Elizabeth A. Stanko, eds. London and New York: Routledge, 1989: 13–45.

Radzinowicz, Leon, and Roger Hood. "The American Volte-Face in Sentencing Thought and Practice." In *Crime, Proof, and Punishment: Essays in Memory of Sir Rupert Cross*. C. F. H. Tapper, ed. London: Buttersworths, 1981: 127–43.

Rafter, Nicole Hahn. *Partial Justice: Women in State Prisons, 1800–1935*. Boston: Northeastern University Press, 1985.

———. "Introduction: The Development of Feminist Perspectives on Crime." In *International Feminist Perspectives in Criminology: Engendering a Discipline*. Nicole Hahn Rafter and Frances Heidensohn, eds. Buckingham, UK: Open University Press, 1995.

Randa, Laura E., ed. *Society's Final Solution: A History and Discussion of the Death Penalty*. Lanham, MD: University Press of America, 1997.

Rapoport, Miles S. "Restoring the Vote." *The American Prospect*, August 13, 2001: 13–14.

Reeves, Helen, "Victim Support Schemes: The United Kingdom Model." *Victimology* 10.1–4 (1985): 678–86.

———. "Afterward." In *Victims of Crime: A New Deal?* Mike Maguire and John Pointing, eds. Buckingham, UK: Open University Press, 1988.

Reggio, Michael H. "History of the Death Penalty." In *Society's Final Solution: A History and Discussion of the Death Penalty*. Laura E. Randa, ed. Lanham, MD: University Press of America, 1997: 1–11.

Reinelt, Claire. "Moving onto the Terrain of the State: The Battered Women's Movement and the Politics of Engagement." In *Feminist Organizations: Harvest of the New Women's Movement*. Myra Marx Ferree and Patricia Yancey Martin, eds. Philadelphia: Temple University Press, 1995.

Reiner, Robert. "Media Made Criminality: The Representation of Crime in the Mass Media." In *The Oxford Handbook of Criminology*. 2nd ed. Mike Maguire, Rod Morgan, and Robert Reiner, eds. Oxford: Clarendon Press, 1997: 189–231.

Reitz, Kevin R. "Sentencing." In *The Handbook of Crime and Punishment*. Michael Tonry, ed. New York: Oxford University Press, 1998: 542–62.

———. "The Disassembly and Reassembly of U.S. Sentencing Practices." In *Sentencing and Sanctions in Western Countries*. Michael Tonry and Richard S. Frase, eds. Oxford: Oxford University Press, 2001: 222–58.

Reitz, Kevin R., and Curtis R. Reitz. "Building a Sentencing Reform Agenda: The ABA's New Sentencing Standards." *Judicature* 78.4 (January–February 1995): 189–95.

Rennison, Callie Marie. "Intimate Partner Violence, 1993–2001." *Bureau of Justice Statistics; Crime Data in Brief*. Washington, DC: U.S. Department of Justice, February 2003.

Rhode, Deborah L. *Justice and Gender: Sex Discrimination and the Law*. Cambridge: Harvard University Press, 1989.

Richardson, Genevra. "Judicial Intervention in Prison Life." In *Accountability and Prisons: Opening Up a Closed World*. Mike Maguire, Jon Vagg, and Rod Morgan, eds. London: Tavistock Publications, 1985.

———. "From Rights to Expectations." In *Prisons After Woolf: Reform Through Riot*. Elaine Player and Michael Jenkins, eds. London: Routledge, 1994.

Rifkin, Janet. "Mediation in the Justice System: A Paradox for Women." *Women & Criminal Justice* 1.1 (1989): 41–54.

Rigby, Michael. "Number of Presidential Pardons Declining." *Prison Legal News*, December 2003: 39.

Robbins, Ira P. "Managed Health Care in Prisons as Cruel and Unusual Punishment." *Journal of Criminal Law and Criminology* 90.1 (Fall 1999).

Roberts, Julian V. "American Attitudes About Punishment: Myth and Reality." In *Sentencing Reform in Overcrowded Times: A Comparative Perspective.* Michael Tonry and Kathleen Hatlestad, eds. New York: Oxford University Press, 1997: 250–59.

Roberts, Julian V., and Loretta J. Stalans. "Crime, Criminal Justice, and Public Opinion." In *The Handbook of Crime and Punishment.* Michael Tonry, ed. New York: Oxford University Press, 1998: 31–57.

Roberts, Julian V., Loretta J. Stalans, David Indermauer, and Mike Hough. *Penal Populism and Public Opinion: Lessons from Five Countries.* Oxford: Oxford University Press, 2003.

Robin, Gerald D. "Forcible Rape: Institutionalized Sexism in the Criminal Justice System." *Crime and Delinquency* 23 (April 1977): 136–53.

Rock, Paul A. *A View from the Shadows: The Ministry of the Solicitor General of Canada and the Making of the Justice for Victims of Crime Initiative.* Oxford: Clarendon Press, 1986.

_____. "Governments, Victims and Policies in Two Countries." *British Journal of Criminology* 28.1 (Winter 1988): 44–66.

_____. *Helping Victims of Crime: The Home Office and the Rise of Victim Support in England and Wales.* Oxford: Clarendon Press, 1990.

_____. *Constructing Victims' Rights: The Home Office, New Labour, and Victims.* Oxford: Oxford University Press, 2004.

_____. "Victims, Prosecutors and the State in Nineteenth Century England and Wales." *Criminal Justice* 4.4 (2004): 331–54.

Rogers, Alan. "'Success – At Long Last': The Abolition of the Death Penalty in Massachusetts, 1928–1984." *Boston College Third World Journal* 22.2 (2002).

Roland, David L. "Progress in the Victim Reform Movement: No Longer the 'Forgotten Victim'." *Pepperdine Law Review* 17.1 (1989): 35–58.

Rose, Gordon. *The Struggle for Penal Reform: The Howard League and Its Predecessors.* London: Stevens and Sons Limited, 1961.

Rose, Vicki McNickle. "Rape as a Social Problem: A Byproduct of the Feminist Movement." *Social Problems* 25.1 (October 1977): 75–89.

Rosen, Ruth. *The Lost Sisterhood: Prostitution in America, 1900–1918.* Baltimore: Johns Hopkins University Press, 1982.

Rosenberg, Gerald N. *The Hollow Hope: Can Courts Bring About Social Change?* Chicago: University of Chicago Press, 1991.

Rosenman, Samuel, ed. *The Public Papers and Addresses of Franklin D. Roosevelt.* Vol. 3. New York: Random House, 1938.

Rothman, David J. *Conscience and Convenience: The Asylum and Its Alternatives in Progressive America.* Boston: Little, Brown and Co., 1980.

_____. "Social Control and the State." In *Social Control and the State.* Stanley Cohen and Andrew Scull, eds. New York: St. Martin's Press, 1983: 106–17.

_____. *The Discovery of the Asylum: Social Order and Disorder in the New Republic.* Rev. ed. Boston: Little, Brown and Co., 1990.

Rothman, David J. "The Crime of Punishment." *The New York Review of Books,* February 17, 1994: 36.

Rotman, Edgardo. "The Failure of Reform: United States, 1865–1965." In *The Oxford History of the Prison: The Practice of Punishment in Western Society.* Norval Morris and David J. Rothman, eds. New York: Oxford University Press, 1995: 169–78.

Royal Commission on Capital Punishment, 1949–1953. *Report.* London: HMSO, September 1953.

Rueschemeyer, Dietrich. "Sociology of Law in Germany." *Law & Society Review* 5.2 (November 1970): 225–37.

Ruggie, Mary. "Workers' Movements and Women's Interests: The Impact of Labor-State Relations in Britain and Sweden." In *The Women's Movements of the United States and Western Europe*. Mary Fainsod Katzenstein and Carol McClung Mueller, eds. Philadelphia: Temple University Press, 1987.

Ruggiero, Vincenzo, Mick Ryan, and Joe Simon, eds. *Western European Penal Systems: A Critical Anatomy*. London: Sage 1995.

Rusche, Georg, and Otto Kirchheimer. *Punishment and Social Structure*. New York: Columbia University Press, 1939.

Ruth, David E. *Inventing the Public Enemy: The Gangster in American Culture, 1918–1934*. Chicago: University of Chicago Press, 1996.

Ruth, Henry, and Kevin R. Reitz. *The Challenge of Crime: Rethinking Our Response*. Cambridge, MA: Harvard University Press, 2003.

Rutherford, Andrew. *Prisons and the Process of Justice: The Reductionist Challenge*. London: Heinemann, 1984.

————. *Transforming Criminal Policy: Spheres of Influence in the United States, The Netherlands and England and Wales*. Winchester, UK: Wayside Press, 1996.

Ryan, Mick. *The Acceptable Pressure Group – Inequality in the Penal Lobby: A Case Study of the Howard Lobby and RAP*. Farnborough, UK: Saxon House, 1978.

————. *Politics of Penal Reform*. Harlow, UK: Longman, 1983.

————. "The Woolf Report: On the Treadmill of Prison Reform?" *The Political Quarterly* 63.1 (January 1992): 50–56.

Ryan, Mick, and Tony Ward. "From Positivism to Postmodernism: Some Theoretical and Strategic Reflections on the Evolution of the Penal Lobby in Britain." *International Journal of the Sociology of the Law* 20 (1992): 321–35.

Saenz, Adolph. *Politics of a Prison Riot: The 1980 Prison Riot, Its Consequences and Aftermath*. Corrales, NM: Rhombus Publishing Co., 1986.

Sampson, Anthony. *The Changing Anatomy of Britain*. New York: Random House, 1982.

Sarabi, Brigette. "ALEC in the House: Corporate Bias in Criminal Justice Legislation." *Prison Legal News*, January 2002: 1–4.

Sarat, Austin. "Narrative Strategy and Death Penalty Advocacy." *Harvard Civil Rights–Civil Liberties Law Review* 31 (1996): 353–81.

————. "Capital Punishment as a Legal, Political, and Cultural Fact: An Introduction." In *The Killing State: Capital Punishment in Law, Politics, and Culture*. Austin Sarat, ed. New York: Oxford University Press, 1999.

————. *When the State Kills: Capital Punishment and the American Condition*. Princeton: Princeton University Press, 2001.

————, ed. *The Killing State: Capital Punishment in Law, Politics, and Culture*. New York: Oxford University Press, 1999.

————, ed. *Pain, Death, and the Law*. Ann Arbor: University of Michigan Press, 2001.

Sasson, Theodore. "William Horton's Long Shadow: 'Punitiveness' and 'Managerialism' in the Penal Politics of Massachusetts, 1988–99." In *Crime, Risk and Insecurity: Law and Order in Everyday Life and Political Discourse*. Tim Hope and Richard Sparks, eds. London and New York: Routledge, 2000: 238–51.

Savage, Stephen P., Rob Atkinson, and Lynton Robins, eds. *Public Policy in Britain*. Basingstoke, UK: Macmillan, 1994.

Savelsberg, Joachim J. "Knowledge, Domination, and Criminal Punishment." *American Journal of Sociology* 99.4 (January 1994): 911–43.

Savelsberg, Joachim J., Ryan King, and Lara Cleveland. "Politicized Scholarship? Science on Crime and the State." *Social Problems* 49.3 (2002): 327–48.

Schabas, William A. "The Abolition of Capital Punishment from an International Law Perspective." Paper presented at "Convergence of Criminal Justice Systems–Bridging the Gaps," International Society for the Reform of Criminal Law, The Hague, August 24–28, 2003.

Schafer, Stephen. *Compensation and Restitution to Victims of Crime.* 2nd ed. Montclair, NJ: Patterson Smith, 1970.

Schechter, Susan. "The Future of the Battered Women's Movement." *Aegis*, Summar/Autumn 1980: 20–25.

———. *Women and Male Violence: The Visions and Struggles of the Battered Women's Movement.* Boston: South End Press, 1982.

Scheerer, Sebastian. "The New Dutch and German Drug Laws: Social and Political Conditions for Criminalization and Decriminalization." *Law & Society Review* 12.4 (Summer 1978): 585–606.

Scheingold, Stuart A. *The Politics of Rights: Lawyers, Public Policy, and Political Change.* New Haven: Yale University Press, 1974.

———. *The Politics of Law and Order: Street Crime and Public Policy.* New York and London: Longman, 1984.

———, ed. *Politics, Crime Control, and Culture.* Aldershot, UK: Ashgate/Dartmouth, 1997.

———. "Constructing the New Political Criminology: Power, Authority, and the Post-Liberal State." *Law and Social Inquiry* 23.4 (Autumn 1998): 857–95.

Scheingold, Stuart A., Toska Olson, and Jana Pershing. "Sexual Violence, Victim Advocacy, and Republican Criminology: Washington State's Community Protection Act." *Law & Society Review* 28.4 (1994): 729–63.

Schiraldi, Vincent, and Judith Greene. "Reducing Correctional Costs in an Era of Tightening Budgets and Shifting Public Opinion." *Federal Sentencing Reporter* 14.6 (May/June 2002): 332–36.

Schlanger, Margo. "Beyond the Hero Judge: Institutional Reform Litigation as Litigation." *Michigan Law Review* 97 (May 1999).

Schlosser, Eric. "The Prison-Industrial Complex." *The Atlantic Monthly*, December 1998.

Schmidt, Janell D., and Lawrence W. Sherman. "Does Arrest Deter Domestic Violence?" *American Behavioral Scientist* 36.5 (May 1993): 601–09.

Schmitt, Frederika E., and Patricia Yancey Martin. "Unobtrusive Mobilization by an Institutionalized Rape Crisis Center: 'All We Do Comes from Victims'." *Gender & Society* 13.3 (June 1999): 364–84.

Schneider, Elizabeth M. "The Dialectic of Rights and Politics: Perspectives from the Women's Movement." In *Feminist Legal Theory: Readings in Law and Gender.* Katharine T. Bartlett and Rosanne Kennedy, eds. Boulder, CO: Westview Press, 1991.

———. *Battered Women and Feminist Lawmaking.* New Haven: Yale University Press, 2000.

Schneider, Eric C. Review of Mary E. Odem, *Delinquent Daughters: Protecting and Policing Adolescent Female Sexuality in the United States, 1885–1920. Journal of Social History* 30 (Summer 1997): 987–88.

Schrag, Peter. "A Quagmire for Our Time." *The American Prospect*, August 13, 2001: 28–33.

Schuck, Peter H. "Public Law Litigation and Social Reform." *Yale Law Journal* 102.2 (May 1993): 1763–86.

Schultz, LeRoy G. "The Violated: A Proposal To Compensate Victims of Violent Crime." In *Considering the Victim: Readings in Restitution and Victim Compensation.* Joe Hudson and Burt Galaway, eds. Springfield, IL: Charles C. Thomas, 1975.

SchWeber, Claudine, and Clarice Feinman, eds. *Criminal Justice Politics and Women: The Aftermath of Legally Mandated Change.* New York: The Haworth Press, 1985.

Schwed, Roger E. *Abolition and Capital Punishment: The United States' Judicial, Political, and Moral Barometer.* New York: AMS Press, Inc., 1983.

Scraton, Phil, ed. *Law, Order and the Authoritarian State: Readings in Critical Criminology.* Milton Keynes, UK: Open University Press, 1987.

———. "Unreasonable Force: Policing, Punishment and Marginalization." In *Law, Order and the Authoritarian State: Readings in Critical Criminology.* Phil Scraton, ed. Milton Keynes, UK: Open University Press, 1987: 145–89.

Scraton, Phil, Joe Sim, and Paula Skidmore. *Prisons Under Protest.* Buckingham, UK: Open University Press, 1991.

Searles, Patricia, and Ronald J. Berger. "The Feminist Self-Defense Movement: A Case Study." *Gender & Society* 1.1 (March 1987): 33–60.

Sebba, Leslie. "The Victim's Role in the Penal Process: A Theoretical Orientation." *American Journal of Comparative Law* 30.1 (1982): 217–40.

Sen, Rinku. "The First Time Was Tragedy, Will the Second Be Farce?" *Color Lines* (Fall 2000).

Shapiro, Bruce. "Victims & Vengeance: Why the Victims Rights Amendment Is a Bad Idea." *The Nation,* February 10, 1997: 11–19.

———. "Capital Offense." *The New York Times Magazine,* March 26, 2000: 19–20.

Shapiro, Karen A. *A New South Rebellion: The Battle Against Convict Labor in the Tennessee Coalfields, 1871–1896.* Chapel Hill: University of North Carolina Press, 1998.

Shapland, Joanna. "The Victim, the Criminal Justice System, and Compensation." *British Journal of Criminology* 24.2 (April 1984): 131–49.

———. "Victims and the Criminal Justice System." In *From Crime Policy to Victim Policy: Reorienting the Justice System.* Ezzat A. Fattah, ed. New York: St. Martin's Press, 1986.

Sharp, Elaine B. *The Sometime Connection: Public Opinion and Social Policy.* Albany: SUNY Press, 1999.

Sherman, Lawrence W. *Policing Domestic Violence: Experiments and Dilemmas.* New York: Free Press, 1992.

Sherman, Lawrence W., and Richard A. Berk. "The Specific Deterrent Effects of Arrest for Domestic Assault." *American Sociological Review* 49 (1984): 261–72.

Sim, Joe. *Medical Power in Prisons: The Prison Medical Service in England, 1774–1989.* Milton Keynes, UK: Open University Press, 1990.

———. "'We Are Not Animals, We Are Human Beings': Prisons, Protest, and Politics in England and Wales, 1969–1990." *Social Justice* 18.3 (Fall 1991): 107–29.

Sim, Joe, Vincenzo Ruggiero, and Mick Ryan. "Punishment in Europe: Perceptions and Commonalities." In *Western European Penal Systems: A Critical Anatomy.* Vincenzo Ruggiero, Mick Ryan, and Joe Sim, eds. London: Sage, 1995: 1–23.

Simon, Jonathan. *Poor Discipline: Parole and the Social Control of the Underclass.* Chicago: University of Chicago Press, 1993.

———. "They Died with Their Boots On: The Boot Camp and the Limits of Modern Penalty." *Social Justice* 22.2 (1995): 25–48.

———. "From the Big House to the Warehouse: Rethinking Prisons and State Government in the 20th Century." *Punishment & Society* 2.2 (April 2000): 213–234.

———. "Fearless Speech in the Killing State: The Power of Capital Crime Victim Speech." *North Carolina Law Review* 82 (May 2004).

Simon, Jonathan, and Christine Spaulding. "Tokens of Our Esteem: Aggravating Factors in the Era of Deregulated Death Penalties." In *The Killing State: Capital Punishment in Law, Politics, and Culture*. Austin Sarat, ed. New York: Oxford University Press, 1999: 81–113.

Simonsen, Clifford E. "Federal Bureau of Prisons." In *Encyclopedia of American Prisons*. Marilyn D. McShane and Frank P. Williams, III, eds. New York and London: Garland Publishing, 1996.

Skocpol, Theda. *Protecting Soldiers and Mothers: The Political Origins of Social Policy in the United States*. Cambridge, MA: The Belknap Press of Harvard University Press, 1992.

Skolnick, Jerome H. *The Politics of Protest*. New York: Ballantine Books, 1969.

———. "On Controlling Torture." In *Punishment and Social Control*. 2nd ed. Thomas G. Blomberg and Stanley Cohen, eds. New York: Aldine de Gruyter, 2003: 213–29.

Skowronek, Stephen. *Building a New American State: The Expansion of National Administrative Capacities, 1877–1920*. Cambridge: Cambridge University Press, 1982.

Smart, Carol. *Feminism and the Power of the Law*. London and New York: Routledge, 1989.

Smith, David Michael. "The Death Penalty Capital of the Western World." *Peace Review* 13.4 (December 2001): 495–501.

Smith, Rogers. *Civic Ideals: Conflicting Visions of Citizenship in U.S. History*. New Haven: Yale University Press, 1997.

———. "Substance and Methods in APD Research." *Studies in American Political Development* 17.1 (Spring 2003): 111–15.

Smith, Steven Rathgeb, and Susan Freinkel. *Adjusting the Balance: Federal Policy and Victim Services*. Westport, CT: Greenwood, 1988.

Snacken, Sonja, Kristel Beyens, and Hilde Tubex. "Changing Prison Populations in Western Countries: Fate or Policy?" *European Journal of Crime, Criminal Law and Criminal Justice* 3.1 (1995): 18–53.

Snare, Annika, and Ulla Bondeson. "Criminological Research in Scandinavia." In *Crime and Justice: An Annual Review of Research*. Vol. 6. Michael Tonry and Norval Morris, eds. Chicago: University of Chicago Press, 1985.

Snider, Laureen. "Criminalization: Panacea for Men Who Assault Women but Anathema for Corporate Criminals." In *Social Inequality, Social Justice*. Dawn H. Currie and Brian D. MacLean, eds. Vancouver: Collective Press, 1994: 101–24.

———. "Towards Safer Societies: Punishment, Masculinities and Violence Against Women." *The British Journal of Criminology* 38.1 (Winter 1998): 1–39.

———. "Female Punishment: From Patriarchy to Backlash?" In *The Blackwell Companion to Criminology*. Colin Sumner, ed. Oxford: Blackwell Publishers, 2003.

Soetenhorst, Jacquelien. "Victim Support Programs: Between Doing Good and Doing Justice." In *Crime and Its Victims: International Research and Public Policy Issues*. Emilio C. Viano, ed. New York: Hemisphere, 1989.

Sontag, Deborah. "Fierce Entanglements." *The New York Times Magazine*, November 17, 2002: 52.

Sowle, Stephen D. "A Regime of Social Death: Criminal Punishment in the Age of Prisons." *New York University Review of Law and Social Change* 21.3 (1994–95): 497–565.

Sparks, Anne. "Feminists Negotiate the Executive Branch: The Policing of Male Violence." In *Feminists Negotiate the State: The Politics of Domestic Violence*. Cynthia R. Daniels, ed. Lanham, MD: University Press of America, 1997.

Sparks, Richard F. *Research on Victims of Crime: Accomplishments, Issues and New Directions*. Rockville, MD: National Institute of Mental Health, Center for Studies of Crime and Delinquency, 1982.

———. "State Punishment in Advanced Capitalist Countries." In *Punishment and Social Control*. 2nd ed. Thomas G. Blomberg and Stanley Cohen, eds. New York: Aldine de Gruyter, 2003: 19–44.

Sparrow, Bartholomew H. *From the Outside In: World War II and the American State*. Princeton: Princeton University Press, 1996.

Spelman, William. "The Limited Importance of Prison Expansion." In *The Crime Drop in America*. Alfred Blumstein and Joel Wallman, eds. Cambridge: Cambridge University Press, 2000.

———. "What Recent Studies Do (and Don't) Tell Us About Imprisonment and Crime." In *Crime and Justice: A Review of Research*. Vol. 27. Michael Tonry, ed. Chicago: University of Chicago Press, 2000.

Spierenburg, Pieter. *The Spectacle of Suffering: Executions and the Evolution of Repression*. Cambridge: Cambridge University Press, 1984.

Spohn, Cassia, and Julie Horney. *Rape Law Reform: A Grassroots Revolution and Its Impact*. New York: Plenum Press, 1992.

Stanko, Elizabeth A. "Victims R US: The Life History of 'Fear of Crime' and the Politicisation of Violence." In *Crime, Risk and Insecurity: Law and Order in Everyday Life and Political Discourse*. Tim Hope and Richard Sparks, eds. London and New York: Routledge, 2000: 13–30.

Stanton, Elizabeth Cady. "There Will Be No Gallows When Mothers Make the Laws." In *Voices Against Death: American Opposition to Capital Punishment, 1787–1975*. Philip English Mackey, ed. New York: Burt Franklin & Co., 1976: 121–22.

Starrs, James E. "A Modest Proposal to Insure Justice for Victims of Crime." *Minnesota Law Review* 50 (1965): 285–310.

Stastny, Charles, and Gabrielle Tyrnauer. *Who Rules the Joint? The Changing Political Culture of Maximum-Security Prisons in America*. Lexington, MA: D.C. Heath, 1982.

Steiker, Carol S. "Capital Punishment and American Exceptionalism." *Oregon Law Review* 81 (2002).

Steiker, Carol S., and Jordan M. Steiker. "Should Abolitionists Support Legislative 'Reform' of the Death Penalty?" *Ohio State Law Journal* 63 (2002).

———. "Judicial Developments in Capital Punishment Law." In *America's Experiment with Capital Punishment: Reflections on the Past, Present, and Future of the Ultimate Penal Sanction*. 2nd ed. James R. Acker, Robert M. Bohm, and Charles S. Lanier, eds. Durham, NC: Carolina Academic Press, 2003: 55–83.

Stern, Vivien. *Bricks of Shame: Britain's Prisons*. 2nd ed. London: Penguin Books, 1989.

———. "The Future of the Voluntary Sector and the Pressure Groups." In *Prisons After Woolf: Reform Through Riot*. Elaine Player and Michael Jenkins, eds. London: Routledge, 1994.

_____. *A Sin Against the Future: Imprisonment in the World*. Boston: Northeastern University Press, 1998.

Stith, Kate, and José A. Cabranes. *Fear of Judging: Sentencing Guidelines in the Federal Courts*. Chicago: University of Chicago Press, 1998.

Stith, Kate, and Steve Y. Koh. "The Politics of Sentencing Reform: The Legislative History of the Federal Sentencing Guidelines." *Wake Forest Law Review* 28 (1993): 223–90.

Stout, Edward, and John H. Stein. "Victim Justice: A New Balance." *The NOVA Newsletter* 14.8–12 (1990).

Strang, Heather. *Repair or Revenge: Victims and Restorative Justice*. Oxford: Clarendon Press, 2002.

Strange, Carolyn. "Murder and Meanings in U.S. Historiography." *Feminist Studies* 25.3 (Fall 1999): 679–98.

Studer, Marlena. "Wife Beating as a Social Problem." *International Journal of Women's Studies* 7.5 (1984): 412–22.

Sturm, Susan P. "Resolving the Remedial Dilemma: Strategies of Judicial Intervention in Prisons." *University of Pennsylvania Law Review* 138 (1990): 805–912.

_____. "Lawyers at the Prison Gates: Organizational Structure and Prison Advocacy." *University of Michigan Journal of Law Reform* 27.1 (1993).

Sullivan, Larry E. *The Prison Reform Movement: Forlorn Hope*. Boston: Twayne Publishers, 1990.

Sullivan, Robert R. *Liberalism and Crime: The British Experience*. Lanham, MD: Lexington Books, 2000.

Surette, Ray. *Media, Crime, and Criminal Justice: Images and Realities*. Pacific Grove, CA: Brooks/Cole, 1992.

Sutton, Jo. "The Growth of the British Movement for Battered Women." *Victimology: An International Journal* 2.3–4 (1977–78): 576–84.

Szymanski, Anne-Marie. "Horse Thieves, Vigilantes, and the Reduction of Crime Rates in Nineteenth Century America." Policy History Conference of the *Journal of Policy History*, Clayton, MO, May 30–June 2, 2002.

T., Anna. "Feminist Responses to Sexual Abuse: The Work of the Birmingham Rape Crisis Centre." In *Victims of Crime: A New Deal?* Mike Maguire and John Pointing, eds. Buckingham, UK: Open University Press, 1988: 60–64.

Taggart, William A. "Redefining the Power of the Federal Judiciary: The Impact of Court-Ordered Prison Reform on State Expenditures for Corrections." *Law & Society Review* 23.2 (1989): 241–72.

Tak, Peter J. "Sentencing and Punishment in The Netherlands." In *Sentencing and Sanctions in Western Countries*. Michael Tonry and Richard S. Frase, eds. Oxford: Oxford University Press, 2001: 151–87.

Tak, Peter J., and Anton M. van Kalmthout. "Prison Population Growing Faster in the Netherlands Than in the United States." In *Penal Reform in Overcrowded Times*. Michael Tonry, ed. Oxford: Oxford University Press, 2001.

Takagi, Paul. "The Walnut Street Jail: A Penal Reform to Centralize the Powers of the State." In *Punishment and Penal Discipline: Essays on the Prison and the Prisoners' Movement*. Tony Platt and Paul Takagi, eds. San Francisco: Crime and Social Justice Associates, 1980: 48–56.

Talbot, Margaret. "The Executioner's I. Q. Test." *The New York Times Magazine*, June 29, 2003: 30.

Talvi, Silja J. A. "Cashing in On Cons." *In These Times*, February 28, 2005: 16.

Teeters, Negley. *The Cradle of the Penitentiary: The Walnut Street Jail at Philadelphia, 1773–1835*. Philadelphia: Lippincott, 1935.

Teeters, Negley, and John D. Shearer. *The Prison at Philadelphia, Cherry Hill: The Separate System of Penal Discipline: 1829–1913*. New York: Columbia University Press, 1957.

Tham, Henrik. "Law and Order as a Leftist Project? The Case of Sweden." *Punishment & Society* 3.3 (July 2001): 409–26.

Thomas, J. E., and Richard Pooley. *The Exploding Prison: Prison Riots and the Case of Hull*. London: Junction Books, 1980.

Thompson, E. P. *Whigs and Hunters: The Origins of the Black Act*. New York: Pantheon, 1975.

Tierney, Kathleen J. "The Battered Women Movement and the Creation of the Wife Beating Problem." *Social Problems* 29.3 (February 1982): 207–20.

Tilly, Charles. "Reflections on the History of European State-Making." In *The Formation of National States in Western Europe*. Charles Tilly, ed. Princeton: Princeton University Press, 1975: 3–83.

———. *From Mobilization to Revolution*. Reading, MA: Addison Wesley, 1978.

Tomes, Nancy. "A 'Torrent of Abuse': Crimes of Violence Between Working-Class Men and Women in London, 1840–1875." *Journal of Social History* 11.3 (Spring 1978): 328–45.

Tomlins, Christopher L., and Bruce H. Mann, eds. *The Many Legalities of Early America*. Chapel Hill: University of North Carolina Press, 2001.

Tonry, Michael. *Malign Neglect: Race, Crime and Punishment in America*. New York: Oxford University Press, 1995.

———. "Racial Disparities Getting Worse in U.S. Prisons and Jails." In *Sentencing Reform in Overcrowded Times: A Comparative Perspective*. Michael Tonry and Kathleen Hatlestad, eds. New York: Oxford University Press, 1997: 220–227.

———. "Rethinking Unthinkable Punishment Policies in America." *UCLA Law Review* 46.6 (August 1999): 1751–91.

———. "Punishment Policies and Patterns in Western Countries." In *Sentencing and Sanctions in Western Countries*. Michael Tonry and Richard S. Frase, eds. Oxford: Oxford University Press, 2001: 3–28.

———. "Symbol, Substance, and Severity in Western Penal Policies." *Punishment & Society* 3.4 (October 2001): 517–36.

———. *Penal Reform in Overcrowded Times*. Oxford: Oxford University Press, 2001.

———. *Punishment and Politics. Evidence and Emulation in the Making of English Crime Control Policy*. Devon, UK: Willan Publishing, 2004.

———, ed. *The Handbook of Crime and Punishment*. New York: Oxford University Press, 1998.

Tonry, Michael, and Richard S. Frase, eds. *Sentencing and Sanctions in Western Countries*. Oxford: Oxford University Press, 2001.

Tonry, Michael, and Kathleen Hatlestad, eds. *Sentencing Reform in Overcrowded Times: A Comparative Perspective*. New York: Oxford University Press, 1997.

Tonry, Michael, and Joan Petersilia. "American Prisons at the Beginning of the Twenty-First Century." In *Crime and Justice: A Review of Research*. Vol. 26. *Prisons*. Michael Tonry and Joan Petersilia, eds. Chicago: University of Chicago Press, 1999: 1–16.

Törnudd, Patrik. "Sentencing and Punishment in Finland." In *Sentencing Reform in Overcrowded Times: A Comparative Perspective*. Michael Tonry and Kathleen Hatlestad, eds. New York: Oxford University Press, 1997.

Travis, Jeremy, and Christy Visher, eds. *Prisoner Reentry and Crime in America*. Cambridge: Cambridge University Press, 2005.

Travis, Lawrence F., III. "The Politics of Sentencing Reform." In *Sentencing Reform: Experiments in Reducing Disparity*. Martin L. Forst, ed. Newbury Park, CA: Sage, 1982: 59–89.

Turow, Scott. "To Kill or Not to Kill." *The New Yorker*, January 6, 2003.

Twentieth Century Fund Task Force on Criminal Sentencing. *Fair and Certain Punishment*. New York: McGraw-Hill, 1976.

Twentieth Century Fund Task Force on the Law Enforcement Assistance Administration. *Law Enforcement: The Federal Role*. New York: McGraw Hill, 1976.

Tyler, Tom R., and Robert J. Boeckmann. "Three Strikes and You Are Out, but Why? The Psychology of Public Support for Punishing Rule Breakers." *Law & Society Review* 31.2 (1997): 237–65.

Uggen, Christopher, and Jeff Manza. "Democratic Contraction? Political Consequences of Felon Disenfranchisement in the United States." *The American Sociological Review* 67.6 (December 2002): 777–803.

_____. "Lost Voices: The Civic and Political Views of Disenfranchised Felons." In *Imprisoning America: The Social Effects of Mass Incarceration*. Mary Pattillo, David Weiman, and Bruce Western, eds. New York: Russell Sage Foundation, 2004.

Uit Beijerse, Jolande, and Renée Kool. "The Traitorous Temptation of Criminal Justice: Deceptive Appearances? The Dutch Women's Movement, Violence Against Women and the Criminal Justice System." In *Gender, Sexuality and Social Control*. Bill Rolston and Mike Tomlinson, eds. Bristol, UK: The European Group for the Study of Deviance and Social Control, 1990: 253–73.

Ungar, Sanford. *FBI*. New York: Atlantic, Little & Brown, 1975.

United Kingdom, Home Office. *Compensation for Victims of Crimes of Violence*. London: HMSO, 1964.

_____. *Crime, Justice and Protecting the Public: The Government's Proposals for Legislation*. London: HMSO, 1990.

_____. *Custody, Care and Justice: The Way Ahead for the Prison Service in England and Wales*. London: HMSO, 1991.

U.S. Bureau of Justice Statistics, U.S. Department of Justice. *Survey of State Prison Inmates, 1991*. Washington, DC: U.S. Department of Justice, Bureau of Justice Statistics, 1993.

_____. *Sourcebook of Criminal Justice Statistics 1996*. Washington, DC: GPO, 1997.

_____. *Sourcebook of Criminal Justice Statistics, 1997*. Washington, DC: GPO, 1998.

_____. *Correctional Populations in the United States, 1996*. Washington, DC: U.S. Department of Justice, 1999.

_____. *Prison and Jail Inmates at Midyear 2002*. Washington, DC: U.S. Department of Justice, April 2003.

U.S. Commission on Civil Rights. "Battered Women: Issues of Public Policy; Proceedings of a Consultation Sponsored by the U.S. Commission on Civil Rights." Washington, DC, January 30–31, 1978. Washington, DC: U.S. Commission on Civil Rights, 1978.

U.S. Department of Justice. "Capital Punishment, 1981." Washington, DC: GPO, 1982.

_____. *Attorney General's Task Force on Family Violence*. Washington, DC: GPO, 1984.

U.S. House, Subcommittee No. 2 of the Committee on the Judiciary. "Abolition of Capital Punishment." 86th Congress, 2nd Session (May 5, 1960).

Useem, Bert, and Peter Kimball. *States of Siege: U.S. Prison Riots, 1971–1986*. New York: Oxford University Press, 1989.

Useem, Bert, Raymond V. Liedka, and Anne Morrison Piehl. "Popular Support for the Prison Build-up." *Punishment & Society* 5.1 (January 2003): 5–32.

Van Blad, John, Hans Mastrigt, and Niels Uildriks. "Hulsman's Abolitionist Perspective: The Criminal Justice System as a Social Problem." In *The Criminal Justice System as a Social Problem: An Abolitionist Perspective*. John van Blad, Hans Mastrigt, and Niels Uildriks, eds. Rotterdam: Erasmus Universiteit, 1987.

Van Dijk, Jan. "Ideological Trends Within the Victims Movement: An International Perspective." In *Victims of Crime: A New Deal?* Mike Maguire and John Pointing, eds. Buckingham, UK: Open University Press, 1988.

Vandiver, Margaret. "The Impact of the Death Penalty on the Families of Homicide Victims and of Condemned Prisoners." In *America's Experiment With Capital Punishment: Reflections on the Past, Present, and Future of the Ultimate Penal Sanction*. 2nd ed. James R. Acker, Robert M. Bohm, and Charles S. Lanier, eds. Durham, NC: Carolina Academic Press, 2003: 613–45.

Van Koppen, Peter J. "The Dutch Supreme Court and Parliament: Political Decisionmaking Versus Nonpolitical Appointments." *Law & Society Review* 24.3 (1990).

Van Swaaningen, René. "Feminism, Criminology and Criminal Law: Troublesome Relationships." In *Gender, Sexuality and Social Control*. Bill Rolston and Mike Tomlinson, eds. Bristol, UK: The European Group for the Study of Deviance and Social Control, 1990: 211–37.

———. *Critical Criminology: Visions from Europe*. London: Sage Publications, 1997.

Van Swaaningen, René, and Gerard de Jonge. "The Dutch Prison System and Penal Policy in the 1990s: From Humanitarian Paternalism to Penal Business Management." In *Western European Penal Systems: A Critical Anatomy*. Vincenzo Ruggiero, Mick Ryan, and Joe Sim, eds. London: Sage, 1995.

Van Zyl Smit, Dirk. *Taking Life Imprisonment Seriously in National and International Law*. The Hague and New York: Kluver Law International, 2002.

Vernon, John. "The Wickersham Commission and William Monroe Trotter." *Negro History Bulletin* 1 (Jan.-Mar. 1999).

Vogel, Mary E. "The Social Origins of Plea Bargaining: Conflict and the Law in the Process of State Formation, 1830–1860." *Law & Society Review* 33.1 (1999): 161–246.

Von Drehle, David. *Among the Lowest of the Dead: Inside Death Row*. New York: Fawcett Crest, 1995.

Von Hentig, Hans. "The Criminality of the Negro." *Journal of the American Institute of Criminal Law and Criminology* 30 (March–April 1940).

Von Hirsch. *Doing Justice: The Choice of Punishments; Report of the Committee for the Study of Incarceration*. New York: Hill and Wang, 1975.

———. "The Future of the Proportionate Sentence." In *Punishment and Social Control: Essays in Honor of Sheldon L. Messinger*. Thomas G. Blomberg and Stanley Cohen, eds. New York: Aldine de Gruyter, 1995.

———. "Sentencing Reform in Sweden." In *Sentencing Reform in Overcrowded Times: A Comparative Perspective*. Michael Tonry and Kathleen Hatlestad., eds. New York: Oxford University Press, 1997.

———. "The Swedish Sentencing Law." In *Principled Sentencing: Readings in Theory and Policy*. Andrew Von Hirsch and Andrew Ashworth, eds. Oxford: Hart Publishing, 1998.

_____. "The Project of Sentencing Reform." In *Sentencing and Sanctions in Western Countries*. Michael Tonry and Richard S. Frase, eds. Oxford: Oxford University Press, 2001.

Von Hirsch, Andrew, and Ashworth, Andrew. "Law and Order." In *Principled Sentencing: Readings in Theory and Policy*. Andrew von Hirsch and Andrew Ashworth, eds. Oxford: Hart Publishing, 1998.

Vorenberg, James. "Decent Restraint of Prosecutorial Power." *Harvard Law Journal* 94.7 (May 1981): 1521–73.

Wacquant, Loïc. "Suitable Enemies: Foreigners and Immigrants in the Prisons of Europe." *Punishment & Society* 1:2 (October 1999): 215–32.

_____. "Deadly Symbiosis: When Ghetto and Prison Meet and Mesh." In *Mass Imprisonment: Social Causes and Consequences*. David Garland, ed. London: Sage Publications, 2001.

_____. "The Advent of a Penal State Is Not a Destiny." *Social Justice* 28.3 (2001): 11–87.

Wagner, Gerard, and Fred Cohen. "Attica: A Look at the Causes and the Future." *Criminal Law Bulletin* 7 (1971): 832–36.

Wald, Karen. "The San Quentin Six Case: Perspective and Analysis." In *Punishment and Penal Discipline: Essays on the Prison and the Prisoners' Movement*. Tony Platt and Paul Takagi, eds. San Francisco: Crime and Social Justice Associates, 1980: 165–75.

Waldo, Gordon P., and Raymond Paternoster. "Tinkering With the Machinery of Death: The Failure of a Social Experiment." In *Punishment and Social Control*. 2nd ed. Thomas G. Blomberg and Stanley Cohen, eds. New York: Aldine de Gruyter, 2003: 311–52.

Walker, Donald R. *Penology for Profit: A History of the Texas Prison System, 1867–1912*. College Station: Texas A&M University Press, 1988.

Walker, Samuel. *A Critical History of Police Reform*. Lexington, MA: Lexington Books, 1977.

_____. *In Defense of American Liberties: A History of the ACLU*. New York: Oxford University Press, 1990.

_____. *Taming the System: The Control of Discretion in Criminal Justice, 1950–1990*. New York and Oxford: Oxford University Press, 1993.

_____. *Sense and Nonsense About Crime and Drugs: A Policy Guide*. Belmont, CA: Wadsworth Publishing Co., 1994.

_____. *Popular Justice: A History of American Criminal Justice*. 2nd ed. New York: Oxford University Press, 1998.

_____. *In Defense of American Liberties: A History of the ACLU*. 2nd ed. Carbondale: Southern Illinois University Press, 1999.

Walkowitz, Judith R. "Review Essay. The Politics of Prostitution." *Signs* 6.1 (Autumn 1980): 123–35.

Ward, David A. "Inmate Rights and Prison Reform in Sweden and Denmark." *The Journal of Criminal Law, Criminology and Police Science* 63.2 (1972): 240–55.

_____. "Sweden: The Middle Way to Prison Reform?" In *Prisons: Present and Possible*. Marvin E. Wolfgang, ed. Lexington, MA: D.C. Heath, 1979.

Ward, Tony. "Symbols and Noble Lies: Abolitionism, 'Just Deserts,' and Crimes of the Powerful." In *Abolitionism: Towards a Non-Repressive Approach to Crime*. Herman Bianchi and René van Swaaningen, eds. Amsterdam: Free University Press, 1986.

_____. "Review Essay on *Prisons Under Protest*." *Social Justice* 18.3 (1991): 225–29.

Warren, Dorian T. "The Intersection Between Voting Rights and Criminal Justice: The National Black Organizational Response to Felon Disenfranchisement." Unpublished paper on file with author, June 2000.

Warrior, Betsy. "Divided But Not Defeated: The Battered Women's Movement in Britain." *Aegis*, January–February 1979: 4–6.

Webb, Sidney, and Beatrice Webb. *English Prisons Under Local Government*. New York: Longmans, Green and Co., 1922.

Websdale, Neil S. "Predators: The Social Construction of Stranger-Danger in Washington State as a Form of Patriarchal Ideology." *Women and Criminal Justice* 7.2 (1996): 43–68.

Weed, Frank J. "Organizational Mortality in the Anti-Drunk-Driving Movement: Failure Among Local MADD Chapters." *Social Forces* 69.3 (March 1991): 851–68.

————. *Certainty of Justice: Reform in the Crime Victim Movement*. New York: Aldine de Gruyter, 1995.

Weeks, Kent M. "The New Zealand Criminal Injuries Compensation Scheme." *Southern California Law Review* 43 (1970): 107–21.

Weigend, Thomas. *Assisting the Victim: A Report on Efforts to Strengthen the Position of the Victim in the American System of Criminal Justice*. Freiburg: Max Planck Institute for Foreign and International Criminal Law, 1981.

————. "Prosecution: Comparative Aspects." In *Encyclopedia of Criminal Justice*. Vol. 3. Sanford H. Kadish, ed. New York: New Press, 1983: 1296–1304.

————. "Sentencing and Punishment in Germany." In *Sentencing and Sanctions in Western Countries*. Michael Tonry and Richard S. Frase, eds. Oxford: Oxford University Press, 2001: 188–221.

Weir, Angela, and Elizabeth Wilson. "The British Women's Movement." *New Left Review* 148 (November/December 1984): 74–103.

Weir, Margaret, ed. "Ideas and Politics: The Acceptance of Keynesianism in Britain and the United States." In *The Political Power of Economic Ideas: Keynesianism Across Nations*. Peter A. Hall, ed. Princeton: Princeton University Press, 1989: 53–86.

————, ed. *The Social Divide: Political Parties and the Future of Activist Government*. Washington, DC, and New York: Brookings Institution and Russell Sage Foundation, 1998.

Welch, Bud. "Speaking Out Against the Execution of Timothy McVeigh." In *Machinery of Death: The Reality of America's Death Penalty Regime*. David R. Dow and Mark Dow, eds. New York: Routledge, 2002.

Welch, Michael. *Punishment in America: Social Control and the Ironies of Imprisonment*. Thousand Oaks, CA: Sage, 1999.

Welch, Paige. "Prison Rape Elimination Act 2003 Signed Into Law; Commission To Be Formed Soon." *Prison Legal News*, March 2004.

Welch, R. "Developing Prisoner Self-Help Techniques: The Early Mississipi Experience." *Prisoner Law Monitor* 2 (October 1979): 118–22.

Welsh, Wayne N. *Counties in Court: Jail Overcrowding and Court-Ordered Reform*. Philadelphia: Temple University Press, 1995.

Western, Bruce. *Punishment and Inequality in America*. New York: Russell Sage Foundation, forthcoming 2006. Manuscript on file with author, June 2005.

Western, Bruce, and Sara McLanahan. "Fathers Behind Bars: The Impact of Incarceration on Family Formation." *Contemporary Perspectives in Family Research* 2 (2000): 307–22.

Western, Bruce, and Becky Pettit. "Incarceration and Racial Inequality in Men's Employment." *Industrial and Labor Relations Review* 54.1 (2000): 3–16.

Whitcomb, Debra, et al. *An Exemplary Project: Stop Rape Crisis Center, Baton Rouge, Louisiana*. Washington, DC: National Institute of Law Enforcement and Criminal Justice, 1979.

White, Aaronette M. "Talking Feminist, Talking Black: Micromobilization Processes in a Collective Protest Against Rape." *Gender & Society* 13.1 (February 1999): 77–100.

———. "I Am Because We Are: Combined Race and Gender Political Consciousness Among African American Women and Men Anti-Rape Activists." *Women's Studies International Forum* 24.1 (2001): 11–24.

Whitman, James Q. *Harsh Justice: Criminal Punishment and the Widening Divide Between America and Europe*. Oxford: Oxford University Press, 2003.

Whittlesey, Donna. "Feminist Models for Offender Treatment." *Aegis*, Winter/Spring 1980.

Wiener, Martin J. *Men of Blood: Violence, Manliness and Criminal Justice in Victorian England*. Cambridge: Cambridge University Press, 2004.

Wilhelm, Daniel F., and Nicholas R. Turner. *Is the Budget Crisis Changing the Way We Look at Sentencing and Incarceration?* New York: Vera Institute of Justice, June 2002.

Wilkins, Leslie T. "Crime and Criminal Justice at the Turn of the Century." In *Readings in Criminal Justice*. Richter H. Moore, Jr., Thomas C. Marks, Jr., and Robert V. Barrow, eds. Indianapolis: The Bobbs-Merrill Company, Inc., 1976.

Williams, Bob. "Mississippi Death Row Conditions Unconstitutional; Sweeping Reforms Ordered." *Prison Legal News*, April 2004: 26–27.

Williams, Linda Faye. "Race and the Politics of Social Policy." In *The Social Divide: Political Parties and the Future of Activist Government*. Margaret Weir, ed. Washington, DC, and New York: The Brookings Institution and Russell Sage Foundation, 1998: 417–63.

Wilson, James Q. "Prison in a Free Society." *Public Interest* 117 (1994): 34–40.

Wilson, James Q., and Joan Petersilia, eds. *Crime*. San Francisco: ICS Press, 1995.

Wilson, Richard J. "The Influence of International Law and Practice on the Death Penalty in the United States." In *America's Experiment with Capital Punishment: Reflections on the Past, Present, and Future of the Ultimate Penal Sanction*. 2nd ed. James R. Acker, Robert M. Bohm, and Charles S. Lanier, eds. Durham, NC: Carolina Academic Press, 2003: 147–65.

Wilson, Ross. "ACC 1997: A Fairer Scheme or a Breach of the Social Contract?" *New Zealand Journal of Industrial Relations* 22.3/23.1 (December 1997/February 1998): 301–10.

Wilson, Theodore. "The Kefauver Committee 1950." *Congress Investigates, 1792–1974*. Arthur M. Schlesinger, Jr., ed. New York: Chelsea House Publishers, 1975: 353–82.

Wilson, Walter, ed. *The Selected Writings of W. E. B. DuBois*. New York: Signet Classics, 1970.

Windlesham, Lord. *Responses to Crime*. Vol. 1. Oxford: Clarendon Press, 1987.

———. *Responses to Crime*. Vol. 2. *Penal Policy in the Making*. Oxford: Clarendon Press, 1993.

Wjpijewski, Jo Ann. "Death and Texas." *The Nation*, July 30, 2001: 20–22.

Wolfe, Bertram H. *Pileup on Death Row*. Garden City, NY: Doubleday, 1973.

Wolfgang, Marvin E. "Victim Compensation in Crimes of Personal Violence." In *Considering the Victim: Readings in Restitution and Victim Compensation*. Joe Hudson and Burt Galaway, eds. Springfield, IL: Charles C. Thomas, 1975.

Wolfgang, Marvin E., and Marc Reidel. "Race, Judicial Discretion, and the Death Penalty." *The Annals of the American Academy of Political and Social Science* 407 (1973): 119–33.

Woodhouse, Owen. "Personal Injury Legislation in New Zealand." *International Labour Review* 119.3 (May–June 1980): 321–34.

Woodiwiss, Michael. *Crime, Crusades and Corruption: Prohibition in the United States, 1900–1987*. Totowa, NJ: Barnes and Noble, 1988.

Woods, Laurie. "Litigation on Behalf of Battered Women." *Women's Rights Law Reporter* 5 (1978): 7–33.

Woodward, C. Vann. *Origins of the New South, 1877–1913*. Baton Rouge: Louisiana State University Press, 1951.

Wool, Jon, and Don Stemen. *Changing Fortunes or Changing Attitudes? Sentencing and Corrections Reforms in 2003*. New York: Vera Institute of Justice, March 2004.

Work, Monroe N. "Negro Criminality in the South." *The Annals of the American Academy of Political and Social Science* 49 (September 1913): 74–80.

Wright, Boyd. "What About the Victims? Compensation for the Victims of Crime." In *Considering the Victim: Readings in Restitution and Victim Compensation*. Joe Hudson and Burt Galaway, eds. Springfield, IL: Charles C. Thomas, 1975.

Wright, Erik Olin, ed. *The Politics of Punishment*. New York: Harper and Row, 1973.

Wright, Julian H., Jr. "Life-without-parole: An Alternative to Death or Not Much of a Life at All?" *Vanderbilt Law Review* 43 (March 1990): 529–68.

Wright, Paul. "Citizen Anti-Crime Initiatives? How the Gun Lobby Bankrolls the War on Crime." In *The Celling of America: An Inside Look at the U.S. Prison Industry*. Daniel Burton-Rose, Dan Pens, and Paul Wright, eds. Monroe, ME: Common Courage Press, 1998.

Wright, Ronald F. "North Carolina Prepares for Guidelines Sentencing." In *Penal Reform in Overcrowded Times*. Michael Tonry, ed. Oxford: Oxford University Press, 2001.

————. "Flexibility in North Carolina Structured Sentencing, 1995–1997." In *Penal Reform in Overcrowded Times*. Michael Tonry, ed. Oxford: Oxford University Press, 2001.

Yarbrough, Tinsley E. "The Alabama Prison Litigation." *Justice System Journal* 9.3 (1984): 276–290.

Young, Jock. "The Failure of Criminology: The Need for a Radical Realism." In *Confronting Crime*. Robert Matthews and Jock Young, eds. London: Sage, 1986: 4–30.

————. "Radical Criminology in Britain: The Emergence of a Competing Paradigm." *British Journal of Criminology* 28.2 (Spring 1988): 289–313.

Young, Marlene A. "The '80s: NOVA's Decade of Success; The '90s: Planning for Future Achievement." *The NOVA Newsletter* 14.2 (1990): 1–4.

Young, Warren. "Influences Upon the Use of Imprisonment: A Review of the Literature." *The Howard Journal* 25.2 (May 1986): 125–36.

Young, Warren, and Mark Brown. "Cross-National Comparisons of Imprisonment." In *Crime and Justice: A Review of Research*. Vol. 17. Michael Tonry, ed. Chicago: University of Chicago Press, 1993: 1–49.

Zalman, Marvin. "The Courts' Response to Police Intervention in Domestic Violence." In *Domestic Violence: The Changing Criminal Justice Response*. Eve S. Buzawa and Carl G. Buzawa, eds. Westport, CT: Auburn House, 1992.

Zander, Michael. *Cases and Materials of the English Legal System*. 5th ed. London: Weidenfeld & Nicolson, 1988.

Zdenkowski, George, and David Brown. *The Prison Struggle: Changing Australia's Penal System*. Ringwood, Australia: Penguin Books Australia, 1982.

Zedner, Lucia. "Victims." In *The Oxford Handbook of Criminology*. Mike Maguire, Rod Morgan, and Robert Reiner, eds. Oxford: Clarendon Press, 1994: 1207–46.

———. "In Pursuit of the Vernacular: Comparing Law and Order Discourse in Britain and Germany." *Social and Legal Studies* 4 (1995): 517–34.

———. "Wayward Sisters: The Prison for Women." In *The Oxford History of the Prison: The Practice of Punishment in Western Society*. Norval Morris and David J. Rothman, eds. New York: Oxford University Press, 1995: 329–62.

———. "The Pursuit of Security." In *Crime, Risk and Insecurity: Law and Order in Everyday Life and Political Discourse*. Tim Hope and Richard Sparks, eds. London and New York: Routledge, 2000.

Zimmerman, Jane. "The Penal Reform Movement in the South during the Progressive Era, 1890–1917." *The Journal of Southern History* 17.4 (1951): 462–92.

Zimring, Franklin E. "Imprisonment Rates and the New Politics of Criminal Punishment." Conference on "The Causes and Consequences of Mass Imprisonment in the USA." New York University School of Law, February 26, 2000.

———. "Imprisonment Rates and the New Politics of Criminal Punishment." *Punishment & Society* 3.1 (January 2001): 161–66.

———. *The Contradictions of American Capital Punishment*. New York: Oxford University Press, 2003.

Zimring, Franklin E., and Richard S. Frase. *The Criminal Justice System: Materials on the Administration and Reform of the Criminal Law*. Boston: Little, Brown and Co., 1980.

Zimring, Franklin E., and Gordon Hawkins. *Capital Punishment and the American Agenda*. Cambridge: Cambridge University Press, 1986.

———. *The Scale of Imprisonment*. Chicago and London: University of Chicago Press, 1991.

———. *Incapacitation: Penal Confinement and the Restraint of Crime*. New York: Oxford University Press, 1995.

———. "Toward a Principled Basis for Federal Crime Legislation." *The Annals of the American Academy of Political and Social Science* 543 (January 1996): 15–26.

———. *Crime Is Not the Problem: Lethal Violence Is*. New York: Oxford University Press, 1997.

Zimring, Franklin E., Gordon Hawkins, and Sam Kamin. *Punishment and Democracy: Three Strikes and You're Out in California*. Oxford: Oxford University Press, 2001.

Zoomer, Olga J. "Policing Woman Beating in the Netherlands." In *Women, Policing, and Male Violence: International Perspectives*. Jalna Hanmer, Jill Radford, and Elizabeth A. Stanko, eds. London and New York: Routledge, 1989.

Zorza, Joan, and Laurie Woods. *Analysis and Policy Implications of the New Domestic Violence Police Studies*. New York: National Organization for Women Legal Defense and Education Fund, 1994.

INDEX

Other Books in the Series (*continued from page iii*)